W9-BXL-678

THE CRITICAL TEMPER

THE

*A Survey of Modern Criticism
from the Beginnings*

THE CRITICAL HERITAGE

In Three Volumes

VICTORIAN LITERATURE,

CRITICAL TEMPER

on English and American Literature
to the Twentieth Century

MARTIN TUCKER
General Editor

Volume III

AND AMERICAN LITERATURE

FREDERICK UNGAR PUBLISHING CO.
NEW YORK

Second Printing, 1973

CONTRIBUTING EDITORS

General Editor, Martin Tucker

OLD ENGLISH LITERATURE

Martin Tucker
Long Island University

MEDIEVAL LITERATURE

Robert Raymo
New York University

ELIZABETHAN AND JACOBEAN LITERATURE

Irving Ribner
*State University of New York
at Stony Brook*

SHAKESPEARE

Paul N. Siegel
Long Island University

MILTON, AND NEOCLASSICAL LITERATURE

John T. Shawcross
University of Wisconsin

ROMANTIC LITERATURE

Frances K. Barasch
*Bernard Baruch College
of The City University of New York*

VICTORIAN LITERATURE

Wendell Stacy Johnson
*Hunter College
of The City University of New York*

AMERICAN LITERATURE

Ray C. Longtin
Long Island University

v

CONTENTS

AMERICAN LITERATURE 229
Ray C. Longtin, editor

BIBLIOGRAPHIC NOTE

Below the introductory paragraph for each writer included in these volumes, the reader will find bibliographic entries of standard editions and biographic studies published through 1967. The scheme of these entries is as follows:

The standard edition (or editions) of the writer's work is placed first; in certain selected cases a study of a single work, as distinct from the collected edition of an author's work, will be found in the bibliographic listings; occasionally there is no listing when no standard work exists. Following the list of editions is the standard biographic study. In cases where scholarly biography has been particularly active, or literary issues remain in the realm of disputation and/or doubt, several biographical sources may be noted.

Abbreviations used in the entries are: *repr.* for reprint; *rev.* for revision; *ed. for* "edited by"; *tr.* for "translated by"; *n. d.* for no date of publication listed; *n. p.* for no place of publication listed.

The abbreviation BC/Longmans, Green means: published for the British Council by Longmans, Green of London The abbreviation *CHEL* means: The Cambridge History of English Literature.

In citation of books throughout the text, the place of publication is always given, with the exception of Oxford University Press and Cambridge University Press, where the places of publication are readily identifiable. Places of publication for The Clarendon Press at Oxford, as well as the New York offices of Oxford University Press and Cambridge University Press, are notated.

PERIODICALS USED

Listed below are titles, their abbreviations, if any,
and place of publication.

	The Academy (later The Academy and Literature), London
Adel	The Adelphi, London
ABR	American Benedictine Review, Latrobe, Pennsylvania
	American Imago, Boston
AL	American Literature, Duke University Press, Durham, North Carolina
AM	The American Mercury, New York
	The Proceedings of the American Philosophical Society, Philadelphia
AQ	American Quarterly, University of Pennsylvania, Philadelphia
AmR	The American Review, New York
AmS	The American Scholar, Washington, D.C.
	Anglia, Tübingen, Germany
At	The Atlantic Monthly (later The Atlantic). Boston
Boston Univ. Stud. in Eng.	Boston University Studies in English, Boston
	The Proceedings of the British Academy, London
BR	The Bucknell Review, Lewisburg, Pennsylvania
BJRL	The Bulletin of the John Rylands Library, Manchester, England
CambJ	The Cambridge Journal, Cambridge, England

CR	The Centennial Review of Arts and Science, Michigan State University, East Lansing, Michigan
CE	College English, Champaign, Illinois
	Commentary, New York
	The Commonweal, New York
CL	Comparative Literature, University of Oregon, Eugene, Oregon
Criterion	The Criterion, London
CQ	The Critical Quarterly, London
	Criticism, Wayne State University, Detroit, Michigan
	Delaware Notes, University of Delaware, Newark, Delaware
	The Dial, Chicago, then New York
	Discourse, Moorhead, Minnesota
DR	The Dublin Review, Dublin (since 1961 The Wiseman Review, London)
	Encounter, London
Eng	English, The Magazine of the English Association, London
	English Institute Essays, New York
ELH	English Literary History, Johns Hopkins University, Baltimore, Maryland
EM	English Miscellany, Rome, published for The British Council, London
ES	English Studies, Amsterdam, the Netherlands; *also* Englische Studien
	English Studies Today, Oxford (International Conference of University Professors of English, 1950)
Essays and Studies	Essays and Studies by members of the English Association, Oxford
EIC	Essays in Criticism, Oxford
Glasgow Univ. Publications	Glasgow University Publications, Glasgow, Scotland

Harpers	Harper's Magazine, New York
HJ	The Hibbert Journal, London
	History, London
HdR	The Hudson Review, New York
HLQ	The Huntington Library Quarterly, San Marino, California
	The Proceedings of the Second Congress of the International Comparative Literature Association, Chapel Hill, North Carolina
IER	Irish Ecclesiastical Record, Dublin
Irish Monthly	The Irish Monthly Magazine, Dublin
JAAC	The Journal of Aesthetics and Art Criticism, Cleveland, Ohio
JEGP	The Journal of English and Germanic Philology, University of Illinois, Urbana, Illinois
JHI	Journal of the History of Ideas, Princeton, New Jersey
JR	The Journal of Religion, Chicago
K-SJ	Keats-Shelley Journal, New York
KR	The Kenyon Review, Kenyon College, Gambier, Ohio
Library	The Library, London
LL	Life and Letters (later Life and Letters Today), London
List	The Listener (now The Listener and BBC Television Review), London
L&P	Literature and Psychology, University of Massachusetts, Amherst, Massachusetts
	Mediaeval Studies, University of Toronto, Toronto, Canada
	Papers, Michigan Academy of Science, Arts and Letters, Ann Arbor, Michigan
	Modern Language Association, see PMLA
MLN	Modern Language Notes, Baltimore, Maryland

MLQ	The Modern Language Quarterly, University of Washington, Seattle, Washington
MLR	The Modern Language Review, Cambridge, England
MP	Modern Philology, Chicago
Month	The Month, London
NR	The National Review, London
NEQ	The New England Quarterly, Boston
	News, A Review of World Events, London
	The New York Review of Books, New York
	Nineteenth-Century Fiction, Berkeley, California
NAR	The North American Review, Boston, then New York
NQ	Notes and Queries, London
	The Open Court, Chicago
PQ	Philological Quarterly, University of Iowa, Iowa City, Iowa
	Poetry, Chicago
Poetry R	The Poetry Review, London
PMLA	Publications of the Modern Language Association of America, New York
QJS	The Quarterly Journal of Speech, New York
QQ	Queen's Quarterly, Queen's University, Kingston, Ontario, Canada
QR	The Quarterly Review, London
	Research Studies, Washington State University, Pullman, Washington
RES	The Review of English Studies, London
PTRSC	The Proceedings and Transactions of the Royal Society of Canada, Ottawa, Canada
	The Transactions of the Royal Society of Literature of the United Kingdom, London
Sat	The Saturday Review of Literature (now The Saturday Review), New York

	Scrutiny, London
SwR	The Sewanee Review, University of the South, Sewanee, Tennessee
SQ	The Shakespeare Quarterly, New York
SS	Shakespeare Survey, Cambridge, England
	The South Atlantic Quarterly, Duke University, Durham, North Carolina
Spec	The Spectator, London
Sp	Speculum, Cambridge, Massachusetts
	Stanford University Publications in Language and Literature, Palo Alto, California
SN	Studia neophilologica, Uppsala, Sweden
	Studies in English, University of Texas, Austin, Texas
SEL	Studies in English Literature, 1500–1900, Tulane University, New Orleans
SP	Studies in Philology, Chapel Hill, North Carolina
	Studies in the Renaissance, New York
Texas Studies in Lang. and Lit.	Texas Studies in Language and Literature, University of Texas, Austin, Texas
TLS	The Times Literary Supplement, London
TDR	Tulane Drama Review (now TDR, The Drama Review), New York University, New York
Tulane Studies in Eng.	Tulane Studies in English, Tulane University, New Orleans
Univ. of California. Publications in Eng.	University of California Publications in English, Berkeley, California
UKCR	The University of Kansas City Review, Kansas City, Missouri
UTQ	The University of Toronto Quarterly, Toronto, Canada

Univ. of Wisconsin Studies in Lang. and Lit.	University of Wisconsin Studies in Language and Literature, Madison, Wisconsin
	Victorian Newsletter, New York University, New York
	Victorian Poetry, West Virginia University, Morgantown, West Virginia
	Victorian Studies, Indiana University, Bloomington, Indiana
West Virginia Univ. Studies	West Virginia University Studies, Morgantown, West Virginia
	The Transactions of the Wisconsin Academy of Sciences, Arts and Letters, Madison, Wisconsin
YR	The Yale Review, Yale University, New Haven, Connecticut

VICTORIAN LITERATURE

Wendell Stacy Johnson, editor

MATTHEW ARNOLD
1822-1888

Son of the eminent Dr. Thomas Arnold, who was headmaster of Rugby School, Arnold was educated at Balliol College, Oxford, was for a few years private secretary to Lord Lansdowne, and became an inspector of schools. His first volume of poetry, *Empedocles on Etna, and Other Poems*, appeared in 1849; other editions of his verse were published in 1852, 1853, 1858, and 1867. In the 1860's Arnold turned from the writing of poetry to the writing of literary and social criticism: his critical studies include *On Translating Homer* (1861), *Essays in Criticism* (1865), *On the Study of Celtic Literature* (1867), *Culture and Anarchy* (1869), *St. Paul and Protestantism* (1870), *Friendship's Garland* (1871), *Literature and Dogma* (1873), *Mixed Essays* (1879), *Discourses in America* (1885), and *Essays in Criticism, Second Series* (1888). By the time of his sudden death, in Liverpool, he had become one of the most influential of Victorian writers on religion, education, and literature, as well as having established his claim to being considered among the leading English poets of his time. Arnold wanted no biography of himself to be written, and no complete life has yet appeared.

C. B. Tinker and H. F. Lowry, eds., *The Poetical Works of Matthew Arnold* (1950)

R. H. Super, ed., *The Complete Prose Works of Matthew Arnold* (1960-), 5 vols. published; edition in progress

PERSONAL

Trained in those chosen places of beauty and high tradition, Winchester and Oxford, with all the strength of his father's influence at Rugby, he was always attached to the English ideal: to the ideals of Milton and of Burke. A scholar, a man of the world, a government official, his affections were not narrow, not provincial; but they were not cosmopolitan, not unsettled. His heart was at home in the quiet dignity and peace of an English life, among the great books of antiquity, and the great thoughts of "all time and all existence." Hence came his limitations; not from prejudice, nor from ignorance, but from a scrupulous precision and delicacy of taste. No one loved France more than he; no one abhorred more than he "the great goddess Aselgeia." He reverenced the German seriousness, depth, moderation of life and thought; he disliked and ridiculed pedantry, awkwardness, want of

3

humour and of grace. In all his criticism, the same balance between excess and deficiency appears: he was a true Aristotelian. And so, when it is said that Arnold was not a poet of profound philosophy, not a thinker of consistency, or not a man whom we can classify at all, the only answer is a *distinguo*. It was Arnold's work to find beauty and truth in life, to apprehend the meaning and moral worth of things, to discriminate the trivial from the grave, and to show how the serene and ardent life is better than the mean and restless. His poetry, then, is not didactic; but meditative, in the classical sense, it is.

Lionel Johnson
Post Liminium (London: Mathews, 1911), pp. 295-96

Arnold's failures in judgment were many, as they must have been with a man who took upon himself his peculiarly ungrateful task. T. S. Eliot tells us that Arnold was not a revolutionary and not a reactionary, but that does not mean he was neutral: rather, he tried to make the past of Europe march with the future. Arnold did not believe that he lived in the period of stasis which Mr. Eliot says was his; indeed, he saw it as a time when all the old orders were breaking up, the order of the Reformation and of the French Revolution as well as the order of ecclesiastic feudalism. From each he desired to conserve the best, and consequently he gets his drubbing from all parties, many of them deserved. He sought to conciliate epochs and that is something that history but no single man can successfully do. Yet Arnold's eclectic and dialectical method has its vitality exactly because it is the method of history.

Lionel Trilling
Matthew Arnold (New York: W. W. Norton, 1939), p. xiii

Matthew Arnold is a particularly complicated instance of the conflict between disinterestedness and action, art and practical criticism. In him the struggle begins early; it rises in an uneven intensity, creating crises large and small the entire length of his career; there are moments in which it abates astonishingly and moments in which it is wholly suspended, with happy result; and the conflict is unsettled at the very end. If Arnold had outlived the acute phase of the Irish crisis which began in 1885, he might have added another collection or two of literary and social essays wise and temperate and even perhaps an admirable elegy, on the death, suppose, of Cardinal Newman—the most suggestive theme for an elegy that the century might have offered him. Arnold's work in the Education Department was a notable complicating factor. He did not become interested in the large issues that his daily work presented until he was almost forty; he then began to put forward extremely specific proposals for the reform first of elementary and then of secondary education. . . . Arnold was led on from educational criticism to a general criticism of politics and society; from proposals concerning the part of the social structure which he knew as an expert to the rest of the structure concerning which he knew scarcely more than Ruskin himself. He did not allow for the vast difference between his accurate and always accumulating knowledge about education and his vague notions about, let us say, the history of the English middle class or of the Church of England. Arnold was never a learned man; and he did not have the learned man's methods of inquiry or his scruples about judging in areas where his knowledge was scanty. So he passed lightheartedly from the practical criticism of the expert to the practical criticism of the artist wandering beyond his true scope.

In his poetry and in his literary criticism and indeed in not a few social essays, he succeeds in communicating with his contemporaries on issues that are comparable in importance with those which Browning illuminated, remaining as Browning did within the terms of art. His case becomes yet more interesting as we recognize him capable of extraordinary success and extraordinary failure within the bounds of a single work, often a poem or a brief essay. The style which for a space has been beautifully even and accomplished will suddenly break into pieces; the impeccable manner sustained long enough to have seemed second nature will suddenly exhibit some gross and incredible flaw; or the structure will be perfectly disinterested and some detail will crop up drenched in controversial or petulant personal feeling. Such incoherences, artistic disasters, indicative of a divided mind and spirit, may occur in any of the genres that Arnold practiced and in any period of his career, although—as might be expected from what has been observed in other writers—they are more frequent in the later years.

E. K. Brown
Matthew Arnold: A Study in Conflict (Chicago:
Univ. Chicago Pr., 1948), pp. 181-83

POETRY

The full acceptance of Arnold's poetry has yet to come. And in order that it may come in our time, we should be careful not to overpraise him, not to credit him with qualities that he never had. His peculiar distinction is his unfailing level of thoughtfulness, of culture, and of balance. Almost alone amongst our poets since Milton, Arnold is never incoherent, spasmodic, careless, washy, or *banal*. He never flies up into a region where the sun melts his wings; he strikes no discords, and he never tries a mood for which he has no gift. He has more general insight into the intellectual world of our age, and he sees into it more deeply and more surely than any contemporary poet. He has a trained thirst for nature; but his worship of nature never weakens his reverence of man, and his brooding over man's destiny. On the other hand, he has little passion, small measure of dramatic sense, but a moderate gift of movement or of colour, and—what is perhaps a more serious want—no sure ear for melody and music.

Frederic Harrison
Tennyson, Ruskin, Mill, and Other Literary Estimates
(New York: Macmillan, 1900), p. 107

"The poet," Mr. Saintsbury writes of him (and it sums up the matter), "has in him a vein, or, if the metaphor be preferred, a spring, of the most real and rarest poetry. But the vein is constantly broken by faults, and never very thick; the spring is intermittent, and runs at times by drops only." Elsewhere Mr. Saintsbury speaks of his "elaborate assumption of the singing-robe," a phrase very happily critical. Arnold felt—no man more deeply —the majesty of the poet's function: he solemnly attired himself to perform it: but the singing-robe was not his daily wear. The ample pall in which Tennyson swept, his life through, as to the manner born; the stiffer skirts in which Wordsworth walked so complacently; these would have intolerably cumbered the man who protested that even the title of Professor made him uneasy. Wordsworth and Tennyson were bards, authentic and unashamed; whereas in Arnold, as Sir William Watson has noted,

> Something of worldling mingled still
> With bard and sage.

There was never a finer worldling than Matthew Arnold: but the criticism is just.

Arthur Quiller-Couch
Studies in Literature, First Series
(Cambridge Univ. Pr., 1918), p. 239

If I am right, then, in concluding that Arnold's influence, both in England and in America, since his death has resided in his poetry rather than in his prose, it should be remarked in passing how few are the poems on which this influence rests. Posterity is capricious about what it remembers. We have almost forgotten Arnold's ambitious attempts in poetry. *Merope* is for scholars, and *Empedocles,* except for its lyrics, is a curiosity. The college student, the lover of English poetry, the browser in literature are moved to admiration by a half-dozen lovely lyrics. "Tell Mat," said Tennyson, "not to write any more of those prose things like *Literature and Dogma* but to give us something like his *Thyrsis,* or *The Forsaken Merman.*" Possibly *The Forsaken Merman* has been more admired than any other single poem of Arnold's. Swinburne's worship of this poem is the voice of the world. . . .

There is a basis, then, for the belief that Matthew Arnold's poetry is still a living force. To many it will always seem remote. "Too cold for me," a lover of poetry once remarked. Yet I—though this is but the witnessing of one—repeatedly discover men and women who are fond of Arnold's poetry. They say little of this. How can you describe what Arnold does for you? Yet faith in his poetry does exist. "I think," Mr. Henry Nevinson says, "his influence is increasing." And Mr. Noyes compares Arnold's lyrics to certain poems of Tennyson's, in respect to their enduring qualities:

> I believe that the best poetry of Tennyson (such a poem as *In Memoriam*) will always have a great influence on a certain quiet section of the public—the section that happens to make the opinion of posterity! . . . The same applies to the poetry of Matthew Arnold.

Those who seek emotional peace will not turn to Arnold. He is for the unflinching, and, perhaps, only for the strong. But he is honest, and he never offers second-best. Above all, he can, in things of the spirit, lead from darkness to reasonable light. George Eliot once confessed that of all modern poetry Arnold's was most steadily *growing* upon her. Her experience is shared by many readers of poetry.

> "It is to him and Clough," says George Woodberry, "that the men of the future will come who desire to find the clearest expression of the most cultivated and thoughtful men of our generation."

Stanley T. Williams
Studies in Victorian Literature (New York:
Dutton, 1923), pp. 91-93

It has been denied that he had any poetic inspiration at all. It is sometimes held that his subject-matter is incapable of poetic treatment, and again that he had no metrical skill, and no ear. How these writers explain away his great poetic accomplishment is hard to discover. I think him a poet highly inspired and highly gifted; there is no other way of accounting for much of his poetry. But by temper as well as training he is almost a fifth- or fourth-century Athenian set down in nineteenth-century England. That, and not merely his brooding over a lost faith, is his disequilibrium. Intensely aware of the dignity and beauty possible to human society he sees the bulk of his countrymen in a religious prison-house; great masses of the people, and legions of little children even, slaves to factories and mines, and without even a slave's security or a slave's value to an owner; and such serenity and beauty as there once had been for the more fortunate in society now rapidly being dissolved by new elements. Despite this he breathes an Attic spirit in his own work; in his poetry there is a mature wisdom appealing to the elemental and universal in man.

Carleton Stanley
Matthew Arnold (Toronto: Univ. Toronto Pr., 1938), p. 39

Arnold cannot escape the impeachment of being "made"; T. S. Eliot calls him academic, which is much the same thing. Those who are moved by his effort to come to grips with important problems, to think as well as feel in verse, to transmute emotion into thought, thought into emotion, are inclined to overlook the frequent failure of the effort, the lapses into prosiness and stiff intellectuality. But there is one mood that assures Arnold the lyric gift—the mood of self-commiseration. Then the stiffness vanishes and he becomes truly a poet. In the face of the frequent strictures on Arnold's cacophony, on his insensitivity to music (attested to by his friends), he is primarily a *musical* poet. Spengler tried to give a pejorative meaning in the phrase "the musical man"—implying a decadence in the yearning, in the infinite aspiration of the music of Beethoven and Wagner. The word *decadence* means little enough, but there is a truth in the assimilation which Spengler makes of the "musical" to the "Faustian" man. The particular kind of pain and pity, the particular kind of aspiration of Arnold's poetry, expressing itself in a lovely legato so unlike the tight, crabbed movement of the bulk of his verse, is best contained in music. Chopin gives us its excess; we find its perfection in certain pieces of Mozart—in the viola quintet in G Minor; and Arnold, like Mozart, though in a less remarkable way, could set off self-pity by the knowledge of the gaiety of health, that gaiety which Stendhal, perhaps Mozart's greatest admirer, found to be one of the first of virtues; in Arnold's mind there is always the vision of the day when wits were clear beside the sparkling Thames and when the merry Grecian coaster breasted the waves.

But the mood of self-pity, set off by the knowledge of gaiety, producing the best of his poetry, is the very mood Arnold undertook to banish from himself. He refused to be of the race of Chateaubriand's René which Sainte-Beuve had scorned because it cherished and proclaimed its unhappiness.

Lionel Trilling
Matthew Arnold (New York: W. W. Norton, 1939), p. 139

Arnold never shrieks like Tennyson in parts of *Maud*, nor bellows like Browning in *Pacchiarotto*. He had also a clearer mind, more intellectual honesty, more sense of practical reality—as we might expect in a poet whose more active temper turned him also into a critic, a religious controversialist, and an inspector of Nonconformist schools from Yarmouth to Pembroke and from Yorkshire to the Thames, having his children born in lodging-houses and living himself on buns hastily eaten in class-rooms before astonished schoolchildren. "Not here, O Apollo, were haunts meet for thee."

And so, though Arnold remains in many ways a typical Victorian, a poet struggling with a preacher, he is, I think, less tiresome in his pulpit than Tennyson or Browning. If his greater fastidiousness, his stronger sense of truth, his practical activities prevented him from writing so much poetry, they prevented him also from writing so much bad poetry. And there is a further important difference: Arnold is poignantly conscious of the conflict in himself. It tears him, and he sees it, and it becomes in our eyes all the more painful, but also the more moving—not a muddle, but a battle; not stupid, but tragic. For Arnold was indeed at war with himself; the artist in him with the moralist, the Greek poet with the Hebrew prophet, the lover of Byron and passion and the beauty of the South with the disciple of Wordsworth and knowledge and the sternness of the North. For some, Arnold is a pedant and a prig: really, he was something much more human and more unhappy.

F. L. Lucas
Ten Victorian Poets (Cambridge Univ. Pr., 1940), pp. 40-41

If the poet in Arnold was reluctant to abandon hope for the spark from heaven, the man found it increasingly difficult to refuse the solicitations of his age that he should assume a conspicuous place in its life. The career of a public servant under an expanding program of government education carried with it responsibilities to Victorian society which could not be ignored. The transformation of the artist into the man of letters was a phenomenon of the times from Carlyle to William Morris; and in Arnold's case the process was materially abetted by a variety of external circumstances, not the least decisive among which was his appointment in 1857 to the Professorship of Poetry at Oxford. His subsequent poetry, nearly all of it in the elegiac mode and much of it purely occasional in nature, reflects the author's final refusal to accept for himself the concept of the alienated artist at home only within the domain of his art.

With the exception of *Thyrsis, Rugby Chapel* and *Obermann Once More* are the most memorable poems of Arnold's later period. In them we find the author making the choice henceforth to speak with a public voice. Like others of the elegies, *Rugby Chapel*, dated 1857 but not published until ten years later, directs a retrospective glance on the influences which shaped the poet's faculties. And how noteworthy it is that at this turning point in his career the son should have felt impelled to celebrate Thomas Arnold's memory after fifteen years of silence! For if the scholar-gipsy is correlative to the poet's inner awareness, Arnold of Rugby as certainly exemplifies the ascendency of an outer or social awareness.

E. D. H. Johnson
The Alien Vision of Victorian Poetry
(Princeton, N. J.: Princeton Univ. Pr., 1952), p. 205

Arnold's poetry has always been appreciated and enjoyed by select readers, but it can hardly be called popular, and it has always seemed a little dry, and even artificial, to many. It separated itself from the main movement of popular Victorian poetry; it lacked the sunset glow of Romanticism by which Tennyson flourished (and inversely Browning) and by whose fading light Rossetti and Swinburne shone. . . .

The limitation of this poetry, both in bulk and in scope, has been a handicap. His subjects were often intensely personal, even while he aimed at disinterested objectivity and deplored personal revelation; other subjects were remote from general interest—"The Church of Brou," for example, the Obermann poems, "Tristram and Iseult" and "Balder Dead"—or he could not make them seem interesting. Often when we expect him to be at his best he falls short; there is a palpable failure, a notable element is lacking. This is especially true with those rich commonplaces so frequent among all worshipers of Apollo, which without a certain energy or delicacy of language become mere banalities, but which may sometimes mysteriously and unpredictably become poetry. On the other hand, so many of his poems have so many excellences that it is unfair to complain when he falls short of the *very best*, as he would say—unfair to seem to question them and likewise to take advantage of them for analytical dissection; unfair, until analysis reveals unsuspected values. His poetry has an air of deliberateness; he aimed at the grand manner, with its "simplicity" and "severity"—two most difficult qualities to achieve—and as a corollary it seems to want warmth, glow, passion.

Paull F. Baum
Ten Studies in the Poetry of Matthew Arnold
(Durham, N. C.: Duke Univ. Pr., 1958), pp. x-xii

Edith Sitwell has said that those who like Matthew Arnold "dislike poetry." Without for a moment subscribing to anything implied by this remark one may admit that people who like their poetry "pure" will not find many things in Arnold to their taste. Poetry was too closely related to life in Arnold's view for him to be interested in mere Sitwellian patterns. But beyond this one may concede that Arnold does not have more than about a dozen really fine poems. I would list them as follows: "The Strayed Reveller," "The Forsaken Merman," "Empedocles on Etna," "To Marguerite—Continued," "Tristram and Iseult," "Sohrab and Rustum," "Philomela," "The Scholar-Gypsy," "Thyrsis," "Dover Beach," and "Stanzas from the Grande Chartreuse." As will be evident from these titles, what Arnold needed in order to produce a good poem was a passionate apprehension of a theme and an image or myth in which to embody that theme. In some of his later poems, like *Balder Dead* and *Merope*, he had an image or myth but no passionate apprehension of the theme. (Indeed, he started with the myth and didn't seem to know what the theme was.) On the other hand, in many of his early poems, like "The Buried Life" or "A Summer Night," he had a theme which he felt passionately but had no adequate image or myth in which to embody it. Hence he resorted to a poetry of statement or, more properly, to a kind of rhetoric. It is this poetry especially which I am sure Miss Sitwell dislikes. I do not dislike it, for I feel that the total body of Arnold's poetry constitutes one large complex myth which, although containing an unusually large amount of *dianoia* or thought, is quite adequately rendered through character, scene, and significant action so as to establish for us a viable poetic world. I would point out that Arnold himself always approached poetry in this way. He never wrote analyses or interpretations of individual poems. In his essays on Wordsworth, Byron, Shelley, Keats, Gray, Milton, Homer, and Dante there is no discussion of either the form or the meaning of any particular work by these authors. What he is always interested in is the quality and scope of the poetic vision as a whole.

A. Dwight Culler
Poetry and Criticism of Matthew Arnold
(Boston: Houghton Mifflin, 1961), p. x

From the days of his dandyish youth to his eminent middle age, Arnold is inclined to take serious problems for his subjects, and our complaint about his dealing with these problems does not concern the solemnity of the subject but rather his hesitation or simple pomposity of tone and the incompleteness of his treatment. Time and again his work seems thin and partial, not whole and decided. When he preaches dogma Arnold loses his poet's voice, for he has neither the fixed Weltanschauung to give it conviction nor the ability to suspend the doubts he feels. Happily, a least, he is not long willing, like a versifying Carlyle, to shout down his own misgivings.

But when Arnold speaks in soliloquy that sufficiently clarifies his vacillating mind, in the poetic *I* that implies no demanding *you*, no audience to edify, he can achieve at least a personal integrity. And when he speaks in monologue he can, at best, give objective form to his sense of man's alienation from and conflict with his environment. By using dramatic and fictional means, too, he can reveal a double vision in the contrasts between the voices of men, or between the voice of the actor and that of the narrator. If there is a danger of his oracles' being unconvincing and his soliloquies too indecisive, the poet who lives between two worlds, the poet of two minds, is true by indirect means to his imagination: when Arnold's poetry embodies the inner dialogue of his mind it recognizes the tyranny of time and yet asserts an order that transcends all temporal change; it celebrates both the society of human beings, with its bond of love, and the longing for a buried life, for isolation from the noisy crowd of others; it praises natural force and the idea of Nature, and it sees steadily the danger to humanity of natural coldness, natural strength. . . .

Whereas his prose criticism uses rhetorical and "poetic" devices to persuade, his poetry is in some ways less inspirational and more truly critical than the prose—more stringently critical of ideas and their implications. But this criticism is indirect, and it involves the feelings along with the intelligence. In fact, for all his abstract language, Arnold's is an imaginative, a "feeling" intelligence: he is not often either witty or incisive, even in his prose. And he is always at least half aware, as we must be, that his most literal-sounding lines about greenwoods and battleplains, sunlight and shadow, dry land and sea, have to do with the persistent question of man's relation to the mysterious world of nature which he fears and worships, controls and serves; with the questions of man's relation to other men, his isolation from or identity with his fellows, and of man's relation to himself, of the alienation of his consciousness from his innermost being.

His dialogue between poet and critic results in momentary steadiness as well as wholeness, in the control of tone without which poems are not consistent and whole, when Arnold retains but submerges his conflicting (or at least contrasting) ideas and impulses about such matters in the forms of fiction, drama, and imagery: when his voice is that not of the poetic critic but of the profoundly and subtly critical poet. It is then that he reconciles the several voices, the several minds, with which most intelligent Victorians, and fragmented modern men as well, must speak.

Wendell Stacy Johnson
The Voices of Matthew Arnold (New Haven:
Yale Univ. Pr., 1961). pp. 139-41

After the failure of every attempt to escape from himself Arnold is left with only one thing to do. He must hover in the void, in one direction waiting for the lightening to strike, the dawn to come, and in the other direction sternly and implacably criticizing all present cultural forms as false. Through his strategy of withdrawal from practical involvement, he attains at last what he has sought from the beginning. Arnold's final platform is the absence of God.

The Scholar-Gipsy best expresses this stance. Arnold's gypsy lives in the rhythm of the perpetual round of the seasons. The ebb and flow of nature is his milieu. His constant alignment toward the spark which has not yet fallen gives him stability in the midst of movement, continuity in the midst of succession. Like the Scholar-Gypsy, Arnold postpones indefinitely the attempt to repossess the buried life, but he recognizes that an escape from fluctuation can be obtained by the rejection of every life less than the buried life, and by a permanent orientation toward the infinite distance where it lies.

In the end Arnold no longer faces toward the lost past, but toward the future return of the divine spirit, a return which he can almost see, as he waits in passive tension, renouncing everything here and now for the sake of something which never quite, while he lives, is actual and present. In *Obermann Once More* the ghost of the Swiss solitary tells Arnold that the dawn of the new world is about to come, and the poet, in what is perhaps the most hopeful passage in all his work, imagines that he sees the morning break—but over there, at a distance, high in the mountains where all things begin. The glimpse of this distant dawn, a dawn which still remains just in the future, is the final prize of Arnold's patient repudiation of everything else:

> And glorious there, without a sound,
> Across the glimmering lake,
> High in the Valais-depth profound,
> I saw the morning break.

> J. Hillis Miller
> *The Disappearance of God* (Cambridge, Mass.:
> Harvard Univ. Pr., 1963), pp. 268-69

CRITICISM

Much of what passes for literary criticism is a very perishable branch of literature. Most of Arnold's essays in this kind remain as sound, vital and interesting to-day as when they were written. By their virtue he probably exercises thirty years after his death a more constant and important influence upon current literary opinion and taste than any English critic living. The persistence of his critical force in literature is ascribable in the main to three causes. . . . he did not attempt a chronicle of all the popular and transitory work issuing from the press; he carefully selected for comment men and books which he thought had some mark of immortality about them; he assembled, as he says, a group of persons illustrating the "admirable riches of human nature." In the second place, he conveyed along with the firm and delicate delineations of his subjects an irresistibly stimulating sense of his own fine delight in them—that indispensable personal gusto of the interpreter which excites the envy of the reader, stimulates his curiosity, and makes him feel that, until he shares it, he is excluded from one of the exquisite pleasures of the world. The third and perhaps most distincitve cause of Arnold's durability is in the number and the soundness of the literary principles and the general ideas which he states and illustrates.

> Stuart P. Sherman
> *Matthew Arnold: How to Know Him*
> (Indianapolis, Ind.: Bobbs-Merrill, 1917), pp. 132-33

No English or American critic since Coleridge has had a more extensive influence than Matthew Arnold. For his influence has operated in at least three ways. He was, in one sense, something of a spokesman for nineteenth-century poetic taste. Secondly, through Arnold, more cosmopolitan ideas became readily accessible to English-speaking critics and readers; after becoming current, these have passed unobtrusively into much of the criticism of the past forty years, including that which now looks back on Arnold himself as either academically ineffectual or else as an evil spirit representing "romantic" tastes in style. Lastly, much of the modern defence of the central educational value of literature rests—where the defence is impressive—on classical premises resurrected and popularized, however vaguely and sketchily, by Arnold.

Arnold's main significance as a critic lies . . . in his constant support of the dignity of critical thinking; his attempt to lift the view of the English-speaking reader toward a wider, more cosmopolitan range; his reapplication of classical criteria; and, above all, his courageous attempt, in an increasingly hostile environment, to reassert the traditional value of literature. Through him, English criticism, which had subsided into mediocrity after Coleridge and Hazlitt, became reanimated and broadened. It became aware of the alert critical intelligence at work in mid-nineteenth-century France, and was reminded once again of the wide aims of classical theory. As a result, Anglo-American criticism of the twentieth century took on a new range and sophistication. Through Irving Babbitt and Paul Elmer More, some of Anold's ideas were systematized into the "New Humanism," which turned militantly upon both the romantic art and the scientific naturalism of the nineteenth century. Following Arnold, such critics looked back to some classical values but, unlike Arnold, they interpreted them with a quite unclassical dogmatism and openly didactic bias. Critics of a very different sort from the "New Humanists" took stands which, though some of them were not aware of it, had first been made possible for modern English and American criticism by Arnold. More formalistically minded critics, in England and especially America, drew suggestions from both classical and nineteenth-century French critical sources. Without Arnold, either directly or through such disciples as Irving Babbitt, their attention to such sources might not have spread so rapidly. Arnold's frequently voiced charge that the English are not critically minded became one of the clichés of modern criticism. And despite his strong antagonism to Arnold, the chief critical writer since World War I, T. S. Eliot, found himself—as he took the place of Arnold—following the procedure if by no means the opinions of his predecessor, and employing a prose style strikingly similar in its conscious, urbane simplicity and its occasional irony.

Walter Jackson Bate
Criticism: The Major Texts (New York:
Harcourt, Brace, 1952), pp. 437-38

Matthew Arnold, poet and critic, should be seen steadily and seen whole. The poet is familiar and his reputation is not in doubt. While Arnold has never had the popular appeal of his great contemporaries, his verse, less mannered and less voluminous, has withstood change of taste and fashion better than much of theirs. But the poetry is only a part of his varied achievement, and Arnold the prose-writer is not well known. In his Harvard lectures of 1930 Mr. Garrod remarked that clever young men no longer read Arnold's criticism and that they would be wiser and no less clever if they did. *Essays in Criticism* and the Introduction to Ward's *English Poets* may still provide critical counters like "high seriousness," "the grand style" and "poetry as criticism of life," but the lectures on Homer and the mass of his social, religious and educational writings remain scattered and largely un-read. There are to-day signs of a change of heart and of a growing sense that these writings are worth rediscovering, because Arnold has a way of antici-pating problems which are our concern as well as his. Here is a writer whose main object was to make the critical study of literature a guide to the business of living; one who saw in this study a training ground for clear thought and a field for the free play of ideas—and the ideas thus acquired he brings to bear on the wider issues of education, politics and religion. A critic of European outlook who believed in a culture based on the attempt "to learn and propagate the best that is known and thought in the world" is likely to furnish tracts for our time as well as for his own.

In range, sanity and intelligence Arnold's critical writings are outstanding in Victorian literature. His temper is no less serious than Carlyle's or Ruskin's, but the touch is lighter and the tone less hysterical. The spirit of gaiety so signally absent from his poetry found its natural outlet in his prose. Nor is it fair to isolate the purely literary criticism from the rest. Literature is not for Arnold a thing apart; it must take its place beside re-ligion, politics and education in establishing the enlightened way of life for which he fought. That is the special quality of his writings about it. Culture, a term we have come to regard with some suspicion, is for Arnold the study of perfection moving "by the force, not merely or primarily of the sci-entific passion for pure knowledge, but also of the moral and social passion for doing good." He is as far removed as Dr. Johnson from the sterile posi-tion of the aesthete. "A fine culture is the complement of a high reason: it is in the conjunction of both with character and energy, that the ideal for men and nations is to be placed." Great poetry must be a criticism of life because a poetry of revolt against, or indifference towards, moral ideas is a poetry of indifference towards life.

John Bryson
Introd. in *Matthew Arnold: Poetry and Prose*
(Cambridge, Mass.: Harvard Univ. Pr., 1954), pp. 13-14

Viewed negatively, Arnold's criticism is directed against both the Utilitarian and the Romantic position. (By the term "Utilitarian" we wish to compre-hend not merely the school properly so called but also the various associated movements of liberal reform.) Naturally, the Romantics loom larger in the literary essays and the Utilitarians in the essays on society, but both are present in that great fact with which Arnold everywhere has to deal, the French Revolution; and his principal antagonist, the Dissenting mentality, is a compound of the two. Positively, his criticism is an attempt to fashion a large objective image of human culture—of the "best that is known and thought in the world"—which shall be as a palladium to the English people; and for this purpose, though he recognizes that England has a slender continuing tradition of this culture, he goes to sources which are as remote from England as possible, to the culture of Greece and Rome as removed in time, to the continent of Europe as removed in space. He appeals, as did Newman in his quest for a similar center of authority, to the note of "apostolicity," or the judgment of history, and to the note of "catholicity," or the judgment of the whole human race.

A. Dwight Culler
Poetry and Criticism of Matthew Arnold
(Boston: Houghton Mifflin, 1961), p. xviii

WALTER BAGEHOT

1826-1877

Banker, economist, journalist, and literary critic—Bagehot had one of the most versatile minds in his century. His *English Constitution* (1867) is an excellent analysis of government, *Physics and Politics* (1872) one of the best attempts to apply the newly discovered principles of evolution, and *Lombard Street* (1873) a keen introduction to finance. In his *Literary Studies* (1879), collected from essays published in the *National Review*, are sane treatments of Shakespeare, Wordsworth, Scott, Dickens, Tennyson, and Browning.

Homer A. Watt and William W. Watt
A Dictionary of English Literature (New York:
Barnes & Noble, 1945), p. 15

E. I. Barrington, ed., *The Works and Life of Walter Bagehot* (1915), 10 vols.
William Irvine, *Walter Bagehot* (1939)

Bagehot's strong point, indeed, is insight into character: what one of his critics has called his "Shakespearean" power of perceiving the working of men's minds. To possess that power a man must be a bit of what it harshly called a cynic. He must be able to check the sentimentalist tendency to lose all characterization in a blaze of light. His hero-worship must be restrained by humor and common sense.

Leslie Stephen
NR (London) (August, 1900), p. 941

Mr. Bagehot is not only an original writer, but he presents you with his thoughts and fancies in an unworked state. He is not an artist; he does not stop to elaborate and dress up his material; but having said something which is worth saying and has not been said before, this strange writer is content to say something else. There is more meat on Mr. Bagehot's bones for the critic than on almost anybody else's. . . .

Augustine Birrell
Miscellanies, 2nd Ed. (New York: Scribner's, 1902), p. 133

Varied interests gave to his mind a universality which is rare in literature but of incomparable value. It may seem, on a superficial view, that Bagehot dissipated his energies over too wide a field, that if he had concentrated on criticism, or on economics, he might have attained the highest possible reputation in one of these narrower spheres. That would be to mistake the quality of the man and to misjudge the proper value of criticism. The opinion of such a man on one literary topic is worth the life-work of a solitary pedant. This universality, combined with . . . regularity . . . gives him that *centrality* of mind which, on a different scale, he had admired in Béranger: "He puts things together . . . they group themselves in his intelligence insensibly round a principle . . . the man has attained to be himself; a cool oneness, a poised personality, pervades him." Such was the character of Bagehot himself; it omits only his wit and humor, and these may be left to take care of themselves.

Herbert Read
The Sense of Glory: Essays in Criticism
(Cambridge Univ. Pr., 1929), p. 202

What Bagehot aspired to do . . . was of course to see things, with scientific detachment, exactly as they are; and doubtless in considerable degree he succeeded. As a matter of fact his ideas have a color, a vitality, a motive force entirely their own, and looking back over these ideas we must conclude that they proceeded from an imagination that was profoundly realistic, deeply penetrated with a sense of the comic and the humorous, and in a peculiar manner critical and ingenious. Bagehot saw life not sentimentally, nor idyllically, nor fantastically, but with a deep insight into its true character and a delightful perception of its absurdities and contradictions. He was also capable of conceiving great truth, human, moral, and spiritual, but with a quality of imagination which, despite its excellence, has somewhat limited his scope. . . . What Bagehot really enjoyed, and what he usually produced, was a clever and epigrammatic truth. Never ceasing to protest that real verity is dull and tedious, he always made it vivid and exciting. He loved to call sterling virtues by cynical names, to find sage council in muddling stupidity, to clothe sound, inescapable common sense in fantastic and exotic dress. The substance of his thought is sanity itself, its idiom is cleverness, wit, humor, irony. . . . Among nineteenth-century thinkers Bagehot was perhaps not one of the greatest, yet he was certainly one of the most universal. . . . In an age of various and widespread confusion he applied with cool common sense and keen penetration an ancient and profound philosophy to an immense variety of problems, both old and new.

William Irvine
Walter Bagehot (London: Longmans, Green, 1939), pp. 280-84

We are looking for a man who was in and of his age, and who could have been of no other: a man with sympathy to share, and genius to judge, its sentiments and movements; a man not too illustrious or consummate to be companionable, but one, nevertheless, whose ideas took root and are still bearing; whose influence, passing from one fit mind to another, could transmit, and can still impart, the most precious elements in Victorian civilization, its robust and masculine sanity. Such a man there was: and I award the place to Walter Bagehot.

G. M. Young
Today and Yesterday (London: Rupert Hart-Davis, 1948), pp. 240-41

His "robust and masculine sanity," though won at a certain price, relates him to his time: his opinions as contrasted with his doubts were for the most part those of his intelligent contemporaries. . . . But in the way in which he used his mind, his insights, and his intuition, he was far ahead of his own day. There have been many excellent observers of the contemporary scene before him, from Chaucer down through Hazlitt. Bagehot was one of those rare men of real intellect who recognize that analysis is as worthy of a man's best powers as advocacy, that modern society has achieved a complexity which makes it as important to know where it stands and what its constituency is, as where it is going or where it should go. He is the true ancestor of our modern view that the knowledge of what a society is really like, what drives it, what checks it, what distorts its judgment, cannot be gleaned from statistics or mere facts alone, but is as much the province of the literary and imaginative arts as of the moral and metrical sciences.

Alastair Buchan
The Spare Chancellor (East Lansing, Mich.: Michigan State Univ. Pr., 1959), pp. 263-64

Walter Bagehot's character—its freshness and originality—is clearly reflected in his style. "You receive stimulation from him," wrote Woodrow Wilson, "and a certain feeling of elation. There is a fresh air stirring in all his utterances that is unspeakably refreshing. . . . But you know what you lack in Bagehot if you have read Burke. You miss the deep eloquence which awakens purpose. You are not in contact with systems of thought or with principles that dictate action, but only with perfect explanation." Wilson's criticism is peculiarly apposite, for Bagehot was something of a cynic, and as Leslie Stephen has written, "the cynic's merit is to see faults." . . . Walter Bagehot's specific merits as a literary critic are similar to those which characterize him as a writer in general, and his vividness, originality, and wit are especially welcome in what is so often an arid field. His attempts to formulate general theories of literature are, however, somewhat unhappy, for he lacked the requisite training and reading, but for sudden flashes of insight into a writer's genius he is hard to equal.

Norman St. John Stevas
Walter Bagehot (Bloomington, Ind.: Indiana Univ. Pr., 1959), pp. 31-34

The current intellectual fashion in cultural and social matters calls for simplicity and activism. The subtleties, complications and ambiguities that, in the past two or three decades, have been the mark of serious thought are now taken to signify a failure of nerve, a compromise with evil, an evasion of judgment and responsibility. One is reminded of the distinction between the "once-born" and the "twice-born"; the once-born, simple and "healthy-minded," having faith in a beneficent God and a perfectible universe; the twice-born in awe of His mystery, impressed by the recalcitrance of society and the anomalies of social action.

In Walter Bagehot one may see a reconciliation of the two modes. A political commentator who stopped just short of being a political philosopher, a social critic without the appurtenances of today's sociologist but with more imagination and wisdom, accorded the title of "The Greatest Victorian" in an intellectual competition that has not since been equalled, Bagehot was not only, as he said, "between sizes in politics," he was between sizes in everything. He was that rare species of the twice-born who could give proper due to the rights and merits of the once-born. And he did so not by a denial of his own nature but by virtue of the very subtleties, complications and ambiguities that informed his nature.

Gertrude Himmelfarb
New York Review of Books (May 6, 1965), p. 18

CHARLOTTE BRONTË
1816-1855

[Patrick Brontë] had married in 1812 and by 1822 his wife was dead and he was left with six children, Maria, Elizabeth, Charlotte, Patrick Branwell, Emily Jane and Anne, of whom the eldest was eight and the youngest not yet two years of age. Natural disposition aggravated by poverty and misfortune had made him almost as gloomy and silent as the graves that neighbored the melancholy house. The children roamed the moors, and amused themselves with writing. They got some instruction from the father, and when they had grown beyond him the elder girls were sent to a cheap, subsidized boarding-school for the daughters of clergymen. Of this institution it is enough to say that it killed Maria and Elizabeth, that it nearly killed Charlotte, and that it served as the model for Lowood in *Jane Eyre*. When Charlotte was nearly fifteen she was again sent to a boarding-school. A little later, Charlotte returned as a kind of teacher, with Emily and Anne as pupils. . . . In February 1842 the two elder sisters . . . went as pupils to the Pensionnat Heger in Brussels. There Charlotte found herself attracted by Constantin Heger, a man of thirty-three, with considerable gifts and a powerful personality. The death of the aunt who kept house brought the girls back to Haworth. Emily took over the household duties, and Charlotte went back to Brussels in 1843 to teach English in the Heger establishment. But the arrangement failed. Heger had attracted her both as a man and as the expounder of life and literature, and in a year she was home again, very unhappy. To her beloved professor Charlotte then wrote the four letters first completely printed in 1913. They are, as we should expect, full of deep feeling honorably expressed. . . . In 1846, Charlotte, Emily and Anne united in producing *Poems by Currer, Ellis and Acton Bell*. The volume was not successful. Charlotte then embodied some of her experiences in a novel, *The Professor*, which was rejected. . . . In *Jane Eyre* by "Currer Bell" (1847) Charlotte Brontë found herself. Naturally, she chose a story of unhappy experience and troubled love. . . . Branwell drugged himself to extinction in 1848. Before that year closed Emily too was gone. Anne herself died in the next year. . . . *Shirley* (1849) was begun in the first excitement of success; it was finished in utter bereavement. . . . After visits to London, where she received much appreciation and encouragement, Charlotte found recuperation, and her temperament underwent some steeling. She then took up the theme she had essayed in *The Professor*. *Villette* (1853) is a remembrance of Brussels, but the story is told by an artist, not by a sufferer. . . . Two chapters of a novel called *Emma* were all that she left. She had married her father's curate, A. B. Nicholls, in 1854, and in 1855 she was dead before she was thirty-nine, when happiness seemed at last to be coming.

George Sampson
The Concise Cambridge History of English Literature
(Cambridge Univ. Pr., 1941), pp. 787-89

T. J. Wise and J. A. Symington, eds., *The Shakespeare Head Brontë* (1932-1938), 8 vols.

Elizabeth Gaskell, *The Life of Charlotte Brontë* (1857), 2 vols.

PERSONAL

She was pure, utterly and marvelously pure from sentimentalism, which was (and she knew it) the worst vice of the Victorian age. Mr. Leslie Stephen said that, "Miss Brontë's sense of humor was but feeble." It was robust enough when it played with sentimentalists. But as for love, for passion, she sees it with a tragic lucidity that is almost a premonition. And her attitude was by no means that of the foredoomed spinster, making necessity her virtue. There was no neccesity. She had at least four suitors . . . and she refused them all. Twice in her life, in her tempestuous youth, and at a crisis in her affairs, she chose "dependance upon coarse employers" before matrimony. . . . She was shrewd, lucid, fastidious, and saw the men she knew without any glamor. . . . I do not say that Charlotte Brontë had not what is called a "temperament"; her genius would not have been what it was without it; she herself would have been incomplete; but there was never a woman of genius who had her temperament in more complete subjection to her character; and it is her character that you have to reckon with at every turn.

May Sinclair
The Three Brontës (London: Hutchinson, 1933), pp. 79-80

Jane Eyre

She discovered the secret of hiding the sensational in the commonplace: and *Jane Eyre* remains the best of her books (better even than *Villette*), because while it is a human document written in blood, it is also one of the best blood-and-thunder detective stories in the world.

G. K. Chesterton
The Victorian Age in Literature (Oxford Univ. Pr., 1913), p. 71

The melodrama of *Bleak House* itself seems sober compared with that of *Jane Eyre*. Not one of the main incidents on which its action turns but is incredible. It is incredible that Rochester should hide a mad wife on the top floor of Thornfield Hall, and hide her so imperfectly that she constantly gets loose and roams yelling about the house, without any of his numerous servants and guests suspecting anything: it is incredible that Mrs. Reed, a conventional if disagreeable woman, should conspire to cheat Jane Eyre out of a fortune because she had been rude to her as a child of ten; it is supremely incredible that when Jane Eyre collapses on an unknown doorstep after her flight from Rochester it should turn out to be the doorstep of her only surviving amiable relations.

David Cecil
Early Victorian Novelists (Indianapolis, Ind.:
Bobbs-Merril, 1934), pp. 126-27

Jane Eyre deserved its success. Its story, which seems to have been based on a tale read by Charlotte a few years earlier, though melodramatic, is exciting without undue absurdity, remarkably easy to read, and difficult to lay down. The characterization is vigorous and, in general, reconcilable with the reader's experience, the book has enormous vitality, and even a characteristic . . . that interferes with the development of character and action— her persistent moralizing—fell agreeably on the ears of most readers. . . . Charlotte, in *Jane Eyre*, had absorbed her material sufficiently to let her art work freely; and in the person of the heroine she unfolded a tale of passion that was unique at that time in its honesty and in its curious but unmistakable impression of innocence. In her picture of the development of Jane Eyre's love, Charlotte revealed herself as a prose poet.

Lawrence and E. M. Hanson
The Four Brontës (Oxford Univ. Pr., 1949), pp. 223-24

The discovery and revelation of . . . fineness of fibre is this novel's triumph. There is no character in any novel of the eighteen-forties whom the reader knows as intimately as Jane Eyre: and it is an intimacy at all levels—alike with the fiery spirit and the shivering child.

Kathleen Tillotson
Novels of the Eighteen-Forties (Oxford Univ. Pr., 1954), p. 313

GENERAL

It is true she has limitations, most obvious in *Shirley*, but to be found in a measure in all her books; a kindly benevolent outlook upon life there is not. Some of her pictures of men and women were grotesque even when written; they are doubly grotesque to-day without being far enough away from us to enable us to feel that she is giving us a picture of a bygone era. But when all limitations are conceded, there still remain to us great books, full of interest, of imperishable character drawing. Jane Eyre and Lucy Snowe, Rochester and Paul Emanuel, with a number of minor characters are all drawn with a master touch. . . . These books must be read if only for their style, if only for their fine passionate phrases, they must be read still more for their fine moral and intellectual qualities, for the stern sense of duty that belongs to them, the scorn of all meanness and trickery, the wonderful grasp of the hard facts of life, of the stern facts of our being.

Clement K. Shorter
Charlotte Brontë and Her Sisters
(New York: Scribner's, 1905), pp. 233-34

Her books are not about men like Dickens', nor about man like Thackeray's, but about an individual man. With her the hero or more frequently the heroine for the first time steps forward and takes a dominating position on the stage; and the story is presented, not through the eyes of impersonal truth, but openly her own. . . . Charlotte Brontë's imagination is stimulated to create by certain aspects of man's inner life as that of Dickens or Thackeray by certain aspects of his external life. As Thackeray was the first English writer to make the novel the vehicle of a conscious criticism of life, so she is the first to make it the vehicle of personal revelation. She is our first subjective novelist, the ancestor of Proust and Mr. James Joyce and all the rest of the historians of the private consciousness. And like theirs her range is limited to those aspects of experience which stimulate to significance and activity the private consciousness of their various heroes and heroines. . . . Charlotte Brontë fails, and fails often, over the most important part of a novelist's work—over character. Even at her best she is not among the greatest drawers of character. Her secondary figures do not move before us with the solid reality of Jane Austen's: seen as they are through the narrow lens of her heroine's temperament, it is impossible that they should. And the heroines themselves are presented too subjectively for us to set them in the round as we see Maggie Tulliver or Emma Bovary. Nor is her failure solely due to the limitations imposed by her angle of approach. Since she feels rather than understands, she cannot penetrate to the inner structure of a character to discover its basic elements. . . . Formless, improbable, humorless, exaggerated, uncertain in their handling of character—there is assuredly a great deal to be said against Charlotte Brontë's novels. So much, indeed, that one may well wonder if she is a good novelist at all. All the same she is; she is even great. Her books are as living today as those of Dickens; and for the same reason. They have creative imagination of the most powerful kind, able to assimilate to its purpose the strongest feelings, the most momentous experiences.

David Cecil
Early Victorian Novelists (Indianapolis, Ind.:
Bobbs-Merrill, 1934), pp. 120-21, 132, 135

The comic, in short, made no great appeal to Charlotte Brontë: life to her was too real, too earnest; and she was certainly not one to subscribe to "the vile English tradition that humour is a literate quality," though in much of her prose she complied only too willingly with what was then the golden rule, that a facetious lightness is the perfection of style—without, however, achieving lightness. The comic side of the Brussels adventure is inevitably more apparent to that critical onlooker, the reader, than to either Crimsworth or Lucy Snowe, or to Charlotte Brontë, for whom those two were too much herself to be viewed so disinterestedly. Some detachment is indispensable for any glimpse of the underlying comedy of things, and detachment was more than she could arrive at in her view of a world in which she had endured and agonized. Charlotte Brontë detested Fielding; she could never see through the ironical nonchalance to his tender humanity. It is a wonder that she could put up with Thackeray's besetting levity, as well as his humour and satire. As to the repugnance which she felt towards Jane Austen, it has been well pointed out that she herself was too often a fit subject for that lady's raillery. Her failings in other respects were not unconnected with her lack of that alert eye for the grotesque which not only gives the positive delight of laughter, but also ensures sanity and proportion. Yet perhaps Charlotte Brontë had still more genius, certainly more intensity of genius, than either her predecessor, Jane Austen, or George Eliot, her successor.

Ernest A. Baker
The History of the English Novel, Vol. VIII
(London: Witherby, 1936), pp. 62-63

Aside from partial sterilization of banal Gothic by dry factuality and humor, Charlotte goes on to make a much more important—indeed, a radical— revision of the mode: in *Jane Eyre* and in the other novels . . . that discovery of passion, that rehabilitation of the extra-rational, which is the historical office of Gothic, is no longer oriented in marvelous circumstances but moves deeply into the lesser known realities of human life. This change I describe as the change from "old Gothic" to "new Gothic." The kind of appeal is the same; the fictional method is utterly different. . . . The first Gothic writers took the easy way: the excitement of mysterious scene and happening, which I call old Gothic. Of this Charlotte Brontë made some direct use, while at the same time tending toward humorous modifications (anti-Gothic); but what really counts is its indirect usefulness to her: it released her from the patterns of the novel of society and therefore permitted the flowering of her real talent—the talent for finding and giving dramatic form to impulses and feelings which, because of their depth or mysteriousness or intensity or ambiguity, or of their ignoring or transcending everyday norms of propriety or reason, increase wonderfully the sense of reality in the novel.

Robert B. Heilman
in *From Jane Austen to Joseph Conrad*, eds. R. C. Rathburn
and Martin Steinmann, Jr. (Minneapolis, Minn.: Univ. Minnesota
Pr., 1958), pp. 131-32

EMILY BRONTË

1814-1848

All the Brontës scribbled poetry secretly, and in 1845 Charlotte found and read Emily's manuscripts. To judge by her later emendations of her sister's poems, Charlotte never completely understood them any more than she understood Emily herself, but she at least realized in them the presence of an untrammeled, mystical lyricism which she knew neither she nor Anne possessed. The poems were intensely personal, and Emily was furious at having them read, but after much persuasion she agreed to let

Charlotte publish them. To Emily's poems Charlotte added some of her own and Anne's, and in May 1846 *Poems*, by Currer, Ellis, and Acton Bell (the pseudonyms they chose preserved their own initials) was published at the expense of the sisters. Only two copies were sold, and there were but three reviews of the little collection. After this each of the sisters began a novel. . . . Emily and Anne [were] successful in getting their first novels accepted, and in December, 1847, a joint book appeared, containing Anne's *Agnes Grey* and Emily's only novel, *Wuthering Heights*; neither work attracted much attention. . . . As inspiration in her masterpiece [*Wuthering Heights*], one of the great works of genius in English fiction, Emily drew equally on her own emotional, introverted nature and on the wild and mysterious moorland around her for the story of the passionate Cathy and her savage lover Heathcliff, whose love lasts through their lives and beyond their death and burial in the quiet churchyard on the moors. But *Jane Eyre* and the still greater *Wuthering Heights* brought to the novel an introspection and an intense concentration on the inner life of emotion which before them had been the province of poetry alone.

Thomas Marc Parrott and Robert Bernard Martin
A Companion to Victorian Literature (New York:
Scribner's, 1955), pp. 160-62

H. W. Garrod, ed., *Wuthering Heights* (1930)
C. W. Hatfield, ed., *Complete Poems of Emily Brontë* (1941)
Lawrence and E. M. Hanson, *The Four Brontës* (1949)

Wuthering Heights

It is futile to talk of *Wuthering Heights* as a literary model. Books like that are miracles incapable of repetition. It is a queer book—quite unlike anything we have seen or imagined. It is more than odd; it is entirely abnormal. . . . But an exceptional book like this, coming upon us unasked, stirs up our easy conventions. It seems to reveal new worlds in human nature; it strikes us dumb before the wonder and mystery of living. The writer who can achieve this has no call to justify her position in literature.

Marjorie Bald
Women-Writers of the Nineteenth Century
(Cambridge Univ. Pr., 1923), pp. 98-99

Emily Brontë's imagination is as intense as that of Dickens. Like him, she can sweep us with a stroke of the pen into a world more living than the one we know. But her achievement is more wonderful than that of Dickens. For her world was harder to vitalize. . . . Her genius is all fire and air: it can set the pulse of life throbbing in incredible vagaries of feeling: give the most aerial conception a local habitation and a name. . . . Style, structure, narrative, there is no aspect of Emily Brontë's craft which does not brilliantly exhibit her genius. The form of *Wuthering Heights* is as consummate as its subject is sublime. So far from being the incoherent outpourings of an undisciplined imagination, it is the one perfect work of art amid all the vast varied canvases of Victorian fiction.

David Cecil
Early Victorian Novelists (Indianapolis, Ind.:
Bobbs-Merrill, 1934), pp. 180, 202

Wuthering Heights does not, I think, provide the Aristotelian purgation of the emotions by pity and terror. Its stern story does not move us to these warm human emotions. Rather we feel raised to the level of somber grandeur and intensity which the book displays; we feel set free, it is true, in body, soul and spirit—but free not from ourselves, only to be more of whatever of grandeur our selves have to offer.

Phyllis Bentley
The Brontës (London: Barker, 1948), p. 102

The structure of *Wuthering Heights* is as different and unconventional as the theme. How could it be otherwise? New wine should not be poured into old bottles. Though there are superficial awkwardnesses and old-fashioned conventions in the point of view, this seems to be the inevitable way of telling such a story. The structure provides yet another analogy with Elizabethan drama, for it is consciously organized like a five-act tragedy, with breaks always indicated at the appropriate points. The method of telling the story, "in terms of autobiography thrice involved," as William Dean Howells said, is necessary for this structure. Mr. Lockwood, the relative nonentity who records the story as told to him by Ellen Dean, lives in the community only a few months before Heathcliff dies; yet representing, as he does, normal humanity, and experiencing enough of the confusion of Wuthering Heights to make him believe anything about these creatures, and being the audience before whom their past is unfolded, a past which is broken into segments by Ellen's or Mr. Lockwood's interruptions, he lends credibility to the events and serves as a curtain marking off the divisions of the story. . . .

As careful as she was in constructing the story, so meticulous was Emily Brontë in maintaining unity of place and tone. The reader never leaves the moors, once he has arrived there with Mr. Lockwood. He travels between Wuthering Heights and Thrushcross Grange; he sees the graves on the hillside and catches an occasional glimpse of Peniston Crag; he knows where the road to Gimmerton branches off from the road with which he is well acquainted, but never does he follow that road to the outer world. When Mr. Earnshaw travels to Liverpool, when Heathcliff disappears, when Isabella escapes, when Edgar goes to get Isabella's son, the reader remains on the moors, awaiting their return or news of their death. Wuthering Heights, Thrushcross Grange, and the rippling moors between—these are the physical bounds of the story. And so with the tone. No comic scenes or characters lighten the dramatic intensity of the action. Even Joseph is more ironic than comic, and Mr. Lockwood's occasional facetious comments are outside the action and have no influence upon it. Though incapable of understanding the book, Charlotte Brontë sensed the power attained through this unity: "Its power fills me with renewed admiration; but yet I am oppressed; the reader is scarcely ever permitted a taste of unalloyed pleasure; every beam of sunshine is poured down through black bars of threatening cloud; every page is surcharged with a sort of moral electricity."

Wuthering Heights is not the "work of immature genius," "awkwardly and illogically constructed," a study of "unnatural passion"; nor is it, I believe, the "one perfect work of art amid all the vast varied canvases of Victorian fiction." In theme and structure, however, it is the product of a mature artist who knew what effects she wished to achieve and possessed the ability to carry her scheme through to a logical and satisfying conclusion. Her theme of the relationship between love and hate is universal in its significance; her structure, if not unique in English fiction, is the ideal one for this story which could not be confined within the relatively narrow bounds of the drama.

Melvin R. Watson
Nineteenth-Century Fiction (September, 1949), pp. 95, 100

Emily Brontë's single novel is, of all English novels, the most treacherous for the analytical understanding to approach. It is treacherous not because of failure in its own formal controls on its meaning—for the book is highly wrought in form—but because it works at a level of experience that is unsympathetic to, or rather, simply irrelevant to the social and moral reason. One critic has spoken of the quality of feeling in this book as "a quality of suffering":

> It has anonymity. It is not complete. Perhaps some ballads represent it in English, but it seldom appears in the main stream, and few writers are in touch with it. It is a quality of experience the expression of which is at once an act of despair and an act of recognition or of worship. It is the recognition of an absolute hierarchy. This is also the feeling in Aeschylus. It is found amongst genuine peasants and is a great strength. Developing in places which yield only the permanent essentials of existence, it is undistracted and universal.

We feel the lack of "completeness," which this critic refers to, in the nature of the dramatic figures that Emily Brontë uses: they are figures that arise on and enact their drama on some ground of the psychic life where ethical ideas are not at home, at least such ethical ideas as those that inform our ordinary experience of the manners of men. They have the "anonymity" of figures in dreams or in religious ritual. The attitude toward life that they suggest is rather one of awed contemplation of an unregenerate universe than a feeling for values or disvalues in types of human intercourse. . . . Emily Brontë's book has been said to be nonphilosophical—as it is certainly non-ethical; but all philosophy is not ethics, and the book seizes, at the point where the soul feels itself cleft within and in cleavage from the universe, the first germs of philosophic thought, the thought of the duality of human and nonhuman existence, and the thought of the cognate duality of the psyche.

Dorothy Van Ghent
The English Novel: Form and Function
(New York: Holt, Rinehart, and Winston, 1953), pp. 153, 170

GENERAL

Emily Brontë's poetry, which is at once explicit and profound, with sense finely annealed to cadence, is the most essential poetry ever written by a woman in the English tongue. Her mind, far more daring than Charlotte's, soared above particular creeds and attained in a few momentary manifestations those universal forms of thought common only to minds of the first order. . . . *Wuthering Heights* remains, the towering rock of Charlotte's metaphor, extremely definite, completely achieved, and of an amazing unity of tone. . . . *Wuthering Heights*, with its unerring unity of conception and its full catharsis of the emotions of pity and terror, is one of the very few occasions on which the novel has reached the dignity of classical tragedy.

Herbert Read
Reason and Romanticism (London: Faber and Gwyer, 1926), pp. 180-81, 184

Emily may have had no more sense of form for form's sake than Charlotte; she may have no more dramatic instinct; but she had an instinct for the ways of human passion. She knew that passion runs its course, from its excitement to its climax and exhaustion. It has a natural beginning and a natural end. And so her scenes of passion follow nature. She never goes back on her effect, never urges passion past its climax, or stirs it in its exhaustion. In this she is a greater "realist" than Charlotte.

May Sinclair
The Three Brontës (London: Hutchinson, 1933), p. 231

As Maeterlinck finely put it, nothing ever happened to Emily Brontë, and yet everything happened. "It was as if everything happened to her more personally and more profoundly than to others, for everything that she perceived or heard of was transformed into thoughts and feelings, into compassionate love, into admiration, into adoration of life. . . ." Emily has suffered from the cranks and monomaniacs as much as Charlotte from the philistines. Better to admit that she was not as other women are, and by patiently weighing what she said in verse or prose try to fathom her meaning. If her ideas are often remote, nothing could be more lucid than her language. Careful analysis and comparison of her famous story and her poetry, especially by those whose interests have given them a sympathetic understanding of the visionary flights in both, are likely to be the most effective method of interpreting Emily Brontë. For it is obvious that she was a mystic; not deeply versed in mystical lore, but a mystic by natural disposition. She was one of those to whose rapt gaze the world about them seems to melt away and give place to the deeper realities of the world beyond.

Ernest A. Baker
The History of the English Novel, Vol. VIII
(London: Witherby, 1936), pp. 66-67

Emily remains a subjective artist; and her six crowning poems ["There let thy bleeding branch atone," "Cold in the earth," "Death," "Julian M. and A. G. Rochelle," "No coward soul is mine," "Often rebuked, yet always back returning"] mark the very peak in English of the subjective poetical philosophy of life. But when she tries to dramatize and *socialize* this private vision by the creation of characters, the narrowness of her perception is made clear. It is for this reason that the *Gondal* cycle, like the story of *Wuthering Heights*, reveals certain discrepancies of theme and certain unrealities of human behavior. Like Nietzsche, whom she much resembled and whom in her fierceness of thought she anticipated, Emily was unable to realize the implications of her ideas within the context of a traditional society. It is always man alone that she sings and celebrates, or man in the single relationships of passion. But when she begins to imagine all those other contacts and responsibilities which the human person forms in passing through society, her writing is often immature and melodramatic. The shadow of the misanthropist Byron invalidates her thought even at that distance. . . . But what she achieved—what still remains positive—is something of no insubstantial order. Through her six great poems she must be considered as one of our major poets, while a larger number of other pieces reveal her as an interesting minor poet. As to *Wuthering Heights*—even though one may not assent to the judgment that pronounces it a flawless work of fiction—to have conceived the bare idea of it, the notion of a novel that should be poetic through its symbolic drama, rather than through any verbal graces—this itself is an innovation and an act of faith so unusual in the mundane art of novel-writing that its example will intrigue and fascinate us always.

Derek Stanford
Emily Brontë, Part II (London: Peter Owen, 1953), pp. 270-71

ELIZABETH BARRETT BROWNING
1806-1861

Until some time after she married Robert Browning, Elizabeth Barrett was much better known and more highly regarded as a poet than her husband. A semi-invalid in her dominating father's London household, she read widely and wrote the *Essay on Mind, with Other Poems* (1826), a translation of *Prometheus Bound* (1833), *The Seraphim and Other Poems* (1838), and a slim volume entitled simply *Poems* (1844). Her verse was admired by the younger poet with whom she escaped to Italy after their marriage in 1846. As Mrs. Browning she published *Sonnets from the Portugese*, love poems addressed to her husband and now her best-known work (1850); *Casa Guidi Windows*, named for the Brownings' house in Florence and inspired by the Italian struggle for national independence (1851); *Poems before Congress* (1860); her most ambitious work, *Aurora Leigh* (1857); and *Last Poems* (1862).

Oxford Standard Authors *Poetical Works of Elizabeth Barrett Browning* (1904)
Gardner B. Taplin, *The Life of Elizabeth Barrett Browning* (1957)

Browning's worship of his wife's memory ought not to influence our estimate of Elizabeth Barrett Browning as a poetess. Strangely enough, or perhaps not strangely, when one considers the nature of popular taste, Mrs. Browning's reputation as a poet during her lifetime was much greater than her husband's. Not until after her death, when he left Florence and settled in London, was he known to a wide public in England. Her reputation, however, has persisted, less for the intrinsic merits of her poetry than for the romance of her marriage, and the reverence, touching upon idolatry, in which her memory was enshrined by her husband.

Irene Cooper Willis
Elizabeth Barrett Browning (London: Gerald Howe, 1928), p. 96

Today the world's main interest in Elizabeth Barrett Browning lies in her love story and her eloquent, lively letters: as poet she now ranks well below her husband. But in her own time, and for many years after, this was not so. The world agreed with Browning in placing her higher than himself. Then, for some forty years or more, her reputation was low. It is probable that we of this generation value her with more accuracy; admitting that a lack of sustained strength is, to an appreciable extent, atoned for by the sensitive quality of her writing. Indeed, a modern poet and critic, whose judgment most of us place very high in poetic perception, has gone so far as to assert —at least in private—that Mrs. Browning is a "finer" poet than her husband. Her handicap was, he considers—a handicap particularly exemplified in *Aurora Leigh*—an experience comparatively narrow.

Dorothy Hewlett
Elizabeth Barrett Browning (London: Cassell, 1953), p. xiii

Probably Elizabeth Barrett Browning's poetry will never again be loved by a great many. . . .

But it is worth a greater effort to tune in than most readers now make. Literary historians might turn their attention to Mrs. Browning's technical experiments in versification, which time has not only justified but proved extremely influential. Biographers, on the other hand, might give her private life a rest. Ordinary readers who read for pleasure might discover some odd delights. Mrs. Browning's poetry is often wilful and sometimes very silly, at times inelegant, at times grotesquely violent; the dramatic action is always weakly sustained, and the unity of the whole is defective. But she had strong powers of heart and mind: a force of emotion so great as to make many poets of higher fame look namby-pamby by comparison; a hard-hitting wit, a brilliant originality, great technical invention and audacity, a towering imagination and an associative faculty so nimble that it leaps over the gaps left by her incoherent construction. And behind all these was a consciousness spreading further than human life and human time, a range of sympathy from the chaffinch to the cherubim.

Alethea Hayter
Mrs. Browning (London: Faber and Faber, 1962), pp. 244-45

ROBERT BROWNING
1812-1889

Born in South London and educated privately, Browning inherited his father's love of painting and music as well as poetry. His first ambitious poem, *Pauline,* was published anonymously in 1833, and was followed, after the poet had spent two years travelling in Europe, by *Paracelsus* (1835); a tragedy he wrote for the actor Macready, *Strafford* (1837); and the difficult long poem *Sordello* (1840). Browning's earliest verse was marked by extremely personal subject matter—partly the result of Shelley's influence—and idiosyncratic style; but with the poems of *Bells and Pomegranates* (collected in 1846), he began to write in the dramatic form for which he was to become best known. Although *Christmas Eve and Easter Day* (1850) sees religion from the poet's own point of view, the volumes of *Men and Women* (1855) and *Dramatis Personae* (1864) consist of dramatic monologues, and the long poem generally considered Browning's masterpiece, *The Ring and the Book* (1868-1869), tells its story of violence and death mostly in such monologues. The Italian setting in this work shows Browning's interest in the country to which he had moved upon his marriage to Elizabeth Barrett in 1846. Possibly the subject of a delicate woman's escape from tyranny and a prison-like home reflects, as well, the personal experience of Mrs. Browning's elopement with the poet. Later volumes of poetry are *Balaustion's Adventure* (1871), *Prince Hohenstiel-Schwangau* (1871), *Fifine at the Fair* (1872), *Red Cotton Nightcap Country* (1873), *Aristophanes' Apology* (1875), *The Inn Album* (1875), *Pacchiarotto, and How He Worked in Distemper; with other Poems*

(1876), *La Saisiaz* (1878), two series of *Dramatic Idyls* (1879 and 1880), *Jocoseria* (1883), *Ferishtah's Fancies* (1884), *Parleyings with Certain People of Importance in their Day* (1887), and *Asolando* (1889). After his wife's death in 1861, Browning returned to England with their son. He came to be regarded, in the last twenty years of his life, as one of the foremost English poets, second in reputation only to Tennyson among his contemporaries.

F. G. Kenyon, ed., *Works of Robert Browning* (1912), 10 vols.
H. W. Griffin and H. C. Minchin, *The Life of Browning* (1910)
William C DeVane, *A Browning Handbook* (1935)

Personal

We may come to think of him as a poet who struggled bravely to gain an insight into the hidden soul of things—fought his way towards a light that by turns eluded and blinded him. And, meanwhile, what a world he created may some day be again revealed even to the most intelligent of us—its colour, its abundance of life, its palpitating vigour, its movement that goes glorying in its own rapidity and strength. When we look below outward things in that world, we may come to see some of our own troubles and pleasures, our own most modern doubts and certainties, faithfully mirrored or forecast with a marvelous accuracy.

F. R. G. Duckworth
Browning: Background and Conflict (New York:
E. P. Dutton, 1932), p. 213

In the course of his long career as a poet he had suffered more than most poets from the excesses of both contumely and laudation. He triumphed over both at last, but not before the laudation had done damage to the quality of his poetic achievement. To his later contemporaries his poetry and his presence had become the very symbols of heartiness, courage, and faith. Some of his spirit has lingered to us who live in a disenchanted world. Yet the critics of our own day are inclined to disregard much of what Browning says, and to fasten intently upon how he says it. He is now seen to have been a pioneer and a revolutionist in the art of the new psychological poetry, a century before his time; and this aspect, at least, of his present fame would have delighted Robert Browning.

William Clyde DeVane
A Browning Handbook, 2nd Ed. (New York: Appleton-
Century-Crofts, 1955), p. 38

Men and Women

Probably the very qualities which led to the formation of Browning societies in his lifetime—his interest in abstract problems, his discussion of the thoughts which were agitating his own generation—will tell against him in another age, concerned with other problems of its own, and his poetry will never live by virtue of sheer intrinsic beauty, like the poetry of Shelley or Keats, but insight into character must surely have its value in any age, and if in years to come men relegate *Paracelsus* and *Sordello* to the topmost shelves of their libraries, it is difficult to believe that they will ever impoverish themselves by forgetting . . . Fra Lippo Lippi, and Bishop Blougram, and all the rest of Browning's noble portrait gallery of *Men and Women*.

G. E. Hadow
Introd. in *Browning's Men and Women*
(Oxford Univ. Pr., 1911), p. xxii

What, one would . . . like to know, did Elizabeth think of the fact, curious enough in all conscience, that of the fifteen poems in *Men and Women* whose inspiration may be attributed to the married life of the poet, twelve at least portray love frustrated or incomplete? For even *The Guardian Angel* has its sediment of dissatisfaction; and as for the remarkable *Love Among the Ruins* (written in Paris the day after *Childe Roland*), it is only on a vast substructure of pride and ambition overthrown that unity in love is therein achieved. Alone amongst these poems, *By the Fireside* offers us a glimpse of that tranquil and impassioned harmony which might seem to be the inevitable sequel to the love letters: and it may have been a wish to redress, belatedly, the balance of so unexpected a reckoning that caused Robert Browning, a bare ten days before the books were finally printed, to add the laboured poem *One Word More* which appears there as epilogue and dedication to E. B. B.

Betty Miller
Robert Browning (London: John Murray, 1952), p. 201

The Ring and the Book

This, I repeat, is the excellence of Browning's genius—fulness of creative power, with imagination in it like a fire. It does not follow that all it produces is poetry; and what it has produced in *The Ring and the Book* is sometimes, save for the meter, nothing better than prose. But this is redeemed by the noble poetry of a great part of it. The book is, as I have said, a mixed book—the central arena of that struggle in Browning between prose and poetry. . . .

Stopford Brooke
The Poetry of Robert Browning
(New York: Crowell, 1902), p. 413

The Ring and the Book is a great receptacle into which Browning poured, with an affluence that perhaps is excessive, all his powers—his searching for truth, his passion, his casuistry, his feeling for beauty, his tenderness, his gift of pity, his veiled memories of what was most precious in his past, his hopes for the future, his wordly knowledge, his unwordly aspirations, his humor, such as it was, robust rather than delicate.

Edward Dowden
Robert Browning (London: Dent, 1904), p. 267

The Ring and the Book is at once the largest and the greatest of Browning's works, the culmination of his dramatic method, and the turning-point . . . of his style.

Arthur Symons
An Introduction to the Study of Browning, rev. Ed.
(London: Dent, 1906), p. 150

If on such an occasion as this—even with our natural impulse to shake ourselves free of reserves—some sharp choice between the dozen different aspects of one of the most copious of our poets becomes a prime necessity, though remaining at the same time a great difficulty, so in respect to the most voluminous of his works the admirer is promptly held up, as we have come to call it; finds himself almost baffled by alternatives. *The Ring and the Book* is so vast and so essentially gothic a structure, spreading and soaring and branching at such a rate, covering such ground, putting forth such pinnacles and towers and brave excrescences, planting its transepts and chapels and porticos, its clustered hugeness or inordinate muchness, that with any first approach we but walk vaguely and slowly, rather bewilderedly, round and round it, wondering at what point we had best attempt such entrance as will save our steps and light our uncertainty, most enable us to reach our personal chair, our indicated chapel or shrine, when once within. For it is to be granted that to this inner view the likeness of the literary monument to one of the great religious gives way a little, sustains itelf less than in the first, the affronting mass; unless we simply figure ourselves, under the great roof, looking about us through a splendid thickness and dimness of air, an accumulation of spiritual presences or unprofaned mysteries, that makes our impression heavily general—general only—and leaves us helpless for reporting on particulars. The particulars for our purpose have thus their identity much rather in certain features of the twenty faces—either of one or of another of these—that the structure turns to the outer day and that we can, as it were, sit down before and consider at our comparative ease. . . . There are innumerable things in *The Ring and the Book*—as the comprehensive image I began with makes it needless I should say; and I have been above all appealed to by the possibility that one of these, pursued for a while through the labyrinth, but at last overtaken and then more or less confessing its identity, might have yielded up its best essence as a grateful theme under some fine strong economy of *prose* treatment.

Henry James
Notes on Novelists (New York: Scribner's, 1914), pp. 385-86

Browning's "central meaning," it seems clear, was his vision of humanity (which is at the same time a vision of Spirit at work in the world) as he presents it most directly in Book III of *Sordello* and in the *Epilogue* to *Dramatis Personae*. He restates the idea, though in less direct terms, in introducing his masterpiece, *The Ring and the Book*. . . . Here again he is speaking in his own person. He might have chosen to tell the story simply and from his own point of view, he says, "Landscaping what I saved, not what I saw. . . ." Instead, he prefers to work as a "Maker-see," causing us to witness the event and draw our own conclusions.

Donald Smalley, ed.
Introd. in *Poems of Robert Browning* (Boston:
Hougton Mifflin, 1956), p. xxii

It is certainly a valid criticism of *The Ring and the Book* that good and evil are not sufficiently interfused. Our judgment is forced from the beginning, whereas it would seem to be peculiarly the genius of a poem treating different points of view toward the same story to treat each point of view impartially, allowing judgment to arise out of the utmost ambiguity.

But such a criticism raises the question whether facts really can speak for themselves; whether a poet can, with the mere accumulation of prosaic details and a workable middle style seldom rising to passages which can in themselves be called poetry, achieve the high transcendental meaning Browning wanted. For he wanted nothing less than to portray in Pompilia the most exalted saintliness (Dante's Beatrice was not, I should imagine, beyond his mark), revealing itself amid and by means of the ordinarily vicious human motives and judgments. The poetry, the total illumination, lies in the dynamism of the whole scheme, really in the backward glance, the reader's sense of having come a long way.

However we measure Browning's achievement, his aim—to make poetry rise out of prose and spirituality out of the world's common clay, to meet in other words the conditions for modern intellectual and moral conviction as Tennyson in the *Idylls*, Arnold in *Sohrab* and Morris in *Sigurd* do not— would have to be the aim, I should think, of any genuinely modern literature. If his method seems to pertain more closely to the novel than to poetry, so much the better for my point.

Robert Langbaum
The Poetry of Experience (New York:
Random House, 1957), p. 135

GENERAL

[Browning's] method is, to penetrate by sympathy rather than to portray by intelligence. The most authoritative insight is not the poet's or the spectator's, aroused and enlightened by the spectacle, but the various heroes' own, in their moment of intensest passion. We therefore miss the tragic relief and exaltation, and come away instead with the uncomfortable feeling that an obstinate folly is apparently the most glorious and choiceworthy thing in the world. This is evidently the poet's own illusion, and those who do not happen to share it must feel that if life were really as irrational as he thinks it, it would be not only profoundly discouraging, which it often is, but profoundly disgusting, which it surely is not; for at least it reveals the ideal which it fails to attain.

This ideal Browning never disentangles. For him the crude experience is the only end, the endless struggle the only ideal, and the perturbed "Soul" the only organon of truth. The arrest of his intelligence at this point, before it has envisaged any rational object, explains the arrest of his dramatic art at soliloquy. His immersion in the forms of self-consciousness prevents him from dramatizing the real relations of men and their thinkings to one another, to Nature, and to destiny. For in order to do so he would have had to view his characters from above (as Cervantes did, for instance), and to see them not merely as they appeared to themselves, but as they appear to reason. This higher attitude, however, was not only beyond Browning's scope, it was positively contrary to his inspiration. Had he reached it, he would no longer have seen the universe through the "Soul," but through the intellect, and he would not have been able to cry, "How the world is made for each one of us!" On the contrary, the "Soul" would have figured only in its true conditions, in all its ignorance and dependence, and also in its essential teachableness, a point against which Browning's barbaric wilfulness particularly rebelled. Rooted in his persuasion that the soul is essentially omnipotent and that to live hard can never be to live wrong, he remained fascinated by the march and method of self-consciousness, and never allowed himself to be weaned from that romantic fatuity by the energy of rational imagination, which prompts us not to regard our ideas as mere filling of a dream, but rather to build on them the conception of permanent objects and overruling principles, such as Nature, society, and the other ideals of reason. A full-grown imagination deals with these things, which do not obey the laws of psychological progression, and cannot be described by the methods of soliloquy.

We thus see that Browning's sphere, though more subtle and complex than Whitman's, was still elementary. It lay far below the spheres of social and historical reality in which Shakespeare moved; far below the comprehensive and cosmic sphere of every great epic poet. Browning did not even reach the intellectual plane of such contemporary poets as Tennyson and Matthew Arnold, who, whatever may be thought of their powers, did not study consciousness for itself, but for the sake of its meaning and of the objects which it revealed. The best things that come into a man's consciousness are the things that take him out of it—the rational things that are independent of his personal perception and of his personal existence. These he approaches with his reason, and they, in the same measure, endow him with their immortality. But precisely these things—the objects of science and of the constructive imagination—Browning always saw askance, in the outskirts of his field of vision, for his eye was fixed and riveted on the soliloquizing Soul. And this Soul being, to his apprehension, irrational, did not give itself over to those permanent objects which might otherwise have occupied it, but ruminated on its own accidental emotions, on its love-affairs, and on its hopes of going on so ruminating for ever.

The pathology of the human mind—for the normal, too, is pathological when it is not referred to the ideal—the pathology of the human mind is a very interesting subject, demanding great gifts and great ingenuity in its treatment. Browning ministers to this interest, and possesses this ingenuity and these gifts. More than any other poet he keeps a kind of speculation alive in the now large body of sentimental, eager-minded people, who no longer can find in a definite religion a form and language for their imaginative life. That this service is greatly appreciated speaks well for the ineradicable tendency in man to study himself and his destiny. We do not deny the achievement when we point out its nature and limitations. It does not cease to be something because it is taken to be more than it is.

George Santayana
Interpretations of Poetry and Religion
(New York: Scribner's, 1900), pp. 211-14

One of the very few critics who seem to have got near to the actual secret of Browning's optimism is Mr. Santayana in his most interesting book *Interpretations of Poetry and Religion*. He, in contradistinction to the vast mass of Browning's admirers, had discovered what was the real root virtue of Browning's poetry; and the curious thing is, that having discovered that root virtue, he thinks it is a vice. He describes the poetry of Browning most truly as the poetry of barbarism, by which he means the poetry which utters the primeval and indivisible emotions. "For the barbarian is the man who regards his passions as their own excuse for being, who does not domesticate them either by understanding their cause, or by conceiving their ideal goal." Whether this be or be not a good definition of the barbarian, it is an excellent and perfect definition of the poet. It might, perhaps, be suggested that bar-

barians, as a matter of fact, are generally highly traditional and respectable persons who would not put a feather wrong in their head-gear, and who generally have very few feelings and think very little about those they have. It is when we have grown to a greater and more civilised stature that we begin to realise and put to ourselves intellectually the great feelings that sleep in the depths of us. Thus it is that the literature of our day has steadily advanced towards a passionate simplicity, and we become more primeval as the world grows older, until Whitman writes huge and chaotic psalms to express the sensations of a schoolboy out fishing, and Maeterlinck embodies in symbolic dramas the feelings of a child in the dark.

Thus, Mr. Santayana is, perhaps, the most valuable of all the Browning critics. He has gone out of his way to endeavour to realise what it is that repels him in Browning, and he has discovered the fault which none of Browning's opponents have discovered. And in this he has discovered the merit which none of Browning's admirers have discovered. Whether the quality be a good or a bad quality, Mr. Santayana is perfectly right. The whole of Browning's poetry does rest upon primitive feeling; and the only comment to be added is that so does the whole of every one else's poetry.

G. K. Chesterton
Robert Browning (New York: Macmillan, 1903), pp. 184-85

Between *Dichtung* and *Wahrheit* there was, indeed, in Browning's mind, a [close] affinity. . . . His imagination was a factor in his apprehension of truth; his "poetry" cannot be detached from his interpretation of life, nor his interpretation of life from his poetry. Not that all parts of his apparent teaching belong equally to his poetic mind. On the contrary, much of it was derived from traditions of which he never shook himself clear; much from the exercise of a speculative reason which, though incomparably agile, was neither well disciplined in its methods nor particularly original in its grasp of principles. But with the vitalising heart of his faith neither tradition not reasoning had so much to do as that logic of the imagination by which great poets often implicitly enunciate what the after-thinker slowly works out. The characteristic ways of Browning's poetry, the fundamental joys on which it fed by no means define the range or the limits of his interpreting intellect, but they mark the course of its deepest currents, the permanent channels which its tides overflow, but to which in the last resort they return.

C. H. Herford
Robert Browning (New York: Dodd, Mead, 1905), p. 282

With the exception of Shakespeare, any other English poet could now be spared more easily than Browning. For, owing to his aim in poetry, and his success in attaining it, he gives us much vital truth and beauty that we should seek elsewhere in vain; as he said in the *Epilogue* to *Pacchiarotto*, the strong, heady wine of his verse may become sweet in process of time.

William Lyon Phelps
Robert Browning: How to Know Him (Indianapolis, Ind.:
Bobbs-Merrill, 1915), p. 70

What a creature of contradictions he seems to-day to look back on!—a poet who now sings like an angel, now talks like poor Poll; who could write magnificent dramatic monologues, and yet dramas (like *A Blot in the 'Scutcheon*) that maunder beyond belief; whose psychology is at once so subtle and so superficial; who bared his soul to the world in a hundred transparent disguises and yet denounced, with a peck at Shakespeare, the mere notion that he could unlock his heart; who garbed himself in eccentricity, and yet fled at first sight from the coasts of Bohemia. One doubts at times his claim to be called a poet at all. Why did he not write in prose?

> Blown harshly keeps the trump its golden cry?
> Tastes sweet the water with such specks of earth?

Often, alas, it does not; but we can separate good from bad. Indeed we must. And, after all, to the author of things like *The Lost Mistress, Love among the Ruins, A Toccata of Galuppi's, Porphyria's Lover, Childe Roland*, and *St. Martin's Summer*, much may be forgiven, even his complete works.

F. L. Lucas
Eight Victorian Poets (Cambridge Univ. Pr., 1930), p. 37

Above all, Browning recognized modern scepticism. He places no reliance on creeds which pass all understanding or faiths founded on the miraculous. He trusts God only as far as his own eyes and intuitions. He was an old man when Renan noticed that such was the tendency of nineteenth-century thought and feared that we should have to return to credulity or lose our ideals. "Je le dis franchement, je ne me figure pas comment on rabâtira, sans les anciens rêves, les assises d'une vie noble et heureuse." The English poet had no such fears. Altogether, one might have expected that Browning would become the hero of the iconoclasts.

At one time, it looked as if he would attain to that "bad eminence." In 1865, even before he had published his "murder poem," he learns from Chapman and Hall that the young men are inquiring for his books, some of which had languished almost unread for a quarter of a century. In 1867 young Oxford proposed him as Matthew Arnold's successor to the professorship of poetry, and in order that he might be qualified, the older men granted him an M.A. by diploma (26 June). In October 1868 Balliol made him an honorary fellow. In 1871 he was offered the Lord Rectorship of

Glasgow University. In 1877 *The Inn Album* was translated into German. In June 1879 Cambridge conferred on the poet a D.C.L. In 1881 F. J. Furnivall founded the Browning Society and its publications so far stimulated the book-lovers' interest, that people paid enormous prices for the original volumes which he had printed at private expense and given away. In 1887 W. G. Kingsland published *Robert Browning, Chief Poet of the Age.* So it would seem that at last we have found one of the pioneers of the twentieth century.

Yet such a conclusion is very questionable. It will be noticed that the more adventurous admirers then and now who might have relished his unconventionality and introspection, do not cultivate his optimism nor his learned sympathies. Even *The Ring and the Book* was more discussed than read, and more read than imitated. Besides, there is something unsubstantial about the homage which Browning enjoyed, but by which he was not deceived. He seems to have realised that his reputation was founded on what one might call the discipleship of a cult. Outside a small group of kindred spirits, he was a household name only to those who subscribed to the Browning Society, or considered themselves superior to the critical powers of the common herd. He was so sensitive to this estrangement that he refused the most advantageous invitations to publish in magazines; because he would thus obtrude his poems on the adventitious reader. Nor was he deceived by the university honours, which he accepted with reluctance. They were a tardy recognition of his erudition, industry and high moral tone. In fact his life was more a source of interest than of inspiration.

Why had he lost touch with the deeper, more spiritual influences which shape the thoughts of the future? There are several answers and they will help us to realise the delicacy and elusiveness of literary adjustments. In the first place, as he grew older, his literary indiscretions became more and more unpardonable. In 1845 his intimate friend, Carlyle, had the foresight as well as insight to give "that prodigious advice of his, to write your next work in prose." In later life Browning did sometimes so draft his monologues, but he could not resist turning them into verse because, even to the end, he was blessed with a genius for flashing out into occasional phrases of sublimely vivid poetry. But, unlike Tennyson, he was not blessed with a talent of self-criticism, and some of his lines are more prosaic than *Paradise Lost* at its pamphleteering worst, and some of his rhymes out-Ingoldsby Ingoldsby. H. H. Hatcher claims that less than one out of every hundred of his 34,746 rhymes is unusual; yet the peccant examples quoted by his apologist are unforgettable. His freakishness lacks a sense of humour, and that defect is always remembered against a writer.

H. V. Routh
Towards the Twentieth Century
(New York: Macmillan, 1937), pp. 110-11

In the sixty years that have passed since Browning's death, his poetic reputation has varied as widely as in his lifetime. The pendulum of critical opinion has again swung violently from one extreme to the other. In particular, Browning has suffered, along with Tennyson, from the general reaction to Victorianism and all its works which has characterized the opening decades of the twentieth century. There are signs that the nadir has been reached, and that a juster and truer appreciation of the Victorian epoch is at hand. But we are still in the wake of that inevitable shift of literary evaluation which marks the transition from one generation to the next. . . .

Though we must look to the future for an impartial evaluation of Victorian literature, it is evident that Browning, with the possible exception of Carlyle, had a more robust and sinewy mind than any of his contemporaries. He is a great humanist; and however deeply and broadly he quarries in the mine of the thoughts and emotions of men and women, the vein never runs thin, though it may lead at times through tortuous tunnels. The horizons of an intellect of such power and fertility are vast; and linked with this amplitude is the gift of communicating the joy and tingle of his contact with life. In this respect he allies himself with Chaucer, Fielding, and Scott. Like theirs his interest in humanity is unflagging, and while he does not maintain their objectivity of representation, he probes deeper than any of his forerunners into the inner springs of character.

William O. Raymond
The Infinite Moment and Other Essays in Robert Browning
(Toronto: Univ. Toronto Pr., 1950), pp. 3, 17

He was, to use his own definition, an objective poet where Shelley was a subjective one. As such his appeal was to the aggregate human mind and his concern with the doings of men. So, though unsuccessful as a playwright, he was, primarily and always the poet of the dramatic situation, and a "fashioner" before he was a "seer." Shelley took only from nature what struck out most abundantly and uninterruptedly his inner light and power. Browning took much more, but not, in parnassian fashion, merely for the sake of the men and scenes and cities he described. He viewed nature and humanity with ceaseless curiosity and sympathy, trying over in his poetry ever fresh combinations of character and landscape, but always with the view of discovering some secret that lay behind them. Had he pursued the course on which he embarked in *Pauline* he would have continued to lay bare his own heart in the hope of discovering the secret there; had he pursued the false trail struck in "Christmas Eve" he would have ceaselessly argued about the ultimate nature of experience and lost his clue in a welter of mere ratiocination. As it was he embodied ever and again in fresh poetry his flashes of comprehension concerning the relations of the trinity, Love, Knowledge and Faith, which came thickest in his early maturity, but which did not desert him in his long years of outwardly barren living, and which returned with renewed strength in the years immediately before his death. Browning had indeed a philosophical message, though not one of the kind the Browning Society was looking for. The secret, he tells us again and again, is to be found in man's experience, not in abstraction but in the welter and richness, in the violence and colour, in the love and beauty of the world itself.

J. M. Cohen
Robert Browning (London: Longmans, Green, 1952), p. 193

Browning . . . asserted that intuition is the ultimate means of knowledge, and that the faculty which enables the artist to approach truth is imaginative insight. In his own case these faculties operated most successfully through a form of dramatic perception in which the fact and its ulterior meaning become fused into unity by a single act of apprehension. But with the decline of dramatic sensibility in his later work, fact and meaning draw apart, so that he depends increasingly on the rationalizing intellect to set up correspondence between them. Whether the successes of his middle period are attributable to the glow of emotional maturity, or to the perfecting of a suitable form, or to both, it is only in the poems of these years (and perhaps occasionally in the Indian summer of *Asolando*) that we find the inner and outer consciousness held in equipoise. In the later poetry as in the early efforts, the split in awareness is manifest.

E. D. H. Johnson
The Alien Vision of Victorian Poetry (Princeton, N. J.:
Princeton Univ. Pr., 1952), p. 143

There may be gaps in the statement that Browning was no artist, but it remains basically true. And he was not a poet of vision. His eyes, calm as Elizabeth found them, are not those of a visionary. He saw what the common man sees. He saw it a thousand times more vividly, and presented it with unparalleled richness and warmth, but the world so presented is still the world in which we spend our sensual days. Here and there he passes beyond —to a vision of the creative process in *Paracelsus*, of the love of Christ in *Saul* and *Christmas-Eve*, of courage confronting evil in *Childe Roland*. But it is much more than "the cloudy border of his base" that Browning "spares to the foiled searchings of mortality." Only in the one great exceptional region does he out-top knowledge—in love and the radiant spirit of woman: in Balaustion and Pippa, Pompilia and Caponsacchi, and in the great love-lyrics, where also he sometimes brings about a miracle of art. Love was to Browning what nature was to Wordsworth and the heavenly vision to the mystic poets. It is only in his love poetry that his philosophy achieves its full significance, and it is no accident that it occasionally does so through the medium of a perfect art-form.

For genius, the indefinable—Browning certainly had it. He was possibly the greatest genius who wrote mainly within the Victorian period. But he was born with an unspecialized genius, one that had to be directed into the field of poetry. Such unspecialized genius is undoubtedly a force of nature, with all its characteristics of creativeness, fecundity, grotesqueness, imperfection. This accounts too for Browning being, even within the chosen region, a little uncertain as to his own essential quality, whether he were land-animal or sea-animal: I have called him amphibian with special reference to a number of his poems, but the label has some significance as a description of his literary tendencies.

What have we then? A huge formless genius, a limited art, unchallenged supremacy in love poetry. There is one final thing to say about him. He was the first and greatest of the modern poets. Now this is a different kind of statement from the last one. It does not make him a poet at all. The stream of "poetry" runs continuously on in its deep changeless traditional course through Tennyson, Arnold, the Rossettis, Swinburne, Meredith, Yeats, Thompson, Alice Meynell, Bridges, de la Mare, Davies, Flecker, Brooke, Belloc, Chesterton, Gould, Graves, Nichols, Hodgson, Thomas, Frost, Masefield, Wolfe, Roy Campbell, Andrew Young. But Browning broke violently through the banks of this stream, and started a new line of advance. It led through Hopkins, Hardy, Housman, the later Yeats, Owen, Eliot, Palmer, Muir, Edith Sitwell, Richard Church, Ruth Pitter, Auden, Spender, Day Lewis, MacNeice, and others too numerous to mention. It has produced, notably in Hardy, Eliot and Church, work of great interest and importance. But generally it dispenses with form, relying on epigram; it neglects the audience, and rejoices in eccentricity: as a line of advance it cannot continue to offer an alternative to traditional poetry; indeed it now shows signs of disappearing into the sand. To vary the metaphor, just as Browning was an excrescence on the tree of nineteenth-century poetry, so "modern poetry" is an excrescence on the age-old tree of literature. Some of it has a vitality of its own, and may live on, but the greater part of the gnarled mass will wither and die. So of Browning: more of him will die than of other poets. But enough of him will remain to remind the world that he was, somehow, after all, one of the chief glories of a very great period of English literature.

Henry Charles Dufferin
Amphibian (London: Bowes and Bowes, 1957), pp. 304-6

His romanticism, then, was too much for his Christianity, but his psychic insecurity, combined with the pressure of the Victorian compromise, was too much for his romanticism. Perhaps, however, he owed his success as a nineteenth-century prophet to his ability to combine the *Andrea del Sarto* and *Pisgah-Sights* themes in a single gospel of vigorous inactivity. By means of the former he satisfied the Victorian desire for earnest moral effort, confident vitality, progress, service, muscular drive toward "ideals." By means of the latter he soothed the Victorian dread of any really fundamental change. There was a ringing challenge to be up and doing—with no danger of disturbing the constituted order. As if they were riding a mechanical horse in a gymnasium, his disciples could enjoy plenty of virile exercise without the disquietude of going anywhere in particular.

Hoxie N. Fairchild
Religious Trends in English Poetry, Vol. IV
(New York: Columbia Univ. Pr., 1957), p. 166

He rarely attains the tragic vision; he does not succeed in creating the serene character; he is unable to communicate religious truth mystically ("Saul," for example). It might be said that he descends with Dante into hell, achieves purgatory, but never quite attains paradise.

When these shortcomings are acknowledged, however, there is yet much to justify calling him a major poet. In his work there is range, depth, intensity, irony, paradox, wit, whimsy, and humor. He grasped sympathetically and penetratingly numerous points of view extending from skepticism ("Fear and Scruples") to cautious affirmation ("Fra Lippo Lippi"). His characters range in complexity from the naïve simplicity of Pippa to the sophisticated subtlety of Bishop Blougram. He treats love as mere lust in Ottima; and in Pompilia, although he never achieves the etherealized vision of Dante's Beatrice, he approaches it. The objectivity, hence the honesty, with which he dramatizes ideas and emotions within his scope, gives him breadth of appeal and provides a vision of life that should remain meaningful. It would be difficult to find in the nineteenth century a more comprehensive and penetrating poet. . . .

Browning's ability to maintain a consistency of tone in poems so different as "Bishop Blougram's Apology" and "Andrea del Sarto" is a psychological and artistic achievement. Sometimes one device becomes the chief, though never the only, means of drawing a poem together. In "Andrea del Sarto," symbol, precisely formulated and carefully controlled, is particuarly effective. Both "Fra Lippo Lippi' and "Bishop Blougram's Apology" are unified by the coherency of an argument, which, characteristic of Browning's casuistic poems, serves purposes other than argumentative. Argument provokes character revelation and stimulates emotional reaction. In "Bishop Blougram's Apology" it serves as a dialectical drama which brings the poem into oneness. Browning's most characteristic and effective unifying device is irony. More than any other, it creates the tension found in all his best monologues. Particularly adapted to treating both conflict and multiple vision, it permits Browning to achieve unity without sacrificing his artistic detachment. Irony gives his work objectivity, complexity, intellectuality, intensity, seriousness, and humor, placing him in the "wit" rather than the "soul" tradition.

Browning's poetry as a whole is of uneven value. Much in the seventeen volumes which he wrote need not be salvaged, nor indeed, preserved. A considerable portion may be prized, not for its "philosophy" as the Browning societies would have it, but for its effectiveness in communicating a significant vision of life in a structure capable of stimulating diverse aesthetic responses. Browning's scope, intensity, and vividness assure his being read long after his early devotees have found other and more exciting inspiration for their "positive thinking."

Roma A. King
The Bow and the Lyre (Ann Arbor, Mich.: Univ. Michigan
Pr., 1957), pp. 136, 150-51

Browning's mature techniques in the treatment of character were developed rather slowly, through trial and error, in a series of long poems, stage plays, and experimental dramas—dating from the time of *Pauline* (1833) to the year of the *Dramatic Romances and Lyrics* (1845). In a series of twenty character-revealing dramatic monologues, composed between 1844 and 1871, Browning richly exploited the lessons that he had learned in his early experiments and stage dramas. Various dramatic, imagistic, verbal, syntactical, and prosodic devices are employed in these twenty poems to create impressions of character: the devices tend to work coordinately, and to achieve intense effects. . . .

First, it would seem to be clear that Browning himself was a poet who paid the utmost attention even to the minutiae of his artistry, and that he was able to fuse the complex elements of his art again and again to create desired effects in his finest poems.

Second, it would seem to be equally clear that character itself is of key importance in Browning's art in the dramatic monologue form. This is not to say that all of the poet's monologues are of equal importance as character portraits, or indeed that any one monologue need be viewed as a character portrait alone. But much of Browning's true achievement becomes clear when we consider certain monologues in the light of his treatment of character—and it is in this light, and in rereading these monologues with close attention to their details, that we may come to a new understanding of them.

Park Honan
Browning's Characters: A Study in Poetic Techniques
(New Haven: Yale Univ. Pr., 1961), pp. 312-13

SAMUEL   BUTLER
1835-1902

> Butler was born in Nottinghamshire and, after taking a Cambridge degree, spent five years on a sheep ranch in New Zealand; he returned in 1864 to England, where he made a career as an essayist and satirist. His works include a well-known utopian vision of the future, *Erewhon* (1872), its title an anagram on "nowhere"; a series of critical pieces on religion and science in the sixties and seventies (he continued to attack Darwin's theories until late in his life); pamphlets on Shakespeare's sonnets (1899) and on Homer (1897), arguing that the latter was a woman; prose translations of the *Iliad* (1898) and the *Odyssey* (1900); *Erewhon Revisited* (1901); and the posthumously published novel of late Victorian family life *The Way of All Flesh* (1903). More than on his essays and notes on travel, society, and literature, or on his verse and his translations, Butler's reputation rests on the first and last of these.

> Henry Festing Jones and A. T. Bartholomew, eds., *Works* (Shrewsbury Edition) (1923-1926) 20 vols.
> Henry Festing Jones, *Butler: A Memoir* (1919), 2 vols.
> Philip Henderson, *Butler: The Incarnate Bachelor* (1953)

The mainspring of his life was the determination of a thwarted and diminished ego to fulfil itself, to set itself on high, to triumph in complete liberty and power over the forces that threatened to crush it. But his mind was at once too intuitive and too speculative to permit the struggle to remain a merely personal one. What concerned him was to establish his nature, his aspirations and their fulfilment upon a philosophic basis, to identify them with the nature, the aspirations, the fulfilment of all humanity—and more than that—with the fulfilment of the universe. Only so could he be safe and mankind be safe. He and all humanity stood or fell together. His struggle became generalized, symbolic, tremendous. His theories are all rooted in his personal struggle, and in his ardent and brilliant attacks on entrenched and fossilized authority, on pedantry, bigotry and humbug wherever he detected them, he was revenging himself magnificently for the wrong they had done him in the person of his father.

All philosophies are subjective and all contain truth, but none are true, and their proportion of objective value and applicability varies greatly. There was a fundamental sanity and vigour in Butler, a strong sense of reality, a keen analytical faculty and a power of turning accepted ideas upside down and inside out in order to get a fresh view of them, which amounted to an innovation in method and resulted in some of his most "future-piercing" conceptions. This method had its genesis in the vigorous protest of his own spirit against the traditional implications that threatened to stifle it. His thought, nourished by the complex subjectivity of an unusually brilliant, versatile and realistic nature, is so rich in objective values that it has more truth for us today than it had for his contemporaries. He was far more sensitive both to what had been thought and to what would be thought than to what was being thought.

Clara G. Stillman
Samuel Butler: A Mid-Victorian Modern
(New York: Viking, 1932), p. 12

Mr. Bernard Shaw wrote of Samuel Butler in his preface to *Major Barbara*, in 1906, as being "in his own department the greatest English writer of the latter half of the nineteenth century. It drives one almost to despair of English literature," he went on to say, "when one sees so extraordinary a study of English life as Butler's posthumous *Way of All Flesh* making so little impression. . . . Really, the English do not deserve to have great men."

Wherein does Butler's claim to recognition consist? The first answer is, in originality and depth. Sir Grafton Elliot Smith has said that the inertia of tradition and public opinion and the lack of courage to defy them when evidence fails to conform to them, seem to be potent to blind all but the ablest and most fearless of men to facts which are really patent. Butler was sensitive to such facts in a way that ought to be normal but is at the opposite pole from being average. He was a man of deeply sensitive feeling: this emerged in deep passions, but there was latent in him titanic strength which was largely used in controlling himself and pretending to be unmoved. The records of Butler reveal a heart hungry to love and be loved. From his childhood, he was thwarted by father, mother, sisters and all the people whom convention represented to be sympathetic. He was ready to acquiesce in the ways of the world, but conscientiousness made it clear to him that the ways of the world—many of the most approved ways of the world—were contrary to the truth. He came to be Zoroastrian in his worship of the truth and his hatred of the lie, but he was always unflinching in avoiding the attitude of the prig. This constant struggle between two positions apparently opposed constitutes the chief difficulty in the way of his being understood.

It has been truly pointed out that genius is simply this sensitiveness to truth in experience: it is simply eminent ability: the form in which it finds expression is not necessarily dictated to be any particular one. It was really by historical accident that Shakespeare was a dramatist, Newton a scientist, and Wren an architect. In Butler's case the eminent ability came out in great versatility.

R. F. Rattray
Samuel Butler (London: Duckworth, 1935), pp. 7-8

Like his fellow-Victorians, the deepest need of his nature was to escape from the reality of his own existence; only he escaped by means of ideas, and they by means of emotions. He was a pioneer idealogue. His mind was his refuge; and he lived secure amongst its shadows and fantasies. Where for instance Dickens shaped his turbulent appetites into creatures of darkness and light, making a melodrama of them, Butler shaped his into thought and made a utopia of them.

Malcolm Muggeridge
The Earnest Atheist (New York: Putnam's, 1937), p. xii

Butler knew that his "dream" was a fiction. In *Erewhon* the bounds of Utopia must be crossed before Higgs can find a new religion. In *The Way of All Flesh* the Erewhonian creed has become a timid reality. Butler returned to his "dream" with renewed passion in *Erewhon Revisited*, in a last wishful look at a binding faith of the future. But it was the fable of Ernest, bridge-builder, which culminated the efforts of those nineteenth-century writers who had tried to revitalize Victorian religion through their novels. The form of Ernest's dream was a typical Victorian compromise; the essence of his doubts, his reliance on a truth of feeling, his relativism, and his insistence on "naturalness" were Victorian as well as modern; Ernest's severance of all ties and bonds, and his ultimate repudiation of the hallowed Victorian institutions, the family, the church, and the school, were new. Samuel Butler bridged Victorian dissent and modern alienation. Unbeknown to him, his "crossing" was successful. He transported the "Nowhere" of *Erewhon* into the bounds of the modern novel.

J. C. Knoepflmacher
Religious Humanism and the Victorian Novel
(Princeton, N. J.: Princeton Univ. Pr., 1965), pp. 294-95

"LEWIS CARROLL" (CHARLES LUTWIDGE DODGSON)

1832-1898

A lecturer in mathematics at Oxford, and an amateur artist and photographer, Charles Dodgson achieved fame under his pseudonym as the author of *Alice's Adventures in Wonderland* (1865), written to amuse a little girl, and its sequel *Through the Looking Glass* (1872). He also wrote a nonsense poem *The Hunting of the Snark* (1876), and *Sylvie and Bruno* (1889-1893). His books have come to be regarded not only as classics for children but as remarkable and influential works of imagination.

Works: Nonesuch Library (1949)

S. Dodgson Collingwood, *The Life and Letters of Lewis Carrol* (1898)

It must seem a curious thing that there has been so little serious criticism of the Alices, and that so many critics, with so militant and eager an air of good taste, have explained that they would not think of attempting it. Even Mr. De La Mare's book, which made many good points, is queerly evasive in tone. There seems to be a feeling that real criticism would involve psycho-analysis, and that the results would be so improper as to destroy the atmosphere of the books altogether. Dodgson was too conscious a writer to be caught out so easily. For instance it is an obvious bit of interpretation to say that the Queen of Hearts is a symbol of "uncontrolled animal passion" seen through the clear but blank eyes of sexlessness; obvious, and the sort of thing critics are now so sure would be in bad taste; Dodgson said it him-self, to the actress who took the part when the thing was acted. The books are so frankly about growing up that there is no great discovery in translat-ing them into Freudian terms; it seems only the proper exegesis of a classic even where it would be a shock to the author. On the whole the results of the analysis, when put into drawing-room language, are his conscious opinions; and if there was no other satisfactory outlet for his feelings but the special one fixed in his books the same is true in a degree of any original artist.

William Empson
Some Versions of Pastoral (London:
Chatto and Windus, 1935), p. 253

More than fifty years have passed since January 14th, 1898. They have seen the gradual growth of an imposing *corpus* of Lewis Carroll literature which has testified to ever-increasing interest on both sides of the Atlantic. Yet two of the most valuable contributions to an understanding of C. L. Dodgson appeared in the year of his death. The Rev. T. B. Strong, subsequently Bishop of Oxford, writing from intimate knowledge, contributed to the *Cornhill* of March, 1898, a cool and lucid analysis of the man and his works that has not been displaced as criticism, though it has been very charmingly supplemented by Mr. Walter de la Mare's long and delightful essay pub-lished in 1932. He wrote of him as one who had "paroxysms" of work when he was "apt to forget his meals, and toil on for the best part of the night," admitted that "to a large extent, especially in his later years," he lived as a recluse, but added that "those who knew him ceased to find it puzzling" that he had produced the "Alice" books: "There was always the same mind displayed in his talk."

Derek Hudson
Lewis Carroll (London: Archibald Constable, 1954), p. 11

The *Alice* books will undoubtedly continue to be read on many different levels. But the true reader who is also the true lover will not be too con-cerned with the travesties, the ambiguities, and the double meanings hidden below the surface. He will not feel driven to solve the metaphysical implications about rabbit holes, caucus-races, croquet games, mad tea-parties and a pack of cards; nor will he be compelled to work out the moves which prove that *Through the Looking-Glass* is a prolonged chess game which the white pawn, Alice, finally wins. He will not care that the two books have yielded almost as many quotations as the Bible, Shakespeare's plays, or Pope's and Byron's poems. Those who come to these books with no preconceived ideas and without too much purpose will find the same enjoyment in the unexpected turns of the stories and the uncanny twists in speech as the author had in making them. Here is that wildness and wittiness, that unfolding imagination which, in the mind of a genius, is transformed into magic. Here, in short, is the most enchanting as well as the most inexhaustible literary fairy tale ever composed.

Louis Untermeyer
Introd. in *Alice's Adventures in Wonderland and
Through the Looking Glass* (New York: Collier, 1962), pp. 10-11

THOMAS CARLYLE
1795-1881

Carlyle is one of the earliest Victorian writers and was in his time one of the most influential. The son of a poor Scottish stonemason, he began at fourteen his studies for the ministry in the University of Edinburgh. His loss, there, of his Calvinistic faith is represented in the central chapters of *Sartor Resartus*, which reveal how deep the author's depression and need to affirm some value in life had been. In 1826 he married the brilliant Jane Welsh; the Carlyles lived for eight years at lonely Craigenputtock in Scotland, and then, until 1866, in the Chelsea district of London. In the 1820's Carlyle was writing essays and translations from the German, but he became well known only with the publication (1833-1834) of his philosophical, autobiographical, quasi-fictional, and frequently perplexing *Sartor Resartus*. This work was followed by his second version of *The French Revolution: A History* (1837), the first version having been inadvertently destroyed in manuscript by a servant of John Stuart Mill; a pamphlet on *Chartism* (1840), revealing Carlyle's early sympathy with the working class; a series of lectures, *On Heroes, Hero-Worship, and the Heroic in History* (1841); *Past and Present* (1843), unfavorably contrasting the England of the nineteenth century with that of the fourteenth; *Oliver Cromwell's Letters and Speeches* (1845); the *Latter-Day Pamphlets* (1850), which display Carlyle's increasingly bitter and reactionary temper; *The Life of John Sterling*, a biography that lacks the author's extreme mannerisms of style; the massive and ambitious *History of Friedrich II of Prussia, called Frederick the Great*, in six volumes (1858-1865); and the posthumously published *Reminiscences*, edited by J. A. Froude (1881).

H. D. Traill, ed., *Works* (Centenary Edition, 1896-1899), 30 vols.
David A. Wilson, *Carlyle* (1923-1934), 6 vols.

PERSONAL

His life's work was to "hold the mirror up to Nature," and beckon his fellows to working instead of fighting, as the one way to make life in the world worth living. As the war-wearied Chinese learned from the wise—Confucius and others—to be rational and despise the killers, so may we wild men of the West be taught by Voltaire and Goethe, Carlyle and Tolstoy, to be ashamed of slaughter and abhor to fight.

His preaching of peace is none the less wise because it is also sometimes funny. By instinct he was fearless and pugnacious; but the folly and wickedness of strife was the best lesson he learned from religion in his boyhood, and it was ratified on refflection and practised. In private life he was a peacemaker, and patient without weakness.

He spoke so freely on so many things that it is easy to find inconsistencies. They never troubled him, for logic was his servant, not his master, and his theory of the Universe was that there never can be any theory complete. It is stupid to doubt his sincerity. That is his supreme attainment. His philosophy had nothing new; but he was the Rembrandt of writers; and in the great pen-portrait gallery of his works there may here and there loom greater men than himself, but not one more amusing.

David Alec Wilson
Carlyle Till Marriage (London: Kegan Paul, 1923), p. xii

Carlyle was an earthborn spirit, a Titan, groaning under the Etna of his dark obsessions; his attempts to scale those heavens of serene contemplation to which Goethe and Emerson attained were always defeated; always he fell back into his mud-element with outcries of despair. In him, as in Rembrandt, the sense of beauty was deficient, and the lovely light of reason shone but dimly and fitfully on his mind. "His power of expression," Jowett said of him, "outran his real intelligence, and constantly determined his opinion." But it is for his expression, not for his opinion, that many set so high a value on his writings—for that splendour and music, of which, since the seventeenth century, Carlyle was one of the greatest masters. Carlyle's failure to impose his narrow, rigoristic, moralistic, joyless Annandale view of the world upon the world, added an element of tragedy to his deeply tragic sense of life. He suffered also the deeper tragedy of those who attempt to deify the Universe; who personify it as a God to find that they have made a Devil of it. Their cosmic piety plunges them into such abysses of moral contradiction that it becomes, as many believe it became with Carlyle, a mask of atheism and dark despair.

Carlyle was a "sick giant," as Emerson said of him; and "if genius were cheap," Emerson added, "we might do without Carlyle, but in the existing population, he cannot be spared." With this final verdict of his life-long friend, let us take leave of him as we see him walking with David Masson in the park one evening, under his extraordinary tall, broad-brimmed hat, which gave him the air of an old magician, and gazing up at the stars that were growing brighter as the daylight faded. He spoke of the infinite beauty and harmony of the Universe; but soon the old prophetic fury seized him; he began to denounce the irreverent, mocking spirit of the age. Too much jest, too much irony and laughter, too much sniggering at things! And then, as if remembering his own wild satirical torch-dancings, he paused, and giving a shrug of self-disgust: "Ah," he exclaimed, "I have given too much in to that myself!"; and the proud, melancholy old man walked on, lost in his life-long dialogue under the earnest stars with Death, Judgment and Eternity.

Logan Pearsall Smith
Reperusals and Re-Collections (London:
Archibald Constable, 1936), pp. 220-21

It appears that the leaders of Victorian culture were still living on the inspiration of the romantic movement, but each applied it to his own world in his own way. They looked within themselves for a divine pattern on which to model their thoughts; they looked on conduct for a reflection of that pattern, describing what they saw so as to make it fit in with their ideal. They tried to adjust ethics to metaphysics. There is a rather ignoble temptation to belittle the achievement of these geniuses whom we can no longer imitate. They were great as artists and yet greater as a moral force. Whoever is scholar enough to yield to their magic, must also yield to their high sense of duty. Yet their influence will not stay with the admirer because these moralists protest too much. None wholly convinced themselves, nor their contemporaries, much less us. They express a tension, a yearning, not a realisation. They show us how they think we ought to live, not how we can live.

Carlyle is conspicuous amongst these figures because he is the most aggressively practical of them all. He insists as vigorously as any on the evidence of his own conscience, but much more vigorously on the evidence of his eyes, that is to say, on conduct as observed in past and present events. He asserted the superiority of the "poorest historical fact" over fiction, even over imaginative poetry. He was so intolerant of "windy sentiments" that he would not tolerate any theories at all. As such he exercised an enormous influence in the 'forties and 'fifties. He got as close as he could to life without renouncing his visions. He was a realist in ideals. But he is much more significant for us as a realist who could not substantiate his ideals. Thanks to his pragmatism he ended by finding himself in a false position. In fact, towards the end of his life he seemed to fear that he would become as he described his contemporaries, "destitute of faith and terrified at scepticism." For instance, earnest and adventurous thinkers in the 'fifties and 'sixties were trying to explain the mysteries and anomalies of human nature by tracing its origin. Carlyle did not examine or even consider their hypothesis, though crowded with facts. He merely betrayed the animosity inspired by fear, caricaturing their conclusions as "man made chemically out of *Urschleim* or a certain blubber called protoplasm." On another occasion, near the end of his life, when Froude remarked that one could believe only in a God who did something "with a cry of pain which I shall never forget, he said, 'he does nothing.' "

So Carlyle joins the other great Victorians of the earlier period who lost heart or effectiveness because they clung to their inward convictions. His failure completes the impression that there was something specially uncongenial and disconcerting in that epoch, from which we perhaps are still suffering.

H. V. Routh
Towards the Twentieth Century (New York:
Macmillan, 1937), pp. 134-35

A prophet, I maintain, Carlyle was to his generation, the most potent voice of the spirit in reaction against a mechanical view of society, against a too great faith in the findings of an economic science which claimed infallibility, which claimed to have discovered the laws governing both the production and the distribution of wealth. His friend and enemy J. S. Mill, who, Carlyle complained to Espinasse, in conversation used to insist on "having everything demonstrated," came to recognize in his *Autobiography* "the proper distinction between the laws of the Production of Wealth, which are real laws of nature, dependent on the properties of objects, and the modes of its distribution which, subject to certain conditions, depend on human will." Macaulay, too, in his speeches modified the extreme faith in *laissez-faire* which he had announced with so entire confidence in his review of Southey's *Colloquies on Society*. But as a prophet I feel that Carlyle lost the faith which gives inspiration to what the prophet says. It is not only that he grows angry. He ceased, Espinasse complains, to give close study to the problems. There is a measure of *a priori* judgement in his pronouncements on the subjects with which he deals in the *Latter Day Pamphlets*. "He says over and over," Emerson complained, "for months, for years, the same thing." It is true of what he writes also. "He is terribly earnest but never serious—that is, never *in earnest*" was the judgment passed on him by G. M. Hopkins. The difference is not at once obvious but is, I think, real. Carlyle is "in earnest" up to the writing of *Past and Present* because he believes he can persuade those he is appealing to. In what came later his manner is as "earnest" as ever, even more so, but it has lost the note of hope and conviction. If one has come to regard one's fellow men with "abhorrence mingled with pity," one may be willing to hail any dictator who can secure order and find work for all.

H. J. C. Grierson
Proceedings of the British Academy (1940), pp. 324-25

Sartor Resartus

It is often complained that Carlyle's doctrine of renunciation and duty, which is the final message of *Sartor*, and his ideal of a Blessedness which agrees to renounce all claim upon the world's gifts of happiness, fame or what not, while consecrating life and labor to the world's betterment, is narrow and incomplete. Doubtless it is so. To no man is it given to see and to appropriate in the form of experience the whole truth. Surely it is enough for one book that for thousands of readers it has helped to sharpen insight, strengthen veracity and encourage devotion of purpose to noble ends.

William Savage Johnson
Thomas Carlyle: A Study of His Literary Apprenticeship 1814-1831
(New Haven: Yale Univ. Pr., 1911), pp. 120-21

In interpreting the new ideas, especially those of Kant and Fichte, Thomas Carlyle played the greatest part. Victorian Protestantism—often a Calvinistic Protestantism—found in him a renewer of the old religious doctrines, in fresh terms, and in such forms as would commend themselves to men who had lost their moorings in the orthodox faith and wished to believe without retaining the old supernaturalism. In Carlyle's transcendentalism, as notably expressed in *Sartor Resartus*, they found the substance of the old religion in a new form: predestination, and God's providence, now appeared in the German doctrine of the progressive unfolding of the Divine Idea in history; the Calvinist's "elect" were now the Heroes, on which Carlyle lectured; the middle-class Protestant reverence for work seemed amply justified in Fichte's emphasis on the moral deed, rather than on the pretensions of the understanding or the longing for "happiness"; nature— always a snare and a delusion to the religious—was now seen as, in one sense, an unreal "appearance," since time and space are merely relative, and in another sense, as the raw material with which man was to express his true self through work; and God, who had seemed so remote and incomprehensible, was now an inner spiritual Will or Self, mysteriously at work in nature and in man.

Charles Frederick Harrold, ed.
Introductory Survey in *English Prose of the Victorian Era*
(New York: Oxford Univ. Pr., 1938), pp. xliv-xlv

It would be absurd to claim to find the unity of a novel by James in the wonderful *olla podrida* that makes up *Sartor Resartus*, and yet I do believe the book displays artistic form, not only of theme and style but also, and even basically, of that sort of structure involving relationships between distinct characters participating in a series of actions demanded by a plot moving to a preconcerted judgment about life. In short, *Sartor Resartus* deserves to be recognized as a true novel, and not just the sort of book we call a novel because no other term fits. But it is true that Carlyle discharged all of his gifts indiscriminately into the book in an excess of bitterness at his failure to win literary recognition, as though he would create in spite of his inexperience and the indifference of the world, so that the structural merit of the book may easily fail to strike the reader who first notices the bewildering mixture of philology, topical and universal satire, literary and historical allusion, philosophy, irony, humor, anger, and buffoonery. . . .

The Philosopher, the Editor, the Hofrath or the reader inasmuch as he has become implicated in the meaning of the Clothes-Philosophy, all are marked by the common fate of man, a fate symbolized by the unexpected, sudden disappearance of Teufelsdröckh—an end Carlyle constantly stressed by his favorite quotation, with which he concluded the climax of *Sartor Resartus*:

> We *are such stuff*
> As dreams are made of, and our little Life
> Is rounded with a sleep!

In the face of his world, which was much like ours in its quest for secure values, Carlyle was determined not to fade and leave not a wrack behind. *Sartor Resartus*, firm in its artistic unity, remains as the inspired vision of a magician whose labors now are ended.

John Lindberg
Victorian Newsletter (Spring, 1960), pp. 20, 22-23

The French Revolution

Carlyle's fashion being entirely his own, *The French Revolution* resembles no other history. It is an epic in prose, flashing with the lightning and reverberating with the thunder of stormy events. You feel that something is really happening and that the course of the world has taken a new direction. Setting out from a conviction that "the history of the world is the biography of great men," he produced both a thrilling story and a collection of marvelously vivid portraits.

George Sampson
The Concise Cambridge History of English Literature
(Cambridge Univ. Pr., 1941), p. 698

In power of graphic description and portraiture, whether of battle, human incident, or distinguished personality, Carlyle has no superior in English. Moreover, the energy of his utterance, especially in such a work as *The French Revolution*, is the energy of a Titan. There is also his humor, "his mountain mirth," as Emerson called it; for we are not to forget that the wrath of the sage often ended in explosions of laughter over his own extravagances, proving after all that he had more fellowship with Rabelais than with Swift.

Frederick William Roe, ed.
Victorian Prose (New York: Ronald Pr., 1947), p. 5

Frederick The Great

We must remember Carlyle's worship of force. He had been preaching all his life a form of the doctrine, might is right; and, as was usual with him, the doctrine had grown more extreme under contradiction and opposition. Thus we have the *Nigger Question* and the *Iliad in a Nutshell*. There is an element of truth in the doctrine, and under Carlyle's original application of it there had been a well-marked moral foundation, so that it could have been in many cases altered to read, "right is might." He meant not merely that "Providence is on the side of the heaviest battalion," but quite as much that the battalion is heaviest because Providence is on its side. In other words, he believed that the forces of the universe are moral forces and that true and permanent success mean being in harmony with them. As time went on however the qualifications were gradually stripped off, and latterly what Carlyle worshipped was little better than naked force. Now, in all the eighteenth century he could hardly have found a better example of successful force than Frederick. Destitute as he was of the piety of Carlyle's previous hero, he was at least an eminently successful governor, and Carlyle respected nothing so much as the faculty for the genuine government of men, not what he would have called sham government, the kind of government which follows while it seems to lead. If Frederick had not created a state, he had raised it from a position bordering on insignificance to one not far from the front in the European system. Moreover, this state was peculiarly interesting to Carlyle, for he saw in Prussia the future head of Germany, and in Germany a possible leader of Europe. These reasons induced him to turn to Frederick, and perhaps tempted him to clothe Frederick with attributes which were not all his.

Hugh Walker
The Age of Tennyson (London: Bell, 1914), pp. 21-22

Past and Present

We may feel that Carlyle's constructive powers are underestimated, but we must admit that he is more effective when he tells us what is the matter, than when he tells us what we shall do. But, in spite of such faults *Past and Present* has continued to exert an influence from 1843 to 1923. "There is nothing like it," said Arthur Hugh Clough. Its eloquence was partly responsible for Kingsley's novel, *Yeast*. It roused thousands of Englishmen from inertia to a fresh consideration of social conditions. The fierceness of the denunciation stung Philistine reformers out of their complacency. What if Carlyle did, as Henry James said, scold like an angry governess? He made men look about them more thoughtfully.

> "I hope," Carlyle wrote his mother, "it will be a rather useful kind of book. It goes rather in a fiery strain about the present condition of men in general, and the strange pass they are coming to; and I calculate it may awaken here and there a slumbering blockhead to rub his eyes and consider what he is about in God's creation."

This is the sum of the matter: a word from Carlyle was a call to action. He does battle against *laissez-faire*. "Ay," he said, "by God, Donald, we must help them to mend it!"

Stanley T. Williams
Studies in Victorian Literature
(New York: E. P. Dutton, 1923), p. 39

GENERAL

As for the mere "art" of writing in verse, or for that matter in prose, Carlyle, as we have seen, troubled himself but little. If he could once see his facts "blazing," and was sure of their spiritual significance, the outward dress of words became to him a negligible detail. This was a dangerous laxity upon his part, no doubt; but his extraordinary native gift for expression made him reckless of all theories of style. But in his theory of the function of the imagination he is at one with most of the great creative artists who have tried to communicate in words their sense of the significant in art.

Bliss Perry
Thomas Carlyle: How to Know Him (Indianapolis, Ind.:
Bobbs-Merrill, 1915), p. 66

The greatness of the writer imposes recognition even by those who withstand the thinker and the man. Carlyle is one of the most spirited poets of modern England. When his words have exhausted all their practical effects, Carlyle will continue to live as a poet. The imperfections of his artistic instinct, the failures of his sense of rhythm, precluded his writing verse; but all other qualities of poetry, the essential qualities of poetry, were his. His vision of the world is that toward which the poets of the romantic generation had striven: a perception of the spiritual in the material. But the universality, the might and the lofty vistas of German idealism gave to Carlyle's vision, while he was at the very beginning of his literary career, a breadth and a clearness beyond comparison. His imagination lived so freely under the sense of the unreality of time and space, that every spectacle he pictured had its double aspect of reality and dream. To his eyes, hazy depths revealed themselves behind the configurations of nature and history; the particular details are bathed in haze, and, of a sudden, they melt into it and disappear; and from the darkness of death, the past surges suddenly into view, still alive. Such swift appearances and disappearances intoxicate the mind with a penetrating, magnificent obsession; and the poetry and the mystery of the beyond flow into all the aspects of the real more intimately than with any other writer. No poet has had in a higher degree, sublimity of imagination; no poet has with greater power evoked the infinite, or the eternal silences which lie behind the transitory sights and sounds of life.

To its unexampled power of metaphysical dissolution, Carlyle's imagination joins the specifically English gift of concrete force and picturesque energy. It is as capable of concentrating its shining rays upon picture after picture, as of dissolving these pictures. The intellectual vigor of narrative and description, the precision of detail, the expressive richness of idiom make Carlyle's style one of the most intense there are. His style is as effective upon the senses as upon the intelligence, upon those senses, at least, which are not, in the narrow connotation, sensual, those senses which are a part of the mind and of the muscular energy. The sudden relaxations and irruptions, the broken rhythms of this style, its discordant harmony, its profound congruence with the vehemence, the bitterness, the irony and the humor of the thought it conveys, make it a unique instrument, the work of a unique temperament, an instrument which adds an unforgettable note to the choir of English prose. Like his doctrine, Carlyle's art has its weaknesses and its limitations; in both art and doctrine, the deepest quality, the quality which will best assure the duration of Carlyle's work, is force, that energy which is capable of violating ideas, of subjugating them without inducing them to obedience or discipline; but capable, too, without striving for or achieving the perfectly beautiful, of eliciting from the world and from the soul fragments marvelous in their beauty.

Louis Cazamian
Carlyle, tr. E. K. Brown (New York: Macmillan, 1932), pp. 285-86

The present writing is in the midst of post-war turmoil such as provoked Carlyle's social criticism. England, the birthplace of machine industry, may become its victim, as everywhere production outstrips distribution and consumption, with unemployment on a scale that threatens a world-wide breakdown of capitalism. Thoughtful men question the wisdom of seeking further command over nature until means have been devised to prevent fools and knaves from misusing in war and peace the terrifying powers already unloosed by science. The cry is for strong government. Growing doubt of the capacity of the average man to rule himself through his representatives is driving a desperate world to the experiments of Fascism and Communism. In the crisis he foresaw, Carlyle is being remembered. Editions of translated excerpts from his writings in 1920, 1921, and 1922 accompanied the rise of Fascism to power in Italy. Mr. Shaw's *Apple Cart* has preached to England, in the manner of *Frederick the Great*, the parable of a patriot king striving to protect the people from their elected rulers, who will not turn the powers of science and industry to their welfare. Germany, under the frightful strain of war ruin, reparation payments, and economic and political instability, is imbibing courage from selections from Carlyle that have sold to the extent of 300,000 copies since 1926.

Will the author of *Past and Present* be read so widely in England and America? The chastened mood of the moment is auspicious. The dogmas of democracy and *laissez faire* are shaken. Science, especially the physics that tried Carlyle's faith, no longer speaks the language of crass materialism. Moral responsibility, lately out of fashion, begins to be perceived as the indispensable cement of a fast disintegrating society. The great public is listening to writers who say incompletely and imperfectly what Carlyle said with unparalleled brilliance and cogency. If Victorian clouds do not shroud his lightnings, it may next turn to him. In our partially aroused state we have need of his obstinate faith that the modern world contains resources for its own salvation. The stupendous scale of the contemporary scene dwarfs our thinkers. We must await men of Carlyle's range and stature for the achievement of a social synthesis, if procrastination has not already put it beyond human capacity. Until Titans arise, we will look with envy and regret at the lost opportunity of a generation that had a Carlyle.

Emery Neff
Carlyle (New York: W. W. Norton, 1932, repr. New York:
Russell and Russell, 1968), pp. 268-69

Few Victorian literary reputations have survived into the twentieth century more uncertainly than that of Thomas Carlyle. Those of his writings that were most topical appear, very naturally, most outdated; the industry that burrowed through a mass of rubbish to discern veritable facts about Cromwell and Frederick the Great seems almost ridiculous in face of the small army of assistants busy with card-indexes ranked behind the modern historian; the famous style that electrified his contemporaries stands forbidding as a roadblock between Carlyle and modern readers. His philosophy, as far as it is understood, is likely to seem a blend of platitudes ("Work alone is noble") and of apologies for dictators.

None of the unfriendly criticisms made of Carlyle is without truth; yet, added together, they make a picture that is grotesquely inaccurate. To appreciate Carlyle the reader today must make a greater effort than is required of him by any other Victorian writer: but the rewards are correspondingly great. The style that seemed to bristle so formidably, when viewed from a too-respectful distance, proves to have a surprising resilience and friendliness once we have ventured into the midst of it: it has, indeed, less the effect of a *style* than of a man speaking to other men—stammeringly at times it may be, upon occasion finding difficulty in fitting words to the fiery shape of his ideas, but possessing unquestionable fine eloquence and passion. And the prophetic message that Carlyle felt himself destined to give to the world; that too has its meaning for those who live in the age of atomic power, though not quite in the form that Carlyle conceived it. More clearsighted than any other British thinker of his century, he saw that the Age of Machinery (as he called the Industrial Revolution) spelled the doom of *laissez-faire* in politics and economics. He offered in opposition to the measured optimism about a slow but inevitable increase in human prosperity felt by Victorian Conservatives, Liberals and Radicals alike, a very different vision:

> In the days that are now passing-over us, even fools are arrested to ask the meaning of them; few of the generations of men have seen more impressive days. Days of endless calamity, disruption, dislocation, confusion worse confounded: if they are not days of endless hope too, then they are days of utter despair. For it is not a small hope that will suffice, the ruin being clearly, either in action or in prospect, universal. There must be a new world, if there is to be any world at all! That human things in our Europe can ever return to the old sorry routine, and proceed with any steadiness or continuance there; this small hope is not now a tenable one. These days of universal death must be days of universal new-birth, if the ruin is not to be total and final.

These words were written during years of revolutionary upsurge and social change: have they not some relevance to our own time also?

Julian Symons
Introd. in *Carlyle: Selected Works, Reminiscences,
and Letters* (Cambridge, Mass.: Harvard Univ. Pr., 1963), pp. 9-10

ARTHUR HUGH CLOUGH

1819-1861

As a student at Rugby School, Clough was influenced by Dr. Thomas Arnold, and at Oxford he was close to Dr. Arnold's son Matthew, the poet. Clough resigned an Oxford fellowship in 1848, having scruples about subscribing to the Articles of the Church of England. He then travelled, wrote, and worked in London as examiner in the Education Office; he died, and is buried, in Florence. Clough's verse is marked by a questioning of religious and other beliefs and an earnest seeking after truth. His long poems are *The Bothie of Tober-na-Vuolich* (1848), *Amours de Voyage* (1858), and the posthumously published *Dipsychus* and *Mari Magno*.

H. F. Lowry, A. L. P. Norrington, and F. L. Mulhauser, eds., *Poems* (1951)

F. L. Mulhauser, ed., *Correspondence* (1957), 2 vols.

PERSONAL

. . . Clough, just as he is finer than most of his poetry, is more interesting than most of his life. He had, one may say, two ruling passions—one, for going his own way and thinking his own thoughts; the other, for going, and for thinking, straight. The moral conscientiousness of the model pupil of Arnold is of no great interest: young prigs, never rare, were particularly plentiful then. But the intense intellectual conscientiousness into which it grew is a far rarer quality: it remains one of the central things in the worth of Clough's poetry and in the unhappiness of his life.

F. L. Lucas
Eight Victorian Poets (Cambridge Univ. Pr., 1930), p. 60

Arthur Hugh Clough was far more than a "poet of doubt"—the role in which posterity has been most inclined to remember him. He was emphatically not a weak, indecisive Thyrsis whose piping took such a troubled sound that he drooped and died because he could not make up his mind about the nature and purposes of God. Nor did he confine his contemplations to matters of religion. On the contrary, he was profoundly and actively interested in political economy, in international politics, in social reform, in education, in love (almost a third of his poetry is concerned with love and marriage, a fact virtually ignored by many of his critics and biographers), and—perhaps most deeply of all—in literature.

Clough was preëminently a thinker. Without minimizing his lyrical ability (which was considerable), one may fairly say that it is as a logician and an alert observer of facts that Clough excelled. He never allowed theoretical speculation to carry him away from the earth, and he was specially gifted at seeing two sides to every proposition and weighing the pros and cons of every question. These capacities, which Clough shared with John Stuart Mill, may perhaps be recognized more readily in his prose than in his poetry.

Buckner B. Trawick
Selected Prose Works of Arthur Hugh Clough
(Birmingham, Ala.: Univ. Alabama Pr., 1964), p. 1

POETRY

The Devil, save for one scene in which he catches from his opponent the trick of unrhyming monologue, the Devil of *Dipsychus* is—after Butler and Byron—the best satirist our literature can shew in that order of satiric verse of which *Hudibras* and *Don Juan* are the supreme examples. It is a reproach to our criticism that a satire so gay and so going should be so little read. The truth is that nearly all Clough's readers have been of the wrong sort; they have been dull persons—clergymen with doubts, and theologically minded laymen—and they have liked only Clough's dull parts.

H. W. Garrod
Poetry and the Criticism of Life (Cambridge, Mass.:
Harvard Univ. Pr., 1931), p. 125

It should first be noted that he produced only one poem worth considering, *The Bothie of Tober-na-Vuolich*. This orginial and spirited composition is most significant, partly because it is full of promise, and partly because that promise was not fulfilled. Perhaps no work has celebrated more felicitously the true spirit of academic youth. Clough, like nearly all Arnold's favourable pupils, has been accused of being a prig. *The Bothie* is redolent of College culture, yet it is absolutely free from priggishness. Even the adaptation of the hexameter is so natural and lighthearted that it hardly seems to be the achievement of an Homeric scholar, who could interpret the prosody of the *Iliad* and the *Odyssey*. And again, though *The Bothie* is the work of a studious poet, and celebrates a studious fraternity, yet no other English poem gives a better sense of the open air, and the joys of health and strength among streams and mountains. Nor is it easy to find another scholarly composition, in which the humour is so unsophisticated. Above all, the poem culminates in action. It tells how an Oxford scholar discovered that the end of culture is to be natural and started on his manhood in that spirit. Thus the poem has a value which transcends literary criticism. It turns the reader towards this most intimate and pressing problem, the conduct of his own life, and plays upon his own motives and aims with the clear and inspiring light of art.

Why did Clough never surpass this achievement; nor even repeat it? His university career sapped his inspiration, and in tracing this decline, we see how impossible it is for any man to play his proper part in the material world unless he understands his place in the spiritual world, and can clearly see where his soul owes its allegiance. When he went up to Oxford he was amply armed against Newmanism by Dr. Arnold. But, like all the gifted and imaginative Oxonians of this generation, he was soon converted to the great tractarian's earnestness, to his dream of a devout and God-fearing England, strong in the universality and divine authority of the unsectarian

pre-Lutheran Church, glorious in its sumptuous symbolism, its mystic communion and human fellowship, its historicity, its humanism, and its duty
of self-examination—all so attractive to a schoolboy who kept a diary. No
young man of Clough's temperament could be true to himself without hover-
ing between this appeal to his idealism and the rather austere Calvinism and
religious isolation which he had previously been taught to prize as the
earthly crown of the Christian gentleman.

So Clough's thoughts were unsettled, his buoyancy and creativeness oppressed, his academic studies distracted. Then came the inevitable reaction.
He found himself unmistakably searching here and there for definite proofs,
for authorization which will stand the test of logic, and modern experience,
and so discovering the joy of exercising his brain in the disposal of his life.
In order to make a free choice in his religion he fell under the tyranny of his
intellect—the alternative was to fall under the tyranny of Rome. As was
usual in the England of those days this new spirit came to a head in conflict
with an old institution, the subscription to the Thirty-nine Articles. "It is
not so much from any definite objection to this or that point, as a general
dislike to subscription, and a strong feeling of its being a bondage and a
very heavy one and that may cramp and cripple one for life."

H. V. Routh
Towards the Twentieth Century (New York:
Macmillan, 1937), pp. 168-69

It is perhaps unfortunate that Arthur Hugh Clough chose verse as the vehicle
for his perplexities: although he desired to write "poetry" he was not sufficiently an artist to be much interested in making *poems*. At times he can
be very refreshing when he seems to be working toward a poetry of seriously witty conversation not unlike that of W. H. Auden's lighter vein.
Usually, however, he accepted the dominant Victorian fallacy that poetry is
the prophetic utterance of bards who have made up their minds about the
great mysteries; and since he could *not* make up his mind about them his
efforts to write what the age called "true" poetry were largely stultified. For
that very reason, however, his poems are rewarding for anyone who wishes
to understand the spiritual difficulties of the period.

Rather too much has been said of how Dr. Arnold, completing the work
begun by Arthur's formidable mother, made him a morally overstrained
young prig. The fact provides a partial explanation of one element in his
character, but it should not be made the starting point for a Stracheyan
exposure of the absurdities of Victorian seriousness. Clough deserves to be
treated with much sympathy and respect. The problems which disturbed
him were well worth worrying about. He was a highly intelligent man with
a natural bent toward cheerfulness, clarity, intellectual honesty, and wholesome realism; but the age pulled him in too many different directions to

enable him to fulfill his best potentialities. Only a very great mind could have synthesized all the disparate thoughts and feelings which beset him.

Hoxie N. Fairchild
Religious Trends in English Poetry, Vol. IV
(New York: Columbia Univ. Pr., 1957), p. 505

We are in a better position to value Clough today. For one thing, we are more accustomed to and more tolerant of unconventional poetic styles, in fact we often find them a tonic. And then in a number of ways we are tougher than our predecessors; we can follow Clough's penetrating psychological insights without fear; we can delight in (and also heed) the subtly-planted shafts of his irony because we are not shocked. We can take heart from his compassion because we ourselves find the human predicament too complex for neat classifications. In short, we can read Clough as an astringent, and often a very exciting astringent, where his own generation found him alarming, odd, or merely depressing.

Mr. Graham Greene has said of Clough, or, rather, made his hero in *The Quiet American* say: "He was an adult poet in the nineteenth century. There weren't so many of them." And he has prefaced the book with a quotation from Clough which shows typically this adult wisdom and insight:

> I do not like being moved; for the will is excited; and action
> Is a most dangerous thing; I tremble for something factitious,
> Some malpractice of heart and illegitimate process;
> We are so prone to these things, with our terrible notions of duty.

It is this quality of adultness which gives Clough his modern ring. He will not be discovered through the anthologies. The poems chosen to represent him there do not convey his scale; the range and power and originality of his most serious work.

Katharine Chorley
Arthur Hugh Clough (Oxford Univ. Pr., 1962), p. 7

It is true that Clough lacked the variety of Tennyson, Browning, and Arnold, and the originality of Hopkins. His refusal to utilize medieval legend and classical myth, the limited scope of his characters, the predominantly subjective and skeptical nature of his poems, and the plainness of his style give his work less diversity than that of his major contemporaries. But on a second or third reading, with special attention to the narrative poems of 1848-50, one comes to recognize an unexpected range and depth. Clough was amazingly aware of both himself and his age, and alert to the newest developments of thought that spring up at the point of intersection. His notation of anti-heroism and the loss of identity was not only early but perceptive: he saw most of the causes. No one struck more forcefully at the amoral character of a worldly society. But Clough's major insight was psychological. He explored subtleties of feeling that included paradoxical emotions, followed the devious twistings of inner debate, and knew the dumb sense of thwarted effort and lost opportunity. His range of observation is reflected in his range of form: satire, comedy, and romance; sensuous description; philosophical lyric; and the dialectic of reason. And he created a style equal to his need. His control of syntax, denotation, and tones of voice, especially the tone of irony—all in natural idiom and flexible rhythmš —was skillful enough to project his complex experience. He did not succeed, perhaps, as often as Tennyson, Browning, and Arnold, but he left behind him a distinguished body of work.

In addition to its intrinsic virtues, Clough's poetry has the further attraction of contemporary relevance. We welcome his special capacity, so rare in his own age, for double vision. He could see at least two sides to every question. (He could even see two sides of seeing two sides of every question.) He could sympathize with Hewson, Claude, and Dipsychus, admire them and praise them, and at the same time allow the critical spirit to expose their limitations. Here, as in shorter poems like "It is true, ye gods, who treat us," "That there are powers above us I admit," or—significant title—"Thesis and Antithesis," he had the ability attributed by Eliot to the metaphysicals, and by inference to the moderns of recognizing "implicit in the expression of every experience . . other kinds of experience which are possible." This gift of dipsychian vision saved him from both the simplifications and the didacticisms of his contemporaries, and now makes him a living poet in the 1960s.

Walter Houghton
The Poetry of Clough (New Haven: Yale Univ. Pr.,
1963), p. 226

From time to time references have been made to the satiric poetry of Arthur Hugh Clough, but up to now there has been no real exploration of this subject. The only essay of any length on the topic is that by Humbert Wolfe, who, unfortunately, spent most of his time and space attempting to demonstrate that Clough's "innate satirical genius" was destroyed in the struggle to rid itself of "the swaddling-clothes of Arnoldism, and of all the honourable and clogging pieties of the period." There have also been references from time to time to the "modernity" of Clough's poetry, but, again, this subject has not been fully explored, the most recent and satisfying treatment up to the present being Walter Houghton's analysis of the reasons for Clough's unpopularity in his own day. That these two facets of Clough's poetry should receive the notice of some critics is not surprising, but the fact that the close connection between them has not attracted more attention is. In terms of his poetic method and manner, it is his satirical poetry (as distinguished from his lyric) that resembles most closely the poetry of our own time. . . . Rejecting the lofty, graceful style of Victorian poetry, he writes his satiric poems in a vigorous, masculine style, employing irony, ambiguity, and indirection, qualities that his contemporaries did not particularly admire or, in some cases, understand. It is this style, with its resultant ironic tone, that gives his satiric poetry its characteristic "modern" note. His three long poems, the *Bothie, Amours*, and *Dipsychus*, readily demonstrate this. . . .

The qualities that mark the shorter satiric poems are those that are found in the three long ones and illustrate the nature of his achievement in this genre. If we postulate effectiveness of communication, intensity of tone, depth of insight, and sharpness of vision as attributes of successful satire, then Clough's place as a satiric artist is assured. With his preciseness of diction, scrupulous employment of imagery, skillful handling of rhythm and meter, and "modern" tone, he manages to convey with considerable force the reformative intent that is the basis of his satiric writing. When to these verbal qualities are added those of his own character—his positive naturalism and liberal thought—we can see why he would appeal to modern readers who, caught in the "terrible division" of their age, respect and respond to poetry that speaks decisively and unashamedly in praise of the great and good, of nobleness, learning, and piety.

Michael Timko
Victorion Poetry (April, 1963), pp. 104-5, 114

PROSE

This, then, is the value of Clough's prose, that we have in more direct fashion than in his poetry his study and his practical rejection of the creeds of his day, together with his reliance upon a high and honest hopefulness. It is doubt, yet faith; skepticism, yet belief. All this is set forth in the prose. Each idea has its expression also in the poetry, in such poems as *The New Sinai, Say Not the Struggle Nought Availeth, Alteram Partem*, or *Qua Cursum Ventus*. But these should guide the student who is interested in Clough's mind to the prose: to the *Letters*, and to the frank confession written at the last, in the *Notes on the Religious Tradition*, which bears as a text the first stanzas of *Through a Glass Darkly*. In this essay we find Clough's final word. Much of the essay is in the mood so characteristic of him:

> "Lay not," he says, "your hand upon the veil of the inner sanctuary, to lift it up; go, thou proselyte of the gate, and do thy service where it is permitted thee. . . . When the veil is raised? . . . Who knows?"

Stanley T. Williams
Studies in Victorian Literature (New York:
E. P. Dutton, 1923), p. 252

WILLIAM WILKIE COLLINS
1824-1889

A friend of Dickens who is sometimes called the first English writer of the detective story, Collins was an artist and journalist, but his great success was achieved with two popular novels of mystery, *The Woman in White* (1860) and *The Moonstone* (1868). He is a master of suspenseful plotting, and his influence as a literary craftsman has been considerable on other mystery writers.

Kenneth Robinson, *Wilkie Collins: a Biography* (1951)
Nuel P. Davis, *The Life of Wilkie Collins* (1956)

Collins's best novel—or, at any rate, the only one of Collins's novels which every one knows—is *The Woman in White*. Now *Bleak House* is the novel in which Dickens most closely approaches Collins (and after *Bleak House, Little Dorrit* and parts of *Martin Chuzzlewit*); and *The Woman in White* is the novel in which Collins most closely approaches Dickens. Dickens excelled in character; in the creation of characters of greater intensity than human beings. Collins was not usually strong in the creation of character; but he was a master of plot and situation, of those elements of drama which are most essential to melodrama. *Bleak House* is Dickens's finest piece of construction; and *The Woman in White* contains Collins's most real characterization. Every one knows Count Fosco and Marion Halcombe intimately; only the most perfect Collins reader can remember even half a dozen of his other characters by name. . . .

The one of Collins's books which is the most perfect piece of construction, and the best balanced between plot and character, is *The Moonstone*; the one which reaches the greatest melodramatic intensity is *Armadale*.

The Moonstone is the first and greatest of English detective novels. . . . Sergeant Cuff, far more than Holmes, is the ancestor of the healthy generation of amiable, efficient, professional but fallible inspectors of fiction among whom we live today. And *The Moonstone*, a book twice the length of the "thrillers" that our contemporary masters write, maintains its interest and suspense at every moment. It does this by devices of a Dickensian type; for Collins, in addition to his particular merits, was a Dickens without genius. The book is a comedy of humours.

T. S. Eliot
Selected Essays 1917-1932 (New York:
Harcourt, Brace, 1932), pp. 374-77

When all is said, it is as a story that *The Woman in White* has most interest. It was the story-tellers—Scott and Cooper and Dumas—that Collins cared for most among novelists; and he usually chose to write in an unadorned style, relishing most such prose as that of Byron's letters. Since Collins himself belongs among the great story-tellers rather than among the great novelists, *The Woman in White* well opens with this thrilling sentence: "This is the *story* of what a Woman's patience can endure, and what a Man's resolution can achieve."

Clyde K. Hyder
PMLA (June, 1939), p. 303

This larger range of the novel now began to include the novel of crime, in which the interest lay not in retribution but in detection . . . the chief master of this art in England is William Wilkie Collins. . . . In Wilkie Collins the unravelling of the skein of crime is the work, not of the hand of the law, but of some person with a compelling interest in the elucidation. Sometimes there is no crime, but only a mystery. The same skill is lavished on both; and Wilkie Collins has never been excelled as a contriver of complicated plots. His first outstanding success, *The Dead Secret* (1857), was followed by the unsurpassed "thriller," *The Woman in White* (1860). Other successes are *No Name* (1862), *Armadale* (1866), *The Moonstone* (1868) and *The Law and the Lady* (1875). Wilkie Collins has the power of generating an atmosphere of foreboding, and of imparting to natural scenes a desolation which suggests depression and horror of spirit. The beginnings of his books are sometimes so tremendous that the conclusion fails to maintain the level. This is true, for instance, of *Armadale*. The main defect of the Wilkie Collins method is an abuse of machinery—not indeed of the machinery of detection, but of the machinery of narration. We get diaries, papers, memoirs, confessions, and so forth, which, designed to give verisimilitude, end in giving tedium.

George Sampson
The Concise Cambridge History of English Literature
(Cambridge Univ. Pr., 1941), p. 796

CHARLES DICKENS

1812-1870

When Charles Dickens was twelve years old his father was put into the Marshalsea, a London debtors' prison, and he himself had to work in a warehouse; the family fortunes soon improved, so that he could return to school and then, at fifteen, work in a lawyer's office, but Charles never forgot his early poverty and shame. He began publishing humorous sketches when he was twenty-one, and many of them were collected as *Sketches by Boz* (1836). Throughout his career he was concerned with periodicals, as both contributor and editor, and virtually all of his works were published serially. These include—with the dates given for publication in book form—the *Pickwick Papers* (1836), *Oliver Twist* (1838), *Nicholas Nickleby* (1839), *The Old Curiosity Shop* (1841), *Barnaby Rudge* (1841), *American Notes* (1842), *A Christmas Carol* (1842), *Martin Chuzzlewit* (1844), *Dombey and Son* (1848), *David Copperfield* (1850), *Bleak House* (1853), *Hard Times* (1854), *Little Dorrit* (1857), *A Tale of Two Cities* (1859), *Great Expectations* (1861), *Our Mutual Friend* (1865), and the uncompleted *Mystery of Edwin Drood* (1870). A prolific and extremely popular writer in his own day, Dickens has always appealed to a large reading public. His extravagances and sentimentalism, his use of flat and sometimes grotesque characters, of melodrama, and of coincidence within his plots have made some critics consider his art to be badly flawed; but a tendency of modern criticism has been to recognize the vitality of his stylistic extravagances, to forgive the passages of sentimentality for the sake of his moral perceptiveness, to find psychological truth in his grotesques, dream-like power in his melodrama, and a coherent sense of the complex unpredictable interrelationships of real life in his plots, with all their complications and coincidences. Dickens is now generally accepted as one of the great English novelists.

Arthur Waugh, Walter Dexter, *et al.*, eds. *The Nonesuch Dickens* (1937-1938), 23 vols.

John Forster, *The Life of Charles Dickens* (1872-1874), 3 vols.

Edgar Johnson, *Charles Dickens: His Tragedy and Triumph* (1952), 2 vols.

PERSONAL

He was in a sense a superficial man; his emotions were easily stirred, and —as with easily stirred waters—were not very profound; sentiment with him was apt to degenerate into sentimentality, tragedy to become melodrama, comedy to become farce; these things both in his life and in his books. He was not a scholar, for which, of course, he was in no way to blame, and his judgments of literature and of art cannot be called otherwise than middle-class. In all his instincts and ambitions he was of the state of life in which he was born, middle-class; he showed this in his art as well as in his life. It must not be thought that we are using the term middle-class as one of opprobrium, but it is distinctly, and in this case truly, definitive.

Set in the balance against these defects his gifts weigh far the heavier. We cannot sum them up better than by repeating Carlyle's eulogium. "The good, the gentle, high-gifted, ever-friendly, noble Dickens—every inch of him an Honest Man." How great praise that from how great a source!

W. Teignmouth Shore
Charles Dickens and His Friends (London:
Cassell, 1909), pp. 322-23

Admittedly there are features in him which we could wish different. His perpetual moral preoccupation tends to destroy the artistic illusion. We should have liked to find in his work certain more sensitive and more profound characters: for these existed in those days, as the novels of George Eliot and Meredith prove. Granted. But, reverting to Chesterton's simile, we should not take our stand with the man before the hippopotamus, or springtime or the sun or the moon, and wish they had been a little different. Dickens was Dickens, as Balzac was Balzac. Let us move respectfully round these giant monuments, and after the pleasures of analysis, let us savour the undiluted joy of loving them.

André Maurois
Dickens, tr. Hamish Miles (New York: Harper, 1935), p. 164

No grown-up person can read Dickens without feeling his limitations, and yet there does remain his native generosity of mind, which acts as a kind of anchor and nearly always keeps him where he belongs. . . . Nearly everyone, whatever his actual conduct may be, responds emotionally to the idea of human brotherhood. Dickens voiced a code which was and on the whole still is believed in, even by people who violate it. It is difficult otherwise to explain why he could be both read by working people (a thing that has happened to no other novelist of his stature) and buried in Westminster Abbey.

When one reads any strongly individual piece of writing, one has the impression of seeing a face somewhere behind the page. It is not necessarily the actual face of the writer. I feel this very strongly with Swift, with Defoe, with Fielding, Stendhal, Thackeray, Flaubert, though in several cases I do not know what these people looked like and do not want to know. What one sees is the face that the writer *ought* to have. Well, in the case of Dickens I see a face that is not quite the face of Dickens's photographs, though it resembles it. It is the face of a man of about forty, with a small beard and a high colour. Hs is laughing, with a touch of anger in his laughter, but no triumph, no malignity. It is the face of a man who is always fighting against something, but who fights in the open and is not frightened, the face of a man who is *generously angry*—in other words, of a nineteenth-century liberal, a free intelligence, a type hated with equal hatred by all the smelly little orthodoxies which are now contending for our souls.

George Orwell
Critical Essays (London: Secker and Warburg, 1946), pp. 54-56

Pickwick Papers

It is when one comes to consider *Pickwick* as a novel that the trouble arises. Professor Sylvère Monod has said that it is not *un véritable roman* in the sense in which the word is used today, and G. K. Chesterton declared that "it is not a novel at all." Even Forster described it as "a series of sketches." Other writers have been content to regard it as an entertainment, or a monstrous kind of periodical; while critics who exult about the place of *Tristram Shandy* in "the history of the novel" have boggled over the *Pickwick Papers*.

All this is questionable. It is quite as much a novel as most works written in the twentieth century which have exploited all the looseness and freedom of fiction, and it is even more of a novel than many earlier works, also written in the tradition of *Don Quixote* or *Gil Blas*. To judge it by limitations which were not formulated until halfway through the nineteenth century, and which still cannot be applied to half our English novelists, living or dead, is to nullify one's criticism completely.

Of course the real merits of *Pickwick* have little to do with whether or not one wishes to call is a *novel*. Its bright comedy, its good humour and its raciness of style, are something apart from its form. But these qualities themselves have often been undervalued, just because critics have felt that *Pickwick* was in a class by itself. . . . In writing of *Pickwick* in his essay, "Dickens: The Two Scrooges," Edmund Wilson . . . devotes most of his time to the lamentable interpolated stories, and dismisses the humour as "the aspect . . . that is best known." Yet, as well as coming at the end of the eighteenth-century tradition, *Pickwick* deserves to be considered seriously as Dicken's first novel.

Of course, this is not to say that the book was not largely improvised, but that improvisation itself may be an art, and that if it produces something permanent it is creative. The form of *Pickwick* was not carpentered but grew. It took shape like a genie from a bottle. It may be clumsy and disjointed, but it has movement, and once it gets under way a controlling mind behind it of immense persuasiveness and definite character. It has direction rather than form, a story rather than a unified plot, and its success is not only due to the impression of abundance it gives, but to a definite sense of completeness.

K. J. Fielding
Charles Dickens: A Critical Introduction
(New York: David McKay, 1958), pp. 17-18

Oliver Twist and *Nicholas Nickleby*

The three novels with which Dickens had now established his literary eminence all glow with his characteristic endowments. They are bursting with vitality. *Pickwick Papers* had swiftly ripened to an affectionate hilarity that made Dickens a master of luminous humor unexampled by any writer since Shakespeare. *Oliver Twist* blazes with a sulphurous melodrama in which horror is fused with angry pathos. *Nicholas Nickleby* mingles the indignation of *Oliver* with the loose, sprawling comedy of *Pickwick*. But their differences are only the flashing facets of a many-sided brilliance. For deep in all three there already runs the vein of social criticism that was to become dominant in Dickens's entire career. They share a unity of viewpoint and of underlying purpose that makes them logically related in the great unfolding of Dickens's powers. . . .

Nickleby, however, lacks the essential unity and coherence that blankets all of *Oliver* with its heavy evil—evil that is no melodramatic embroidery on the workhouse and slum themes, but part of the very canvas. In *Nickleby*, on the other hand, the diverse threads are loosely woven together, its varied scenes and crowds of characters related to each other in a sprawling picaresque improvisation in the eighteenth-century tradition of *Tom Jones* and *Roderick Random*. And yet, no more than *Tom Jones*, is the story really lacking in structure. It opens when the indigent widow, Mrs. Nickleby, arrives in London with her children, the youthful Nicholas and Kate, to seek the aid of her husband's brother Ralph. He has no intention of parting with a penny more than he can help, but he sees a chance to use Kate as a decoy with the wastrels to whom he lends money. His cynical exploitation of the charms of his pretty niece while her brother Nicholas is got out of the way, his later machinations against the heiress Madeline Bray, and Nicholas's return to foil these schemes, provide a plot almost as involved as that of *Oliver Twist*. For plot purposes, however, it hardly matters *where* Nicholas is; his experiences as a teacher in Yorkshire with Squeers and as an actor in Portsmouth with Vincent Crummles are purely arbitrary. Dotheboys Hall gives Dickens the chance to expose the schools, but Nicholas's life would have been little different had he never seen the place. And Kate might as well have been a seamstress or a governess as a milliner at Mme. Mantalini's and a companion to Mrs. Wititterly.

But the triumphant achievement of the book is that these gratuitous interludes start into a life so far exceeding their structural importance as to represent, in fact, *Nicholas Nickleby*'s most vivid claim upon our memories.

Edgar Johnson
Charles Dickens: His Tragedy and Triumph, Vol. I
(New York: Simon and Schuster, 1952), pp. 273, 285

Martin Chuzzlewit

Martin Chuzzlewit...has certain weaknesses. The first chapter, which traces the history of the Chuzzlewits, is an absurd rigmarole after the manner of Henry Fielding in *Jonathan Wild*. It also seems to include some forgotten topical satire which missed its aim. Its main fault, after that, is the plot. In construction it is undoubtedly the weakest of Dickens's works, and the worse for an ambition to weave a mystery round the curmudgeonly old

Martin Chuzzlewit, who is transformed into a universal benefactor by the final number. Its closing scene, in which all the characters are re-united, is a triumph of theatrical conventionality which would have shamed Vincent Crummles.

It is not even as well planned as *Nickleby* and it has the disadvantage that, being intended as a satire on ordinary life, it needs to be more realistic. It is true that, after he had finished, Dickens said that he had tried "to resist the temptation of the current Monthly Number, and to keep a steadier eye on the general purpose and design" (*Preface*), but this is by no means clear from the story. It is true, too, that the manuscript shows that by the end of the third number he had already decided on "Old Martin's plot to degrade and punish Pecksniff in the end." Yet it is not well worked-out. The situation in which a father (Anthony Chuzzlewit) who so loves his son that he forgives him even when he knows that the son is plotting his murder, was taken from Le Sage's *Gil Blas*; and it should be remembered that, as much as *Pickwick* and more than his other first five novels, *Chuzzlewit* was still written in the tradition of the glorious shelf-full of eighteenth-century novels that Dickens had first read in childhood.

As much as any of his books, too, it is written with a moral purpose. It may be unnecessary to labour this point, but it is impossible to understand Dickens without it, and no one can question that this was his purpose in *Martin Chuzzlewit*. . . .

The best things in the novel, in fact, were not planned but grew and flourished naturally. Mrs. Gamp and Pecksniff, especially, developed in a manner Dickens himself had not foreseen. "As to the way in which these characters have opened out," he wrote of them, "that is to me one of the most surprising processes of the mind in this sort of invention. Given what one knows, what one does not know springs up; and I am as absolutely certain of its being true, as I am of the law of gravitation—if such a thing be possible, more so." Such, says Forster revealingly, "was the very process of creation," with "all his important characters." Both Mrs. Gamp and Pecksniff were founded on real people, and, given what he knew of them, Dickens felt that almost by a natural law he could show what they would say or do in any possible circumstances.

K. J. Fielding
Charles Dickens: A Critical Introduction
(New York: David McKay, 1958), pp. 75-77

Dombey and Son

The total achievement of *Dombey and Son* makes it one of Dickens's great books. With a creative vitality hardly surpassed by any of the books between it and *Pickwick*, it leaves all its predecessors far behind in structural logic, intellectual power, and social insight. His writing until now is the work of a brilliantly inspired youthful writer; *Dombey* is the first masterpiece of Dickens's maturity. Readers may prefer individual scenes in *Nickleby, Oliver,* or *Martin Chuzzlewit* to individual scenes in *Dombey*—although it is debatable that they contain anything really better than Captain Cuttle and Mr. Toots—but no one could say critically that they are better books. The problem of building a unified plot around a central theme so imperfectly tackled in *Chuzzlewit* is triumphantly solved in *Dombey.* None of Dickens's later books exhibit the loose improvisation with which he had begun; their elaboration is not that of planlessness but of a vast cathedral. And with *Dombey,* above all, Dickens has achieved a form by means of which he can convey the more detailed and philosophic social criticism that was to animate his work in the future.

Edgar Johnson
Charles Dickens: His Tragedy and Triumph, Vol. II
(New York: Simon and Schuster, 1952), p. 643

Across the social picture are ruled the ruthless lines of the new order, symbolized in the railway. It links high and low, devastates Camden Town, uproots Stagg's Gardens, provides employment for Mr. Toodle, bears Mr. Dombey from grim past to grimmer future, and finally obliterates Carker. Its appearance on each of the four carefully spaced and placed occasions is emphasized by a volcanic upsurge in the style, by description much overflowing its narrative function. In these descriptions may be discerned the fascination of the new as well as the horror of the strange; but the tone is mainly that of dread. Twice the railway is used to highlight the darker thoughts of hero and villain, thoughts of fear and hate and death. The train is seen only as destructive, ruthless, an "impetuous monster," a "fiery devil." There is no suggestion of hope, of social progress. This colouring of gloom and horror may derive from the over-riding mood of the novel; it may be a picturesque reflection of contemporary doubts; but more probably, from the evidence of the later novels, it represents a persistent shade in Dickens's own social view, which contains at least as much pessimism as optimism, and always more of the visionary than of the reformer.

The social criticism in *Dombey and Son* cannot be abstracted from the novel, and even such disengaging as is attempted here perhaps distorts it. It is pervasive, unformulated; not documentary in origin or usefulness; no purposeful journeys or reading of newspaper reports lie behind it, and it is not a convenient source for social historians. Partly for this reason, that it is inseparable, it assists instead of disturbing the firm unity of the design. It is part of the "Idea of the world" which protects Dickens from being "prevailed over the world's multitudinousness."

Kathleen Tillotson
Novels of the Eighteen-Forties
(Oxford Univ. Pr., 1954), pp. 200-201

David Copperfield

With the next novel, *David Copperfield*, we reach the peak of achievement. "Of all my books I like this best," said its author, who, on finishing it, felt that he was "dismissing a portion of himself into the shadowy world." Matthew Arnold and John Ruskin were agreed in preferring it to all the others. The reading world of that day had no notion that the story was in great part autobiographical, but in 1859 we find Dickens admitting to William Howitt that he had worked many childish struggles and experiences into the narrative. . . .

Though there is no main plot in *David Copperfield,* there are a whole crop of sub-plots connected with the machinations of Uriah Heep, Miss Murdstone, the amours of Steerforth, the disparity in age of the Strongs and the mystery of Betsey Trotwood's husband. They enrich but do not affect the narrative to any appreciable degree.

Una Pope-Hennessy
Charles Dickens (London: Chatto and Windus, 1945),
pp. 342-43

No book of Dickens is so difficult to assess fairly as *David Copperfield.* It was the author's own favourite; and, of course, it is very much closer to his own experience than any of his other works. This means that the impression of abounding life, in which the whole of Dickens's work is so rich, is particularly strong; but it also means that the subtle kinds of falsification, which beset him—sentimentality, cheap resentment, and unreal victories over half-imagined evils—all these and other faults are present in a virulent form.]To strike a critical balance here is difficult: the book is certainly a readers' favourite, as well as the author's. It is vastly enjoyable both for the simple and the discriminating. Everybody can appreciate Mr. Micawber, but what can the critic say about him? All criticism naturally tends to concentrate on the topics about which the most interesting things can be said. No doubt these topics tend to coincide, in a rough and ready way, with the greatest literary achievements. But there are exceptions. To read of Mr. Micawber is, as Chesterton said, like receiving a blow in the face. It is a deeply-felt experience, but it is not susceptible of analytic description. It follows that any detailed critical discussion of *David Copperfield* will tend to be unbalanced because it is impossible to give appropriate space to Micawber.

It is certain that the book has been widely loved. I suspect also that, more than most of Dickens's works, it has been read with the same spirit that the author writ. A character like Micawber almost annihilates differences of intellect and education in the readers. And the whole easy, fond reminiscent tone, slightly tinged with self-mockery, and rather more strongly tinged with self-pity, is very attractive, at times, to everyone. *David Copperfield* answers a very common requirement with supreme—perhaps unequalled—appropriateness. It does so by means of two almost opposite qualities, by the incredible clearness of the nostalgic pictures it presents, and by its marked tendency to fantasy. That is, it continually evades the consequences of its own assumptions; it lacks the inner logic of Dickens's most distinguished works.

A. O. J. Cockshutt
The Imagination of Charles Dickens
(New York Univ. Pr., 1962), pp. 114-15

Bleak House

The book . . . illustrates very well Dickens's unconscious disregard of anything in the way of rules or regularity in literary art. If he thought of such things at all, he probably regarded himself as exempt—as did Napoleon in the case of morals. He conducts the story in an in-and-out fashion partly as told impersonally and partly as related supposedly by Esther Summerson. But he doesn't bother to limit Esther Summerson to the kind of ideas and the kind of language that Esther Summerson would, or could, have used. Her personality is maintained by a few little mincing phrases and by a sort of modest decorum of sentiment, but when she needs it she is given all the humour and power of Charles Dickens. The voice is Esther's, but the jokes are Dickens's! Nothing is more false in art than to make a fictitious personage speak out of his character, as if Mr. Pickwick suddenly talked cockney, or Sam Weller dropped into French. But, as usual, Dickens "gets away with it." Few, if any, readers ever bother whether Esther is in character or not; many no doubt think her a mighty humorous girl and that she ought to have written books.

Stephen Leacock
Charles Dickens (New York: Doubleday, Doran, 1934)
pp. 162-63

What Dickens has done here, in fact, has been to create the novel of the social group, used as an instrument of social criticism. Though to a certain extent, in *Vanity Fair*, Thackeray had anticipated him, Thackeray used his story more in the spirit of *Everyman* or *Pilgrim's Progress*, as a moral commentary upon human nature, hardly more than suggesting that people's lives were shaped and twisted by social institutions. But Dickens had from the beginning of his career been deeply concerned with institutions, although at first he was able to do no more than sandwich his attacks on them between episodes of melodrama and comedy or relate them to his story only by implication. With *Dombey and Son* he had attempted a more integral suffusion of social criticism and narrative, but for all its successes *Dombey* achieves neither the scope nor the depth of *Bleak House.* . . .

From one point of view this is a gain in "realism," but from another it is an artistic loss. For if there is a danger of Dickens's intricate structures seeming contrived and overmelodramatic, with their missing documents and hidden sins rising up out of the past, there is also a strength in tightness and intensity of development. This advantage Dickens potently exploits by creating a sense of taut inevitability that deepens immeasurably the emotional impact. The movement of *Bleak House* becomes a centripetal one like a whirlpool, at first slow and almost imperceptible, but fatefully drawing in successive groups of characters, circling faster and faster, and ultimately sucking them into the dark funnel whence none will escape uninjured and where many will be crushed and destroyed. In pure emotional power *Bleak House* ranks among Dickens's greatest books.

Edgar Johnson
Charles Dickens: His Tragedy and Triumph, Vol. II
(New York: Simon and Schuster, 1952), pp. 764-65

Hard Times

There is little truly representative of Dickens in *Hard Times* (1854), beyond the sincerity and ardour with which he champions the unfortunates bleeding under the wheels of modern industrialism. Taine, misguidedly though not incomprehensibly, chose to annotate the book as a typical example of Dickens's novels. But the proper place for *Hard Times* is with the pamphleteering literature of Carlyle and Ruskin, to the former of whom it was dedicated, whilst the latter gave the book a cordial welcome, not refraining, however, from pointing out how much more effective it would have been, as a controversial tract, had the writer used "severer and more accurate analysis." But this was asking the impossible of Dickens.

Ernest A. Baker
The History of the English Novel, vol. VII
(London: Witherby, 1936), p. 297

Hard Times is not a difficult work; its intention and nature are pretty obvious. If, then, it is the masterpiece I take it for, why has it not had general recognition? To judge by the critical record, it has had none at all. If there exists anywhere an appreciation, or even an acclaiming reference, I have missed it. In the books and essays on Dickens, so far as I know them, it is passed over as a very minor thing; too slight and insignificant to distract us for more than a sentence or two from the works worth critical attention. Yet, if I am right, of all Dickens's works it is the one that has all the strength of his genius, together with a strength no other of them can show—that of a completely serious work of art. . . .

The inspiration is what is given in the title, *Hard Times*. Ordinarily Dicken's criticisms of the world he lives in are casual and incidental—a matter of including among the ingredients of a book some indignant treatment of a particular abuse. But in *Hard Times* he is for once possessed by a comprehensive vision, one in which the inhumanities of Victorian civilization are seen as fostered and sanctioned by a hard philosophy, the aggressive formulation of an inhumane spirit. . . .

All this is obvious enough. But Dickens's art, while remaining that of the great popular entertainer, has in *Hard Times*, as he renders his full critical vision, a stamina, a flexibility combined with consistency, and a depth that he seems to have had little credit for. . . .

The final stress may fall on Dickens's command of word, phrase, rhythm and image: in ease and range there is surely no greater master of English except Shakespeare. This comes back to saying that Dickens is a great poet: his endless resource in felicitously varied expression is an extraordinary responsiveness to life. His senses are charged with emotional energy, and his intelligence plays and flashes in the quickest and sharpest perception. That is, his mastery of "style" is of the only kind that matters—which is not to say that he hasn't a conscious interest in what can be done with words; many of his felicities could plainly not have come if there had not been, in the background, a habit of such interest.

F. R. Leavis
The Great Tradition (New York: G. W. Stewart,
1948), pp. 227, 246

It is generally acknowledged by Dr. Leavis and others that the Trade Union scenes are not satisfactory; though Dickens achieved one stroke of prophetic insight, when, in Bounderby's interview with Blackpool, he showed the subconscious sympathy between owners and Trade Unions linked against individualistic workers.

The parallel between Bounderby's and Blackpool's matrimonial troubles is unconvincing; and one feels that probability, psychology and everything else had been sacrificed to symmetry. The last chapter summarises in a few hundred words events which might fill a whole novel. Here Dickens's sense of superiority of life to fact, which is the guiding star of the novel, up to this point, seems ironically to have deserted him. Gradgrind could almost have written the chapter himself.

There are then, it seems to me, sound reasons against considering *Hard Times* a masterpiece. But it remains a work of great distinction, which performed for the first time the very important imaginative task of integrating the factory world into the world of nature and of humanity.

A. O. J. Cockshutt
The Imagination of Charles Dickens
(New York Univ. Pr., 1962), p. 141

Little Dorrit

Little Dorrit is one of the three great novels of Dickens' great last period, but of the three it is perhaps the least established with modern readers. When it first appeared—in monthly parts from December 1855 to June 1857—its success was even more decisive than that of *Bleak House*, but the suffrage of later audiences has gone the other way, and of all Dickens' later works it is *Bleak House* that has come to be the best known. As for *Our Mutual Friend*, after having for some time met with adverse critical opinion among the enlightened—one recalls that the youthful Henry James attacked it for standing in the way of art and truth—it has of recent years been regarded with ever-growing admiration. But *Little Dorrit* seems to have retired to the background and shadow of our consciousness of Dickens.

This does not make an occasion for concern or indignation. With a body of work as large and as enduring as that of Dickens, taste and opinion will never be done. They will shift and veer as they have shifted and veered with the canon of Shakespeare, and each generation will have its special favorites and make its surprised discoveries. *Little Dorrit*, one of the most profound of Dickens' novels and one of the most significant works of the nineteenth century, will not fail to be thought of as speaking with a peculiar and passionate intimacy to our own time.

Little Dorrit is about society, which certainly does not distinguish it from the rest of Dickens' novels unless we go on to say, as we must, that it is *more* about society than any other of the novels, that it is about society in its very essence. . . .

The imagination of *Little Dorrit* is marked not so much by its powers of particularization as by its powers of generalization and abstraction. It is an imagination under the dominion of a great articulated idea, a moral idea which tends to find its full development in a religious experience. It is an imagination akin to that which created *Piers Plowman* and *Pilgrim's Progress*. And, indeed, it is akin to the imagination of *The Divine Comedy*. Never before has Dickens made so full, so Dantean, a claim for the virtue of the artist, and there is a Dantean pride and a Dantean reason in what he says of Daniel Doyce, who, although an engineer, stands for the creative mind in general and for its appropriate virtue: "His dismissal of himself [was] remarkable. He never said, I discovered this adaptation or invented that combination; but showed the whole thing as if the Divine artificer had made it, and he had happened to find it. So modest was he about it, such a pleasant touch of respect was mingled with his quiet admiration of it, and so calmly convinced was he that it was established on irrefragable laws." Like much else that might be pointed to, this confirms us in the sense that the whole energy of the imagination of *Little Dorrit* is directed to the transcending of the personal will, to the search for the Will in which shall be our peace.

Lionel Trilling
The Opposing Self (New York: Viking, 1955), pp. 50-51, 64

Great Expectations

Great Expectations, in comparison with Dicken's besetting carelessness, is a masterpiece of verbal art, whether in narrative and description or in the dialogue. It is not more than half as long as his average novel; and whatever else this thriftiness indicates, it is a sign that Dickens kept his characters in their place, and did not let them display themselves for the sake of display, as was too often his wont, in the novel next to follow, for instance. He evidently saw his ending from the very first, and from time to time put in little hints of what was in store; as when Pip tells Miss Havisham that he only knows how to play beggar my neighbour, and she bids Estella, "Beggar him." It is almost as clear a warning as the later injunction, "Love her, love her, love her!" which is again as ominous as the notice Pip receives when there are other dangers about, "Don't go home!" The presentiments and intuitions, for instance, which somehow convince Pip that Jaggers's housekeeper is Estella's mother, and that her father is Magwitch, are among the links scattered all over the story which hold it firmly together. One thing they make clear and definite, that Estella was meant to be his bane and not his blessing: the altered ending falsified everything.

Ernest A. Baker
The History of the English Novel, Vol. VII
(London: Witherby, 1936), p. 313

GENERAL

It is clearly impossible that so flawed a talent should ever produce a book of any consistent merit. But certain aesthetic conditions suit it better than others; the Picaresque form, for instance. *Pickwick* is far from being Dickens' best book, but it is the freest from his structural faults. For since it is avowedly a story of heterogeneous adventures only connected together by a central figure, it does not require that framework of conventional intrigue with which Dickens has felt it necessary to cumber up the more "orthodox" novels of *Bleak House* and *Great Expectations*. If you have little gift for form, the wisest thing to do is to write a book with as little form as possible. Again, he does best when he writes from a child's point of view. Children are instinctive, they have strong imaginations, vivid sensations; they see life as black or white, and bigger than reality, their enemies seem demons, their friends angels, their joys or sorrows absolute and eternal. They do not look at life with the eyes of the intellect or of the instructed observer, they are not ashamed of sentiment: in fact they see life very like Dickens. And he has an extraordinary understanding of them. He does fail over them when he is describing them from the outside, when he is exploiting their pathos and charm.)His angel children are among the more revolting of his sentimental wallowings; but when he takes their standpoint as that from which to survey the rest of the world, he is triumphantly successful. The first halves of *Great Expectations* and *David Copperfield* are among the profoundest pictures of childhood in English letters. Who that has read it can forget the vast, sinister marsh of *Great Expectations*, with the convict rising like a giant of fairy-tale from its oozy banks; and the forge with its entrancing sparks; and kindly, clumsy Joe Gargery and Mrs Gargery, that comic ogress, as they appear to the wondering, acute six-year-old gaze of Pip? But better still are the first one hundred and sixty pages of *David Copperfield*, the best Dickens ever wrote, one of the very best things in the whole of English. Here for once Dickens seems not only living, but lifelike; for though the world that he reveals is more exaggerated, lit by brighter lights, darkened by sharper shadows than that of most grown-up people, it is exactly the world as it is seen through the eyes of a child. . . .

Like the writers of the old moralities, Dickens peoples his stage with virtues and vices, and like them he does it gaily, presenting them as no frigid abstractions, but as clowns and zanies thwacking their bladders, exuberant in motley and bell.

And with the convention of the old moralities his novels have their universal application. Dickens' gospel is crude; but it is not slight or shallow. The truth it enshrines is a universal truth. In every country, every walk of life, human beings feel the beauty of the primary generosities, the evil produced by their absence. So that in every country, every walk of life Dickens strikes a responsive chord in the hearts of mankind.

David Cecil
Early Victorian Novelists (Indianapolis, Ind.:
Bobbs-Merril, 1934), pp. 64-66, 73

Chief among [his limitations] was his inability to see far below the outward and visible idiosyncrasies of mankind; what was said on the same deficiency in Scott applies exactly to Dickens. On this side, no two writers are more fundamentally akin. James Oliphant put the truth rather too aggressively, and in a manner open to misunderstanding: "The prime defect of Dickens was the lack of insight into character." Carlyle was less severe and a good deal more accurate in his famous complaint that, instead of fashioning his characters, as Shakespeare did, from the heart outwards, "your Scott fashions them from the skin inwards, never getting near the heart of them!" And he would have said the same of Dickens. . . . Perhaps Shakespeare alone united the all-seeing eye and the penetrating vision which at the same time discerns the inmost life, if others have had some smaller share of this universalizing power. But it must be conceded that your Scott and your Dickens, although they do not expose the inner mechanism, do not often go wrong in reading the dial-face on which its workings are registered. . . . How much [Dickens] did ignore is less apparent because of the vividness with which all the rest is given; he seizes the salient and striking with such gusto and vigour that the reader may fail to notice that the inner reality has escaped. It is just here that his grip on personality fails. The distinctions of character which stare him in the face are purely external. The deeper differences between one consciousness and another consciousness are a sealed book to Dickens. He knows there is the deeper difference and the deeper affinity; but he cannot put his finger on the place and show what it really amounts to. It was a fault often observed in his readings, or rather in his acting of scenes from his novels, that "he isolated his parts too sharply." He isolated them in his mind; he could not help it. To him, humanity consisted of an infinite number of individuals, all different, and it was this multifariousness that absorbed his whole attention. His characters do not react upon each other; in truth, they do not act at all, they only behave, and show off their unlikeness one to the other. . . .

However they may have originated, these imaginative figures are substantiated by their own dramatic integrity and by the potent engine of his realistic art, the Defoe-like accumulation of detail, true as eyesight, and the harmonious, if sometimes stagy, atmosphere which is evolved from his vivid though it may be visionary picturing of their surroundings. Ultimately, all partake of a certain reality, all become more than probable; they are. And, after all, Mrs. Gamp and Sam Weller, not to speak of Pip and David Copperfield, are inherently nothing like so improbable as Charles Dickens. His fertility in creations that have this durable substance extorts the comparison with Shakespeare.

Ernest A. Baker
The History of the English Novel, Vol. VII
(London: Witherby, 1936), pp. 326-27, 330

Of all the great English writers, Charles Dickens has received in his own country the scantiest serious attention from either biographers, scholars, or critics. He has become for the English middle class so much one of the articles of their creed—a familiar joke, a favorite dish, a Christmas ritual—that it is difficult for British pundits to see in him the great artist and social critic that he was. Dickens had no university education, and the literary men from Oxford and Cambridge, who have lately been sifting fastidiously so much of the English heritage, have rather snubbingly let him alone. . . .

As for criticism, there has been in English one admirable critic of Dickens, George Gissing, whose prefaces and whose book on Dickens not only are the best thing on Dickens in English but stand out as one of the few really first-place pieces of literary criticism produced by an Englishman of the end of the century. For the rest, you have mainly G. K. Chesterton, who turned out in his books on Dickens some of the best work of which he was capable and who said some excellent things, but whose writing here as elsewhere is always melting away into that peculiar pseudo-poetic booziness which verbalizes with large conceptions and ignores the most obtrusive actualities. Chesterton celebrated the jolly Dickens; and Bernard Shaw offset this picture by praising the later and gloomier Dickens and insisting on his own debt to the author of *Little Dorrit* at a time when it was taken for granted that he must derive from such foreigners as Ibsen and Nietzsche.

Chesterton asserted that time would show that Dickens was not merely one of the Victorians, but incomparably the greatest English writer of his time; and Shaw coupled his name with that of Shakespeare. It is the conviction of the present writer that both these judgments were justified. Dickens —though he cannot of course pretend to the rank where Shakespeare has few companions—was nevertheless the greatest dramatic writer that the English had had since Shakespeare, and he created the largest and most varied world. It is the purpose of this essay to show that we may find in Dickens' work today a complexity and a depth to which even Gissing and Shaw have hardly, it seems to me, done justice—an intellectual and artistic interest which makes Dickens loom very large in the whole perspective of the literature of the West.

Edmund Wilson
The Wound and the Bow (Boston:
Houghton Mifflin, 1941), pp. 1-3

Technique is vision. Dickens' technique is an index of a vision of life that sees human separatedness as the ordinary condition, where speech is speech *to* nobody and where human encounter is mere collision. But the vision goes much further. Our minds are so constituted that they insist on seeking in the use of language an exchange function, a delivery and a passing on of perceptions from soul to soul and generation to generation, binding them in some kind of order; and they insist on finding cause and effect, or *motivation*, in the displacements and encounters of persons or things. Without these primary patterns of perception we would not have what we call minds. And when these patterns are confused or abrogated by our experience, we are forced, in order to preserve some kind of psychic equilibrium, to seek them in extraordinary explanations—explanations again in terms of mutual exchange and cause and effect. Dickens saw his world patently all in pieces, and as a child's vision would offer some reasonable explanation of why such a world was that way—and, by the act of explanation, would make that world yield up a principle of order, however obscure or fantastic—so, with a child's literalism of imagination, he discovered organization among his fragments.

Dorothy Van Ghent
The English Novel (New York:
Holt, Rinehart, and Winston, 1953), pp. 127-28

Many critics have attacked or rejected Dickens—often by implication or innuendo—for three clearly unjustified reasons. Some critics have really attacked not Dickens but the Dickensians, not his writings but the excessive adulation of them. No doubt the admirer and student of Dickens will find himself in strange company at times, amid not only responsible historians and critics but also obsessed antiquarians, enthusiastic name droppers, and sentimental rhapsodizers. Not all readers of Dickens also read Dostoevsky or Henry James, nor need they. But enough readers have taken Dickens seriously as an artist to answer such objection. . . .

Other critics have looked not for Dickens' strengths but only for his weaknesses. They have condemned him for those of his early works in which he often either relied too fully on the cruder conventions of earlier fiction or gave too much freedom to his own still imperfect genius. They have condemned him for overobvious irony and satire, and clumsy picaresque plots; or for oversimple morality and melodrama, and false emotionalizing and uncontrolled verbal fancy. Dickens undeniably had these faults, especially at first, but they are the faults of his creative ambition and imagination. They are the faults of a novelist who never feared to take chances artistically to say what he wished to say, who never had the artistic discretion of Jane Austen, who knew her limitations and made her successes within them. . . .

Still other critics have set up a limited definition of the novel and by it have determined that Dickens was no novelist and therefore no artist. They have decided that the novel is not romance but reality, not myth but history; that is is not symbolic but literal and not poetic but prosaic. Hence they would have action always probable, behavior always explainable in everyday terms; they would have style decorous and restrained, speech the speech of normal men and women, and characters moved only by the ordinary springs of human behavior, by the ordinary human desires for fame and fortune, money and matrimony.

Judged wholly by any or all of these views, Dickens fails artistically. But they are all one-sided, they all take too limited a view of Dickensians, of Dickens, and of prose fiction. A roll call of past and present criticism of Dickens shows that his work has seriously engaged the minds of many important critics and writers of the last hundred years, and the range and depth of their reaction to Dickens show how much more there is to him than the obvious faults of his early work, or the obvious merits of that work. Also, recent theorists of fiction—for example, Northrop Frye, who in *Anatomy of Criticism* sees prose fiction as having four forms: novel, romance, confession, and anatomy—demand either a more generous definition of the novel or, more usefully, a sharper sense of the different types of prose fiction, of which the novel is only one. Seen through the work of such critics and of such theorists of fiction, Dickens stands as a meaningful and critically challenging creative artist in prose.

Lauriat Lane
The Dickens Critics (Ithaca, N. Y.:
Cornell Univ. Pr., 1961), pp. 2-3

"GEORGE ELIOT"
(MARY ANN EVANS CROSS)
1819-1880

Mary Ann Evans was born in Warwickshire. A plain and timid girl, she devoted herself to music, religion, and the study of languages. In 1846 she published her translation from the German of Strauss's *Leben Jesu*, an unorthodox life of Christ. A few years later she became assistant editor of the liberal *Westminster Review*; she came to know many London writers and intellectuals, including the rationalist Herbert Spencer, through whom she met George Henry Lewes. Lewes, a journalist, was separated from his wife, although the couple could not be divorced, and in 1854 he and Miss Evans told their friends that they intended to live together. The woman generally described as the most morally sensitive among the Victorian novelists—and George Eliot is at heart a moralist—lived for twenty-four years in what many if not most of her contemporaries regarded as sin; but she always thought of herself as being truly if not legally married and referred to Lewes as her husband. During this time her novels and verse were written and published, all under her masculine pseudonym: *Scenes of Clerical Life* in 1858, *Adam Bede* in 1859, *The Mill on the Floss* in 1860, *Silas Marner* in 1861, *Romola* in 1863, *Felix Holt* in 1866, *The Spanish Gypsy, a Poem* in 1868, *Middlemarch* in 1871-1872, and *Daniel Deronda* in 1876. It is sometimes said that among her novels *Middlemarch* is the masterpiece, but others as well have been praised highly by modern critics. Lewes died in 1878, and Miss Evans married a younger man, John Cross, seven months before her own death in 1880.

Works: Warwick edition (1901-1903), 12 vols.

John W. Cross, *George Eliot's Life as Related in Her Letters and Journals* (1885), 3 vols.

Lawrence and Elisabeth Hanson, *Marian Evans and George Eliot: a Biography* (1952)

PERSONAL

The time for romance had passed away as the century grew older, and men and women were facing the strenuous life that met them with the rise of the scientific spirit. Even the excitement of the Oxford Movement had died down, and it was succeeded by a much more general excitement over the new physical interpretation of man and nature, or what was considered such. Science and religion came into violent opposition, and men's beliefs became shattered. It was here that George Eliot's calm judgment was so useful. She seemed to take the ordinary life and convert its ordinariness into something bigger and better. She did not controvert, but she showed that there was truth above the struggles, and also showed that there was a spiritual element running through all the events of life without which they would be incomprehensible. This, for those who were puzzled and troubled over the conclusions that Darwin's and Huxley's reasoning led to, was the greatest possible solace and help. We are not so concerned about science and its relation to the religious and moral life in these days, or at least we approach the question of the reconciliation rather differently. But though our approach may be different, we can still appreciate George Eliot's ethical background; and the way in which she traces how men's actions are bound up with the happenings of their forefathers and race, is associated with those laws of evolution and heredity that were coming to be so seriously taken into account.

Elizabeth S. Haldane
George Eliot and Her Times (New York:
Appleton-Century-Crofts, 1927), p. 322

Fifty years ago it was fashionable to say that George Eliot was unread because she was so ponderously intellectual and didactic. This critical cliché sprang partly from efforts to magnify current favorites by depreciating the Victorian giants. Of *Middlemarch*, which is generally accepted today as one of the greatest novels of its time, Edmund Gosse could only say that it was a "remarkable instance of elaborate mental resources misapplied, and genius revolving, with tremendous machinery, like some great water-wheel, while no water is flowing underneath." W. E. Henley professed himself uncertain whether George Eliot's books were novels disguised as treatises or treatises disguised as novels; and his mot that they seem to have been dictated "to a plain woman of genius by the ghost of David Hume" leaves us wondering which author he was more ignorant of. In criticism like this the clever epigram and the gibe at her horse-faced ugliness (rarely noticed by those who knew her) took the place of specific comment on her books, which obviously required more intellectual effort than those of Stevenson or Kipling.

After World War I, as the other Victorians were rediscovered, George Eliot remained in eclipse. Her insistence on moral principle in the universe bored a generation that had done with morality; her subtle analysis of temptation meant nothing where there was no such thing as sin. Youthful readers lost in admiration of *Antic Hay* and *The Green Hat* found her view of life mournful. Their new materialism denied the inevitable consequences that play so large a part in George Eliot's books; modern technology seemed fairly bent to control man's destiny, and he intended to shape the consequences to suit himself. The height of this confidence marked the low ebb of her reputation.

Today her concern with the intellectual and ethical no longer damns her as an artist. "It is precisely because she was a mind . . . that she interests us now," writes Mr. V. S. Pritchett. And it is because of her moral insight that Dr. F. R. Leavis places her squarely at the center of *The Great Tradition*, which begins in his uncompromising style: "The great English novelists are Jane Austen, George Eliot, Henry James, and Joseph Conrad." He points out that James "did actually go to school to George Eliot," whose moral seriousness "qualified her for a kind of influence that neither Flaubert nor the admired Turgènev could have." Professor Geoffrey Tillotson declares that one could overrate *Middlemarch* only "by saying that it was easily the best of the half-dozen novels of the world."

Gordon Haight, ed.,
The George Eliot Letters (New Haven:
Yale Univ. Pr., 1954), pp. ix-x

Adam Bede

The massy line of the book is deflected toward the end. ("The mirror," George Eliot says, "is doubtless defective; the outlines will sometimes be disturbed, the reflection faint or confused.") By Mrs. Poyser's clock, Hetty's last-minute reprieve cannot really be timed with a time integral to the rest of the novel, nor can Adam's marriage with Dinah. Henry James says of these events that he doubts very much "whether the author herself had a clear vision" of them, and suggests that the reason may be that George Eliot's perception

> was a perception of nature much more than of art, and that these
> particular incidents do not belong to nature (to my sense at least);

by which I do not mean that they belong to a very happy art . . .
they are a very good example of the view in which a story must
have marriages and rescues in the nick of time, as a matter of
course.

We should add Arthur Donnithorne's return in his interesting and picturesque ill-health. Hetty's reprieve, the marriage of Dinah and Adam,
Arthur's reconstruction through such suffering as Arthur is able to suffer—
these are no compensation for and no real "illumination" of the tragedy of
Hetty. They are the artificial illumination which so many Victorian novels
indulged in, in the effort to justify to man God's ways or society's ways or
nature's ways. But still there is left the ticking of the oak-cased clock, rubbed
by human "elbow-polish," that paces the book through its greater part: the
realization of value, clean as the clock-tick, radiant as the kitchen of Hall
Farm, fragrant as the dairy; and the tragic realization of the loss of however
simple human values, in Hetty's abandoned footsteps as she seeks the dark
pool and caresses her own arms in the desire for life.

Dorothy Van Ghent
The English Novel (New York:
Holt, Rinehart, and Winston, 1953), pp. 180-81

Middlemarch

George Eliot's knowledge of law and social problems was gained by laborious reading. Legal questions were submitted to a friend who stood high in
the practice of law, to "guard against errors." It was to such conscientious
preparation as this, coupled with the "insight into soul" which was the author's natural gift, that *Middlemarch* owes its strength as a portrayal of
English life in the middle of the nineteenth century. It is a novel without a
plot, but it needs none. All the characters posses a strong individuality and
are so vividly painted that they leave a lasting impression as of people we
have known. Its purpose is to show how the social conditions of modern
times operate to balk the lofty aspirations and well-meant endeavors of
those whose ideals are above the ordinary.

Charles S. Olcott
George Eliot: Scenes and People in Her Novels
(London: Cassell, 1911), pp. 168-69

Middlemarch (1872) is undoubtedly the best novel of this period. It tells
again of the revolt of noble aspirations and intellectual ambitions, cramped
in the philistinism of Victorian life. Nor are the characters much below
George Eliot's best. Dorothea Brooke is another Romola in her purity and
singleness of aim, her self-devotion, her need of experience, and her patient
willingness to do all that her duty requires of her. Casaubon illustrates bril-

liantly and bitterly a favourite opinion of hers "that the deepest disgrace is to insist on doing work for which we are unfit—to do work of any sort badly." Another fine piece of work is the way Rosamond Vincy, Lydgate's expensive and selfish wife, plays her part as a foil to Dorothea's devotion and altruism. As these and other personages with their many connections must slip into situations which multiply their troubles, test or purify their motives and expose the futility and malevolence of provincial life, we can well pardon the narrative for stretching to an unconscionable length and involving no less than four distinct intrigues—more than Thackeray ventured to elaborate in the longest of his long serials. The novel was more successful than *Adam Bede* and the authoress received, as she records in her Journal, "many deeply affecting assurances of its influence for good on individual minds." Then why does the work seem to us to be heavy and at times even wearisome? Because it is dated. We have (or think we have) outlived those old bad times. So we note that George Eliot is repeating herself.

H. V. Routh
Towards the Twentieth Century (New York:
Macmillan, 1937) pp. 273-74

There have been fluctuations in the critics' estimate of the value of *Middlemarch* in relation to George Eliot's other novels. It was a success on its first publication and George Eliot wrote in her journal, 1 January 1873:

> No former book of mine has been received with more enthusiasm—not even *Adam Bede*.

During her lifetime it continued to be reckoned among the best of her novels. But when her total work was assessed immediately after her death it was the fashion to assert that she never recovered her creative vitality after *Romola* and that her best work is the work of her first period. In 1887, R. H. Hutton was exceptional in his opinion that:

> None of George Eliot's tales can compare with *Middlemarch* for delicacy of detail and completeness of finish—completeness as regards not only the individual figures but the whole picture of life delineated—and for the breadth of life brought within the field of the story.

That opinion is shared by most modern critics, and to-day *Middlemarch* is commonly agreed to be the author's masterpiece. . . .

In *Middlemarch* George Eliot presents a world too various and too absorbingly interesting and amusing for the total effect of the book to be melancholy—the selection of experience in it represents the typical sorrows of ordinary human beings, but it represents no less vividly the common human joys. And, as with all successful works of art, there is an over-balance of delight which comes from the contemplation of work well done.

Joan Bennett
George Eliot: Her Mind and Art (Cambridge Univ. Pr.,
1948), pp. 160, 180

Daniel Deronda

Daniel Deronda sold as well or better than *Middlemarch*, but the "inner circle" of Marian's admirers were beginning to ask one another uneasily whether "her method was not now too calculated, her efforts too plainly premeditated." Some there were, like Henry James, who remained a very "Deronda of the Derondists, for my own wanton joy, which amounts to saying that I found the figured, coloured tapestry always vivid enough to brave no matter what complications of stitch." But others there were also—Swinburne amongst them—who thought that *Daniel Deronda* showed, as did *The Spanish Gypsy*, "how much further and more steadily and more hopelessly and more irretrievably and more intolerably wrong it is possible for mere intellect to go than it can be for mere genius." But then it was Swinburne who "discovered" Charlotte Brontë to be so much greater than George Eliot; and to-day we might be inclined to reverse the verdict, to regard George Eliot, "the type of intelligence vivified and coloured by a vein of genius," as preferable to Charlotte Brontë's "type of genius directed and moulded by a type of intelligence," for the Brontës are become a trifle outworn, whilst *Middlemarch* and even *Daniel Deronda*—for all its absurdities—have been unduly neglected. *Daniel Deronda* was George Eliot's last novel. In a letter to Dr. Albutt, as early as 1873, she had said "some time or other, if death does not come to silence one, there ought to be a deliberate abstinence from writing, a self-judgment which decides that one has no more to say"; and, it seems, now this time had come.

Anne Fremantle
George Eliot (New York: Macmillan, 1933), pp. 130-31

The religion of heredity or race is not, as a generalizable solution of the problem, one that George Eliot herself, directly challenged, could have stood by. In these inspirations her intelligence and real moral insight are not engaged. But she is otherwise wholly engaged—how wholly and how significantly being brought further home to us when we note that Deronda's racial mission finds itself identified with his love for Mirah, so that he is eventually justified in the "sweet irresistible hopefulness that the best of human possibilities might befall him—the blending of a complete personal love in one current with a larger duty. . . ."

All in the book that issues from this inspiration is unreal and impotently wordy in the way discussed earlier in connexion with Dorothea—though

Middlemarch can show nothing to match the wastes of biblicality and fervid idealism ("Revelations") devoted to Mordecai, or the copious and drearily comic impossibility of the workingmen's club (Chapter CXLII), or the utterly routing Shakespearean sprightliness of Hans Meyrick's letter in Chapter LII. The Meyricks who, while not being direct products of the prophetic afflatus, are subordinate ministers to it, are among those elements in George Eliot that seem to come from Dickens rather than from life, and so is the pawnbroker's family: the humour and tenderness are painfully trying, with that quality they have, that obviousness of intention, which relates them so intimately to the presiding solemnity they subserve.

No more need be said about the weak and bad side of *Daniel Deronda*. By way of laying due stress upon the astonishingly contrasting strength and fineness of the large remainder, the way in which George Eliot transcends in it not only her weakness, but what are commonly thought to be her limitations, I will make an assertion of fact and a critical comparison: Henry James wouldn't have written *The Portrait of a Lady* if he hadn't read *Gwendolen Harleth* (as I shall call the good part of *Daniel Deronda*), and, of the pair of closely comparable works, George Eliot's has not only the distinction of having come first; it is decidedly the greater.

F. R. Leavis
The Great Tradition (New York: G. W. Stewart, 1948), pp. 84-85

GENERAL

It is said that George Eliot is not very widely read nowadays, that the author of *Adam Bede* and *The Mill on the Floss*, who for years was regarded as one of the greatest of English novelists, has fallen from her high estate. Certainly, after the death of Thackeray and Dickens there was left no writer whose reputation among the critics, or whose popularity with the public was at all commensurate with hers. But now. . . .

Great writers are apt to suffer these vicissitudes of fortune. They are not immune, even the most illustrious of them, from the caprice of changing fashion and altered conditions of life. In an age of iconoclasts, their very greatness is an invitation, an incitement to those who would attract attention to themselves and gain a facile notoriety by decrying the heroes of a former generation. In an age in which Shakespeare, to say nothing of Scott and Dickens, is no longer looked on as sacrosanct, it would be surprising to find that George Eliot had wholly escaped such unflattering attentions. The truth is, however, that George Eliot has been the object not so much of attack as of neglect—a far worse fate.

J. Lewis May
George Eliot (Indianapolis, Ind.: Bobbs-Merrill, 1930), p. 5

In spite of the variety of her talents and the width of her scope, in spite of the fact that she is the only novelist of her time who writes on the scale of the great continental novelists, the only novelist who holds the same conception of her art which is held today, her reputation has sustained a more catastrophic slump than that of any of her contemporaries. . . . For though she is nearer to us in form and subject than the other Victorians, in point of view she is quite as distant. Indeed, we find her point of view even more alien. This is natural enough. An exclusively moral point of view is, at any time, a bleak and unsatisfying affair. Life is altogether too complex and masterful and mysterious to be ordered into tidy little compartments of right and wrong; and any attempt so to order it inevitably leaves a good deal outside that is both interesting and delightful. Moreover, George Eliot's compartments are conspicuously inadequate ones. The virtues of her admiration, industry, self-restraint, conscientiousness, are drab, negative sort of virtues, they are school teachers' virtues. George Eliot does confront human nature a little like a school teacher; kindly but just, calm but censorious, with birchrod in hand to use as she thinks right, and lists of good and bad conduct marks pinned neatly to her desk. And when we see all the vivid disorderly vitality of human nature ranged before her for carefully measured approval or condemnation, we tend to feel rebellious and resentful. . . .

George Eliot's loss of reputation is not wholly undeserved. . . . Though like Tolstoy she is an interesting critic of life, though she constructs well like Jane Austen, though like Dickens she creates a world, yet when we set her achievement in any of these lines beside those of these famous competitors, we feel something lacking. Somehow we are dissatisfied.

It is easy to see why she fails to stand a comparison with Tolstoy. Her vision of life is smaller. . . . Even in *Middlemarch*, there are certain things she does not see. Her assiduously intellectual view made her oblivious of the irrational instinctive aspects of human nature. She can enter into its deliberate purposes and its conscientious scruples, but not into its caprices, its passions, its mysticism. . . . Constructed within so confined an area of vision, it is inevitable that her criticism of life is inadequate. Compared to Tolstoy's it seems petty, drab, provincial. *Middlemarch* may be the nearest English equivalent to *War and Peace*, but it is a provincial sort of *War and Peace*.

David Cecil
Early Victorian Novelists (Indianapolis, Ind.:
Bobbs-Merrill, 1934), pp. 300-301

Her passion was the condition of her art. To evolve and eternalize a world of beauty was her high purpose. Her good sense would have held her to familiar material even if her own inclination and ability had not been determined from her memories: she wished to help common humanity. Consequence follows cause; selflessness and love for others are noble ideals;

dreams guide the soul. So Maggie Tulliver lost herself but gained freedom. That her freedom ends in death is sad, but life is sad and always ends in death, George Eliot would have replied, though she would have removed this sadness by improving conditions, by universal sympathy. So Romola dropped the burden from her heart in bearing burdens of others. So Marner found his life through the child he served. So Esther Lyon relinquished a fortune for something better. Dinah's life is exalted; Hetty's is condemned. Dorothea failed and Lydgate failed because conditions were wrong; and if in *Middlemarch* is the greatest expansion of her doctrine that urges common good through unselfishness, in *Deronda* she went further afield, giving a savior to a race other than her own, as in the *Gypsy* she had instanced a noble attempt of one who would have delivered his tribe but failed through conditions. In the triumphs or failures of her characters the struggle is between duty and inclination; or the struggle may be between conception of an ideal and lack of means to achieve the ideal.

Her characters are everyday characters—clergymen, carpenters, squires, housewives, young girls, old maids, children of the middle class, chiefly and best—because the everyday man or woman is the normal man or woman she knew, and through whom the world must move upward. She had learned from Wordsworth the art of firing her imagination through simple, homely folk; she had learned from Dante the worth of accurate representation; and her imagination, enlivened through memory, had its power through early keenness of vision and a consciousness which, like that of Sophocles, saw life steadily and whole.

This consciousness, unlike that of most Victorian novelists, made her an intellectual writer. Analysis, she said, comes before synthesis. Dissecting her humanity for motive and act—hers and Lewes's interest in the new science of psychology made the dissection more enjoyable—she understood, from the evidence at least, better than most writers those hidden inner springs of complex characteristics that propel word and deed. An artist, she synthesized, created, other men and women, some of whom live as universal types. Though created for the idea which rules her story, they bleed blood, not sawdust; they are developed from brain out; not from a portrait, inward.

Blanche Colton Williams
George Eliot (New York: Macmillan, 1936), pp. 318-19

From one point of view her novels continue in the tradition evolved from Fielding, but which had gradually become less picaresque and more strictly narrative. She tells a story with a beginning, middle and end. The main interest is focussed on a small group of characters the development of whose fortunes is laid out. They move towards a crisis or tangle which is unravelled before the end so that in the last chapter a *dénouement* is reached.

All the fortunes with which the reader has been concerned are tidied up. . . .
But from another point of view George Eliot is an innovator. The organic
or living form of her novels, within the expected framework, is different
from anything that had gone before. It resembles, in some respects, Jane
Austen's form in so far as the central characters are deeply rooted in their
social environment which determines their story as much as does their individual character. The difference is that the social environment is wider,
more complex, made up of a greater variety of minor characters drawn
from many more social and economic levels, and also that the display of
this outer circle or environment is more conscious. Jane Austen took her
social *milieu* for granted; its manners and traditions were, for her, as little
open to question as the laws of nature. George Eliot was aware of the
ethical, religious and social conventions of the world she paints as a
product of history, evolved in time and changing with time. She was consciously interested in the pressure all these exert on individual lives and in
the existence of a problem concerned with resisting or succumbing to that
pressure. She shares the modern consciousness of man in a changing and
developing society. Consequently, the organic form of her novels—an inner
circle (a small group of individuals involved in a moral dilemma) surrounded by an outer circle (the social world within which the dilemma has to
be resolved)—is more significant than in any preceding fiction. Furthermore, her perception of individual human beings is more complex than that
of her predecessors. She never suggests a simple division of characters into
good and bad. The individual, like the environment, has evolved and is
evolving; his or her behaviour at any given moment is the inevitable result
of all that has gone before; therefore, while the action can itself be judged,
both in relation to its consequences and to its aesthetic beauty (an action
that pleases or displeases) the doer is not presented judicially but compas-
sionately. In her discourse George Eliot sometimes deviates from this attitude and her novel suffers accordingly. But whenever her reflective powers
are in due subordination to her creative gift, wherever, as usually happens in
the dialogue, she responds to her characters rather than thinks about them,
the reader feels with them and the total effect of her novel is an increase of
understanding and of compassion.

Joan Bennett
George Eliot: Her Mind and Art
(Cambridge Univ. Pr., 1948), pp. 100-101

George Eliot's greatness is of a different kind from that she has been generally credited with. And by way of concluding on this emphasis I will ad-
duce once again her most intelligently appreciative critic, Henry James:

> She does not strike me as naturally a critic, less still as naturally
> a sceptic; her spontaneous part is to observe life and to feel it,

to feel it with admirable depth. Contemplation, sympathy and faith—something like that, I should say, would have been her natural scale. If she had fallen upon an age of enthusiastic assent to old articles of faith, it seems to me possible that she would have had a more perfect, a more consistent and graceful development than she actually had.

There is, I think, a complete misconception here. George Eliot's development may not have been "perfect" or "graceful," and "consistent" is not precisely the adjective one would choose for it; yet she went on developing to the end, as few writers do, and achieved the most remarkable expression of her distinctive genius in her last work. . . . And her profound insight into the moral nature of man is essentially that of one whose critical intelligence has been turned intensively on her faiths. A sceptic by nature or culture—indeed no; but that is not because her intelligence, a very powerful one, doesn't freely illuminate all her interests and convictions. That she should be thought depressing (as, for instance, Leslie Stephen thinks her) always surprises me. She exhibits a traditional moral sensibility expressing itself, not within a frame of "old articles of faith" (as James obviously intends the phrase), but nevertheless with perfect sureness, in judgments that involve confident positive standards, and yet affect us as simply the report of luminous intelligence. She deals in the weakness and ordinariness of human nature, but doesn't find it contemptible, or show either animus or self-deceiving indulgence towards it; and, distinguished and noble as she is, we have in reading her the feeling that she is in and of the humanity she presents with so clear and disinterested a vision. . . .

For a positive indication of her place and quality I think of a Russian; not Turgenev, but a far greater, Tolstoy—who, we all know, is pre-eminent in getting "the spirit of life itself." George Eliot, of course, is not as transcendently great as Tolstoy, but she *is* great, and great in the same way. . . . Of George Eliot it can in turn be said that her best work has a Tolstoyan depth and reality.

F. R. Leavis
The Great Tradition (New York: G. W. Stewart,
1948), pp. 123-24

There are, it seems to me, two principal dangers to which the novelist deeply interested in the ways of society is exposed. One of these dangers is described by Mr. Edwin Muir in a comment he makes about the novels of H. G. Wells and John Galsworthy. "To Mr. Wells and Mr. Galsworthy," he writes, "society is essentially an abstract conception, not an imaginative reality; they do not recreate society, therefore, in their novels, they merely illustrate it, or rather their ideas about it. . . . To them society is there full grown as an idea at the beginning; it is not created by the characters, rather it creates them; but at the same time it is always beyond them, exists as a thing in itself, and cannot be adumbrated completely except by employing the arts of exposition." The other danger is illustrated in the novels of Thackeray. Here there is no question of an abstract conception of society and of characters who are merely deduced from that conception. As Mr. Muir further observes, "Thackeray sets his characters going, he exhibits them continuously in a present not verbal but psychological, and at the end a picture of society has sprung up before our eyes." But one should add that at the end of the Thackeray novel the characters he has so magnificently created tend to lose their identity and to disappear into the limbo of Vanity Fair. George Eliot, not the least accomplished of the Victorians in the art of compromise, avoids these two extremes. In *Middlemarch*, for instance, her vision of society and her vision of the individual never split asunder. They are bound together by an interlocking of the particular and the general, of the concrete and the theoretical, by a method of social analysis that has been refined into a subtle and complex art.

Claude T. Bissell
ELH (September, 1951), p. 239

The reason for this emphasis on the positive movement is, I believe, that George Eliot is always concerned with asserting and exploring the moral evolution of mankind. In fact, if we were to adopt her own use of the motto, we might select one from among those with which she so meticulously prefaced her books and chapters of books and allow it to stand as a general thematic statement for all of her novels. Since it implies not only theme but image and structure as well, no motto would be more apt than the last part of the verse which she herself apparently wrote for chapter xli of *Felix Holt*:

> . . . the soul can grow
> As embryos, that live and move but blindly,
> Burst from the dark, emerge regenerate,
> And lead a life of vision and of choice.

The use of the motto now strikes the twentieth-century reader as a quaint Victorian habit which, because it is too suggestive of the text prefacing a sermon, could better have been omitted. And, happily, it can be omitted. For obviously no mere motto could ever begin to suggest what image, theme, and structure have artistically created in the novels of George Eliot.

That George Eliot is a highly conscious artist should at this point be so obvious as to need no further comment. Also superfluous is the observation that she is as much concerned with making her reader see and feel as with making him think, in short, that she wishes to aid her reader in his struggling movement toward vision. A final word which does, however, remain to be said, even though it has been said before, is that *Adam Bede* is a great novel and that *Middlemarch* is one of the greatest novels ever written.

Reva Stump
Movement and Vision in George Eliot's Novels
(Seattle, Wash.: Univ. Washington Press, 1959), p. 216

Her vision too seems as much modern as Victorian. Not that she seems modern in the way that Hemingway, Huxley, Lawrence do, but she does not seem as distinctly Victorian as Thackeray or Charlotte Brontë. We feel that, without quite coming to its center, she touches upon our consciousness, that her vision and many of the techniques attendant upon it are close to our own. If there is sometimes rather obvious pathos or moralism, or an obnoxiously virtuous heroine, there is much more that is congenial to our sense of the world: the studies in disenchantment, the psychological analysis, the seriousness with which she took her art. "It was really George Eliot who started it all," said D. H. Lawrence. "It was she who started putting all the action inside." Lawrence was speaking relatively, of course; George Eliot never went so far as someone like Virginia Woolf in putting all the action inside.

Her place in the history of English fiction, however, does not indicate her relevance for us—that she is at (or very nearly at) the center of the central tradition of English fiction. By central tradition I do not mean to suggest the best or most authentic tradition, but simply the one that has been most widely and most successfully cultivated. That tradition has been defined in part by F. R. Leavis in *The Great Tradition*, and the awareness of continuity and unity is all about us. Richardson, Fielding, Jane Austen, George Eliot, Trollope, Conrad, James, Forster—perhaps preeminently Jane Austen, George Eliot, and James.

Jerome Thale
The Novels of George Eliot (New York:
Columbia Univ. Pr., 1959), p. 9

The recent revival of interest in George Eliot, largely inspired by the publication in 1954 of the first volumes of Professor Gordon S. Haight's *The George Eliot Letters*, has resulted in a sizable amount of literary criticism and scholarship. Yet, for the most part, individual critical attempts to deal with George Eliot's writings have been singularly onesided. Critics have either concentrated on a close scrutiny of the formal aspects of her art, or, increasingly aware of her importance as a thinker whose work was really meant to be "philosophic," have examined George Eliot's early essays and reviews in order to reconstruct the ideology later exemplified in her novels in the light of Darwin, Huxley, Comte, Mill, Lewes, Spencer, Hennell, Strauss, or Feuerbach. Both approaches have yielded valuable and illuminating results. And yet they have somehow perpetuated the illusion that George Eliot's art and ideology are best examined in separation, that two divorced "principles" govern her novels, and that these principles, the one artistic and the other intellectual, must remain irrevocably apart. Thus, a fine critic of George Eliot's "form" seems compelled to argue defensively that the neglect of the "strictly formal features" of her fiction merits an exclusive attention to her art, while an equally able expositor of the philosophical implications of George Eliot's determinism is betrayed into self-consciousness when in his otherwise excellent discussion, he admits that he treats "George Eliot as a philosopher rather than an artist."

George Eliot successfully transmuted ideas into the form and structure of her novels; it is seldom sufficiently emphasized that this transmutation is in itself a key to her "art."

J. C. Knoepflmacher
Religious Humanism and the Victorian Novel
(Princeton, N. J.: Princeton Univ. Pr., 1965), pp. 24-25

EDWARD FITZGERALD

1809-1883

FitzGerald was a man of leisure, a friend of writers, and a translator. One work of his, a paraphrase as much as a translation, gives him a place in the history of English literature: his *Rubáiyát* (1859), based on the verse of the twelfth-century Persian Omar Khayyám, is one of the most often-quoted Victorian poems. A mixture of philosophic reflection and hedonism, it contains a large enough number of memorable lines and passages to account for its enduring popularity. FitzGerald revised his work, and the Rubáiyát was re-issued in 1868, 1872, and 1879.

George Bentham, ed., Variorum edition (1903), 7 vols.
Alfred M. Terhune, *The Life of FitzGerald* (1947)

We may be thankful for so simple, so tenderhearted, so ingenuous a life; we may feel that the long, quiet years were not misspent which produced, if so rarely, the delicate flowers of genius. To enrich the world with one imperishable poem, to make music of some of the saddest and darkest doubts that haunt the mind of man—this is what many far busier and more concentrated lives fail to do. To strew the threshold of the abyss with flowers, to dart an ethereal gleam of the encircling gloom, to set a garland of roses in the very shrine of death, to touch despair with beauty—this is to bear a part in the work of consoling men, of reconciling fate, of enlightening doom, of interpreting the vast and awful mind of God. Truth itself can do no more than hint at the larger hope—"It is He that hath made us."

A. C. Benson
Edward FitzGerald (New York: Macmillan, 1905), p. 201

There is much to be said for the freedom which FitzGerald invariably exercised in recasting a work, and he often defended his method in letters to friends. He protested that a translation cannot be literal and at the same time retain the spirit of the original; and, above all, the spirit must be retained. "The live Dog better than the dead Lion" or "better a live Sparrow than a stuffed Eagle," he declared. To appreciate the validity of his contention, one has merely to compare his *Rubáiyát* with a literal translation. Mr. Payne's version, for example, although interesting for its attempt to reproduce the very idiom and rhythms of the Persian, is so painfully literal as to be worthless from the standpoint of art. And FitzGerald has had his champions—many of them. One, Hugh Walker, observes that the number of translations which are likely to maintain a permanent position in English literature thus far might be limited to five: the Authorized Version of the Bible, Chapman's Homer, Pope's Homer, FitzGerald's *Rubáiyát,* and Jowett's Plato. Not one of these, he points out, attempts a literal translation.

The approval of FitzGerald's poems by *all* types of readers, from tyro to pundit, is its best defense, if any defense is required. With the exception of the Bible, FitzGerald's *Rubáiyát* is probably quoted more frequently than any other work in English literature. Despite the strictures of pedants, a term which excludes most scholars, the *Rubáiyát* has become one of the immortal poems of the language.

Alfred McKinley Terhune
The Life of Edward FitzGerald (New Haven:
Yale Univ. Pr., 1947), p. 223

ELIZABETH CLEGHORN GASKELL
1810-1865

[Mrs. Gaskell] was a novelist who knew two worlds. Before her marriage in 1832, to the Reverend William Gaskell, a Unitarian minister, she lived in the charming village of Knutsford in Cheshire; afterward in the tempestuous manufacturing city of Manchester. She treated the petty problems of the village in a series of sketches for Dickens' magazine, *Household Words* (1851-3); in book form they became *Cranford* (1853), a "novel" which combines some of the rural felicity of Goldsmith's *Vicar of Wakefield*, the calm satire of Jane Austen's *Emma*, and the restrained realism of Mary Mitford's *Our Village*. She also grappled with the more vital problems of the city. Better acquainted than either Disraeli or Dickens with industrial conditions in the "hungry forties," she shocked England in *Mary Barton* (1848) with her depiction of Henry Carson, the relentless employer. At the end of *North and South* (1855) employer John Thornton awakens to the need for better understanding of labor's problems—a theme which the author emphasizes in both books. In *Ruth* (1853) she pondered a different problem, the struggle of a milliner's apprentice, once seduced, to become respectable in Victorian society. Mrs. Gaskell's best-known non-fiction work is a sympathetic biography of Charlotte Brontë (1857).

Homer A. Watt and William W. Watt
A Dictionary of English Literature (New York:
Barnes and Noble, 1945), p. 115

Clement Shorter, ed., *Novels and Tales* (1906-1919), 11 vols.

Annette B. Hopkins, *Elizabeth Gaskell: Her Life and Work* (1952)

During the twenty years of her literary life, Mrs. Gaskell wrote five novels, a biography, the group of sketches which she called *Cranford,* several poems, and more than forty articles and short works of fiction. To note her advance in these years one has but to compare *Libbie Marsh's Three Eras* with *Cousin Phillis,* or *Mary Barton* with *Wives and Daughters.* Her stories of the weird and the grotesque will probably never be popular; they serve chiefly as an indication of her great imaginative powers, which she largely repressed in the works by which she will be best known—*Cranford, Wives and Daughters, Cousin Phillis,* and the like.

Her chief general contributions to literature were those she made in the social novel and in the delineation of village life and customs in Victorian England. Her chief particular contributions were her incomparable characterizations of spinsters and doctors and servants, her excellent use of dialect, and her sympathetic understanding of the views of English working-men. In the first of these she has no near rival in English literature; in the second she did much to add to a realistic presentation of characters by giving a correct representation of their conversations; and in the last she set the mode for others, until in time men became recognized as human beings and not as worthless chattels. To have done any one of these things would have been to live; to have done all three, and to have done them well, will insure her a lasting place among the worthies of English literary history.

Gerald de Witt Sanders
Elizabeth Gaskell (New Haven: Yale Univ. Pr., 1929), p. 144

The fault with Mrs. Gaskell's work is that her intensity is veiled by the general excellence of her writings as a whole. Her range is too wide to admit of any outstanding peak. It is easy to criticize her for falling short of a standard which she never set up for herself, and by doing this we damn things in which we should rejoice. Mrs. Gaskell knew the extent of her powers, and she was sufficiently discriminating to know when to stop writing. She was a good writer, and a writer who is consistently good deserves a high place in the realm of letters. Although not a first-rate novelist like Fielding, Scott, or Thackeray, she produced first-rate novels.

When the future ceases to respect high intentions, and social quarrels between masters and men have ceased, *Ruth* and *Mary Barton* may seem primitive to caustic retrospection's eye. *Cranford, Wives and Daughters,* and *Sylvia's Lovers,* her best books, will escape that critical argus, because they approach the ideal of a good story-teller—whose true function, we take it, is to be an artist rather than a commentator on life.

It is difficult to assign a place to Mrs. Gaskell in English letters. In a drawing-room of the 'fifties her most fitting situation would be on a sofa, between Charlotte Brontë and Anthony Trollope, from which she would cast side-glances at Dickens and Wilkie Collins.

The lapse of time since her death has added greatly to the early prestige of her work. Nowadays, with a broader vision, we may forgive and condone those initial defects for which the period in which she wrote is to blame. New and attractive editions of her books are frequent, and it is something to know that after sixty years her work is alive: she is read.

A. Stanton Whitfield
Mrs. Gaskell (London: Routledge, 1929), pp. 213-14

Throughout Mrs. Gaskell's work the idea of understanding is strong and pervasive. It is precisely this idea which fired her early phase of social indignation and mellowed her later period of detached and observant humour. There is nothing spectacular about her work or personality. In an age of literary brilliance this unassuming yet steadfast luminary tended to be dimmed by the proximity of the great surrounding planets, her contemporaries. Yet at her best her writing reflects virtues not easily found among those with even the greatest reputations. They embody her own remedy for the attainment of human happiness. Her prescription, by no means new, was to her mind simple and obvious, compounded from three basic elements. It contained Faith, Hope and Charity. To her as well, the greatest of these was Charity.

Yvonne ffrench
Mrs. Gaskell (Denver, Colo.: Alan Swallow, 1949), p. 107

THOMAS HARDY

1840-1928

Thomas Hardy, last and one of the greatest of Victorian novelists, was born in Dorset on June 2, 1840, in the center of the Wessex country which later figured in his works. . . .

He tried unsuccessfully to publish his poems, but even after they were rejected he continued writing them. . . . Hoping that it would sell better than poetry he turned his hand to fiction. . . . *Desperate Remedies*, 1871, his first published book, is a contrived, melodramatic murder story. . . . The first of his many novels of country life, *Under the Greenwood Tree*, 1872, shows in a pleasant little idyll how deeply Hardy understood rustic ways. *A Pair of Blue Eyes*, 1872-3, is a romantic tragedy which alternates between Cornwall and London. . . . The success of these last two novels brought a commission to write a serial for the *Cornhill Magazine; Far from the Madding Crowd,* published anonymously in 1874, was Hardy's first masterpiece. . . .

Hardy still preferred poetry to fiction, but he felt compelled to write stories to support himself, for he had married and given up architecture in 1874. . . . His next work, *The Hand of Ethelberta*, 1875-6, is a "society" novel. . . . In *The Return of the Native, 1878,* he looked again to the land as a source of his power; the two major "characters" are Eustacia Vye, who broods with a tragic passion over the heath on which she lives, and the heath itself, which symbolizes the blind forces of nature against which she rebels.

The Trumpet-Major, 1880, is a light-hearted love story of the period of the Napoleonic Wars. . . . *Two on a Tower*, 1882, shocked his audience with the frankness of its treatment of sexual passion in a woman. Over the pages of *The Mayor of Casterbridge*, 1886, hangs the shadow of an inexorable fate . . . , but for all its gloom it is one of Hardy's most powerful novels. *The Woodlanders*, 1886-7, is the quietly beautiful story of a simple countryman. . . . *Wessex Tales,* 1888, *A Group of Noble Dames*, 1891, and *Life's Little Ironies*, 1894, are the major collections [of stories].

His novels culminated with the two greatest, *Tess of the D'Urbervilles*, 1891, and *Jude the Obscure*, 1896. The second part of the title of *Tess* is *A Pure Woman*, to show what Hardy thought of his heroine. . . . *Jude* shows the horrible decline of a man and woman drawn together by sexual desire and torn apart by the disaster it entails. . . . Hardy announced in 1896 that *Jude* was his last novel, and turned with relief to the writing of vigorously intellectual and experimental lyrical poetry which many critics think is at least as great as his novels.

Thomas Marc Parrott and Robert Bernard Martin
A Companion to Victorian Literature (New York:
Scribner's, 1955), pp. 194-97

Works (1912-1913), 23 vols.

Florence E. Hardy, *The Early Life of Thomas Hardy 1840-1891* (1928); *The Later Years of Thomas Hardy 1892-1928* (1930)

Carl J. Weber, *Hardy of Wessex* (1940)

FICTION

There is, of course, no denying, nor any need to deny, that the thread of which the Wessex novels and poems are woven is a dark one of "pessimism"; but what matters in art is not so much the name of the material, as its quality. Optimism is exactly on all fours with pessimism, romanticism with classicism, if all are equally shallow; there is, in actual life, nothing to choose between Micawber and the melancholy Jacques. Thus what it is that redeems Hardy is, almost obviously, the tragic richness of his pessimism, the humanity, the sympathy which he brings to it. To say tragic, is in itself to say something big. . . . Though the great tragic writers throughout history can be counted on the fingers, and to put Hardy among them would be to presume upon posterity, it is by his relationship with them that he must be tried and condemned, or crowned.

Bonamy Dobrée
The Lamp and the Lute (Oxford Univ. Pr., 1929), p. 22

As we consider the great structure of the Wessex novels it seems irrelevant to fasten on little points—this character, that scene, this phrase of deep and poetic beauty. It is something larger that Hardy has bequeathed to us. The Wessex novels are not one book, but many. They cover an immense stretch; inevitably they are full of imperfections—some are failures, and others exhibit only the wrong side of their maker's genius. But undoubtedly, when we have submitted ourselves fully to them, when we come to take stock of our impression of the whole, the effect is commanding and satisfactory. We have been freed from the cramp and pettiness imposed by life. Our imaginations have been stretched and heightened; our humour has been made to laugh out; we have drunk deep of the beauty of the earth. Also we have been made to enter the shade of a sorrowful and brooding spirit which, even in its saddest mood, bore itself with a grave uprightness and never, even when most moved to anger, lost its deep compassion for the sufferings of men and women. Thus it is no mere transcript of life at a certain time and place that Hardy has given us. It is a vision of the world and of man's lot as they revealed themselves to a powerful imagination, a profound and poetic genius, a gentle and humane soul.

Virginia Woolf
The Common Reader, Second Series
(London: Hogarth Press, 1932), p. 257

Bitter and hard as he conceived life to be, Hardy himself was never hard, nor, save in a rare impulse of exasperation, was he bitter. The burning flame of his charity blazed all the higher for the infinite and unrelieved blackness of the universe, in which it was the solitary gleam of light.

David Cecil
Hardy the Novelist (London: Constable, 1943), pp. 156-57

The literary historian and the modern novelist alike can benefit from a study of Hardy's anti-realism and occasional symbolist experiments; they can discover in Hardy ways of escaping inanimate drabness. But it would be absurd to read into Hardy's anti-realism any profound metaphysical intentions, or into his symbolist experiments the complex aesthetic intentions of Conrad. . . . In the end he did write, and seemingly with full consciousness of what he was doing, three very great novels: *Tess of the D'Urbervilles, The Mayor of Casterbridge*, and *Jude the Obscure*. . . . Less austere and less ambitious than Conrad, Hardy confined himself to our unregenerate longing for happiness and our common destiny of suffering.

Albert J. Guérard
Thomas Hardy: The Novels and Stories (Cambridge, Mass.:
Harvard Univ. Pr., 1949), pp. 158-59

The Return of the Native

Hardy has combined "character and environment." Not always are the two so remarkably interwoven as in the novel under consideration; not always is the influence of environment so strong in affecting character. And, environment apart, not always does Hardy put so many great characters in one story as in *The Return of the Native*. In many of his novels there is one great character about whom the action revolves: witness Tess, Michael Henchard, Jude. In *The Return of the Native* there are three characters that so constantly participate in the action, and are so fully developed and so vividly portrayed, that they are equally impressed on the reader's memory. They are not only thoroughly real, not only true to life, they possess that individuality which depends upon no merely outward and accidental features but upon the multitude of acts, thoughts, and emotions, which, inextricably combined, make up life's "web of mingled yarn." The ability to create true and memorable characters, characters who remain with us always as vividly as if we had known them in life, is one of the certain marks of greatness in a novelist. Nowhere in Hardy is this greatness more abundantly demonstrated than in *The Return of the Native*.

Albert C. Baugh
Introd. in *The Return of the Native* (New York:
Macmillan, 1928), pp. xviii-xix

The world did not acknowledge it, but a masterpiece of English literature had appeared. It is Hardy's most nearly perfect work of art. . . .

The manifold points of interest that this Egdon tragedy possesses have in the course of sixty years and more become generally appreciated. The novel has long outlived the blind criticism of 1878 and has become one of the classics of English fiction.

Carl J. Weber
Hardy of Wessex (New York: Columbia Univ. Pr., 1940), pp. 73, 77

The Mayor of Casterbridge

In his next novel, Hardy tried to dispense with the crude fatalistic machinery of *Two on a Tower*, external events persistently interfering with human intentions, and to imagine a man bringing sorrow and disaster on himself through his own defects of character. *The Mayor of Casterbridge* (1886) reverts in some measure to the causative structure of George Eliot's novels, which were expositions of determinism, her characters bearing their destinies within them in the master-tendencies of their appetites and wills. The conflict is transferred to the inner arena, and the adversary is now ancient habits, rooted impulses, uneradicated vices. In the upshot, Henchard is reduced to impotence: the destiny within him triumphs, and he is humbled to the dust. It is not so much that free will is an illusion, autonomy of the self a figment, as that every free act is turned to derision, through the effects of bygone failures, and of fresh misfortunes that no foresight or effort can avert. For the habit of detecting malice behind every accident was too strong for Hardy to keep within the limits proposed, and *The Mayor of Casterbridge* is as bitter an exposure of "the machinery contrived by the gods" for stultifying mortal activities as any of the preceding novels. It is clear, however, that he thought he had succeeded in presenting a man whose egotism and obstinacy are the sole agents of his ruin. But, apart from these extraneous interventions, the odds are piled up beforehand. Henchard is not a fair specimen of normal, albeit unregenerate man. He is the deliberate embodiment of a vice or overwhelming propensity, combined with fatuous self-confidence, such as Aeschylus made the sure instrument of tragedy. Hardy's fatalism, in short, is simply transferred from outside to inside. Whereas he was wont to weight the dice against his characters in their external circumstances, this time he weights the individual himself. Henchard is one who can never master an insubordinate temperament. He has striking abilities, many virtues, he is generous and soft-hearted; but the ungovernable devil in him keeps breaking out, and, though he knows his own failings, no one better, secures the upper hand in the direst emergencies. This is no study of gradual moral corruption, like Flaubert's of Madame Bovary or

George Eliot's of Lydgate. It is the pursuit of a man's original sin to the bitter end, like *Jude the Obscure*, where, however, there is more attention to the inner life; here the psychology is rudimentary.

Ernest A. Baker
The History of the English Novel, Vol. IX
(London: Witherby, 1936), pp. 45-46

Tess of the D'Urbervilles

It is not drama now that Hardy wants, but pathos. It is not the conflict of wills among antagonists chosen for their strength. It is the struggle of weakness and innocence in the clutch of circumstance. And this accounts for the transcendent appeal of the story of Tess. No matter how much we may admire the cunning workmanship of the earlier novel, no matter how breathlessly we may have followed the march of destiny in the story of Eustacia Vye, embracing in our concern the desperate nostalgia of Eustacia, the jealous motherliness of Mrs. Yeobright, the unworldly aspirations of Clym —we cannot feel for any of these the simple love and grief that Tess inspires; no fates of theirs can make us so cry out against the cruelty of life. It may be an irony hard for the artist to stomach. Not all his orginality of conception, not all the devices of structural art, not all the resources of his wisdom and science avail him so well with the mass of his readers as the direct appeal of one heart to another.

I do not wish to imply that *Tess* is in any way inferior in art to *The Native*. But it is an art supremely free from self-consciousness, and making the reader uncommonly at ease. And quite irrespective of the degree of art displayed, the fact remains—let it be palatable or unpalatable to artist or critic—that the greatest element of appeal in *Tess* is the pathos inherent in its story, and after that the heat of feeling with which the author traces the suffering of his heroine. And it is this pathos, and this heat of feeling—voicing itself in accents of great beauty—that makes the superiority of *Tess*, I will not say merely to *The Native*, but to any other English novel of its period.

Joseph Warren Beach
The Technique of Thomas Hardy (Chicago:
Univ. Chicago Pr., 1922), p. 185

At the end of the book, with the "Aeschylean phrase" on the sport of the gods, we feel again that intrusion of a commentary which belongs to another order of discourse. The gibbet is enough. The vision is deep and clear and can only be marred by any exploitation of it as a datum in support of abstraction. We could even do without the note of "ameliorism" in the joined hands of Clare and Tess's younger sister at the end: the philosophy of an evolutionary hope has nothing essential to do with Tess's fate and her common meaning; she is too humanly adequate for evolutionary ethics to comment upon, and furthermore we do not believe that young girls make ameliorated lives out of witness of a sister's hanging.

What philosophical vision honestly inheres in a novel inheres as the signifying form of a certain concrete body of experience; it is what the experience "means" because it is what, structurally, the experience *is*. When it can be loosened away from the novel to compete in the general field of abstract truth—as frequently in Hardy—it has the weakness of any abstraction that statistics and history and science may be allowed to criticize; whether true or false for one generation or another, or for one reader or another, or even for one personal mood or another, its status as truth is relative to conditions of evidence and belief existing outside the novel and existing there quite irrelevant to whatever body of particularized life the novel itself might contain.

Dorothy Van Ghent
The English Novel (New York:
Holt, Rinehart, and Winston, 1953), p. 197

Jude The Obscure

The story as it progresses has an accompaniment of emotional significance as obvious as that of *Tess of the D'Urbervilles*. But the indignation with the tragic fashion of existence is not here hot and flaming, but cold and bitter and almost cynical. It is brought into disconcerting prominence by being personified in Jude's son, one of the most daring, and certainly one of the most dreadful, imaginations in literature. This horrible boy seems unconsciously aware of the whole dismal past of human existence, and seems also to see nothing in the future but endless repetition of the same futility of suffering. But his part is not merely one of gratuitous commentator, the action of the story takes its final tragic turn from his interference. That interference of his is a thing of such nightmare horror, that it depends simply on the mood in which one reads of it or thinks of it, whether it is to seem appalling or only grotesque. At any rate, like the boy himself, it is not easily forgotten; and, as a matter of technique, one can only be astonished at the way the mood which surrounds the whole story is concentrated into this formidable small boy, and, by his means, inextricably woven into the narrative texture. Even so, however, this formal condensation of the mood is not enough to counteract the tremendous emphasis it takes from being so personified. The emphasis is too great for the form of the book as a whole to contain. The mood breaks out, not quite unmanaged, but by no means completely mastered; it "chews the bit and fights against the reins." There has been a weakness of artistic control; and, when such perilous stuff is to be dealt with, it is only by a triumphant and utterly unquestioned mastery over the substance that art can properly be said to achieve itself.

Lascelles Abercrombie
Thomas Hardy (London: Martin Secker, 1912), pp. 164-65

One cannot leave this great and terrible book without noting the power that has kept remorselessly to one theme, that has held the attention unswervingly upon one character, that has refused to lighten the burden of the story by the factitious means of making that character, or indeed any person in the book, attractive, appealing, or anything but dumb and commonplace, and that has carried through the whole study in monotone. In moments of cool analysis one may be tempted to ask whether it is not the author himself who has doomed his puppets to disaster, for there is little individuality in the several characters who are differentiated one from another by little save differences in opinion. But the unquestionably powerful impression made is an answer to that criticism.

Samuel C. Chew
Thomas Hardy, Poet and Novelist (New York:
A. A. Knopf, 1928), pp. 73-74

It is right, with *Jude*, to speak of a failure of total imaginative organization, and it is easy enough to point to places that are false, or ill-judged, or merely embittered. But the parts are greater than the whole. There are scenes between the two protagonists whose psychological veracity still may astonish, and there are longer and and shorter passages of tenderness and of penetration that only a novel such as Hardy here conceived could find place for. Finally—to re-establish its connection with the preceding novels —the opening book of *Jude* is Hardy's finest narrative of a countryman's struggle toward the civic milieu: something needed to complete the pattern of his work. And the grave, retrospective irony that pervades the opening owes its authority to the later memorable rendering of that milieu: bewildering, tantalizing, frustrating, disappointing, and in the end insupportable. It is a grim but necessary complement to the simpler, more affirmative novels.

Douglas Brown
Thomas Hardy (London: Longmans, 1954), p. 100

POETRY

The poems are thoroughly modern, too; their persons do not belong to romance or story, but to recognizable, everyday species of the present; and the turn of the psychology, though comment and moralizing are avoided, frequently implies some typical modern questioning of received notions. The whole body of the poems of this kind will perhaps include twice as many as those to which I have alluded; several are not obviously tragical, some have a humorous twist. But they stand out pretty clearly from the rest of Hardy's poems, and form a natural group; and they are poems [of "eminently psychological art"] which, it seems to me, deserve a special place in our literature.

Lascelles Abercrombie
Thomas Hardy (London: Martin Secker, 1912), pp. 182-83

If he must dwell on the slopes of Parnassus rather than at the top, we must still remember that even so he dwells far above the average person and above many writers whose popularity is greater than his. It is difficult to say that had his horizon been narrower, his experimentation less, he would have achieved greater intensity and a higher stature as an artist. But it is to such a conclusion, I think, that one must necessarily come. He looked at too many men whose lives were spiritually barren and did not concentrate on the few whose natures merited continuous study. He tried too many poetic forms to wrest from any one its greatest potentialities. His intellectual restlessness took him far afield, but because he looked in the wrong direction he did not find that calmness of spirit, the depth of which would perforce have revealed itself in his work. He had a certain measure of calm to be sure, but he could not conscientiously invest man with enough dignity or with a great enough stature to permit him to look up to him, even beyond him to the stars, and past the stars into those dark spaces between. And it is those interstellar spaces that tease one beyond thought. He saw man too much in his workaday guise and failed to see the dreams and visions that even to the most seemingly prosaic person give a quality beyond the ordinary. He gives us what we might call the summation of folk wisdom, but that has its limitations as well as its power. He was content to be a realist, and like realists, he suffers from a limited vision that tends to turn him into a sentimentalist. And there is a large element of the sentimental in Hardy. An idealist not only sees all that the realist sees, but his vision is great enough for him to see beyond mere terrestrial manifestations to something greater, as Dante and Milton were able to do. Too often he was content with man as he shows himself to the world and not as he shows himself to himself when he knows he is unobserved; when he struggles with his frustrations and refuses to let them keep him from new and greater experiences of life. Although Hardy never mistakes facts for knowledge, he sometimes mistakes knowledge for wisdom.

James Granville Southworth
The Poetry of Thomas Hardy (New York:
Columbia Univ. Pr., 1947), p. 233

It seems possible to say rather easily, and with substantial if not chronological accuracy, what is Hardy's place in English letters. Tennyson and
Browning are orthodox in their piety, and we will say they are early Victorian poets; if Tennyson's orthodoxy sometimes wavers, it is not enough to
keep him from being Poet Laureate. But Hardy is a disaffected religionist,
and we will say he is a late Victorian poet. The age which we style Victorian
is not so sure and pure as many of its critics have wished to think; it is
entitled to a major poet with something like the modern temper. Hardy is
that poet, and the age becomes more reputable for having him.

John Crowe Ransom
Selected Poems of Thomas Hardy
(New York: Macmillan, 1961), pp. xxxii-xxxiii

GERARD   MANLEY   HOPKINS

1844-1899

As a student at Oxford, Hopkins was influenced briefly by his tutor Walter
Pater, more by the critical writing of John Ruskin, and most of all by the
religious precepts and example of John Henry Newman. He was received
into the Roman Catholic church by Newman in 1866, and two years later
he became a Jesuit. For a time he gave up drawing and poetry, both of
which he loved; ordained in 1877, he dedicated himself to his priestly and
scholarly vocation, being appointed Professor of Classics at University
College, Dublin, in 1884. But he returned to poetry, devoting his talent
largely to religious ends, as early as 1875 when, moved by the account of
how five German nuns had died in a shipwreck, he began his ambitious
"The Wreck of the Deutschland." The originality and the passionately personal style of this and almost all his later poems made editors unwilling to
publish him. Upon his death his unpublished verse was left in the care of
his friend and correspondent Robert Bridges, the Poet Laureate, who at
last edited an almost complete collection of it in 1918. The influence of
this poetry and Hopkins's critical reputation have grown so since the second
decade of the twentieth century that Hopkins is now often thought of as
either the first of the major modern poets or one of the great—and some
critics would say the greatest of—Victorian poets. Markedly individual in
his manner, using archaic and dialectal words, invented terms, ellipses of
syntax, intense and startling images, he seems to be in harmony with modern literary tastes. But Hopkins also shares certain qualities, such as
extreme self-consciousness, a deeply serious concern about the relations of
man, nature, and God, and an extremely ambivalent feeling about all kinds
of natural imagery, with his Victorian contemporaries. Less than fifty
years after the first volume of his work was posthumously published, it is
possible to claim for him a place as one of the major English poets of the
nineteenth century.

W. H. Gardner and N. H. Mackenzie, eds., *Poems of Gerard Manley Hopkins* (4th ed., 1967)

John Pick, *Gerard Manley Hopkins, Priest and Poet* (1942)

PERSONAL

Victoria died. Edward VII mounted the throne for a belated convivial reign. George V succeeded him. In 1913 Robert Bridges was appointed poet laureate. In 1915 he published his wartime anthology, *The Spirit of Man*, containing seven poems by Gerard Hopkins, and, three years subsequently, the first edition of Hopkins' collected poems. It was the right moment. England, after four years of toil and conflict, was in the mood to listen to the voice of a new poet whose absolute sincerity made cheap the accustomed counters of expression, and whose earnestness transcended his native era and his creed.

This is not to say, however, that the whole nation instantly read and welcomed him. Even in 1918 Hopkins' public was a confined one, for many readers were estranged by what seemed to them an extravagant form and an obscure content in his work. The first edition of his poems did not sell out until ten years had passed. "Are there many who care, or will learn to care, for the poetry of Gerard Hopkins?" asked one critic. "Probably not. It seems impossible that poetry should ever follow the direction of his teaching. . . ." Even as he raised this question, those most precise and subtle attributes that give Hopkins' writing its ascendancy today—the indefatigable intellect, the quality of emotional reserve and of withholding, the alert sense of words—were beginning to exert their power on a maturing generation.

Eleanor Ruggles
Gerard Manley Hopkins: A Life
(New York: W. W. Norton, 1944), pp. 12-13

The Wreck of The Deutschland

Hopkins wrote the "Deutschland" from an intuition of will and intellect, but Mr. Eliot wrote the *Waste Land* from an intuition of emotions and impressions which eschew the logic of ideas. Hopkins will also differ from other poets of to-day who have attempted a sensuous intuition only. But however obscure the intellectual intuition of his appeal, yet it does not leave his work mere skeletal thought loosely covered with laboured prettiness and rhythmical arabesques, but rather an intimate fusion wrung from imperishable blows, an interior and subtle rhythm which, in the final analysis, make his lines inevitably ring true.

The Wreck of the Deutschland stands, as Dr. Bridges has pointed out, "chronologically as well as logically in front of his book, like a great dragon folded in the gate to forbid all entrance." It is a poem which shares the mysteriousness of Thompson's *Mistress of Vision*, the mysticism of *The Hound of Heaven*, and that indefinable, impalpable, dramatic starkness of the *Prometheus* of Aeschylus.

G. F. Lahey
Gerard Manley Hopkins (Oxford Univ. Pr., 1930), p. 108

Like some great landmark, *The Wreck of the Deutschland* cleaves sharply between two very definite periods of Hopkins's work, between his early verse and his great poetry, between Oxford and the Society of Jesus. And this new and great power differs from the earlier poetry in far more than mere metrical resources and technical richness. The advance in thought is even greater. The examination of one of his Oxford poems makes this immediately clear. . . .

After we have read this first really great poem of Hopkins, we can well address him with the words of his contemporary, Francis Thompson:

> God has given thee visible thunders
> To utter thine apocalypse of wonders.

John Pick
Gerard Manley Hopkins, Priest and Poet
(Oxford Univ. Pr., 1942), pp. 50-51

When all allowances have been made . . . it will be found that *The Wreck of The Deutschland* has a completeness, an intellectual and emotional unity, a subtlety and variety of verbal orchestration which are unique not only in English but also, we believe, in the literature of the world. It is essentially a poem to be read aloud; but like a sonata, it demands not a little interpretive skill. Its qualities are not to be gauged in one or two hasty, possibly peevish, readings. It is tart wine, but it mellows with keeping. The majority of sensitive readers will probably experience at first a mixture of attraction and repulsion. They will be attracted by what Father Lahey has called "the many marvellous lines which spangle the whole poem"—an unfortunate saying, which gives an erroneous impression of mere accidental and extrinsic felicity; they will be repelled by the strangeness of its individual style. It is by now generally recognized, however, that familiarity with Hopkins's style dispels much of the strangeness without destroying the value of his innovation. The infinite variety of "The Deutschland" is in some measure due to its difficulty. As we re-read the poem, we are continually surprised by new aspects of its poetry, but we do not exhaust its intellectual possibilities. In Dixon's words, it is "enormously powerful." It takes possession of the mind, fascinates, puzzles, exasperates, allures and recaptures it once again. Some may be, indeed have been, disturbed by the fervent irrationalities of its Trinitarianism and Marianism, its so-called martyrolatry and saint-worship; they may, at first, resent the insidious persuasiveness of its appeal; but they will probably be forced to agree with Longinus that it is not to persuasion but to ecstasy that passages of extraordinary genius carry the hearer. To the ardent Catholic the poem must always stand as one of the loftiest expressions of both the central problem and the crowning glory of his creed—the problem of tragedy and the triumph of faith. To others it will perhaps rather suggest the tragedy of faith and the triumph of pure poetry. There are things in this poem which will never please the prejudiced, the occasional, the superficial and the uninformed reader. Moreover there will, perhaps, always be some people of taste and judgment who, like Robert Bridges, will be unable to pronounce it uniformly successful. Yet with an ever-growing number of serious students of literature it will undoubtedly take the rank it deserves beside the *Nativity Ode, Lycidas, Intimations of Immortality*, and *The Hound of Heaven*.

W. H. Gardner
Gerard Manley Hopkins, Vol. I
(Oxford Univ. Pr., New Edition, 1958), pp. 69-70

The Windhover

I shall . . . consider a sonnet by Gerard Manley Hopkins, *The Windhover, to Christ our Lord*, as a more evident example of the use of poetry to convey an indecision, and its reverberation in the mind. . . .

I am indebted to Dr. Richards for this case; he has already written excellently about it. I have little to add to his analysis, and use it here because it is so good an example.

Hopkins became a Jesuit, and burnt his early poems on entering the order; there may be some reference to this sacrifice in the *fire* of the Sonnet. Confronted suddenly with the active physical beauty of the bird, he conceives it as the opposite of his patient spiritual renunciation; the statements of the poem appear to insist that his own life is superior, but he cannot decisively judge between them, and holds both with agony in his mind. *My heart in hiding* would seem to imply that the *more dangerous* life is that of the Windhover, but the last three lines insist it is *no wonder* that the life of renunciation should be the more *lovely*. *Buckle* admits of two tenses and two meanings: "they do buckle here," or "come, and buckle yourself here"; *buckle* like a military belt, for the discipline of heroic action, and *buckle* like a bicycle wheel, "make useless, distorted, and incapable of its natural motion." *Here* may mean "in the case of the bird," or "in the case of the Jesuit"; *then* "when you have become like the bird," or "when you have become like the Jesuit." *Chevalier* personifies either physical or spiritual activity; Christ riding to Jerusalem, or the cavalryman ready for the charge; Pegasus, or the Windhover.

Thus in the first three lines of the sestet we seem to have a clear case of the Freudian use of opposites, where two things thought of as incompatible, but desired intensely by different systems of judgments, are spoken of simultaneously by words applying to both; both desires are thus given a transient and exhausing satisfaction, and the two systems of judgment are forced into open conflict before the reader. Such a process, one might imagine, could pierce to regions that underlie the whole structure of our thought; could tap the energies of the very depths of the mind. At the same time one may doubt whether it is most effective to do it so crudely as in these three lines; this enormous conjunction, standing at it were for the point of friction between the two worlds conceived together, affects one rather like shouting in an actor, and probably to many readers the lines seem so meaningless as to have no effect at all. The last three lines, which profess to come to a single judgment on the matter, convey the conflict more strongly and more beautifully.

William Empson
Seven Types of Ambiguity (New York: Harcourt, Brace, 1931), pp. 284-86

"The Windhover: To Christ our Lord" is the greatest of Hopkins' poems of this period, greatest in the implications of its subject, greatest in its metrical accomplishment. . . .

The octet is an onomatopoeic and emphatic recreation of the flight of the windhover in its magnificent and triumphant career. Instrumental in its music, it moves with the rhythm of flight: it starts with a swirl, soars, whirls again, and then banks with the wind. . . .

From the opening "I caught this morning morning's minion" to "the achieve of, the mastery of the thing" the poet is in an ecstasy of amazement at the mastery and brilliant success of the windhover—a beauty so great that it is difficult to imagine any that has its equal.

But there is a beauty far, far greater. And the sestet is devoted to a revelation of a beauty beyond this beauty, a beauty which is "a billion times told lovelier, more dangerous" than the purely natural and triumphant flight. And whence comes this achievement which is more than achievement, this mastery which is more than mastery?

It is in the act of "buckling," when the windhover swoops down, when its flight is crumpled, when "brute beauty and valour and act, oh, air, pride, plume" in an act of self-sacrifice, of self-destruction, of mystical self-immolation send off a fire far greater than any natural beauty:

> Brute beauty and valour and act, oh, air, pride, plume, here
>> Buckle! AND the fire that breaks from thee then, a billion
> Times told lovelier, more dangerous, O my chevalier!

Nor is this to be wondered at, for this is true even in humble little things—is true of everything: the sheen of common earth shines out when the plough breaks it into furrows; and fire breaks from fire only in the moment of its own destruction:

> No wonder of it: sheer plod makes plough down sillion
> Shine, and blue-bleak embers, ah my dear,
>> Fall, gall themselves, and gash gold-vermillion.

John Pick
Gerard Manley Hopkins, Priest and Poet
(Oxford Univ. Pr., 1942), pp. 70-71

For some time, after so much discussion and analysis of "The Windhover," critics have shown a growing ennui. "The Windhover" was, in Gerard Manley Hopkins' opinion, (and he was no mean critic of himself and others) simply "the best thing" he had ever written. Yet today a definite contraction of enthusiasm for the poem is evident, mixed, often enough one suspects, with glowering suspicions of swindle. A statement of Mr. G. D. Klingopulos may be taken as typical: "The poet appears to have had difficulty in drawing significance out of the marvelous opening description, and seems to stretch the meaning to a rhetorical pattern which has raised difficulties of interpretation."

"The Windhover," indeed, has raised difficulties of interpretation. Explications various, contradictory and, above all, subtle, have been proliferated until no student of poetry can now approach the poem without first girding his loins for a task. My purpose in this paper, however, is to assert that the difficulties of "The Windhover" have been manufactured by its critics, and that "The Windhover" is not a difficult poem, only a rich one. I further contend that these difficulties, manifold as they have become, have all arisen from a single error: a refusal on the part of its interpreters to explore the poem, fully and patiently, on its literal level of meaning before erecting their structures of "further meaning.". . .

The first important reading of "The Windhover" was made in 1926 by I. A. Richards. Almost every misreading, as I would call them, which has followed derives from this influential and, admittedly, perceptive article. . . .

The reading of Mr. William Empson is, as he tells us himself, heavily indebted to that of Dr. Richards. Mr. Empson uses the poem as a "clear example" of his seventh type of ambiguity which is that where the ambiguous sense functions as "a fundamental division in the writer's mind. . . ."

What we need now is a reading that sufficiently emphasizes the "literal" meaning; and for that we must turn to the work of Professor John Pick. Let me say that, whereas I think Professor Pick has read the poem quite accurately, his, no doubt intentionally, brief treatment does not give us that depth of significance which the sheer amount of criticism that this poem has called forth leads us to expect. . . .

I feel I must reject Mr. Empson's suggestion, followed by Mr. McLuhan and others, that "buckle" can be taken either in the indicative or imperative moods. (In fact Mr. McLuhan reads it exclusively as an imperative.) While, according to grammatical form, it can indeed be either, when the literal meaning is restored to its primary position and emphasis, the imperative is excluded by the context. On the literal level, the bird (brute beauty, etc.) is "here", i. e. "now" buckling . . . My contention is "The Windhover" "has raised difficulties of interpretation" because, led either by a rationalistic pre-conception of what the psychology of a believer must be or by a bent towards the subjective, its critics have plunged too directly into its moral or religious significance without giving due weight to the poet's anxiety to "render the object." The realism of Hopkins drove him to place meaning in *things* first, to seek to utter *things* in such terms that they remain fully themselves while revealing the very pattern of being in all its orders. He often failed; but in this poem that gives us the soaring grandeur and perilous swoop of the kestrel as a paradigm of the universe, he came as near success as anyone has a right to expect.

F. X. Shea
Victorian Poetry (Autumn, 1964), pp. 219, 229-30, 238-39

GENERAL

Gerard Manley Hopkins died in 1889. He was one of the most remarkable technical inventors who ever wrote, and he was a major poet. Had he received the attention that was his due the history of English poetry from the 'nineties onward would have been very different. But that is a fanciful proposition: it would be extravagant to suppose that he would have received such attention even had his poems been generally accessible. Even now that they have been so for a dozen years, we see that it is possible for respected critics, writing about them with the consciousness of authority, to exhibit conspicuously in public a complete and complacent obtuseness, and yet arouse no remark: that is the measure of Hopkins' originality. . . .

The strength and subtlety of his imagery are proof of his genius. But Victorian critics were not familiar with such qualities in the verse of their time. The acceptance of Hopkins would alone have been enough to reconstitute their poetic criteria. But he was not published in 1889. He is now felt to be a contemporary, and his influence is likely to be great. It will not necessarily manifest itself in imitation of the more obvious of his technical peculiarities (these, plainly, may be dangerous toys); but no one can come from studying his work without an extended notion of the resources of English. And a technique so much concerned with inner division, friction, and psychological complexities in general has a special bearing on the problems of contemporary poetry.

He is likely to prove, for our time and the future, the only influential poet of the Victorian age, and he seems to me the greatest.

F. R. Leavis
New Bearings in English Poetry (London:
Chatto and Windus, 1932), pp. 150, 192-93

Even in the years of his richest production we have a sense of a poet driving himself too hard, of an almost unbearable excitement, superbly mastered. But it was not his religious devotion in itself that was at fault, still less that "chastity of mind" of which he wrote that it "seems to lie at the very heart and be the parent of all other good, the seeing at once what is best, the holding to that, and the not allowing anything else whatever to be even heard pleading to the contrary." He may have practised his ideal too rigorously. But his lesson to modern poets consists as much in the purity of his self-dedication as in his technical originality. "So few people," he complained once, "have style, except individual style or manner." The one he earned; with the other he was lavishly endowed.

TLS (June 10, 1944), p. 283

To create an English and Catholic convention of poetry and poetic language: this was too grand an order for one Victorian poet. The experiments are yet more important than the achievement; the comparative failures more interesting than the good whole poems.

The ideal of poetry must be to instress the inscapes without splintering the fabric of the universe, and, expressionally, to make every word rich in a way compatible with the more than additively rich inclusive structure of the whole poem.

In Hopkins' poems, the word, the phrase, the local excitement, often pulls us away from the poem. And in the more ambitious pieces, the odes as we may call them ("The Wreck," "Spelt from Sibyl's Leaves," "Nature is a Heraclitean Fire"), there is felt a discrepancy between texture and structure: the copious, violent detail is matched by no corresponding mythic or intellectual vigor. Indeed, both the Wrecks are "occasional," commissioned pieces which Hopkins works at devotedly and craftfully, as Dryden did at his *Annus Mirabilis*, but which, like Dryden's poem, fail to be organisms. Hopkins wasn't a storyteller, and he was unable to turn his wrecks into myths of Wreck: they remain historical events enveloped in meditations. "The Bugler-Boy" and other poems suffer from the gap between the psychological naïveté and the purely literary richness. To try prose paraphrases of the middle poems is invariably to show how thin the thinking is. Hopkins' mind was first aesthetic, then technical: he thought closely on metaphysical and prosodic matters: his thinking about beauty, man, and Nature is unimpressive.

The meaning of the poems hovers closely over the text, the linguistic surface of the poems. The rewarding experience of concern with them is to be let more and more into words and their linkages, to become absorbed with the proto-poetry of derivation and metaphorical expansion, to stress the inscapes of our own language.

Austin Warren
Gerard Manley Hopkins: By the Kenyon Critics
(Norfolk, Conn.: New Directions, 1945), p. 88

The definitive and comprehensive critical work on Hopkins is yet to be written, although W. H. Gardner has come closest to it. In one respect the prospective critic is at a real advantage. He can assume the permanence and importance of Hopkins without needing to defend him at length against Bridges' charges of obscurity, oddity and religious sensualism: this job has already been adequately done. The extent and pervasiveness of Hopkins' influence in itself has prepared readers for understanding his poetry. In a true sense, he has become part of the poetic tradition.

Maurice Charney
Thought (June, 1950), p. 320

When this Epilogue was first written, some ten years ago, it included the following words:

> The best of the later, deeply-pondered critical studies of Hopkins (those of G. F. Lahey, F. R. Leavis, André Bremond, D. Sargent, and B. W. Kelly) have all sought to establish the fact that Hopkins was not merely an interesting experimentalist and innovator in the technique of poetry; they have proved that he is entitled to be acknowledged as a complete and successful poet.

That it should still be necessary to enunciate this claim points to an unhealthy state of criticism, a tendency to pay too much attention either to the manner and technique of poetry or to the matter alone—an extraordinary inability to comprehend poetry as it really is, that almost mystical *compositum* of thought, emotions, and form. . . . Before drawing our final conclusion we must say a last word about Hopkins' faults. That he left so many poems unfinished was partly his misfortune and partly to his credit: he refused to substitute putty and rubble for genuine inspiration. The peculiar nature of his mind and inner experience made it necessary for him to fuse, adapt, twist and sometimes distort the elements of his native language; and at rare times idiosyncrasy led him into oddity or extravagance. Yet the truth of Erigena's saying, that "a vice is but a spoilt virtue and can have no separate existence," is in this case so curiously demonstrated that the task of absolute critical discrimination becomes well-nigh impossible: what seems good to one reader may seem bad to another. All the critic can do is to expound the processes of thought and expression, indicate the general solipsist tendency, and leave the individual educated reader to form his own judgment on this word or that construction. We must repeat, however, that most of this poet's awkwardness and difficulty disappears when we have taken the trouble to master his idiom. His style is not for imitation, because it is doubtful whether the same combination of qualities will ever be found again in one man.

When the clamour of protest and approval has died down, these facts about our subject will, we believe, emerge clearly: that by his unique personality and character, merging good living with high thinking; by his interpretation of beauty and duty, touching man to the very quick of his being; by his power of speech at once sweet and strong, melodic and harmonic; by his skill in architectonic and execution; by the stimulus he gave to the ethical and creative purposes of poets yet to be—by these and other qualities Gerard Manley Hopkins has certainly earned the distinction of being called a *major poet*; and in his finest moments he is assuredly one of our greatest.

W. H. Gardner
Gerard Manley Hopkins, Vol. II
(Oxford Univ. Pr., New Edition, 1958), pp. 368, 377-78

THOMAS HENRY HUXLEY
1825-1895

Huxley was trained as a scientist and, in his writing and lecturing, devoted himself to popularizing the achievement of science. From 1846 to 1850 he was assistant surgeon on the ship *Rattlesnake*. Returning to England to become a writer of monographs, a lecturer, and a defender of scientific education, he argued with Bishop Wilberforce on the evolution of species —Huxley called himself "Darwin's bulldog"—with Matthew Arnold on modern education, and with Gladstone on the literal accuracy of the Bible. He invented the word *agnostic* to describe his own view that one cannot know the truth about the supernatural doctrines of religion; he was always concerned, as a skeptic about miracles and as an inductive experimenter, with what truths might or might not be proved. Between 1863 and 1880 a number of his lecture series were published, and he became known by these, rather than his monographs, to the general reading public.

Leonard Huxley, *Life and Letters* (1900), 2 vols.
Clarence Ayres, *Huxley* (1932)

Throughout the papers on social subjects which fill portions of the first, third, and ninth volumes of the *Collected Essays*, criticism is followed by definite suggestion. And so it was with all matters, both practical and speculative, with which he dealt; the order of his mind was architectonic. To regard Huxley as a compound of Boanerges and Iconoclast is to show entire misapprehension of the aims which inspired his labours. In Biology his discovery of the structure of the Medusæ laid the foundations of modern zoology; his theory of the origin of the skull gave a firm basis to vertebrate morphology; and his luminous exposition of the pedigree of man imported order where confusion had reigned. In the more important matter of Education he formulated principles whose adoption would bring out the best that is in every scholar, and inspire him with love of whatever "is of good report"; while his invention of the laboratory system of zoological teaching has been adopted with the best results in every school and university of repute. In Theology he separated the accidental elements from the essential, leaving as residuum a religion that, coordinated with the needs and aspirations of human nature, would find its highest motive and its permanency in an ethic based on sympathy.

Edward Clodd
Thomas Henry Huxley (New York: Dodd Mead, 1902), pp. 244-45

The work of Huxley's life, carried on with unflagging zeal and undiminished powers almost to the day of his death, is a symmetrical and finished whole. Beginning with primeval protoplasm, the "physical basis of life," it ranges through the long perspectives of the animal kingdom to man as the noblest outcome of organic evolution. To man as an individual, to thinking man as a member of an organized society, and to man as "Nature's rebel," with deeply implanted ethical and religious sentiments, waging continual war against the stern realities of the cosmic process.

Huxley's researches as a comparative anatomist and embryologist would alone entitle him to a conspicuous place among his contemporaries. And when to this we add his championship of evolution, his labours in the cause of education, his contributions to sociology and ethics, he stands, an unique figure, among those who brought about that Scientific Renascence for which the Nineteenth Century will be memorable as long as the human race endures.

J. R. Ainsworth Davis
Thomas H. Huxley (London: Dent, 1907), pp. 252-53

The qualities which prevented Huxley from being the patient, profound author of a unified philosophical system, made him a great debater and powerful foe of religious orthodoxy—almost a Voltaire. He knew how to seize the dramatic situation, how to pick his foes, and he was never so efficient as when in a fight. His imposing store of knowledge, his gift for image and epigram, could be matched by few representatives of the Church. Their weak replies were quickly forgotten, his ringing words remembered, and the authority of God steadily decreased. So effective was Huxley in controversy that his judgments have become historical judgments and we estimate many of his foes by what he said of them.

It was not only popular theology that Huxley undermined, to an immeasurable degree, but the morality resting on that theology. This consequence he did not intend or foresee, and he would have been horrified at the very idea, for he was a thorough Victorian in morality. But a man's principal achievements are often indirect, and in this case Lilly, Mallock,

Balfour and others were correct in predicting that Huxley's views were pointing straight toward moral confusion, if not to chaos; for it is difficult if not impossible for human beings to believe in moral laws, when they do not believe in a Law-giver. "Morality, in Professor Huxley, I can well believe is strong enough to hold its own," said W. S. Lilly in 1886. "But will it be strong enough in Professor Huxley's grandchildren?" The answer to this question is in the novels of the grandson, Aldous Huxley. Agnosticism and the "hypothesis that animals are automata" and the doctrine that morality is independent of theology are the views held by the people of *Antic Hay, Those Barren Leaves* and *Point Counter Point*. Of course, the war, the "machine age" and other factors helped to produce such types of character, but the unbelief of Professor Huxley had a considerable influence.

But we must end on a positive note because Huxley was on the whole a positive and creative figure. He was a great scientist, and a great exponent of scientific method and scientific education. He not only made his own discoveries but did as much as any one man to give the world a genuine sense of science. His doubts have made us more honest, his courage has made us more courageous. We may be too subtle or too cynical now, to appreciate his ardent, evangelical nature. The battle has been won. Scientists no longer need to be prophets and they can afford to be dull.

Houston Peterson
Huxley, Prophet of Science (London:
Longmans, 1932), pp. 313-14

[His] lectures are gems of lucid expression and still appear perennially in the composition books as models of exposition. No writer on science has succeeded better in striking the tenuous balance between the ponderosity of technical jargon and the self-conscious breeziness which too often characterizes the popularizings of the science-for-the-millions school.

Homer A. Watt and William W. Watt
A Dictionary of English Literature
(New York: Barnes and Noble, 1945), p. 148

In his *Autobiography: Methods and Results*, Huxley notes with a biologist's interest in heredity that he inherited a quick temper, tenacity, and artistic aptitude from his father, and from his mother swiftness of apprehension, which he seems to have valued most—and rightly, for, joined with the clarity which he later made a test both for truth and for style, it lies at the very basis of his mind and character. He had the coolness, the sureness, the self-confidence which clarity and swiftness bestow. He was always mobilized for action. He never hesitated, was never less than himself. In fact, he was not so much the patient solver of problems as the prodigious performer—the rapid and voluminous reader, the ready and eloquent speaker, the facile and felicitous writer. He possessed the obvious virtues in nearly as much splendour as Macaulay, and was almost as magnificently adequate to his age. Like Macaulay also, he remained personally modest but gratified his self-esteem by taking his duties and his world very seriously. In fact, he had some of Macaulay's faults, but he had them in less extreme degree. He was less inclined to formularize himself and his goods for mass production. He felt somewhat less, one suspects, the need of having a stream of ready-made thoughts going through his head at all times like a Fourth-of-July parade. He was probably more patient in groping for an idea or in grappling with a problem. He certainly did not retreat from difficult subjects. Metaphysics was one of his natural elements. Here he differed from Macaulay and resembled Voltaire. He had Voltaire's combativeness, his eager curiosity about facts and theories, his heroic but often negative and incredulous common sense, which sometimes closes the mind to large and daring conceptions.

William Irvine
Apes, Angels, and Victorians (London:
Weidenfeld and Nicolson, 1955), p. 8

CHARLES KINGSLEY
1819-1875

The son of an Anglican clergyman, Kingsley was himself ordained shortly after taking a Cambridge degree. He was associated with the Broad Church party, and his combination of protestant vigor with sympathy for the struggles of the laboring class against social injustice came to be labelled "muscular Christianity." Although his first published work, a poetic drama about St. Elizabeth entitled *The Saint's Tragedy* (1848) reveals little of such interests, the novels *Alton Locke* (1850) and *Yeast* (1851) deal with working men and with Chartism—the laborer's movement for reform— from the point of view of a Christian Socialist. In 1853 Kingsley published his novel about early Christianity, *Hypatia*, and in 1855 appeared his anti-Catholic novel of Elizabethan England, *Westward Ho!* His other works include *Glaucus*, about the zoology of the seashore (1855), *The Heroes*, a re-telling of Greek myths for children (1856), a novel about an epidemic, *Two Years Ago* (1857), *Andromeda and Other Poems* (1858), his popular fairy tale *The Water Babies* (1863), another historical novel, *Hereward the Wake* (1866), letters from the West Indies collected under the title *At Last* (1871), and *Prose Idylls, New and Old* (1873). From 1860 to 1869 he was Regius Professor of Modern History at Cambridge, and it was during this time—in 1864—that he accused John Henry Newman of believing that truthfulness was not a virtue for a Roman

Catholic priest, provoking a reply and a controversy out of which came Newman's *Apologia pro Vita Sua*. Kingsley lectured in America in 1874; he died, soon after returning to England, in his Hampshire parish.

Life and Works (1901-1903), 19 vols.
Una Pope-Hennessy, *Canon Charles Kingsley* (1948)

Charles Kingsley was a glowing flame that dazzled his day and generation and then burned out, all too soon. His influence is subtle, based in part upon his unique personality and in part upon his message. Although a disciple of Thomas Carlyle in social and political theory and of Frederick Denison Maurice in theology, he was a man whose independent mind and forceful personality made a peculiar contribution to the problems of his day. He was not a social democrat, in the way in which that word was understood in his day, but he had a spacious spirit capable of taking to itself the needs and rights of the lower classes. He was no revolutionist, seeking to destroy the safeguards of society; he believed as firmly as did Disraeli in the House of Lords. While not seeking to upset the social and political standards of his time, he called the socially privileged to the full and appropriate responsibility of their class. Kingsley was neither thoroughgoing scientist, nor theologian, nor historian, and though he did not hesitate to enter the domains of each, it was not as a final authority nor as an exact teacher, but rather as the fervid poet whose vivid imagination lighted up those regions of knowledge for the people about him, as the rising sun gilds the horizon and announces the dawn of a new day. . . . Kingsley's collected poems comprise a volume in themselves, yet there was more poetry in him than ever came out. He was too active a man to write much poetry. *The Saint's Tragedy* was written before he became involved in the social, political, and religious controversies, and the promise he showed then of becoming a dramatist of power gave rise to Bunsen's hope that Kingsley might continue Shakespeare's historical plays. Even had he possessed the intellectual genius to do so, the temperament of a man like Kingsley would have kept him from fulfilling that promise. Something of a deep critical discernment, of balanced temper and strict self-command is necessary to make a supreme dramatist. However, his very limitations of temperament, while interfering with his dramatic promise, made him a good lyric poet. Toward the close of his career he expressed his opinion that besides *Hypatia* his poems would probably be all of his literary work that would survive. Happily, his prediction has not come true, and we believe that Kingsley has a place commensurate with his genius among the immortals. Some men's writings are the greatest part of them, and posterity studies their lives through a spirit of curiosity excited by their works. In a sense this is true of Kingsley, but in a truer sense many are reading Kingsley's literary works because of the indelible impression his personality

made upon his fellow men, for whom, in all his activities, he labored. His
life in itself was a poem of deep lyric passion.

Stanley E. Baldwin
Charles Kingsley (Ithaca, N. Y.: Cornell Univ. Pr., 1934),
pp. 174, 193-94

Kingsley was not a realist. . . . Muscular fiction emanated from sentimentalism, not from any sound moral philosophy; Kingsley's did, at any rate,
however much it owed to Carlyle's new valuations of manliness, courage,
and the capacity for doing things. Its sources were in the eighteenth-century
novel of sentiment, which likewise aped at times the epical strain.

Ernest A. Baker
The History of the English Novel, Vol. VIII
(London: Witherby, 1936), p. 76

Born in the same year as the Queen, Kingsley typifies the Victorian man
as closely as she presents the Victorian woman. He shared most of her
fundamental principles. He believed in England, in the Empire, in the Established Church; in the ennobling influence of womanhood and the sanctity of the home; in a good God guiding the universe and each of its
individual inhabitants; in the spiritual brotherhood of men within a benevolent aristocracy; in evolutionary progress and the compatibility of science and religion. Most of the great literary figures of the nineteenth century
were rebels against or thinkers in advance of their time. Kingley's influence
was due in large part to his not being a thinker at all. He suffered all the
torments endured by the average man of the period in his struggle with a
changing universe; he differed from the average man in the courage with
which he faced the problems of the day and the volubility with which he
discussed them. He made for himself solutions which were shallow but
convincing to hundreds because of their power for comfort and because of
the enormous vitality and sincerity behind his presentations. His power in
his time and his significance to succeeding generations lies in this, that he
was not so much an artist as a fluent English gentleman.

Margaret Farrand Thorp
Charles Kingsley (Princeton, N. J.:
Princeton Univ. Pr., 1937), pp. 1-2

Kingsley's *Alton Locke* (1850) is the kind of minor novel that remains
with us less for its intrinsic worth than for its exposure of certain conditions
which continue to make us feel guilty. In this century, Orwell's *1984,* a
much different type of book in virtually every way, will one hundred years
from now be read with the same kind of galling curiosity. Kingsley's
theme is the familiar one that bread is not sufficient. But here the theme is

set forth not by a conservative anxious to avoid the questions raised by the Chartists and Luddites, but by a man sympathetic to the working-man's cause. Through the fortunes and misfortunes of Alton Locke, Kingsley claims that political and social freedom for the worker—including the vote and better working conditions—must never be separated from religious feeling.

Frederick Karl
An Age of Fiction (New York: Farrar, Straus, 1964), p. 333

RUDYARD KIPLING
1865-1936

During the twenty-five years before the First World War, Kipling was probably the most popular writer in the English-speaking world. Since 1920 his stock has fallen and today, in a tangle of contradictory opinions, it is hard to form a true picture of either his popularity or his merit. Into his verse he poured the ingredients which make for popular acclaim—the conventional inspirationalism of *When Earth's Last Picture is Painted* and of the inevitable *If*; the solemn pomp of the *Recessional*; the travel-folder exoticism of *Mandalay*; the drum-beat heroism of *Danny Deever, Gunga Din*, and *Fuzzy-Wuzzy*. He was a versifier of tremendous vigor and facility and, even when he lards the lines with Cockney vulgarisms, the movement seldom halts. At his best, as in *McAndrew's Hymn*, he wrote real poetry. But because *If* has been framed in too many bedrooms and *Mandalay* murdered in too many barrooms, many will deny this. Fewer deny Kipling's skill as a story-teller in prose. He was born in Bombay and spent most of his early life in India. On that complex land he drew for much of his fiction, treating his material partly with the authenticity of an honest journalist, partly with the mystery of a born romantic—mingling the gay humor of the British Tommy with the inscrutability of the dark-skinned native. These qualities mark Kipling's first collection of short-stories, *Plain Tales from the Hills* (1888), and the best of his novels, *Kim* (1901). Other short-stories appear in *Mine Own People* (1891), *The Day's Work* (1898), and *Traffics and Discoveries* (1904). Kipling was also a master of stories for children, as in *The Jungle Books* (1894-5), *Stalky and Co.* (1899), and *Just So Stories* (1902).

Homer A. Watt and William W. Watt
A Dictionary of English Literature (New York: Barnes and Noble, 1945), pp. 163-64

Works: Bombay Edition (1913-1938), 31 vols.
C. E. Carrington, *The Life of Rudyard Kipling* (1955)

His work nobly enforces those old-fashioned virtues of man which, it is to be hoped, will never go out of fashion—to do one's duty, to live stoically, to live cleanly, to live cheerfully. Such lessons can never be taught too often, and they are of the moral bone and fibre of Mr. Kipling's writing. But with them go the old-fashioned vices of prejudiced Toryism. . . .

As a writer Mr. Kipling is a delight; as an influence he is a danger. Of course, the clock of Time is not to be set back by gifts ten times as great as Mr. Kipling's. The great world movement will still go on, moving surely, if slowly, and with occasional relapses, in the direction which it has always taken, from brute force to spiritual enlargement. But there are influences that speed it along and others that retard. It is to be regretted that Mr. Kipling's influence should be one of those that retard.

Richard Le Gallienne
Rudyard Kipling: A Criticism
(London: John Lane, 1900), pp. 160, 162-63

The tendencies . . . of the first period are still active in the third—the shift from observation to reminiscence is still going on, the delight in an escape from life still runs alongside of delight in life itself. There is still further widening of sympathetic psychology; a continued increase in the subtlety of personal intervention, in general excellence and delicacy of the narrative art. The suggested story reaches its climax, as does the unintelligible story. Satire, at least of the bitter sort, has largely disappeared. While, then, the same formula holds: increase in Imagination and Sense of Form; decrease in self-assertion; escape from overpowering Sense of Fact: it is also true that the force of these tendencies has not been sufficient to effect a transformation. Kipling remains to the end what his training and his personality made him at the beginning of his career. His greatness still lies, not in his reasoning power, not in his moral interpretation or criticism of life, not in his sense of form, but rather in his sense of fact, vivid, concrete, and humanly interesting; in a power of imagination closely related to this sense of fact; in an emotional or even sensational appeal; and in intensity, in vital energy. With the single exception of Chaucer, he is the most powerful personality of all those who have expressed themselves in the short-story.

Walter Morris Hart
Kipling The Story Writer
(Berkeley, Calif.: Univ. California Pr., 1918), p. 220

As far as can be judged at present, the elements in Mr. Kipling's work which have won him popularity are the least important, the most ephemeral. It will only be possible to give him his rightful place when the political heats of his day have become coldly historical. But to us, the successive generation, he has a value that may well be permanent, apart from his language, which itself deserves to live. He has indicated an attitude towards life which, to us groping for a solid basis, may serve, if not for that basis itself, then as a point of disagreement. He deals, after all, with the enduring problems of humanity, the problems out of which all religion, all real poetry must arise. Moreover, he provides a solution which those of his own cast of mind—and they are many, though most may be unaware of it— will greet with satisfaction, and even with that sense of glamour, of invigoration, which it is partly the function of good literature to give.

Bonamy Dobrée
The Lamb and the Lute (Oxford Univ. Pr., 1929), p. 65

If his genius did not fail, neither did his influence decrease. The English-speaking peoples continued to read him and there is no present indication of their ceasing to do so. This is a fact, however much anyone may like or dislike it. It is true that his last collection of stories met with a marked falling off in response. But, in my judgement, that is due to the fact that he was attempting something too difficult for many of his readers and almost, perhaps, for himself. . . . But the popularity of his other work has not been in the least affected. Kipling is still read, and read widely and with pleasure, and therefore, since he is essentially a man with a doctrine to preach, has a formative effect on innumerable minds. He is a great artist. He is a political philosopher with a passionate belief in his own conclusions and an unsurpassed power in recommending them to the minds of others. Because he is both these things he is an historical force which we ought to endeavour to evaluate in all its aspects.

Edward Shanks
Rudyard Kipling (New York: Doubleday, 1940), pp. 15-16

Much of Kipling's work may have been faulty; it was didactic, it was mannered, it was intricate; it showed up vast lacunae in his mind and in his way of thinking; if he had an infallible eye and an infallible ear, he had by no means always an infallible taste; his worst fell disastrously below his best. But—he brought the universe before the multitude, he had a note in his music for every listener, he threw his pearls to every corner of the market-place. He covered the world and carried it as a toy in his hand; if his own heart remained hidden, he had looked closely into the hearts of others—and he shared his knowledge of them freely. And whether or not his knowledge were inspired and whether or not it were knowledge, he made it seem—so very often—as if it were the absolute Logos of God. In the wide humanity of his dealings he touched everyone sometime somewhere. Whether or not he will return to his own, to mount again that pinnacle which he once justly occupied, will depend on the accidents of time and chance; but quite certainly it will not be for lack of the essential qualities. They may be hidden, they may be obscured by that dense veil of Kipling he drew over everything he wrote; but they are there, the search for them is made very pleasant and even the veil itself is a charming thing in which to lose oneself.

Hilton Brown
Rudyard Kipling (New York: Harper, 1945), p. 228

One reason for Kipling's power as a good bad poet I have already suggested —his sense of responsibility, which made it possible for him to have a world-view, even though it happened to be a false one. Although he had no direct connection with any political party, Kipling was a Conservative, a thing that does not exist nowadays. Those who now call themselves Conservatives are either Liberals, Fascists or the accomplices of Fascists. He identified himself with the ruling power and not with the opposition. In a gifted writer this seems to us strange and even disgusting, but it did have the advantage of giving Kipling a certain grip on reality. The ruling power is always faced with the question, "In such and such circumstances, what would you *do?*" whereas the opposition is not obliged to take responsibility or make any real decisions. Where it is a permanent and pensioned opposition, as in England, the quality of its thought deteriorates accordingly. Moreover, anyone who starts out with a pessimistic, reactionary view of life tends to be justified by events, for Utopia never arrives and "the gods of the copybook headings," as Kipling himself put it, always return. Kipling sold out to the British government class, not financially but emotionally. This warped his political judgment, for the British ruling class were not what he imagined, and it led him into abysses of folly and snobbery, but he gained a corresponding advantage from having at least tried to imagine what action and responsibility are like. It is a great thing in his favour that he is not witty, not "daring," has no wish to *épater les bourgeois.* He dealt largely in platitudes, and since we live in a world of platitudes, much of what he said sticks. Even his worst follies seem less shallow and less irritating than the "enlightened" utterances of the same period, such as Wilde's epigrams or the collection of cracker-mottoes at the end of *Man and Superman.*

George Orwell
Critical Essays (London: Secker and Warburg, 1946), p. 113

There are certainly things to be disapproved of in Kipling's writings. . . . The worse faults, as the strongest evidences of original genius, are in the first half of his work. His later tales deserve more impartial study than they have received. If Kipling "limps" in them, as Mr. Edmund Wilson avers, it is because he has traveled a long way. "Shrunken" I cannot accept; to me his stature is increased.

J. M. S. Tompkins
The Art of Rudyard Kipling
(London: Methuen, 1959), pp. 258-59

Criticism has not yet come to terms with Kipling: the man and his works symbolise a part of British political and social history about which his countrymen have an uneasy conscience. . . . At the root of every assessment of Kipling lies the problem of his morality. In 1941 the two most famous critics in England and America chose quite independently to consider his status. T. S. Eliot . . . asked us to reconsider the fashionable verdict on the great imperialist. He met with an unequivocal response. Raymond Mortimer, Peter Quennell, Graham Greene, G. W. Stonier, Hugh Kingsmill, and *Scrutiny* in the person of Boris Ford echoed each other's disgust; and in America Lionel Trilling denied that Eliot could claim Kipling for the Tory tradition, "a tradition which is honoured by Dr. Johnson, Burke, and Walter Scott. . . . He has none of the *mind* of the few great Tories. His Toryism had in it a lower middle-class snarl of defeated gentility." . . . Auden and Orwell characteristically refused to sing in harmony but took as proved the usual charges against Kipling's social and moral philosophy; and Desmond MacCarthy's encomium at Kipling's death, though judicious, was restrained.

On the other side of the Atlantic, however, Edmund Wilson, writing at the high-noon of American liberalism, gave a verdict which has become orthodoxy. He found much to praise in the young Anglo-Indian journalist and in the dark stories of Jamesian complexity written in his last years— "the Kipling that nobody read.". . .

It is in the study of the texture of his prose that the next advance in understanding him must be made. . . . Like Miss Tompkins I believe that until now the critics have underestimated and misunderstood the nature of Kipling's work.

Noel Annan
Victorian Studies (June, 1960), pp. 323-24, 348

EDWARD LEAR
1812-1888

His ambition was to be a Pre-Raphaelite painter, and Lear's water colors are still justly admired. But his fame attaches rather to his nonsense verse —the first volume of which was published in 1846—and especially his limericks. Modern readers and critics have sometimes found in this verse a surrealistic and profoundly revealing strain; and the appeal to both adults and children of his resolutely illogical poems remains widespread.

Angus Davidson, *Edward Lear* (1939)

In Lear's nonsense-world it is not his drawings, but his poems, which take first place. Here again—with the exception, as we have already seen, of the limericks—he invented something entirely new. In his poems, pure and absolute nonsense as they are, he yet found a vehicle for the expression of his deepest feelings, paradoxical though this may seem: and this is the often unsuspected secret of their peculiar power to move others. It is not only that Lear had an "extraordinary mastery of rhythm," as Mr. Maurice Baring calls it. "It is quite different," he points out, "from the neat clashing rhymes of most writers of humorous poetry. Poems like "The Owl and the Pussy-Cat" have an *organic* rhythm. That is to say, the whole poem (and not merely the separate lines and stanzas) forms a piece of architectonic music. . . . Behind this sense of rhythm—which makes itself felt, too, in the best of his water-colours—there lies the emotional force that is an essential quality of all true poetry, a force that is derived from life itself. Even in some of the limericks, light-hearted as they are, there is, if one chooses to think of it, a foundation of human experience. . . . Lear, clearly, was much influenced by Tennyson—more than merely to the extent of using his metres (the "Yonghy-Bonghy-Bó," for instance, is in the metre of "Row us out from Desenzano"; "My Aged Uncle Arly" in that of "The Lady of Shalott"; "Calico Pie" in that of "Sweet and Low," etc.) But he did not burlesque him: his poetry, rather, is in the nature of a burlesque of bad romantic poetry of the popular kind. While good poetry confines the reader to the poet's own point of view at the moment, bad poetry, by the use of vague images, allows the reader to interpret it in his own way and in accordance with his own associations. Lear suggests very often the kind of effect attained by this use of vague images: yet his own images are always perfectly clear and conscious. His poetry might be called the "reductio ad absurdum" of Romanticism. It is here that he has some slight resemblance to the Surrealists, who have claimed him as one of themselves—together with Dante, Shakespeare ("dans ses meilleurs jours"), Hugo, Poe, Baudelaire, and other distinguished writers of the past. The "automatic writing" of Surrealism, indeed, with its "absence of all control exercised by reason and all aesthetic or moral preoccupation" is a "reductio ad absurdum" of the Romantic theory of Inspiration: but Lear's writing is intended to be absurd, whereas that of the Surrealists is not. Lear's effects are deliberate, carefully thought out, selective.

Angus Davidson
Edward Lear (New York: E. P. Dutton, 1939), pp. 195, 200

We are safe with Lear because he is himself safe. Pussy-cat or not, the marriage was made, and the sanity which results from it turns upon those three things, laughter, poetry and religion, inwardly experienced and whole-hearted, which appear . . . in tantalizing combination when we cannot hope to work out their inter-relationship. We can only suppose that they have some affinity, each working out its own form of union and balance in the mind.

Elizabeth Sewell
The Field of Nonsense
(London: Chatto and Windus, 1952), pp. 180-81

THOMAS BABINGTON MACAULAY
1800-1859

"The great apostle of the Philistines," as Matthew Arnold called him, was born at Rothley and educated at Cambridge. His essay on Milton (1825) was the beginning of a literary career; but Macaulay had a political career as well, serving as a Whig member of Parliament, a legal advisor in India, and—until 1841, when the Melbourne government fell—as Secretary-at-War. In 1842 he published his popular *Lays of Ancient Rome.* The five volumes of his major work, the *History of England from the Accession of James II,* appeared between 1848 and 1861, the last edited by his sister and published posthumously. This lively and novelistic history, combining strong Whig prejudices with a vivid literary style, has appealed to readers less, perhaps, for its historical accuracy than for its detailed and dramatic writing. The author was made first Baron Macaulay of Rothley in 1857.

Works (1905-1907), 9 vols.
George O. Trevelyan, *The Life and Letters* . . . (1876), 2 vols.

When all has been said, it remains true that Macaulay gave a new life and meaning to the historical Essay. He made it a vehicle through which thousands of people, who would never have read history at all, have acquired in a pleasurable way some acquaintance with great characters and events. These essays are probably the best of their kind in Europe. And there can be no doubt that they will live. Only it is much to be desired that, when they are used for purposes of education, students should be warned against the errors which many of them contain. On a higher level than any but the very best of the Essays, stand those five biographies which Macaulay wrote for the *Encyclopædia Britannica*—those of Atterbury, Bunyan, Goldsmith, Johnson, and the younger Pitt. All these are mature and careful pieces of work, quieter and more restrained in style than the Essays, but hardly less attractive. They show Macaulay as a master of artistic condensation. Taking into account their merits both of matter and of form, we should be safe in affirming that, as a writer of short biographies, Macaulay has not been surpassed, if he has been equalled, by any English writer. The life of the younger Pitt, in particular, calls for unqualified admiration. It was written in the January of 1859, the year of his death; and he never wrote anything better. It is a sample of what he could have done in the History if he had reached that period, and it must enhance our regret that the History remained a fragment.

Richard C. Jebb
Macaulay (Cambridge Univ. Pr., 1900), pp. 43-44

Something can be said for every view of him. But wherever the emphasis of our esteem may fall, none of his work is slight enough to be over-shadowed by any other part of it. He lies in Poet's Corner; and in number, perhaps, those who know him by his stirring *Lays* overtop any other body of his admirers. But the tribute of his College to his various qualities of mind is that which must be followed here. In a judgment so broad it may not be easy to preserve unity. Yet there are, it seems to me, unique traits of genius which reveal themselves in all the aspects of his many-sided life.

At the present time the opinion of men of letters regarding him runs strongly in the direction of criticism. All are agreed that the man himself is an ornament to our literature and our public life. It is agreed, too, that there are few in this century whose work, despite high literary qualities, has been so little over the heads of the people. His influence does not stay in the closet but reaches the forum; and he is welcome wherever he is known. But yet, as Aristotle has said of Plato, when both our friends and the truth are dear to us, the truth must be preferred; and round the in-trinsic value of Macaulay's work vigorous and penetrative criticism con-tinues to gather. His own critical judgment is assailed; the knife he did so much to sharpen is turned upon himself. His new and striking departure in historical method is condemned on the witness of its result. His poetry, it is said, is an exotic growth, his style a gaudy mannerism. To much of this indictment we must consent; but our consent will not always be un-qualified. For there are faults and faults. There are faults which greatly serve the ends of truth by defining her limits more closely; there are schol-ars' errors which touch the imagination with all the force of truth; there are those errors of reaction which goes to an extreme, but still of reaction from what is false, which in every sphere of knowledge have been the footsteps of progress. From some of these, and from lesser, defects no one will clear Macaulay. His was a mind whose strength was closely allied to its weakness; which was too brilliant to be cautious, and too quick to be profound. His faults therefore lie side by side with his merits. Yet from every repeated appeal to his work, from weighing what is best in it against its acknowledged blots, we return with a conscious right to the assertion that, despite many failings, time will vindicate a great and an immortal name.

D. H. Macgregor
Lord Macaulay (London: C. J. Clay, 1901), pp. 3-4

Faults he has, many and grave. The splendid rhetoric, that carries his reader on to so many heights, too often distorts the truth or conceals the awkward fact which would spoil it. Macaulay the politician was not in this respect serviceable to Macaulay the historian: the evil fruit of the hustings too often beguiled him. The natural vigour of his temperament had always caused him to see men and their motives over-much in black and white, and the habits of party oratory tended to intensify still more these lights and shades. So he must paint James wholly bad and William wholly good: so he must contrast Marlborough's genius—"the red coat and eagle eye of the victor of Blenheim," which he never lived to draw—against the black shade of unbroken avarice and treachery. To this rhetoric his natural ear for fine-sounding synthesis the more inclined him. He, who cared for music but little when he heard it in a concert room, loved it in words and could never resist its charm. . . .

Yet when all is said and done, Macaulay was too honest a man to be perpetually unjust, even to Tories. . . . He loved the Whig cause and those who fought for it, but he loved England more.

Arthur Bryant
Macaulay (New York:
Appleton-Century-Crofts, 1933), pp. 106-7, 110-11

It is not difficult to understand why Macaulay's writing, so abundant and downright in substance, so highly coloured and so strongly cadenced, should have taken contemporaries captive. Nor is the reaction less comprehensible. When Ruskin, three years before Macaulay's death, spoke of "the beautiful, quiet, English" of Sir Arthur Helps, he anticipated the change of taste that was rapidly setting in. Macaulay is loud. He writes as if his purpose was less to convince than to silence his readers: not to win their agreement but to force their assent. Naturally, the new age rebelled, the more hotly perhaps because the large unlettered public was faithful, not caring whether their favourite was a bad historian, as Seeley said; a bully, as John Morley said; or that his verses sometimes made Matthew Arnold cry out in pain. That revolt has long died away. The last shot was fired by Lytton Strachey when he spoke of the Philistine on Parnassus. On Parnassus, truly. But it was no Philistine who wrote,

> Heard on Lavernia Scargill's whispering trees,
> And pined by Arno for my lovelier Tees;

or who could say of Dante what Dante has said of Virgil:

> Vagliami il lungo studio e il grande amore.

G. M. Young
Macaulay: Prose and Poetry
(Cambridge, Mass.: Harvard Univ. Pr., 1952), pp. 7-8

It is no longer for his political opinions but for his history that Macaulay is chiefly remembered. As late as 1881, John Morley, who did not care greatly for Macaulay, said that his historical works found throughout England and the colonies in the library between Shakespeare and the Bible, had, more than any other books, determined the direction of men's conception of history. The great period of English history for Macaulay was that between the Revolution of 1688 and the Reform Bill of 1832, a period in which England established the three great Whig principles—the right of the people to change their sovereign, the superiority of the Parliament to the king, and religious toleration along with an established church. All three of these represented compromise, but compromise had led to national prosperity and success, improvement in the conditions of living, and a prospect of almost limitless progress in the future. On the contrary side, Macaulay detested mobs and radicals. He believed in Parliament but did not care to have the suffrage extended beyond that provided in 1832. As the English historian, D. C. Somervell, says, "His views were moderately 'advanced' in the 'twenties, and somewhat old-fashioned in the 'fifties, but they were the same views."

In his prose style Macaulay strove to be clear. Sometimes his style is mannered, but always there is perfect organization and lucid structure. His chief mannerism is balance and antithesis, which he sometimes extends to sentences and even to whole paragraphs. There is an oratorical sonorousness about his sentences even when there is a lack of the simpler rhythms. Lytton Strachey, who in his biographies followed Macaulay's historical method of building up details and constructing a sparkling narrative, accused Macaulay of sacrificing exactness to his style of utterance. "When he wished," says Strachey, "to state that Schomberg was buried in Westminister Abbey he *had* to say that 'the illustrious warrior' was laid in 'that venerable abbey, hallowed by the dust of many generations of princes, heroes and poets.' There is no escaping it; and the incidental drawback that Schomberg was not buried in Westminster at all, but in Dublin is, in comparison with the platitude of the style, of very small importance."

John Wilson Bowyer and John Lee Brooks, eds.
The Victorian Age: Prose, Poetry, and Drama, 2nd Ed.
(New York: Appleton-Century-Crofts, 1954), pp. 28-29

GEORGE MEREDITH

1828-1909

Born in Portsmouth and eduucated partly in Germany, Meredith began his writing career as a journalist and for 35 years read manuscripts for a London publisher. His marriage, in 1849, to the daughter of the novelist

Thomas Love Peacock was unsuccessful and ended after nine years when she left him, eloping with the painter Henry Wallis. It inspired the writing of *Modern Love*, a series of poems about unhappy marriage, published in 1862, a year after her death. Although this is Meredith's most ambitious work in poetry, his other volumes of verse—published in 1851, 1887, 1888, 1892, 1898, 1901, and 1909—include a number of often anthologized lyrics. Yet Meredith is probably best known as a novelist, one who uses the poet's techniques of verbal play and elaborate imagery along with the novelist's methods of psychological revelation. His first works of fiction were the oriental fantasy *The Shaving of Shagpat* (1855) and a burlesque on the Gothic tale, *Farina* (1857); these were followed by the "problem" novels about well-born English men and women, the first few containing strongly autobiographical elements: *The Ordeal of Richard Feverel* (1859), *Evan Harrington* (1861), *Sandra Belloni* (1864), *Rhoda Fleming* (1865), *Harry Richmond* (1871), *Beauchamp's Career* (1876), *The Egoist* (1879), *Diana of the Crossways* (1885), *One of Our Conquerers* (1891), *Lord Ormont and His Aminta* (1894), and *The Amazing Marriage* (1895). His one historical novel was *Vittoria* (1867). Meredith's lecture-essay *On the Idea of Comedy*, a discussion of the "comic spirit" that illuminates the satirical purpose in much of his fiction, has been influential. But as a novelist he was not popular in his own day; and his complex, sometimes obscure style, especially in the relatively late novels, has made him a rather special taste even for modern readers who recognize his importance. Although *Richard Feverel* and *The Egoist* are generally accepted as major achievements, Meredith is still probably one of the least known of the great Victorian novelists.

Memorial Edition (1909-1912), 27 vols.

Lionel Stevenson, *The Ordeal of George Meredith* (1953)

PERSONAL

Even individual eccentricity . . . seems to him governed by actual laws; therefore capable of innate mental comprehension. He means that not only would he be able to account for it in a chance character, but that if he himself had been forming that character from his own mind, it would still have displayed the same eccentricities. Though each human being, he says, is born with something no one else has ever had, that something is just as much the result of laws and as much subject to them as the commonest trait. Besides this, the progress of humanity is not merely the result of individual individuality, but also of the individuality of the race, the individuality of nature's law. Nothing, says the novelist of types, is an exception; many things are unknown.

Finally, we come to the last point of his outlook. We must clearly understand that he claims the vantage ground of the spirit of aloofness—which has been called the comic spirit. He views us all from a height, and therefore he views us all together, and all at the same time. He sees influences at work which are unknown to the actors themselves; he sees fate's slow, vast sweep which can be observed only from above the tempestuous fight; he sees the mysterious sixth sense, which sways mankind with sympathetic movements. The intense grip of life's gigantic panorama prevents his view from becoming warped. The comic spirit is the smile of infinity on the efforts and yearnings of finity: it is the look of eternity on time.

Richard H. P. Curle
Aspects of George Meredith
(London: Routledge, 1908), pp. 14-15

We find a mind of wondrous richness, subtle, fecund, nimble, forceful, an abiding *vivida vis*—the passion of the poet, the vehemence of the orator, the serene wide outlook of the philosopher, the arch-smile of the Comic votary, the phantasy of the Euphuist, the wittiness of the Athenian, combined in one prodigious mental whole. It took some four men of supreme talent to produce the genius of Meredith. He is, first, the poet described by Shakespeare—looking into himself—with his eye in a fine frenzy rolling, with his fiery glance that gazes at both earth and heaven, and misses neither the richness of the universal mother nor the glories of the firmament, neither the infinitely great nor the infinitely small, bodying forth in his imagination shapes unseen before, giving the vital flesh and blood to insubstantial phantoms, impassioned with a romantic glow, writing not sonnets but whole novels to a mistress's eyebrow, gifted with the reasoning powers of a mathematician, the calculation of a chess master, and the profundity of a philosopher. There is the finest subtlest equipoise in this felicitous union. Poetic rapture, bordering as always upon madness, is compatible with the view that civilisation is based on commonsense; romance will hold no truce with sentimentalism; the wit is quintessential wisdom. He has a noble charity and a generous patience, he is intense and earnest, he jests at all the world, and sometimes at himself. He illustrates better than any since Shakespeare that impetuous mental energy which Matthew Arnold deemed the source of our literary greatness. Indeed, the aptest parallel to Meredith at his greatest in pregnancy of thought, opulence of language, lyric fervour, and tenseness of the mind, is a Shakespearean sonnet. No man has ever been endowed with richer gifts. The gods have heaped their favours on him, and he is to outshine all mortals—but on one condition. Cassandra was inspired with prophetic vision, but none was to believe her. Meredith was to have all gifts of mind, but it was ordained that few should understand him.

J. H. E. Crees
George Meredith (Oxford: Blackwell, 1918), pp. 182-83

The Ordeal of Richard Feverel

The Ordeal of Richard Feverel is not a wholly satisfactory book. The writer's sense of the tragedy of human existence is so keen that it borders on cruelty. Self-slain, his characters seem not the less almost hounded to ruin. But to realize the greatness of the book, we need only to reflect how intolerable the story would become if shrunk to the canvas of an inferior writer. We may not find the story likable; but we cannot, unless we are idiots, read and be blind to its power. In view of this first of his novels we might question whether the author's outlook on life will grow broad-based enough to support his burden of sensitiveness; but we know him already as a poet and not a transcriber—one who is not boxed in with his characters but sees them against a great background of earth and of air.

Mary Sturge Gretton
The Writings and Life of George Meredith
(Cambridge, Mass.: Harvard Univ. Pr., 1926), p. 42

When Meredith began *The Ordeal of Richard Feverel*, he had behind him *The Shaving of Shagpat* and *Farina* and the 1851 edition of *Love in the Valley,* all three rarefied distillations of life in the manner of allegory and pastoral. The characters and the incidents were derived from reality and were translatable again into actual life, but they were clothed in the metaphor of poetic romance. He was now concerned to give his fiction a local habitation, to show human passion at play in nineteenth-century English settings. In *The Ordeal* he achieved some of his finest scenes of pathos and tragedy. . . .

The ornamental framework of the novel possesses a certain charm, though one would prefer a more Doric simplicity, and it does remind one that the novelist is not naïve—that he is wiser than the Wise Youth, that he sees with scientific analysis the fallacy of Sir Austin, the pretender to scientific wisdom, that he can discourse philosophically of life's passions, in short, that he draws on the disciplines of reason and common sense. But the psychological beauty is what transcends these. As we live in Richard's thoughts we feel anew that youth, adventure, love are magical qualities. We are forced relentlessly to admit that life may be a ruthless destroyer of the magic; and yet, in the paradox of tragedy, we perceive that through the chill, melancholy disillusionment about his own volatile nature and the mutability of a star-crossed fate man may still apprehend, however poignantly, a beauty which is not mutable.

Walter F. Wright
Art and Substance in George Meredith
(Lincoln, Neb.: Univ. Nebraska Pr., 1953), pp. 147, 161

The Egoist

For the most part the earlier novels had begun with something more or less directly concerning the immediate action of the story, but with *The Egoist* we start with one of those subtle studies which call for more thought on the part of readers than the vast majority of them care to expend on the merely literary aspect of their fiction. In a sense each of the novels, from *The Egoist* onwards, is a study of the many-sided marriage problem, is in a more accentuated degree than usual an examination of the relation of the sexes.

The Egoist is a marvellous book as much for its diverse portraitures as for its remorseless delineation of an egoism fostered by circumstance to an astounding degree. . . . Nowhere in the preceding volumes had Mr. Meredith made such rich use of his wonderful powers of psychological analysis, although perhaps in each of the novels, from *Richard Feverel* onwards, are to be found indications of the use to which those powers might be put.

Walter Jerrold
George Meredith (London: Greening, 1902), pp. 141-43

The Egoist is something entirely different from what the critic supposed it to be. It is not a story in the ordinary sense, it is a study in character; its author used the methods not of the novelist, but of the dramatist; he treated language as if it were in a plastic rather than in a fixed state, that is, he discarded the rules of the prose writer and availed himself of the privileges of the poet; and finally he did not aim so much to amuse as to instruct, for the purpose of the book is to make the reader turn his criticising eye inward upon himself, rather than outward upon his fellowman.

Elmer James Bailey
The Novels of George Meredith: A Study
(New York: Scribner's, 1907), p. 134

The Egoist remains the masterpiece. This central comedy combines the excellences of the earlier and the later ones. The subject is as serious as that of any of Meredith's books, though it does not share the grave seriousness that shadows some of the later ones by reason of the tragic issues. The protagonist is a man of social dignity and fair morality, though greatly open to the shafts of the imps. He is as worthy a subject for comic treatment as the Misanthrope. In such a man, the comic traits of humanity are worth minute and careful study. Associated with him, and affected by his eccentric movements, are several other characters of weight, whose fortunes we follow with the deepest concern. But *The Egoist* has the advantage of leavening the seriousness of the later comedies with the amusing qualities of the early ones. The invincible conceit of Sir Willoughby, as we have seen, his desperate shifts and embarrassments, his self-delusion at the beginning of the story, and his vain ingenuities at the end, make him much more laughable than Fleetwood or Victor Radnor. . . . I have little doubt that *The Egoist* will become for English readers, what it is said to be now for the French, the representative novel of Meredith. If it be true that comedy was Meredith's characteristic genre, *The Egoist* must be his masterpiece. It is at once the most perfect in design and the most comprehensive in material of all his novels, and consequently of all his works. We could lose everything else of Meredith, and we should have in *The Egoist* an epitome of his philosophy and his art. *The Egoist* is to Meredith what *Hamlet* is to Shakespeare.

Joseph Warren Beach
The Comic Spirit in George Meredith
(London: Longmans, Green, 1911), pp. 220-23

Richard Feverel is a young man's experiment, and therein lies a good deal of its attractiveness. In *The Egoist*, the maestro controls his orchestra with a life-learned ability to obtain his effects of tone and interpretation.

Siegfried Sassoon
Meredith (New York: Viking, 1948), p. 148

With Meredith's *The Egoist* we enter into a critical problem that we have not before faced. . . . That is the problem offered by a writer of recognizably impressive stature, whose work is informed by a muscular intelligence, whose language has splendor, whose "view of life" wins our respect, and yet for whom we are at best able to feel only a passive appreciation which amounts, practically, to indifference. We should be unjust to Meredith and to criticism if we should, giving in to the inertia of indifference, simply avoid dealing with him and thus avoid the problem along with him. He does not "speak to us," we might say; his meaning is not a "meaning for us"; he "leaves us cold." But do not the challenge and the excitement of the critical problem as such lie in that ambivalence of attitude which allows us to recognize the intelligence and even the splendor of Meredith's work, while, at the same time, we experience a lack of sympathy, a failure of any enthusiasm of response? . . . What Desmond McCarthy said of Meredith might be said of Milton: "It must be remembered in reading Meredith that half his touches are not intended to help you to realize the object so much as to put power into the form." The statement applied to Meredith makes only a fumbling kind of sense, inasmuch as it divides the "form" from the "object," and what we see as failure in Meredith is just this division of form and object, the division of the elegant pattern and splendid style of the book from potential meaning, from potential relationships between characters and thus potential relationships with ourselves. Applied to Milton, it has a good deal more sense, and the difference lies here. One feels that, in a highly special and deeply meaningful way, the Miltonic style *is* "the object"; one feels that the verbal manipulation is the mind's desperate exhibition of its independence and strength, working on the plastic stuff of the word in a frightful vacuum of other stuff adequately tough to reward the worker's gift and exertion—

the mind is with its "back to the wall," so to speak, in the position of Lucifer; one feels that this is the moral kinetics which, in Milton, is profoundly "the object," and that the "power" of Milton's language is the same as that satanic power which moved a causeway through empty space from hell to earth. We cannot say so much of Meredith. Style is here a brilliant manner, and, with some embarrassment—for we would not be without the pleasures Meredith provides—we would quote Dr. Middleton on style in the author's own admirably intelligent style:

> "You see how easy it is to deceive one who is an artist in phrases. Avoid them, Miss Dale; they dazzle the penetration of the composer. That is why people of ability like Mrs. Mountstuart see so little; they are bent on describing brilliantly."

Dorothy Van Ghent
The English Novel
(New York: Holt, Rinehart, and Winston, 1953), p. 194

POETRY

Of his poems . . . the last two volumes, *Odes in Contribution to the Songs of French History*, and *A Reading of Life*, are extremely involved, and many other poems scattered throughout various volumes share an identical fate. His faults of this kind are accentuated to a great degree in his poetry, which, when obscure, is as far as I am concerned, simply impossible of comprehension. I am quite prepared to hear that it is disgraceful of me to admit any such thing, but it is so—and I am not alone. . . .

But it is a thankless busines to speak of faults, which, after all, mainly arise from striking qualities. I am quite sure that there are more than I could mention, but I am quite sure they are largely the outcome of a powerful mind's individuality. For at heart Meredith is essentially sane and filled with the great and eternal thoughts. . . . It is not by any means altogether unfitting that those very words he applied to Shakespeare should themselves be applied to him—

> Thy greatest knew thee, Mother Earth; unsoured
> He knew thy sons. He probed from hell to hell
> Of human passions, but of love deflowered
> His wisdom was not, for he knew thee well.

Richard H. P. Curle
Aspects of George Meredith
(London: Routledge, 1908), pp. 300-302

There are those who would counsel you to begin your study of Meredith with *Modern Love* . . . : and here their counsel may easily be wiser than mine, personal taste interfering to make me wayward. As a poetic form, the sonnet-sequence—even when turned as Meredith turns it, from quatorzain to seizain—is (unless handled by Shakespeare) about the last to allure me. I should add, however, that Meredith's use of the sixteen-line stanza in *Modern Love* is exceedingly strong and individual: and that in the past hundred years few quatorzains, or sonnets proper, will match his *Lucifer in Starlight.* . . . As a subject, the relations of the husband, the wife and the other man, especially when rehearsed by the husband, have usually (I state it merely as a private confession) the same physical effect on me as a drawing-room recitation. I want to get under a table and howl. From the outset the recital makes me shy as a stranger pounced upon and called in to settle a delicate domestic difference; and as it goes on, I start protesting inwardly, "My dear sir—delighted to do my best . . . man of the world . . . quite understand . . . sympathetic, and all that sort of thing. . . . But really, if you insist on all this getting into the newspapers. . . . And where did I put my hat, by the way?" In short—take the confession—with the intricacies and self-scourgings of *Modern Love* I find myself less at home than with the franker temptations of St. Anthony, and far less than with the larger, liberally careless amours of the early gods.

Sir Arthur Quiller-Couch
Studies in Literature, First Series
(Cambridge Univ. Pr., 1918), p. 179

He is a considerable poet, but only a great poet at moments. These moments give him greatness because of that originality of his. When he does blaze and hack his way through to beauty, it is a new beauty of his own that is of the utmost value to the reader because it adds something unique to his experience. Wrestling with a body of profound and original thought, and having to create for himself a new tradition, a new set of symbols, Meredith had to work under the most difficult conditions, and those difficulties, combined with certain weaknesses we have already noted, are frequently too much for him. But when he overcomes them his triumph is all the greater. The somewhat stoical and rationalistic creed, disdaining passion as it did, he set himself to express, made his task all the harder, for passion is the friend of poetry. As we have seen, it is the impelling force of emotion that we miss in so much of his work, and the lack of it is largely the secret of its weakness.

J. B. Priestley
George Meredith (New York: Macmillan, 1926), p. 110

Freed the fret of thinking, he would revert to the semi-pagan self of his prime—pagan in acceptance of the life-giving and joy-giving power of nature. And it may be that this is the essential part of him which survives.

Most of his finest poems are inspired by the connection of human life and passion with the life of nature, and it is only when they stand in direct contact with nature that the characters in his novels put on their full grandeur and charm. The enduringness of his work depends on this rather than his interest in analysing character and conduct, his delight in linguistic dexterity and epigrammatic display, and his abounding humour. As a delineator of womanhood he stands alone in modern literature. But he has also given us a heightened consciousness of nature which differs from other poets of the nineteenth century, whose effects are, I think, mainly pictorial. The great moments in their writing seem held by an imperishable stillness. Meredith is unlike them through his association with movement. He is with us in the lark ascending, in the cloud shadow flying to the hills on a blue and breezy noon, in the flush and fervour of eastern clouds at daybreak, and when evening has brought the shepherd from the hill. In many a mutation of weather and landscape he has made "the thing at heart our endless own." Others have shown a sanctioning star above the troubled world of men. The star of Meredith burns and is alive with constant fire. He is the poet of nature in action and the joy of earth. At any season of the year he stands the test of being thought about when one is out of doors. For the outdoor element in him has the oxygen of aliveness in it. I was once asked what I meant by saying that I liked the idea of Meredith though I couldn't always enjoy what he wrote. I was too young then to be able to frame the answer which has since become apparent to me. It is that the idea of Meredith means a sense of being fully alive. To be at one's best is to be Meredithian.

Siegfried Sassoon
Meredith (New York: Viking, 1948), pp. 262-63

GENERAL

Even when his inspiration fails him, his writing is so brilliant, that brilliance and versatility of intellect have been generally supposed his chief title to fame. It argues no lack of appreciation of this rich intellectual endowment to say that, when Meredith's achievement is estimated as a whole, it occupies a secondary place. His inspiration appears to lie in his poetic grasp, the intensity of realisation with which he holds to the main issue and keeps it living, in defiance of the tangles of complexity he is for ever weaving every side of it, and which might have been expected to prove fatal to the life within. Again and again you may put your finger on speeches which come neither from character nor situation, but are plainly forced upon both by a critical reaction on the part of their author; and yet the effect of the character itself will not be appreciably marred. It is, in fact, just because the central life is so convincingly represented, that it becomes possible to detect these superficial inconsistencies. And what is true of the characters is equally true of the composition in its wider aspects. In spite of all its twists and turns, its pausing by the way, its return for analysis and counter-analysis, the underflow of passion asserts itself irresistibly, and, once the reader will consent to trust to it, carries him triumphantly along.

M. Sturge Henderson
George Meredith: Novelist, Poet, Reformer
(New York: Scribner's, 1907), p. 316

Beyond the merely unintelligent, two large classes of George Meredith's critics remained. The first class consisted of those who in no way underestimated the importance of the problems with which Meredith set himself to deal, but demanded that their philosophy and their fiction should be served to them in separate dishes. The novel, said they, was quite unsuited to be a channel of ethical teaching. To say that was, in Meredith's view, to sign the death-warrant of fiction—"to demand of us truth to nature, excluding Philosophy, is really to bid a pumpkin caper." He contended that, to be in any way credible, a transcript of later nineteenth-century life must portray the inner as well as the outer; men's minds were probing, mining, testing themselves and all they encountered; groping, individually and collectively, in search of new ideals and inspirations on nebulous borderlands of knowledge; apprehending laws for human existence that had, as yet, no formulae. Intuitive discoverers—the poets—had transcribed now and again some phrase of pure truth; but these isolated fragments had been regarded by the nineteenth century as *objets d'art*, adorable specimens for museums, rather than as vital revelations. Meanwhile the rank and file had been infected with those blank misgivings, those obstinate questionings, which at the beginning of the century had been confined to the poets. Consequently the problem novel was in vogue. How, George Meredith asked, could the chasm between muddy trapesings and "the shining table-lands" be bridged except in a novelist who should unite the poet's vision with sturdy sense of social and political progress—accept humanity with "the stem, the thorns, the roots, and the fat bedding of roses" that in so doing he might envisage its flower? The second class of objectors, while sympathizing both with Meredith's themes and his attitude to them, were alienated by obscurities of style that seemed to them unworthy and even perverse. Why, they asked, should the man who could write *Modern Love* and the *Hymn to Colour* miss out connectives and relative pronouns, invert conditional clauses, use adjectives as substantives or substantives as adjectives? The explanation required by these objectors consists, mainly in the fact that Meredith, failing in the younger years of his life to win an adequate public for his works, took to writing for himself—to addressing his own intelligence—and, in doing so, greatly overestimated the agility of other people's minds. . . .

Brilliance and versatility of intellect have been, mistakenly, supposed to be Meredith's chief endowment. His inspiration, really lies in his poet's grasp, the intensity of realization with which he holds his main issue and keeps it living, in defiance of the web of complexity he for ever was weaving every side of it—a web which must have strangled any but the strongest heartbeat within.

Mary Sturge Gretton
The Writings and Life of George Meredith
(Cambridge, Mass.: Harvard Univ. Pr., 1926), pp. 11-13

His work is obviously without that universality, that appeal on many different levels, which mark that of a Homer, a Cervantes, a Shakespeare, or, in their own fashion, a Dickens, a Molière. It is not merely that his work does not reach perfection, for the work of greater men is equally faulty, but that in spite of its richness, its breadth and depth, it lacks, just as he himself lacked, that four-square humanity which we expect from the supreme masters. He will never be everybody's man. A whole range of emotions never seems to have found its way into his work, which wants that charity, that brooding tenderness for man as man, which would endear it to whole populations as yet unborn. But, when all is said and done, he remains a giant, even though a giant somehow so twisted by pride and wilfulness that he appears of lesser stature. He touches greatness at an extraordinary number of points. No English writer of his century cast a wider net; he is a philosopher, poet, and novelist; he challenges Thackeray and James on the one side of his work just as he challenges Browning and Swinburne on the other; and whatever he touches he makes his own; his thought is his own, so is his poetry, and as for his fiction, it is original in every particular, in scope, form, matter, manner and style. His blend of philosophy and poetry, wit and rhapsody, comedy and romance, is unique, and there are moments when overpowered by his breadth and force, we see in him the only writer of the last two centuries who can be placed by the side of Shakespeare.

J. B. Priestley
George Meredith (New York: Macmillan, 1926), pp. 198-99

George Eliot has lost the unexampled hold she once had on the intelligent reader; and Meredith, superior people affirm, is already out of date. His windmills, they say, have all been overthrown: there are no sentimentalists now, women have asserted their freedom, their equality, and so on through the catalogue of his watchwords and war-cries. But Meredith was never in date. His portrayal of life, whatever its demerits, is peculiarly untrammelled by considerations of time. Those critics who complain that he dates, that he was a mere Victorian depicting an age that has disappeared, and those who, on the other hand, imagine that, because he stood aloof, he knew nothing and had nothing to say of the age in which he lived, not merely cancel each other out, but also illustrate the truth, that he saw what were the permanent characteristics of his countrymen, their virtues and their failings, and judged them by the standard of what they might be. He reviewed the present in the light of the future, as befitted the apostle of spiritual evolution. Nor was his vision of an evolving society, an evolving race, restricted to such narrow objects as women, for instance, have recently attained. He would not admit, even to-day, that women have won their emancipation, or have reached that level in a fully civilized society in which Comedy can flourish and their wits keep mankind in the right road. The anti-grundyism and flouting of convention that rejoice many hearts at the present time are possibly not a sign of "noble strength on fire" or of true freedom, which according to Meredith must be based on a whole-hearted belief in the orderliness as well as the goodness of Nature. He believed in taking counsel not of the sensations but of the intelligence: "I let the former have free play but deny them the right to bring me to a decision." Sentimentalism is now a byword, thanks to Meredith, who gave it a name. Everybody now is as afraid of being thought a sentimentalist as of being found wanting in a sense of humour. Whether the thing itself is dead is a very different matter. Congenital vices of human nature do not disappear at the touch of a conjurer's wand. It would be more than rash to say that Meredith has been fully assimilated and done with: the very opposite might be as plausibly maintained. For what we have received we are indebted to the ideas in his novels and in his poems, and those ideas have plenty of work to do still.

Ernest A. Baker
The History of the English Novel, Vol. VIII
(London: Witherby, 1936), pp. 380-81

George Bernard Shaw had his word about Meredith, . . . and it is the one which suggests our final insight into the figure Meredith presents. Recounting a visit he had paid to Box Hill, Shaw said: "He had supported the reactionary candidate in a recent election, imagining that he represented the principles of the French Revolution, and Meredith was apologetic when I explained to him that my Fabianism was the latest thing. He was a relic of the Cosmopolitan Republican Gentleman of the previous generation."

While enjoying the image Shaw presents us, we note something other than comic in Meredith's fumbling, at the end of the century, for the principles of the French Revolution. Meredith was expressing the two sides of his nature: the romantic and the enthusiast of reason. Reason is the hinge that connects Meredith the political thinker with Meredith the artist. The adherent of reason, in his view, is the safe leader of men, but this adherent, in his novels, is fascinatingly ambivalent and indeed gives way in the '90's, in the decade of Nietzsche in England, to the romantic man of will. If Meredith failed to recognize that Fabianism was the latest thing, perhaps the explanation is that he was not so much a political participant, in any of the restrictive meanings of the term, as a man for whom acceptance of social responsibility meant exercise—in the light of his own needs—of moral and critical imagination. Despite all that has been said, it was the novel, and to a lesser extent the poem, that was his field of action and of thought. And in the '90's, the principles of the French Revolution were still more useful to him for creating the moral dimension of his art than were those of Fabianism. Shaw's comment on Meredith's political ineptitude suggests something of central importance: however eager Meredith was to be known as a historian, as a "political pundit," or for that matter as a military strategist, his commitment was to art, not to history or politics or military science. However eagerly he attempted to speak from other points of view, it is as an artist-moralist that he made his claim for survival, and it is as such that we see him now.

Norman Kelvin
A Troubled Eden
(Palo Alto, Calif.: Stanford Univ. Pr., 1961), pp. 215-16

JOHN STUART MILL
1806-1873

Social critic, economist, political and philosophical essayist, Mill had one of the most flexible and comprehensive minds of the nineteenth century. One tag applied to him, "the saint of rationalism," suggests his warmth of personality and his clarity of reason, his interest in both human values and logic. He was reared and educated on the rigid principles of his philosophically radical father, James Mill, and of the great Utilitarian Jeremy Bentham: he began reading Greek at three and was formidably learned by the time of adolescence, but, as Mill observes in his celebrated *Autobiography,* his training left no place for aesthetic concerns, for human affections, or for any emotion at all. Yet, to some extent influenced by the divergent views of Carlyle and other more Romantic contemporaries, he developed beyond the narrow Utilitarianism of his father. Another major influence on his life was Harriet Taylor, a married woman with whom he fell in love at the age of 24 and whom he at last married, after her husband's death, in 1851. For much of his life he was employed in the India House, where his father was an official. His important works include *A System of Logic* (1843), the influential *Principles of Political Economy* (1848), *Thoughts on Parliamentary Reform* (1859), the great essay *On Liberty,* which is the single most important exposition of modern political liberalism (1859), *Considerations on Representative Government* (1861), *Utilitarianism* (1863), *Auguste Comte and Positivism* (1865), *On the Subjection of Women* (1863), and two posthumously published volumes, the remarkable *Autobiography* (1873) and *Three Essays on Religion* (1874).

F. A. Hayek, ed., *Collected Works* . . . (1963-   ); edition in progress
Michael St. John Packe, *The Life of John Stuart Mill* (1954)

GENERAL

He was from his youth upwards devoted to the spread of principles which he held to be essential to human happiness. No philanthropist or religious teacher could labour more energetically and unremittingly for the good of mankind. He never forgets the bearing of his speculations upon this ultimate end. Whatever his limitations, he brought the whole energy of a singularly clear, comprehensive, and candid intellect to bear upon the greatest problems of his time; and worked at them with unflagging industry for many years. He was eminently qualified to bring out the really strong points of his creed; while his perfect intellectual honesty forced him frankly to display its weaker side. Through Mill English Utilitarianism gave the fullest account of its method and its presuppositions. . . . He virtually answers in the *Logic* the question, what are the ultimate principles by which the Utilitarians had more or less unconsciously been guided.

Leslie Stephen
The English Utilitarians, vol. III
(London: Duckworth, 1900), p. 74

Mill's is a mind vigorous, free, frank: keen, but never cold. Here—agree or disagree with what he says—is that rare thing, perfect fairness; a candour that refuses nothing and keeps nothing back, in most unusual conjunction with an enthusiasm burning with sure unwavering flame. To read Mill is to be in contact with an intelligence of the first order, which cuts through the sloppy, the flabby and the merely sentimental and annihilates the taker of words for things, but cuts, always, in order to make, not break. He never dodges; he always states the whole case, points against as fully as points for; he never leaves his own opinion in doubt, or omits any of the stages in the process by which that opinion has been reached. His is a wholly realistic intelligence, and a completely unconventional one. Not a trace in it of Victorian complacency.

It belongs, of course, to its period. He believed in historic development, at a time when few did; but he could not forsee its course. His concern, in the main, is with ideas and forces that are independent of period, and when the modern reader least agrees with him, he will find himself confronted with a case that has to be met. Nor are his ideas as old-fashioned as many suppose. Let those who ask what he has to do in a series dedicated to the foundation layers of Socialism recall that he was the first British writer of accepted standing to treat Socialism with serious respect, and assign to it a commanding importance. Let them remember, further, that he shook the very foundations of the "classical" economics of his day when he, first, proved that Distribution did not rest on immutable laws, quasi-physical in character, as was then taken for granted, but was an affair of human will, alterable so soon as men willed to alter it; and, second, when he publicly threw overboard his own earlier acceptance of Ricardo's theory of the Wages Fund. His political contribution was hardly less significant. Because he believed, with passion, in freedom of action and of thought for everyone, he saw, and showed to a previously blind generation, that the vast majority of men, and all women, were in his day, suffering from a denial of that freedom. For women and for working men he fought, tirelessly; against privilege, in all its forms, as against the vulgar gospel of getting on, he fought, as tirelessly.

Mary Agnes Hamilton
John Stuart Mill (London: Hamish Hamilton, 1933), pp. 12-13

Mill is not one of the Victorian masters of imaginative prose, like Carlyle, Ruskin or Newman, whose thought is inseparable from a passionate personality and whose style, consequently, reflects the movement and color of a poetic mind. Mill has passion, at times profound passion, but it is so highly intellectualized that it is felt only by those readers most capable of sustained interest in ideas, which are often abstract and are expressed with scrupulous regard for the laws of logic. His life, however, was the opposite of what Carlyle, in a letter to his brother, called it (he had been reading the *Autobiography*): "the life of a logic-shopping engine, little more of human in it than if it had been done by a thing of mechanized iron." Speculation upon the processes and presuppositions of thought were a necessity for Mill, but there never lived a man with a loftier or more disinterested devotion to the public good. His writings, without exception, are dedicated to the enlightenment and emancipation of his fellow men. "He is the only writer in the world," wrote John Morley in an eloquent tribute (*The Death of Mr. Mill*), "whose treatises on highly abstract subjects have been printed during his life-time in editions for the people, and sold at the price of railway novels. . . . Perhaps the sum of all his distinction lies in the union of stern science with infinite aspiration, of rigorous sense of what is real and practicable with bright and luminous hope." And again, upon the anniversary of Mill's birth, Morley wrote (1906): "Nobody who claims to deal as a matter of history with the intellectual fermentation between 1840 and 1870 or a little longer, whatever value the historian may choose to set upon its products, can fail to assign a leading influence to Mill. . . .

Mill's own prose would be greater, perhaps, if it had, along with its other virtues, Macaulay's vitality or Carlyle's individuality and color. But though he understood that imagination was as essential for literary greatness as pure intellect, he was himself deficient in imagination, as he was in sheer energy. Being, however, one of the clearest and wisest minds of his time, with something to say—"the grand requisite of good writing"—and possessing an extraordinary command of the ordinary resources of language, Mill holds a place with the Victorian masters of prose. It was his mission in life, he said, to "build the bridges and clear the paths," and for this indispensable work his style is eminently adequate.

Frederick William Roe, ed.
Victorian Prose (New York: Ronald Pr., 1947), pp. 215, 218

On Liberty

Although Mill called *On Liberty* "a kind of philosophic textbook of a single truth," it was really more of a hymn or incantation. It was intended rather to excite than to persuade. There were a dozen other names he might have given it, but he deliberately chose the one among all others which in every age has most surely caused men to perform intellectual somersaults. The essay was, in genesis, Harriet's early paper on "Toleration," elaborated in her lifetime, dressed in Mill's most graceful prose, and authorized from the depths of his sage majestic knowledge. But of course that was not all. It was intended as the consummation of their life together, a joint statement of the values to be borne in mind while urging the onward progress of mankind towards perfection. Mill added to it his entire personality. It knitted up the nebulous aspirations running through his works, and proclaimed the unity underlying all his thought. Its roots ran back through the solid ground of Anglo-Saxon Puritanism, to draw their nourishment from the distinctive feature of Christian civilization, the power and importance of personal identity. The pulse of the book invoked Mill's constant ideal of human intercourse, an Athenian society tempted by the Socratic frame of mind. . . .

He did his best to rescue his own age. He failed, and an age of darkness followed. But the stuff he handled was imperishable. Liberty could not for ever be outmoded.

> The worth of a State, in the long run, is the worth of the individuals comprising it; and a State which . . . dwarfs its men, in order that they may be more docile instruments in its hands even for beneficial purposes, will find that with small men no great thing can really be accomplished; and that the perfection of machinery to which it has sacrificed everything, will in the end avail it nothing, for want of the vital power which, in order that the machine might work more smoothly, it has preferred to banish.

When authority, in whatever form, had done its worst. When men were tired of being led obediently to ruin; it was then, Mill thought, that the teachings of the *Liberty* would have their greatest value. "And," he added, "it is to be feared that they will retain that value a long time."

Michael St. John Packe
The Life of John Stuart Mill
(New York: Macmillan, 1954), pp. 400, 406

WILLIAM MORRIS
1834-1896

Morris was born in Walthamstow, a suburb of London. He went to Oxford intending to become a priest but at the university became interested in literature and art. One of his closest college friends was Edward Burne Jones, the painter, and both young men were influenced by Ruskin in their love of medieval subjects and of Gothic design. Morris started in 1856 the *Oxford and Cambridge Magazine,* defending the interests and style of the Pre-Raphaelite artists—D. G. Rossetti contributed several poems—but the periodical lasted only a year. With Burne Jones and Rossetti he worked at the Oxford Union murals, which soon faded since none of the artists was practiced in fresco technique. In 1859 he married Jane Burden, who was to become Rossetti's favorite model. Although Morris was a man of many talents and interests, a designer of fabrics and stained glass, a printer and publisher, and in the last several decades of his life a political orator and active socialist, he is important in the history of English literature as a poet. Among his principal poetic works are *The Defence of Guenevere,* a volume of poems on medieval subjects (1858); the classical *Life and Death of Jason* (1867); *The Earthly Paradise,* including medieval, classical, and Icelandic materials (1868-1870); the saga *Sigurd the Volsung* (1876); and the revolutionary *Poems by the Way* (1891). Morris also wrote prose romances, including *The House of the Wolfings* (1889), lectures on art and socialism, the medieval and yet political prose tale *The Dream of John Ball* (1888), and a Utopian vision of England in the future, *News from Nowhere* (1890). In part, perhaps, influenced by the development of Ruskin's career, he came more and more to be concerned with economic and social reform. But Morris never lost his love for design or poetry, and in the last year of his life he produced the beautifully printed and decorated Kelmscott edition of Chaucer.

Collected Works, ed., May Morris (1910-1915), 24 vols.

J. W. Mackail. *The Life of William Morris* (1899), 2 vols.; rev. 1907, repr. 1950

There is, perhaps, no single work by William Morris that stands out as a masterpiece in evidence of his individual genius. He was not impelled to give peculiar expression to his own personality. His writing was seldom emotionally autobiographic as Rossetti's always was, his painting and designing were not the expression of a personal mood as was the case with Burne-Jones. But no one of his special time and group gave himself more fully or more freely for others. No one contributed more generously to the public pleasure and enlightenment. No one tried with more persistent effort first to create and then to satisfy a taste for the possible best in the lives and homes of the people. He worked toward this end in so many directions that a lesser energy than his must have been dissipated and a weaker purpose rendered impotent. His tremendous vitality saved him from the most humiliating of failures, the failure to make good extravagant promise. He never lost sight of the result in the endeavour, and his discontent with existing mediocrity was neither formless nor empty. It was the motive power of all his labour; he was always trying to make everything "something different from what it was," and this instinct was, alike for strength and weakness, says his chief biographer, "of the very essence of his nature." To tell the story of his life is to write down the record of dreams made real, of nebulous theories brought swiftly to the test of experiment, of the spirit of the distant past reincarnated in the present. But, as with most natures of similar mould, the man was greater than any part of his work, and even greater than the sum of it all. He remains one of the not-to-be-forgotten figures of the nineteenth century, so interesting was he, so impressive, so simple-hearted, so nearly adequate to the great tasks he set himself, so well beloved by his companions, so useful, despite his blunders, to society at large.

Elizabeth Luther Cary
William Morris: Poet, Craftsman, Socialist
(New York: Putnam's, 1902), pp. 1-2

It was the Middle Ages as he *saw* them in architectural and pictorial remains and in the pictures conjured up in his mind by Froissart and Malory and Chaucer that fascinated him. . . . His early lyrics, or what survive of them in the volume of 1858, *The Defense of Guenevere and Other Poems*, have not the close, heavy atmosphere of Rossetti's, but the purpose of the poet is the same—the rendering of an intense, passionate, unwavering mood. Malory and Froissart have equally enthralled him, the romantic, passionate dreams of the Middle Ages and the passionate, if brutal, realities which Froissart presents in such sharp contrast to the dreams. And for Morris both *were* dreams, vivid and sharp, into which he threw himself with the same passionate ardour with which Scott had lived in the world of the old ballads, but the ardour is more purely that of the artist, more that of Keats in *La Belle Dame sans Merci*, which was, he said later, the germ of all the poetry of his group. Scott's poems are a substitute for the life of action from which he was cut off; he divines through the ballads the men of whom they told, and they are genial, burly men such as he still meets. Morris lives more entirely in the picture and the dream, a world of bright colours and expressive gestures, and persons seen as in tapestries and frescoes, vivid but in two dimensions only; and he lives as in a dream the life of fierce loves and hates which for him is the whole life of the Middle Ages he had loved from a boy and the Scandinavian heroes whom he came to love. . . . To my mind, the best of Morris's poetry is lyrical, for in the intenser mood of which song is the expression one misses these other qualities less. In the long poems from *Jason*, through *The Earthly Paradise* to even *Sigurd the Volsung*, one is a little oppressed by the monotony of the mood, the one mood of love and longing and regret. He was never again quite so vivid, so intense, so dramatic as in *The Defence of Guenevere* and *Sir Peter Harpdon's Ball* (a parallel in its Pre-Raphaelitic realism to *My Sister's Sleep*) and *Shameful Death* and *The Haystack in the Floods*; never made more telling use of passionate, expressive gesture. . . . Nor was he ever again quite so boyishly, so delightfully romantic as in some of the ballads with refrains—*Two Red Roses across the Moon* and *The Eve of Creçy* and *The Sailing of the Sword.* . . .

But it will not quite do to say with the late Mr. Dixon Scott that the effect of these poems was a kind of accident, due to the vividness with which Morris saw and painted, that he had no cunning of word and rhythm, and that his later, more diffuse poetry is altogether of another kind. . . . The mood of the early poems is the mood of the later, if never again expressed with such dramatic intensity, in such sharp, vivid pictures.

H. J. C. Grierson
Lyrical Poetry from Blake to Hardy
(London: Hogarth Pr., 1928), pp. 107-09

Morris has "faced the facts." This is the paradox of him. He seems to retire far from the real world and to build a world out of his wishes; but when he has finished the result stands out as a picture of experience ineluctably true. No full-grown mind wants optimism or pessimism—philosophies of the nursery where they are not philosophies of the clinic; but to have presented in one vision the ravishing sweetness and the heart-breaking melancholy of our experience, to have shown how the one continually passes over into the other, and to have combined all this with a stirring practical creed, this is to have presented the *datum* which all our adventures, worldly and other-worldly alike, must take into account. There are many writers greater than Morris. You can go on from him to all sort of subtleties, delicacies, and sublimities which he lacks. But you can hardly go behind him.

C. S. Lewis
Rehabilitations and Other Essays
(Oxford Univ. Pr., 1939), pp. 54-55

In examining the basic ideas of Morris's literary works one finds that his observations regarding life, history and art are in distinct agreement with his views concerning the individual and society under varying conditions. One will note, too, that these views led him eventually to the cause of the people—to an attempt to repurify decadent modern civilization—and that the ideas which pervaded his earlier poetry were not lost sight of, but found a richer and fuller expression in poetry and prose of his later years. . . . As time went on he was to believe more and more firmly in a coming great change, or revolution, within society. In the preceding chapter we have noted that as early as March, 1874, Morris had certainly been thinking of the "revenge of the Gods" against modern civilization.

What Morris did was to fit the ideas of Norse mythology into his own creed. That it helped him to become the Pagan which he afterward claimed to be, there can be little doubt.

Lloyd Wendell Eshleman
A Victorian Rebel (New York: Scribner's, 1940), p. 128

Morris's poetry presents something of a problem to the twentieth century. This large body of romance literature includes a number of the most famous stories of Europe, told in verse that is never less than adequate, and often extremely beautiful. It belongs to a still larger body of quasi-medieval nineteenth-century romance, a kind of poetry which for more than a century has contributed one of the dominant strains to English literary sensibility. Morris's own contribution to this literature is both in bulk and quality very considerable, and up to about 1914 the number of cheap reprints indicate that it was also extremely popular. Yet to the common reader of to-day it is "a legend emptied of concern" . . . . Morris's poetry is unrelated to contemporary experience in a way that medieval romance and earlier epic is not. Medieval romance took its contemporary readers, no less than us, into a dream-world. But it dealt with ideas—about love, chivalry, and supernatural forces—in which its readers really believed. . . . Morris's *Jason* or *The Water of the Wondrous Isles* mean nothing beyond themselves; they show us figures on a tapestry, in which it would be idle to look for any further significance; and they have no more relation to nineteenth-century life than Morris's tapestries have to nineteenth-century methods of industrial production. It is the same with Morris's epic. *Beowulf* and the *Iliad* are interpretations of the heroic age, not indeed for the heroic age itself, but at least for a world in which much of the heroic ethos survived. The *Aeneid*, as an example of the literary epic, uses the old heroic themes but relates them to its own time by a conscious contemporary political purpose. Morris's Sigurd simply takes a heroic theme and restates it in his own idiom, but only as an example of a world that no longer exists and of values that have passed away. . . .

The attempt to adapt ancient heroic legends to the contemporary atmosphere could hardly result in more than the painful snuffle of Tennyson's blameless king. In such an age, if poetry is not to lose a great deal of its range of subject and emotion, it can hardly do other than accept a frank archaism, the treatment of themes from age past, unrelated to any modern reality, as samples of what mankind has been, or has dreamed about, and may perhaps again. So Yeats believed; and the modern poets who have not thought as he did have achieved excellence at the cost of a painful restriction both of themes and rhythms. Morris as a narrative poet is in much the same position as he is as a craftsman—one who keeps alive an obsolete skill, which seems hardly likely to mean much to the world he lives in, but which may nevertheless be keeping the door open for some necessary re-expansion of the artist's range, in some future that we cannot at the moment foresee.

Graham Hough
The Last Romantics (London: Duckworth, 1947), pp. 113, 132-33

JOHN HENRY NEWMAN
1801-1890

The son of a London banker, Newman experienced a religious conversion when he was fifteen, not long before entering Trinity College, Oxford. In 1824 he was ordained a priest in the Church of England and became curate of St. Clement's; four years later he was named vicar of St. Mary's, the Oxford University church, where he made his reputation as a brilliant preacher. Newman also wrote verse during this period, including his well-known hymn "Lead, Kindly Light." After 1833 he was associated with the leaders of the Oxford Movement, the so-called Tractarians who wanted the Anglican church to reaffirm its apostolic and catholic nature. Although John Keble's sermon on "National Apostasy" marked the beginning of this movement and Professor Edward Pusey was by some considered its leader, so that the new "high church" men were also known as "Puseyites," Newman came to be the group's most eloquent spokesman. He also proved to be its most controversial, when he issued his Tract XC, arguing that even the anti-Roman Catholic parts of the Anglican thirty-nine articles of faith could, on historical grounds, bear a truly catholic interpretation. In 1843 he resigned his living at St. Mary's and his Oxford fellowship, and in 1845 he became a Roman Catholic, being ordained priest in that church the following year. From then until his death he was concerned, in writing and speaking, with the Catholic faith, especially with its place in England, and with Catholic higher education. Replying to a published remark of Charles Kingsley's in 1864 to the effect that Newman believed "truth for its own sake had never been a virtue with the Roman clergy," he became engaged in an exchange out of which came his autobiography and defence of his religious position, the *Apologia pro Vita Sua*. Along with this great work of 1864, Newman's major writings are *The Arians of the Fourth Century* (1833); *An Essay on the Development of Christian Doctrine*, during the writing of which the author was converted to the Church of Rome (1845); *Loss and Gain: The Story of a Convert*, his first novel (1848); *Lectures on the Present Position of Catholics in England* (1851); *The Idea of a University*, extremely influential lectures on higher education delivered upon the proposed founding of an Irish Catholic university (1852); *Callista*, an historical novel (1856); *The Dream of Gerontius,* his most ambitious poem (1866); *Verses on Various Occasions* (1868); and *An Essay in Aid of a Grammar of Assent* (1870). In 1879 he was created cardinal.

C. F. Harrold, ed., *Works* (1947-1949), 10 vols.
C. F. Harrold, *Newman: A Study of His Mind, Thought and Art* (1945)

PERSONAL

John Henry Newman is indeed himself a remarkable instance of one of his own most characteristic contentions, that the same object may be seen by different onlookers under aspects so various and partial as to make their views, from their inadequacy, appear occasionally even contradictory. . . .

While to some Newman is . . . before all things a religious philosopher—and he has often been compared with Pascal—there are others, like Lord Morley, who appear to see in him little more than a great master of English prose who is hardly to be reckoned a thinker at all. By yet others he has been placed in the category of the great ecclesiastical writers in history, the eloquence and force in some of his later sermons suggesting a comparison with Bossuet, his personal charm and delicate balance of mind recalling Fénelon. English Catholics think of him primarily as the great defender of their religion against Mr. Kingsley, Dr. Pusey, and Mr. Gladstone; as the man who has annihilated by his brilliant irony both High Church Anglicanism and the bombast of Exeter Hall in the lectures of 1849 and 1851. Yet the champion who entered the lists on behalf of the Roman claims in 1849 is still hailed by many as the founder of modern Anglicanism. There are, on the other hand, thousands for whom Newman's writings belong, to use Dean Stanley's phrase—"not to provincial dogma, but to the literature of all time." He is for them the author of the Oxford Sermons, with their matchless insight into human nature; the religious poet who wrote the *Dream of Gerontius and* "Lead, kindly Light"; while the *Apologia* belongs in their eyes to the literature of self-revelation, not to apologetic. To others, again he is the theologian who has an almost unequalled knowledge of the first three centuries of Church history. . . .

His belief in God, in another life, in the Church, was unwavering. Yet when Huxley said that he could compile a primer of infidelity from Newman's writings, those who knew them best saw at once the grounds for such a misreading. The sceptic's mind was vividly present to Newman's imagination. History witnessed in his eyes to "the all-corroding, all-dissolving scepticism of the intellect in religious enquiries." He saw to the full the plausibility of the case which might be made out against the truths he most deeply believed. Of all points of faith he felt, as he has told us, that the being of God was most encompassed with difficulty. He believed in the divinity of the Catholic Church. Yet he saw so clearly the human element in it that he sometimes alarmed even those who agreed with him by the closeness with which his mind could approach the line which separated the human from the Divine. His deepest convictions were compatible with a keen sense of all that told against them. Mr. Hutton notes a parallel quality in his literary style—its presentation of currents opposed to its steady, onward, main drift.

Wilfrid Ward
The Life of John Henry Cardinal Newman, vol. I
(London: Longmans, 1912), pp. 2-3, 16

The character of Newman is as perpetually discoverable as a great book. Readers will always be fascinated by his personality, by his style, and by his insights into perennial problems in faith and in the nature of religious ideas. So complex are his personality and intellect, so fertile are the paradoxes and suggestions in his thought, that he will long continue as a potent if at times an enigmatic influence. He will exert an influence by the exploitation, by the very perversion, of his teachings. His disciples will continue to deduce from his works many conclusions which they do not contain. This has happened to many another great writer; it has happened to Plato and Aristotle, to Goethe and to Hegel; it has happened, of course, to Christianity itself. With the passing of time and the rise of new exigencies of the spirit, men will ignore those books of Newman which no longer bear a living utility, and will adapt to their needs those elements in his thought which retain their vitality. Indeed, it is quite possible, as Sarolea declared, that "the influence of Newman will be in proportion as he is more ingeniously misunderstood."

We have seen how his admirers have sought to link him with evolutionism, with pragmatism, with skepticism, with Modernism. Newman has even been seen as an anticipator of Freud, in his emphasis on how childhood experiences mold and direct our egos, how they later became idealized, and how we forget the painful and the evil in them: "n'est-ce pas la thèse même du psychologue de Vienne?" asks Seillière. More plausible is the attempt to trace parallels between Newman and Bergson. That there was an *influence* can hardly be proved. There is, however, as Cronin shows, "a fruitful field of comparison between the illative sense and the Bergsonian intuition," and Newman's insights into the problem of knowledge are again discovered to be prophetic of theories to flourish after his own day. But Newman's greatest seminal force will lie in the sphere of religious truth. His weight will increasingly be felt on the side of anti-immanentism, in the direction of greater and subtler and more enlightened supernaturalism. In a letter she wrote in 1929, Evelyn Underhill declared very succinctly that "it is really better to face up at once to what a genuinely Catholic religious philosophy teaches than to temporize with half-Christian pantheistic-immanentist books. . . . [One] has got to make the transition from 'God in everything' to 'everything in God.' " In the reaction from nineteenth- and early twentieth-century "socializing" and "historicizing" of Christianity, Newman's works, both as truly understood as a fruitfully and ingeniously "misunderstood," will doubtless be a major contribution.

C. F. Harrold
John Henry Newman
(London: Longmans, Green, 1945), pp. 374-75

Apologia pro Vita Sua

Plainly . . . both much of Newman's life and various segments of his taste and personality have been left out of the *Apologia* or too briefly mentioned for their importance to be realized. Yet we must not overstress the point. We must balance the loss of range and fullness against the gain in concentration. By excluding all which did not bear directly upon his ideas of religious truth (together, of course, with their concomitant emotional attitudes and reactions), Newman was able to achieve a powerful artistic unity. The *Apologia* as it stands carries an impact not to be attained in a wider and looser framework. And the unity is the unity of Newman's life from his first conversion in 1816 to his last in 1845. It is the central line. How did it happen that this man who started as an Evangelical lost his Calvinism, became an Anglo-Catholic, and then went to Rome? And in that process what and how was he thinking and feeling? That is the *Apologia*. And there is no question that such a rigid focus, like a strict adherence to classical unities, gains compelling attention.

We have not yet, however, come to the main issue or issues. In asking, "How good is the *Apologia?*" we may dismiss the difficulties of reading and balance the limitations of range against the intensity of vision. But there remain other considerations that are decisive. Taking it simply as it stands, we want to know two things, and they correspond, naturally enough, with the dual character of the book. So far as it is an apology, did Newman tell the truth? So far as it is a work of psychological analysis, did he reveal the inner movement of his mind? In both cases, of course, there is also the question of style, but my judgment on that has been given. Whether for defence or for revelation, Newman's writing in the *Apologia* seems to me of the highest order. Is he to be praised as highly for the truth of his account and the fullness of his self-analysis? . . .

He could not distinguish and arrange and relate his motives into a consistent pattern, but he was exceptionally aware of himself. And for our part, we come away with a vivid and consistent sense of personality. *Why* he did this or did that may be doubtful, and often is, but we never doubt that *this* man would have acted in precisely *that* way. This conception of biography, so easily undervalued by an age of scientific analysis, has perhaps never been better stated than by Newman himself when he explained what he meant by a "Life":

> I mean a narrative which impresses the reader with the idea of moral unity, identity, growth, continuity, personality, . . . of the presence of one active principle of thought, one individual character flowing on and into the various matters which he discusses, and the different transactions in which he mixes.

Walter Houghton
The Art of Newman's Apologia
(New Haven: Yale Univ. Pr., 1945), pp. 93-94, 112

The *Apologia pro Vita Sua* is not the autobiography of Newman from 1801 to 1845. It tells us nothing of the family life, the student activities, the intellectual and artistic interests of its complex subject. Nor is it even a spiritual autobiography of those years except in a limited sense. We must turn to the *Letters and Correspondence*, with their "Autobiographical Memoir," to supplement the bare account given in the *Apologia* of Newman's conversion to Evangelical Christianity. The *Apologia* is primarily a work of rhetoric designed to persuade a body of readers or "judges," English, Protestant, and suspicious of a convert to an unpopular religion, that Newman, whom Kingsley had made a symbol of the Catholic priesthood, was a man not of dishonesty but of integrity. Newman chose autobiography as his method because of his lifelong English preference of the concrete to the abstract, his vivid realization of the role in persuasion of personal influence: "I am touched by my five senses, by what my eyes behold and my ears hear. . . . I gain more from the life of our Lord in the Gospels than from a treatise *de Deo.*" "The heart is commonly reached, not through the reason, but through the imagination, by means of direct impressions, by the testimony of facts and events, by history, by description. Persons influence us, voices melt us, looks subdue us, deeds inflame us." It was his conversion to Catholicism after a long puzzling delay, many predictions of the event, and even charges of treachery to the Church of England that had created the atmosphere of suspicion in which his character had been impugned. Therefore he would confine the autobiography principally to a brief explanation of how he arrived, to begin with, at what so many regarded with suspicion and fear: Anglo-Catholic principles; and to a detailed one of how, having accepted them and devoted himself to propagating them, he became convinced that the principles which had led him thus far must lead him farther still, into the Catholic Church. "I am but giving a history of my opinions, and that, with the view of showing that I have come by them through intelligible processes of thought and honest external means" (p. 27).

If that history of opinions, in spite of its limited scope, has so much of the richness and variety of great autobiography, it is because Newman held that the means by which we arrive at belief, all of which he would try to chronicle for his own life so far as that was possible, were multiform and complex.

Martin J. Svaglic
PMLA (March, 1951), p. 138

GENERAL

Mark Pattison, in a judgment which is well known, held that the force of Newman's dialectic, and the beauty of his rhetorical exposition, blinded one to the narrowness of their basis. "Newman assumed and adorned the narrow basis on which Laud had stood two hundred years before. All the grand development of human reason, from Aristotle down to Hegel, was a sealed book to him." This judgment, coming from one who was not only the most learned man of his time, but who also knew Newman well, cannot be disputed. None the less, its terms invite us to remark the insight and the foresight with which Newman's mind worked on the materials at its disposal. He has given unrivalled literary illustration to the conception of a University as a place of education, and again to the process by which a living idea is developed under the action of many minds and through long ages of history. To say that he was primarily a rhetorician is not to deny that he was also an independent thinker, and a thinker, moreover, who in some important respects reached forward rather than back. . . . Human nature and human needs remain unaffected by anything so contingent as philosophy, and the use which Newman made of his own gifts renders him a singularly effective witness to the truth that, among the sources of strength and consolation open to mankind, the highest place cannot be claimed by literature. Nor is it in the realm even of theology that he will exercise his most abiding influence. The aspirations of the religious consciousness change but little, and few have given them more poignant expression. The most eloquent Christian teacher of nineteenth-century England, he has that in him which is beyond eloquence. There are moments when his simplest words come to us charged with an unearthly import, as straight from out the region where he loved to dwell.

Bertram Newman
Cardinal Newman (New York: Century, 1925), pp. 211-12

Newman has secured a place in most histories of nineteenth century literature, but the treatment of him there is hopelessly inadequate, leaving, as it does, the impression that he will be found an admirable stylist by those who have the courage to struggle through thirty-odd volumes of "theology." The result is obvious: Newman is in grave danger of sinking into that literary limbo where dwell the "great unread." He will find high company there, no doubt, Milton, Dryden, and Johnson among them: but that is meager consolation to those who decline to accept him as merely a tradition whose voice was music to our grandfathers and now has gone down the wind, forever. If Newman had a perfect style and wrote with persuasiveness, grace, and unfailing insight on subjects that hold an abiding interest for men and women wholly apart from creed, then it seems worth while to discuss him as a man of letters, to try to appraise his merits and defects; to estimate the value of his work as literature; to find his place, as Matthew Arnold would say, in his century; and finally, to consider his significance to our generation.

Joseph J. Reilly
Newman as A Man of Letters
(New York: Macmillan, 1927), p. ix

He had a comprehensive doctrine about the world, man's place in it, and how he ought to live. This took the religious form of Roman Catholic Christianity, and its metaphysical form was that the whole universe was one integrated system. In making us accept that view of life, particular doctrines and distinctive methods of presentation or argument stand, as we have seen, essentially related; each encourages the reader to accept the other. As for the methods themselves, the central point of this whole enquiry is that they do not merely state Newman's outlook, but they display it. They fuse together to be a picture with the qualities that he wants us to see in the world. All the time a variety of techniques—metaphor and analogy, discussions of meaning, carefully chosen examples—steadily tend to make the controversial non-controversial, so that we are not coerced by any "smart syllogism" into accepting Newman's conclusions in the abstract, but brought imperceptibly to a living understanding of his creed. The continuous texture of his work modifies our receptivity until we find ourselves seeing the world as he sees it. To this end all the parts of his work act in conjunction. Tone, forms of argument, illustration and example, imagery and manipulating senses integrate to make something which has a single unified impact on the reader; and the impact is not that of a formal argument, but in its fullness and vividness more resembles that of a work of art, something which can make the reader find more in his experience, see it with new eyes, because for a while it constitutes his whole experience.

John Holloway
The Victorian Sage (London: Macmillan, 1953), p. 201

WALTER PATER
1839-1894

An Oxford graduate, Pater early became a fellow, then a tutor, and spent most of his life at the university. His interests were always in the fine arts and in literature; from the mid-sixties he was particularly concerned with the art of the Renaissance, and he came to be identified with the vaguely defined "aesthetic" art and poetry of Morris, the later Rossetti, and Swinburne—art and poetry in some ways deriving from, and yet in radical contrast to, that of the "Pre-Raphaelite" forties and early fifties. Pater's most widely known works are his collection of essays on *The Renaissance* (1873, revised 1888), a novel about ancient Rome, *Marius the Epicurean* (1885), *Imaginary Portraits* (1887), and *Appreciations* (1889).

Works (1910), 10 vols.

A. C. Benson, *Walter Pater* (1906)

One does not praise his works as the perfection of style; there is a limpidity and lucidity of prose style—prose as used by Newman, by Matthew Arnold, by Ruskin in chastened moods,—to which no style that depends upon elaborateness and artifice can attain; but it may fairly be claimed for Pater that he realised his own conception of perfection. The style is heavy with ornament, supple with artifice. It is not so much a picture as an illumination. For sunlight there is stiff burnished gold; it is full of gorgeous conceits, jewelled phrases; it has no ease or simplicity; it is all calculated, wrought up, stippled; but it must be considered from that point of view; it must be appraised rather than criticised, accepted rather than judged.

To feel the charm it is necessary to be, to some extent, in sympathy with the philosophy of Pater. We see in him a naturally sceptical spirit, desiring to plunge beneath established systems and complacent explanations; and this, in common with an intense sensibility to every hint and intimation of beauty, apprehended in a serious and sober spirit; not the spirit that desires to possess itself of the external elements, but to penetrate the essential charm. Yet it is not the patient and untroubled beauty of nature, of simple effects of sun and shade, of great mountains, of wide plains, but of a remote and symbolical beauty, seen by glimpses and in corners, of which he was in search—beauty with which is mixed a certain strangeness and mystery, that suggests an inner and a deeper principle behind, intermingled with a sadness, a melancholy that is itself akin to beauty.

A. C. Benson

Walter Pater (New York: Macmillan, 1906), pp. 215-16

His view of art, as expressed in *The Renaissance,* impressed itself upon a number of writers in the 'nineties, and propagated some confusion between life and art which is not wholly irresponsible for some untidy lives. The theory (if it can be called a theory) of "art for art's sake" is still valid in so far as it can be taken as an exhortation to the artist to stick to his job; it never was and never can be valid for the spectator, reader or auditor. How far *Marius the Epicurean* may have assisted a few "conversions" in the following decade I do not know: I only feel sure that with the direct current of religious development it has had nothing to do at all. So far as that current—or one important current—is concerned, *Marius* is much nearer to being merely due to Pater's contact—a contact no more intimate than that of Marius himself—with something which was happening and would have happened without him.

The true importance of the book, I think, is as a document of one moment in the history of thought and sensibility in the nineteenth century. The dissolution of thought in that age, the isolation of art, philosophy, religion, ethics and literature, is interrupted by various chimerical attempts to effect imperfect syntheses. Religion became morals, religion became art, religion became science or philosophy; various blundering attempts were made at alliances between various branches of thought. Each half-prophet believed that he had the whole truth. The alliances were as detrimental all round as the separations. The right practice of "art for art's sake" was the devotion of Flaubert or Henry James; Pater is not with these men, but rather with Carlyle and Ruskin and Arnold, if some distance below them. *Marius* is significant chiefly as a reminder that the religion of Carlyle or that of Ruskin or that of Arnold or that of Tennyson or that of Browning, is not enough. It represents, and Pater represents more positively than Coleridge of whom he wrote the words, "that inexhaustible discontent, languor, and home-sickness . . . the chords of which ring all through our modern literature."

T. S. Eliot
Selected Essays, 1917-1932
(New York: Harcourt Brace, 1932), 356-57

As a sample judgment we may take this from Paul Elmer More:

> Paterism might without great injustice be defined as the quintessential spirit of Oxford emptied of the wholesome intrusions of the world—its pride of isolation reduced to sterile self-absorption, its enchantment of beauty alembicated into a faint Epicureanism, its discipline of learning changed into a voluptuous economy of sensations, its golden calm stagnated into languid elegance.

Along with the stress in all these studies on Pater's aestheticism went the stress on the so-called impressionistic character of his criticism. The Humanists have been particularly bitter against him as an impressionist, by which they mean a person who substitutes for a sound interpretation or judgment of a work of art his own purely personal impressions. This view of his criticism is predominant in practically all the works from Thomas Wright to the present. It has combined with the stress on his aestheticism to give us the picture of a critic who stands apart from the main stream of English critical thought, and indulges his own charming fancies without any solid foundation of critical judgment. The praise given by Oliver Elton, who called him "our greatest critic since Coleridge," was distinctly out of line with the prevailing view.

In the last few years, however, we have had signs that the tide is turning. In 1931 there appeared a distinguished study by A. J. Farmer of *Walter Pater as a Critic of English Literature*; and in 1933 came an analysis by Miss Helen H. Young, *The Writings of Walter Pater, a Reflection of British Philosophical Opinion from 1860-1890*. In these studies, full credit is given not only to Pater's emotional sensitivity, and to his cultivated sense of style, but to the substratum of thought which underlay his whole work. He begins to appear not merely as an aesthete and a stylist but as a thinker.

For our own sakes this better understanding should be encouraged. We cannot afford to dismiss with impatience so sensitive and discriminating a man of letters as Walter Pater because he is a step behind and a step ahead of the modern temper.

Ruth C. Child
The Aesthetic of Walter Pater
(New York: Macmillan, 1940), pp. 4-5

Decorative prose of any kind, . . . arouses little enthusiasm in our day; and perhaps no one but Yeats could in 1936 have boldly transcribed the Gioconda passage as poetry. Yet that is probably what it was—the only kind of poetry possible to a man like Pater, without the energy of self-dramatisation necessary for full creative work. Pater's practice of the genre is distinguished by a sense of order and control that is rare in prose poetry.

He is open to the charge of preciosity and affectation, and his deliberate obliviousness of most of the interests of mankind will always be viewed with impatience by those who demand a more obvious kind of effectiveness. We have shown, I suppose, that it was psychologically inevitable, a part of Pater's basic longing for home as a place enclosed and sealed against the turbulence of the outside world. Historically, the important thing to say is that this withdrawal was necessary. There were more than enough influences at work in late Victorian life to drag the arts into the commonplace of day-to-day existence. In an age that was boiling up for the Boer War and the windy degradation of the daily press it was necessary that a small group of hierophants should keep the sacred flame burning in some still retreat. It was not perhaps particularly good for their own health; the atmosphere of shrines is notoriously insalubrious. But it is not a very profitable exercise to estimate the value of an attitude like Pater's apart from its effect; its justification is that in a world not inclined to be sympathetic to such delicate plants, it has continued to exist; and continues to represent a certain phase of our culture. And it would be a mistake to suppose that Pater's preoccupations were altogether apart from the main stream of cultural development. One might reply to objections against Pater's achievement in the words he himself uses about criticism:

> In truth the legitimate contention is, not of one age or school of literary art against another, but of all successive schools alike, against the stupidity which is dead to the substance, and the vulgarity which is dead to form.

Graham Hough
The Last Romantics (London: Duckworth, 1947), p. 173

COVENTRY PATMORE
1823-1896

Patmore published a first book of verse in 1844, contributed to the short-lived Pre-Raphaelite magazine *The Germ* (1850), and brought out the four parts of his long poem *The Angel in the House* (the last part, *The Victories of Love*, can also be described as a sequel) between 1854 and 1863. He became a Roman Catholic in 1864, and his later poetic volume, *The Unknown Eros* (1877) represents the shift from smooth domestic verse to a rugged, even harsh, style and a virtually mystical strain. Patmore also produced criticism of both art and literature, collected in *Principle in Art* (1889) and *Religio Poetae* (1893).

Frederick Page, ed., *Poems* (1949)
Frederick Page, *Patmore: A Study in Poetry* (1933)

He did not quite reach his aim, but even Catullus has scarcely done that. The peculiar beauty of his verse is not to every one's taste; if it were he would have that universal attractiveness which we have admitted that he lacks. But he wrote, with extreme and conscientious care, and with impassioned joy, a comparatively small body of poetry, the least successful portions of which are yet curiously his own, while the most successful fill those who are attuned to them with an exquisite and durable pleasure.

It is much to his advantage that in a lax age, and while moving danger-
ously near to the borders of sentimentality, he preserved with the utmost
constancy his lofty ideal of poetry.

Edmund Gosse
Coventry Patmore (New York: Scribner's, 1905), p. 212

Tennyson and Browning, Arnold, Swinburne—yes, and Meredith—are
more excellent poets than Patmore. He was a learned theorist in metre,
but neither a gifted singer nor an expert one.

He praises apprehension at the expense of comprehension, and upon
apprehension he narrowed his aim. Yet now and then, beside his penetrating flashes, Browning's experimental psychology wears but a half-serious
look, as of a clever game; Tennyson's *In Memoriam* keeps, indeed, its
seriousness, but as the pathetic side of its inadequacy to its theme; while
even the noble philosophies of Arnold and Meredith (though we return
to them) are momentarily stunted in a glimpse of more tremendous heights.

The publication of the *Odes* (or, to give the volumes their titles, of *The
Unknown Eros* and *Amelia*), in 1877-8, closed Patmore's career as a poet.
Already he had moved from Heron's Ghyll to Hastings, and in 1891 he
moved again to Lymington. To these later years, which he spent almost
as a recluse, belong his prose writings, with their clear grasp of eternal
principles and their indiscriminate ferocity against all contemporary hopes
and strivings.

Sir Arthur Quiller-Couch
Studies in Literature, Third Series (New York:
Putnam's, 1930), pp. 140-41

Patmore, when he had once found himself, did not go outside his own
domestic, civic, and interior life for the occasions of his poetry. Thus there
can be no other greatness in his poetry than there is in loving justice and
mercy and beauty, and in the belief that they exist infinitely. To say this
is to make a very humble and a very proud claim for Patmore. It is to
admit that, unlike all the great English poets except Wordsworth, he does
not entertain us with spectacle, and it claims that he is with Wordsworth.

Frederick Page
Patmore: A Study in Poetry (London:
Oxford Univ. Pr., 1933), p. 184

Even at its best Patmore's poetry is spoilt by ugly inversions and elisions,
inexcusable considering the freedom of the form. But in these last Odes,
we are hardly aware of such faults: the thought is irredeemably fused in
the expression, and the result is true poetry of the rarest and perhaps the

highest kind—metaphysical poetry such as Lucretius, Dante, Donne, Crashaw and Wordsworth wrote.

Herbert Read
In Defence of Shelley (London:
Heinemann, 1936), pp. 108-9

If, because of his limited output, his comparatively narrow range when compared with Tennyson or Browning, the absence of virtuosity in his poetry, and the touches of perverse temper in some of his works, he cannot be ranked in the first flight of Victorian poets, he is surely at the top of the second class. He is more dynamic and a richer poet than Christina Rossetti; he has more to say than Clough; he is more profound and more imaginative than Elizabeth Barrett Browning; he is more consistent and passionate than Barnes. His poetry may well be an acquired taste; yet it is possible to feel of it, as it is of the work of few of these others, that there is still much more to be learnt of it, and felt of it, that it contains a world of insight and experience whose significance is likely to increase rather than diminish as the generations pass.

J. C. Reid
The Mind and Art of Coventry Patmore
(London: Routledge, 1957), p. 325

When Patmore is not intolerably bad he can be very exciting. He would, however, be the first to insist that the merit of his writing cannot be considered separately from the merit of what he says. . . .

He would have been enraged by A. E. Housman's remark: "Nobody admires his best poetry enough, though the stupid Papists may fancy they do. But I should say as little as possible about his nasty mixture of piety and concupiscence." His best poetry, he would have insisted, embodied that love-doctrine which his critic describes so unsympathetically. True, Patmore sometimes writes excellent poems without riding his special hobby —*Winter, The Toys, The Azalea, Departure*—and it may well have been such pieces that made the famous little chill run up and down Mr. Housman's spine. It would seem perverse, however, to say that Patman writes good poetry only when he is *not* expressing the ideas which are supremely important for him and which he thinks should be supremely important for everyone. A reasoned evaluation of Patmore's work must depend very largely on whether his religious philosophy actually *is* "a nasty mixture of piety and concupiscence." If so, he was not the sort of poet that he aspired to be.

Hoxie Neale Fairchild
Religious Trends in English Poetry, Vol. IV,
(New York: Columbia Univ. Pr., 1957), p. 317

CHRISTINA ROSSETTI
1830-1894

Combining her celebrated brother's love of color and cadence with her mother's deeply religious nature, Christina Rossetti wrote fantastic, sensitively lyric, and devotional verses. Educated at home, she lived a solitary life—she was twice engaged but never married—and became a virtual recluse in her later years. She published her first volume of poetry in 1847; *Goblin Market and Other Poems* in 1862; *The Prince's Progress and Other Poems* in 1866; *Sing-Song: A Nursery Rhyme-Book* in 1872; and collections in 1881, 1890, and 1893. Her poems, in some respects comparable with Dante Gabriel Rossetti's, can both fall into a more sentimental strain and achieve more rhythmic vigor and freedom. A final volume of her *New Poems* was edited by another brother, William Michael, in 1896.

William Michael Rossetti, ed., *Poetical Works* (1904)
Mary F. Sandars, *The Life of Christina Rossetti* (1930)

Goblin Market

In common with other such enduring works of art as *The Faerie Queene, Gulliver's Travels,* and *Alice in Wonderland, Goblin Market* has many levels of meaning. At the narrative level it offers a charming and delicate fairy tale to delight a child, if a somewhat precocious one. At the symbolic and allegorical level, it conveys certain Christian ethical assumptions. At the psychological level, it suggests emotional experience universally valid.

Unlike the other long autobiographical poems we have been examining, this one, Christina's masterpiece, has no hero. No fiery intellectual such as is found in *Convent Threshold,* no poet-lover similar to the one who first shares and then shatters the speaker's earthly paradise in *From House to Home,* no tardy and loitering prince failing to make hymeneal progress grace this work. It can hardly be said to have a heroine, for the sisters, Laura and Lizzie, between them share the narrative interest. Golden-haired, ivory-skinned, "like two blossoms on one stem," they seem but different aspects of the same maiden. They may in fact be regarded as Christina's version of sacred and profane love. For once in her poetry, she presents love in large, abstract, general terms. But although the individual contours are lacking, no poem of hers is more clearly based upon personal experience.

Despite the fact that William remembered that he had often heard her say she did not mean anything profound by this fairy tale and it was not to be taken as a moral apologue, he himself freely admitted finding "the incidents . . . suggestive," and in his comments about the poem encouraged an interpretation at a deeper level than that of a fairy tale fantasy. Although modern critics have been inclined to drop the whole matter of meaning and to regard the poem as a Pre-Raphaelite masterpiece which combines a realistic use of detail with the vague symbolism and religiosity of *A Blessed Damozel*, in interpreting the poem it would seem more fruitful to pay attention to William's various hints and admissions, particularly since Christina herself, for reasons of her own, wished to discourage explication. Indeed, these very reasons are what give the poem its organizing principle.

Once *Goblin Market* is read as the complex, rich, and meaningful work it actually is, the prevalent critical view that the poem has the bright, clear, obvious pigmentation and the lightly woven surface texture of a Pre-Raphaelite painting will no longer be tenable. An analysis of the poem in the light of the emotional facts in Christina's life will reveal that the symbolism, vague and suggestive as it may appear, actually has the same underlying contact with reality that her other poems display. Ford Madox Ford once remarked that, although love among the Pre-Raphaelites was a romantic and glamorous affair of generalizations, Christina alone regarded it concretely and individually. . . .

One of Christina's leading concepts begins to emerge: the paradox of love as both destroyer and redeemer. Nowhere is this concept dramatized with more striking originality and imaginative power than in *Goblin Market*; but what distinguishes this long narrative poem from the many short lyrics expressing the same idea is that here human rather than divine love is the agent of redemption.

Lona Mosk Packer
Christina Rossetti (Berkeley, Calif.:
Univ. California Pr., 1963), pp. 140-41, 149

GENERAL

Probably the first impression one gets from reading the *Complete Poetical Works* of Christina Rossetti, now collected and edited by her brother, Mr. W. M. Rossetti, is that she wrote altogether too much, and that it was a doubtful service to her memory to preserve so many poems purely private in their nature. The editor, one thinks, might well have shown himself more "reverent of her strange simplicity." For page after page we are in the society of a spirit always refined and exquisite in sentiment, but without any guiding and restraining artistic impulse; she never drew to the shutters of her soul, but lay open to every wandering breath of heaven. In comparison with the works of the more creative poets her song is like the continuous lisping of an æolian harp beside the music elicited by cunning fingers. And then suddenly, out of this sweet monotony, moved by some stronger, clearer breeze of inspiration, there sounds a strain of wonderful beauty and flawless perfection, unmatched in its own kind in English letters.

Paul Elmer More
Shelburne Essays [Third Series]
(Boston: Houghton Mifflin, 1905), p. 124

The English Romantics had failed, and the points they insisted on were neglected by the world till in 1862 Christina Rossetti published *Goblin Market and Other Poems*, and by her triumph paved the way for her brother, for Swinburne, and the Victorian Romantics generally. In many aspects the position was anomalous. Here was a woman extraordinarily straitlaced and Puritanical, who yet assured the success of what was afterwards abused as "The Fleshly School," by an absolutely blameless volume finishing with a section of Devotional Poems.

In all ways Christina Rossetti is a unique and remarkable figure. Genius is generally expected to entail weakness in some direction, and to require people around its possessor to act as ministering angels; yet here was a woman of rare genius whose life was spent in suffering, yet in ministering to others.

In the pauses of writing magnificent poetry she would trudge out in thick boots and short skirts—neither being then fashionable—to visit the poor and sick, or to pay a visit to a Home for Fallen Girls of which she was an associate. . . .

There is pathos in the mere circumstances of her life. She who had longed for, yet rejected love, went about everywhere with her mother and two aunts. . . . Her life . . . is in many ways a sad one, but it had great compensations in the intense mutual love between Christina Rossetti and her family, and the satisfaction denied to thousands who long for it of doing one thing supremely well.

Mary F. Saunders
The Life of Christina Rossetti (London:
Hutchinson, 1930), pp. 20-21

The Pre-Raphaelite part of Christina Rossetti's verse, like the verse of Dante Gabriel, of William Morris, and, with certain exceptions, of Swinburne, is as essentially Victorian as a Baxter print or a Tenniel cartoon. To say this is to belittle none of these things. "Victorian" will soon cease to be a term of reproach. But when we turn to [her] great lyrics . . . we find in them that timeless quality inherent in the purest poetry; and we realise that no influences, no factors, no impressions outside the frontiers of her own inviolate soul could have given to those lyrics their penetrating eloquence, their perdurable music, their austere loveliness.

Dorothy Margaret Stuart
Christina Rossetti (London: Macmillan, 1930), p. 188

DANTE GABRIEL ROSSETTI
1828-1882

Son of an Italian political refugee who devoted himself to interpreting Dante's allegory, Rossetti was a painter of mystical and sensuous women —and the leading spirit in the "Pre-Raphaelite Brotherhood" of artists— as well as a poet. Some of his early verse, including "The Blessed Damozel," was published in the 1850 Pre-Raphaelite journal *The Germ*. In 1860, already an artist with a reputation and patrons, he married his delicate model Elizabeth Siddal. Less than two years later she died of an overdose of laudanum, leaving Rossetti so stricken with grief and possibly remorse that he buried his unpublished poetry in her coffin. Nine years afterward, in poor health and financial difficulties, he allowed friends to disinter her body and recover the poems, which were published in 1870. Although the poet-painter had issued his translations of *The Early Italian Poets* in 1861, the 1870 volume was the one that made him famous, and the one that exposed him to attack—in an 1871 article by Robert Buchanan—as one of the "fleshly school of poetry." Rossetti was ill-prepared mentally to withstand such attack, and a good part of his life was spent in deep depression. He published his *Ballads and Sonnets* in 1881 and died the following year.

William Michael Rossetti, ed., *Works* (1911)
Oswald Doughty, *A Victorian Romantic* (1949)
Rosalie Glynn Grylls, *Portrait of Rossetti* (1964)

PERSONAL

To the muddled Victorian mind it seemed vaguely suitable that the artist should be melancholy, morbid, uncontrolled, and generally slightly deranged. It was a complement of the somewhat earlier popular tradition that to be "understanding" one must be also an invalid, and to be "pure," impoverished. This mischievous misconception found its fulfilment in the 'nineties when, in London and Paris, at any rate, most of the considerable artistic figures were in fact consumptive or perverted or epileptic or in some way enough debased to give colour to the impression that Art was the lily that flowered from the dung-heap.

In Rossetti's own day, no doubt, not a little of the adulation he aroused came from this romance of decay—a sort of spiritual coprophily characteristic of the age. Even now we are inclined to think of him with melancholy tolerance and to say, "If he had not been improvident and lethargic, how great an artist he might have been," as we say of the war poets, "If they had not been killed. . . ." But it seems to me that there we have the root cause of Rossetti's failure. It is not so much that as a man he was a bad man—mere lawless wickedness has frequently been a concomitant of the highest genius—but there was fatally lacking in him that *essential rectitude* that underlies the serenity of all really great art. The sort of unhappiness that beset him was not the sort of unhappiness that does beset a great artist; all his brooding about magic and suicide are symptomatic not so much of genius as of mediocrity. There is a spiritual inadequacy, a sense of ill-organisation about all that he did.

But if he were merely a psychopathic case and nothing more, there would be no problem and no need for a book about him. The problem is that here and there in his life he seems, without ever feeling it, to have transcended this inadequacy in a fashion that admits of no glib explanation. Just as the broken arch at Glastonbury Abbey is, in its ruin, so much more moving than it can ever have been when it stood whole and part of a great building, so Rossetti's art, at fitful moments, flames into the exquisite beauty of *Beata Beatrix.*

Evelyn Waugh
Rossetti: His Life and Works (New York:
Dodd, Mead, 1928), pp. 226-27

But after all, as the Japanese proverb says, "It is better to be a crystal and be broken, than to be perfect like the tile upon the housetop." The crystal that was Rossetti, came to a shattered end; but the visions that found life within it, live still. Like Blake, he was poet and painter in one; and, like Blake, he saw the world ablaze with all its colours, not as a colour-blind pattern of moral blacks and whites. The English writers of his age tended to have too much conscience and too little artistic conscience: he was needed. Through him, this "great Italian," as Ruskin called him, "tormented in the inferno of London," Italy gave to the England of Tennyson what she had given before to the England of Chaucer and, again of Shakespeare, a sense of beauty, naked and not ashamed. In him the green wealth of the Southern vine was wedded to our Northern elm, and bore its fruit under the frown of harsher skies. Life denied him much, gave him much only to take it back again; his fate may seem a failure and a tragedy; yet in words of his own, that might serve for his epitaph, he has recorded all the hopes he cared or dared to cherish—and those at least were not in vain:

> Crave thou no dower of earthly things
> Unworthy Hope's imaginings;

To have brought true birth of Song to be
And to have won hearts to Poesy,
Or anywhere in the sun or rain
To have loved and been beloved again
Is loftiest reach of Hope's bright wings.

F. L. Lucas
Dante Gabriel Rossetti (Cambridge Univ. Pr.,
1933), pp. xxxiii-xxxiv

The House of Life

If in Rossetti's art—painting and poetry—there is often the fragrance of incense rather than of flowers, it is not necessary to cry, *Retro me*. There are many who scent evil in all that they do not like or do not understand; and if to the object of their dislike or misunderstanding there is a background of shadow, they flee at once with horror and fear. Is this attitude (one may ask) any more healthy than the alleged unhealthiness of that which they fled from? There is a beauty of night and a beauty of daylight; there is a sweetness of perfume which is not the perfume of flowers. It is not that one is purer or cleaner or wholesomer than the other; it is that they are different, and perhaps the chief difference is simply that between nature and art. If it suit any reader's fancy or conscience to prefer one to the other, we can only say that it is so, taking care that the moral judgment does not conceal an artistic judgment.

Finally, however, we come to this latter judgment. Below the large utterance of the great poet's best work there are two kinds of beauty to be recognized, which may be called "natural" and "artistic." These do not exist alone, but are often interwoven or juxtaposed even in single passages. Other terms might be "simple" and "complex." The purity and grace of the former make it especially attractive to us, not to speak of the ease with which it is apprehended. For these and other reasons we may instinctively prefer it, but we need not erect this preference into a prejudice against the deliberate or conscious artistry of those poets who, like Virgil and Milton and, in their lesser way, Tennyson and Rossetti, do not quite conceal the fact that they are artists. Here lies the true charge against Rossetti as poet— excess of artistry. Too often one feels that sense of strain which Hazlitt felt in Milton. The rack and torture of composition become a little too apparent. Partly it is a matter of inadequate expression; partly also of the matter to be expressed. The density as of a hothouse atmosphere, the oversweetness as of tuberoses, the pervading effect of artificiality—such, where they are found, constitute the most serious charge against "The House of

Life." If in any degree I have succeeded in disengaging them from the complaint of moral unwholesomeness, I have done more than I could hope.

Paull Franklin Baum, ed.
The House of Life (Cambridge, Mass.:
Harvard Univ. Pr., 1928), pp. 33-34

The pursuit of love becomes first an unconscious and then a conscious pursuit of death when the mind fails to externalize itself sufficiently to maintain a balance between life and the dream. Rossetti's tremendous energy broke away from the Siren voices again and again, by expressing his deepest desires in creative art. There is no essential contradiction between his recognition of himself, "I loved thee ere I loved a woman, Love," without the title "To Art" and with it, for art is ultimately the embodiment of a man's alter-ego, whose most fundamental desire is an ideal Love. The amazing group of sonnets entitled *The House of Life* has had a stifling effect on the most careful and sensitive readers simply because of the terrific energy of the poet's creative resistance of death, and this is in the verbal texture as well as the dominant moods.

The raptures of the love recorded in *The House of Life* began to recede like an ebbing flood of moonlit sea which discloses a ghastly shore. The pursuit of the fleshly paradise leads always down to "devious coverts of dismay" they are one with those "charnel caves" screened by flowers, above which sing the sirens. The preoccupation with death and remorse for lost life which makes yet heavier the resonant gloom of this great sonnet sequence is the reflection of the poet's mystical failure. A true mystic in worshipping beauty would overcome fear and remorse at last by the illumination which succeeds the shadow of death. Rossetti could gain no surer foothold on spiritual freedom than "The One Hope"—of re-union, but that was a straw he clung to with the strength of a drowning man. He had dragged his heaven down to earth, environed himself with the fleshly paradise, and before he could gain his freedom it vanished like that paradisal feast which the oriental ruler gave to the youths before drugging them; when they awoke they believed that they had been in heaven; but they had gone no further than the palace of pleasure.

R. L. Mégroz
Dante Gabriel Rossetti: Painter Poet of Heaven and Earth
(London: Faber and Gwyer, 1928), pp. 315-16

GENERAL

Two things strike at once all who feel Rossetti's power, whether in attraction or repulsion. No English poet of his standing, except Gray, has left so slender a body of verse, and hardly any of it is second-rate or superfluous. Again, it is curiously underivative. There are traces of Elizabethan and Jacobean influence in the rhythms; Dante has cast a spell over his mind, and he has loved Keats and admired the early Browning; but he speaks with his own voice, and that voice is new. This novelty appertains both to his matter and to his technique. He wrote of spiritual things in the most definite and concrete sensible imagery. "Like Dante, he knows no region of spirit which shall not be sensuous also, or material." He sees the truth of emotion and thought not in metaphors, but in sharply realized pictures. His style again, whether in ballad or sonnet or lyric, is elaborate, subtle, and strange. He aims at a simplicity which is attained at the expense of infinite art. . . .

Rossetti, if he can scarcely be placed among the greater poets, had an influence more potent and pervasive than many of the great. He intoxicated his contemporaries, and the effect may be seen in Swinburne and Morris. There is a ridiculous side to it, which H. D. Traill caught in his deadly parody of "Sister Helen"; but there is also a rare and not easily defined beauty. He wrote ballads, but he was not a ballad-maker, lyrics, but he was not a singer; he is always the artificer, working with arabesques and inlays and strange jewels and rich intractable substances. "The dwelling-place," says Walter Pater, "in which one finds oneself by chance or destiny, yet can partly fashion for oneself; never properly one's own at all, if it be changed too lightly; in which every object has its associations—the dim mirrors, the portraits, the lamps, the books, the hair-tresses of the dead, and visionary magic crystals in the secret drawers, the names and words scratched on the windows, windows open upon prospects the saddest or the sweetest; the house one must quit, yet taking perhaps, how much of its quietly active light and colour along with us!—grown now to be a kind of raiment to one's body, as the body, according to Swedenborg, is but the raiment of the soul—under that image the whole of Rossetti's work might count as a *House of Life.*"

John Buchan
Introd., in *Dante Gabriel Rossetti: Poems*
(London: Nelson, 1934), pp. x-xiii. This essay was also
printed in Buchan's *Homilies and Recreations* (London, 1926)

Perhaps Rossetti's greatest fault is that he works his metal too much, and is too easily satisfied that the metal is gold. "If he suffers for anything," says Mr. Elton, "it is his economy, as most writers do for their superfluity. Rossetti's formidable will puts everything ten times through the alembic. Nothing is easy for him, and he cannot make us think it has been easy." Of the two qualities he demanded in a sonnet, brains and music, most unenthusiastic critics will find the former lacking. The fundamental brainwork of conception is applied too often with strenuous energy to a subject we cannot admit as quite justifying the effort. The brainwork of persistent artistry overtowers that of original intelligence. His thought is all feeling— this is his "mysticism." His gift is music, not brains. And in his deliberate conscious devotion to what he conceives to be his gift—if we are to accept quite unreservedly what may have been only a casual remark—he runs to the extreme of laborious pretense and mere idiosyncrasy. Seldom indeed is he insincere, for his devotion is real enough, and almost the weakest of his sonnets is hallowed, for art, by his intensity. If, as has been said, he unconsciously substitutes tenseness for intensity, the *faux bon* for the *vraie vérité*, we must admit that this is not an altogether damning fault, and we must be extraordinarily careful lest we forget that his best work, that by which any poet is to be finally judged, rises clearly above his weakness. His deficiency—in spite of the regal greatness his immediate friends felt in his bodily presence—is the lack of a great spirit. It is this which keeps him from the circle of the highest poets. His impulsive swift power, an advantage in youth, really prevented him from fully maturing; and that, with the terrible experiences upon which the same impulsive swift power drove him, left him at the end an unfinished man. A great poet, a great artist in two arts, we must grant him to be, and, yes, in the special realm of his peculiar genius, that dark forest of the mysteries of death and life and brooding beauty, lighted with the passion of love earthly and divine, there a great spirit is his, too.

> Shall birth and death, and all dark names that be
> As doors and windows bared to some loud sea,
>   Lash deaf mine ears and blind my face with spray;
>   And shall my sense pierce love,—the last relay
> And ultimate outpost of eternity?

This is his struggle and his artistic achievement.

Paull Franklin Baum, ed.
The House of Life (Cambridge, Mass.:
Harvard Univ. Pr., 1928), pp. 57-58

A mind so powerfully self-centered as Rossetti's needed as many links as possible with the external world, to prevent its very vitality turning inward and consuming it. Rossetti balanced the introversion of his mind by his personal attractiveness which enabled him to be rich in friendship, and in his creative work he achieved the same object by his intuitive sympathy with individuals. This was largely involved in a fine dramatic sense. The remote and dreamlike imagery of his best romantic poems is generally charged with dramatic sympathy. The same is true of the best of the early water-colours. He realizes the human heart. This is why the pictures are often so much like poems, and why other poets were stimulated by them. A third means of externalizing the mind is in intellectual contemplation, which, as we have seen, colours his poetry. This synthetical process of the mind is closely united with his visionary view of human destiny, sometimes tinged with satire, as in the sonnet "On Refusal of Aid Between Nations." Here there is no irony, but in "The Burden of Nineveh" and "Jenny" the satire is slightly ironical. The early version of "Jenny," which lacked the dramatic sympathy of the mature version, was probably inspired by Alfred de Musset who, in "Rolla" and "Souvenir," and even in lighter pieces like "Mimi Pinson" has affinities with Rossetti. It would be easier to argue from Rossetti's work that he was French than that he was Italian.

R. L. Mégroz
Dante Gabriel Rossetti: Painter of Heaven and Earth
(London: Faber and Gwyer, 1928), p. 308

The significance of Rossetti's work for the sensibility of the *fin-de-siècle* is very great. It inaugurates that period of emotional unrest in which satisfaction is sought in the traditional religious symbolism, but is not found, since the symbols have been emptied of almost all their traditional religious content. We begin to discern for the first time the figure of the conscious aesthete, deliberately pursuing beauty—

. . . how passionately and irretrievably
In what fond flight, how many ways and days.

His confused and partial return to the medieval concept of an ideal love, dominating the whole of life, is a genuine enrichment of the content of poetry. The bread-and-butter treatment of sexual themes, the "passionless sentiment" of Tennyson, is replaced by something which, for all its divagations, is a more adequate version of experience. The concept of a love which can never be satisfied by its simple bodily objects is not absorbed by Rossetti as it was by Dante into any total scheme of life: and this, together with the association between love and death, and the conflict between "soul's beauty" and "body's beauty," have often been written off as ethical eccentricities of the decadence. We must acknowledge in post-Freudian days that their psychological significance is more permanent. Rossetti is attacking some of the central neuroses of our culture. It is true that his progeny in the nineties did not amount to much: but the impasse in which he ultimately found himself provided the starting-point for the work of Yeats. Rossetti's turning away from science, sociology and progress into the analysis of his own soul led him into a *selva oscura* from which the only outlet is a dim, half-earthly, half-religious hope: in Yeats this faint hope gives rise to a tireless exploration of new possibilities of experience.

Graham Hough
The Last Romantics (London: Duckworth, 1947), pp. 81-82

As painter and as poet, Dante Rossetti represents something of the old Pre-Raphaelite strain and more, perhaps, of the later tendency. At his most characteristic, he combines the two interests, one in religious or moral subjects realistically portrayed, and one in earthly, even voluptuous, images artfully realized. *The House of Life* includes a sonnet on "St. Luke the Painter," whose art "looked through [symbols] to God" instead of achieving, as later painters did, only the "soulless self-reflection of man's skill"—and this sentiment is pure Ruskin. And, of course, *The House of Life* also includes such earthly, fleshly lyrics as "Silent Noon."

Finally, if Rossetti's pictures often have extremely literary purposes, either illustrating or telling stories, his poems often have extremely visual qualities which are purely pictorial; we are probably less likely to "read" his simple physical images as psychologically or morally or philosophically symbolic than we are the images of any other important Victorian poet. The parallels observed here may support Rossetti's own inclination to think of himself as a poet who painted. Certainly he is a literary artist. But the accent hovers between the two words in that ambiguous phrase when we consider his work as a whole.

Wendell Stacy Johnson
Victorian Poetry (Winter, 1965), p. 18

JOHN RUSKIN

1819-1900

Ruskin was educated at home by his Scottish-born parents and early developed, along with a Calvinist conscience, a love for landscape and for painting. His first volume of *Modern Painters*, a defence and extended appreciation of the great English artist Turner, with animadversions on other painters, was published in 1843, to be succeeded by four more, increasingly broad ranging digressive volumes in 1846, 1856, and 1860. A brilliant and extremely influential, if dogmatic, theorist and critic of the fine arts, Ruskin came to be more and more concerned with economic and social issues. The dark, erratic side of his genius is suggested by the history of his unconsummated marriage to Euphemia Gray, annulled after five years, his proposal of marriage to a girl thirty years younger than he, his fierce attacks on the art of Whistler, and the intermittent insanity of his late years. But that Ruskin is a genius his great impact upon minds as diverse as Morris, Proust, Gandhi, and Frank Lloyd Wright suggests, and critics have been as admiring of his most impressive passages as they have been perplexed by his inconsistencies. Ruskin's major works include, along with the volumes of *Modern Painters, The Seven Lamps of Architecture* (1849), *The Stones of Venice,* in three volumes (1851-1853), *Pre-Raphaelitism* (1851), *Unto This Last* (1862), *Sesame anl Lilies* (1865), *The Crown of Wild Olive* (1866), *Time and Tide* (1867), a series of letters to working men entitled *Fors Clavigera* (eight volumes, 1871-1884), and the serially published autobiography *Praeterita* (1885-1889). He was sometime Slade Professor of Art at Oxford, the founder of a vaguely medieval socialist "Guild of St. George," and an active lecturer as well as a prolific writer. Ruskin's very considerable literary output has been collected and annotated in one of the most admirable redactions of any nineteenth-century writer, the Cook and Wedderburn edition.

Edward T. Cook and Alexander D. O. Wedderburn, eds., *Works* (1903-1912), 39 vols.

Edward T. Cook, *The Life of John Ruskin* (1911), 2 vols.

PERSONAL

The interest of Ruskin's life is the interest of a personality, and I want you to try to regard him in that light, and not either as a prophet, or a reformer, or an art-critic, or a writer. He was all these things by turns—they were but the guises which this restless and ardent temperament assumed. As a prophet, he was unbalanced and unconvincing, because he had depth rather than width of view. He did not see the whole problem. He saw clearly enough into the hearts of like-minded people, but he was essentially a partisan, and condemned what he did not understand as severely as he condemned what he hated. He took, from his education and his sheltered life, a meagre view of the world. He had little sympathy with robust strength, and wide tracts of human nature, at its bluntest and soundest, were entirely obscure to him. And thus his reprobation was so extravagant that it made no appeal, not even the appeal of shame and terror, to those whom he inveighed against most fiercely. Then too he did not even do justice to his age; he overlooked one of the best and strongest forces of the time—the resolute search for truth, the stern determination of the scientific spirit not to generalise till it has investigated. He went wrong himself in every department of his work, from his passion for generalisation and his acquiescence in incomplete investigation. What made his protests ineffectual was that he believed himself to have a perfectly analytical mind. His mind was indeed analytical, when he applied it to questions which he understood, and to workers with whom he sympathised. But he had no notion of just comparison, and when his sympathy was not enlisted he could not even analyse. He had the power of putting vague personal preferences into language superficially exact, and this was a terrible snare to him and to his followers, who believed that they were getting logical reasons when they were only getting instinctive predilections. Yet I am far from saying that as a prophet his work was thrown away. He was no ascetic . . . and thus he was able to see the dangers of the materialism that is not uplifted by the concurrence of the soul. But he felt that the invariable comfort in which he lived to some extent invalidated his message. "If I had lived in a garret," he once wrote, "then I could have preached that Queen Victoria should do the same." But . . . he accepted with a sort of unquestioning loyalty the precise standard of material luxury in which he had been himself brought up, and he regarded any extension or development of this as base and degrading. Yet he was here in the main right, because he saw that the bane of the age is its impatience of simplicity, its worship of success, its preference of comfort, and its mistaking the quality of pleasure. . . .

A. C. Benson
John Ruskin (New York: Putnam's, 1911), p. 201

Ruskin began writing in earnest at the age of seven. He ceased sixty years later, after a final attack of madness forced him to lay down his pen. In the interim he published more than forty books, several hundred lectures and articles, and with the accuracy of a solitary fanatic recorded in his diaries every thought, image, and emotion which crossed his consciousness. Many of his works are ill-organized and incomplete, fragments of a larger, never-realized design which constantly shifted with the growth of his thought. Some are trivial; yet none is lifeless, for he brought to his most trifling digression the energy and undisciplined abundance of his genius. The variety of subjects he wrote about is astonishing, but no less so than the individuality of his point of view. . . . The wonder of Ruskin is both his disorder and oneness —the triumph of a unified vision over an often divided and ravaged mind. . . . His thought has a way of spilling over from book to book, advancing and recoiling, but always emanating from a central core of perception that has a life and form of its own. One seems to have wandered without a guide into a vast gallery where finished masterpieces hang alongside hasty sketches, titles of objects are misleading, the rooms arranged at random and the partitions dividing them arbitrarily placed. No single work can be understood apart from the others, and the whole is as remarkable as it is at first glance unintelligible.

John D. Rosenberg
The Darkening Glass (New York:
Columbia Univ. Pr.. 1961), pp. xi-xii

GENERAL

My generation shun Ruskin's emotive rhetoric, because they know from experience that emotive rhetoric is a drug which can make most men and women everywhere believe anything.

In the last quarter of the nineteenth century thousands of men and women drank Ruskin's rhetoric and having drunk called eagerly for more. My generation who will not drink rhetoric demand a calm parade of arguments and statistical facts; and so they read not Ruskin's *Fors Clavigera*, but Wells' *Outline of History*, and *The Work, Wealth and Happiness of Mankind*. . . . The difference is in the presentation; and that arises because the men in the street to-day want Wells' presentation and not Ruskin's.

Ruskin voiced not only his own secret fears and disquietudes, but also the secret disquietudes, fears and discontents of his age. As conditions have not improved but grown more menacing since he laid down his pen in 1889, the fears and discontents of our age are still those of the nineteenth century. That is why Ruskin's work belongs to the living present and is not yet part of the dead past.

R. H. Wilenski
John Ruskin (New York: Stokes, 1933), p. 368

Ruskin had, and still has, a singular power of enthralling and inspiring his listeners. In spite of his scoldings, his despairs, his egoism, his flashes of unreasoning hatred for railways and other mechanical deformities of modern life, he captivated multitudes in his day. His great repute rose in his early forties, about the time he turned from criticism of art to social questions. A book of "Selections" exhibited purple patches from earlier work, and purple they were. In all his earlier works he was prone at set moments to elaborate a page or two of spectacular prose, pulsing with color, glowing with ornament, in long symmetrical balance of clauses, but borne forward on a strong current of musical cadence. Such occur in "The Mountain Glory" in the fourth volume of *Modern Painters*, and "St. Mark's" in the second volume of *Stones of Venice*. Beneath them rises and falls the regular rhythm of Old Testament English, and of the longer ground swell of Dr. Johnson's essays, which the family used to read aloud to beguile the time on their long journeys, and whose music had entered deeply into Ruskin's impressionable young mind.

English education was still in large measure oral—Ruskin's especially—and men wrote as if they were speaking, with the sound of their words tingling or thundering in their ears. Some of Ruskin's best writing originated as lectures. For several years he was Professor of Fine Art at Oxford. He was a fluent talker in public and private. All of which accounts for the irresistible but easy momentum of his style. It reflects, too, something of the magnetic presence often described by his hearers—the tall, auburn-haired, well-groomed figure, rather attractive than good-looking, with the direct, intense, but kindly blue eye, and the invariable blue cravat.

But his personal power proves itself most in the devoted following which rose in response to his teaching and personality. Ruskin Societies sprang up all around. Books about him still multiply. No other literary man has been honored with so monumental an edition of his works as that by Cook and Wedderburn, with its thirty-eight volumes, its master index volume, and its reproductions of his drawings.

His purple luxuriance of manner he abandoned when he came to grips with social problems. It enraged him if anyone praised that earlier skill, for he thought it had blinded them to his ideas. The change was to his advantage, for he launched forth at his best with the lithe and unimpeded energy of the stripped athlete in *Unto this Last* and *Crown of Wild Olive*.

With his other terrible handicaps, he had perhaps too many distracting talents, but out of the litter of his disordered career emerges the single powerful figure of a teacher and prophet who ranks with Carlyle and Dickens as a regenerator of the Victorian world.

Charles Grosvenor Osgood
The Voice of England (New York: Harper, 1935), pp. 521-22

Wherever we open his works we are liable to find prolixity, prejudice and a choice assortment of manias and phobias; but everywhere there is evidence of intellectual power and a delicate and practised sensibility. It is easier to illustrate this by examples chosen from outside his own particular field. The critique of visual appearances to which Ruskin devoted so much of his time is, as he practised it, almost a new genre: there is nothing with which it can be compared. In other fields it is easier to estimate his status at once. His political writings, unprofessional and emotional as they are, probably did more than anyone's to awaken a new social conscience in the uncritical believers in *laisser-faire*. In the passages on literature that are scattered through his writing we are constantly compelled, in spite of frequent disagreement, to acknowledge the energy and acuteness of his judgments. . . .

It is in employing . . . imaginative and descriptive powers on the visual appearance of things that Ruskin's originality lies. Minds of this degree of delicacy and range had applied themselves before to ideas and to literary form, but never before to the appearance of nature, and their representation in art. The individual criticisms in *Modern Painters* are nearly always from the representational point of view, and many people would doubt nowadays how far this kind of criticism is worth doing. (All painting, even the most abstract, is nevertheless some kind of commentary on visual appearances; and Ruskin is dealing mostly with descriptive artists.) What cannot, however, be doubted is that Ruskin is not repeating studio or academy commonplaces, that he has really looked both at pictures and at the natural world: and this is clear even in the most pedestrian pieces of criticism.

Graham Hough
The Last Romantics (London: Duckworth, 1947), pp. 3, 5-6

In fields of art and of social and political economy, Ruskin wrote more or less steadily for over sixty years. Like De Quincey, he took infinite pains with his prose, and consequently some of it, more especially the earlier, has the taint of artifice, to be seen in ornamental flourish of phrase or purple patch. An epithet is forced for the sake of alliteration or a phrase for balance, and paragraphs sometimes wind up with "grand closings," as Ruskin liked to call them. Even his extraordinary "capacity for rhythmic cadence" is at times carried to the length of making his style more regularly measured than is consonant with the nature of prose. His sentences, too, often run to extreme lengths and become overcrowded with details; and in the larger matters of structure he is, again like DeQuincey, one of the most digressive of writers.

But with all allowance for faults, his style remains, at its best, a great style. It moves, in Ruskin's literary life, through at least three phases, though the reader never can be sure when the earlier Ruskin will anticipate the later or the later remind him of the earlier. The earlier style is the most famous. It is the work of a man with a soul of a poet and the eye of the painter. It is rich in color, in imagery, and in rhythm; and it accomplishes marvelously lovely effects with ordinary words in ordinary collocations. There is nothing freakish about it. It is simply the expression of one who has been caught up into a seventh heaven of beauty. The middle style,—the style of *Unto This Last*, for example—is more difficult to describe because its art is better concealed. It has cast aside the earlier rigidities and formal devices. Its sentences as well as its rhythms are shorter, and its thought is more concentrated. The intensity is not less, but it is better controlled. The typical writing of the third manner of which *Fors Clavigera* and some of the later lectures are examples, is a still different thing. It is often flat and uninspired, weakly garrulous and didactic or merely petulant and sometimes hysterical,—the wearisome grumblings of a tired and disappointed old man. But when the imagination of the embattled veteran is aroused his language reminds the reader of Swift or Carlyle. He has then at his command a fierce and merciless satire, a pungent criticism of the stupidity and pusillanimity of mankind, a sweeping denunciation of the shams and corruptions of modern life, such as sometimes come from a writer who has reached an age and an eminence whence he assumes the privilege freely to indulge in "sputters of sulphur" as he lectures humanity. Whatever his manner, Ruskin could and did manage it, repeatedly, with superb mastery.

Frederick Roe, ed.
Victorian Prose (New York: Ronald, 1947), p. 319

Modern Painters: Their Superiority in the Art of Landscape Painting to all the Ancient Masters proved by Examples of the True, the Beautiful, and the Intellectual from the Works of Modern Artists, especially from those of J. M. W. Turner, Esq. R.A.—is one of the most presumptuous, most poetic, most brilliant, yet most wrongheaded volumes ever published by a very young man. Ruskin was twenty-four, and at a single stroke now established himself in the forefront of modern English art critics.

Peter Quennell
John Ruskin: The Portrait of a Prophet
(New York: Viking, 1949), p. 30

Ruskin's own judgment . . . is that . . . his real work began in 1856, the year of *Modern Painters* III and IV. . . . These volumes mark the end of Ruskin's apprenticeship. They cut the landscape feeling down to its true dimensions; it was a valuable element in humanity, but its utility was severely limited.

From then on his message was: "Clear society of injustice. Give children a decent environment to grow in. Give workmen a chance to express themselves. Then you will have your art, but not before."

At one and the same time he wanted all men to be artists and denied that great art was possible in the nineteenth century. . . . For Ruskin, beauty was a destination and a guide, but he knew the road was paved with sweat and stones. Before society could expect beauty from its workmen, it had first to feed, clothe, and house them properly.

On this new target Ruskin leveled the same weapons which had helped and hindered him in his early battles, an imagination fertile in the invention of theories both sensible and nonsensical, an eye that saw what was before it, and a willingness to change a theory if it did not fit the facts. In his social works there is the familiar blend of wisdom and folly that characterizes his art criticism, folly when he indulged in loose speculation, wisdom when he reported what he saw.

Fundamentally Ruskin was a sensitive reporter, not an artist, not an economist, least of all a philosopher. . . .

He left as a heritage, not a pseudo-scientific explanation of history, but a social conscience which is worth more than a dozen economic systems and which will outlast all of them. He saw what we are too often prone to forget. In the words of Charles Beard, he demonstrated to all who were willing to heed that economics is not a science but a branch of ethics.

Francis G. Townsend
Ruskin and the Landscape Feeling (Urbana, Ill.:
Univ. Illinois Pr., 1951), pp. 80, 82

It was a struggle between the truth that had been revealed to him by Turner and the truth that he had discovered under the indirect guidance of Thomas Carlyle. To those who love art Carlyle may appear as Ruskin's evil genius;

to those who love humanity in the mass, he may be seen as the guardian angel.

Joan Evans
John Ruskin (London: Jonathan Cape, 1954), p. 418

ROBERT LOUIS STEVENSON
1850-1894

> Stevenson left his native Scotland because of ill-health, married in California, and spent the latter part of his life in Samoa, where he died. He wrote travel sketches, essays, adventure tales, and children's verse; his reputation with modern critics has been sustained largely by his prose. Some of his best-known volumes are *Travels with a Donkey* (1879), *Virginibus Puerisque* (1881), *New Arabian Nights* (2 vols., 1882), *Familiar Studies* (1882), *Treasure Island* (1883), *Dr. Jekyll and Mr. Hyde* (1886), *Kidnapped* (1886), *The Black Arrow* (1888), *The Master of Ballantrae* (1889), *The Wrong Box, The Wrecker,* and *The Ebb-Tide,* all with Lloyd Osbourne (1889, 1892, 1894), *Weir of Hermiston* (1896), and *St. Ives* (1897).
>
> *Works,* Tusitala Edition (1923-1927), 35 vols.
>
> Graham Balfour, *The Life of Stevenson* (1901), 2 vols.

The finest papers in *Across the Plains,* in *Memories and Portraits,* in *Virginibus Puerisque,* stout of substance and supremely silver of speech, have both a nobleness and a nearness that place them, for perfection and roundness, above his fiction, and that also may well remind a vulgarised generation of what, even under its nose, English prose can be. But it is bound up with his name, for our wonder and reflection, that he is something other than the author of this or that particular beautiful thing, or of all such things together. It has been his fortune (whether or no the greatest that can befall a man of letters) to have had to consent to become, by a process not purely mystical and not wholly untraceable—what shall we call it?—a Figure. Tracing is needless now, for the personality has acted and the incarnation is full. There he is—he has passed ineffaceably into happy legend. This case of the figure is of the rarest and the honour surely of the greatest. In all our literature we can count them, sometimes with the work and sometimes without. The work has often been great and yet the figure *nil.* Johnson was one, Goldsmith and Byron; and the two former moreover not in any degree, like Stevenson, in virtue of the element of grace. Was it this element that fixed the claim even for Byron? It seems doubtful; and the list at all events as we approach our own day shortens and stops. Stevenson has it at present —may we not say?—pretty well to himself, and it is not one of the scrolls in which he least will live.

Henry James
Notes on Novelists (New York: Scribner's, 1914), pp. 24-25

The companionable author, whether great or small in intellectual stature, is of more value to you who possess him than any of his books. I had almost said, than any book. Especially does this appear to be true in the case of Robert Louis Stevenson, who has written no long sustained great work of art, but whose literary production as a whole makes him the fluent, easy, sympathetic, encouraging companion *par excellence*, whom to know, in his good and in his less good, is always a personal and companionable experience. For if he has left us no very great books, he has instead left us himself, and that more completely and confidingly, and hence, to those who like him, more enjoyably, than perhaps any other modern writer. He lives as a part of everything he writes, naturally, without subtlety, though in many a different dress and pose for which his fancy and his genial egotism gave him the zest.

Richard A. Rice
Stevenson: How to Know Him (Indianapolis, Ind.:
Bobbs-Merrill, 1916), p. 3

Let us . . . praise Stevenson for his real determination and for that work of his which we can approve as well as love. To love uncritically is to love ill. To discriminate with mercy is very humbly to justify one's privilege as a reader.

It is sufficient here to maintain that Stevenson's literary reputation, as distinct from the humanitarian aspect of his fortitude, is seriously impaired. It is no longer possible for a serious critic to place him among the great writers, because in no department of letters—excepting the boy's book and the short-story—has he written work of first-class importance. His plays, his poems, his essays, his romances—all are seen nowadays to be consumptive. What remains to us, apart from a fragment, a handful of tales, and two boy's books (for *Kidnapped*, although finely romantic, was addressed to boys, and still appeals to the boy in us) is a series of fine scenes—what I have called "plums"—and the charm of Stevenson's personality. . . .

Stevenson . . . was not an innovator. We can find his originals in Wilkie Collins, in Scott, in Mayne Reid, in Montaigne, Hazlitt, Defoe, Sterne, and in many others. No need for him to admit it: the fact is patent. "It is the grown people who make the nursery stories; all the children do, is jealously to preserve the text." That is what Stevenson was doing; that is what Stevenson's imitators have been doing ever since. And if romance rests upon no better base than this, if romance is to be conventional in a double sense, if it spring not from a personal vision of life, but is only a tedious virtuosity, a pretence, a conscious toy, romance as an art is dead. The art was jaded when Reade finished his vociferous carpet-beating; but it was not dead. And if it is dead, Stevenson killed it.

Frank Swinnerton
R. L. Stevenson (New York: Doran, 1923), pp. 188-90

My tremendous enthusiasm for much of his prose work cannot be matched
. . . by any such feeling for his verse. He himself called his formally published
verse—*A Child's Garden, Underwoods, Songs of Travel, Ballads*—mere
pithy talk in rhythm. In Trudeau's copy of *Underwoods* he wrote:

> Some day or other ('tis a general curse)
> The wisest author stumbles into verse.

Yet to see the best of it as negligible would be another error. Standard anthologies usually give him space and notice, justly enough, in the same
category as Kipling, Henley, Poe. In more fugitive work he often adjusted
verses into grace and connotation or found a string of phrases that cling
significantly to the memory. . . .

He loved great poetry—Virgil, Milton, Marvell—like a mistress, and that
very passion kept him from great affection for his own. He would have been
first to agree that his literary validity would suffer little if he had never
published a line of verse.

But it was very high indeed in other aspects—the thought is always
frustrating—still rising when he died, so it can do without the ultimate
versatility. Few of the prose writers who knew their craft best were poets in
the same class. This validity of Louis's lay in fascinated industry that
warmed words into coming alive in his hands; in devotion so intense that
writer and words grew indistinguishable; in intelligent, organic ambition not
for himself but for his beloved medium. It all culminated—glowing, eccentric, and whalebone-strong—in the parson's glimpse of Janet trampling
the clothes; Pew tapping on the frozen road; Utterson and Poole listening
at the laboratory door; the Durie brothers' quarrel; Hermiston hearing of his
wife's death. . . . If literary fashion, as arbitrary as the cut of next year's
evening gowns, keeps people from reading such things for their own delight
and wonder, the more fools they.

J. C. Furnas
Voyage to Windward (New York: Sloane, 1951), pp. 454-55

ALGERNON CHARLES SWINBURNE
1837-1909

Swinburne's mother was the daughter of the Earl of Ashburnham and his
father was an admiral. As a child he was delicate but energetic. He read
voraciously both before and during his student years at Balliol College,
Oxford. At the university he was inspired by Pre-Raphaelitism in art
and revolutionary ideas in politics. But he was also affected by a desire to
defy social conventions and by a love of alcohol; in 1860 he left Oxford
without having taken a degree. He then spent a part of his time on the

continent. But after 1879 he lived with, and was cared for by—virtually nursed and guarded by—the critic Theodore Watts-Dunton. Swinburne's first volume, in 1860, consisted of two verse plays, *The Queen Mother and Rosamond*. His literary output from then until his death was very great, including *Atalanta in Calydon* (1865), *Chastelard* (1865), *Poems and Ballads* (1866), *A Song of Italy* (1867), a critical study of *William Blake* (1868), *Songs Before Sunrise* (1871), *Bothwell* (1874), a study of *George Chapman* (1875), *Essays and Studies* (1875), *Erechtheus* (1876), *A Note on Charlotte Brontë* (1877), *Poems and Ballads: Second Series* (1878), *Songs of the Springtides* (1880), a volume of parodies, *The Heptalogia* (1880), *A Study of Shakespeare* (1880), *Mary Stuart* (1881), *Tristram and Other Poems* (1882), *A Century of Roundels* (1883), *Marino Faliero* (1885), *A Study of Victor Hugo* (1886), *Locrine* (1887), *Poems and Ballads: Third Series* (1889), *A Study of Ben Jonson* (1889), *The Sisters* (1892), *Astrophel and Other Poems* (1894), *Rosamund: Queen of the Lombards* (1899) and *The Duke of Gandia* (1908). Published after Swinburne's death were *Charles Dickens* (1913), *Posthumous Poems* (1917), and the fragmentary novel *Lesbia Brandon* (1952).

Edmund Gosse and T. J. Wise, eds., *Complete Works* (1925-1927), 20 vols.

Edmund Gosse, *The Life of Algernon Charles Swinburne* (1917)

Samuel C. Chew, *Swinburne* (1929)

PERSONAL

It is only by emphasising his impulse for revolt and his impulse for submission that we can attain to any consistent realisation of his character. It is only by constantly referring his poetry to these two dominant characteristics, or rather to the conflict or balance between them, that we can evolve any useful theory of his literary value.

It will be admitted, I presume, that the most durable of all Swinburne's works are *Atalanta in Calydon*, the "Hertha" group of *Songs before Sunrise*, and the second series of *Poems and Ballads of 1876*. In all these works a perfectly co-ordinated balance between revolt and submission is conveyed.

Harold Nicolson
Swinburne (New York: Macmillan, 1926), p. 16

Years passed. Swinburne's fame increased, but his popularity and magnetism were on the wane. It was discovered that this revolutionary poet held on some points distinctly conservative views; that this great romantic preserved an eminently classic attitude as regards form and the canons of prosody; that his boldest attempts were often a feat of consummate art; that this lyrist and this pamphleteer was also a critic and a scholar. His way of life, which had at one time been wild and irregular, suddenly became deplorably quiet. He had retired to a "dull suburban villa" with a dull friend, and, being now stone-deaf, seemed sealed to all outward influences. Newspapermen and literary gossips, who had so often stated that the poet was at death's door, resented that he should live up to his seventy-third year. His lack of interest in the younger generation was manifest, and Oscar Wilde was an unwelcome guest at The Pines. The older generation, especially, among whom he had created such a sensation grew to dislike and even to hate him as one hates one's old illusions, enthusiasms or indignations. So the legend got about that Swinburne was stale and dull and old-fashioned. It is still current nowadays, and the exquisites of the modern school affect to see in him the last and perhaps the worst of the Victorians.

He was however essentially a modern. He is far more akin to Proust and Gide, Lawrence, Huxley or Joyce than either Tennyson, Browning, Leconte de Lisle, Zola, Meredith or Hardy. He sowed the seeds from which grew Pater, Wilde and the whole decadent school; but he went further than these. In refusing to suppress some of the deepest sexual tendencies of his nature he was un-Victorian; in the simple, straight-forward manner in which he treats and records those impulses, he is as unlike Wilde as is possible. His political ideas are out of date; but his sensibility is modern. And by the way in which he embodied this sensibility in perfect works of art he is the superior of most moderns. This rhetorician was in a sense truer and subtler than Meredith; this romantic, more realistic than Hardy. The time will come when this much will be recognized as the truth concerning the author of *Lesbia Brandon, A Year's Letters, Poems and Ballads*, and *Solomon's Vision of Love*. And it will then be the turn of some of his most recent critics to look old-fashioned.

Georges Lafourcade
Swinburne: A Literary Biography (London: Bell, 1932), pp. x-xi

POETRY AND DRAMA

As a poet, nothwithstanding his genius and labour, it must be said he found the world inhospitable. The measure of praise that he won has gone no further than the acknowledgment of the victory of a poetic power that could not be denied; it has not much increased with years; it has never been adequate, just or intelligent. There is, perhaps, the consciousness of this in the concluding words of his remarks on his collected verse, which he addresses to his friend and house-mate through these latter years: "It is nothing to me that what I write should find immediate or general acceptance; it is much to know that, on the whole, it has won for me the right to address this dedication and inscribe this edition to you." The poet, like all men of simple greatness, is free, it would seem, from the desire for applause, but not from the human want of some loving comradeship in his art. There are, in the wide world, here and there a few—a number that will increase ever with passing generations and is even now perhaps manyfold greater than the poet knows—in whose hearts his poetry is lodged with power.

G. E. Woodberry
Swinburne (New York: McClure Phillips, 1905), pp. 115-17

Swinburne's two long verse narratives show his powers at a height only excelled in a score of his best short poems, since whatever the narrative form refused to him which the lyric could not have done—and that was little—the old tales of Tristram and Balen made up for it, and he interwove with them the richest of his own spirit-stuff. *Tristram of Lyonesse* followed two years after *Songs of the Springtides,* and with them represents a brilliant middle period in Swinburne's art, when, in the earlier forties of his age, he was able to combine the ardour of *Songs Before Sunrise* with the richness of the first *Poems and Ballads.*

Edward Thomas
Algernon Charles Swinburne (London: Martin Secker, 1912), p. 211

None of the obvious complaints that were or might have been brought to bear upon the first *Poems and Ballads* holds good. The poetry is not morbid, it is not erotic, it is not destructive. These are adjectives which can be applied to the material, the human feelings, which in Swinburne's case do not exist. The morbidity is not of human feeling but of language. Language in a healthy state presents the object, is so close to the object that the two are identified.

They are identified in the verse of Swinburne solely because the object has ceased to exist, because the meaning is merely the hallucination of meaning, because language, uprooted, has adapted itself to an independent life of atmospheric nourishment. In Swinburne, for example, we see the word "weary" flourishing in this way independent of the particular and actual weariness of flesh or spirit. The bad poet dwells partly in a world of objects and partly in a world of words, and he never can get them to fit. Only a man of genius could dwell so exclusively and consistently among words as Swinburne. His language is not, like the language of bad poetry, dead. It is very much alive, with this singular life of its own. But the language which is more important to us is that which is struggling to digest and express new objects, new groups of objects, new feelings, new aspects, as, for instance, the prose of Mr. James Joyce or the earlier Conrad.

T. S. Eliot
Selected Essays, 1917-1932 (New York: Harcourt Brace, 1932), p. 285

When Swinburne died in 1909, he had for several years been recognized as the greatest living English poet. He was, however, generally regarded as little more than a master of technique, except by such unusual critics as William Morton Payne. During recent years the traditional complaints of lack of thought and remoteness from human interests have recurred. Writers like Oliver Elton, Edmund Gosse, T. Earle Welby, Harold Nicolson, and Samuel C. Chew have, however, emphasized the preëminence of *Songs before Sunrise* and of Swinburne's later volumes, particularly the second series of *Poems and Ballads*. The poet of liberty has to some extent overshadowed the poet of passion. A superb lyrist he remains. . . .

Time winnows the false from the true. The good that a writer creates is likely to live after him, the evil to perish. We need no longer be shocked by Swinburne's poems. His political views do not now concern us in the same way as they did our fathers. Contemporary criticism is likely to go astray precisely because it is contemporary—and hence temporary, though dealing with permanent values. Religious ideals and social standards change. But beauty transcends all creeds and critical doctrines. Fortunately it cannot be confined by the shibboleths of scholiasts or cabined within the boundaries of a system. As a great lyric poet, in spite of singular limitations, Swinburne is sure of that immortality destined for those shining ones whose names are cherished for their creation of beauty.

Clyde Kenneth Hyder
Swinburne's Literary Career and Fame (Durham, N. C.:
Duke Univ. Pr., 1933), pp. 268-69

CRITICISM

Swinburne has long been out of fashion. Of the great English poets he remains the most unappreciated, and the reasons are not hard to find. Born in 1837, he lived till 1909, surviving by eight years the queen who had acceded to the throne in the year of his birth. His virtuosity was dogma, but his strength had become labor and sorrow, and the glow was gone. The shifting and resettling of taste was seismic, as it had been at the beginning of the nineteenth century, and those who seemed to follow his tracks only drew attention to the change. . . .

Taste, fashion, shifting sensibility, the modern temper, and other theoretical considerations apart, Swinburne has many virtues that have never been adequately recognized. As a translator, for instance, he could have ranked with the great masters. . . .

As a parodist, Swinburne has received a certain amount of recognition but hardly his due. No careful reader of *Specimens of Modern Poets: The Heptalogia* could fail to concede that he is, quite simply (to use his own phrase), the greatest parodist who ever lived. . . .

Swinburne also had satiric and epigrammatic gifts of a high order. He was not a Martial lost in Putney, and he published little that could properly be termed satirical, but if he had set his sights in that direction, he might have won a reputation. . . .

The absurd prose style of his later period requires no comment beyond Edward Thomas' observation that if De Quincey and Dr. Johnson had "collaborated in imitating Lyly they must have produced Swinburne's prose." Yet his early prose was an instrument of beauty. . . .

Swinburne's criticism has rendered several distinct services to literature, and the study of his complete correspondence will make clear for the first time the intimacy of his involvement and the depth and range and sureness of his learning. . . . With remarkable tact, he could separate the good from the bad, the weak from the strong. "In the whole range of literature covered," T. S. Eliot once wrote of the essays on the Tudor and Stuart dramatists, "Swinburne makes hardly more than two judgments which can be reversed or even questioned." The same claim, with not much more qualification, might be made of the whole *corpus* of his criticism. . . .

Swinburne was a thinker. Tennyson, describing him as a "reed through which all things blow into music," failed to point out that in the best poems all things also blow into meaning. These poems nearly always embody "fundamental brainwork," as Rossetti called it, and it is inaccurate and unjust to say that in them the sound obscures the sense: *Atalanta in Calydon; Erechteus*; "The Triumph of Time," "A Leave-taking," "Itylus," "Anactoria," "Hymn to Proserpine," "Ilicet," "The Garden of Proserpine," "Hesperia," and a few others in the first *Poems and Ballads*; the "Prelude," "Super Flumina Babylonis," "Hertha," "Genesis," "To Walt Whitman in America," "Siena," and one or two more from *Songs before Sunrise*; nearly all of *Poem and Ballads*, Second Series, the finest of his volumes of poems: "Thalassius" and "On the Cliffs"; "By the North Sea"; "Tristram of Lyonesse" and "Adieux à Marie Stuart"; several of the exquisite *Century of Roundels*; "A Midsummer Holiday" and "A Ballad of Sark"; "To a Seamew," "Neap-Tide," and all the Border Ballads; "A Nympholept," "A Swimmer's Dream," "Elegy" ("Auvergne, Auvergne"); "The Tale of Balen"; "A Channel Passage" and "The Lake of Gaube."

Cecil Lang, ed.
The Swinburne Letters, Vol. I (New Haven:
Yale Univ. Pr., 1959), pp. xiii, xv-xix

It is unfortunate for Swinburne's reputation as a critic that he failed to arrange a logical presentation of his ideas; but he was not a formal aesthetician. Beneath his flamboyancies we find principles balanced between freedom and control, wisdom and emotion, the ideals for an art created by dedicated men transmuting the resistant materials of an imperfect, various, and sullied world. It is typical of his honesty and perspicacity that he refused to regard criticism as a fine art. He believed that criticism is important and he tried to do literature a service with his own; but he would not rank it with poetry. His critical ends were practical, often journalistic, and feverishly of the moment; in depth of perception and accuracy of judgment, and in a faithful application of his principles, he makes his mark. H. W. Garrod has said, ". . . there is more truth in two pages of Swinburne than in twenty of Taine." Since he moved between a fervent romanticism stimulated by the Elizabethans, by Lamb, Blake, Hazlitt, Shelley, Gautier, and Hugo, and the constants of a classicism derived from Greek literature and from Jonson, Dryden, and Arnold, it has been easy for his readers to miss the fact that his insights were struck from a set of basic critical and aesthetic standards, and that many of his preoccupations were those which continue to aggravate the serious artist well into the twentieth century. To realize the accuracy of this statement, we need only to review Yeats's troubled concern over the fragmentation of life and his quest for "unity of being," his awareness of the divided nature of the arts, of the phases of the creative mind and its enigmatic wavering between the broad spectrum of the subjective and the objective inspirations, and his resolution of the issues between artist and public achieved with no little pain through the assembling of a private mythology. All of these concerns were Swinburne's too. The aim of art, he believed, was to enable both artist and perceiver to transcend the immediate fragmented world and achieve repose, "the supreme pause of soul and sense," as he wrote of Rossetti, "where we feel and accept the quiet sovereignties of a happy harmony and loyal form, whose service for the artist is perfect freedom."

Robert L. Peters
The Crowns of Apollo (Detroit, Mich.:
Wayne State Univ. Pr., 1965), pp. 27-28

ALFRED, LORD TENNYSON
1809-1892

Tennyson was born in Lincolnshire, the son of an abstracted and moody father who was rector of Somersby. In 1827 he and his brother Charles published, anonymously, *Poems by Two Brothers*. From 1828 to 1831 he was at Trinity College, Cambridge, where he met and formed a deep friendship with Arthur Henry Hallam; with Hallam he travelled to Spain in 1830. In the same year he published *Poems Chiefly Lyrical*. In 1832 another volume of *Poems* appeared, to be met by some hostile criticism. A year later, in Vienna, Hallam died. The reception of the poems, but perhaps even more the death of his dearest friend—as *In Memoriam*, the great elegiac poem about death and grief, reveals—so affected Tennyson that he published nothing more during a "ten years' silence," until 1842. Then another volume of *Poems* (in fact, two volumes) appeared. In 1847 the poetic narrative about feminism and marriage, *The Princess*, was published. 1850 was a turning point in the poet's life: he married, he allowed a version of *In Memoriam* to be made public, though at first anonymously; and he was appointed Poet Laureate by Queen Victoria. From this time on his reputation was assured, and Tennyson became one of the most popular of Victorian poets. His volumes of verse include the *Ode on the Death of the Duke of Wellington* (1852), *Maud* (1855), the first four *Idylls of the King* (1859), *Enoch Arden and Other Poems* (1864), *The Holy Grail and Other Poems*, making up four more of the idylls (1869), *Gareth and Lynette and Other Poems*, with two further idylls (1872), two verse dramas, *Queen Mary* (1875) and *Harold* (1876), *Ballads and Other Poems* (1880), *The Cup, The Falcon*, and *Becket*, all plays (1884), *Tiresias and Other Poems*, including the last idyll to appear, "Balin and Balan" (1885), *Locksley Hall Sixty Years After and Other Poems* (1886), *Demeter and Other Poems* (1889), and *The Death of Oenone and Other Poems*, a posthumous volume (1892). In 1883 he was elevated to the peerage as Baron Tennyson. By the time of his death he was widely regarded as the greatest poet of his day, and that judgment has been concurred in by at least a good many modern scholars and critics.

Hallam Tennyson, ed., Eversley Edition (1907-1908), 9 vols.

Hallam Tennyson, *Alfred, Lord Tennyson: A Memoir* (1897)

Paull F. Baum, *Tennyson Sixty Years After* (1948)

Jerome Hamilton Buckley, *Tennyson: The Growth of a Poet* (1960)

PERSONAL

He stands on the edge of the abyss; he looks with faltering eyes into the dark, and the thin voice of death, the sobbing of despair, the cries of unsoothed pain tell him that the dark is not lifeless, that there is something beyond and above and around all, and that the same eternal, awful Power which laughs in the sunlight, which touches the flower with the distilled flush of the heavenly ray, is as present in darkness as in light, and bears upon his unwearied shoulder the infinite multitude of stars and suns, and enfolds all things within himself.

On the one hand beauty, the beauty that triumphs over the petty, busy handiwork of man, and on the other mystery, the mystery from which man comes and into which he goes.

A. C. Benson
Alfred Tennyson (New York: E. P. Dutton, 1907), p. 216

He had a large, loose-limbed body, a swarthy complexion, a high, narrow forehead, and huge bricklayer's hands; in youth he looked like a gypsy; in age like a dirty old monk; he had the finest ear, perhaps, of any English poet; he was also undoubtedly the stupidest; there was little about melancholia that he didn't know; there was little else that he did. . . .

Baudelaire was right in seeing that art is beyond good and evil, and Tennyson was a fool to try to write a poetry which would teach the Ideal; but Tennyson was right in seeing that an art which is beyond good and evil is a game of secondary importance, and Baudelaire was the victim of his own pride in persuading himself that a mere game was

> le meilleur témoignage
> que nous puissions donner de notre dignité.

Thus if Tennyson embarrasses us by picturing Paradise as an exact replica of Somersby Rectory or Torquay, he has at least a conception, however naïve, of a *good* place, and does not, like Baudelaire, insist that its goodness and badness are unimportant, for all that matters is its novelty, to be attained at whatever cost by a cultivation of hysteria with delight and terror.

W. H. Auden, ed.
A Selection from the Poems of Alfred, Lord Tennyson
(Garden City, N. Y.: Doubleday, Doran, 1944), pp. x, xix

Tennyson is Victorian in his ardent, widespread, slightly frightened interest in science. He is Victorian in his religious doubts and fears, in his burning need of reassurance that God is merciful and immortal life is assured. He is Victorian in his attitude to women: an attitude of worship, puritanism and condescension. He is Victorian in his class-consciousness, in his insularity, his jingoism. But he is, above all, Victorian in his sense of mission. For while Tennyson possessed the evident weaknesses of his age, he was also endowed with its strength. His poethood was, to him, a responsibility; his Laureateship was a heaven-sent duty. His gift of words demanded that he should lead his countrymen in the paths of rectitude. In *The Princess* he suggested the true relation between the sexes; in *In Memoriam* he showed the progress of the pilgrim-soul to God. In the *Idylls of the King* he showed sense at war with soul, the virtue of an ideal moral code; in countless narrative and circumstantial poems, in his dramas, in his descriptive verse, he exalted England and patriotism. He felt, as he told Agnes Weld, his niece, that his every word "should be consecrated to the service of Him Who had touched his lips with the fire of Heaven," that he must "speak in God's name to his age." And more: "to try and find out what God had made him to be, and then to resolve to be that very self, and none other, was his constant aim. . . . No man ever came nearer than he did to perfect truthfulness."

Tennyson's sense of mission embraced more than poetry: it included every action of his life. He determined to be a living example of rectitude. Every morning he had prayed God "to strengthen my resolution to embrace all opportunities of doing good, to make me diligent in the duties of my calling." And he had achieved his unparalleled prestige not only by his gift of words, but by his living example: by his domestic felicity, his unswerving morality, his support of the persecuted and promising, his dignity, his spiritual presence, his sense of pastoral dedication. "However we rank him," wrote Stephen Gwynn in 1899, "we are grateful to the man merely for having existed."

After the death of Tennyson, Gladstone asked Jowett: "Whom shall we make Laureate?" and Jowett answered: "Don't make anyone Laureate. Nobody expects it." The Laureateship remained unfilled until 1896. It was an extraordinary tribute to the poet who had conferred an honour on his office. And it was this sense of vocation in life and in art, this sense of heaven-sent mission in deed and in word, that had made Tennyson unique among our Laureates: that had made him the Pre-eminent Victorian.

Joanna Richardson
The Pre-Eminent Victorian (London: Jonathan Cape, 1962), pp. 292-93

In Memoriam

This haunting wail of fear and loneliness piercing at moments through the undertones of *In Memoriam* echoes a note which runs through all the poetry of Tennyson, and which, when once apprehended, beats with pitiful persistence on the heart. It is a cry that mingles with the mystery of wide spaces, of sullen sunsets or of sodden dawns; the cry of a child lost at night time; the cry of some stricken creature in the dark, "the low moan of an unknown sea. . . ."

The age of Tennyson is past; the ideals which he voiced so earnestly have fallen from esteem. The day may come, perhaps, when the conventions of that century will once again inspire the thoughtful or animate the weak. But for the moment, it is not through these that any interest can be evoked. And thus, if we consider it reasonable and right that Tennyson should also stand among the poets, let us, for the present, forget the delicate Laureate of a cautious age; the shallow thought, the vacant compromise; the honeyed idyll, the complacent ode; let us forget the dulled monochrome of his middle years, forget the magnolia and the roses, the indolent Augusts of his island-home; forget the laurels and the rhododendrons.

Let us recall only the low booming of the North Sea upon the dunes; the grey clouds lowering above the wold; the moan of the night wind on the fen; the far glimmer of marsh-pools through the reeds; the cold, the half-light, and the gloom.

Harold Nicolson
Tennyson (Boston: Houghton Mifflin, 1923), pp. 272-73, 302-3

Here at least he speaks his own mind in response to the most significant experience of his life. And yet Tennyson, reading the poem to Knowles, said: "It is a very impersonal poem as well as personal. There is more about myself in 'Ulysses.' . . . The different moods of sorrow as in a drama are dramatically given. . . . 'I' is not always the author speaking of himself, but the voice of the human race speaking through him." Even in this work, then, he thwarts the reader's inclination to suppose that he seriously means what he says. In XXXVII, after an important group of lyrics on the relation between private faith and revealed religion, Melpomene apologizes to Urania for having "darkened sanctities with song":

> For I am but an earthly Muse,
>   And owning but a little art
>   To lull with song an aching heart,
> And render human love his dues.

Similarly in XLVII, after rejecting absorption into "the general Soul" in favor of personal immortality, he reminds us that these lays are merely

> Short swallow-flights of song, that dip
> Their wings in tears, and skim away.

The familiar sequence on the doubts raised by evolutionary science is anxiously broken off in LVII:

> Peace; come away: the song of woe
>   Is after all an earthly song.
>   Peace; come away: we do him wrong
> To sing so wildly: let us go.

He dodges every vital issue that he raises, yet would have us believe that "Like Paul with beasts, I fought with death."

"It's too hopeful, this poem, more than I am myself," said Tennyson to Knowles. "I think of adding another to it, a speculative one, bringing out the thoughts of the 'Higher Pantheism' and showing that all the arguments are about as good on one side as another, and thus throw man back more on the primitive impulses and feelings." It is probably safe to assume that we come closest to Tennyson's real thought when he is not thinking—when he is least systematically argumentative about theology and metaphysics and relies most completely on his subjective emotions. His creed begins and ends in "I have felt."

Hoxie Neale Fairchild
Religious Trends in English Poetry, Vol. IV
(New York: Columbia Univ. Pr., 1957), pp. 113-14

The Prologue to *In Memoramiam* was written last; in fact, it is dated 1849. Quite wisely Tennyson did not try to make the introduction to his elegy like an overture. No matter how hard he might have tried, he would have been unable to summarize or suggest the themes treated in the poem. So instead, the Prologue is the last stage in Tennyson's "way of the soul." The one thing that the Prologue makes clear is that there is no intellectual advance in *In Memoriam*: the dichotomy between faith and science, or between wisdom and knowledge as adumbrated in Section CXIV, remains unresolved:

> We have but faith: we cannot know,
> For knowledge is of things we see;
> And yet we trust it comes from thee,
> A beam in darkness: let it grow.

The progress within the elegy, as the Prologue suggests, is an emotional one; intellectually the speaker is just as uncertain as he was when the elegy began. Faced with a world in which scientific progress was outstripping spiritual progress, the poet desired something of spiritual value to fall back on. But the antagonism between science and religion—and of all English poets Tennyson was probably the most keenly and vitally aware of the scientific advancements in his own day—forbade his intellectual acceptance of a doctrine that could not be proved either through the senses or by the mind. What he learned from the experience of Hallam's death and of elegizing his friend was that no religious assertion is possible; what he does affirm, then, is not God but love. For this reason the Prologue invokes the "Strong Son of God, immortal Love," as evidence that the elegy does not find renewal of faith in God but spiritualizes, indeed Christianizes poetically, the poet's love for Hallam.

Once more Tennyson speaks deprecatingly of the early lyrics in his elegy, calling them "wild and wandering cries, / Confusions of a wasted youth." Undoubtedly he refers not only to the beginning sections of his elegy but also to all his early poetry composed before and soon after Hallam's death. By the time that the Prologue was written and "In Memoriam" finished, Tennyson was ready to say farewell to the subjective vein that had characterized his verses. From this time onward the "I" in his poetry would become "we," and Tennyson as laureate would speak as the official poetic voice of England.

Clyde de L. Ryals
Theme and Symbol in Tennyson's Poems to 1850
(Philadelphia: Univ. Pennsylvania Pr., 1964), pp. 268-69

Maud

The public and the critics were bewildered by the unorthodox *Maud*. The periodical critics attacked strenuously. They disapproved of the metrical experiments and of Tennyson's apparent indorsement of not only the

Crimean War, but war in general. Tennyson undoubtedly meant that the youth found a way to rehabilitate himself in martial immolation for the public good, but the public extended his meaning (about which he had not made himself clear) to include approval of the idea of war.

Gladstone in 1859 condemned *Maud* as the "least popular, and probably the least worthy of popularity," of Tennyson's poems. He pointed out that, contrary to the poem's doctrine, modern war caused more mammon-worship than did peace. But in 1878 Gladstone apologized for not having called attention to the metrical virtuosity of the poem, while overemphasizing its sociological implications. This change in opinion typifies the history of *Maud's* reputation.

But the immediate response was not entirely unfavorable. The poem was praised on publication by Henry Taylor, Ruskin, Jowett, and the Brownings. Edward FitzGerald considered it Tennyson's best poem after 1842. T. S. Eliot reflects modern appreciation of its metrics by saying that *Maud* and *In Memoriam* are examples of "the greatest lyrical resourcefulness that a poet has ever shown." And Roy P. Basler, in his analysis of the poem, illustrates Tennyson's anticipation of many of the concepts of Freud and Jung.

Maud was one of Tennyson's favorites among his own poems. Although his high hopes for it were dashed by the unfavorable reception, he never ceased to defend it. Tennyson was ultra-sensitive about criticism, and especially about criticism of *Maud*. When asked to read his own poetry, he usually chose either *Maud,* the *Ode on the Death of the Duke of Wellington,* or *Guinevere.* He blamed *Maud's* poor reception partially on the inability of people to read his poem properly. He wrote his brother-in-law Charles R. Weld that in order properly to appreciate *Maud*, it was necessary to hear the author read it, because he alone, through his dramatic reading with full voice and ample lungs, could give full effect to the long sweeps of metre. Many testimonials confirming Tennyson's own opinion of his ability to read *Maud* effectively have been left by the poet's friends. Anne Thackeray Ritchie, for instance, said that his reading of *Maud* was like harmonious thunder and lightning.

Later generations have realized that Tennyson was justly proud of his varied metres for the different moods of the speaker. But like *In Memoriam* and *The Princess*, this not-so-long poem is not often read now in its entirety. It is the separate lyrics which appear in anthologies, not the entire poem.

George O. Marshall
A Tennyson Handbook (New York: Twayne, 1963), pp. 130-31

But *Maud*, which meant so much to the poet who read it so passionately and which contains poetry as lovely and technically perfect as any he wrote, has generally been judged to be an imperfect work of art. Most readers will agree with those critics who, like Mr. Eliot, locate its imperfection in the character of the emotion which flows from the frenetic hero. Distorted and disproportionate to its objects as they appear in the poem, the hero's feeling prevents the reader from identifying with him fully and sympathetically, despite the fact that such identification is almost required by the nature of the poem. On the other hand, the poet does not provide any compensating frame of objectifying judgment by means of which the reader might gain more perspective on the hero and thus a more detached but more understanding and compassionate view of him. The autobiographical reasons for this aesthetically unsatisfactory state of affairs are clear. The feelings Tennyson wished to express in the poem were essentially personal, but, because he could not admit that they were, he had to embody them in an ostensibly dramatic story which would obscure, while it yet remained in formulaic correspondence with, the real private objects of experience which had given it rise. The result was that for him and his speaker the queer disjointed story told in the poem had a hidden emotional dimension which it cannot have for the reader, who must remain perplexed and perhaps annoyed by its insistent and inexplicable manifestation in the poem. The dramatic mask brought still other difficulties: it relieved Tennyson of any moderating sense of responsibility (which otherwise he might have felt) for the exaggerated sentiments expressed, while at the same time, perhaps, it encouraged him to still further exaggeration as a means of convincing himself (and others) that it was after all not he but his distraught hero who spoke. Let the hero rant as he chose, Tennyson in his deep sympathy could still see nothing really out of bounds, so that he was in fact surprised and hurt when others did. (His own intense readings of the poem, significantly, almost always greatly increased his audience's feeling for the hero.)

But this brings us to a more basic point: it was not the fact that the poem was drawn from Tennyson's own experience which caused the trouble but the fact that because he was not emotionally free of that experience he saw it in inadequate perspective.

Ralph Wilson Rader
Tennyson's Maud: The Biographical Genesis
(Berkeley, Calif.: Univ. California Pr., 1963), pp. 115-16

The Idylls of the King

"Tennyson," says Matthew Arnold, in that relentless, even voice of his, "with all his temperament and artistic skill, is deficient in intellectual power. . . ."In a word, Tennyson preached too much, without well knowing what to say; and the surplice he dressed his Muse in finally proved her winding-sheet.

Secondly, the charge will run, just as he could not think deeply, he could not feel deeply either. He has no passion, only pathos. *Elaine* or *Oenone* is pathetic, not tragic. *Maud* shrieks when it tries to thunder. "Tears, idle tears, I know not what they mean"— precisely, cries the Devil's Advocate, Tennyson didn't know; but Byron knew, and the tears of Baudelaire were never "idle. . . ."

Thirdly, it will be said, Tennyson cannot create character. His plays, for all the labour they cost him, are long dead and buried now. Nor can Lady Clara Vere de Vere or the Lord of Burleigh pretend to be very lively in the year 1930; they feel their age, poor things.

Nor, fourthly, continues the Denying Spirit, is Tennyson a master of long narrative either, like William Morris. The *Idlls of the King* have no epic quality; their very name betrays them—Malory made into "Idylls"!—the spear of Malory's Lancelot twisted into a china shepherd's crook! Where the action of the story should hurry the reader on, Tennyson's style with its slow, over-polished perfectness is always holding him back, always crying, "Stay a moment; I am so beautiful." And as a picture of the real savagery of the Middle Ages, the *Idylls of the King* are about as adequate as a fancy-dress ball or a parish pageant. "We read at first Tennyson's *Idylls,*" writes Carlyle to Emerson, "with profound recognition of the finely elaborated execution, and also of the inward perfection of vacancy and, to say truth, with considerable impatience at being treated so very like infants, though the lollipops were so superlative. . . ."

That is what the Devil's Advocate says nowadays, when he has troubled to read Tennyson at all; or even when he has not. And what is the answer? The answer is, I think, that the Devil's evidence contains much truth; but not the whole truth; and in fact does not prove his case. Tennyson still remains a great poet, even though he may not have been a great thinker, nor a master of passion, nor of character, nor of long narrative. For he has other gifts, supreme gifts, of eye and ear and tongue. He is a great landscape-painter, and a great musician. He wrote many bad things, calculated to please his own age and now perished with it—so, for that matter, did Shakespeare. But he had style; and style, though it may not at once win the day for a poet, can win him eternity.

F. L. Lucas
Eight Victorian Poets (Cambridge Univ. Pr., 1930), pp. 11-14

In short, what survives in Tennyson is the painter and musician. The same, after all, is true of another great English poet—Spenser (save that Spenser's was a far less varied and a narrower mind). "Tennyson's new book," writes Browning in 1870 of the *Holy Grail* volume, "is all out of my head already. We look at the object of art in poetry so differently! Here is an Idyll about a knight being untrue to his friend and yielding to the temptation of that friend's mistress after having engaged to assist him in his suit. I should judge the conflict in the knight's soul the proper subject to describe: Tennyson thinks he should describe the castle, and the effect of the moon on its towers, and anything *but* the soul." It is like a thrush scratching its head over the queer nocturnal habits of a nightingale. Yet there is no law that poets must prefer souls to moons. Some may feel that Tennyson's moons—such moons as watch the dying Arthur, or Lancelot's coming to the tower of Carbonek—show fewer marks of age by now than most of Browning's souls. Possibly Tennyson was wrong to attempt the *Idylls* at all, for his genius was not epic. But he was hardly wrong to avoid psychology, for his genius was not dramatic either. A writer can seldom do everything: we should be grateful if he is wise enough to concentrate on what he can do well. Yet fault has been found even with Shakespeare for having no new ideas—only verbal witchery. It is always possible to complain of a vine that it does not bear peaches—or Apples of Knowledge.

F. L. Lucas
Tennyson: Poetry and Prose (Oxford Univ. Pr., 1947), p. xv

Whether it be as an escape from actuality through dream or madness, or as an escape into higher truth through vision and the quest, the central emphasis in Tennyson's poetry develops from an inner rather than an outer awareness, from the life of the imagination rather than from a sense of responsibility to society. For the conflict between the appearance of the external world and the reality of the individual consciousness which we have found to be the real theme of the *Idylls of the King* runs through nearly all the more serious poems of Tennyson's later period. . . .

Yet the imagination not only conceives, it also shapes; and so it is that for Tennyson inner awareness finally becomes allied with the artistic act as well as with the apprehension of philosophic truth. The source of all true inspiration is within the intuitional consciousness of the individual. This sense of the immateriality of the outward show, of the strangeness and mystery that always lie just under the appearance of things, of the unknowableness of the human mind in its instinctual perceptions is the germinal impulse in virtually all of Tennyson's best poetry. Hence his uneasy conviction that the age with its obsessive materialism could not really supply him the materials with which to work; hence also his recognition of the subterfuges that were necessary in order to get Victorian society to listen to his message.

For these reasons Tennyson's genius was most at home when employed on traditional legends of proven narrative and moral interest, which could yet be made exemplificatory of deeper implications for the reader who cared to look below the surface.

E. D. H. Johnson
The Alien Vision of Victorian Poetry
(Princeton, N. J.: Princeton Univ. Pr., 1952), pp. 63, 65-66

The *mythagogues* of Tennyson's youth had made Arthur a sun god, a fertility cult hero, and it is possible that Tennyson may be recalling this facet of his hero's character. At any rate, this emphasis, in the various songs, on the natural world is in accordance with the general plan of the *Idylls* in which the events move through the four seasons of the year. A symbolism of natural forces moves through the poem, woods, and waters, storm and mist. . . .

The vision of society led by a hero mysteriously come from the unknown, and of the world of sense commanded by a spiritual power arising from the deep, is crossed and threatened by natural forces. Sometimes, as in Lynette's song, or in the opening of *Guinevere,* they rejoice with the ideal. Sometimes as in the songs of Vivien, and Tristram, though neutral in themselves, they can be used by sinful men, and threaten to corrupt right order.

> This fire of Heaven,
> This old sun-worship, boy, will rise again,
> And beat the cross to earth, and break the King
> And all his Table.

In the last analysis, the natural order itself, being subject to decay, undermines the achievement of Arthur. Reasons are given for the breakup of Logres—Merlin's surrendering his wisdom to the mere sensuality of Vivien, Lancelot's betrayal of honour to sensuality—but the imagery of the creeping year which runs all through the poem suggests that, to Tennyson, the mere fact of being in time ensures a downfall of the ideal itself.

Valerie Pitt
Tennyson Laureate (London: Barrie and Rockliff,
1962), pp. 214-16

GENERAL

Tennyson, though much of his work is no doubt destined to be shed in the course of time, as is so much of all workers except the very greatest, has stamped his name for ever on English literature as *the* poet, the one dominant poet of the long Victorian era, and as one of the chief lyrists in the whole of our poetic roll. He is destined to share with Milton the crown of consummate mastery of poetic diction. As a poet of nature he stands beside Byron, Keats, Shelley, and Wordsworth. Byron is the poet of mountains and oceans, Shelley of clouds and air, Keats of the perfume of the evening, Wordsworth of the meaning and mysteries of nature as whole. And so Tennyson is the poet of flowers, trees, and birds. Of flowers and trees he must be held to be the supreme master, above all who have written in English, perhaps indeed in any poetry. The meanest flower that blows does not inspire in Tennyson thoughts so deep as it did to Wordsworth, but Tennyson has painted them all—flowers, wild and cultivated, trees, herbs, woods, downs, and moors—with the magic of a Turner. He spoke of trees and flowers, from the cedar of Lebanon to the hyssop that groweth on the wall. As flowers, hills, trees, and rivers uttered to Wordsworth a new moral Decalogue, so they seemed to Tennyson, as they did to Turner, radiant with a fanciful beauty which no man had seen before. If we cannot claim for Tennyson the supreme place of a poet of man's destinies, or as one of the creative masters of our literature, he has for ever clothed the softer aspects of the world of man and nature with a garment of delicate fancy and of pure light.

Frederic Harrison
Tennyson, Ruskin, Mill and Other Literary Estimates
(New York: Macmillan, 1900), pp. 46-47

So we may hold that the thought of Tennyson is not so well bestowed in the argumentative poems (like that which Mr. Gladstone refuted in the *Nineteenth Century*) as in some of those where he uses mythology, the legends of *Tithonus* or the *Holy Grail*, to convey his reading of the world. The difference between the two kinds of thought is very great; and the nobler kind is not discourse but vision. It does not lend itself.

One need not be afraid to defend the "thought" of Tennyson on the lower ground either. But there is not much to be gained for his poetry in this way. Much of his reasoning is opinion, as good as that of other thinkers, but not founded as most of Wordsworth's is on certain and irrefragable knowledge. It is generally far above the range of ordinary didactic poetry, but much of it has suffered through lapse of time and the change of fashions, and has become antiquated like the *Essay on Man*. What is least injured in this way, what best retains its value as philosophy, is the poem of the *Ancient Sage*, which is based on experience like that of Wordsworth's; and the wisdom of the *Ancient Sage* is summed up in the sentence that "nothing worthy proving can be proved."

William Paton Ker
Tennyson (Cambridge Univ. Pr., 1909), pp. 24-25

It is probable, then, that Tennyson's permanent place will be with poets like Milton, Pope, and Keats, who—different as they are in many respects —are alike in being distinguished as artists rather than thinkers, and in communicating ideas which they have derived from contemporary movements rather than struck out for themselves. But he is far nearer to Milton than to Pope and Keats, in respect to the fact that his thought, if not highly original, has passed through the imaginative processes of a truly powerful mind. As to his lyric art, which I am not considering here, at its best it need fear comparison with no other poet whatsoever. He can not be to any other generation precisely what he was to his own; on the other hand we have seen that his comparative strangeness to our literary thought is due to certain special tendencies which we may assume to be temporary.

Raymond MacDonald Alden
Alfred Tennyson: How to Know Him (Indianapolis, Ind.:
Bobbs-Merrill, 1917), pp. 366-67

Were an anthology of Tennyson's poetry to be compiled for the purpose of including only such poems as can appeal directly to the literary taste of to-day, the result might well be both curious and illuminating. . . . Were I myself to make such a selection, I should from the first be tempted to reject the *Idylls of the King,* the *Idylls of the Hearth,* or at any rate *Enoch Arden, Dora* and *Sea Dreams,* the "Keepsake" verses, most of the ballads and dramatic pieces, and some of the later theological compositions. I should also, I think, reject both the *Locksley Halls.* On the other hand, I should include all the "Classical" poems, with the exception of *Lucretius* and *The Death of Oenone.* I should include nearly all the early Romantic poems, together with the *Kraken* and the *Ode to Memory*; I should give *The Vision of Sin* and *The Palace of Art* in their entirety; I should include *The Northern Farmer,* while rejecting the other dialect poems; I should give the lyrics from *The Princess* while omitting the main narrative; I should include the whole of *The Two Voices* and *Maud* and nearly the whole of *In Memoriam*; I should give *Boadicea* and the other experiments in quantity; and finally, I should retain practically all the occasional poems, the dedications, epitaphs and such pieces as *The Daisy* and *Will Waterproof's Lyrical Monologue.*

Tennyson, if my guess is right, suffered twenty years of agony. That agony burned up and out in *Maud* with the anger of a great funeral-pyre. Certainly there remained the force that could blaze into *Lucretius* and at the last could write in *Crossing the Bar* a poem as nobly simple as Landor's farewell to life. Nevertheless something died with *Maud* and thereafter Tennyson wrote because he most brilliantly could and not because he could none other.

If so much is admitted, must we then admit that Tennyson is not one of the permanent Thrones of English verse? Must we confess that while Shakespeare's last play was *The Tempest* and Wordsworth grew from strength to strength, Tennyson, falling from his high estate as he aged, abdicated? Emphatically no. There is enough poetry of major beauty and significance in Tennyson to rank him with all but the five or six greatest of all. He came when the Lake School was sinking into silence. For half a century his single flame illuminated a dark and disastrous period of English history—dark and disastrous because it was steadily and remorselessly destroying the old civilization without creating a new.

Humbert Wolfe
Tennyson (London: Faber and Faber, 1930), p. 58

Tennyson wrote to instruct as well as to delight. Consequently the didactic value of his work is uncommonly high. In numerous ways he offers noble lessons on the meaning and conduct of life; while from his luminous mind revealing rays of light fall on the darkest mysteries. He could not, it is true, open up, like Shakespeare, the tragic depths of the human heart; nor did he, after the fashion of Robert Browning, "eat sin like bread and drink iniquity like water" and transmute them into powerful poetry. He was more after the manner of Sir Walter Scott, at home within the orbit of conventional life, though surely not without a touch of his heroic quality; and also like the great Scottish romanticist he found it much easier to rise into the upper reaches of the ethical and the ideal. Still, where and how we find him, he held, and with a tenacity quite his own, that all art, and not the least poetry, must be made subservient to the highest moral and spiritual purposes of life.

William Muir Auld
The Mount of Vision (New York: Macmillan, 1932), p. 10

We admire, as profoundly as our elders did, his gift of language, his power of the swift and often brilliant phrase, his nearly perfect lyric style; we acknowledge his moments of insight; we feel his charm and wonder at his magic. Yet we seem unable to forget the "bad Tennyson," the drossy part. This is in some sense a judgment on him, because he chose to identify himself so closely with the peculiarly transient characteristics of his time, which we, and those who come after us, can comprehend only by means of the historical imagination and with which we can feel little sympathy. An unhappy irony. But it is also a judgment on us if we cannot—or until we can—dissociate his weakness from his strength and cherish the immortal part.

Paull F. Baum
Tennyson Sixty Years After (Chapel Hill, N. C.:
Univ. North Carolina Pr., 1948), p. 296

It was no wonder that learned critics attacked "the poverty of his thought" or that intellectual liberals, like Lord Acton, found his metaphysics airy, his knowledge indefinite and his reasoning loose. But to many others who passed with him through those revolutionary years, the fact that one who could comprehend so clearly the challenge of materialism, was able to maintain with such simplicity of conviction the indispensable elements of spiritual faith, was of immense comfort and significance. When lapse of time enables Tennyson's work to be seen in true perspective, this may well be found not the least important of his contributions to our spiritual heritage. It may also be realized that his instinctive simplicity of approach and concentration on fundamentals, enabled him to foresee, though, like Tiresias, he was powerless to prevent, the disasters which an ill-directed materialism was destined to bring upon the world.

The same simplicity of approach marked the poet's political thought. The "Passion for the Past," which influenced him so powerfully, made him, like Scott, essentially conservative in outlook and gave his love of England a mystical intensity. He was obsessed by the fear, which steadily increased during the latter part of his life, that the weakening of individual morality and religious faith must lead to international chaos, of which, indeed, at the end of his life, he clearly foresaw the imminence. This and his intense patriotism led him to see in the close knitting together of the British Empire, under the guidance of "our crowned Republic's crowning common sense," and in co-operation with the greater republic beyond the Atlantic, the best hope for an orderly development of world progress.

Whatever may be true of Victorian liberalism, even a superficial study of the Victorian press and literature must dispel the obstinately maintained illusion as to the complacency of the age as a whole and of Tennyson its prophet. In fact the period spanned by the poet's life was one of continuous and violent controversy, political, religious and philosophical. Catholic Emancipation; the extension of the franchise; the repeal of the Corn Laws; Chartism and the Continental Revolutions; the shadows falling across Britain's Imperial path from India, from the France of Napoleon the Third, from Czarist Russia, from Fenian Ireland, from the young German Empire; the schism in the Church caused by the Tractarian Movement; the renewal of the Roman controversy which followed the secession of Ward, Newman and Manning; the fierce dissensions accompanying the rise of free thought and agnosticism; the turmoil of scientific discovery and material progress —these form the background against which Tennyson's work and particularly that of the last half of his life, must be studied.

His reactions were in no way tepid or complacent—in fact they exposed him increasingly to attack from the Rationalists, Radicals and Little Englanders. Yet in spite of this, in spite of growing doubts as to the value of the *Idylls of the King*, and of almost universal agreement amongst the critics as to the ineffectiveness of his dramatic venture, he retained unchallenged to the end of his long life the position of National Poet which he had won for himself with *In Memoriam*.

Charles Tennyson
Alfred Tennyson (New York: Macmillan, 1949), pp. 539-41

What saved him, at last, was that he felt his predicament even if he did not thoroughly comprehend it. He saw the crisis of art and society as a war of values, a matter of conscience. He does not theorize about it nor arrive at systematic principles. Yet in viewing the function and origin of conscience, he offers a more complex and subtler insight than T. H. Huxley, who supposed conscience to be merely a social monitor, the inner voice of social obligations. For Tennyson, it is more primitive and more powerful, arising in partly unconscious levels of the mind and presenting to the reason and the will an ambiguous scene of unreconciled motives and values. In Tennyson's anatomy of conscience, our human action upon nature and society meets a crisis of the divided will, which cannot be healed until it frees itself from fantasy and despair. That freedom Tennyson could not really win. His failure accurately represents the continuing crisis of our culture.

Walt Whitman, who liked Tennyson, discerned that "his very doubts, swervings, doublings upon himself, have been typical of our age." The price that Tennyson pays for being a "representative" poet is great. He suffers our disease and our confusion. He triumphs not as a master but as a victim. It is a vicarious role, and upon him we heap our detested sins. If the circumstances of his breeding, his generation, and his temperament had made him a convert to Catholicism, socialism, or theosophy, he might have written more interestingly to us. He might have been admired to the extent that he escaped the general malaise. But he kept to the mid-stream of his culture. As a result, he works out remorselessly the fatal consequences of the romantic tradition, bankrupts its style by his lavish expenditures, and reduces its intellectual ambitions to the accidents of individual perceptions and personal blindness. After him the deluge, the spreading chaos of "modern art." He is one of its makers.

There is no Tennyson tragedy. The themes of frustration can scarcely amount to that, and the tragic order of values is lacking. Besides, the victim himself, though not our father, turns out to be a well-remembered uncle, and no hero. Yet there was in him, as Hawthorne instantly perceived, "the something not to be meddled with," as he moved with the shuffling gait of a man whose injury cannot be healed and who makes of it, by force of will, the secret of his strength.

Arthur J. Carr
UTQ (July 1950), p. 382

If the epithet "major poet" has any meaning, Tennyson cannot be denied the essential attributes of majority: dedication to the poet's calling, command of his medium, range of vision, capacity for growth, magnitude of performance, and place in a tradition as one who, consciously indebted to a literary past, in turn influences the course of subsequent poetry. Tennyson had from the beginning the deepest sense of vocation and the awareness of a verbal power strong enough to compel his unwavering commitment. He mastered his craft by constant exercise and tireless experiment, and his technical successes in many different genres were numerous partly because his productivity was sufficiently ample to allow a large margin for error. Yet his long-sustained dexterity would have been of little avail had it not served the needs of his ever-changing sensibility. Though seldom directly subjective, his work—read as a whole and, as far as possible, in chronological order— is the faithful record of his development from the wondering child of Somersby to the ancient sage of Aldworth, from the aestheticism of the Cambridge period to the moral realism of the *Idylls of the King*, from the social confidence of "Locksley Hall" to the disillusion of its sequel, from the doubt of *In Memoriam* to the quiet assent of the last lyrics. *In Memoriam* runs through a complete cycle of despair and recovery, meaningful in itself as a way of the soul; *Maud* creates its own little world, where love is the one antidote to madness; and the *Idylls* calls into new self-subsistence a mythology in which a social order rises, flourishes, and declines. Still, for all their vitality as separate entities, each of these draws freely on the established conventions of English and classical poetry; each, taking its new place in literary history, looks knowingly back to its antecendents in a similar genre. . . .

The distinction that his critics have repeatedly drawn between the bard of public sentiments and the earlier poet of private sensibilities is ultimately untenable. For there was no real break in Tennyson's career; from the beginning he felt some responsibility to the society he lived in, and until the end he remained obedient to the one clear call of his own imagination. His development depended not on a sacrifice of the personal vision, but on the constant interaction between public knowledge and private feeling. From first to last his best poetry raised a psychological protest against the commonplace fact he knew with the intellect or acutely perceived with the senses. In the perspectives of evolutionary theory, he saw perpetual movement as the law of life; but with all his own passion of the past, he intuited a lost order of values, a peace—both aesthetic and religious—untouched by the bewildering changefulness and relativity of the world.

Jerome Hamilton Buckley
Tennyson: The Growth of A Poet (Cambridge, Mass.:
Harvard Univ. Pr., 1960), pp. 254-55

The Blakean distinction between contrary and negation is basic to Tennyson's perception of the world and thus to his poetry. Every quality, every manifestation of the sensual world, inevitably implies its contrary. It follows that, so long as human life continues, this pair may not finally be resolved to a third term of synthesis. Rather, they exist in constant dialectic tension; they do not destroy each other, as do negations. Life and death, reality and appearance, the unity and multiplicity of "The Mystic": man must recognize and accept their mutual existence, not seeking to simplify them by denying one or the other. He must give each its due until, balanced, "like, unlike, they sing together / Side by side." Thus he achieves a necessary harmony, an apparent stability, in a world he yet knows as a bewildering flux of multiplicity. . . .

Tennyson's world is ever in constant contrary process. As many critics have commented, in nearly every poem reality lies beyond its sensual manifestation. "This double seeming of the single world" is the theme of more than "The Ancient Sage," in which this formula appears. . . . The poet is never certain that he is "heir to all the ages, in the foremost files of time"; in "Supposed Confessions" he asks, "Oh! wherefore do we grow awry / From roots which strike so deep?" He laughed pityingly at the story of a Brahman who had smashed a microscope which showed him animalcules fighting in a drop of water. "As if we could destroy facts by refusing to see them," he commented. "Nature, red in tooth and claw" is always behind his hope, almost a plea, that man may realize the highest within himself. Without this hope, he felt, man would find life impossible, "reel back into the beast."

Accordingly, in *In Memoriam*, he built his hope into a faith. But it is clear that even in that poem the reconciliation of contraries is not a final answer. Section CVI ("Ring Out, Wild Bells") is, in its context, as desperate as it is triumphant, an incantation designed to create hope as much as a prophecy of its realization. Its mixture of faith and a larger fear was set forth long before the old man of the second "Locksley Hall" was to speak of "Evolution ever climbing after some ideal good, / And Reversion ever dragging Evolution in the mud."

Allan Danzig
PMLA (December, 1962), pp. 578, 583

Having no central allegiance the Victorian had no sense of what to exclude —he had, in short, no taste. Swinburne presents us with the poetic apotheosis of bad taste, but for any other poet, for a more serious poet, the position was not less difficult for being largely unrealised.

We need not then attempt to explain or justify Tennyson's failures in terms of too close an alignment with a stodgy public, or again as the result of a fastidious withdrawal from the real problems of his age. The disintegration of a culture under the pressure both of intellectual and social change affected both Tennyson and his readers, and it robbed both of standards of judgment by which to measure their achievement. And yet the measure of

Tennyson's importance is increased by the difficulties of his background. He did not succumb to temptation as Arnold and Swinburne, in their different ways, succumbed. Against the shift and instability of the period he built a central poetic tradition which served his successors as a support. Dr. Leavis quite rightly shows that Yeats emancipated himself from the Tennysonian convention, but the fact remains that the convention was there for Yeats to use and develop until he was mature enough to discard it. It is after all only small poets who allow themselves to be imprisoned by the style and the sensibility of their predecessors, and Yeats was not a small poet. But even the great need support when they begin: the Tennysonian tradition supported not only Yeats but Eliot, whose poetry with its exploitation of associations, its cadences like a tired voice falling to silence, its movement from significant complexes of images to paradoxical balances of words and verbal definitions, is more Tennysonian than perhaps Eliot himself realises. It is the measure of a poet that he expands the possibilities of the language. That Tennyson did so while creating and maintaining a poetic tradition which the first mass audience in the world could accept, and in which it found comfort was in itself, a considerable achievement. That he did so in a cultural situation unpropitious to literature, suggests an unusual greatness.

Valerie Pitt
Tennyson Laureate (London: Barrie and Rockliff,
1962), pp. 269-70

The great gift of Turner and Tennyson to art was the expression of effect in terms of outward objects: each was aware of what T. S. Eliot in his well-known essay on *Hamlet* has called the objective correlative. "The only way of expressing emotion in the form of art," writes Mr. Eliot, "is by finding an 'objective correlative'; in other words, a set of objects, a situation, a chain of events which shall be the formula of that *particular* emotion; such that when the external facts, which must terminate in sensory experience, are given, the emotion is immediately evoked." Turner found it very early, as his drawing of Mont Cenis testifies, and Tennyson was already using the "talking landscape" as early as "Mariana." Thus regarded, Turner becomes the godfather not only of the impressionists (as he is now generally regarded) but also of the abstract expressionists, and Tennyson stands as the major precursor in the first half of the nineteenth century of the modern English symbolists.

In his treatment of certain themes, then, Tennyson is modern; but as I have said, in form he is distinctly nineteenth-century. He inherited a certain artistic tradition and attempted to work with its techniques. Although these techniques had adequately served his predecessors, Tennyson had the misfortune to be born in a time when the old tradition had, under the impact of science, begun to decay. He fully realized the precarious state of his times, and he sought to translate into his art all his misgivings about the society of which he was a part. Yet he had not a suitable means for expressing his disaffection with contemporary society or his desire for a more congenial reality. There is, consequently, a curious texture in Tennyson's art: he is like a man of the mid-twentieth century in the dress of a century earlier. The effect is not ludicrous; rather, it is sad and tensile, as though he were seeking to liberate himself from the bonds of form. His art is melancholy because it looks backward and forward, with regret for a vanished past and often with apprehension to a fearful future.

Clyde de L. Ryals
Theme and Symbol in Tennyson's Poems to 1850
(Philadelphia: Univ. Pennsylvania Pr., 1964), pp. 274-75

WILLIAM MAKEPEACE THACKERAY
1811-1863

Thackeray was born in Calcutta; in 1817, after his civil servant father's death, he was sent to England to be educated. He spent less than a year at Cambridge, travelled to Germany, studied law, and at last devoted himself to the study of art and to journalism. In 1836 he married (his wife was to be confined, six years later, to a mental institution), and the next year he began his career as a writer. Most of Thackeray's work was published serially, often in periodicals, and much of it he himself illustrated. His books, with dates of first (serial) publication, are *The Yellowplush Papers* (1837-1838), *Catherine* (1839-1840), *A Shabby Genteel Story* (1840), *The Great Hoggarty Diamond* (1841), *The Ravenswing* (1843), *The Luck of Barry Lyndon* (1844—revised and published in 1856 as *The Memoirs of Barry Lyndon, Esq.*), *Notes of A Journey from Cornhill to Grand Cairo* (1846), *The Book of Snobs* (1846-1847), *Vanity Fair* (1847-1848), *The History of Pendennis* (1848-1850), *The History of Henry Esmond, Esq.* (1852), *The Newcomes* (1853-1855), *The Rose and the Ring* (1855), *The Virginians* (1857-1859), *The Roundabout Papers* (1860-1863), *Lovel the Widower* (1860), *Philip* (1861-1862), and the posthumously published *Denis Duval* (1864). In 1859 Thackeray became editor of the *Cornhill Magazine*. He died, in 1863, in his London home.

George Saintsbury, ed., *The Oxford Thackeray* (1908), 17 vols.
Gordon N. Ray, *Thackeray: The Uses of Adversity* (1955)
Thackeray: The Age of Wisdom (1958)

PERSONAL

In a profounder respect, too, his life had prepared him to be a novelist by giving him the remoteness that permits perspective. From the day when, as a six-year-old-child, he had left his doting family and traveled half around the world to live among strangers and suffer loneliness and a measure of actual cruelty, he had remained an alien and an onlooker in life. . . . By the time he had survived . . . recurrent blows of destiny, he was justified in regarding life with disillusionment.

And yet he had not become a thorough-going cynic. His cynicism was nothing more than a shell, beneath which his natural generosity and sensitiveness were as active as ever. In his misfortunes he had encountered unselfish kindness as well as cold indifference, and its rarity had made him cherish it all the more. The schoolboy whose intensest delight had been the spangled fantasies of the pantomine had carried over into manhood not only an enthusiasm for the theater in its most implausible extravagances but also a tendency to look at actual life as a serio-comic melodrama.

Lionel Stevenson
The Showman of Vanity Fair (New York:
Scribner's, 1947), pp. 152-53

Vanity Fair

From the beginning of chapter xliv, when Sir Pitt *fils* comes to stay in Curzon Street, to the great catastrophe itself, the artist is thoroughly inspired, the rider has settled to the race, and is getting every possible effort out of the horse. . . . In these hundred pages—they come to about that in closely printed editions—there is not a line, not a phrase that is weak or wrong. There is nothing like them anywhere—one may know one's Balzac pretty well and look in vain for their equal in him, while anywhere else it is simply vain even to look. The variety, the intensity, the cool equal command, are not only unmatched, they are unmatched in novel-literature; and the circumstances preclude their being matched in any other. Most novelists stray into fields where they are strangers, and get hedged or ditched: some keep to known but limited ground and are monotonous. Thackeray here . . . cannot go wrong. The very Sedley-Osborne scenes throw up what is now the main plot—the "splendour and misery" of Becky—like the Porter scene in *Macbeth* or the Fool and Edgar in *Lear*. The visit to Queen's Crawley; the irruption of Becky into the "highest circles"; her double management of Sir Pitt and Lord Steyne; the charade; the plot; its defeat by Lady Jane's innocent agency; the great catastrophe itself; the almost greater negotiations about the duel; the comic justice of the Coventry Island appointment—all these with minor things hardly less wonderful in their way, do the part of the matter. And the manner plays up in unfailing provisions of style and atmosphere, of satire, and pathos, and humour, and "criticism of life. . . ."

Vanity Fair then, is not perhaps Thackeray's best book but it can hardly be denied that it contains his best long passage. And this is almost a book in itself in quantity as well as in quality, for you might print it so as to fill and fill handsomely, one of the usual French volumes in yellow paper covers. When he had finished it, he had not finished his work or taken possesion of all his property: but he had lodged his "proofs," his titles, his diploma-piece—once for all.

George Saintsbury
A Consideration of Thackeray (Oxford Univ. Pr., 1931),
pp. 174-76

Beyond . . . literary influences, however, there were sources for the story in his own life. The opening scene at Miss Pinkerton's Academy reflected something of his early school days in Chiswick; the Indian background of Jos Sedley and Captain Dobbin and the O'Dowds was full of reminiscences of the Thackeray and Becher and Webb clans. A good many of the names and allusions had already appeared in his earlier writings—*The Yellowplush Papers, The Life of Major Gahagan, Mrs. Perkin's Ball.* This habit of carrying characters over from one story to another was evidence of the the strong reality that his creations had in his imagination, and gave them an equally strong reality to any faithful reader. In conjunction with his overt use of well-known persons as models for some of his secondary characters, it gave rise to the assumption that his central ones also were portraits of people he knew.

Out of all these elements was *Vanity Fair* shaped. And whatever uncertainty and experimentation may have befogged its inception, its successive monthly numbers soon established it as an organic masterpiece of fiction, and its author as one of the leading novelists of his time.

Lionel Stevenson
The Showman of Vanity Fair (New York:
Scribner's, 1947), p. 154

Henry Esmond

The History of Henry Esmond, Esq., a Colonel in the Service of her Majesty Queen Anne, written by himself (1852), stands on a separate pinnacle from the rest of Thackeray's novels; though not the greatest, it is the most perfect in shape and style, and it occupies the same position among historical novels by any authors whatsoever. It was most carefully prepared; in fact, it was the first of his novels which he planned in detail before commencing to write. He was almost as familiar with the period chosen as with his own lifetime, and till the eve of his death he nursed the idea of writing a history of the age of Anne. Recently he had been immersed in it afresh in preparing his *Lectures on the English Humorists,* which he published a year later in 1853. It came to him as second nature to write in a style which, without actual archaism, expressed the very mind and soul of the period. In short, the book is written with all the apparatus of a historical memoir by a contemporary, and with an art such as might have been expected of a man of letters who was a friend of Steele and Addison. Though he speaks for the most part in the third person, that man is the autobiographer; and Thackeray succeeded in the difficult task of making him a real, concrete character; Henry Esmond is, in truth, one of Thackeray's great creations.

Ernest A. Baker
The History of the English Novel, Vol. VII
(London: Witherby, 1936), p. 367

Anthony Trollope, who liked to commend an edifying morality in other people's writing, declared that *Henry Esmond* was by far the best of Thackeray's novels. "The lesson," he said, "is salutary from beginning to end. The sermon truly preached is that glory can only come from that which is truly glorious, and that the results of meanness end always in the mean." For that and other reasons he once told Thackeray that *Esmond* was so much his best work that there was none second to it. The latter replied, "That was what I intended." And although at certain other times Thackeray said that he believed *Vanity Fair* was his best work, he is also on record as saying that he was willing to let his reputation stand or fall by *Esmond*. It is to be doubted, however, that he liked it chiefly for its high morality, for he went on to tell Trollope, somewhat jokingly we may presume, that Henry was a prig. Nevertheless many subsequent critics have agreed with Trollope, and of all Thackeray's books *Esmond* has become required reading for school children. George Saintsbury allowed himself to be so transported with delight that he could declare: "A greater novel than *Esmond* I do not know; and I do not know many great books." From this unequivocal praise it will be the duty of this chapter to dissent slightly. Yet if *Esmond* is not Thackeray's greatest novel it is his greatest work of art and certainly one of the best of all historical novels. He attempted a rare and difficult feat and he accomplished it triumphantly.

John W. Dodds
Thackeray: A Critical Portrait (New York:
Oxford Univ. Pr., 1941), p. 160

GENERAL

Thackeray possessed in a greater measure than any other English writer the *style coulant,* which Baudelaire ascribed in dispraise to George Sand. His words flow like snow-water upon the mountainside. He could no more restrain the current of his prose than a gentle slope could turn a rivulet back upon its course. His sentences dash one over the other in an often aimless succession, as though impelled by a force independent of their author. The style, as employed by Thackeray, has its obvious qualities and defects. It is so easy that it may be followed by the idlest reader, who willingly applies to literature the test of conversation. The thread of argument or of character is so loosely held that it need not elude a half-awakened attention. On the other hand, the style must needs be at times inaccurate and undistinguished. The solecisms of which he is guilty, and they are not few, may readily be forgiven. It is more difficult to pardon the frequent lack of distinction, especially as in *Esmond* Thackeray proved that he could write, if he would, with perfect artistry. But the method of his more familiar books seems the result less of artifice than of temperament. He seldom gives you the impression that he has studied to produce a certain effect. An effect is there, of course, facile and various, but beyond his management. He is so little conscious of his craft, that he rarely arrives at the right phrase, thus presenting an obvious contrast to Disraeli, who, often careless in composition, yet sowed his pages with pearls of speech which time cannot dim. But how little do we take away from the most of Thackeray beyond a general impression of gentlemanly ease!

Charles Whibley
William Makepeace Thackeray (New York:
Dodd, Mead, 1903), pp. 234-35

Matthew Arnold did not think him a great writer, though he was impelled to admit, "at any rate, his style is that of one"; all that Ruskin had to say of Thackeray (in "Fors Clavigera") is that "Thackeray settled like a meat-fly on whatever one had for dinner, and made one sick of it"; and to-day, though depreciation of the novelist comes mainly from the decadent school, yet only a few months since one of the most brilliant of the younger novelists stated that he had nothing to learn from Thackeray or Dickens.

It is, of course, easy to point out Thackeray's faults as a novelist. He was often careless; he would kill a character in one chapter and bring him to life again a hundred pages further on, and commit a score of such blunders; and he would often interrupt the narrative to give tongue to his own reflections. "And there is a sermon, and great deal of love and affection from Papa," he concluded a letter to his daughters; and the same remark applies to his books. . . .

When Allingham said to Thackeray that a certain story of Dickens might be improved by a man of good taste with a pencil in his hand, by merely scoring out this and that, "Young man," interrupted Thackeray, affecting an Irish brogue, "you're threading an the tail 'a me coat. What you've just said applies very much to your humble servant's things." Whereupon Allingham and Father Prout protested there was not a line too much in Thackeray's novels, and, as regards the best works of the author, the protest is true. It would be a dangerous precedent for any writer to follow, but in Thackeray's case, had the story been strictly adhered to, the books would have been less fascinating; it is the digressions, the personal touches, the little weekday sermons, that invest the novels with much of their charm— "Like the songs of the chorus," says Mr. Andrew Lang, "they bid us pause a moment over the wider laws and actions of human fate and human life."

Lewis Melville
William Makepeace Thackeray (Garden City, N. Y.:
Doubleday, Doran, 1928), pp. 252-53

Thackeray is the first novelist to do what Tolstoy and Proust were to do more elaborately—use the novel to express a conscious, considered criticism of life. He has generalised from the particular instances of his observation to present his reader with a systematic philosophy of human nature.

It was a great innovation—his unique precious contribution to the development of the novel. And of course it gives his books a force unshared by any, however full of genius, that deal merely with particulars. It may be a narrow view—Thackeray's was—but even a narrow view of so big a subject is something pretty big; only a creative imagination of a high power could work on so large a scale; choose for its ground so huge an area of experience, assimilate to its own colour so different and varied a mass of facts. And the impression it makes on the reader is proportionately formidable. Here is no mere picture of Tom or Dick or Harry, he feels, here is a coherent and considered view of that common man of whom Tom and Dick and Harry are only individual examples. This is how Thackeray looked on his life, this is how I could look on my life if I chose. And he is in consequence stirred to a more serious response than could be raised in him by the record of a mere particular instance. . . .

The truth is—and it is the first truth to be realised in arriving at any estimate of Thackeray's achievement—that he was born in the wrong period. He is the only important Victorian novelist who was. No doubt an age of stricter critical standards would have improved the books of Dickens and Charlotte Brontë; their plots would have been better constructed, their characters truer to actual life. But these would only have been negative improvements; they would not have increased their positive value. For this positive value arises, not from good construction or realistic verisimilitude, but from imaginative force. And for the development of imaginative force no age could have provided more favourable conditions than the Victorian. Thackeray's strength, on the other hand, lies not in imaginative force, but in his power of construction and his insight into the processes of human nature. Moreover, it needs for its full expression an atmosphere of moral tolerance. His genius, in fact, and his age, were always pulling him different ways. And he yielded to the age.

David Cecil
Early Victorian Novelists (Indianapolis, Ind.:
Bobbs-Merrill, 1935), pp. 69, 97-98

This odd mixture of assurance and diffidence was to be seen also in the novel itself. The modest sub-title, labeling it "pen and pencil sketches"; the elaborate pretense that the author was but a "puppet-master," displaying the antics of dolls rather than the behavior of human beings; the ironical asides to the reader, dissociating the author from the serious emotions of the characters —all these were symptoms of embarrassment and efforts to prepare a way of escape if the public and critics should prove adverse. On the other hand, the same sub-title implied that the author ambitiously took the whole of "English society" to be his province; and the pose of the puppet-master and ironic commentator implied that he considered himself an omniscient analyst, aloof from mere mortal limitations. The resulting oscillations between impartiality and prejudice, between sympathy and sneering, between sentiment and cynicism, were bound to exasperate many readers; but the creative power behind the mannerisms was real enough to compel attention for the story and belief in the reality of the personages in spite of the author's own insistence upon their being marionettes.

Few novelists ever had a more thorough apprenticeship. He had learned the art of writing through ten grueling years of journalism for every type of publication and in a wide variety of forms—burlesques, travel-articles, short stories, criticism of books and pictures, factual reporting. His style, while remaining strongly individual, had become flexible, exact, and easy. To be the investigator of English society—whether in the narrow or wide sense of the word—he was qualified by the range of his experience. Birth and education made him at home in the caste which Dickens and many of the other contemporary novelists observed only as outsiders, and yet he had also seen much of the seamy side of life. Without entirely losing his insular notions, he had become more cosmopolitan than his rivals; he knew France as intimately as England, had lived many months in Germany, had thoroughly explored Ireland and the Near East. If great fiction needs to be based on wide knowledge of mankind, he was equipped to produce it.

At the present day the place of Thackeray's novels in the regard of Englishmen, and perhaps also of Americans, has its interest for any historian of critical reputations. Most of the critics whose work achieves print dislike or slight them, and give us the impression that they speak for everybody. . . . On the chance evidence of [a] dozen people, . . . his novels are still honoured and read. . . . To be in and out of the turnstile of a public library is, I claim, a proof that a novel is alive, and well alive. Of Thackeray's novels, *Vanity Fair* and perhaps *Esmond* would by that test be found still in motion.

> Geoffrey Tillotson
> *Thackeray the Novelist* (Cambridge Univ. Pr., 1954), p. ix

The reader's estimate of Thackeray's view of life has much to do with his final evaluation of Thackeray's work. Dr. F. R. Leavis, to whom moral strenuousness and intellectual rigorousness are all-important, dismisses him as "a greater Trollope," since by the standards of "the great tradition" he is judged morally equivocal and intellectually incoherent. Even a sympathetic critic like Mr. V. S. Pritchett cannot bring himself to regard Thackeray's view of life as other than superficial and hence awards him the consolation prize of being "the supreme impressionist among the English novelists." Yet readers from the relaxed, tolerant, workaday world have always thought of Thackeray as a sage and will presumably go on doing so. Joyce Cary speaks for them, when he writes during a discussion of Dickens:

> Thackeray was a strong and wise man. When in his letters he describes himself as weak and procrastinating, we have the measure of his strength, in what he expected of himself. He saw and grimly accepted a treacherous and insecure world where indeed there were love and goodness, but no security for either.
>
> Dickens, far greater in genius, as he was more nervous, more passionate, more sensitive, unbalanced sometimes almost to madness, could not accept Thackeray's world and hated to be reminded of its real existence. He had to live in his dreams, his personal melodrama, drugged with glory, in doses that had to be increased every year.

Certainly Thackeray is a major novelist. He has the essential "density, weight, and richness" to endow his work with "that deep, moving, shaking impact of personality for which we turn to the abiding poets and writers of the world." But at the same time he is a highly idiosyncratic writer, whose books captivate some while they alienate others. Moreover, he is also intensely English, and consequently, as Zola once pointed out, "so difficult to understand" for those who are not his fellow-countrymen. Hence the proportion of his work which remains significant varies greatly from one reader to another. To devoted Thackerayans, who in W. C. Brownell's words "read 'Philip'—or even 'Lovel the Widower'—without finding a dull page," everything that he wrote is absorbing. Professor Tillotson, the most accomplished spokesman for such readers in our time, draws many effective illustrations, indeed, from just these neglected books. The non-Thackerayan who concerns himself seriously with the masterworks of the English tradition will want to know at any rate such representative early stories as "Mr. Deucease at Paris," *The Great Hoggarty Diamond*, "Denis Haggerty's

Wife," and *Barry Lyndon; The Book of Snobs*, because of the influence
it has had on English thought and manners; his four great novels, *Vanity
Fair, Esmond, The Newcomes*, and *Pendennis*; and the best of his ballads, *The Rose and the Ring*, and *The Roundabout Papers*, together with
some sampling from his travel books, *Punch* papers, and letters, for their
revelation of his delightful private character. From the closer winnowing of
those who apply the highest standards of world literature, *Vanity Fair* and
Esmond at least survive; and these two central classics, into which Thackeray put the best of himself, suffice to guarantee his enduring fame.

Gordon N. Ray
Thackeray: The Age of Wisdom 1847-1863
(New York: McGraw-Hill, 1958), pp. 430-31

FRANCIS THOMPSON
1859-1907

Francis Joseph Thompson was born on the sixteenth of December, 1859,
the second son of Charles Thompson, a physician, and Mary Turner Morton. Intending Francis to become a priest, Dr. Thompson, a Roman
Catholic convert, sent him to Ushaw College, near Durham; but after
seven years his teachers decided that, although he had been a good boy
and pious, his absentmindedness, timidity, and poor health disqualified him
for the priesthood.

Then for six years his father sent him to study medicine at Owens College in Manchester, but he was irregular in attendance, preferring the
public galleries, the libraries, and the cricket-field, and failed three times
in his medical examination. While he was attending Owens College, his
mother gave him a copy of De Quincey's *Confessions of an English Opium
Eater*, with the unexpected result that he himself soon began taking opium.
He learned in his medical course hardly more than how to secure the drug.

Failing in further attempts to find a vocation for his son, Dr. Thompson
advised him to enlist in the army. But Francis was unable to pass the
physical examination, and slipped off to London. There he collected books
for dealers, polished shoes, and did odd jobs, falling more and more into
disrepute and sleeping in the streets. A shoemaker and church-warden
rescued him temporarily and gave him light tasks in his shop. There, on
the back of old account books, he scribbled an essay, "Paganism New and
Old," and some poems, which he sent to Wilfrid Meynell, editor of the
Roman Catholic periodical, *Merry England*. Yet even the churchwarden's
patience was exhausted when Thompson let a shutter fall and injure a
customer. After a good many months had passed, he found one of his
poems published in *Merry England*, and wrote to inquire whether there
had been some mistake. Meynell, who had recognized the excellence of
the work of the new contributor and had tried unavailingly to locate him,
arranged for an interview.

Thereupon Thompson came under the loving care of the Meynells, who
secured for him permission to spend a while with the monks of Storrington
Priory. With improved health and self-control, he found a good deal of

energy to write and an opportunity to place poems, reviews, and essays.

His first volume, *Poems*, attracted considerable attention when published in 1893. Though referred to by one critic as "the poet of a small Catholic clique," he was generally regarded as a new poet of genuine distinction. *Sister Songs* (1895), written for the Meynell children, was less sympathetically received. . . .

From 1893 to 1897 Thompson lived near the Capuchin Monastery at Pantasaph in Wales. There he sometimes walked with Coventry Patmore, the Roman Catholic mystic, whose influence is found in *New Poems* (1897), his third and last volume of poetry. His later life was given to journalism and reviews.

Thompson died of consumption on November 13, 1907, and was buried in Kensal Green.

John Wilson Bowyer and John Lee Brooks
The Victorian Age (New York: Appleton-Century-Crofts,
1954), p. 830

Wilfrid Meynell, ed., *Works* (1913), 3 vols.; repr. (1937) one vol.
Everard Meynell, *Life* (1913)

Viola Meynell, *Francis Thompson and Wilfrid Meynell* (1952)

Francis Thompson is one of the greatest mystical poets of English, and therefore of European literature. If one begins the adventurous exploration of the poetry of Christian love, very soon in one's mental travels the focus shifts from English literature to Latin civilization, and that is a rich amalgam of pagan and Christian elements. Donne and Crashaw alone ensure the discovery of the middle ages. Shelley and Patmore will not allow us to ignore Greek sources. In trying to trace the links between the mediæval literature and the renaissance literature one inevitably discovers that half the Greek influence was Asiatic in origin, and that this half has the same character as the decadent pagan art and religion which was absorbed by mediæval Christianity and transmuted into an energizing strength of romance. No appreciative reader of Francis Thompson's poetry can fail to realize the strain of oriental opulence which is that pagan life transfigured by countless poets and mystics.

R. L. Mégroz
Francis Thompson (London: Farber and Gwyer, 1927), p. viii

Thompson's was a bold adaptation of St. Paul's exhortation: "Be ye other Christs." As a poet, he strove to restore the beauty that was creation's before sin defaced it. And in his essay, "Form and Formalism," he boldly states his aim:

> Theology and philosophy are the soul of truth; but they must be clothed with flesh, to create an organism which can come down and live among men. Therefore Christ became incarnate to create Christianity. Be it spoken with reverence, a great poet who is like-

wise a great thinker does for truth what Christ did for God, the Supreme Truth.

Whoever fails to understand this ideal of Thompson cannot hope to grasp the meaning of his poetry or the significance of his portrait.

Terence L. Connolly
Francis Thompson: In His Paths (Milwaukee, Wisc.:
Bruce, 1944), p. 199

ANTHONY TROLLOPE
1815-1882

> One of the most prolific and most popular of Victorian novelists, Trollope was the son of the even more prolific novelist Mrs. Frances Trollope. He combined a successful career in the General Post Office with a life of constant literary labor, writing lightly satirical novels about the country lives of squires and ecclesiastical figures, about politicians and ladies. Among the best-known of his many books are the five Barsetshire novels —*The Warden* (1855), *Barchester Towers* (1857), *Doctor Thorne* (1858), *Framley Parsonage* (1861), and The Last Chronicle of Barset (1867)—the four Plantagenet Palliser novels—*Can You Forgive Her?* (1864), *Phineas Finn* (1869), *Phineas Redux* (1874), and *The Prime Minister* (1876)—*The Eustace Diamonds* (1873), and the writer's frank and lively *Autobiography* (1883).
>
> Michael Sadleir, ed., Shakespeare Head Edition (1929), 14 vols.
> Michael Sadleir, *Trollope: A Commentary* (1927, rev, 1945)

Let is be clear from the outset that Trollope's expression of the mid-Victorian spirit has always the limitation of class and background congenial to his taste. He is the chronicler, the observer and the interpreter of the well-to-do, comfortable England of London and the English shires. The industrial north, whence came the wealth that gave the period prosperity, is beyond his range of vision, and deliberately so. Newman, Darwin, Arnold and Ruskin—with all that these names imply of spiritual struggle, of scientific discovery, of the philosophies of education, of beauty, and of economic ideals—might never have lived in the world he made so peculiarly his own. Wherefore, to speak of Trollope's mid-Victorians is to accept the limits that he set upon himself; to claim for him unrivalled skill as social interpreter is to assume that it is skill within those limits.

When Trollope speaks for mid-Victorianism he does not merely make involuntary expression of the *Stimmung* of his own time. His portrayal of actuality is often literal and conscious, and this particularly with scenes of country-house life, sporting and social. . . .

It has been the great misfortune of the mid-Victorian that, amid the jeers provoked by their few insincerities, their manifold virtues of energy, generosity and self-scarifice have been forgotten. The snobs and the hypocrites were not more numerous among them than in any other generation; but during the mid-Victorian age this small minority sat, by hazard of historical evolution, in seats of prominence and sought by argument to create a moral code from a mere opportunism. Thus it was that the ostentatious *Tartufferie* of the few obscured the quiet merits of the many. Of the thousands of English families who lived their lives in contented and industrious well-being, who from principle alone and by self-denial strove to fulfil their own high standard of personal integrity, no tradition has been formed. Whatever their faults, their heavinesses and their self-delusions, these mid-Victorians were neither slothful nor blasé. To them life brought daily opportunity of adjusting self-indulgence to self-discipline. They held bravely to the pursuit of an ideal; they were warm in their genuine faith, if not in the well-doing of human nature, at least in its capacity for well-doing.

Of this acquiescent but scrupulous section of his countrymen Anthony Trollope is at once the mouthpiece and the unconscious advocate. In the face of his simplicity, his courage and his humour it is impossible to deny to mid-Victorian England qualities none the less admirable for being unspectacular. In Trollope's England is neither portentousness nor rococo ornament; Trollope himself was neither prig nor moraliser. Who shall persist, against the evidence of his work and of his personality, in regarding as hypocritical, purse-proud and vulgar the epoch of which his fiction was so conspicuously a product, of which his *Autobiography* is so unmistakably a voice?

Michael Sadleir
Trollope: A Commentary (Boston:
Houghton Mifflin, 1927), pp. 5, 24-25

It is not the place here to argue whether the modern novel has gained in symbolism what it has lost in matter of fact. Writers like Mr. Arnold Bennett, Mr. Swinnerton, and others are still with us, supplying us with all the facts that we need. But the novelist as poet—the one great advance that the English novel in the last thirty years has made—implies so many added qualities, so many fresh defects, that another world from the definite actual world of Trollope has to be encountered.

This at least we can say, that a certain attitude of almost lazy disappointment in and disapproval of life betrayed by the modern novelist would be altogether foreign to Trollope's view. He knew well how harsh and cruel and ugly life could be, but no experience of his own prevented him from finding life the most inspiriting, man-making, soul-rewarding experience. He savoured it with all the blood in his body from the first years when, neglected in body and despised in soul, he stumped down the muddy lanes to a school that he loathed, to the last years when he knew that his popularity was gone and his race was run.

His satire sprang from his humorous scorn of his own oddities and failures; of that deeper and more modern irony that implies that life has done the individual a desperate and impertinent injury, an irony that has its source in an affronted egotism, he knew nothing at all.

That is why he is the rest and refreshment to us that he is. His affections are natural and logical. He restores our own confidence, calls in our own distrust, laughs at our vanity without scorning us, and revives our pride in our own average humanity.

Hugh Walpole
Anthony Trollope (New York: Macmillan, 1928), p. 199

It is scarcely possible to review or even to assess the work of a man who wrote so much as Trollope wrote, who created so large a world, comprehending people of such variety, and people so completely conceived. So much of what delights must be left out; not only because a thorough analysis of his work would equal his own output in length, but also because much of his quality—quality which showed itself variously in pathos, humour, penetration, delicacy or what one might describe as a sense of human right feeling—cannot best be apprehended through description; it is communicable only from Trollope direct to the reader.

One can only say that Trollope, besides creating a world for his readers, also contrives by his writings to give an added substance to the existing world: he acts as a stereoscope so that the living world becomes more completely three dimensional to us after we have read his books. If the title of artist can be allowed to those who know little about heaven, but who can give greater substance to earth, then Trollope earns that title.

To those who love Trollope this is a matter of only dialectical importance; it is enough for them that he will never fail to divert; to delight with his comedy and acuteness, to stimulate with his wisdom and experience and to open the heart with his tenderness and understanding.

Beatrice Curtis Brown
Anthony Trollope (Denver, Colo.: Alan Swallow, 1950), p. 100

OSCAR WILDE
1856-1900

Unfortunately, Wilde is sometimes thought of primarily as the victim of The Marquis of Queensbury's prosecution in a trial for homosexual offenses. His record includes various triumphs. He was an important figure in the "aesthetic" eighties—at Oxford, in the late seventies, he was inspired by both Ruskin and Pater—he was a witty conversationalist. and an amusing lecturer, in England and America; he was a novelist of sorts (*The Picture of Dorian Gray*, 1891), and, most important, he was a dramatic writer who could produce both the pagan tragedy *Salomé* (1893) and the comedies of high wit, *Lady Windermeres Fan* (1893), *A Woman of No Importance* (1894), *An Ideal Husband* (1899), and *The Importance of Being Earnest* (1899). The last of these is the most enduring play written in the Victorian period and a comic masterpiece worthy to stand with the best works in the English tradition of Congreve and Sheridan.

Works (1908), 14 vols.
Hesketh Pearson, *The Life of Wilde* (1946)

The Importance of Being Earnest

Shakespeare gave to the English stage a comedy as full of poetic passion as great tragic art, Ben Jonson the comedy of humours, and Congreve and his fellows the true comedy of manners, but Wilde in his one masterpiece brought into the same company of excellence the comedy of pure fun.

John Drinkwater
The Muse in Council (London: Sidgwick and Jackson,
1925), p. 229

In spite of the polished brilliance of its paradoxical dialogue and the sure pace of its surprising action, *The Importance of Being Earnest* . . . never transcends, as a work of art, the incomplete or the trivial. Its tone is that of satire, but of a satire which, for lack of a moral point of view, has lost its sting. . . . With more experience as a writer of comedies, Wilde might have outgrown the contemptible destiny of too farcical plots just as he had already outgrown the too contemptibly vengeful destiny of the problem play.

Edouard Roditi
Oscar Wilde (Norfolk, Conn.: New Directions, 1947), pp. 138-39

How is a bubble to be described and analysed? It may burst before you have done more than observed its rainbow lights and perceived how beautifully round it is. . . . To sit down like a man in a laboratory and inspect this play through a magnifying glass is to deprive it of its charm and stamp oneself as a humourless fool. . . . The play is a piece of pure frivolity.

St. John Ervine
Oscar Wilde (New York: Morrow, 1952), pp. 286-87

GENERAL

It is sometimes held that Wilde is saved by his wit. By all accounts it was delightful in private life: in literature there is nothing that reveals more constantly the unsureness of his taste. These slightly withered epigrammatic

impertinences must have been invaluable over the dinner-table, where no
doubt they had served several times before finding their way into print:
but they have an air of incurable social smartness; and of all things social
smartness is the most impossible to combine with the emotional and sensual
intensity at which Wilde is aiming in *Dorian Gray* (This is why his only
consummate success is in farce, in *The Importance of being Earnest*, where
the smartness is part of the fun.) Apart from this intermittent crackle of
epigram, *Dorian Gray* is an utterly humourless book.

Graham Hough
The Last Romantics (London: Duckworth, 1947), p. 200

Wilde does not seem to have believed . . . that only new and confused art-
forms could express the novelty and confusion of modern life. Like Baudelaire, he tended to adhere to traditional forms, even to revive them; he is
more neo-classical, closer to Byron or even Pope, especially in his orderly
handling of narrative, than Tennyson or Browning, much as Baudelaire was
closer to Racine or Malherbe than to Victor Hugo or Musset. And this very
art involves a complex body of critical beliefs which it illustrates more or
less clearly. It is thus for his criticism that Wilde deserves most certainly to
be honored as a master of modern literature.Here, his ideas are clearly and
fully expounded, in all their novelty. Two or three generations of writers
have now been influenced by them, directly or indirectly, either by reading
Wilde or by inheriting various concepts of his esthetics from such disciples
as Stefan George or André Gide. And to realize Wilde's stature as a critic,
we need but return, from his dialogues, to the work of some other critics of
his generation or of the next two decades. Saintsbury is but a reliable and
sensible scholar; Charles Whibley, a charming enthusiast with exquisite taste
but vague principles; Sir Edmund Gosse, a first-class columnist for the Sunday supplements; Sir Arthur Quiller-Couch, an unbelievably sentimental
fuddy-duddy who is content to state that a poem is good because, after
twenty or more years of knowing it, he is still moved to tears by its beauty.

   Matthew Arnold had indeed laid the foundations of a serious and academically sound tradition of English Romantic criticism which became the
heritage, in the Universities, of a number of competent scholars and was
kept alive, in literary journals, by a few more scholarly critics among whom
the most brilliant was perhaps Walter Bagehot. But Ruskin's followers,
almost without exception, had become either sentimental moralizers whose
taste rapidly degenerated into a vague socialism of arts and crafts, or equally
vague esthetes who gasped before Gothic or Renaissance monuments as,
Baedeker in hand, they wandered from Amiens to Venice or from Florence
to Chartres. Most of Pater's followers too, inspired by his tastes rather than
by his few principles, had become archaeologists or classical scholars, or else
rather hedonistic or intellectually irresponsible decadents and impressionists.

In all the confusion of late Victorian criticism, where the soundest sought refuge in mere scholarship and the most perceptive, such as Arthur Symons, often seemed content with a sort of spinelessly enthusiastic literary journalism, Oscar Wilde's ingenious, imaginative and vigorous dialectical thought appears monumental. Few critics in our own more critical age are gifted with his scholarship, his acumen, his stylistic brilliance, his masterful authority that never condescends to the coy false modesty which mars much of Eliot's criticism, and especially with Wilde's sense of philosophical structure, which places him at once in the same class as Matthew Arnold and Coleridge.

Edouard Roditi
Oscar Wilde (Norfolk, Conn.: New Directions, 1947), pp. 5-6

He has become an influence over successive generations of youth. To many thousands of young men and women he had provided a key to at least partial liberation, an opening to new vistas of thought. The very fact that they should pass rapidly beyond "the Wilde stage" is a sign of the stimulating nature of his ideas. And that quality itself arises out of the impulses within his nature which motivated his restless shifting, his apparent inconsistencies and contradictions, all finally united in the search for personal liberation.

For the essential link in Wilde's thought and action, the goal to which all his intentions turn, is to be found in his doctrine and practice of individualism. Around this idea of the individual human being, the autonomous and free personality, all his activities revolve, and from it stem, on one side or the other his apparently contradictory tendencies. At the height of his pleasure-seeking folly, in the depths of his pitiful suffering, in his arrogance and his humility, he still sought the free development of his own self. In the pagan worship of pleasure and the Christian cult of pain he finds alike an essentially personal salvation; but Jesus and the Greek philosophers are valid for him only in so far as they are prophets of individualism, while in the inaction preached by the Chinese sages he sees the way for each man to become perfect. The impulse of art and thought he seeks within, and to the inner world of the imagination he gives a far deeper importance than to the external world of society, which is merely the background against which the individual acts his drama, criticism is primarily a way in which human consciousness can be extended. The general values of social morals he despises, but the code of manners that smooths the intercourse of equal individuals he values, while in Socialism he sees a means to divest the individual of those burdens of property and power which prevent him from realising his own nature. His very debaucheries and follies are means of individual experience, and therefore, while they may be rejected, should never be regretted. Each man, declares Wilde, should seek to make himself perfect, but he can do this only from within, by living in the personal world that has been given to him and by following his own inner laws and impulses.

To this one belief he held consistently in all his apparent inconsistencies of life. It became the standard by which he measured all life and thought and art; it became his single rule of conduct and determined his philosophy.

And, in the last analysis, when we have considered all his various acts and attitudes, it is here that Wilde's real value remains, in his consistently maintained search for the liberation of the human personality from all the trammels that society and custom have laid upon it. All the rest is intentions, the intentions of a man struggling to realise his own greatness, and finding it completely only in failure.

George Woodcock
The Paradox of Oscar Wilde (New York:
Macmillan, 1949), pp. 249-50

AMERICAN LITERATURE

Ray C. Longtin, editor

LOUISA MAY ALCOTT
1832-1888

Born Nov. 29 in Germantown, Pennsylvania, the daughter of Amos
Bronson Alcott; *Flower Fables* written in 1848 (published 1852);
served as a nurse in the Civil War; first novel *Moods* published in 1864;
editor of Merry's Museum, a children's magazine in 1867; other novels
are *Little Women* (1868) and *Little Men* (1871); died March 6, in Boston.

Edna D. Cheney, ed., *Louisa May Alcott: Her Life, Letters and Journals*
(1889)
Madeleine B. Stern, *Louisa May Alcott* (1950)

PERSONAL

In mind and emotion [Louisa May Alcott] never emerged from adolescence. To the end of her brave beneficent life she was a tomboy, gauche
and shy, abrupt and somewhat harsh in manner, covering her inherent
sentimentality with honest affectations of bluntness. One may like her the
better for all this, as millions have done, but the fact remains that she
never grew up; and this fact is one of the first that an adult intelligence
will discover.

. . . The fact itself is patent enough. It is clearly discernible in Louisa's
photographs, in her handwriting, in the style of her prose and verse. Living
almost always among intellectuals, she preserved to the age of fifty-six
that contempt for ideas which is normal among boys and girls of fifteen.
Loving her father and her father's closest friends devotedly, she took not
the slightest interest in the abstract thought of Bronson Alcott, Emerson,
and Thoreau. To her as to her mother "philosophers" were always rather
ridiculous. She seems to have felt, moreover, that love, marriage, and
child-bearing were interruptions of serious business—although she never
quite made out what the serious business of life really is, unless it be
earning a livelihood. When she wrote for and about adults she wrote badly,
because ignorantly. . . . Louisa endured poverty with courage if not with
patience, and she saw human suffering in some of its most terrible and
pathetic forms, but not even these experiences brought her maturity.

Odell Shepard
NAR (Summer, 1938), pp. 392-93

GENERAL

[Bronson] Alcott, a son of a small Connecticut farmer, got an education peddling "notions" in the plantations of Virginia; and he became both a significant personality, and within the province of education, an interesting thinker: in an age that found Spencer too mystical and difficult, he was a walking embodiment of Plato and Plotinus. Louisa, one of his children, grew up in Bronson's household, worshiped Emerson, and looked upon her father as a well-meaning but silly old man. As a result, the daughter of the philosopher reverted on a lower level to the Yankee peddler: she became a hack writer, purveying lollypops and chocolate cordials to the middle-class market. Her realistic judgment and her bitter, merciless tongue were at the service of a childish fantasy: her fiction took the place in politer circles of the new ten-cent shocker.

Of all Louisa Alcott's books only one has survived for us. It is that which was made possible by the poor and abstemious life her father's silly ways had thrust upon his children in Concord. *Little Women* was the picture of a happy childhood: that was all: yet it contained so much of what a starved childhood would hope for that it became universal. Louisa's imagination offered her nothing that she could pit against this memory: with all its scrimping and penury, the reality had been equal to the heart's desire. All America after the [Civil] War turned to *Little Women*: and why? Was it not because the only meaning of their life had been in child-hood? Maturity had nothing to offer them; it was only before they had started to make a living that they had lived.

Lewis Mumford
The Golden Day (Oxford Univ. Pr., 1927), pp. 161-62

In this tale [*Little Women*] Louisa wrote a book for everybody. A story about adolescents, it had a happy reach above and below the magic border-line of fleeting youth. . . . On its first appearance it was read with joy by men and women as well as by girls and boys. If it has been less read by adults since, it is because they have all had the opportunity to read it earlier. . . .

What draws this diverse public is the love-story and the presentation of the home. People have read *Little Women* avidly not only for its high-keyed romance but also for its gentler and quieter drama of the home. *Little Women* is a romance *par excellence* of family affection. Nothing so simple had ever before or has since been attempted, and this simplicity is one of the things that has made the book a classic.

Also it was the first purely American novel. There had been previously colonial novels, Puritan novels, Indian novels, Southern novels, and New

England novels; but no American novel had appeared up to then. *Little Women* was the first novel written that reflected the Union. Considering the sore time in which it was written, the author's abolitionist background, and her earlier writings, its unbiased attitude toward the war bears noticing. . . . It was a war-story which both sides could read. It flowed through the nation, passing all barriers and acting as one of the great healers of the time. The South, which had hated and anathematized Harriet Beecher Stowe, embraced the abolitionist Louisa May Alcott with unreserved warmth and affection. Southern girls were brought up on *Little Women* as generally as were other girls. They had no thought of the author as other than one of themselves. Louisa May Alcott was everywhere regarded as an American author and *Little Women* as an American book.

Katharine Anthony
Louisa May Alcott (London: Cresset Pr., 1939), pp. 172-73

Little Women was not just "a book for girls"; it was also a novel written in a new, fresh, realistic style. The characters are real human beings, warm and full of vitality. There is a kind of reader identification that only a true novelist can effect: no girl, or woman remembering her girlhood, can read about the March sisters without seeing herself as one of them and identifying some of her own problems with theirs. And for background Miss Alcott gave a true and vivid picture of the times in which she lived—one of the novelist's most important functions.

Marjorie Worthington
Miss Alcott of Concord (Garden City, N.Y.:
Doubleday, 1958), p. 209

AMBROSE BIERCE

1842-1913

> Born June 24 in Horse Cave Creek, Ohio. He joined the 9th Indiana Infantry in 1860. He worked in the government mint in San Francisco in 1866, and during this time contributed material to the *Argonaut & Newsletter*. His first short story, "The Haunted Valley," was published in the *Overland Monthly* in 1871. Also in 1871, he married Mary Day and went to England, returning to San Francisco in 1876. In 1887, he wrote the column "Prattle" in the Sunday *Examiner* and became "literary dictator" of the Pacific Coast. *Can Such Things Be* was published in 1893, and in 1897 he became the Washington correspondent for the *New York American*. He disappeared in Mexico in 1913.

> *Collected Works of Ambrose Bierce* (1909-1912), 12 vols.

> Paul Fatout, *Ambrose Bierce, the Devil's Lexicographer* (1951)

PERSONAL

For his exceeding power in invoking images and emotions of the uncanny and supernatural, we had dubbed Bierce the Shadow Maker, and it was into the shadows not only of death but of an unknown death that he was to pass; for it is unlikely that he can now be of the living, and as improbable that we are ever certainly to know the circumstances of his end. So mysterious a going-forth would have appealed with the greatest zest to his sense of the grimly dramatic. It is almost a certainty that he entered Mexico, then war torn, with the hope of finding death. . . .

It has been both affirmed and denied that he was with Villa at the battle of Torreon. Shortly after that time he passed without authentic trace into the unknown. At the close of the war, prospectors, Mexican officers and our own entire consular force were interrogated for news of his fate, but only silence or the vaguest rumors have come back. The latest report is a verbal one, that of a soldier of fortune in one of the Mexican armies, who asserts that to his positive knowledge Bierce was captured by Carranzista irregulars and shot as a spy. Antedating that assertion is the tale of a San Francisco reporter lately out of Mexico City, who claims that in a restaurant there he met the Mexican leader of a guerilla band who told him of their capture, in 1915, near Icamoli, of a tall, ruddy-faced, white-haired American whom they shot in company with several humbler suspects. The reporter states in addition that the officer bore a small snapshot of Bierce, evidently detached from the passport that he was known to have taken out. But the fact that he (the reporter) could not produce this picture, which patently could have no special value in the eyes of its Mexican possessor, casts doubt on the whole story.

However, it is by all odds probable that he was slain by some such band of guerillas and not in battle, nor, despite his sincere championship of the right to suicide, by his own hand. The shadows have closed on his trail and it is of no very great importance where that trail had its end, whether near some humble village of the plain or up in the bare and desolate mountains of Mexico.

George Sterling
AM (September, 1925), pp. 18, 19

The necessity of living up to the part he created for himself in print accounted for many of the attitudes [Bierce] assumed and, moreover, influenced important events in his life. Such characteristic stunts as the keeping of a skull on his desk and the haunting of moonlit graveyards were obviously not to be taken too seriously. More undermining to his character, however, was the temptation to pose always as a stern, implacable castigator of fools. His striking appearance, his military precision, and his quiet assurance of manner all encouraged him to play a role marked by such petty acts as refusing to speak to friends who had disappointed him, declining to shake hands with professional enemies, and "disintroducing himself" from men of whom he strongly disapproved. His pontifical manner in print inevitably carried over into private life, and he often proved a martinet in dealing with the young writers who looked up to him as their "Master." Moreover, his inherent sensitivity, sufficiently pronounced in itself to make him likely to quarrel with those dearest to him, was lamentably accentuated by his weekly pose in print as "Bitter" Bierce. Otherwise, one cannot understand how a man as kind hearted and sensible as his letters show him to have been could have broken violently with almost all of his friends, his devoted and understanding wife, and his talented sons. His official manner came so to permeate his life that in his moments of frankest self-analysis he had difficulty in dissociating the disappointed idealist from "Almighty God" Bierce of the public print.

Franklin Walker
Ambrose Bierce, Wickedest Man in San Francisco
(n. p., Colt Pr., 1941), pp. 11-12

GENERAL

French in effect . . . is Ambrose Bierce, who in his earlier work displayed a power to move his readers that is little found outside of Poe. Reserve he has, a directness that at times is disconcerting, originality of a peculiar type, and a command of many of the subtlest elements of the story-telling art, but lacking sincerity, he fails of permanent appeal. He writes for effect, for startling climax, for an insidious attack upon his reader's nerves, and often, as in his collection entitled *In the Midst of Life*, he works his will. But he is not true, he works not in human life as it is actually lived, but in a Poe-like life that exists only in his own imaginings. In his later years journalism took the fine edge from his art and adverse criticism of his work turned him into something like a literary anarchist who criticized with bitterness all things established. A few of his novels may be studied with profit as models of their kind, but the greater part of his writings despite their brilliancy can not hope for permanence.

Fred L. Pattee
A History of American Literature Since 1870
(New York: Century, 1915), pp. 379-80

It has been said that Bierce's stories are "formula," and it is in a measure true; but the formula is that of a master chemist, and it is inimitable. He set the pace for the throng of satirical fabulists who have since written;

and his essays . . . are powerful, of immense range, and of impeccable diction. His influence on the writers of his time, while unacknowledged, is wide. Rarely did he attempt anything sustained; his work is composed of keen darting fragments. His only novel is a redaction. But who shall complain, when his fragments are so perfect?

Vincent Starrett
Ambrose Bierce (Chicago: Walter Hill, 1920), p. 38

The time when Bierce should have gained a hearing was between 1890 and 1910. His thinking, though not markedly original, was independent and aggressive and today seems somewhat provocative. He saw fairly straight when he looked at actual conditions, and he said very plainly what he saw. His printed resentment met with no general response. Much of what he had to say was implicit in Bellamy's *Looking Backward* which fascinated the multitude with an explicit picture of a communized Boston before communism had become a pariah in the public mind. It was rather more than suggested in Howell's *A Traveller from Altruria* with its strictures on the ways of the fortunate and its flavor of sugar-coated socialism. But Bierce's methods were more direct and his opinions less hopeful. He did not believe in Arcadias or Utopias or Platonic republics. He rejected communism and socialism, and he was as devastating in his comminatory passages as the plain-spoken objectors in the Platonic Dialogues who are set up for the not always convincing rebuttals of Socrates.

Percy Boynton
More Contemporary Americans (Chigago:
Univ. Chicago Pr., 1927), pp. 90-91

. . . I do not think that Bierce was essentially a man of letters. If he had been he would not have let his chance to leave an important body of work behind him escape. He was essentially a man of action who chose to function in letters. He needed something to fight against to arouse his best powers. The mere act of composition gave him small satisfaction. It has been remarked before, that in spite of his worship of his particular manner of expression, he apparently did not find pleasure in working with words. He was not an artist in words the way Walter Pater was, for instance. He regarded his skill in expression in the same way that a swordsman regards his skill with the rapier. It was a convenient weapon with which to dispose of the fools and rogues he disliked.

In spite of all these reservations it is still possible to regard Bierce as one of the most important writers of his day and a significant figure in American literature. He stands out from every other writer of his generation for his independence, for the fact that he spoke out in meeting in no uncertain terms, and for the originality of his thinking.

C. Hartley Grattan
Bitter Bierce (Garden City, N.Y.: Doubleday,
Doran, 1929), pp. 269-70

Ambrose Bierce stands quite apart and alone. He was no naturalist, no dabbler in science or student of economic forces. He saw neither people nor things; his concern was with neither characters nor with the world; he was housed tight with the indefatigable inventiveness of his cruel and somber fancy. One cannot even surmise by what shocking early experience, by what unhealed wound of the soul he was compelled to evoke again and again eerie astonishment and stark horror. The undoubted influence of Poe accounts for little or nothing. No man can write sixty-eight tales concerned with dread and death and all the last indignities of mortality without an inner compulsion. His power cannot be denied. Again and again he strikes the reader with horror and a kind of ugly and gasping awe; the endings of the tales are often on the edge of the unbearable. Nothing written of the horrors of the World War in recent years surpasses in the sheer exposition of either the death of the body or the corruption of the soul the Civil War tales of Bierce. Only these tales are morally and therefore in the last analysis creatively sterile, because Bierce showed himself conscious of no implication and disengaged no idea. The naked horror sufficed him. That is equally true of the civilian tales and of the later collection: *Can Such Things Be*? He had rare moments of introspective insight: "What mortal can cope with a creature of his dream? The imagination creating the enemy is already vanquished; the combat's result is the combat's cause." But these moments are indeed rare. *The Devil's Dictionary* shows a mind neither agile nor incisive; the satiric definitions are commonplace in substance and muddy in expression. Bierce fancied himself a great radical, but he could not think to the root of any matter. Neither was he an artist in prose. His manner just carries his substance; the dreariest *clichés* did not trouble him. His gift lay wholly in producing that appalling assault upon the nerves by a curt and ingenious presentation of the horrible. That a definite taste for this sort of thing persists is attested by the existence of the Grand Guignol theater in Paris. It is the taste of weary and jaded souls. It is genuine enough and though the writers who minister to it are as sterile as the readers who possess it, Ambrose Bierce must in simple justice be ranked high among the masters of cruelty and horror.

Ludwig Lewisohn
Expression in America (New York:
Harper, 1932), pp. 318-19

No reader, thumbing through [Bierce's] twelve volumes of *Collected Works*, can avoid being struck by their monumental disproportion. As if in a last effort to compensate for the good books he might have written, Bierce padded the set with outdated editorials and stale hoaxes and forgotten polemics, disregarding his habitual distinction between journalism and literature. Frequently the degree of animus seems disproportionate to the issue, and usually the style is disproportionately superior to the subject. *Black Beetles in Amber* (1892) aims at the kind of elegant preservation that Pope accorded his enemies in *The Dunciad*, but Bierce's fluent verse seldom rises very high above its occasion. His prose, on the other hand, has a crisp precision which is almost unparalleled among his contemporaries; his puristic standards of usage, which he may have brought back from England are set forth in his little handbook *Write it Right* (1909). America needed, but did not want, a Swift. It needed the sharp reservations of the satirist, armed like Bierce with the weapon of wit. It wanted only the blunt affirmations of the humorist. "Nearly all Americans are humorous; if any are born witty, heaven help them to emigrate!" exclaimed Bierce. Though many of his satirical sketches suggest that Gulliver might have discovered another Brobdingnag in California, one of his essays laments "The Passing of Satire." His points were too fine, his targets too ubiquitous. His phobias included millionaires, labor leaders, women, and dogs. His values were ultimately the negative values of war.

Harry T. Levin
in *Literary History of the United States,* eds. Robert Spiller *et al.,* Vol. I
(New York: Macmillan, 1948, rev. 1963), pp. 1068-69

CHARLES BROCKDEN BROWN
1771-1810

Born January 17 in Philadelphia, Pennsylvania; he was apprenticed to a Philadelphia lawyer in 1787, but gave up law for literature in 1793, in which year he drifted between Philadelphia and New York. In 1798, he published *Alcuin: A Dialogue* and *Wieland*; in 1799, *Arthur Mervyn*, *Ormond*, and *Edgar Huntley*, and also edited *Monthly Magazine* and *American Review* in New York. *Clara Howard* and *Jane Talbot* were published in 1801. In 1804 he married Elizabeth Linn and entered trade with his brothers, but continued to write as a journalist. He died February 22.

The Novels of Charles Brockden Brown . . . , (1827), 7 vols.

Harry R. Warfel, *Charles Brockden Brown, American Gothic Novelist*, (1949)

He failed to meet the requirements of fiction of a high order; he created only a few strong characters; he was discursive and stilted in diction. . . . In extenuation, we must remember that these novels were written when Brown was a young man—for he was only thirty when the last appeared; that he wrote with fatal rapidity; and that he lacked the wisdom of rejection and the aid of critical advice. In his mature life he repented, too mournfully, of these early novels, and repressed the fancies with which his imagination was stored. Without question, his mind and imagination could produce effective scenes. The author's temperament, especially shown in his youth and early manhood, and his proneness to attacks of melancholy and gruesome fancies, explain largely the characteristics of his fiction. To these individual traits must be added the fashion of the day in literature and his attempts to follow the English imaginative writers who were favorites of the hour.

Annie R. Marble
Heralds of American Literature (Chicago:
Univ. Chicago Pr., 1907), pp. 304-5

[Brown's] books, if they seem to us the crude expression of youth, are the expression of a literature's youth no less than an author's. In workmanship he is far from inefficient, for all his paired adjectives and overbalanced clauses. His language seems to us prolix and pretentious only if we go to it direct, instead of from the reading of his British predecessors. The "penalty" that he paid as citizen of a youthful democracy was more than compensated for: whatver one may think of the British critic's sneer, apropos of Poe, that "Americans are never safe from the pitfalls of a language that is older than their nation." Moreover, Brockden Brown was found remarkable—even in his day and generation—for writing in a style that is nervously instinct with repressed energy. His sentences are short— at times, like most modern writer's monotonously so; but experiment, even literary experiment, is better than stagnation. And yet, immensely inferior to Poe and Hawthorne as artist—a circumstance that might almost be taken for granted—he is inferior to all great story tellers in his sacrifice of universal truth to the situation, the moment. His weird tales never transcend the plausible without always attaining even that quality. What Hawthorne wrote of *Twice Told Tales*—"instead of passion there is sentiment"—applies much more appropriately to *Wieland* and *Mervyn*. Finally, his skilfully presented illusions once explained away, we are left little more than a sordidly mundane reality. In luridness, however, this reality is all-sufficient.

Warren B. Blake
SwR (October, 1910), pp. 435-36

Brown's chief claim to our attention does not lie in what he did, but rather in the preposterous importance which the older literary historians have attached to him. At bottom he was of no more signficance, from the point of view of intrinsic merit or of influence, than Hugh Henry Bracken-ridge. . . .

Brown, fortunately, did not establish a school in American fiction. He left almost no impression at all, not even upon his contemporaries. As Dr. Loshe says, "He remains an interesting, but, as far as novel-writing is concerned, an isolated, figure in the American literature of his time." Godwin and Scott, true enough, borrowed a line or two from him, but many a greater author has borrowed from many a lesser one. To be borrowed from is the least of all literary virtues. What counts is whether a writer is read. Brown was little read even in his life-time. Ten years after his death he was read only by the lazier subscribers to circulating libraries; and today he is completely forgotten by the intelligent reading public, and the literary historians, generally tardy in appraising the true worth of a respectably hollow man, are rapidly catching up with those whom they are supposed to lead.

Charles Angoff
A Literary History of the American People, Vol. II
(New York: A. A. Knopf, 1931), pp. 320, 325

It is true that Charles Brockden Brown, who has the doubtful honor of being the first man in America to try to live by his pen, was more interested in writing books that could sell than in presenting a literature to the new country. His failure came from lack of ability and the colonial habit of mind, not from an attempt to celebrate a nation that was politically preco-cious but socially adolescent, and in its esthetic infancy. He failed because his servile talent could only copy Godwin in ideas and the Gothic romance in plot and atmosphere, and if he is to be read at all, it will only be for his curious perversions of the American scene. He gets space in literary histories that might better be devoted to the state papers, the political controversies, the correspondence, of the really great Americans of his times, and to the faint records of a commencing popular literature of the frontier.

Henry S. Canby
Classic Americans (New York: Harcourt, Brace, 1931),
pp. 60-61

[Brown's novels] are improvisations, and youth is written on their every page. Fatally easy it is to criticise them. He lacked repose, he lacked finish, he lacked the patience that could recast and replan, and he had a stilted Della Cruscan inflation of a style that was extreme even in the ornate period in which they were written. . . . There is another defect, however, more damning. The Englishman John Davis, in his *Travels in the United States* (1798), was the first to point out his utter lack of humor:

> Nature has utterly disqualified him for subjects of humor: Whenever he endeavors to bring forth humor, the offspring of his throes are weakness and deformity. Whenever he attempts humor, he inspires the benevolent with pity, and fills the morose with indignation.

Fred L. Pattee
The First Century of American Literature
(New York: Appleton-Century, 1935), p. 105

[Brown's] novels strike with a quaint sound on the modern ear. The men and women who move across their pages are a little shadowy, for the creation of character is not Brown's special forte. That admirable repository of virtues, Constantia, never quite comes alive, and even her tears (which for all her fortitude, she sheds on occasion) are not enough to make her credibly human. But the obvious shortcomings of these tales make it too easy to adopt a patronizing tone toward them and their author. They are honest work, of serious intention, and still surprisingly readable as sheer narrative. So good a judge as Peacock did not hesitate to call them . . . "unquestionably works of great genius." It seems likely that they will retain their modest place as minor classics from the brave early years of the Republic.

Ernest Marchand
Ormond (New York: American Book, 1937), p. xliv

Charles Brockden Brown was not a great artist; he had no carefully formulated principles of the art of the novelist; but he did know human nature, both from study and from experience. His wide reading in the literature of England, and, indeed, that of other modern countries, had instilled in him almost unconsciously a sense of the rightness of phrase and the correctness of form in the many genres of literary work. In his keen analysis of human motives and his incomparable powers of observation, Brown possessed the elemental foundations for a great novelist. His gift of discerning the hidden springs of human action was a gift that could not be gained from books or experience—it could only come from nature. No doubt Brown early realized that he possessed such talent, which he felt impelled to increase. Although essentially a recluse, he did move among men, and his spongelike senses absorbed all they touched. It was this ability to take in all at one glance that was at the bottom of his power to lay bare the heart of his characters under storm and stress, to create with a Defoe-like realism scenes as powerful as are to be found in any writer, and to picture vividly appropriate physical background against which to portray the high-minded villains, his men of soaring passions and fascinating intellects.

But with this strength there was weakness: Brown's inability to make his characters live. They are shadowy figures moving about in a strange, unnatural world, driven by the weird forces of heaven and earth. Their creator pushes them at will; almost never are their actions the result of the inevitable workings of their own impulses. The scenes in which they move live vividly in the reader's mind long after the names of the characters are forgotten. Then, too, while Brown had the power to build up incomparable scenes and striking episodes, he was never able to resolve those scenes and give them artistic meaning in the whole scheme of the work. They stand out too frequently as mere episodes independent of the main plot. The reader in the end comes to think of Brown as the creator of great scenes, and not the writer of great novels.

David Lee Clark
Charles Brockden Brown (Durham, N. C.:
Duke Univ. Pr., 1952), p. 193

Arthur Mervyn . . . is a cynical book. But the emotions, the operation of mind, back of cynicism are more complex than those that go with mere terror and physical shock. In *Arthur Mervyn* Brown broke out of the mode of psychological melodrama and worked toward a broader and more disturbing image of life. He turned the corner, we may say, from Gothic romance to the more varied prospect of the nineteenth-century novel—a considerable achievement. From another viewpoint we might choose to say that through his steady interest in the perverse irregularities of actual human conduct he challenged the eighteenth century classifications of human nature and psychology. From yet another (not unrelated) we might see his work as creating an image of society and human character as they will be found anywhere, even in America the new found land, that profoundly challenged the new republic's assumptions of progress and civic virtue, its instinct for optimism. But we could not usefully assert any of these things if the novel were as artless as Brown's fiction is usually made out to be. *Arthur Mervyn* is stamped with the seriousness and integrity, and the vitality, of Brown's own intelligence, qualities that make his writing, despite all that divides and discourages us from it, worth our renewed attention.

W. B. Berthoff
AQ (Winter, 1957), pp. 433-34

For the haunted castle and the dungeon [of the Gothic tradition] Brown substitutes the haunted forest (in which nothing is what it seems) and the cave, the natural pit or abyss from which man struggles against great odds to emerge. These are ancient, almost instinctive symbols, the *selva oscura* going back to Dante and beyond, while the cave as a metaphor for the mysteries of the human heart is perhaps as old as literature itself. . . . No reader . . . can fail to perceive that the symbol of the cave is prompted by motives deeper than a mere devotion to the national scene, that it represents with special aptness the black trap of man's own secret guilt and fear. . . .

It should be noticed that the shift from the ruined castle of the European prototypes to the forest and cave of Brown involves a shift not just in the manner of saying what the author is after. *The change of myth involves a profound change of meaning.* In the American gothic, that is to say, the heathen, unredeemed wilderness and not the decaying monuments of a dying class, nature and not society becomes the symbol of evil. Similarly not the aristocrat but the Indian, not the dandified courtier but the savage colored man is postulated as the embodiment of villainy. Our novel of terror, that is to say (even before its founder has consciously shifted his political allegiances), is well on the way to becoming a Calvinist exposé of natural human corruption rather than an enlightened attack on a debased ruling class or entrenched superstitution. The European gothic identified blackness with the super-ego and was therefore revolutionary in its implications; the American gothic (at least as it followed the example of Brown) identified evil with the id and was therefore conservative at its deepest level of implication, whatever the intent of the authors.

Leslie Fiedler
Love and Death in the American Novel
(New York: Criterion Books, 1960), pp. 147-48

WILLIAM CULLEN BRYANT
1794-1878

Born Nov. 3 in Cummington, Massachusetts. *The Embargo* was published in Boston in 1808. He spent one year at Williams College in 1810, and in 1815 was admitted to the bar. He married Frances Fairchild in 1821, during which year *Poems* was published at Cambridge. He became joint editor of the *New York Review* in 1825, assistant editor of the *New York Evening Post* in 1827, and editor-in-chief in 1829. *Poems* was published in New York and London in 1832; *The Fountain and Other Poems* (1842); *The White-Footed Deer and Other Poems* (1846); *Letters of a Traveller* (1850); *Thirty Poems* (1864); *The Iliad of Homer* (1870); and *The Odyssey of Homer* (1871). He died June 12.

Parke Godwin, ed., *The Poetical Works of William Cullen Bryant* (1883), 2 vols.; *Prose Writings of William Cullen Bryant* (1884), 2 vols.

Harry Houston Peckham, *Gotham Yankee: a Biography of William Cullen Bryant,* (1950)

POETRY

There is only one code of honor for the artist—to be true to his vision. Bryant preferred to lead a comfortable life, and be a good journalist rather than a poet, and so he descended from the serene nobility of *Thanatopsis* to the puerile pieties of the *Hymn to the Sea, The Future Life, The Crowded Street* and many other truly orthodox utterances. Even *The Forest Hymn,* perhaps the best of these, says merely the proper and expected thing, offering bland counsels of moderation. . . .

If the passions were indeed the enemies of this poet's "feeble virtue," they never got the upper hand. At least they do not appear in his poetry. It is said that Mr. [William Jennings] Bryan pronounces *To a Waterfowl* the finest American poem—a preference which marks the limitation of his reading or taste; but this, which is no doubt Bryant's best lyric, is also marred by the ever-present and expedient moral. The famous "Truth crushed to earth" quatrain from *The Battlefield* is the only bit of his poetry, after *Thanatopsis,* in which his religiosity rises for a moment to higher ground and assumes something of prophetic dignity.

Bryant was, in short, a man born to be a poet who sacrificed the muse, not to those violent enemies, the flesh and the devil, but to that more insidious one, the world—or, in other words, comfort and respectability. Now and then a brief flash of inspiration disturbed his placidity, but gradually the light went out, until, in his tone-imparting old age, he could not even see that he was sitting in darkness.

Let us be careful whom we honor with monuments. Build one to Poe, who was true to his art whether drunk or sober; to Whitman, who never sold out even to pay his debts; to Whistler, whom neither wrath nor ridicule could swerve from his purpose; to any starveling who keeps faith with the muse and scorns a respectable old age: but not to the deserter, the wearer of ribbons, the tone-imparter.

Harriet Monroe
Poetry (July, 1915), pp. 199-200

. . . Bryant is not one of the world's master-poets. It is not so much that he contributed little or nothing to philosophic thought or spiritual revolution, not altogether that his range was narrow, not that he never created a poem of vast and multitudinous proportions, drama, epic, or tale, not that he knew nature better than human life and human life better than human nature, not that he now and then lapsed from imaginative vision into a bit of sentiment or irrelevant fancy—not either that there is not a single dark saying, or obscure word, construction, allusion, in all his verse, for the judicious to elucidate at a club or in a mongraph. He is not one of the world's master-poets, because he was not pre-eminently endowed with intellectual intensity and imaginative concentration. The character of his whole mind was discursive, enumerative, tending, when measured by the masters, to the diffuse. Thus, among other results, his report of things has given man's current speech but few quotations, of either epigrammatic criticism or haunting beauty. A book could be written on this thesis, but a paragraph must suffice. It is just as well: it is better to realize what Bryant was than to exploit what he was not. [ca. 1917]

William E. Leonard
in *Cambridge History of American Literature*, Vol. I
(New York: Macmillan, 1946), pp. 275-76

Bryant was once thought to be not only our first poet in time but also in degree; today it is clear that two such different men as Poe and Emerson have both surpassed him. Bryant is little read today, although a few of his pieces are imperishable. But his place in American literature is secure, for the following reasons: He is the Father of American Poetry: He is pre-eminently our poet of Nature: He is a master of blank verse: He is a teacher of peace and rest.

There is an elemental quality in his work, that is lacking often in more brilliant writers. His poetry is clear and cold like a mountain lake, and seems to come from an inexhaustible source. There are times when we find him colourless, for he will never satisfy the love of excitement. But in certain moods, when we are weary of doubt and struggle, weary of passion and despair, weary also of cant, affectation, and the straining for paradox —then there is a pleasure in his pathless woods. His calm, cool, silent forests are a refreshing shelter. Some of us, like Hamlet, are too much in the sun; Bryant is a shadowed retreat.

William Lyon Phelps
Howells, James, Bryant and Other Essays
(New York: Macmillan, 1924), pp. 29-30

Conservative in the use of stanzaic devices, careful with his rimes, and an adaptor of such old meters as the alexandrine, poulter's measure, and the eight-stress line, Bryant was, nevertheless, abreast of the times in his defense and use of trisyllabic substitution, in his breaking away from the tyranny of the heroic couplet, and in his deliberate attempt to work out a versification which fitted his needs rather than to shape his message to conform to an inherited verse technique. He is eminently important in the history of American versification because his technique was finished, effective, and truly artistic. Of all American poets, his achievement is most nearly comparable to and worthy of Wordsworth himself.

Gay Wilson Allen
American Prosody (New York: American Book, 1935), p. 52

Misled by [the] changes in American life, by Bryant's own final mediation, and even by such superficial considerations as his patriarchal appearance and august manner, literary historians have often failed to view him in true perspective. Rather, they have read the moderation of these last years into his entire career and have wrongly attributed to him, from first to last, a cold heart and an illiberal brain. The authentic Bryant, viewed historically in his own generation, was not only a sober moralist but an impassioned defender of democracy, an enlightened religious liberal, an early American exponent of Romantic theory, and a discoverer and an exploiter of Romantic themes. Of all these achievements, most ecstatic and therefore most memorable was his discovery of external nature. As passing generations ignore and then forget many aspects of Bryant's work, they remember and ever will remember that he was the poet of Hampshire hills and Berkshire streams, "pulsing" in Whitman's phrase, "the first interior verse throbs of a mighty world—bard of the river and of the wood, ever conveying a taste of open air."

Tremaine McDowell
William Cullen Bryant: Representative Selections
(New York: American Book, 1935), p. lxviii

In spite of manifest deficiencies in Bryant, there are . . . great compensating merits. He had the quality essential to poetic success, a sense of form; and his deficiencies in ideas, diction, and imagery are less important than they might otherwise be because of a highly personal yet valid means of dramatization. Certainly, as do most poets of any time, Bryant wrote much that is worthless. Not a little of such dispensable stuff still appears in anthologies, partly through custom and partly for biographical and historical reason. But if we go to the best of his poetry and use a taste critically fastidious, we find in Bryant a pleasure and a power. He has his place on Parnassus, surely; and what is more, he still speaks to us from it.

George Arms
The Fields Were Green (Stanford, Calif.:
Stanford Univ. Pr., 1953), p. 19

[Bryant's] form and manner are dictated by the analogies and correspondences which the poet, in all his faith in natural order, knows are there. By definition, the dream he interprets cannot be a nightmare. He does not suffer toward his discovery of such analogies and correspondences. He does not have to register his own sense of them. Unlike Wordsworth, he does not have to attend to the intrinsic quality of the scene; unlike Emerson, he does not have to attend to the intrinsic quality of his own response. He finds what has been put there for him to find—neither the scene nor a sense of himself as being somehow involved in the scene, but rather a compound of the two; it is a compound whose authority is guaranteed by the stability and fixity of Nature and its products. His is a cautious, comforting orthodoxy, adapted to the capabilities of the least of his readers.

Roy Harvey Pearce
The Continuity of American Poetry (Princeton, N. J.:
Princeton Univ. Pr., 1961), pp. 208-9

GENERAL

Since [Bryant's] death a serious injustice has been done him by the critics, who have dwelt too exclusively on his work in the field of verse to the neglect of other work in fields perhaps quite as significant. The journalist has been forgotten in the poet, the later democrat who spoke for American liberalism has been displaced by the youthful versifier who described American scenery. For this our belletristic historians, who are so impatient of any incursions into matter of fact, are to blame. Yet to ignore so much of Bryant results in underestimating him, and this serves to explain the thin and shadowy quality of his present reputation. He was a much larger man and more significant than the critics have made him out to be. His active and many-sided life is very inadequately expressed in the slender volume of his verse, excellent as much of that is. The journalist and critic who for fifty years sat in judgment on matters political and economic as well as cultural, who reflected in the *Evening Post* a refinement of taste and dignity of character before unequaled in American journalism, was of service to America quite apart from his contribution to our incipient poetry. He was the father of nineteenth-century American journalism as well as the father of nineteenth-century American poetry. In the columns of the *Evening Post* the best liberalism of the times found a place, inspired and guided by Bryant's clear intelligence. The lucidity of his comment and the keenness of his humanitarian criticism set the editor apart from shriller contemporaries, and made him a power for sanity in a scurrilous generation. But with his death the evanescent character of even the highest journalism asserted itself, and with the fading of his journalistic reputation the earlier Bryant of *Thanatopsis* shouldered aside the Bryant of the *Evening Post,* and an unconscious distortion of his career began, a distortion made easier by the fact that no outstanding work of the later period remained to restore the balance.

Vernon Louis Parrington
Main Currents in American Thought, Vol. II (New York:
Harcourt, Brace, 1930), p. 238-39

GEORGE WASHINGTON CABLE
1844-1925

Born October 12 in New Orleans, Louisiana. The death of his father in 1859 forced him to support his family. In 1863 he enlisted in the 4th Mississippi Cavalry. In 1869, he married Louise S. Bartlett, and in 1871, wrote a column for the *New Orleans Picayune*. He began to write stories and sketches for *Scribner's Monthly* in 1873. His subsequent works— *Old Creole Days* (1879); *The Grandissimes* (1884); and *Silent South* (1885)—aroused Southern resentment for his outspoken views on Reconstruction. Eventually, he moved to Northampton, Massachusetts and there became involved in Home-Culture Clubs and wrote primarily on religious and reform subjects. In 1899, however, he returned to writing romances with *Strong Hearts* and continued with several other volumes of romance until 1918 when *Lovers of Louisiana* was published. He died January 31.

No standard edition of works.

Arlin Turner, *George Washington Cable, a Biography* (1956)

PERSONAL

Cable proclaimed his preference for colored people over white and assumed the inevitable superiority—according to his theories—of the quadroons over the Creoles. He was a native of New Orleans and had been well treated by its people, and yet he stabbed the city in the back, as we felt, in a dastardly way to please the Northern press.

Grace King
Memories of a Southern Woman of Letters (New York:
Macmillan, 1932), p. 60

While memories of the Reconstruction era were still fresh in the South, Cable had launched a determined campaign in behalf of civil rights for Negroes. His efforts were met by a flood of abuse in his section, some of it astonishingly virulent and crude. He was called a traitor to the South, a bastard son attacking for personal gain the sacred institutions of his region. Yet for ten years he continued the debate, exhausting every means within his reach to bring a just solution to the great sore problem. He lectured, he wrote essays, he organized a group of prominent Southerners to publish their views.

Thus at the middle of his career Cable became embroiled in the affairs of his time as few authors have ever done. His convictions were so clear and his devotion to humanitarian reform was so strong that he turned from a satisfying campaign for prison reform and pushed his literary work to the back of his desk while he embarked on a course he knew would set him at odds with the normal spokesmen for his section. He chose this course deliberately and persisted in it against the advice of respected friends. When the cause had been lost as a practical matter, in the early 1890's, he abandoned it regretfully and channelled his reform efforts in the last thirty years of his life to home culture clubs and garden clubs in his new home, Northampton, Massachusetts.

Arlin Turner
George W. Cable (Durham, N. C.: Duke Univ. Pr., 1956), p. ix

GENERAL

As [Cable] was the son and grandson of slaveholders, is it not strange that he should in his *Silent South* and *Freedman's Case in Equity* accord to the blacks social equality with the whites? Born and bred in the land of the Creoles, is it not singular, to put it charitably, that he should have so misrepresented them in his *Creole Days*? Living where the convict lease system was in vogue, knowing as he did the good as well as the bad features of this system, why did he give only a one-sided view to mislead those already prejudiced against it? His Southern friends wondered at this and were disappointed in him. The South, so often misrepresented by Northern writers, felt this blow more keenly, as it was dealt them by one professing to be of their number. He has been called a renegade by some, and many bitter things have been said about him by his own people. . . .

No one can doubt Cable's artistic ability. His style is pure, simple and unadorned, and throbbing with life. He really opened a new field in the world's literature, and to him is largely due the credit of preserving the traditions of a fast vanishing civilization.

Mildred L. Rutherford
The South in History and Literature (Atlanta, Ga.:
Franklin-Turner, 1906), pp. 501, 503

This collection [*Old Creole Days*], together with *Madame Delphine* the sum total of his really distinctive short stories, owes its charm not alone to quaintness and strangeness of materials. It is as redolent of Cable as *The Luck of Roaring Camp* is of Harte. Cable's technique and his atmospheres may have been influenced by the French, but his style—epigrammatic, Gallic in its swift shiftings and witty insinuations, daintily light, exquisitely pathetic at times, exotic always in its flavour of the old Creole city so strange to Northern readers—all this is his own. No one has excelled him as a painter of dainty femininity, as a master of innuendo and suggestion, as a creator of exotic atmospheres. Whether his backgrounds are realistically true we do not ask, and whether his characters are actual types we do not care. They are true to the fundamentals of human life, they are alive, they satisfy, and they are presented ever with exquisite art. *Old Creole Days* stands unique, one of the undisputed masterpieces in the realm of the short story. [ca. 1917]

Fred L. Pattee
in *Cambridge History of American Literature*, Vol. II
(New York: Macmillan, 1933), p. 384

George Washington Cable deserves mention apart from the other popularizers of the Southern gentry, for he more than the other writers of this school has associated himself with a definite region and in his treatment of that region has preserved some flavor of its pioneer past. The pioneer past of Louisiana, Cable's chosen territory, is a Latin past, Cable renders that past rather less justice than does the less well-known raconteur of French America, Grace King, who appreciates to the full the Parisian quality of New Orleans. Cable, although a soldier in the Confederate army (or perhaps *because* he fought on the losing side in the Civil War) throws in his lot with the angels and never misses a chance to correct the fascinating charm, the rollicking gaiety of his Louisiana by the intrusion of impeccable Puritan and abolitionist sentiments. Lafcadio Hearn, himself a dabbler in the legends of New Orleans, hailed *The Grandissimes* as "the most remarkable work of fiction ever created in the South." But in this as in *Old Creole Days* and *Strange True Stories of Louisiana,* the sympathies of the writer are with the quadroons and free men of color for whom he pleads a full social recognition, with the Grandissime of the New South who shamelessly goes into business partnership with his quadroon bastard brother, rather than with the Grandissime of the Old South who holds tenaciously to his belief that "the yankee government is a failure, a driveling failure," and who dies with the cry upon his lips, "Louisiana forever!" But while Cable extols the "progressive" régime which obliterates lines of class and color, he employs for decorative purposes the characters and settings of old Creole society. It is something that the Old World fragrance of that decaying society has been preserved even in the pages of an unsympathetic critic; but always it is a musty fragrance, a decorative, not a vital, element in modern life. [ca. 1927]

Lucy Lockwood Hazard
The Frontier in American Literature
(New York: Barnes and Noble, 1941), pp. 76-77

Like Lafcadio Hearn, [Cable] did not have the creative type of mind. His inspiration had to be fed by continuous surface impressions of the life around him—new turns of phrase, new incidents. These he could fashion into books with all the ingenuity and meticulous care of a Swiss watch maker. But after he left the South he continued to write about it, although he was cut off from all the impressions he had been accustomed to receive from daily contacts with his models, from all new accretions of picturesque incident. His mind was not sufficiently fertile nor his memory vivid enough to supply his lack; and this was a contributing reason why his later books lacked authenticity and vital interest; why they become pale shadows of his early success. In spite of this Cable will always be remembered for two books, *Old Creole Days* and *The Grandissimes,* and also because he is the legitimate father of the literary movement which is producing such splendid fruit in the South today. Cable first, among Southern writers, treated objectively and realistically the life he saw around him, and was first to break the taboo against writing about the Negro. His courage freed the authors who followed him of the necessity of fulsome praise for all things sectional; taught them their right and duty to analyze and portray truthfully, even, if necessary to criticize, the social conditions under which they and those around them live. All this Cable accomplished at the cost of practical ostracism among his own people; so he may well be called the first martyr to the cause of literary freedom in the South.

Edward L. Tinker
AL (January, 1934), pp. 325-26

The connection between right living and good literature was observed easily and naturally by Cable; the reader never feels that the artist in him is inhibited by conscience. Perhaps Cable was diverted from art to some extent by his social interests, but for the falling off which his writing exhibits the final explanation must lie in the nature of his endowment as a writer. In one word he suffered from the fatal flaw of incoherence. From the time when he published his first story, " 'Sieur George," to the futile efforts of his old age, he constantly proved himself incapable of holding his grip on a long narrative. It may be that he would have done better had he emulated Irving and confined his efforts to the shorter tale. Certainly his *Old Creole Days* is his most nearly perfect volume. Yet the gifts which are concentrated in that volume are scattered so richly through *The Grandissimes* and through even some of his less successful novels that he takes rank as one of the best fiction writers of his day. He had the supreme gift of being able to penetrate a subject—not merely expound it or analyze it or make a report on it. He did not attempt to recreate old New Orleans by forcing facts upon the reader; rather he attempted to liberate the atmosphere which should gradually reveal an earlier civilization. He prevailed by wooing his subject instead of belaboring it. He developed a prose style which was masterful in phrase and cadence but soft in its impact. Its secret was not energy but suasion. The mark of his mastery is his effortlessness. He does not seek to grip the reader by intensity but to win him by a species of venial guile. His gentleness occasionally develops into something very like sentimentality but it is presently turned off into quiet jest or whimsicality. His humor, too, is of the sort which lives in harmony with the narrative it is intended to support instead of insisting on a separate maintenance. In short, Cable was a mature and mellowed artist in a day when the youthfulness of our nation was expressed most frequently with far greater show of vitality. The pattern of his art did not always please the popular fancy. The tendril-like spread of his imagination confused readers who were accustomed to stories more obviously derived from a single stalk of action. Yet for readers less insistent upon rigid organization there is a permanent charm in observing the sensitive processes and natural luxuriance which characterized Cable's writing. Ordinarily grouped with the local color novelists by reason of his priority in treating fully the face and fashion of old New Orleans—from levee to mansion. from quadroon to magistrate —Cable excelled most of his colleagues in the genre. By subtle mixture of his material he achieved a range of hue and a variation of tone quite beyond the powers of most of his confrères, who in many cases were content with the quick application of primary colors.

Alexander Cowie
The Rise of the American Novel (New York:
American Book, ca. 1948), pp. 566-67

There is a good deal of highly effective symbolism in [*The Grandissimes*], mostly having to do with light and dark and the ambiguity not only of racial strains but of reality itself. This symbolism (used with equal effectiveness in American literature perhaps only in *Light in August* and in Melville's *Benito Cereno*) stems from the dread and guilt which remain unconscious in most of the characters but is articulated by Honoré when to Frowenfeld he professes himself amazed at "the shadow of the Ethiopian —the length, the blackness of that shadow." We sit, he says, "in a horrible darkness."

Nevertheless the novel should not be regarded as "symbolistic," despite the recent tendency to re-read the older American fiction as dramas of meaning. We do not have in *The Grandissimes* an epistemological symbolism. The book does not ask the intelligence to concern itself with meaning but rather to grasp and cleave to the concrete conditions of life. We have, as in so many American concrete fictions, a realistic novel tending away from strict realism toward the "romance" by way of melodrama.

The symbols are involved in the intricacies of experience but (as in Cable's ancestral Calvinism) they move, not toward ambiguity and multiple meaning, as in symbolistic art, but toward ideology and dialectic.

Richard Chase
KR (Summer, 1956), pp. 377-78

JAMES FENIMORE COOPER

1789-1851

Born September 15 in Burlington, New Jersey, but moved with his family to Cooperstown, New York, in 1790. He entered Yale in 1802 but was dismissed in 1805, and, in 1806, shipped out and was later commissioned as a midshipman. He resigned his commission in 1810 and married Susan Delancey in 1811. His first book, *Precaution* (1820), was written on a dare from his wife. In the following few years he published *The Spy* (1821); *The Pioneers* (1823); *The Pilot* (1823); and *The Last of the Mohicans* (1826). He left with his family for extensive travel in Europe in 1826 and while abroad *The Bravo* (1831) was published. In 1834 he returned to America and published *A Letter to His Countrymen*. Other works followed: *The American Democrat, Homeward Bound,* and *Home as Found* (1838); *The Pathfinder* (1840); *The Deerslayer* (1841); *Satanstoe* and *The Chainbearer* (1845); *The Redskins* (1846); *The Oak Openings* (1848); and *The Sea Lions* (1849). He died September 14 at Cooperstown.

The Works of James Fenimore Cooper (1922), 22 vols.

James Grossman, *James Fenimore Cooper* (1949)

Personal

Like Hugh Brackenridge before him, Cooper was a democrat who criticized the ways of a reputed democracy because of his love for an ideal republic. Too few of his kind have arisen in America; too few who dare to speak their minds unterrified by public opinion. An individualist of the old English breed, he could not be intimidated or coerced in the matter of his rights by any clamor, whether of newspapers or mobs. He had his shortcomings in plenty, both as romancer and critic. Testy, opinionated, tactless, forever lugging in disagreeable truths by the ears, he said many wise things so blunderingly as to make truth doubly offensive, and he hewed at his art so awkwardly as well-nigh to destroy the beauty of his romance. Yet the more intimately one comes to know him, the more one comes to respect his honest, manly nature that loved justice and decency more than popularity. His daily life became a long warfare with his fellows, who exacted of him a great price for his idealism; but later generations should love him none the less for the battles he fought. That America has been so tardy in coming to know him as a man and a democrat, as well as a romancer, is a reflection upon its critical acumen.

Vernon Louis Parrington
Main Currents in American Thought, Vol. II
(New York: Harcourt, Brace, 1930), pp. 236-37

Leatherstocking Tales

What did Cooper dream beyond democracy? Why, in this immortal friendship of Chingachgook and Natty Bumppo he dreamed the nucleus of a new
society. That is, he dreamed a new human relationship. A stark, stripped
human relationship of two men, deeper than the deeps of sex. Deeper than
property, deeper than fatherhood, deeper than marriage, deeper than love.
So deep that it is loveless. The stark, loveless, wordless unison of two men
who have come to the bottom of themselves. This is the new nucleus of a
new society, the clue to a new world-epoch. It asks for a great and cruel
sloughing first of all. Then it finds a great release into a new world, a new
moral, a new landscape.

Natty and The Great Serpent are neither equals nor unequals. Each
obeys the other when the moment arrives. And each is stark and dumb in
the other's presence, starkly himself, without illusion created. Each is just
the crude pillar of a man, the crude living column of his own manhood.
And each knows the godhead of this crude column of manhood. A new
relationship.

The Leatherstocking novels create the myth of this new relation. And
they go backwards, from old age to golden youth. That is the true myth
of America. She starts old, old, wrinkled and writhing in an old skin. And
there is a gradual sloughing of the old skin, towards a new youth. It is
the myth of America. [ca. 1922]

D. H. Lawrence
Studies in Classic American Literature (London:
Martin Secker, 1924), pp. 57-58

Leatherstocking is the happy product of the romantic movement in literature
and the westward movement in history. He incarnates the best qualities of
both parents. He has the sentiment of the romantic hero without his mawk-
ishness; he has the heroism of the frontiersman without his vulgarity. He
is an idealized frontiersman, not in the sense that any of his qualities are
idealized, but in that the combination of these qualities in one individual
unmarred by their corresponding defects, is possible only to the conscious
selection of art, not to the biological selection of nature. He is a frontiersman, but he is not presented as an inevitable product of frontier conditions.
As if to disarm criticism on this point, Cooper has placed beside him un-
desirable frontier types such as the greedy and unscrupulous Hutter, the
boisterous Hurry Harry, Paul the headstrong beehunter, Ishmael the surly
n'er do weel.

It is by the creation of this character, not by any cinema-like ingenuity
of plot complication, that Cooper's Leatherstocking Tales deserve a place
in the history of American literature and in the literature of American his-

tory. But the creation of character does not make an epic. What constitutes the peculiar significance of the Leatherstocking Tales is that the frontier furnishes a theme as well as a character. [ca. 1927]

Lucy Lockwood Hazard
The Frontier in American Literature (New York: Barnes and Noble, 1941), pp. 112-13

It is of course Natty who holds the five [Leatherstocking] novels together and makes them a related series. Cooper's great success is in large part because he has allowed Natty so much diversity in his unity. Between books he changes abruptly and without explanation; yet even when we suspect that he is responding primarily to the needs of the particular story (for whose sake the very details of his biography are often altered), he seems still to illustrate some law of development and growth. Created before the days of petty truth to local color, he absorbs the habits and traits of entirely different regions when they are convenient, as easily as a hero of ancient myth gathers inconsistent cults to himself. It is true, as Mark Twain complains in his witty but parochial essay, "Fenimore Cooper's Literary Offenses," that Natty at times "talks like an illustrated, gilt-edge, tree-calf, hand-tooled, seven-dollar Friendship's Offering in the beginning of a paragraph . . . [and] like a negro minstrel in the end of it." But this misses completely how much Natty's few and rather limited ideas are enriched by the careless profusion of his means of expression. It is in fact Natty's inconsistency—his incisive statements as "I peppered the blackguards intrinsically like," his mixture of superhuman skill in shooting and disregard of elementary precautions, his fluctuations between philosophic indifference and childish showing off—that makes him emerge from the series a magnificent whole, one of the great rounded characters of American literature.

James Grossman
James Fenimore Cooper (New York: Sloane, 1949), pp. 149-50

For at least one section of the reading public [in 1825], . . . Leatherstocking, like Boone, was a symbol of anarchic freedom, an enemy of law and order. Did this interpretation conform to Cooper's intention in drawing the character?

The original hunter of *The Pioneers* (1823) clearly expresses subversive impulses. The character was conceived in terms of the antithesis between nature and civilization, between freedom and law, that has governed most American interpretations of the westward movement. Cooper was able to speak for his people on this theme because the forces at work within him closely reproduced the patterns of thought and feeling that prevailed in the society at large. But he felt the problem more deeply than his contemporaries; he was at once more strongly devoted to the principle of social order and more vividly responsive to the ideas of nature and freedom in the Western forest than they were. His conflict of allegiances was truly ironic, and if he had been able—as he was not—to explore to the end the contradictions in his ideas and emotions, the Leatherstocking series might have become a major work of art. Despite Cooper's failures, the character of Leatherstocking is by far the most important symbol of the national experience of adventure across the continent. The similarities that link Leatherstocking to both the actual Boone and the various Boones of popular legend are not merely fortuitous.

Henry Nash Smith
Virgin Land (Cambridge, Mass.: Harvard Univ. Pr.,
1950), pp. 60-61

[T]he medium of Cooper's mind was subtle enough to permit an attitude of great complexity to take shape. In his political and agrarian novels he enlarged the scope of the novel itself by introducing ideas in a functional and structural way. These ideas became the very substance of the novels. Important as this was technically in the development of the fictional form, the novels remain very incomplete successes because Cooper's personal feelings and imagination never seem wholly involved. In the Leatherstocking tales the reverse is true. The ideas are not present as such, although they may make their presence felt indirectly. Instead the imagination takes over. Natty Bumppo is not a "character,". . . but a symbol thrown up from the depths of Cooper's own response to America, a response that involved both love and revulsion. Natty's love for the land of America is mystical in its proportions, and yet the civilization she was producing seemed a violation of that land itself. Natty's flight across the continent is an unconscious but profoundly realized symbol of Cooper's own recoil. But whereas in the Effingham novels we are mainly conscious of the hatred Cooper felt for the national manners and ideas that he believed had betrayed America's spiritual obligations and possibilities, in the Leatherstocking tales we are aware of that tolerance and charity that was, after all, the prime mover in his complicated attitude.

Marius Bewley
The Eccentric Design (London: Chatto and Windus,
1952), p. 111

[*The Last of the Mohicans*] was not Cooper's own favorite in the [Leatherstocking] series (he preferred *The Deerslayer*), but it has always been the world's, because in it there is defined almost perfectly the basic myth of Leatherstocking. Not merely are elements scattered through the other four romances here gathered together; the good Indian and the bad, the dark

Maiden and the fair, the genteel lover and the stern, tender-hearted father, the comic tenderfoot and the noble red patriarch; these elements are presented in their pure essences. Natty is nowhere more super-eminently his sententious, cool, resourceful self, Chingachgook nowhere more noble or terrifyingly at home in the woods (and his archetypal meanings are here reinforced by Uncas, Cooper's third mythical character, who makes here his only appearance); while Magua is so essentially the bad Indian, "reptile," "fury," "Devil," and Shylock in one, that beside him Cooper's other villains seem scarcely to exist. Cora and Alice (the names themselves are almost mythical), the passionate brunette and the sinless blonde, make once and for all the pattern of female Dark and Light that is to become the standard form in which American writers project their ambivalence toward women.

No chases are more thrilling and absurd, no movement into danger less credibly motivated, no rescues more hair-raisingly ridiculous, no climaxes more operatic than those of *The Last of the Mohicans*. The scenery is almost totally abstract, archetypal; among unnamed trees, two women and their protectors flee before a sinister pursuit, twice resumed, which takes them to the mythic cave of Charles Brockden Brown, behind a rocky waterfall worthy of Scott, and eventually onto the bosom of a wooded lake (Cooper's very own!), the image of which haunts our dreams but can never be discovered by picknicker or fisherman. And in all the magic woods (sometimes more like those of Shakespeare's *A Midsummer Night's Dream* than any native forest), no mosquito bites, no ant crawls; the charmed underbrush itself relents and will not tear the clothes or mar the looks of the two girls who without soap or comb or brush must maintain their symbolic beauty, light and dark, unblemished. Were one of the actors once to sweat or belch or retire to the bushes to relieve himself, the spell would be broken; we would know that all of them were merely flesh. But nothing gives the game away. The Indians talk like mythic Celts out of *Ossian,* the gentry like Fenimore Cooper remembering the genteel British novel, Natty himself like an improbable blend of stage provincial, backwoods preacher, and instinctive sage. The novel is so all of a piece that reality does not intrude.

Leslie A. Fiedler
Love and Death in the American Novel (New York:
Criterion, 1960), pp. 197-98

GENERAL

An ultra-romantic hero, and a more commonplace hero, matched by the ultra-romantic and the more normal heroines; a villain; and a pedant— these are the people to be met in the best Cooper stories, and as the types are named over, his resemblance or indebtedness to Scott is clear. The world he describes is the frontier, and the plot involves a chase, with one moment of horror. The simplicity of these elements is the index of the writer's character. The inventory of his literary equipment is short; he is neither a great bookman, nor a philosopher, nor a historian; he is nothing but a storyteller. After the fashion of practical minds, he observed and represented life as an experience not necessarily complex; in private life he recognized no situation that a prompt application of the ten commandments would not solve. But he had for humanity at large a vast sympathy, for the expression of which his intellectual equipment was inadequate; and he loved his country with a fervor hardly matched again among American men of letters. It was his patriotism that made his success in literature. Whatever he learned from Scott was changed into something new by the complete Americanism of his mind, and the American landscape, his lifelong passion, colored even his pictures of the Old World. To say that he was not an artist, or that he had no style, is to leave his quality untouched. He had American character, which he stamped on everything he wrote, and which he made familiar to all peoples. Through his pages our gaunt pine forests, our charmed lakes, and our mysterious prairies were added once for all to the geography of the human imagination; in his stories a romantic and fast dying race were rescued to the remembrance of every reading nation, so that through him boyhood the world over "plays Indian"; he created the most typical figure in the novel of his age, the frontiersman, and setting him on the most romantic border our civilization recalls, endowed him with American ideals of justice and efficiency, and with something of American fatalism. Leatherstocking is one of the heroic figures of the world's fiction—one of its prizemen; Thackery spoke truth when he said that Cooper deserves well of us.

John Erskine
Leading American Novelists (New York:
Henry Holt, 1910), pp. 128-129

. . . For James Fenimore Cooper nature was not the framework, it was an essential part of existence. He could hear its voice, he could understand its silence, and he could interpret both for us in his prose with all the felicity and sureness of effect that belong to a poetical conception alone. . . .

He knows the men and he knows the sea. His method may be often faulty, but his art is genuine. The truth is within him. The road to legitimate realism is through poetical feelings, and he possesses that—only it is expressed in the leisurely manner of his time. . . . His sympathy is large, and his humour is genuine—and as perfectly unaffected—as is his art. In certain passages he reaches, very simply, the heights of inspired vision.

Joseph Conrad
Notes on Life and Letters (London: Dent, 1921), pp. 76-77

[Cooper's] qualities as a social critic have usually been made to appear as his faults. His directness and vigor of mind caused an uncompromising attitude which often prevented the immediate effectiveness of his writings, but which tends to increase their permanent value. His appreciation of old-world culture made him restless in an American environment; and the prejudices resulting from his blind idealism and his belief in American principles made him violent in his condemnation of corruption in the post-feudal society of Europe. His method, like those of Milton and Carlyle, was one of convinced enthusiasm rather than of measured logic. His writings are at once a reflection and an interpretation of the emerging American civilization about him.

Robert E. Spiller
Fenimore Cooper: Critic of His Times
(New York: Minton, Balch, 1931), p. viii

If we except *The Water Witch,* a minor but original masterpiece, not flawless, perhaps, but still a unit, we find Cooper to be essentially a man of fragments. . . . He embodies a social ideal that in his own lifetime was so far gone in decay that his defense of it cost him his reputation, and that it may scarcely be said to have survived him to the extent of two decades. He displays at his best a rhetorical grandeur of a kind cognate with his social ideals, but habitual rather than understood, and commonly collapsing for lack of support from his action; that is, he displays a great traditional moral sense corroded by the formulary romantic sentiment of his own period, and apparently with no realization that the two are incompatible. On a few occasions he displays great vigor of conception, as in the creation of such plots as *The Sea Lions* and *The Wept of Wish-ton-Wish,* as in the creation of such characters as Leatherstocking and Jason Newcombe, as in the residual feeling of intimacy with which he leaves one, from perhaps a half dozen of novels, with life in frontier and provincial New York. This is a vigor which has little to do with rhetoric, or at least has to do with it but seldom, and which frequently survives a great deal of bad rhetoric: the figure of Leatherstocking emerges from the debris of the five novels in which he was created, independent, authentic, and unforgettable. . . . For the American who desires an education historical as well as literary, and richly literary instead of superficially, the entire work should be exhumed. It is a mass of fragments, no doubt; but the fragments are those of a civilization.

Yvor Winters
Maule's Curse (Norfolk, Conn: New Directions, 1938), pp. 49-50

The drama Cooper constructed for [his] actors on the spatial scene resulted from his trick of poising that scene upon the very brink of time. In the characteristic adventure of a Cooper novel (it is not to be confused with the "plot . . ."), the personality of the Adamic hero is made to impinge upon the products of time: the villages lying a little inland, or on the safer side of the frontier; social institutions, with their precedents and established practices; relationships inherited through the years, thick with intimate histories; complexities, involvements, and corruptions. These appear concretely as the game laws, for example, in *The Pioneers;* as the secret, suspect, early career of Judith Hutter in *The Deerslayer*; as the mixed domestic, erotic, and military Anglo-American relations in *The Spy*. These are things the hero has to cope with in the course of his dramatic life, but which he must eventually stay clear of, if he is to remain faithful to the spatial vision. . . . In those novels where the setting is the untracked American forest, the world always lies all before the hero, and normally, like Huck Finn, he is able to light out again for the "territories."

The principle of survival in his essential character requires him constantly to "jump off" (this was the current phrase)—to keep, as it were, two jumps ahead of time. This was the notion carried by the popular anecdote whereby Daniel Boone, Natty's historic cousin, was made to complain that "I had not been two years at the licks before a d——d Yankee came and settled down *within an hundred miles of me! . . .*"

. . . [This] though by no means the usual focus of Cooper's tiresome, conventional plots, [is] the index to his real achievement. For in the universe of Cooper, as against that of Brockden Brown, space so-to-speak asserts itself against the onslaught of time, with a vigor that is articulated in the new hero's impregnable virtue—and indeed makes that hero's birth and survival possible. [This is] also the mark of Cooper's one great gift, possibly the one gift indispensable to the narrative artist who aspires to transmute American experience into story: the gift for seeing life dramatically as the measurement by conduct of institutions and the measurement by institutions of conduct.

R. W. B. Lewis
The American Adam (Chicago: Univ. Chicago Pr., 1955), pp. 99-100

Usually [Cooper's] rendition of character and setting is unsatisfactory. In characterizing his people he makes the mistake of reporting their etiquette instead of their manners and of judging their propriety instead of their morals. His characters, especially his "females," as he always calls them, are usually sticks. He offers us a great many details about the ship, the house, the carriage, or the town his people are in. And yet unless he has been able to set some swift intrigue or combat in motion, the setting remains—even when thoroughly inventoried—scattered and inert, and fails to develop into that "enveloping action" which in a coherent novel the setting should be.

Not only are Cooper's novels disorganized technically. It was inevitable, given the time and place in which Cooper wrote, that the culture his novels depict should also be disorganized. As Yvor Winters says, Cooper's writings are "a mass of fragments . . . but the fragments are those of a civilization." They are the fragments of a civilization in this way at least: that they established for later writers certain images of American culture and proposed certain ideological and aesthetic ways of understanding American life and representing it. If Cooper is of only secondary importance as an artist, he is of the first importance both as a creator and critic of culture. In his novels and other writings he was both the analyst and the visionary of American conditions. There was always in the back of his mind the idea that each of his novels was a "letter to his countrymen" (the title of one of his studies of the difference between European and American culture). He wanted to be the spokesman of his country, as well as its severest critic, and he thought of his novels as public acts.

Exactly because he conceived of his duty as public and national, and also, of course, because he was among the first on the scene, Cooper was able to formulate some of the principal attitudes and dilemmas of American fiction.

Richard Chase
The American Novel and Its Tradition
(Garden City, N. Y.: Doubleday, 1957), pp. 46-47

Like Freud [in *Moses and Monotheism*], Cooper hoped to recreate the beginning of human society. Unlike Freud, he identified its origins with the earliest stages of American civilization. Interlocking these, he introduced the traditional matter of the American dream and thereby fulfilled his mission as a novelist of the new kind, an American novelist who assisted at the birth of the Nation and who served it by portraying how it might, once purified, lead the way for all mankind. All this he incorporated in a line of action that involved the public and the private life of a single family [the Bush family in *The Prairie*]. For Cooper, like Freud, realized that the forces which animate a tribe of this kind are the same forces which, once harnessed, will compel men and nations to fulfill their highest destiny.

William Wasserstrom
American Imago (Winter, 1960), pp. 436-37

STEPHEN CRANE
1871-1900

> Born November 1 in Newark, New Jersey. His father died in 1880. In 1889 he entered Lafayette College but left and entered Syracuse University in 1890, only to leave the same year when his mother died. He became a free-lance writer in New York City in 1891 and subsequently published *Maggie: A Girl of the Streets* (1892) and *The Red Badge of Courage* and *The Black Riders and Other Lines* (1895). In 1896, he sailed on a filibustering expedition to Cuba, but his ship sank off the Florida coast, after which he went to Greece as a war correspondent. In 1898, he married (?) Cora Taylor and went to live in England, but left in the same year for Cuba as a war correspondent. He returned to England in 1899 and published *War is Kind* in 1900. He died June 5 of tuberculosis in Badenweiler, the Black Forest.

> Wilson Follett, ed., *The Works of Setphen Crane* (1925-1926), 12 vols.
> R. W. Stallman, *Stephen Crane* (1968)

PERSONAL

[Crane] was frail of physique, neurotic, intense, full of a vibrant energy that drove him too fiercely. He was naturally lyrical, romantic, impulsively creative, but his training made him . . . a realist—a depressed realist after Zola. His earliest work was his best, *Maggie: A Girl of the Streets*, a grim and brutal picture of the darker strata of New York City—his most distinctive creation. But he had no patience, no time, for collecting material. He was too eager, too much under the dominance of moods, to investigate, and his later novel, *The Red Badge of Courage*, which purports to be a realistic story of army life in the Civil War, is based upon a kind of manufactured realism that is the product not of observation or of gathered data, but of an excessively active imagination. When he died, though he was but thirty, he had done his work. Despite his lyrical power and his undoubted imagination, his place is not large.

Fred Lewis Pattee
A History of American Literature Since 1870 (New York:
Century, 1915), pp. 397-98

Let it be stated that the mistress of [Crane's] mind was fear. His search in aesthetic was governed by terror as that of tamer men is governed by the desire of women. *Maggie* had represented the terror of an environment tinged by social judgment. In all the Mexican and Texan sketches appears, as in *The Red Badge of Courage*, a vision of man's identity faced by its end, by incomprehensible death. One gets the solid courage of the marshal of Yellow Sky who shoves annihilation from him by a simple statement; the rogue of *A Man and Some Others* dies easily because he is bound by contract to defend his flock. In the true story *Horses* and the fanciful *Five White Mice* one sees Crane himself, recording his own pulse before a shadow which he refused to kneel and worship. He could be afraid, and afraid with all the quivering imagination of an artist—here stood the great death and here, mentally or in flesh, stood he. [1923]

Thomas Beer
Hanna, Crane, and The Mauve Decade
(New York: A. A. Knopf, 1941), p. 96

[One should not] underestimate the courage and sincerity that Crane showed in representing the fatigue and fear rather than the false glamour of battle. But the writing, despite brilliant flecks, is hard and cold. An ultimate lifelessness, a paralysis of some function of the soul is troublingly evident in all he wrote. "Let it be stated that the mistress of this boy's mind was fear," his biographer Thomas Beer writes with great perspicacity. The primal fear of life which psychological analysis reveals in every soul was intolerably heightened in Crane's and probably contributed to his lack of physical vitality and so to his early death. He was drawn to delineate the things he feared—bleak sordidness and poverty and, above all, fear itself. After the success of *The Red Badge of Courage* his position, both critical and economic, was excellent; James Huneker became his friend and his years in England were enriched by association with a group of creative spirits that included Joseph Conrad. Nothing availed. He died before his thirtieth year was completed. He had said not long before: "I'm just a dry twig on the edge of the bonfire." How poignant that is and how true! His work lacks the sap of passion and the vibrancy of music.

Ludwig Lewisohn
Expression in America (New York:
Harper, 1932), pp. 320-21

GENERAL

Crane's courage has entitled him to much praise from our contemporaries, and his pessimism has been congenial to many of them. That may explain why the aridity of his writing and the lack of understanding have been overlooked. He has been singled out among his contemporaries for admiration, and other writers, no less limited, certainly, but of comparable historical importance, have been neglected. Yet Crane does very well as a symbol of the writers of the nineties—talent that flares bravely and is cruelly extinguished; blind, bitter blows against dark evils; struggle and flight, suffering and death.

Granville Hicks
The Great Tradition (New York: Macmillan 1935), p. 163

. . . For all its beauty, Crane's best work was curiously thin and, in one sense, even corrupt. His desperation exhausted him too quickly; his unique sense of tragedy was a monotone. No one in America had written like him before; but though his books precipitately gave the whole esthetic movement of the nineties a sudden direction and a fresher impulse, he could contribute no more than the intensity of his spirit. Half of him was a consummate workman; the other half was not a writer at all. . . . The man who wrote *The Blue Hotel* also wrote more trash than any other serious novelist of his time. Even in buffooneries like his unfinished last novel, *The O'Ruddy*, there is the sense of a wasted talent flowing over the silly improvisation in silent derision. He had begun by astonishing the contemporary mind into an acceptance of new forms; he ended by parodying Richard Harding Davis in *Active Service* and Stevenson in *The O'Ruddy*. Yet it was not frustration that wore him out, but his own weariness of life. His gift was a furious one, but barren; writing much, he repeated himself so joylessly that in the end he seemed to be mocking himself with the same quiet viciousness with which, even as a boy, he had mocked the universe. An old child, it was not merely by his somberness that he anticipated the misanthropy of the twentieth-century novel. Pride and a fiercely quaking splendor mark his first and last apotheosis: he was the first great tragic figure in the modern American generation.

Alfred Kazin
On Native Grounds (New York:
Reynal and Hitchcock, 1943), pp. 71-72

Theme and style in *The Red Badge of Courage* are organically conceived, the theme of change conjoined with the fluid style by which it is evoked. Fluidity and change characterize the whole book. Crane's style, calculated to create confused impressions of change and motion, is deliberately disconnected and disordered. He interjects disjointed details, one non sequitur melting into another. Scenes and objects are felt as blurred; everything shifts in value. Yet everything has relationship to the total structure; everything is manipulated into contrapuntal cross-references of meaning. Crane puts language to poetic uses, which, to define it, is to use language reflexively and to use language symbolically. It is the works which employ this use of language that constitute what is permanent of Crane. Crane's language is the language of symbol and paradox. For example, the grotesque symbol and paradox of the wafer-like sun, in *The Red Badge*; or, in "The Open Boat," the paradox in the image of "cold comfortable sea-water," an image which calls to mind the poetry of W. B. Yeats with its fusion of contradictory emotions. This single image evokes the sensation of the whole experience of the men in their wave-tossed dinghy. But, furthermore, it suggests another telltale significance, one that is applicable to Crane himself. What is readily recognizable in this paradox of "cold comfortable sea-water" is that irony of opposites which constituted the personality of the man who wrote it. It is the subjective correlative of his own plight. It symbolizes his personal outlook on life—a life that was filled with ironic contradictions. The enigma of the man is symbolized in his enigmatic style.

R. W. Stallman, ed.
The Red Badge of Courage (New York:
The Modern Library, 1951), pp. xxxv-xxxvii

Vernon Loggins speaks suggestively of Crane's style as "a meaningful mingling of unexpected and curious words." The famous last sentence of Chapter IX in the *Badge*—"The red sun was pasted in the sky like a wafer"—has been lauded for its brilliance and excoriated for its artificiality. It is, of course, both brilliant and artificial; Crane was a great phrasemaker, but it would be too much to say that he never forced the note. Joseph Hergesheimer has rightly praised the dialect of the *Badge*— not "so much a dialect as it is the flexible and successful record of what promised to be the new language of a new land." Crane was far more of a "marvelous boy" than Chatterton ever was, for his talent was far more genuine. How much he would have developed if he had lived, it is difficult to say; his last work is not, in all its aspects, completely reassuring. In a sense he was one of those persons who do not need to live because they know all the answers beforehand. He pointed the way. He pointed many ways. And it is no disrespect to him to say that he did not in himself take the naturalistic novel very far.

Edward Wagenknecht
Calvacade of the American Novel (New York:
Henry Holt, 1952), p. 216

In the complex of Crane's work the oedipal tensions are so strong as to be his single inner theme, and perhaps his only personal contact with reality after the parental relationships which dominated *Maggie* and *George's Mother*. The drive toward mutilation and wounds upon the onset of maturity extends from the *Red Badge* itself. The concern with war and death—and with a virility that only exists within the shadow of destruction—was just as obviously a shield for the real intensity and compulsive necessity of the inner drives toward the brink of self-immolation. Moreover, . . . the persistent concern with prostitutes and courtesans in his works—from Maggie Johnson herself to the Nora Black of *Active Service* — . . . figured . . . even more directly in his life. Was it in fact an attempt to rescue such unfortunates from the sexual "sin" which still obscured the pure and immaculate mother-symbol of the child's fantasies?

But then, by marrying one of these women, he was also marrying the mother-symbol herself in effect—and plunging directly into the fire. . . . The oedipal child attempts to replace the father as the mother's lover. The real sin is not, after all, the mother's but the child's desire. The real crime at the base of Crane's work was not that of social ostracism but of these incestuous fantasies, of course. And the climax of his story was in almost absolutely classical terms the son's mutilation and destruction: the acknowledgment of his own wrong and of the father's divinity.

That was the real design of his work in remarkably clear statements and, as it were, completely transparent imagery. In transmuting these emotions outward into the ordinary realms of experience, while expressing them with such dramatic brilliance—and even with a sort of ironic comedy that played around the web of infancy which constrained him—Stephen Crane had also completed his function as an artist.

Maxwell Geismar
Rebels and Ancestors (Boston: Houghton Mifflin, 1953), pp. 123-24

To define Crane's naturalism is to understand one of the few perfect and successful embodiments of the theory in the American novel. It illustrates the old truth that literary trends often achieve their finest expressions very early in their histories. *Mutatis mutandis*, Crane is the Christopher Marlowe of American naturalism—and we have had no Shakespeare.

Crane's naturalism is to be found, first, in his attitude toward received values, which he continually assails through his naturalistic method of showing that the traditional concepts of our social morality are shams and the motivations presumably controlled by them are pretenses; second, in his impressionism, which fractures experiences into disordered sensation in a way that shatters the old moral "order" along with the old orderly processes of reward and punishment; third, in his obvious interest in a scientific or deterministic accounting for events, although he does not pretend or attempt to be scientific in either the tone or the management of his fables. Crane's naturalism does not suffer from the problem of the divided stream because each of his works is so concretely developed that it does not have a meaning apart from what happens in it. The meaning is always the action; there is no wandering into theory that runs counter to what happens in the action; and nowhere does a character operate as a genuinely free ethical agent in defiance of the author's intentions. Crane's success is a triumph of style: manner and meaning are one.

Charles C. Walcutt
American Literary Naturalism (Minneapolis, Minn.: Univ. Minnesota Pr., 1956), pp. 66-67

The life of passion and impulse is powerful in the classic writers, but it is deeply sublimated and can thus be represented to us only by symbols that are complex and profound enough to lead us down beneath the surface towards the deeper meanings. But by the time of Crane this fecund source of symbolism has been largely lost, for the simple reason that the conventional morality which overlaid the instinctual life has been openly abandoned. The contrast between overt morality and hidden impulse is no longer a secret, to be represented only indirectly. It has been brought out into the open and has been made the "whole point."

Because Crane always had his eyes on this and related contrasts, he is an ironist. And what he loses in symbolism he gains in irony. He loves to make a wryly observed contrast between conventional morality and the passions which govern actual human conduct; this he does, for example, in *Maggie* throughout, capping the climax with Maggie's brutal and besotted mother condescending to "fergive" her daughter in the name, presumably, of decent Christian ethics. Crane is a master at demonstrating the sometimes wild discrepancies between man's fantasies and ideals, on the one hand, and, on the other, the trapped and fated creature he actually is. From one point of view, the theme of *The Red Badge* and *George's Mother* is the familiar one about the young man who has romantic, adolescent, or egotistic illusions about war or about his place in the world. This theme is commonly carried through, especially in the traditional European novel, by tracing the process of education by which the youth matures and learns to square his thoughts and dreams about reality with reality itself. There is some attempt to do this in *The Red Badge*, particularly at the end, but Crane seems half-hearted about carrying things through to the moral conclusion and inclined to point out and poetically dramatize the discrepancy between illusion and fact, and let it go at that. Many different instances of irony can be found in Crane's stories: for example, the agonizing position of the men in "The Open Boat"—so near to shore and safety and yet so much at the mercy of the sea. To generalize, one might say that the recurring, perhaps obsessive, idea in Crane's writing is that man must believe what is obviously not true—namely, that he is a rational creature whose mind through thought and the imagination of the ideal can control and give significance to human conduct. The truth, Crane believes, is that man is pretty much at the mercy not only of his own illusions but of superior social and cosmic forces and of his own instincts.

Richard Chase, ed.
The Red Badge of Courage and Other Writings by Stephen Crane
(Boston: Houghton Mifflin, 1960), pp. xii-xiii

In a sense, . . . *The Red Badge* is a faithful, though oblique, reflection of the era in which it was written; it expresses certain doubts about the meaning of individual virtue in a world that has become suddenly cruel and mechanical. For this very reason, however, Crane's novel fails to typify the literary tastes of the nineties. Most Americans still regarded literature as an amusing diversion from life rather than an honest image of it, and the most popular writers, such as Thomas Bailey Aldrich, Francis Marion Crawford, and James Whitcomb Riley, were usually the most socially innocuous. More serious novelists like James and Howells strove to be realistic, but they did nothing to deny the prevailing belief that fiction should be refined, unsensational, and concerned with ethical ideals. The canons of genteel taste, formulated by such respected critics as George E. Woodberry, William C. Brownell, Edmund C. Stedman, and Charles Dudley Warner, demanded a lofty tone and a high moral purposefulness. *The Red Badge of Courage* does not simply fail to meet such expectations, it deliberately flouts them; and we may fix one element of Crane's relation to his times by saying that he self-consciously tried to break all the rules of the Genteel Tradition. His inscription in a friend's copy of *Maggie* epitomizes his cockiness: "This work is a mud-puddle, I am told on the best authority. Wade in and have a swim."

Frederick C. Crews, ed.
The Red Badge of Courage (Indianapolis, Ind.:
Bobbs-Merrill, 1964), pp. xii-xiii

RICHARD HENRY DANA, JR.

1815-1879

Born August 1 in Cambridge, Massachusetts. He entered Harvard in 1831, but gave up his studies there in 1834 because of eye trouble. In that year, he sailed as a common sailor on the brig *Pilgrim* to California via Cape Horn. He returned to Harvard in 1836, joining the senior class, and was graduated the following June. In 1840, he published *Two Years Before The Mast* and was admitted to the bar. He married Sarah Watson in 1841 and devoted the remainder of his life to the practice and study of law. He died February 2 in Rome and is buried there in the Protestant Cemetery.

C. F. Adams, *Richard Henry Dana: A Biography* (1890), 2 vols.

We must give Dana credit for a profound mystic vision. The best Americans are mystics by instinct. Simple and bare as his narrative is, it is deep with profound emotion and stark comprehension. He sees the last light-loving incarnation of life exposed upon the eternal waters: a speck, solitary upon the verge of the two naked principles, aerial and watery. And his own soul is as the soul of the albatross.

It is a storm bird. And so is Dana. He has gone down to fight with the sea. It is a metaphysical, actual struggle of an integral soul with the vast, non-living, yet potent element. Dana never forgets, never ceases to watch. If Hawthorne was a spectre on the land, how much more is Dana a spectre at sea. But he must watch, he must know, he must conquer the sea in his consciousness. This is the poignant difference between him and the common sailor. The common sailor lapses from consciousness, becomes elemental like a seal, a creature. Tiny and alone Dana watches the great seas mount round his own small body. If he is swept away, some other man will have to take up what he has begun. For the sea must be mastered by the human consciousness, in the great fight of the human soul for mastery over life and death, in KNOWLEDGE. It is the last bitter necessity of the Tree. The Cross. Impartial, Dana beholds himself among the elements, calm and fatal. His style is great and hopeless, the style of a perfect tragic recorder. . . . [ca. 1922]

D. H. Lawrence
Studies in Classic American Literature (London:
Martin Secker, 1924), p. 116

Interesting evidence of the simplicity and straightforwardness of the style of *Two Years Before the Mast*, which like that of *Robinson Crusoe* so commended it to boys, is found in the fact that quotations from it long formed the material upon oculists' cards for testing the eyesight. [ca. 1917]

Algernon Tassin
in *Cambridge History of American Literature*, Vol. II
(New York: Macmillan, 1933), p. 401

Dana had no gift for yarning, to say nothing of a capacity for the psychological subtleties of a Conrad or the cosmic vision of a Melville. . . . But for sheer, straightforward, unmodified narrative power—austere and utterly restrained—it has not often been surpassed.

Edward Wagenknecht
Cavalcade of the American Novel (New York:
Henry Holt, 1952), p. 31

EMILY DICKINSON
1830-1886

> Born December 10 in Amherst, Massachusetts. She spent the year of
> 1847 at Mount Holyoke Female Seminary. She began corresponding with
> Thomas Wentworth Higginson, her literary mentor, in 1862, and in the
> same year published "Safe In Their Alabaster Chambers" in the *Spring-
> field* (Mass.) *Republican*. Her father died in 1874, and a year later her
> mother was paralyzed. Emily became her nurse until 1882, when her
> mother died. In 1884, Emily suffered the first attack of her fatal illness
> and died two years later on May 15 in Amherst.

> Thomas H. Johnson, ed., *The Poems of Emily Dickinson* (1955), 3 vols.
> Thomas H. Johnson, *Emily Dickinson: An Interpretive Biography* (1955)

PERSONAL

It is a strange combination of delights that Emily Dickinson has left to us,
so direct as to seem obscure, so loving as to seem brusque, so simple as
to seem eccentric. Living amid the velvet hush of American Victorianism,
she blew clarion notes of the shocking truth; a daughter of Puritanism,
she pushed past the rigid image of Fear and took her God confidently
by the hand. The vast love that was her being was never squandered in
such sentimental abstractions as Humanity, Nature, and Religion; it was
profitably, if wantonly, poured out for the individuals and objects that
she knew, her family, her friends, the hired man, all children, her garden,
and the visible symbols of life everlasting. Pomposity and show were
known to her only as absurdities to be shunned; and always, in every
word she wrote, we find that sense of proportion, too significant to be
called a sense of humour, which gave to her most solemn statements an
unvarying charm.

Robert Hillyer
The Freeman (Oct. 18, 1922; repr. in *The Recognition of
Emily Dickinson*, eds. Caesar R. Blake and Carlton
F. Wells (Ann Arbor, Mich.: Univ. Mich. Pr., 1964), pp. 103-4

Emily's poetry, like the art of any original, is a system unto itself.
Whatever theories it holds come after the performance—as the intuitive
Whitman discovered about his own work. Walt and Emily, along with
Forefather Emerson, are the great American rebels; and the woman is
fully the equal of the males. Best of all, we need no biography through
which to apprehend her. She sang her own life and the life of the surrounding world that never caught her. Her poems reveal, in blinding, ecstatic
array, not alone herself, not alone womankind, not alone America, but
oneself, mankind and the universe. And the god she made in her own
image—the "burglar, banker, father"—is the most intimate and irresistible

democrat who has ever come down with Christendom. No church or schism can hold her delirium. It is the most pious and impious of creeds, and has the forest for its aisles, and a circumnavigating altar. The heart of a flying bird, never-for-more-than-a-moment alighting, is the all-in-one and one-in-all. Skepticism is the salt she drops on her tail: sanity catches the insane songster. Then she's off again, and no amount of science, of reason, of ratiocination, can catch her again, unless she employs these dreadful things herself. Only poetry—whatever that may be—can keep up with her. [ca. 1929]

Alfred Kreymborg
A History of American Poetry (New York:
Tudor, 1934), pp. 193-94

POETRY

The poems are disappointing. Critics have echoed Higginson, until Emily Dickinson has figured, often at length, in all the later histories and anthologies, but it is becoming clear that she was overrated. To compare her eccentric fragments with Blake's elfin wildness is ridiculous. They are mere conceits, vague jottings of a brooding mind; they are crudely wrought, and, like their author's letters, which were given to the public later, they are colorless and for the most part lifeless. They reveal little either of Emily Dickinson or of human life generally. They should have been allowed to perish as their author intended.

Fred L. Pattee
A History of American Literature Since 1870
(New York: Century, 1915), pp. 340-41

[Emily Dickinson's] poems are remarkable for their condensation, their vividness of image, their delicate or pungent satire and irony, their childlike responsiveness to experience, their subtle feeling for nature, their startling abruptness in dealing with themes commonly regarded as trite, their excellence in imaginative insight and still greater excellence in fancy. Typical is such a poem as that in which she celebrates the happiness of a little stone on the road, or that in which she remarks with gleeful irony upon the dignity that burial has in store for each of us—coach and footmen, bells in the village, "as we ride grand along." Emily Dickinson takes us to strange places; one never knows what is in store. But always she is penetrating and dainty, both intimate and aloof, challenging lively thought on our part while remaining, herself, a charmingly elfish mystery. Her place in American letters will be inconspicuous but secure. [ca. 1917]

Norman Foerster
in *Cambridge History of American Literature*, Vol. III
(New York: Macmillan, 1933). p. 34

Without gainsaying her fondness both for assonance and for the suspended rhyme (in which words ending in different vowel sounds followed by the same consonant are made to serve), it should be palpable now that in many cases she missed, in her constrained haste, finding even approximately the right word. Her great gift was for poetic thought—a very different thing from the customary nineteenth-century reflecting in verse— since it involved a fusion between her thought and the image which embodied it. But these further poems make even clearer than it was before that she possessed no comparable gift for versification. Her almost standard measure was the familiar ballad stanza, which was also the "common meter" of the hymn books of her heritage. She seems hardly to have been concerned with the possibilities of metrical experiment, and many of her best poems are those wherein the vividness of what she had to say stirred her small stanzas with fresh irregularity. In any such long sequence of her less successful work . . . the cumulative impression cannot escape monotony.

F. O. Matthiessen
KR (Autumn, 1945), repr. in *The Recognition of Emily Dickinson*, eds. Caesar R. Blake and Carlton F. Wells (Ann Arbor, Mich.: Univ. Mich. Pr., 1964), p. 233

Emily's finest poetry may be viewed as the autobiography of a victorious struggle against acute pain that was in a sense madness and threatened total prostration of her personality. Unforgettably she describes her moods of extreme depression. She subtilizes between the various shades of fear, anguish, crisis, numbness, and despair. Her heightened capacity for ecstacy or joy proved, of course, no less an evidence of abnormality than did her extreme sensitivity to human ills. Especially in the love poems and in those numerous pieces neither classified by her editors as love poetry nor obviously such but covertly and fundamentally of this description, one detects signs of her tragic dislocations. This may be seen in such magnificent lyrics as, "After great pain a formal feeling comes," or "There's a certain slant of light On winter afternoons." Emily discloses the history of the lover's madness even more objectively than Robert Burton, author of *The Anatomy of Melancholy*. Even many of the physiological symptoms of such madness she vividly describes, as attacks of fever, frigidity, trembling, numbness, and dizziness. Her poems themselves afford a relentlessly faithful record of a soul which has passed through experiences as pathological in the life of the individual as prison camps infested with torture are pathological in the life of a state.

Henry W. Wells
Introduction To Emily Dickinson (Chicago: Packard, 1947), pp. 35-36

But it is not her achievement as a prosodist, substantial as it is, that gives high rank to Emily Dickinson. It is her tragic vision. She knew that she could not pierce through to the unknowable, but she insisted on asking the questions. Her agonizing sense of ironic contrasts; of the weight of suffering; of the human predicament in which man is mocked, destroyed, and beckoned to some incomprehensible repose; of the limits of reason, order, and justice in human as well as divine relationships:—this is the anguish of the Shakespeare of *King Lear*, and it was shared in like degree among nineteenth-century American writers only by Herman Melville, who also had his war with God. Yet, unlike Melville, she is willing to love the God with whom she is at war. Thus she is a closer spiritual neighbor to Jonathan Edwards, who believed (as she evidently did) that final judgment is not a foreseeable end, but a pronouncement renewed in all moments of existence. . . .

Emily Dickinson was an existentialist in a period of transcendentalism, a movement in her New England which saw the immanence of God in a buttercup, a state which she once or twice in poetry tried to envision. Yet her judgment persistently asserts that neither intuition nor reason can solve the riddle of existence, and in her lifetime only the actress Eleonora Duse lived with a similar artistic effectiveness for audiences. Dickinson assesses the problems of anxiety and loneliness, the extremity of pain and its duration and redemptive quality, and she thereby steadily participated in the issues of existing.

Thomas H. Johnson
Final Harvest (Boston: Little, Brown, 1961), pp. xii-xiii

[Emily Dickinson's] grand theme . . . is Life as it is involved in her life. She declines to take the other option for the egocentric poet: her life as it might be involved in Life. The "I" with which so many of her poems begin, since it is so completely her own, since it is of such a power to make its world flow into and out from it, makes her the most imperious of American poets. Her empire is, in the poems, one over which she has total dominion—her soul. . . .

Without the wilfully "artistic" purpose of Poe, without the wilfully "metaphysical" and "religious" purpose of Emerson and Whitman, without their hope that by committing themselves to a conception of the self in one or another of its manifestations they might save society—Emily Dickinson was able completely and entirely to save herself, thereby to exhibit many of the infinite forms of such salvation for all who might care to look. What she never achieved—nor could try to achieve, one guesses —was a philosophical poetry which, in its submission to traditional and artistic disciplines, would allow the ego to discover its formal relations

to other egos and to celebrate not only the relations but their forms—
the grand myths as it were. . . . For many reasons . . . Emily Dickinson
held close to and thereby most richly developed the egocentric style which
is basic in nineteenth century poetry. This was her triumph.

Roy Harvey Pearce
The Continuity of American Poetry (Princeton, N. J.:
Princeton Univ. Pr., 1961), pp. 182, 186

Emily Dickinson marked a turning point in the American poet's conception of his function. For all her experience of the blaze of noon and the
lightning-flash, for all her knowledge of the flower's ecstasy and the bee's
power, she had to reject the kind of "mysticism" which in Emerson
became mistiness and in Whitman amorphousness. She wrote neither as a
visionary nor as a genius but as a craftsman making order out of the
fragments of mutability. The only question was how durable one's web
was; and durability depended on how well one practiced one's "Trade."
She could only trust with Thoreau and Keats that if the materials and
the art were pure, the result could not be other than wonderful.

Albert J. Gelpi
Emily Dickinson, The Mind of the Poet
(Cambridge, Mass.: Harvard Univ. Pr., 1965), p. 152

GENERAL

Emily Dickinson was not only a lyric poet; she was in a profound sense a
comic poet in the American tradition. She possessed the sense of scale and
caught this within her small compass. A little tippler, she leaned against the
sun. The grave for her was a living place whose elements grew large in stone.
Purple mountains moved for her; a train, clouds, a pathway through a
valley became huge and animate. Much of her poetry is in the ascending
movement, full of morning imagery, of supernal mornings: seraphim toss-
ing their snowy hats on high might be taken as her symbol. Her poetry is
also comic in the Yankee strain, with its resilience and sudden unprepared
ironical lines. Her use of an unstressed irony in a soft blank climax is the
old formula grown almost fixed, yet fresh because it was used with a new
depth. . . .

She seemed to emerge afresh as from a chrysalis in each lyric or even
in each brief stanza; and the air was one which had been evident before
in the sequence of American expression. Emerson had it, as Santayana
noted, in everything he wrote. Whitman had it, and was aware of the
quality: it was that of improvisation. In one way or another every major
American writer had shown its traces, except perhaps Henry James in
the broad spaces of his early novels, but he too turned toward experiment

in the end. Emily Dickinson was another—perhaps the last—of those primary writers who had slowly charted an elementary American literature; and she possessed both the virtues and the failings of her position. Her poetry has an abounding fresh intensity, a touch of conquering zeal, a true entrance into new provinces of verbal music, but incompletion touches her lyricism. Often—indeed most often—her poems are only poetic flashes, notes, fragments of poetry rather than a final poetry. Yet like the others who had gone before her—Whitman, Hawthorne, Emerson, James—she set a new outpost, even though like them she had no immediate effect upon American literature. [ca. 1931]

Constance Rourke
American Humor (Garden City, N.Y.: Doubleday, 1953),
pp. 209-10, 212

[Emily Dickinson] has Hawthorne's intellectual toughness, a hard, definite sense of the physical world. The highest flights to God, the most extravagant metaphors of the strange and the remote, come back to a point of casuistry, to a moral dilemma of the experienced world. There is, in spite of the homiletic vein of utterance, no abstract speculation, nor is there a message to society; she speaks wholly to the individual experience. She offers to the unimaginative no riot of vicarious sensation; she has no useful maxims for men of action. Up to this point her resemblance to Emerson is slight: poetry is a sufficient form of utterance, and her devotion to it is pure. But in Emily Dickinson the puritan world is no longer self-contained; it is no longer complete; her sensibility exceeds its dimensions. She has trimmed down its supernatural proportions; it has become a morality; instead of the tragedy of the spirit there is a commentary upon it. Her poetry is a magnificent personal confession, blasphemous and, in its self-revelation, its honesty, almost obscene. It comes out of an intellectual life towards which it feels no moral responsibility. Cotton Mather would have burnt her for a witch. [ca. 1932]

Allen Tate
The Man of Letters in the Modern World
(New York: Meridian, 1955), p. 226

Emily Dickinson's theology has, obviously, little significance to-day, but her religious experiences are not without interest, simply because she describes and interprets them so personally and honestly. In her poems one feels the vitality of both Puritanism and the revolt against Puritanism; they are alive for us because they were alive for her. Emerson's doctrine of self-reliance takes on substance by virtue of its immediate reality for a real person, even though self-reliance meant for that person merely an isolated life in Amherst, Massachusetts. And what is true of her religious experiences is true of all the others that figure in her poems. Like Thoreau she could find importance in the simplest events of nature, and she was perhaps even more successful than he in communicating her sensitive perceptions to her readers. The limited observations of field and garden furnished themes for many poems and images for many more. And there was, of course, a whole field of experience, closed to Thoreau, that Emily returned to time after time in her poetry. We may not know who her lover was or why she never married him, but surely no American poet has written so movingly of love and renunciation. Sometimes she spoke with the utmost simplicity; sometimes passion merged with religious aspiration in a cry of fierce and almost agonizing intensity. The exaltation of the mystic is in most of her poems, whether her theme is life or death, heaven or hell; but that exaltation rests upon a singularly intense response to altogether human joys and fears.

Granville Hicks
The Great Tradition (New York: Macmillan, 1935), pp. 128-29

In examining the complex pattern of Emily Dickinson's thought we must guard ourselves from attributing to her an undue consistency or an undue solemnity. Her states of mind were not progressive, but approximately simultaneous. She did not move in a systematic fashion from one intellectual position to another, nor set herself to defend a single point of view. Her delight was to test all conceivable points of view in turn. At any moment she was ready to acknowledge in herself the claims of rationalist and mystic, Pyrrhonist and Transcendentalist. A mood of faith that possessed her in the morning might become a matter of delicate mockery in the afternoon, a piercing grief could be sublimated overnight into a rapture of spiritual purgation. She enjoyed every extension of the multiplicity of metaphor. Hence a reader who looks to her for a single attitude invariably finds her inconsistent.

A study of her mind, moreover, is almost sure to risk misrepresentation by its formality. It may point out certain directions that her thoughts took, but it fails to catch the darts and ripples that distinguish their movement. She could write of solemn things without becoming permanently solemn. The swift intuitions of her intelligence were a continual surprise, an adventure, a joy sufficient in itself. She glanced from one to another with the lightness of a metaphysical ballerina. In poetry she found the freedom of mastery. Translated to that realm pain and heartache, like sunset and autumn, became incitements to artistic activity and occasions for artistic triumph. Like her own "Martyr Poets" she discovered "in Art the Art of Peace." There she could obtain sure transport when the everlasting arms proved not to be a "sufficient phaeton." Poetry was her playmate, not her taskmaster, and she came to it with a sparkle in her eye and mischief on her lips.

George Frisbie Whicher
This Was a Poet (New York: Scribner's, 1938), pp. 305-6

[Dickinson] is newly relevant to our contemporary experience. Her sense of the anguish of personal existence and of the precariousness of human life recommends her to a time in which new philosophies of existence have come forcefully to our attention. Her vigor, her curious and reconnoitering mind appeal to a period which has been given too much to apathy and suspicion of the spirited imagination. Her rigorous psychology and her sense of the virtue of definition, of intellectual severity, of the exclusions which the mind must make if it is to preserve its precarious "economy," of the powerful consequentiality of fact and circumstance, of the hostility or indifference of the universe to man—all these attitudes recommend Emily Dickinson to an age which is seeking secular modes of thought more severe, more realistic, and more durable than the easier optimisms which have sometimes characterized American intellectual life.

Richard Chase
Emily Dickinson (New York: William Sloane, 1951), p. 5

[Dickinson's] great talents, to be sure, are those of a highly original sayer, not a seer. To set this emphasis right one more analogy will be cited in conclusion. . . . If significance in literature can be measured by the quantity of metaphor thrown up, as Henry James believed, then her poems on death and immortality represent the summit of her achievement. The novelty and brilliance of her imagery in these [poems] . . . are memorable. Within the context of the individual poems, old and new symbols are maneuvered by the language of surprise so as to illuminate the two profoundest themes that challenged her poetic powers. This reveals her kinship with another article of James' esthetic faith: if the creative writer pushes far enough into language he finds himself in the embrace of thought. By slant and surprise, by wit and a novel reworking of traditional modes, she evolved a way with words that became her instrument of knowing. Committed to nothing but dedicated to a search for truth and beauty, hers was a free spirit for whom living was a succession of intense experiences and art an endless exploration of their meanings. A poet rather than a systematic thinker, she never came up with dogmatic answers. Indeed her most effective verbal strategy was to exploit ambiguity, as in the conflicting attitudes towards her flood subject Immortality.

Charles R. Anderson
Emily Dickinson's Poetry (New York:
Holt, Rinehart and Winston, 1960), pp. 284-85

JONATHAN EDWARDS
1703-1758

> Born October 5 in East Windsor, Connecticut. He entered Yale in 1716 at
> the age of 12 and graduated in 1720. He became a minister in New York
> City in 1722 and was elected a tutor at Yale in 1724. In 1725 he took up
> ministerial duties in Northampton, Massachusetts, and two years later
> married Sarah Pierpont. In 1734 the "Great Awakening," under the influ-
> enec of George Whitefield spread through New England. *A Treatise Con-
> cerning Religious Affections* was published in 1746. In 1750 Edwards was
> dismissed from his parish, and in 1751 he went to Stockbridge as a mis-
> sionary to the Indians. *A Careful and Strict Enquiry into . . . Freedom of
> the Will* was published in 1754. In 1757 he went to Princeton as president
> of the College of New Jersey, and a year later published *The Great
> Christian Doctrine or Original Sin Defended.* He died March 22 in
> Princeton.

> Perry Miller, ed., *The Works of Jonathan Edwards* (1957-), edition in
> progress
> Perry Miller, *Jonathan Edwards* (1949)

. . . Though we may follow Edward's logical system to the breaking point,
as we can follow every metaphysical system, and though we may feel that,
in his revulsion from the optimism of the Deists, he distorted the actual
evil of existence into a nightmare of the imagination—yet for all that, he
remains one of the giants of the intellect and one of the enduring masters
of religious emotion. He had not the legal and executive brain of Calvin,
upon whose *Institutes* his scheme of theology is manifestly based, but in
subtle resourcefulness of reasoning and still more in the scope of his
spiritual insight he stands, I think, above his predecessor. Few men have
studied Edwards without recognizing the force and honesty of his genius.
[ca. 1921]

Paul Elmer More
Shelburne Essays on American Literature (New York:
Harcourt, Brace, 1963), pp. 51-2

As one follows the laborious career of [Jonathan Edwards], a sense of
the tragic failure of his life deepens. The burdens that he assumed were
beyond the strength of any man. Beginning as a mystic, brooding on the
all-pervasive spirit of sweetness and light diffused through the universe,
with its promise of spiritual emancipation; then turning to an archaic
theology and giving over his middle years to the work of minifying the
excellence of man in order to exalt the sovereignty of God; and finally
settling back upon the mystical doctrine of conversion—such a life leaves
one with a feeling of futility, a sense of great powers baffled and wasted,

a spiritual tragedy enacted within the narrow walls of a minister's study. There was both pathos and irony in the fate of Jonathan Edwards, removed from the familiar places where for twenty years he had labored, the tie with his congregation broken, and sent to the frontier mission at Stockbridge to preach to a band of Indians and to speculate on the unfreedom of the human will. The greatest mind of New England had become an anachronism in a world that bred Benjamin Franklin. If he had been an Anglican like Bishop Berkeley, if he had mingled with the leaders of thought in London instead of remaining isolated in Massachusetts, he must have made a name for himself not unworthy to be matched with that of the great bishop whom he so much resembled. The intellectual powers were his, but the inspiration was lacking; like Cotton Mather before him, he was the unconscious victim of a decadent ideal and a petty environment. Cut off from fruitful intercourse with other thinkers, drawn away from the stimulating field of philosophy into the arid realm of theology, it was his fate to devote his noble gifts to the thankless task of re-imprisoning the mind of New England within a system from which his nature and his powers summoned him to unshackle it. He was called to be a transcendental emancipator, but he remained a Calvinist.

Vernon Louis Parrington
Main Currents in American Thought, Vol. II
(New York: Harcourt, Brace, 1927), pp. 366-67

The career of Edwards was on the whole strangely mixed and self-contradictory. Variously gifted as a scientist, philosopher, and poet, he sternly wrought his opulent nature into submission to the God of John Calvin. Possessed of a new mystical vision of divine excellence, he thought to express its splendors in the verbiage of an obsolescent theology, whose decay no human being could have arrested. Yet, confronted with the revivalist phenomena in his own church, he broke with Puritan formalism to follow the path of the impassioned evangelical. He thus became a strong influence in fostering that type of Protestantism which shaped the American mind for more than a century, and which, even in the present age, is still powerful. His enduring literary work is the *Personal Narrative,* in which he crystallized into language of permanent beauty one of the great mystical experiences of the race.

Walter Fuller Taylor
A History of American Letters (New York:
American Book, 1936), pp. 35-36

In the twentieth century, when Edwards's theology is no longer regarded as literally true, it is possible to interpret it as a symbolic expression of the deep psychic forces that pervaded the culture that produced it: to consider it, in other words, not as theology but as poetry. His cosmology has, in fact, a kind of morbid and sinister beauty, resembling that to be found in some of the short stories of Poe and in certain surrealist paintings. As a poet, Edwards foreshadowed the two major themes that occupied the great American writers of the following century. On the one hand his doctrine of "a spiritual and divine light immediately imparted to the soul" pointed toward Emerson and Whitman. On the other hand his intoxication with the idea of omnipotence, the cruelty that it implied, and the overweening pride of logic with which he set out to explain the entire universe, represented tendencies that pervaded the writings of Poe and Melville. If Edwards is judged as an American poet, then only Melville can be said to have surpassed him in depth and intensity of spiritual experience. Indeed, in their basic preoccupations the two men had much in common. That drive of will, both American and Calvinist, which is so conspicuous in Edwards, had its most complete aesthetic embodiment in Melville's Captain Ahab.

Henry B. Parkes
The American People (London: Eyre and
Spottiswoode, 1949), pp. 82-83

Jonathan Edwards is not only the greatest of all American theologians (and philosophers as well), but the greatest of all American writers before the nineteenth century. Such logic, such clarity, such ordonnance (to use a word which T. S. Eliot applied to the sermons of Lancelot Andrewes) are rarely met with in American writing, or in any writing. There is severity, strictness, inexorableness, in Edwards. There are also a love of beauty, a homeliness of illustration, a tenderness, a recognition of the importance of the feelings (which Edwards liked to call the "affections") in the religious experience. There is that rare literary and philosophical (as well as personal) virtue—a balance of head and heart.

Randall Stewart
American Literature and Christian Doctrine
(Baton Rouge, La.: Louisiana State Univ. Pr., 1958), p. 8

Holding himself by brute will power within the forms of ancient Calvinism [Edwards] filled those forms with a new and throbbing spirit. Beneath the dogmas of the old theology he discovered a different cosmos from that of the seventeenth century, a dynamic world, filled with the presence of God, quickened with divine life, pervaded with joy and ecstasy. With this insight he turned to combat the rationalism of Boston, to argue that man cannot live by Newtonian schemes and mathematical calculations, but only by surrender to the will of God, by reflecting back the beauty of God as a jewel gives back the light of the sun. But another result of Edward's doctrine, one which he would denounce to the nethermost circle of Hell but which is implicit in the texture, if not in the logic, of his thought, could very easily be what we have called mysticism or pantheism, or both. If God is diffused through nature, and the substance of man is the substance of God, then it may follow that man is divine, that nature is the garment of the Over-Soul, that man must be self-reliant, and that when he goes into the woods the currents of Being will indeed circulate through him. All that prevented this deduction was the orthodox theology, supposedly derived from the Word of God, which taught that God and nature are not one, that man is corrupt and his self-reliance is reliance on evil. But take away the theology, remove this overlying stone of dogma from the wellsprings of Puritan conviction, and both nature and man become divine. [ca. 1940]

Perry Miller
Interpretations of American Literature (New York:
Oxford Univ. Pr., 1959), p. 127

RALPH WALDO EMERSON
1803-1882

> Born May 25 in Boston, Massachusetts. He graduated from Harvard in 1821. He was ordained at Second Church, Boston in 1829 and in the same year married Ellen Tucker, who died two years later. He resigned from Second Church in 1832 and began his travels in Europe. In 1834, he moved to Concord and a year later married Lydia Jackson. *Nature* was published in 1836, and Phi Beta Kappa address on "The American Scholar" delivered in 1837. In 1838, he delivered the Divinity School Address in Cambridge. *Essays, First Series* was published in 1841. In 1847-1848 he traveled in England and France. In 1856, *English Traits* was published. He traveled in Europe and the Near East in 1872-1873. He died at Concord, April 27.
>
> *The Complete Works of Ralph Waldo Emerson* (1903-1904), 12 vols.
> Ralph L. Rusk, *The Life of Ralph Waldo Emerson* (1949)

PERSONAL

Emerson was a shrewd Yankee, by instinct on the winning side; he was a cheery, child-like soul, impervious to the evidence of evil, as of everything that it did not suit his transcendental individuality to appreciate or to notice. More, perhaps, than anybody that has ever lived, he practised the transcendental method in all its purity. He had no system. He opened his eyes on the world every morning with a fresh sincerity, marking how things seemed to him then, or what they suggested to his spontaneous fancy. This fancy, for being spontaneous, was not always novel; it was guided by the habits and training of his mind, which were those of a preacher. Yet he never insisted on his notions so as to turn them into settled dogmas; he felt in his bones that they were myths. Sometimes, indeed, the bad example of other transcendentalists, less true than he to their method, or the pressing questions of unintelligent people, or the instinct we all have to think our ideas final, led him to the very verge of system-making; but he stopped short. Had he made a system out of his notion of compensation, or the over-soul, or spiritual laws, the result would have been as thin and forced as it is in other transcendental systems. But he coveted truth; and he returned to experience, to history, to poetry, to the natural science of his day, for new starting-points and hints toward fresh transcendental musings.

George Santayana
Winds of Doctrine (London: Dent, 1913), p. 197

Emerson—to vary one of his own metaphors—presented a universe seen through a temperament. We may not like the temperament, and the universe seen through it may appear to us limited, partial, or unreal; but we cannot escape the revelation that the man possessing the one and expounding the other was one of the most friendly, courageous, and serene the world has known. It is hard to recognize in his universe the same one that we behold through the prism of a Hardy, a Strindberg, or a Dostoevsky, and yet, like them, he presented it honestly as he saw it. It is a waste of time to quarrel with genius. It speaks and goes its way. And Emerson would have been the last man to require us to accept his universe without question. He hoped that we would try to make it our own.

Robert M. Gay
Emerson (Garden City, N. Y.: Doubleday, Doran, 1928),
pp. 224-45

Emerson, so cold and shy in his personal relations, was in faith, hope, and creative thinking a white fire burning through convention and all hindering obscurantism. He spoke to the young—as he may again. He sought tinder for his spark; he made tinder; his essential warmth is revealed in his eloquence, where alone he could make literature, but still more in the intellectual emotion of which that eloquence, so often happy in its rhythms, so often phrasing itself in apothegms that have passed into world circulation, was the garment.

Henry Seidel Canby
Classic Americans (New York: Harcourt, Brace,
1931), p. 160

PHILOSOPHY, ESSAYS, GENERAL

What the primitive mind thought of as characteristic of the prophet, [Emerson] extended to all the tribe; this illuminism is one of the earliest of old-world ideas, and had its place in religious development; but now it is little better than an atavistic survival. It involves contempt for experience as the guide of life. Emerson, in this spirit, slighted history, science, art and letters, and religion, the entire recorded life of the race; but civilization is an inheritance, a gift of the past to man, and the individual adds but little to it even by the best faculty and fortune. In setting up the doctrine of the sovereignty of the individual in the form which he employed, he put himself in contradiction to the evolutionary conception of humanity at every point. He had a mind compact of miracle and intellectually he belongs in the age of miracle and not of science.

. . . He is the priest of those who have gone out of the church, but who must yet retain some emotional religious life, some fragment of the ancient heavens, some literary expression of the feeling of the divine. It is because of the multitude of such minds under modern conditions that his *Essays* have had so broad and profound an influence, and the tenderness and veneration with which his memory is widely regarded are due to the peculiarly intimate and personally precious service which he has rendered.

. . . It belongs to primary honesty, therefore, to say that he was not a Christian in any proper use of the word; it is a cardinal fact in considering his relation to the religious changes of the time; rather he was a link in the de-Christianization of the world in laying off the vesture of old religion; but it is plain that no modern mind can abide in his ideas. They were the tent where the Spirit rested for a night, and is now gone; and who can forecast the ways of the Spirit? To those who live in the spirit, he will long be, as Arnold said, the friend; to the young and courageous he will be an elder brother in the tasks of life; and in whatever land he is read he will be the herald and attendant of change, the son and father of Revolution.

George E. Woodberry
Ralph Waldo Emerson (New York:
Macmillan, 1907), pp. 189, 192, 196-97

. . . The phenomenon called Emerson was composed of two elements—the absorption of puritanism and the estrangement from puritanism. The duplication of the phenomenon depended on the transmission of the two constituents, but Emerson transmitted only the second. The old-time faith to which he had owed so much passed from maturity to decadence with tragic certainty and swiftness. A rhetorician would say that he was himself the occasion of the decline, that the plant perished in consequence of the effort it put forth in the creation of its flower. Putting aside such flourishes, it is clear that the followers were in no condition to forego the aid which had proved indispensable to the training of the master, that that aid was in fact withdrawn, and that Emerson himself was a visible occasion, if not in the last analysis, an active cause of its withdrawal.

. . . Emerson's *fame* arrived punctually, and shows no sign of diminution, but his influence, the influence of his central ideas and impulsions, has been curiously prorogued. A hiatus has occurred in the evolution of his power, springing out of an unreadiness on the world's part for the reception of his ideas which the last fifty years seem rather to have increased than abated. Humanity must receive a new and profound charge of the religious spirit before its real pupilage to the waiting master can begin. At the present instant he is hardly in the strong sense a teacher, hardly in the strong sense an example: he is a revelation of capacity, an adjourned hope, an unassured but momentous foreshadowing.

O. W. Firkins
Ralph Waldo Emerson (Boston: Houghton Mifflin,
1915), pp. 372-73

. . . [W]hatever his aesthetic response to nature and to literary art, Emerson was wanting in emotional energy. The passion of the spirit he experienced with a pure strength hard to match in modern times, but the passion of finite humanity burned pallidly within him and consequently failed of outward expression, either in action or in letters. If he had deep feeling, it was too promptly repressed or metamorphosed into the life of the spirit. . . .

. . . [H]is cast of mind was dominantly priestly rather than poetic, mystical rather than aesthetic. He is full of impetuous exaltations, of sudden raptures that carry him far aloft and beyond sight of the familiar terrain of man's life. Beneath his mysticism there is little articulated thought—such thought as Plato's or even Plotinus's—to sustain and direct it. He rises on the wings of faith, not from their high tableland of the mind, but from the flats of daily experience. Even when he lives with us, with home and kindred and nature and art, he is never in the current of human affections but outside of them, contemplating them, on the verge of transcending them. He is always pluming his wings, not for an epic flight, but for a mystical ascenscion to the Highest, where the ways of God do not even need justification, and where the ways of men are forgotten. That absorbed interest in the ways of men—in their actions, thoughts, sensations, passions—which the aesthetic point of view presupposes, was, after all, wanting in Emerson, notwithstanding his resolutions to be a student of the world. He preferred his Plato and his Jesus to his ballads and his Hamlets, and preferred them so markedly that he never quite understood what the ballad-makers and the master of revels had accomplished. Sifting great men to ascertain the constitution of the First Class, he reduced the number sternly to two, Jesus and Shakespeare. Logically he should have reduced the number to one, Jesus, and then have substituted for Him that Oneself whose praises his disciple Whitman was confusedly to sing.

Norman Foerster
American Criticism (New York: Houghton Mifflin,
1928), pp. 104, 109

[Emerson] lacked the temperamental means of letting himself go. In all matters, he had to think several times. The most spontaneous sensation, emotion, passion, had to be weighed before it was committed, even to paper. The deep, fine heart had to consult the intellect before final communication. And what an intellect this was! If the philosopher, seldom complete in himself, interfered with the poet, nevertheless, when they blended, they rendered poems and prose poems of great power and originality. They have a singing eloquence not to be heard in Bryant and Poe. At such times, matter and manner have been caught in an absolute ecstasy. The philosophic poem or poetic philosophy is perfect. One does not care how the perfection was formed, or by what devious hesitations and second thoughts the original fragments were welded.

Technical faults, popular with grammarians and rhetoricians, are apparent on every other page. Such critics have made the most of their opportunities to score against Emerson. Because of his avoidance (it could not have been ignorance) of the rules of syntax in constructing his poems, certain passages have to be read more than once before we dig out their meaning. There are times, surely, when the poet would not have sacrificed a meaning by a closer observance of the rules. Prosodists—another crew of perfectionists—find glaring breaks in Emerson's scansion—an even more risky fault. One barely sets sail along a superbly sustained metre, when a tortured accent or missing foot trips the eye and ear, and a passage has to be re-read for the sake of rhythmic readjustment. Still more irksome is the need of progressing through a series of flying images or aphorisms, some of which refuse to dovetail. Poet and philosopher part, and indulge in a lofty dispute for the rights of priority. The dialectic is dazzling, but the earthly reader is lost in the struggle. Finally, a determination toward complete independence of style often led the poet into fine writing—writing that might have benefited from occasional commonplace or downright banality.

Alfred Kreymborg
Our Singing Strength (New York:
Coward McCann, 1929), pp. 68-69

. . . Unlike the truly great, the influence of Emerson shrinks for most of us as we ourselves develop. May the cause not lie in the two flaws I have pointed out—flaws in the man as in his doctrine in spite of the serene nobility of so much of his life? If with all his wide and infinitely varied reading, noted in his *Journals,* we find his culture a bit thin and puerile, is it not because he himself trusted too much to that theory of spontaneity, of the "spontaneous glance," rather than to the harder processes of scholarship and thinking-through coherently; and if we find him lacking in depth and virility, is it not because he allowed himself to become a victim to that vast American optimism with its refusal to recognize and wrestle with the problem of evil? . . .

If Emerson is still the outstanding figure in American letters, is that not the equivalent of saying that America a century after the *Essays* appeared has not yet grown to mental maturity, and that the gospel it preaches is inspiring only for unformed adolescence—of whatever age—without having risen to a comprehension of the problems of maturity? In Europe, the past has bequeathed not only a wealth of art, but a legacy of evil borne and sorrow felt. Perhaps American letters, like American men, will not grow beyond the simple optimism and, in one aspect, the shallow doctrine of Emerson until they too shall have suffered and sorrowed. Emerson in his weakness as in his strength, is American through and through. He could have been the product, in his entirety, of no other land, and that land will not outgrow him until it has some day passed through the fires of a suffering unfelt by him and as yet escaped by it.

James Truslow Adams
At (October, 1930), p. 492

Pure—the negation of negations, the most stripped and meaningless of concepts. Yet the keyword that unlocks the mystery of [Emerson's] intrepid, sagacious, first-rate mind, a mind that had no commerce with deep, primordial, tragic, human things, an almost abstract, disembodied mind, fine but thin, bloodless and so unclouded, never somber, almost never troubled to its depth because it had no direct contact with the problems and conflicts—nine-tenths of human life—which spring from human passions, relations, longings, triumphs, despairs. . . .

Yet . . . of all the New England Group he alone has a self-sustaining and permanent existence. . . . He was a man among Babbitts and a musician among the dumb. . . . I have written to no purpose if it is not clear that he is in his minor and limited way, a classic. For what is a classic? . . . A classic is simply a writer who has left certain works or even pages which the youth of each generation can and does by some instinctive and passionate reinterpretation make its own.

Ludwig Lewisohn
Expression in America (New York: Harper, 1932), pp. 117, 135

Shifting the focus of the mind from nature as existence to nature as food for spirit, was Emerson's primary aim and his chief argument for idealism. He felt the liberation which poetic imagination brings, but in his eagerness to welcome the achievements of the mind in disregard of matter, he (and most of his friends) went to the absurd lengths of welcoming almost anything that revealed extraordinary power. . . . The transcendentalists shared and abetted the fashion of their day in extending an uncritical sympathy toward almost anything that was unscientific, in their effort to emancipate the spirit from the habits of natural understanding. In this trait, and in general, Emerson represents the golden mean of New England transcendentalism. Though he patronized and sympathized with the reformers and mystics surrounding him, he himself yielded in neither direction; he kept himself aloof, using these ideas and enthusiasms as themes for critical self-cultivation. Not only as a person, but also as an institution, Emerson was both the genial critic and the constructive idealist, combining Yankee humor and sobriety with poetic imagination and freedom. His ability to keep on friendly terms with his intellectual and social environment and tradition made him a great American mediator; his public accepted from him as gospel what in other tones and idioms it repudiated as heresy or humbug.

Herbert W. Schneider
A History of American Philosophy (New York:
Columbia Univ. Pr., 1946), pp. 285-86

[Emerson] was a liberating influence in that he stimulated men to abandon dogmas that had lost their meaning, and gave them courage to rely on themselves. "I unsettle all things," was his own boast. "No facts are to me sacred, none are profane; I simply experiment, an endless seeker with no Past at my back."

But if all men relied on their own "self-supplied" powers without the guidance of dogmas or institutions, was there any guarantee that they would co-operate with each other in a democratic way of life? Would Emerson's self-reliant American display a necessary moral restraint, or would he be predatory and acquisitive? Emerson could denounce the commercialism and the materialistic ambitions of his contemporaries with a Hebraic severity. But although the difference between the self-reliance that was moral and spiritual and that which was predatory and acquisitive was clear enough in his own mind, he did not succeed in making it sufficiently clear in his philosophy; and with his deep-rooted American confidence in the individual and suspicion of authority, he was not willing to recognize that the individual cannot realize all his moral and spiritual potentialities unless he is aided by appropriate social institutions. He had a tendency to evade these problems by retreating into a mystical religiosity that had little relation to the real world. He displayed at times a naïve optimism as characteristic of the America of his time as was his democratic idealism.

Henry B. Parkes
The American Experience (New York:
A. A. Knopf, 1947), pp. 190-91

The ideas of Emerson were . . . merely the commonplaces of the Romantic movement; but his language was that of the Calvinistic pulpit. He was able to present the anarchic and anti-moral doctrines of European Romancism [*sic*] in a language which for two hundred years had been capable of arousing the most intense and the most obscure emotions of the American people. He could speak of matter as if it were God; of the flesh as if it were spirit; of emotion as if it were Divine Grace; of impulse as if it were conscience; and of automatism as if it were the mystical experience. And he was addressing an audience which, like himself, had been so conditioned by two hundred years of Calvinistic discipline, that the doctrines confused nothing, at the outset, except the mind: Emerson and his contemporaries, in surrendering to what they took for impulse, were governed by New England habit; they mistook second nature for nature. They were moral parasites upon a Christian doctrine which they were endeavoring to destroy. The same may be said of Whitman, Emerson's most influential disciple, except that Whitman came closer to putting the doctrine into practice in the matter of literary form: whereas Emerson, as a poet, imitated the poets of the early 17th century, whose style had been formed in congruence with the doctrines of Aristotle, Aquinas, and Hooker.

Yvor Winters
In Defense of Reason (New York: Morrow, 1947), p. 587

The miracle of perception was the life of [Emerson's] vision, and he wished to domesticate it, to teach all men how to live a sympathetic existence and share the power of spirit. He was able to live by his perception, able to live serenely in the optimism generated by a cosmically guaranteed and significant conduct of life. But the basis of his will to believe was correspondence—one of those "profound convictions," he said, "which refuse to be analyzed." For him the angle of vision was religious perspective and correspondence the prism through which his natural eye spiritualized the facts of life. Through it the fire of his piety could infuse the natural facts with the warmth of his desire. To iron-lidded men, however, men who disdained to believe in the possibility of sympathetic existence, the prism was opaque. Among them he knew that the vision he had created was good only as "a lonely faith, a lonely protest in the uproar of atheism." He recognized that in the age of Darwin the age of faith was doomed, that after his generation mysticism would "go out of fashion for a long time," that the reconciler of the next generation would have to create a vision corresponding to the new revelations of science. And knowing that his vision was only a momentary balance in the silent revolutions of thought, he was willing to pass on the burden of seeing and mediation to those who could do it freshly for their time. This willingness to let the generations seek their truth and to make their experiments on life was what he affirmed, and in his own way and for his own time, as much by the effect of his character as by his words, enacted.

Sherman Paul
Emerson's Angle of Vision (Cambridge, Mass.:
Harvard Univ. Pr., 1952), p. 230

Emerson, who did not possess Coleridge's knowledge and power of definition, throws another kind of light on the origins of modern taste. His works are like a continuous monologue in which the genesis of symbolism is enacted over and over. Though he never goes far beyond the breaking of the shell, he exemplifies in the most circumstantial way the new sensibility in the act of emergence. Emerson's failing was a lack of literary purposefulness, but his virtue was honesty. For all his absorption in the ineffable One, he was a faithful reporter of multiplicity. "A believer in Unity, a seer of Unity," he wrote, "I yet behold two." The essential drama of his work was the involuntary drama of his mind: the endless fusion and separation of the elements of his world, issuing in the "fragmentary curve" which was the characteristic structure of his essays. This adumbration of symbolic method is parallel to the concept of symbolism, which comes into being on his pages out of the pressure of the past and the needs of the present. It arises in his frank account of "the perpetual tilt and balance" of matter and mind, which urge their claims upon him like "two boys pushing each other on the curbstone of the pavement." Emerson's vision of symbolic reality was achieved out of the heart of a basic conflict of ideas. To follow the involution of his thought is one way of exploring what symbolism is.

Charles Feidelson, Jr.
Symbolism and American Literature (Chicago:
Univ. Chicago Pr., 1953), pp. 123-24

It is ironic and a little pathetic that so devoted a moralist and so honest a man should have drifted into a position which lays him open to the bad-tempered charge of Yvor Winters that "at the core [he] is a fraud and a sentimentalist," and which is leading increasing numbers of critics and readers to conclude that he is, in Eliot's phrase, "already an encumbrance." The logic of his faith forced him into a comprehensive acceptance that is more irritating than helpful in our disastrous times. In outline, the story of his thought seems an episode from a vanished past—his initial challenge a final eruption of protestant perfectionism thinly disguised as "modern philosophy," his eventual acquiescence close in spirit to what James called soft determinism; both now obsolete stages in evolution of thought that seems unlikely ever to make them tenable again.

Yet the time and attention we still devote to him are not misplaced. We must be careful, as with any artist, to discriminate the quality of the man from his classification as a thinker. We must not, for example, overlook his unique sense of the practical and personal immediacy of ideas, what has been called his "pragmatic mood," because the ideas he chose as weapons are not those we would select; or contemn the spirit of high-minded rectitude in his life and writing because he found it easier than we do to hold that evil will bless—still less, because, to our discredit, we find his sense of duty distasteful; or close our minds, because of changing fashions of speech and opinion, to his memorable formulation of the individualistic principles that still must command our loyalty; or belittle the shrewdness of his *obiter dicta* on the American scene and the human condition to offset that condition he took the road to an agnostic optimism. . . .

Furthermore, it is not true that he has nothing to say to us. Emerson believed in the dignity of human life more unreservedly, almost, than anyone who has ever written. Man possesses, he felt, an unlimited capacity for spiritual growth and is surrounded by influences that perpetually call on him for the best he has of insight and greatness and virtue and love. We think more reanly now, no doubt more truly, of ourselves and our world. But as long as we retain any self-respect, something in us must answer—whatever the second thoughts—to the faith in man that invigorates every page of these volumes. To reject Emerson utterly is to reject mankind.

Stephen E. Whicher
Freedom and Fate (Philadelphia: Univ.
Pennsylvania Pr., 1953), pp. 172-73

Emerson's defects . . . , when they are not the defects of his time and of the inherent nature of his ideas, may fairly be called the defects of his qualities; and, when all is said, they are minor. If we look at the whole body of his work from as near as we can come to his own point of view, remembering that he always aimed at the universal rather than at any particular unity, and that the relation between his various statements is usually organic in the progressive, or dialectic, rather than in any static sense, we can see that his philosophy and his art have a consistency which need not be referred to his character but which inheres fundamentally in the organic metaphor and which is often most present in the tension and dynamic balance of his most contradictory pronouncements. Historically, though he was by no means our greatest literary artist, he was perhaps the most important thinker and writer we have had, the first to make our declaration of cultural independence effective, and the chief pioneer of romanticism (that is to say, of modern thought and art) in this country. We can well afford to forgive him his structural weaknesses and his excessive optimism, which was never merely sentimental, as some critics have assumed. And we owe it to ourselves, if not to Emerson, to remember that we are where we are in the world's culture today partly because we have his high, stooping shoulders to stand upon.

Richard P. Adams
PMLA (March, 1954), p. 130

. . . Emerson [dreamed] that America would develop new ways of life different from the old ways of Europe. He dreamed that the new world would progressively realize the ideals of freedom and democracy enunciated by the Declaration of Independence. And he believed that these American ideals would be realized, not because they were ideal, but because they were appropriate to the facts of American life and to the laws of modern science which were shaping that life. His writing gave expression to the American revolt from the genteel tradition of the European past, to the celebration of the democratic ideals of the American present, and to the formulation of the natural laws and pragmatic attitudes which these implied for the future.

Emerson's "transcendental" philosophy, therefore, was not something borrowed from the abstract ideas of Kant or Carlyle, but something concretely suggested by his own American experience. His revolutionary addresses to the "American Scholar" and the Divinity School reflected his own revolt from the genteel tradition of his youth. His celebration of the discipline of "Nature" and the mysteries of "The Over-Soul" resulted from his own experiences of religious conflict and illumination. And his preaching of active "Self-Reliance," and the facing of "Experience" resulted from his own American experience, and foreshadowed the pragmatism and experimentalism of modern science.

. . . Emerson rejected the authority of tradition—which was essentially a formulation of other people's past experiences—primarily because he believed the conditions of modern American life were so different from those of the "courtly" or "feudal" past as to make the old traditions invalid for the new times. He emphasized the need of intuition and of self-reliance for modern men because the new laws and "traditions" of the new world had not yet been formulated. Rejecting all "paltry empiricism," he appealed, like William James, to "the universal impulse to believe" in "this new yet unapproachable America I have found in the West."

Revolting against past tradition, reflecting present experience, appealing of necessity to the future, Emerson's thought became typically the American philosophy, or "dream."

Frederic I. Carpenter
American Literature and the Dream (New York:
Philosophical Library, 1955), pp. 25, 29

[Emerson's] controlling mode of thought, even in his later and more skeptical years, is a certain form of Optimism and *not* a form of the Tragic Sense, and what I should like to say now is that, however we may ourselves feel about his philosophy, it was one that rested not only on a deep personal experience but on a considered theory of Evil, and moreover that this was a theory by no means peculiar to Emerson, or original with him: on the contrary, it had a long and august tradition behind it in Western thought and analogies with the thought not only of Europe but of the East. To put it very briefly, it is the theory that identifies Evil with non-existence, with negation, with the absence of positive Being. In his own writings Emerson expressed this doctrine first in the famous "Address" at the Divinity School at Harvard in 1838, the manifesto of his heterodoxy. . . .

. . . [This] is not only a philosophical but an essentially religious view, and . . . its sources, to speak only of the West, are in the Platonic and Neo-Platonic tradition and in Christian theology on the side on which it derives from that tradition. . . .

. . . It is superficial to rule out the whole of [Emerson], once for all, on the ground that he lacked the Vision of Evil; to see him as nothing but a transcendental American optimist of the mid-nineteenth century, to fail to see that his view of these things was in a great philosophic and religious tradition; and that he rejected Tragedy not because he was by temperament wholly incapable of tragic insight but because it seemed to him that, as Karl Jaspers has said, "tragedy is not absolute but belongs in the foreground"; it belongs, as he says, "in the world of sense and time," but not in the realm of transcendence. It belongs, let us say, in the world of appearance, of the relative, of illusion; not in the realm of transcendent reality and truth in which Emerson's faith was complete. And perhaps it is only readers who have a comparable faith, who will now accept him as master and guide; accept him as Dante accepted Virgil: "tu duca, tu segnore, e tu maestro."

Newton Arvin
HdR (Spring, 1959), pp. 46-47, 50

In *English Traits* Emerson was wrestling with that whole complex of nineteenth-century ethnology which has since been labeled with opprobrious terms ranging from "proto-Fascist" to simply "mad," and which has shadowed the names of most of its leading exponents. Of course, the term "Emersonian" does not snarl portentously on the page as do "Nietzschean" and "Spenglerian"; rather, it carries with it (and unfairly, I think) an aura of bland impracticality, of something quite harmless and perhaps permanently outdated. . . . To attempt to evaluate Emerson's thought in terms of its specific historical and scientific validity, however, would be to test it against the wrong standard. For Emerson the essence of truth was always a mystery, and the most that he ever hoped to achieve was to catch some aspect of it through the construction of inspired metaphors. He would have been the first to admit that the value of his speculations never transcended their mythological appropriateness. From beginning to end, his method was that of the intuitive seer, boldly asserting today only those thoughts to which he could give an internal assent today, but reserving until tomorrow the assertion of tomorrow's truth. The value of Emerson's thought, therefore, must be measured less by a criterion of true or false than by a criterion of imaginative power and profundity. Examined in this light, we may learn to esteem even his most dogmatic and intemperate utterances. If we must, at the last, deny many of the key elements of what Emerson came to believe, we should not regard this as proving his irrelevance for the modern reader. In the present dark hour it may be well to listen to one who perceived the human world as always standing at the "brink of chaos, always in crisis," and yet who saw in man's perpetual thankfulness for the gift of existence the sign of some coming change. The "whole revelation" which was vouchsafed man, Emerson came finally to acknowledge, was no more than the experience of a "gentle trust"—and yet this experience proved sufficient to cover with flowers the "slopes of this chasm."

Philip L. Nicoloff
Emerson on Race and History (New York:
Columbia Univ. Pr., 1961), pp. 4-5, 257

. . . Emerson was a moral influence and may at some future time be one again; his work contains a system of ideas, and he may be read as demonstrating an intellectual method; but he is also, and in a way crucial to one's understanding of him in these other capacities, a man of words. It is *through* his tone, his metaphors, and his prose rhythms—the "literary" manifestations of his genius—that aspects of his message are conveyed which cannot be understood in any other way. Neglect the literary quality of the work, and one may miss the true meaning of its meaning.

. . . As a prophet, Emerson is apparently seeking to identify the sources of valuable experience, to name and liberate the springs of admirable action. He opens his attention to these in all realms of life: physical, practical, aesthetic, intellectual, moral, mystical. He tries to establish the conditions for initiative in each dimension of experience, to connect these possibilities one with the other, to recommend each separately and together as potential energies for his reader. Finally, as an artist, he seeks to commit the best sense of this manifold message to the local particulars of his discourse. The hope latent in this strategy is that an imaginative response to literary activity will provoke a more direct intuition of his discoveries. The prophetic Emerson may be paraphrased after a fashion by the "understanding": the artist requires a more lively, delicate, and empirical sympathy. And only as this develops in us can we find ourselves prepared to comprehend the prophecy.

Jonathan Bishop
Emerson on the Soul (Cambridge, Mass.:
Harvard Univ. Pr., 1964), pp. 5, 7-8

BENJAMIN   FRANKLIN

1706-1790

Born January 17 in Boston, Massachusetts. In 1718, he apprenticed as a printer to his brother James and, in 1722, the *Dogood Papers* were printed anonymously in the *New England Courant*. In 1723, however, he broke his apprenticeship and ran away to Philadelphia and a year later left for London under the patronage of Governor Keith. In London he published *A Dissertation on Liberty and Necessity, Pleasure and Pain* (1725) and became acquainted with many dignitaries. In 1726, he returned to Philadelphia and, in 1729, bought the *Pennsylvania Gazette*. A year later he married Deborah Read and, in 1731, founded the Philadelphia Library Company. In 1736, he established the Union Fire Company. He invented the open stove in 1742 and established the American Philosophical Society in 1744. In 1749, he founded an academy which later became the University of Pennsylvania. His famous kite experiment and the subsequent invention of the lightning rod took place in 1752. He was appointed Deputy Postmaster General of North America Post in 1753 and was chosen a Fellow of the Royal Society of London in 1756. In 1757, he was appointed colonial agent for the Province of Pennsylvania in London and published *The Way to Wealth*. He was appointed London agent for the colony of Georgia in 1768, New Jersey agent in London in 1769, and Massachusetts agent in London in 1770. In 1774, he was examined by Wedderburn before the privy Council and dismissed as Deputy Postmaster General. His wife died the same year, and in 1775 he returned to America. He presided over the Constitutional Convention of Pennsylvania in 1776, and was appointed one of the committee to frame the Declaration of Independence. In the same year he went to Paris as a commissioner from Congress to the French court. In 1781, he was appointed one of the peace commissioners for the treaty between England and the United States. He left France and returned to Philadelphia in 1785. He died April 17 in Philadelphia.

The Papers of Benjamin Franklin, American Philosophical Society and Yale University (1956-   ), edition in progress
Carl Van Doren, *Benjamin Franklin* (1938)

PERSONAL

. . . Speech and action blend together inextricably to form this fascinating literary figure. [Franklin] moves through the whole length of the eighteenth century, serene and self-possessed, a philosopher and statesman yet a fellow of infinite jest, a shrewd economist yet capable of the tenderest generosities. His wit was often coarse, if not obscene, and, as his latest editor observes, leaves a long "smudgy trail" behind it. Not a little that he wrote and that still exists in manuscript is too rank to be printed. One might wish all this away, and yet I do not know; somehow the thought of that big animal body completes our impression of the overflowing bountifulness of his nature. If wishing were having, I would choose rather that he had not made of his Autobiography so singular a document in petty prudence and economy. Nothing in that record is more typical than the remark on his habit of bringing home the paper he purchased through the streets on a wheelbarrow—"to show," he adds, "that I was not above my business." And for economy, one remembers his visit to the old lady in London who lived as a religious recluse, and his comment: "She looked pale, but was never sick; and I give it as another instance on how small an income life and health may be supported." Possibly the character of his memoirs would have changed if he had continued them into his later years; but I am inclined rather to think that the discrepancy between the breadth of his activities and the narrowness of his professed ideals would have become still more evident by such an extension. The truth is they only exaggerate a real deficiency in his character; there was, after all, a stretch of humanity beyond Franklin's victorious good sense. [1906]

Paul Elmer More
Shelburne Essays on American Literature (New York:
Harcourt, Brace, 1963), p. 66

The Franklin now discoverable in the ten volumes of his complete works is one of the most widely and thoroughly cultivated men of his age. He had not, to be sure, a university training, but he had what serves quite as well: sharp appetite and large capacity for learning, abundance of books, extensive travel, important participation in great events, and association through a long term of years with the most eminent men of three nations. . . . It is absurd to speak of one who has been subjected to the moulding of such forces as a product of the provinces. All Europe has wrought upon and metamorphosed the Yankee printer. The man whom Voltaire kisses is a statesman, a philosopher, a friend of mankind, and a favourite son of the eighteenth century. With no softening of his patriotic fibre or loss of his Yankee tang, he has acquired all the common culture and most of the master characteristics of the Age of Enlightenment—up to the point where the French Revolution injected into it a drop of madness: its emancipation from authority, its regard for reason and nature, its social consciousness, its progressiveness, its tolerance, its cosmopolitanism, and its bland philanthropy. Now this man deserves his large place in our literary history not so much by virtue of his writings, which had little immediate influence upon *belles-lettres*, as by virtue of his acts and ideas, which helped liberate and liberalize America. To describe his most important work is to recite the story of his life. [ca. 1917]

Stuart P. Sherman
in *Cambridge History of American Literature*, Vol. I
(New York: Macmillan, 1946), pp. 91-92

GENERAL

It is to little purpose that certain shortcomings of Franklin are dwelt upon. "There is a flower of religion, a flower of honor, a flower of chivalry, that you must not require of Franklin," said Sainte-Beuve; a judgment that is quite true and quite obvious. A man who is less concerned with the golden pavements of the City of God than that the cobblestones on Chestnut Street in Philadelphia should be well and evenly laid, who troubles less to save his soul from burning hereafter than to protect his neighbors' houses by organizing an efficient fire-company, who is less regardful of the light that never was on sea or land than of a new-model street lamp to light the steps of the belated wayfarer—such a man, obviously, does not reveal the full measure of human aspiration. Franklin ended as he began, the child of a century marked by sharp spiritual limitations. What was best in that century he made his own. In his modesty, his willingness to compromise, his openmindedness, his clear and luminous understanding, his charity—above all, in his desire to subdue the ugly facts of society to some more rational scheme of things—he proved himself a great and useful man, one of the greatest and most useful whom America has produced.

Vernon Louis Parrington
Main Currents in American Thought, Vol. I
(New York: Harcourt, Brace, 1927), p. 178

To call Franklin "one of the greatest masters of English expression" is the veriest nonsense. Almost any one of the Eighteenth Century New England theologians wrote better. Franklin, to be sure, was easier to understand, but there was far less in him worth understanding. His influence on the national letters, in the long run, was probably nil. "He founded no school of literature. He gave no impetus to letters. He put his name to no great work of history, of poetry, of fiction."

But by his international prominence and by the wide circulation of his two-penny philosophy he left a lasting impression on the national culture. In him "the 'lowbrow' point of view for the first time took definite shape, stayed itself with axioms, and found a sanction in the idea of 'policy.' " Thrift, industry, and determination were essential virtues in the building of the nation, but they were not, then or at any other time in history, of sufficient human dignity to build a life philosophy on. Franklin did precisely that for his private life, and by the force of his personality did more than any other man in his day to graft it upon the American poeple. The vulgarity he spread is still with us.

Charles Angoff
A Literary History of the American People, Vol. II
(New York: A. A. Knopf, 1931), pp. 309-10

Only once did Franklin forget his eighteenth century models and touch the spring of the spontaneous, laying bare his soul. It was a happening purely accidental, unpremeditated, unliterary as he conceived of literature: his *Autobiography* was created with no thought of a reading public. Written primarily for his grandchildren, it was poured out hastily in moments snatched from important business. It is Franklin himself undressed for company, at times all but naked. As a result, the book is a *man*: it lives and breathes; it is a classic to be rated with the greatest of the world's autobiographies. And it lives simply because for once Franklin forgot his art. . . .

More and more it is realized now that as a literary figure in our national life Franklin must depend almost wholly upon this single volume of which his own generation knew nothing. It was his "carte de visite," as Walt Whitman would have expressed it, to the generations of Americans to come. By sheer accident it had not been garbed by its author in eighteenth century dress, but had been presented off-hand in the simplicity that is ageless. It is, therefore, Volume One in the book-list of the new America. Its naturalness, its evident genuineness, its atmosphere of nothing withheld, nothing glossed over, its lapses into colloquial diction . . . —all mark it as a pioneer book.

Fred L. Pattee
The First Century of American Literature (New York:
Appleton, 1935), pp. 16-17

Franklin was not one of those men who owe their greatness merely to the opportunities of their times. In any age, in any place, Franklin would have been great. Mind and will, talent and art, strength and ease, wit and grace met in him as if nature had been lavish and happy when he was shaped. Nothing seems to have been left out except a passionate desire, as in most men of genius, to be all ruler, all soldier, all saint, all poet, all scholar, all some one gift or merit or success. Franklin's powers were from first to last in flexible equilibrium. Even his genius could not specialize him. He moved through this world in a humorous mastery of it. Kind as he was, there was perhaps a little contempt in his lack of exigency. He could not put so high a value as single-minded men put on things they give their lives for. Possessions were not worth that much, nor achievements. Comfortable as Franklin's possessions and numerous as his achievements were, they were less than he was. Whoever learns about his deeds remembers longest the man who did them. And sometimes, with his marvellous range, in spite of his personal tang, he seems to have been more than any single man: a harmonious human multitude.

Carl Van Doren
Benjamin Franklin (London: Putnam, 1939), p. 784

The merits of the colonial way of life were most fully exemplified in its representative man, Benjamin Franklin. Franklin was one of those men who achieve distinction by embodying completely the spirit of the society in which they live, rather than by deviating from it or going beyond it. He was the ideal common man of the American world, bold enough to try his hand at everything and unintimidated by professional pretensions of any kind, whether in politics or in science and literature. A human being with certain obvious limitations, having little sense of poetry and no taste for mysticism, endowed with a cool, uncomplicated, and somewhat calculating temperament, he cannot be accounted great by virtue of his concrete achievements in any field; he did not belong to the first rank as a writer or as a scientist or as a statesman. But he applied himself to an astonishing variety of different occupations; and to everything he brought the same refreshing qualities of sanity, realism, tolerance, resourcefulness, and human understanding. He was a great man because of what he was in himself rather than because of any specific accomplishment. This kind of greatness was possible in colonial America not only because of its democratic spirit but also because of the consistency of its intellectual and moral attitudes with its economic and social organization. The individual was able to achieve an integrated personality because he lived in a harmonious society. In his *Poor Richard* aphorisms Franklin could formulate the folk morality of his society without criticism or cynicism; his approval of those bourgeois virtues which brought economic success was only one aspect of his many-sided character, but it was not out of keeping with his other qualities. And it was because Franklin was so completely an American that he could represent America so successfully over a period of more than twenty-five years in European countries. Enjoying European society, and valuing all its qualities of charm and intellectual attainment, Franklin never lost contact with his American background or ceased to appreciate its unique virtues. As a result of his deep-rooted Americanism, this Philadelphia printer and son of a Boston tallow-chandler was able to mingle with European aristocracies and to defend American interests at the British and French courts with a complete self-assurance and sense of equality. He was neither intimidated by Europe nor impelled to depreciate it and attack it.

> Henry B. Parkes
> *The American Experience* (New York:
> A. A. Knopf, 1947), pp. 58-59

. . . In an age when most men wore wigs, he appeared at court bare-headed, his long brown-white hair falling nearly to his shoulders. Ornamental swords, in that age, customarily dangled from the belts of envoys presented to the king. Franklin had no sword. In an age when everyone at court tried to outdo each other with expensive gold and silver buckles attached to his shoes, Franklin made himself distinctive by wearing shoes of plain leather. His plain white stockings contrasted with his gray knee pants and coat. Under his arm he carried a three-cornered white hat which at least one contemporary French lady regarded as a symbol of liberty. On his nose lightly rested one of his most practical inventions, the new bifocal spectacles, which he had made famous.

The simple dignity of a rustic philosopher fitted him naturally and perfectly. In this role, as he well knew, lay his greatest appeal to the elegantly attired courtiers and the bejewelled and painted beauties of France. . . . Long accustomed to ennui from the full-dress parades of visiting envoys, the nobles in this stale old-world palace sensed in Franklin's presence an invigorating breath of the fresh, clean, new-world air of liberty. They were quick to respond with respect, admiration, and (on the part of some of the ladies) adoration for this eminent natural man from the wilderness of the American colonies.

> Richard E. Amacher
> *Franklin's Wit and Folly* (New Brunswick, N. J.:
> Rutgers Univ. Pr., 1953), pp. 4-5

Any view of the American character which is based on a concentration on how Americans make money is bound to be a distortion unless an equal consideration is given to what Americans do with the money they make;

so our conception of Franklin as an individual, and as a pioneer of the American personality, must suffer if we do not keep uppermost in our minds his constant injunctions against miserliness, if we do not emphasize the ideals to which he devoted himself while making money and after he had acquired a moderate fortune. Franklin, in other words, was more typical of America than his *Way to Wealth*, taken by itself, would indicate. Defender of the rights of man, he demanded that men help one another to live better lives. Patron of the arts, sciences and higher learning, he taught by precept and by example that men must endow and maintain schools and colleges to serve men's minds as well as hospitals to care for their bodies. The American blend of practicality and idealism is exemplified by the very combination of his activities: subscriptions in support of churches and a synagogue, and a college library; inventions to produce comfortable homes that were well heated and ventilated and protected from the lightning; support of the movement for the abolition of slavery and sponsorship of a school so that those Negroes who had been freed could learn trades and earn a standard of living equal to that of whites; organization of a fire company and a regular constabulary and also a subscription library; and a proposal for a more direct democracy than we know today.

Bernard Cohen
Benjamin Franklin (Indianapolis, Ind.:
Bobbs-Merrill, 1953) pp. xiv-xv

There are . . . but three parts of the [Autobiography], organically considered: the education in virtue, the principles and methods of the Art of Virtue, and the application of the rules of virtue to public life. Although probably not thus consciously planned, the book has a unity as a tract on the art of being human which it lacks as a mere narrative of a life. Like the autobiographies of Rousseau, Henry Adams, Goethe, and Wordsworth, the subject of the narrative is an alter ego of the author, as much a symbol or projection of his controlling views on the experience of living as it is a portrait of his actual self. The painter's self-portrait usually has the same character: it is as much a product of imagination as of observation. Franklin, like these others, was using this knowledge of the facts of his own life for a purpose which lay beyond the limits of literal reality.

His opening address to "My dear Son" may therefore be taken as but the first of a series of literary devices, common enough at the time but out of fashion now, which Franklin used to establish the factor which T. S. Eliot has called the "objective correlative," a literary counterpart to experience by means of which the author may gain his needed aesthetic detachment without losing the authenticity of the intimate object or event. . . .

From the mass of detail, there gradually emerges a whimsical but consistent character, a sort of New World Tom Jones who has rejected conventional ethical canons and substituted a pragmatic natural morality which can accept life as it comes but at the same time bend and control it through the exercise of a free will granted by a benevolent deity. . . .

The second section, which is the real heart of the book, caused most of the intellectual indigestion which became epidemic among nineteenth century romantics, and is even somewhat difficult for us to accept today. With unbelievable candor, he sets forth his working scheme for improvement in virtue, complete with tables and score sheets, and describes how and for how long he experimented with the scheme himself. His belief that the virtues were individually capable of precise description, and that they could be sharpened one by one by merely giving each a day of concentrated attention, has seemed to later readers a gross violation of fine feeling. It is rather an evidence of clear and consistent thinking in the framework of the empirical rationalism of his time, without the emotional coloring of sentimental humanitarianism.

. . . Actually if one could maintain the benign calm of sweet reason which was so completely at Franklin's command and avoid the self-conscious prudery of his critics, it would be hard to find anywhere a more helpful set of rules and instruments for self-improvement than that which he proposes. But it would also be necessary to share with him that irony and wit which he in turn shared with the other great prose satirists of his day and thereby avoid the subjectivity and emotional coloring which makes the sanest of advice a mockery.

Robert Spiller
Proceedings of the American Philosophical Society
(Aug. 31, 1956), pp. 313-14

PHILIP FRENEAU
1752-1832

Born January 2 in New York. In 1767, he entered the College of New Jersey as a sophomore. In 1771, together with H. H. Brackenridge, he wrote the graduation poem, "The Rising Glory of America." "General Gage's Soliloquy" was published in 1775, the year when he accepted the secretaryship for planters in Santa Cruz, West Indies. In 1778, he voyaged as a supercargo between the Azores and New York and was captured by the British and interned in a British prison ship in New York Harbor. *The British Prison Ship* was published in 1781, and, in the same year, he wrote many revolutionary poems for the *Freeman's Journal*. He shipped out as master of a brig in 1784, but, in 1789, married Eleanor

Forman and left the sea to become a journalist. In 1791, he became the editor of the *National Gazette*, strongly supporting the French Revolution and "Citizen" Genet, until 1793, when the *Gazette* suspended publication. He died Dec. 19 near his New Jersey farm "Mt. Pleasant" in a snow storm.

Fred L. Pattee, ed., *Poems of Philip Freneau, Poet of the American Revolution* (1902-1907), 3 vols.

Lewis Leary, *That Rascal Freneau: A Study in Literary Failure* (1941)

PERSONAL

[Freneau's] life was bitter and turbulent, cast in a bitter and turbulent age; yet he found some grains of comfort in the contemplation of nature and the exercise of the poet's craft. Through it all his heart remained clean and his hands unstained. If he was not a great poet whom all the critics praise, he loved beauty and served it in a careless world among an indifferent people, and it ill becomes America to forget his contribution or deny him some portion of the honor that has fallen generously to others no more deserving.

Vernon Louis Parrington
Main Currents in American Thought, Vol. I
(New York: Harcourt, Brace, 1927), p. 381

Philip Freneau failed in almost everything he attempted. It was partly his own fault, and partly the fault of the restless spirit of his time. Nurtured on books and poetry, he found himself at twenty in a world torn by political and economic stress. There was no place in this world for the life Freneau wanted to live; yet the ideals for which blood was being shed and governments overthrown in the late eighteenth century were just those toward which he strove. Caught mercilessly between the necessity of remaining true to his own highest aspiration and the equally compelling necessity of bending often to degrading means for its attainment, his life was a series of alternating compromises with and escapes from activity in revolutionary America. He was not a political philosopher: he was a poet and too sensitive to personal hurt, too quick to turn in anger on an opponent, to be taken seriously as a measure of the philosophical content of his time. Through all his life Freneau was the young radical who never forgets his quarrel with a world which makes no room for him. As such, he belongs to the twentieth century as well as to the eighteenth, and represents a type of literary failure familiar in almost any age.

But this does not mean that Freneau shall be forgotten. He remains chronologically near the head of every anthology of American verse. "The Wild Honeysuckle" and "The Indian Burying Ground" have become, at least in title, part of the equipment of every man who pretends to knowledge of the pre-Romantic period of English poetry.

Lewis Leary
That Rascal Freneau (New Brunswick, N. J.:
Rutgers Univ. Pr., 1941), p. ix

GENERAL

. . . Not the least of [Freneau's] anticipations was his prophecy of America's empire, and the conscious assumption within himself of so many of the traits of the practical calculating American mind, side by side with its thin mysticism; as if the temperaments of Poe and Franklin were united in one person. Here you shall read lines in glorification of commerce and science, such as our national poet today, if such existed, might write; here you shall see the past disparaged in the classics, and that self-flattering absorption in the present which has sapped the very roots of the New World's imagination. And here too is the fullest expression of that spirit of rebellion and mutual distrust in which the country was unfortunately, if necessarily, founded, and which has clung to it like an inherited taint in the blood, marring the harmony of its development, and suffering a partial expiation in the calamities of the civil war. There is a lesson for us today, and, in more ways than one, a little of humiliation, in the career of our first poet. [ca. 1908]

Paul Elmer More
Shelburne Esays on American Literature (New York:
Harcourt, Brace, 1963), p. 83

. . . Had [Freneau] written half as much he might have written twice as well. That he was something of an artist is shown by the care with which he revised his poems for five successive editions; but his revisions are sometimes actually for the worse. Yet Freneau surpassed all his contemporaries not only in quality but also in sheer quantity and in variety of subject and form. Furthermore, his work presents an almost unique combination of satiric power, romantic imagination, and feeling for nature. At one extreme is the bitter invective of his satires; at the other, the delicate fancy of his best lyrics. . . .

There remains . . . out of Freneau's voluminous product, a small body of work of permanent interest. "The House of Night" deserves remembrance, not only for its pioneer romanticism but also for passages of intrinsic beauty and power; and a score of his lyrics, while far from perfect, are fine enough to deserve a permanent place in our anthologies. What his slender but genuine talent might have produced under more favourable conditions, even a generation later, can only be surmised, but even as it is we have in Freneau the only American poet before Bryant who possessed both imaginative insight and felicity of style. [ca. 1917]

Samuel M. Tucker
in *Cambridge History of American Literature*, Vol. I
(New York: Macmillan, 1933), pp. 181, 183

[Freneau's] chief aesthetic difficulty . . . is that his expansive sympathy, his enthusiasm for what has been called "the cluttered incoherency of the mundane spectacle," his aversion to restraint—all bequeathed him by naturalism—made him unable to select and focus with concentrated intensity truly significant experience in such a way as to stir the reader's imagination, to suggest a symbolic quality. He can seldom, as Browning said, "do the thing which breeds the thought." In most of his poems . . . there is absent that focused vision, that arrangement of life carefully planned to produce a desired effect, that order and harmony, which distinguishes art from experience. He is expansive, rather than intense: that sublime Dantean faculty for "one smiting word and then silence" was never Freneau's. Lack of restraint accounts, also, for his too frequently slipshod metrical and rhyming effects. If a good poem is like a pebble dropped into the still waters of the imagination, wakening ripples there that circle and spread until they lap along the shores of infinity, the average poem of Freneau is like a whole handful of pebbles, thrown carelessly into the "waters of the imagination," wakening ripples there which quickly clash in mere confusion.

Harry Hayden Clark
Poems of Freneau (New York: Harcourt, Brace,
1929), pp. liv-lv

I have every desire to be generous to Freneau, for his character was most amiable. He shared the more liberal vision of America with Paine and Crèvecoeur and was an impassioned friend of the humble and the oppressed. In satires and lampoons he belabored the Federalists and took the part of the people. But these verses are without true life today. It is also possible that in a less turbulent age and in a more cultivated society he might, as he himself rather touchingly pleaded, have been a poet. That, too, is a futile reflection. He is, as things stand, a very minor eighteenth-century writer, more agreeable than his contemporaries because mildly but genuinely touched by the early and restrained romanticism of, let us say, Akenside. He did at least see somewhat poetically the wild honeysuckle and hear the honeybee and the katydid and in "The House of Night" feel for himself the gloom of the Graveyard school of poets. He also wrote blank verse which, fed by the same influences, is not unprophetic of Bryant.

Ludwig Lewisohn
Expression in America (New York: Harper, 1932), p. 41

MARGARET FULLER
1810-1850

Born May 23 in Cambridgeport, Massachusetts. She was educated by her father as a precocious child, reading Ovid in the original at the age of eight. In 1839, she held "conversations" (discussion groups) in Boston and, in 1840, became the editor of *Dial. Woman in The Nineteenth Century* was published in 1845. In 1846, she traveled to Europe and, in 1847, met Angelo Ossoli. Her son was born in the village of Rieti in 1848. She assisted in the Roman Revolution of 1849 and wrote a history of the Revolution in Florence. In 1850, she set sail with her husband and child for America, but vessel was shipwrecked off Fire Island on July 19, and she and her family all perished.

Mason Wade, ed., *The Writings of Margaret Fuller* (1941)

Faith Chipperfield, *In Quest of Love, The Life and Death of Margaret Fuller* (1957)

PERSONAL

As a woman, if we are to consider her socially, we must begin by thinking of her appearance. She had a passionate longing to be beautiful; but apparently no one thought her so. She was rather short, rather heavy, had a lofty but not attractive carriage, opened and shut her eyes oddly, poised her head oddly. Emerson says that at first she "made a disagreeable impression on most persons . . . to such an extreme that they did not wish to be in the same room with her." She grew aware of this with time, though perhaps she did not wholly understand the causes. "I made up my mind," she says "to be bright and ugly."

She was bright enough, but there was too much making up the mind about it, and it did not please strangers, nor even, in the early days, people who knew her well. A tradition of intense dislike still surrounds her name for many who can never get over it.

Gamaliel Bradford
NAR (July, 1919), pp. 109-10

It was by her personality rather than her work that [Margaret Fuller] impressed herself on her generation. But the conquest of a personality by a woman and a daughter of Puritanism was a heroic achievement. It meant the overthrow of respectabilities and sacrosanctities on every hand and a degree of resolution which is not supposed to reside in a truly feminine nature.

There were strange contradictions in her life which were a puzzle to her age. Her inconsistencies of health and fluctuations of energy were baffling to those who knew her best. Though always an invalid, she did the work of three women and sometimes "worked better when she was ill." She gave an impression of abundant vitality and a vast fund of energy. Yet there were moments when her energy strangely foresook her, as when she gave herself up without a struggle to the waves. These things were manifestations of hysteria, and Margaret had long been known to have had a neurotic constitution. According to the Freudian psychology, the source of her hysteria was a secret which she kept from herself, from her own consciousness. "Nature keeps many secrets," she once said, referring to the concealment of her marriage, "that I had supposed the moral writers exaggerated the dangers and plagues of keeping them; but they cannot exaggerate." But the dangers and plagues are greatly enhanced when this conflict with society becomes a conflict within one's own mental life. As Margaret kept the date of her marriage a secret to evade the social censor, she had in earliest childhood undertaken a far more dangerous concealment, the concealment from the inward censor of an erotic element in her love for a deeply reverenced father. Yet with her whole conscious nature, Margaret loved the truth and never ceased from following it. "I feel the strength to dispose with all illusions," she said; "I will stand ready and rejoice in the severest probations." In this kind of ordeal she was profoundly courageous.

Katharine Anthony
Margaret Fuller (New York: Harcourt, Brace,
1921), pp. 210-11

GENERAL

Margaret Fuller's book, *Woman in the Nineteenth Century*, was an epoch-making book and her power to impress her personality and her greatness of soul on those around her did more than anything else to bring the acknowledgment and the recognition that women had an intellectual and spiritual contribution to make, as great as that of men. She blazed new trails; she made many friends, both men and women, in this country and in Europe; she left a trail wherever she went which stimulated thought. It is not what she wrote which makes her life for us a vivid influence today, but what she was, and . . . from a rather tragic childhood to the heroic and tragic end, you feel the sweep of a great personality. She sometimes touched the depths of human sorrow; she sometimes touched the heights of joy and exaltation, but all through there is the strain of indomitable courage and fineness of spirit, which is exhilarating and valuable to us today as it was to those who actually met and knew her.

Mrs. Franklin Delano Roosevelt
Introd. in *Margaret Fuller,* by Margaret Bell (New York: Albert and Charles Boni, 1930), p. 14

Margaret Fuller is mentioned in all histories of American literature, yet as a writer she is as dead as Nahum Tate. Widely accepted in her own day, the first woman in this country, I believe, to attempt and succeed in making a living by her pen, there is not a single page of her writing that is read today, except by the literary antiquarian. She survives wholly as a personality, embalmed in the dislike of Lowell and Hawthorne.

Higginson, it is true, calls her the best literary critic of America. She is not that, she is not even a good literary critic, and for one reason. She could not write. Her style is impossible—dull, inflated, muddy, possessing all the vices and none of the virtues of critical prose. And yet, if one has the patience to wade through it, to discover what she was trying to say, one finds traces of a good critical intelligence.

George E. De Mille
Literary Criticism in America (New York: Dial Pr., 1931), pp. 128-29

[Margaret Fuller] was a whetstone of genius; she possessed the gift of bringing out the brilliance in her friends, and where they lacked talent she made them rise far above their natural limitations. Her crudities and absurdities are those of the pioneer, and are in large measure due to the enthusiasm with which she blazed the trail for those who won greater recognition as they followed in her path. Longfellow, who was no friend of hers and had felt her critical sting, remarked long after her death: "It is easy enough now to say and see what she then saw and said, but it demanded insight to see and courage to say what was entirely missed by that generation." She was a potent force in the Feminist movement; she did much to make the masterpieces of German literature familiar in a country where the language was hardly known when she began the work; she fostered the growth of interest in art; and she proclaimed the dawn of a new day in America, when our literature and art would no longer be derivative and imitative, but rather the unique flowering of our own traditions and culture. She was ahead of her time, yet very much of it. New England's greatest era becomes more understandable in the light of Margaret Fuller's life. Emerson can be read without reference to his historical background, as Shakespeare often is, but Margaret Fuller brings that background to life for us, so that greater figures than she become more clearly defined and better understood.

Mason Wade
Margaret Fuller (New York: Viking, 1940), pp. xv-xvi

BRET HARTE
1839-1902

Born August 25 in Albany, New York. After the death of his father in 1854, he went to San Francisco with his mother, and there worked as a teacher, miner, printer, and editor. *Condensed Novels* was published in 1867, and a year later he became the editor of the *Overland Monthly*, and published "The Luck of Roaring Camp" and "The Outcasts of Poker Flat." In 1871, he moved to New York. He became U. S. Consul at Crefeld, Germany in 1878 and Consul at Glasgow in 1880. In 1885, he moved to London. He died May 5 in Camberley, England.

The Works of Bret Harte (1925), 25 vols.
George R. Stewart, *Bret Harte: Argonaut and Exile* (1931)

PERSONAL

There is . . . no doubt that Bret Harte was, to casual friends and acquaintances, an amiable and companionable person. Nobody has ever alleged that he had vices, unless weakness is a vice; and an amiable weakness, a willingness to give his friends and his public what they desired, characterized his life and his artistic career. The life of English clubs and country-houses evidently demanded nothing which he was not able to give, and his public was, unfortunately, not exacting. So far as it was English, it had a pretty vague notion of the veracity of his replicas of the early Californian sketches. Nor was judgment in the Eastern States of America greatly more discriminating. The man had not only no trouble in disposing of his wares; he had more "orders" than he could fill. So he went down in comfort to the grave, and his most charitable epitaph would include, in some form, the statement that though his only inspiration was outlived by more than thirty years, that was not, directly, his fault; and the remark might fairly be appended that a single inspiration, a single moment of supreme sincerity, is more than is allotted to one in a million of our admirable and progressive species.

Henry W. Boynton
Bret Harte (London: Heinemann, 1905), pp. 77-79

. . . Harte's life is not a tragedy in the older style; in that case he would have died amid a flood of poetry about 1878. In a modern tragedy, he would have slunk off the stage at about the same date, condemned to pass the rest of his life in poverty, obscurity, and bitterness. On the contrary, from 1878 until his health finally broke, his life was a constant progression upwards in every respect; his early years represented a greater literary triumph, his later years a greater triumph of character.

His life in comparison with lives in general was not even a tragedy in the loose sense of the word—a series of mournful events. He achieved a fame equaled by few in his generation. He knew the supreme joy of composing some works of art which have often been judged as close to perfection as man is likely to attain. He had the satisfaction of realizing throughout many years that all over the world thousands of people knew and loved his name and awaited his stories with pleasure. In spite of friends lost, he was successful in establishing a large number of unbroken, warm human relationships. . . . In comparison with drab lives which attain domestic peace and a competency, if this be tragedy, let us have more of them.

George Stewart
Bret Harte (Boston: Houghton Mifflin, 1931), pp. 331-32

SHORT STORIES

. . . Despite the fact that Dickens excelled Bret Harte in depth and scope, there is reason to think that the American author of short stories will outlast the English novelist. The one is, and the other is not, a classic writer. It was said of Dickens that he had no "citadel of the mind"—no mental retiring-place, no inward poise or composure; and this defect is shown by a certain feverish quality in his style, as well as by those well-known exaggerations and mannerisms which disfigure it.

Bret Harte, on the other hand, in his best poems and stories, exhibits all that restraint, all that absence of idiosyncrasy as distinguished from personality, which marks the true artist. What the world demands is the peculiar flavor of the artist's mind; but this must be conveyed in a pure and unadulterated form, free from any ingredient of eccentricity or self-will. In Bret Harte there is a wonderful economy both of thought and language. Everything said or done in the course of a story contributes to the climax or end which the author has in view. There are no digressions or superfluities; the words are commonly plain words of Anglo-Saxon descent; and it would be hard to find one that could be dispensed with. The language is as concise as if the story were a message, to be delivered to the reader in the shortest possible time.

Henry C. Merwin
The Life of Bret Harte (London:
Chatto and Windus, 1911), pp. 343-44

The best deserved portion of Bret Harte's popularity rests upon his sympathetic portrayal of the essential goodness that shines in even the most tarnished specimen of humanity. But even in his revelation of the nobleness that lies sleeping but never dead in the most sordid, Harte is the melodramatist. It is true that he avoids the naive simplicity of painting characters either all black or all white; but he puts them in an equally crude motley of sharply contrasted black and white; his art is not sufficiently subtle to paint in shades of gray. Compare Edwin Arlington Robinson's Flammonde with Harte's Oakhurst, and Oakhurst falls into the category of stage villains with redeeming traits. . . .

If we examine the most famous of Bret Harte's situations, we find that the situations like the characters are composed of violent contrasts. A baby born and reared among miners; a beautiful daughter of joy devoting her life to the care of a helpless paralytic; a simple-hearted man in all innocence offering his pile as a bribe to the jury to release his friend— how much of the appeal of these striking situations depends on the revelation of character in a crisis? How much upon startling incongruity? [ca. 1927]

Lucy Lockwood Hazard
The Frontier in American Literature (New York:
Barnes and Noble, 1941), pp. 190-91

Just as the Greek drama retained to the last some vestiges of choral dancing and its appropriate tone, so the American short story has retained some of the essential qualities of the anecdotal humor of indigenous American "story-telling." From barroom and country store it passed to the pulpit and press and finally became a literature without prolixity, affectation, reverence, or moral conscientiousness—a free and original American short story.

It is when Harte is following this lead most closely that he best succeeds. The attitude and the technique furnish the fundamentals of his art when he has far transcended the simple objective of being "funny." Humor easily passes out of the phase of laughter and becomes a matter of temperament and philosophy, conditioning the whole set of the humorist's mind and governing his soberest behavior. Not only Harte's contrasts and exaggerations but the direct openings and deft endings of his stories, his light tread and smart uninterrupted pace when he is going well, his quick crossing of sentiment with irony or wit, his stripped but comprehensive and exact descriptions, his terse phrase and instinctive avoidance of the "purple passage," indeed his whole style and structure when his subject is within his grasp—all these rise naturally and inevitable out of the kind of humor he has described. And it is all this that constitutes Harte's fundamental contribution to the American short story.

Joseph Harrison
Bret Harte: Representative Selections (New York:
American Book, 1941), pp. cvii-cviii

"The Luck of Roaring Camp" is the father of all Western local color stories; "The Heathen Chinee" begot a progeny of dialect poems. Both represented something new to sophisticated audiences: a romantic, picturesque world; characters as striking as the characters of Dickens and perhaps in part derived from Dickens; a trick of neat paradox that gave scoundrels Raphael faces and endowed bruisers and hard cases with a saving spot of sentiment; a method of story telling that was lean, unpadded, finely calculated. Harte had served a long apprenticeship. He was a finished writer by the time "The Luck" appeared. He was destined to have an influence as great as that of the greatest.

But when Harte left San Francisco in 1871, bound for Boston and the larger world, he had already done all his best work. Money pressures, the demands of a public that always wanted "more like 'The Luck,'" and perhaps a drying-up of his inspiration, forced him into a mold. He went on, the rest of his life, imitating himself. The last twenty-four years of his life he lived abroad, in Germany, in Scotland, and in London where he died. At the end he was a tired, skillful, dependable hack, turning out stories to order and adding a volume every other year or so to his collected works. The best of his achievement lay far back in the seventies.

Wallace Stegner
in Literary History of the United States, eds. Robert Spiller et al, Vol. II
(New York: Macmillan, 1948), p. 867

GENERAL

Bret Harte had visited the gold fields, he had even ridden stagecoaches among them, in the capacity of express messenger, for a period of some weeks. The syrupy tales that he spun out of this acquaintance drifted opportunely before a public relieved of war and facing westward. They were prettily written, between laughter and kind tears. They informed readers enamored of sentiment that even in the Sierras the simpler virtues were imperishable and that humanity remained capable of sweetness on the Pacific slope. So America awarded these romantic Mexicans, quaint miners, and heartbroken harlots the applause and the sobs with which it annually welcomes the announcement that hearts are golden after all.

Our literature thus acquired "Far Western fiction," a pattern of platitudes and conventions seldom broken since 1869. Mr. Harte had presented to us a code of behavior attributable to God's out-of-doors and the lonely peaks. He had invented a dialect even more meretricious, which is current still among his inheritors. Few besides Mark Twain have ventured to dissent from either code or dialect; fewer still have been recognized as dissenting and no dissent has availed much, which is the history of realism in our fiction. Sentiment and fashion abundantly repaid him for a few years, after which he spent a lifetime pathetically rewriting his success. But he had given the nation the nicest possible lens through which to scan its western boundary.

He was not, even in personal behavior, a Westerner. A kind of envy corrodes his letters to his nearest friends—plus a certain frankness in confessing his disasters. He had no generosity; even his praise sneers. He endured fame more eagerly than competitors and grew steadily more covetous of other men's success. No warmth was in him, no capacity to accept a friend's advancement with pleasure. Envy deepens through his relationships, becoming in the end mere bad temper. He seems to have kept no friends, at least in America; what finally ended all his friendships was not so much the loans he forgot or the hospitality he flouted, so much as it was his acetic malice.

Bernard De Voto
Mark Twain's America (Chautauqua, N. Y.: Chautauqua Institution, 1932), pp. 162-63

Bret Harte's literary career ended, to all intents, when he left California in 1871, and it is possible that even his early work has been too highly esteemed. He has been called a stylist of distinction, a master of the short story, and a penetrating student of human nature. Yet it is easy to find flaws in his style, to expose the superficiality of his characterization, and to list many short story writers more dextrous than he. Even his own claim, that he founded a peculiarly western literature, will not bear scrutiny, for he owed much to picturesque writers of other regions, and he portrayed only so much of California life as happened to fit his formula. Yet it is impossible to deny that there is power in his early work, and that something of the frontier does live in these romantic tales. Harte did not found a peculiarly western literature, but he did make a beginning. And then, with the beginning scarcely made, he turned his back on the West and on the hope of literary growth. What he had written, out of a real desire to express the spirit of the region he knew, was, he discovered, merely entertainment for his readers. He accepted—harassed, one must admit, by personal difficulties and financial troubles—the rôle of entertainer, and as an entertainer survived for thirty years his death as an artist.

Granville Hicks
The Great Tradition (New York: Macmillan, 1935), p. 37

NATHANIEL HAWTHORNE
1804-1864

Born July 4 in Salem, Massachusetts. His father died in 1808 at Surinam, Dutch Guiana. In 1813-1814, he was confined at home by an injury to his foot. In 1821, he entered Bowdoin College. *Fanshawe, A Tale* was published anonymously in 1828 and *Twice-Told Tales* in 1837. In 1838, he became engaged to Sophia Peabody and, 1839, became a measurer in the Boston Custom House. He joined the Brook Farm community in 1841, but a year later married Sophia Peabody and settled in "Old Manse" at Concord. He became a surveyor in the Salem Custom House in 1846 and while there published *Mosses from an Old Manse,* but he lost the position in 1849. A series of publications followed: *The Scarlet Letter* (1850); *House of Seven Gables* (1851); and *The Blithedale Romance* and *Life of Franklin Pierce* (1852). He was appointed United States Consul at Liverpool in 1853, but resigned the consulship three years later. In 1858, he took his family to Italy, and while there published *The Marble Faun* (1860). He returned to Concord in 1860 and published *Our Old Home* in 1863. He died at Plymouth, New Hampshire.

George P. Lathrop, ed., *The Complete Works of Nathaniel Hawthorne* (1883), 12 vols.

Randall Stewart, *Nathaniel Hawthorne* (1948)

PERSONAL

Like one of his own characters, he could "never separate the idea from the symbol in which it manifests itself." Yet the idea is always there. He is strong both in analysis and generalisation; there is no weakening of the intellectual faculties. Furthermore, his pages are pervaded with a subtle ironical humour hardly compatible with morbidness,—not a boisterous humour that awakens laughter, but the mood, half quizzical and half pensive, of a man who stands apart and smiles at the foibles and pretensions of the world. Now and then there is something rare and unexpected in his wit, as, for example, in his comment on the Italian mosquitoes: "They are bigger than American mosquitoes; and if you crush them, after one of their feasts, it makes a terrific blood spot. It is a sort of suicide to kill them." And if there is to be found in his tales a fair share of disagreeble themes, yet he never confounds things of good and evil report, nor things fair and foul; the moral sense is intact. Above all, there is no undue appeal to the sensations or emotions.

Rather it is true, as we remarked in the beginning, that the lack of outward emotion, together with their poignancy of silent appeal, is a distinguishing mark of Hawthorne's writings. The thought underlying all his work is one to trouble the depths of our nature, and to stir in us the sombrest chords of brooding, but is does not move us to tears or passionate emotion: those affections are dependent on our social faculties, and are starved in the rarefied air of his genius. Hawthorne indeed relates that the closing chapters of *The Scarlet Letter,* when read aloud to his wife, sent her to bed with a sick headache. And yet, as a judicious critic has observed, this may have been in part just because the book seals up the fountain of tears.

It needs but a slight acquaintance with his own letters and *Note-Books,* and with the anecdotes current about him, to be assured that never lived a man to whom ordinary contact with his fellows was more impossible, and that the mysterious solitude in which his fictitious characters move is a mere shadow of his own imperial loneliness of soul. [ca. 1904]

Paul Elmer More
Shelburne Essays on American Literature (New York:
Harcourt, Brace, 1963), pp. 120-21

[Hawthorne's] youth and early manhood were passed in such surroundings that he was flung directly into the arms of solitude. A naturally sensitive temperament was withdrawn from the world by an impossible arrangement of days. He saw solitude sitting beside his curious mother and dogging the steps of his two reticent sisters. He found solitude in the lonely byways he walked, on the midnight expanse of Lake Sebago where he skated across the pale ice in the moonlight, and in the haunted chamber under the eaves on Herbert St. where he pored over old Puritan chronicles and learned of the Salem witches. His imagination, fostered in such silence, lifted the gray wings of the moth and circled about this native Salem of his where his forefathers had dwelt for so many decades. He lived in the Past, as it were, and the Past is, after all a solitary place peopled only with ghosts.

Herbert Gorman
Hawthorne—A Study in Solitude (New York: Doran,
1927), pp. 17-18

. . . There has grown up, it seems to me, a narrow and lop-sided portrait of one of the greatest, if not the greatest, American novelist [Hawthorne]. That critical portrait is of a man who lived in seclusion throughout his youth in his town of Salem, a seclusion certainly grave, if not morbid, obsessed with the Puritan sense of guilt and haunted by a family curse, writing his wonderful stories that no one knew he had written, working at the dull routine of the Custom House to provide for his family, and emerging in his early middle age, with the publication of *The Scarlet Letter,* to take part in a contemporary world he had scarcely known existed. . . .

. . . He was a great writer and a great man, leading an active and vigorous life of considerable excitement and some hazard. He was an active politician in the Democratic party. . . . He was a skillful journalist. The depth and nature of his political work is mysterious. That is the true mystery of his life. He was forever visiting scenes where explosions had occurred or where violence of some sort was threatened or where smugglers were active. Loneliness and seclusion were his portion, certainly, but they had less to do with his writing and with his view of the world than with his duties in the customs service.

He was probably a government agent [in the years of seclusion].

Robert Cantwell
Nathaniel Hawthorne: The American Years
(New York: Rinehart, 1948), pp. vii-ix, 149

The Scarlet Letter

In method, the romance [*The Scarlet Letter*] was a new thing. Adultery? Yes, but of the actual sin we are told nothing at all. It is inferred: we have indeed to study the text to find what the letter "A" on the woman's breast really stood for. It is a study of results, of the corroding power of a sin concealed and lived with for years. The few characters, really four in number; the concentration upon the single *motif*; the compression; the single dominating atmosphere; the "totality" of effect, to use Poe's term—all this makes it of short-story texture. It accomplishes its end, but it does it by artificial means. The characters are symbols; the dialogue is unnatural; the character Pearl unreal, impossible, despite the claim of the family that she was a careful study of the eldest Hawthorne daughter, Una; the scaffold scene, made to be climactic in the plot is ludicrous. Tragedy was the intent, unrelieved by humor, but emotion is lacking, gripping power, realism. It can be read in cold blood with thoughts only of the method, the literary artifices, the highly finished style.

Fred L. Pattee
The First Century of American Literature (New York:
Appleton, 1935), p. 547

. . . The technique neither of the novelist nor of the allegorist was available to Hawthorne when he approached the conditions of his own experience: he had looked for signals in nature so long and so intently, and his ancestors before him had done so for so many generations, that, like a man hypnotized, or like a man corroded with madness, he saw them; but he no longer had any way of determining their significance, and he had small talent for rendering their physical presence with intensity. . . .

In *The Scarlet Letter,* then, Hawthorne composed a great allegory; or, if we look first at the allegorical view of life upon which early Puritan society was based, we might almost say that he composed a great historical novel. History, which by placing him in an anti-intellectual age had cut him off from the ideas which might have enabled him to deal with his own period, in part made up for the injustice by facilitating his entrance, for a brief time, into an age more congenial to his nature. Had he possessed the capacity for criticizing and organizing conceptions as well as for dramatizing them, he might have risen superior to his disadvantages, but like many other men of major genius he lacked this capacity. In turning his back upon the excessively simplified conceptions of his Puritan ancestors, he abandoned the only orderly concepts, whatever their limitations, to which he had access, and in his last works he is restless and dissatisfied.

Yvor Winters
Maule's Curse (Norfolk, Conn.: New Directions, 1938), pp. 20, 21-22

The Scarlet Letter has four main characters, namely, Hester, Dimmesdale, Chillingworth, and Pearl. Study of their personalities strongly suggests that these are merely aspects of one personality, Hawthorne's. . . .

The deep depression, the dependency upon Hester and his extreme guilt feelings clearly indicate the oral aspects of Dimmesdale's character, which is also Hawthorne's. Hawthorne, too, was often depressed and had many feelings of guilt coupled with an inability to accomplish anything.

The monster, Chillingworth, represents Hawthorne's torturing, tormenting, cruel superego. Some occurrences in Hawthorne's early life explain the cruelty of his superego. . . .

The selfish, wild, uncivilized Pearl, too, is an aspect of Hawthorne's own instinctive urges. She is the id personified. . . .

An analysis of the character of Hester Prynne, coupled with a knowledge of Hawthorne's life, clearly shows that Hester is his mother ideal. . . . Hawthorne had a personality structure with a weak ego, an extremely punishing superego, and very violent libidinal urges. This being the case, what choice did he have but to attempt to find surcease through his mother.

Joseph Levi
American Imago (Winter, 1953), pp. 301-5

. . . In modern times *The Scarlet Letter* has come to seem less than perfect. Other novels, like *Anna Karenina,* have treated the same problem with a richer humanity and a greater realism. If the book remains a classic, it is of a minor order. Indeed, it now seems not quite perfect even of its own kind. Its logic is ambiguous, and its conclusion moralistic. The ambiguity is interesting, of course, and the moralizing slight, but the imperfection persists.

The Scarlet Letter achieves greatness in its dramatic, objective presentation of conflicting moralities in action: each character seems at once symbolic, yet real. But this dramatic perfection is flawed by the author's moralistic, subjective criticism of Hester Prynne. And this contradiction results from Hawthorne's apparent confusion between the romantic and the transcendental moralities. While the characters of the novel objectively act out the tragic conflict between the traditional morality and the transcendental dream, Hawthorne subjectively damns the transcendental for being romantically immoral.

More obviously, Hawthorne imposed a moralistic "Conclusion" upon the drama which his characters had acted. But the artistic and moral falsity of this does not lie in its didacticism or in the personal intrusion of the author, for these were the literary conventions of the age. Rather it lies in the contradiction between the author's moralistic comments and the earlier words and actions of his characters. Having created living protagonists, Hawthorne sought to impose his own will and judgment upon them from the outside. . . . In his "Conclusion" . . . Hawthorne did violence to the living character[s] whom he had created.

Frederic I. Carpenter
American Literature and the Dream (New York:
Philosophical Library, 1955), pp. 63, 69

[W]ithout becoming a myth, *The Scarlet Letter* includes several mythic archetypes. The novel incorporates its own comic-book or folklore version. Chillingworth is the diabolical intellectual, perhaps even the mad scientist. Dimmesdale is the shining hero or to more sophisticated minds the effete New Englander. Hester is the scarlet woman, a radical and nonconformist, partly "Jewish" perhaps (there is at any rate an Old Testament quality about her, and Hawthorne says that her nature is "rich, voluptuous, Oriental." Like many other American writers, Hawthorne is not entirely above the racial folklore of the Anglo-Saxon peoples, which tends to depict tainted women and criminal men as French, Mediterranean, or Jewish—as in Hawthorne's *Marble Faun,* Miriam is Jewish, in Melville's *Pierre* Isabel is French, and in *Billy Budd* Claggart is dimly Mediterranean). Pearl is sometimes reminiscent of Little Red Riding Hood or a forest sprite of some sort who talks with the animals. Later when she inherits a fortune and marries a foreign nobleman, she is the archetypal American girl of the international scene, like the heroines of Howells and James. The subculture from which these discordant archetypes emerge is evidently inchoate and derivative. The symbols do not cohere until they have been made into projections of the faculties of the artist's mind and elements of a quasi-puritan allegory. But to a receptive imagination, they connect *The Scarlet Letter* with universal folklore, as many other novels, good and bad, are connected.

Richard Chase
The American Novel and Its Tradition (Garden City, N. Y.:
Doubleday, 1957), p. 79

If sin may seem to abound more than grace in Hawthorne, and the fall appear more often unhappy than happy, it must be borne in mind that in an inquiry of this sort, we are not concerned with superficial or worldly criteria. If there is spiritual growth, however painfully achieved (and it cannot be achieved without pain), grace can be said much more to abound, and the fall can be said to have been fortunate. Grace much more abounds, for example, and the fall proves fortunate, in *The Scarlet Letter,* though a worldly appraisal would point to a different view.

One of the chief thematic tensions in Hawthorne is the tension between the Puritan and the romantic tendencies. Hawthorne's writings lean in the Puritan direction. But he lived in a romantic age, and his work shows an awareness of the temper of that age. His work is in a sense a "criticism" of that temper, but it is not a criticism which is blind to the romantic fascination, or refuses it a sympathetic hearing.

Randall Stewart
American Literature and Christian Doctrine
(Baton Rouge, La.: Louisiana State Univ. Pr., 1958), p. 83

The Scarlet Letter has essentially the same meaning as nearly everything Hawthorne wrote—the same meaning, that is, if we resort to analytic paraphrase, for in *The Scarlet Letter* that recurrent meaning is incarnated in a symbolism that represents the highest triumph of his art. Hawthorne's inner sphere of reality is really little more than the quiet and pure communion of a human mind and heart with others in love and charity. Using the symbol of a magnetic chain of humanity which, in some ways, corresponds to the Christian idea of a mystical union among the faithful—using this symbol of spiritual fellowship, Hawthorne is always concerned to show the multiple and subtle ways in which the chain can be broken, and the effects this violation has on the human spirit. It is rather as if a Christian novelist were to set out to write a body of fictions dealing with the effects on the human heart of a fall from grace, of the subtle and hidden effects of sin on the soul. But with Hawthorne, the whole drama of which he writes, and which he analyses, is not conceived primarily in terms of sin, at least in the theological sense. His concern with the sanctity and purity of human relationships is ultimately as secular in nature as Henry James's. His interest is focused on an analysis of the barriers which arise between human spirits in a conventional society when its code has been transgressed, and of the subtle poisons that are generated because of those barriers. *The Scarlet Letter* is a study of isolation on the spatial plane. From Hester's and Dimmesdale's original transgression we see widening circles of isolation radiating outwards until Hester is left stranded in the midst of a terrible solitude which, to Hawthorne's thinking, is the negation of reality. Hester is simply cut off from life. And yet, in the subtly woven novel, her guilt is shown to be balanced by that of the surrounding social medium, the intolerant element. The conflict between Hester and the community is the most poised statement Hawthorne ever made of the tension between solitude and society, and at no point does he simplify by allowing the guilt of the one to cancel out the guilt of the other.

Marius Bewley
The Eccentric Design (London: Chatto and Windus,
1959), p. 174

It is Hawthorne who first opens up in our literature, as Melville himself explained, the tragic way; and the greatest of his gothic fictions, the first American tragedy is *The Scarlet Letter*. A "Puritan Faust," it has been called, as if there could be in the United States any other sort of Faust; but it is important all the same to be aware that it was Hawthorne who identified the Puritan experience with the diabolical pact, and cast upon the beginnings of life in America a gothic gloom that not even Longfellow's middlebrow idylls could relieve.

"*O felix culpa!*" is the secret motto of all the novels of Hawthorne after *The Scarlet Letter*, novels in which he tries to relieve the gloom of the tragic vision of his greatest work. But unlike Augustine, Hawthorne comes to feel the fall of man a fortunate calamity not because it leads to the coming of Christ, but because it prepares the ground for marriage and the bourgeois family. It is a bathetic turn: a rejection of that "blackness ten times black" which Melville had discovered in *Mosses from an Old Manse*, in favor of the positive view of life, into which American writers are so often tempted after their first success—and which condemns them to subsequent failure.

Leslie Fiedler
Love and Death in the American Novel (New York:
Criterion Books, 1960), pp. 419, 422

THE SHORT FICTION

Hawthorne's earliest work and, within its compass, some of the best of his work is to be found in his short tales. "The Minister's Black Veil," "The

Birthmark," "The Great Stone Face," "Ethan Brand," "Feathertop" are the sort of stories that tell no story, but create a condition of mind, produce a mood. Every reader can remember the sensation of one of these tales, but you will have difficulty in telling some one else what the tale is about. Hawthorne is a conjurer of moods, a prose-poet. He stands alone in the literature of New England, a verbal melodist without any ethical intention whatsoever, a delicate detached artist, as solitary in Concord as Poe was in New York; symbolizing, if he symbolizes anything, not the Puritan spirit, but the spirit of beauty everlastingly hostile or indifferent to the crabbed austerities and the soul-killing morbidity of Puritan ethics. Neither the philosophic library of Emerson nor the polyglot anthology of Longfellow announces so assuredly as the frail art of Hawthorne that civilization has dawned upon the Calvinistic barbarism of our colonial ancestors. [ca. 1913]

John Macy
The Spirit of American Literature (New York:
The Modern Library, n.d.), p. 94

To the traditional definition of the romance as a love story Hawthorne added a dignity that stemmed from his deep understanding of the relation between man and woman, space and time, comedy and tragedy. Each of his major romances *is* a love story in a sense that may be explained by summing up his view of the rhythms in human experience. . . .

[The] ability to speculate, to rend old patterns, is the prerogative of the man. Normally, his maturity comes through the shocks of love and marriage. For the woman's natural role is to conserve and clothe in time. While she shares some of youth's irresponsibility, as potential childbearer she is automatically linked to time. She needs the man to provide her escape from the ancestral homestead; he needs her to keep him from aimless movement in space. To the man she offers an ambiguous promise of involvement and redemption, passion and purification. If the man will accept her, not deceived or stunned by this ambiguity, he may go on to higher insights, as Dimmesdale does in *The Scarlet Letter*.

The original tragic action may thus be described as a threefold movement: first the parental bond is established; it is broken as the individual proudly asserts his independence from the father and accepts a new bondage to his mate; and finally, after the terrible human cost of sin, agony, and death, some degree of spiritual purification and re-establishment of the original bond is achieved. The sin is a form of adultery, a "commixture" as Hawthorne calls it, in which one set of values is merged with another so that the original functions of the individual are partially inverted. Thus Eve speculates, experiments, and is seduced by her curiosity concerning man's knowledge, while Adam is overcome by the "sinister rib" of female charm. The part of the woman or her surrogate in this action is obviously central. The young man approaches her as a more or less one-dimensional figure. But she is dual: sinner and saint, earthly and heavenly. The vessel containing both poison and possible redemption, she presents a baffling ambiguity of evil and good.

Hawthorne's best stories are all concerned in one way or another with this central situation.

Roy R. Male
Hawthorne's Tragic Vision (Austin, Tex:
Univ. Texas Pr., 1957), pp. 6-7, 9-10

GENERAL

Power . . . is precisely the element most conspicuously lacking in the normal working of [Hawthorne's] imagination. . . . Repeatedly he seems to be on the point of exhibiting power, of moving us, that is to say; but, except, I think, in *The Scarlet Letter,* he never quite does so. His unconquerable reserve steps in and turns him aside. He never crosses the line, never makes the attempt. He is too fastidious to attempt vigor and fail. His intellectual sensitiveness, to which failure in such an endeavor would be acutely palpable, prevents the essay. In the instance of *The Scarlet Letter,* where he does achieve it, he does so as it were in spite of himself, and it is curious that he instinctively re-establishes his normal equilibrium by failing to appreciate his achievement. At least he prefers it to his *House of the Seven Gables.* He is much more at home in amusing himself than in creating something. "I have sometimes," he says, "produced a singular and not unpleasing effect, so far as my own mind was concerned, by imagining a train of incidents in which the spirit and mechanism of the fairy legend should be combined with the characters and manners of familiar life." He was content if his effect was pleasing so far as his own mind was concerned. And his own mind was easily pleased with the kind of process he describes. That is, he follows his temperamental bent with tranquil docility instead of compelling it to serve him in the construction of some fabric of importance. The latter business demands energy and effort. And if he made so little effort it is undoubtedly because he had so little energy. [ca. 1909]

W. C. Brownell
American Prose Masters (New York:
Scribner's, 1929), pp. 69-70

In his special field Hawthorne has no rivals, nor even competitors; it is therefore hard to indicate his place in American literature. He is concerned chiefly with the inner life of the soul, and at his best he ranks high among all masters of spiritual tragedy. In so far as his preoccupation with spiritual things distinguishes him, he represents American Puritanism; he does not, however, represent it completely. He fails to portray its energy in action and its cheerfulness,—the elements of character that Mrs. Stowe delights in and illustrates. That Hawthorne did not himself lack these human qualities is proved by his journals and home records, which show him to have been true man, courageous and lovable, and lighted with the divine fire.

John Erskine
Leading American Novelists (New York: Henry Holt, 1910), p. 273

From the grave difficulties inherent in [Hawthorne's] theme came the inveterate habit of sliding into symbolism and allegory—from this and from the narrowness of his emotional life and the restrictions of his sympathies. The cold thin atmosphere of his work, one comes increasingly to feel, was due not alone or chiefly to the severity of his artistic restraint that forbade all rioting of the senuous imagination; it was due rather to a lack of nourishment, to a poverty of ideas and sensuous imagery. His inveterate skepticism robbed him of much, but his inhibitions robbed him of more. A romantic uninterested in adventure and afraid of sex is likely to become somewhat graveled for matter. Like the Pyncheon fowls, Hawthorne's imagination had suffered from too long inbreeding; it had grown anemic, and every grain of fancy is clucked over and picked at and made much of. Once an idea comes into his head he is loath to let it go, but he must turn it about curiously and examine it from every angle. The striking chapter in *The House of the Seven Gables,* where the death of Judge Pyncheon is played upon so persistently, is only an extreme example of his habitual method. The tongues that wagged over the minister's black veil were no more inquisitive and tireless than Hawthorne's when his imagination is fired by a vivid image. He will not let it go till it is sucked as dry as last year's cider cask. It is the way of one to whom ideas are few and precious. Knowing how little is in the bottle he will linger out the flavor of every drop. Hence his fondness for symbolism, and his frequent lapse into allegory when imagination grows dull. Because Hawthorne was an artist he was saved from the shipwreck that such a method might seem to invite; yet perhaps it is not unreasonable to suggest that he was an artist for the reason that only through the master of a refined technic could his scanty stock of ideas make any show at all.

Vernon Louis Parrington
Main Currents in American Thought, Vol. II
(New York: Harcourt, Brace, 1930), pp. 446-47

In the light of [his] full understanding of the role of the realistic novelist, most critics, in regretting that Hawthorne was not a Fielding or a Balzac, have believed that he failed to come to grips with the life of his age by not portraying such concrete facts as he encountered as an inspector on the docks. But if his art was to fulfil its function by remaining true to what his deepest intuitions had known, there must inevitably have been woven into the texture of his style some thinness and bleakness, the consequences of the long domination of Puritan thought, and of the lack of any developed artistic tradition from which he could start. With all the feverish activity of America around him, there was not the social solidity that Fielding knew, or the manifold gradations between classes that Balzac could analyze. The frequent disproportion between the weight of what Hawthorne wanted to say and the flimsiness of the vehicle he could devise to carry it suggests the nature of the problem to be met by a man of his time who was not content with taking over conclusions from Europe, but was determined to grasp "the usable truth," the actual meaning of civilization as it had existed in America. What Eliot called Hawthorne's "realism" could not depend on a notation of rich surface details; its very starvation made it a truer facing of the tragedy of provincial New England.

F. O. Matthiessen
American Renaissance (New York: Oxford Univ. Pr., 1941), pp. 235-36

It has been truly said that Hawthorne wrote tragedy of a genuinely classical type. And the creation of tragedy, as Matthiessen has pointed out, requires that a writer have insight into the social order and the moral forces at work there. For the tragic theme consists of the maladjustment of the individual to the behavior patterns regulating his relations with fellow individuals. These considerations alone should make evident the fact that a social sense is—and had to be—a fundamental ingredient of Hawthorne's art. Actually, the portrayal of life in the tales and romances is as democratic as anything which nineteenth-century America produced.

Hawthorne conscientiously faced the positive and negative elements in the American equation. In the Puritans he found bleak evidence of the contrast between man's forward-looking and back-sliding. In the society of his own day, and in himself as a member of that society, he observed the same discrepancy in newer guises between what life is and what man would have it. And in reflecting throughout his writing the maladjustments of nineteenth-century America, he achieved one of the finest and truest expressions of a democracy, where in their concern for the decency of human existence men are incessantly striving to adjust the promises of freedom to the permissions of morality.

Lawrence S. Hall
Hawthorne, Critic of Society (New Haven: Yale Univ. Pr., 1944), pp. x, 183

Hawthorne is not sure of his own stand. Perhaps his books are to claim an aesthetic reality; perhaps they merely constitute an "unreal" opposite of the physical world; perhaps they must take refuge in a noncommittal parallelism between Imagination and Actuality. He himself was well aware of one aspect of this indecision—the split within him between the man of "fancy" and the admirer of Trollope. He did not see so clearly that this opposition was transected by another, more debilitating conflict—between the symbolist and the allegorist.

The truth is that symbolism at once fascinated and horrified him. While it spoke to his "sensibilities," it evaded "the analysis of [his] mind." On the one hand, the symbol was valuable precisely because it transcended analytic thought; on the other hand, that very transcendence, with its suggestion of the unconventional, the novel, the disorderly, was potentially dangerous. The letter had "deep meaning," but the letter was scarlet, and Pearl, its embodiment, had no "principle of being" save "the freedom of a broken law." Hawthorne dwells on the elusiveness, the rationally indefinable quality of Pearl, who "could not be made amenable to rules, . . . whose elements were perhaps beautiful and brilliant, but all in disorder; or with an order peculiar to themselves, amidst which the point of variety and arrangement was difficult or impossible to be discovered." Allegory was the brake that Hawthorne applied to his sensibility. For allegory *was* analytic: allegory was safe because it preserved the conventional distinction between thought and things and because it depended on a conventional order whose point of arrangement was easily defined. The symbolistic and the allegorical patterns in Hawthorne's books reach quite different conclusions; or, rather, the symbolism leads to an inconclusive luxuriance of meaning, while allegory imposes the pat moral and the simplified character.

Charles Feidelson, Jr.
Symbolism and American Literature (Chicago: Univ. Chicago Pr., 1953), pp. 14-15

In a review of Hawthorne's life and writings, nothing is more prominent than a quiet, deeply joyful affirmation.To recognize the hand of Providence in the affairs of man, to see the unity in the diversity of the world, to perceive in the forms of Nature a majestic and beautiful Idea, to feel that all these wonderful things are for the instruction and enjoyment of man, and to be assured that beyond is still a higher fruition in man's immortality—these were the basic tenets of Hawthorne's belief as a man, a belief too, permeating all his writings and giving them an abiding substance and worth.

Hubert H. Hoeltje
Inward Sky (Durham, N. C.: Duke Univ. Pr., 1962), p. 561

LAFCADIO HEARN
1850-1904

Born June 27 in Santa Maura, Greece. In 1857, he was placed with his father's aunt in Dublin for rearing. In 1863, he entered St. Cuthbert's College, England, where he lost the sight of his left eye in an accident on the playing field. He took passage in 1869 to New York City, where he arrived penniless. He barely survived in New York and in Cincinnati by doing odd jobs, until he finally learned to set type. In 1873, he wrote feature articles for the *Cincinnati Enquirer* until he was dismissed for openly living with a mulatto woman. He went to New Orleans in 1877 and after some difficulty obtained a position on *The Item*. At this time he began to write for New York magazines and published *Some Chinese Ghosts* in 1887. He spent the years 1888-1889 in the West Indies, often dependent on charity. In 1890, he went to Japan, where he obtained a teaching position in Matsue. In 1891, he married Setsuko Koizumi and, in 1893, moved to Government College at Kumamoto and became a Japanese citizen. In 1894, he received the Chair of English Literature at the Imperial University in Tokyo and subsequently published *Glimpses of Unfamiliar Japan* and *Japan: An Attempt at Interpretation*. He died September 26.

The Writings of Lafcadio Hearn (1922), 16 vols.
Vera McWilliams, *Lafcadio Hearn* (1946)

PERSONAL

From the time when Hearn went to New Orleans as an aged young man to the end of his short career his life was a succession of infatuations with places and peoples. In this aspect his romantic impulse was of the most elemental sort. The spirit of the quest was in it, but it sprang superficially from restlessness, the feeling that beyond the horizon was something fervently to be desired. The Creole life of the gulf port first stirred him as woodland and stream stirred the boy Wordsworth, needing no supplement unborrowed from the eye. Then the sensuous experience fulfilled itself as the dream became everyday reality, and he hungered for new scenes. If he went away, he said, to bleak climes, he could long for New Orleans again; but romance in one's grasp ceases to be romance. Or he could choose a less austere recourse and seek the sunlit life of unfamiliar places. It might be Florida, the West Indies, Southern France. Somewhere else he must feel the thrill of fresh sensation. . . . "If I could only become a consul at Bagdad, Algiers, Ispahan, Benares, Nippo, Bangkok, Nish-Bink—or any part of the world where ordinary Christians do not like to go! Here is the nook in which my romanticism still hides."

. . . Nowhere in his sojournings had he found abundance of beauty and abundance of creative energy too. Everywhere life was compounded of unequal values. Under the most elementary of romantic impulses, the mere impulse of restlessness, he had strayed about the world, and with the larger impulse of the life-quest he had hoped as he went, somewhere to find force and beauty in the balance. In his home in Japan he seemed to have come to an anchorage; but not for long. He must take his boy back to the West for his education; if only to see Japan from a distance he must leave his family provided for and return for a while to the civilization he hated but could not resist. He was buoyed by this prospect when he died.

Percy Boynton
More Contemporary Americans (Chicago:
Univ. Chicago Pr., 1927), pp. 68-69, 73

The biography of a man who snatched a small achievement out of much waste must not scant the deformities of character and the accidents of circumstance. This life, set twisting upon its eccentric course by birth upon the Greek island of Leucadia, and finished by death upon the Japanese island of Honshu, functioned within an unusually limiting set of conditions. Brought up upon a diet of great expectations, the child was betrayed by them and grew up shy, suspicious, and touchy. Deprived of the sight of one eye and disfigured in appearance, the adolescent redoubled his childish faults. Abandoned by his family to suffer some direness of poverty, the young man chewed bitterly upon his misfortunes, and childish and youthful flaws hardened into mature traits. Hearn led always a life that was somewhat strange and occasionally, by the standards of respectability, scandalous. Yet he had the courage of the unencouraged man. He lived to his ultimate fifty-fourth year in a succession of disasters; but he made his way, and he held onto his honesty. As native to him as his faults were his unbudgeable virtues: personal bravery, a stiff integrity, a childlike love of beauty, a naive sympathy for all that lived. He drifted, but in the end he halted the drift and made a pattern of his life as he had made patterns of the disorganized impressions of his senses. An awkward and touching mixture of circumstance and essence—Lafcadio Hearn—and worthy of meditation.

Elizabeth Stevenson
Lafcadio Hearn (New York: Macmillan, 1961), p. xvi

GENERAL

Any good literature, especially the poetic, must be based on reality, must at least incidentally have its running obligato of reality. For literature, again emphasized, vision is the intermediary, the broad, bright highway to fact. Prosaicly, local color requires the local seer. Barred out from this divine roadway to and through the actual universe [by his extreme myopia], the foiled mind of Hearn could choose but one course: to regarment, transform, and color the world, devised and transmitted by others, and reversing the old, *The Logos become Flesh*, rewrite the history of the soul as, *The Flesh become Logos*, for in Hearn's alembic the solidest of flesh was "melted" and escaped in ecstatic clouds of spirit. . . . Except in boyhood, [Hearn] never, with any accuracy of expression or life, saw a human face; at the best he saw faces only in the frozen photographs, and these interested him little.

With creative instinct or ability denied, with the poet's craving for openeyed knowing, and with the poet's necessity of realizing the world out there, Hearn, baldly stated, was forced to become the poet of myopia. His groping mind was compelled to rest satisfied with the world of distance and reality transported by the magic carpet to the door of his imagination and fancy. There in a flash it was melted to formless spirit, recombined to soul and given the semblance of a thin reincarnation, fashioned, refashioned, colored, recolored. . . .

For with Hearn's lack of creative ability, married to his inexperience of happiness, he could but choose the darksome, the tragical element of life, the pathos even of religion as his themes. His intellect being a reflecting, or at best a recombining and coloring faculty, his datum must be sought without and it must be brought to him; his joyless and even his tragic experience compelled him to cull from the mingled sad and bright only the pathetic or pessimistic subjects; his physical and optical imprisonment forbade that objectivation and distant embodiment which stamps an art work with the seal of reality and makes it stand there wholly nonexcusing, or furnishing itself as its own excuse for being.

George Gould

Biographic Clinics, Vol. IV (London: Rebman, 1906), pp. 224-26

[Hearn] had De Quincey's irresoluteness, his jangling nerves, his dominating fancy, his discursiveness, his gorgeous imagination, his oriental soul hampered with the fetters of occidental science. He too was essentially fragmentary in his literary output, a man of intense moods intensely painted, a man of books but of no single, unified, compelling book. One may not read essays like "Gothic Horror" or "The Nightmare Touch," or a passage from "Vespertina Cognitio," and not think of the great English opium-eater. . . .

Like De Quincey, he lingers over the flavor of words, gathering them everywhere he may and gloating over them, tasting them with halfclosed eyes like an epicure, and using them ever delicately, suggestively, inevitably. . . .

His essays, therefore, even as he has intimated, are for the few who are attuned to them, who have sense for delicate suggestion, for "the phosphorescing of words, the fragrance of words, the noisomeness of words, the tenderness, the hardness, the dryness or juiciness of words." Aside from his vision of beauty, his intensity, his suggestiveness of style, he has brought not much. The romancers of the period, a few of them, like Grace King, for example, have felt his influence, but it has not been a large one. He stands almost an isolated figure in his period, an intensely individual soul, a solitary genius like Poe. His place is a secure one. His circle of readers will never be large, but it will always be constant.

Fred Lewis Pattee
A History of American Literature Since 1870
(New York: Century, 1915), pp. 426-28

It is in the light of broad interpretation that we must read the books of Lafcadio Hearn. His is a world of ghosts—of shapes of the mist and colours of the mirage and sounds as of a sea-shell—but within the echoing spaces of that world we shall find beauties as strange and rare as any in literature. And we shall find besides that he has gone before us in naming some of those curious forces by which we are moved. His life was one continuous search, one long endeavour to make even thinner that periphery of the nameless and unknown, and his adventures of the mind brought home strange beauty and precious.

. . . He saw existence as an intricate reciprocity of strange forces; and he recognized these not from the ivory tower of intellectual speculation, but from their constant impingement in all the affairs of living upon his own delicately registering consciousness. Because the artist in him was powerfully active he saw in "the supernatural" but the most beautifully imaginative reconstruction of the natural. Let no one expect to find in his work the gothic, the macabre or the preposterous of *Udolfo* and *The Castle of Otranto*. For his phantoms are but the wistful figures of a mind that knew itself contained within some great unity, and sought by these to people the void of the Unknown. For such a one, however difficult the search for food and shelter, life takes on the aspect of constant adventure in a realm of gold.

Jean Temple
Blue Ghost (London: Jonathan Cape, 1931), pp. 18-20

. . . What, above all, [Hearn] found or seemed to himself to have found in Japan was a beautifully natural and simple practice of certain ancient virtues that are worth more to a contented and dignified human life than all the machinery and culture and conflicts of the West. He never made this point in so many words; he was the least controversial of writers. But this point is in fact his whole point and it is this philosophical implication that tends to uphold the rather frail and fragmentary body of his work. What he was interested in was, as he makes clear in his introduction to "Japanese Buddhist Proverbs," "that general quality of moral experience which . . . must always possess a special psychological interest for thinkers." What he found admirable, what he wanted to convey to the West, to America, in all his best work was the quality of the moral experience of the Japanese people. It was from this point of view that he rendered poem and proverb, retold legends, described landscape and festival. His attempts to blend the Spencerian philosophy with Buddhist mysticism are less sound and less important. He was another in that long list of romantic fugitives, beginning perhaps with Chateaubriand, who fled from the wounds inflicted upon them by their own civilization into a Utopia fancied or real and then described and recounted that Utopia as criticism, corrective, ideal for their countrymen. The close relation of Japanese life to Hearn's delineation of it may be gravely doubted. But the Japan that he conveyed was an exquisite and touching vision and that vision has, both artistically and philosophically, an enduring charm and value.

Ludwig Lewisohn
Expression in America (New York: Harper, 1932), pp. 349-50

"The dominant impression made by his personality," Huneker remarked of Hearn, ". . . is itself impressionistic." A posthumous title, *Diary of an Impressionist* (1911), subsumes his entire work, which—fragile and casual though it be—has extended since his death into a seemingly endless sequence of volumes. The books by which he is most likely to be remembered are the twelve that deal with his adopted country, from *Glimpses of Unfamiliar Japan* (1894) to *Japan: An Attempt at Interpretation* (1904). Their naïve charm has tended to fade in the light of more recent years. Hearn was anything but a shrewd observer of mores or politics, and his ignorance of the language disqualified him from interpreting the literature. His most memorable episodes are descriptions of shrines, gardens, fans, insects, and bric-a-brac. "A land where lotus is a common article of diet," where everything is marshaled in aesthetic order, where egotistical individualism is conspicuous by its absence—as *Kokoro* (1896) reminds us—does not lack attraction. But Japan was already becoming aggressively and mechanically Westernized; while Hearn, who continually warned his students against this unholy synthesis, was swept from his university post in a rising wave of hostility toward Westerners. Tired of lotus-eating, he might have gone back to America if ill health had not finally overtaken him. He never escaped from what he had never found: himself. "Ironically," as Katharine Anne Porter points out, "he became the interpreter between two civilizations equally alien to him."

Harry T. Levin
in *Literary History of the United States*, eds. Robert Spiller *et al*, Vol. II
(New York: Macmillan, 1948), p. 1072

. . . When Hearn came to discover the same pattern recurring in the world of folk tales, legends, and myths, and there saw not only the colorful differences of various lands, peoples, and their cultures, but also the common root from which they grew spontaneously, he accepted them as the manifestation of man's aspiration for the Impossible. After all, they are but versions of dream truths that are "ever the same" the world over, as he explains in his lecture on the supernatural in fiction. They are the cherished prizes of humanity in the quest of the Impossible. . . . As records of these dream truths, folk tales, legends, and myths demand someone to translate them into human terms, someone who is not only a translator but also an artist. It almost seems that Hearn was born to meet this demand. And he succeeded in fulfilling this double role. In approaching his many-colored legends, he could be at once . . . the beholder and . . . the creator. . . . Once Hearn advised his students of literature: "Trust to your own dream-life; study it carefully, and draw your inspiration from that. For dreams are the primary source of almost everything that is beautiful in the literature which treats of what lies beyond mere daily experience." The same applies in his case. In trusting his own dream life he could also trust the dream life of humanity, for with him they are one. Undoubtedly, this is what assures the perennial charm of Hearn's art as a storyteller.

Beong-Cheou Yu
AL (March, 1962), p. 70

OLIVER   WENDELL   HOLMES
1809-1894

Born Aug. 29 in Cambridge, Massachusetts. He graduated from Harvard in 1829 and published "Old Ironsides" in 1830. In 1833, he went to Paris to study medicine and, in 1836, received his M.D. from Harvard. *Poems* was published in 1836. He taught anatomy and physiology at Dartmouth College in 1838. *Contagiousness of Puerperal Fever* was published in 1843. In 1840 he married Amelia Jackson, and, in 1847, he was appointed Professor of Anatomy in the Harvard Medical School. He began *The Autocrat of the Breakfast Table* series for the *Atlantic Monthly* in 1857, and a series of publications followed: *The Professor at the Breakfast Table* (1860); *Elsie Venner* (1861); *The Guardian Angel* (1867); *A Mortal Antipathy* (1885); and *Over the Teacups* (1891). He died Oct. 7.

The Works of Oliver Wendell Holmes (1892-1896), 15 vols.

Eleanor M. Tilton, *Amiable Autocrat: a Biography of Dr. Oliver Wendell Holmes* (1947)

PERSONAL

He believed in good family, in the refinements of wealth, and was an apologist of the privileged whom wealth and opportunity surround with the graces of life to which he was very sensitive. He looked with humorous but distant sympathy on any democratic idea that happened to be current (and a good many queer forms of democratic ideas were current), but he remained closely within the shelter of caste. His point of view is frankly New England, not broadly American, certainly not of a world-social scope. His attitude toward life is that of a gently satirical romantic. He does not understand realism in literature nor the social structure that at bottom unites, say, the Autocrat's landlady with the ancestral advantage which the Autocrat thinks a young man ought to have. The individual specimen of human nature he inspects quizzically, affectionately. He writes for the few, not the many; he addresses those who can catch an idea as it flies. His odd combination of logic and fantasy makes his work a continuous delight; the process of his thought as he unfolds it is fascinating, and he himself watches it with a delighted sense of surprise. He is the most modest of egotists, and, except when he is attacking an enemy (always a generalized intellectual enemy, never a personal one), he suggests rather than asserts. His intellectual curiosity warily eludes closed final statements; to him the universe is going on all the time and was not concluded with the last remark that any of us happened to regard as ultimate. Every imagination that meets his is stimulated to go on thinking about a world that is so full of a number of things. [ca. 1913]

John Macy
The Spirit of American Literature (New York:
Modern Library, n.d.), pp. 168-69

There was a time when Holmes seemed a bold blade enough; he may still seem so in remote levels of the population. From any permanent point of view his prose has the fatal defects of knowingness, of feeble jauntiness, of a total lack in depth of tone. It has lightness and brightness but no body. It is ingenious and adroit. There is a high polish, but the polish is on tin. If there was one quality after which Holmes aimed, it was distinction. Yet distinction is what he inveterately misses. Like higher qualities, which commonly include it, distinction evidently cannot be summoned or sought. Nor has it anything to do, as Longfellow and Holmes illustrate, with conventionally gentle birth and breeding. Conscious fastidiousness, such as Holmes', is wholly alien to it. All through the polite period it escaped, significantly enough, the scholarly, the well-bred, all who by their careful selectiveness in both life and literature seemed, from a superficial point of view to be entitled to distinction, if to little else. The quality belongs, like all other high qualities, to intensity and veracity and to these alone. Here is, if anywhere, the secret of the hopeless withering and wilting of the prose of Holmes. He declared himself a Brahmin; he had light without fire; but his light, too, was not permitted either to blaze or to glow; it only glinted. Distinction of thought and manner should have saved him and it was distinction that he hopelessly missed.

Ludwig Lewisohn
Expression in America (New York: Harper, 1932), pp. 69-70

. . . Oliver Wendell Holmes, whose long life (1809-94) spanned the century, ought to have been a most arresting figure, perhaps the representative man of his age; it is not easy to say why he so often disappoints us. Perhaps it is because he was at the center of so many tendencies and managed to occupy the middle only by achieving a consistent mediocrity.

Holmes stood midway between the vanishing virility of his father's Calvinism and the emerging vitality of his son's militant humanism; what seems to have been available to him from either direction was frequently only the secondary or illusory. The suspicions which clouded his kindly view of human nature lacked the terrible strength which his father, Abiel Holmes, brought to his Calvinist ministry, while his enlightened repudiation of the divine elect took him only as far as the socially eligible, and his replacement of the visible saints by the Boston quality had little of the astringent social philosophy of his son, the Justice. Holmes stood at the heart of his own time. He was, of course, a Harvard man forever, and the class poet par excellence; he was also a respected colleague and friend of the Swiss zoologist, Louis Agassiz. Holmes could listen attentively to the Swedenborgian mystifyings by which the elder James mapped the way of regeneration; he could equally grasp and expound the therapeutic methods by which clinical psychology hoped to accomplish the same thing. He led the attack on the old theology; but he was a competent critic and a great lover of the old literature. His interests were rich and varied; yet what we are apt to find in him is less a synthesis of these interests than a good-humored shrewdness about them all, a solid common sense not deep enough for skepticism, not large enough for faith.

R. W. B. Lewis
The American Adam (Chicago: Univ. Chicago Pr.,
1955), p. 33-34

THE NOVELS

Holmes at the time his novels appeared was a professor of anatomy, a subject of dry bones and dead bodies, and as an anatomist his opinions on psychiatric disorders would not have been considered important to the practicing physicians and psychiatrists. He therefore deliberately and probably shrewdly chose narrative as a medium through which to bring his views before the public. His three stories are poor fiction when judged by modern criteria or compared with the masters of his time—Poe, Thackeray, Balzac, or even Hawthorne of his own literary group. The novels are *Elsie Venner* (1859), *The Guardian Angel* (1867), and *A Mortal Antipathy* (1884). Their plots are simple, almost juvenile and, in two of them, the reader is not disappointed in the customary thwarting of the villain and the coming of true love to its own.

Although *Elsie Venner* enjoyed something of a popular success, literary critics dealt none too kindly with this or with Holmes's subsequent psychological works of fiction that were "tainted with the physiological." Surely Holmes, far more sensitive concerning his literary reputation both as a poet and novelist than about his clinical ability, would not have been pleased that these studies of abnormal characters should be regarded as case histories. In the light of the development of modern psychiatry they remain as testimony to his medical acuity, his knowledge, and his profound psychiatric understanding.

Clarence P. Obendorf
The Psychiatric Novels of Oliver Wendell Holmes
(New York: Columbia Univ. Pr., 1946)

POEMS

At his own level [Holmes] was best as a writer of *vers de societé*. I think of "The Last Leaf," "Contentment," "My Aunt," "Dorothy Q." and the rest: witty poems daring to be almost but not quite sentimental, our pleasure in them deriving in good part from the sense of daring. The sentiments are genuine, but one is quickly made aware that they cannot be too much indulged; that way lay the Romanticism which so disturbed Holmes, perhaps because it was so inviting to him. So the mode is, after a fashion, ironic; but since that which the irony is at once to express and keep at a safe distance—since this is of not much moment in the first place, we are not much involved in taking it seriously in the second place. Holmes's defense against his own feelings is rather simply achieved, because the range of those feelings, themselves already under the control of common sense, is not very large. . . . For the sensibility which is at work in these verses is not that of a poet who would declare that too much profundity is dangerous, but rather of one who was incapable of profundity—and so the proper companion for the "broad-shouldered, out-of-door men" of whom, in reality, he knew very little and cared less. They had not achieved the stage of profundity he, or even his ancestors, had passed. If anything, Holmes, like members of his class, met his ploughmen as they were on the way up and he was on his way down. . . . Holmes's thus was the sensibility of the least common denominator—common sense drained of its portion of *communitas*—and represents still another step downward from, say, a Herrick to an F. P. Adams, a Christopher Morley, or an Ogden Nash: from witticism to jokesterism.

Roy Harvey Pearce
The Continuity of American Poetry (Princeton, N. J.:
Princeton Univ. Pr., 1961), pp. 221-22

GENERAL

He was the last leaf of the New England renascence, and still more intimately of the Calvinistic tree. Holmes was the second American of distinction to pursue an escapist philosophy. Longfellow roamed the high seas and the courts of Europe in order to broaden the culture of his race; Holmes fled back to a former century, or in truth had never escaped it. Holmes diluted the fire and passion of real poets to the niceties of graceful logic. He wrote with the intellect and touches only the intellect. When he descended to the heart, he evoked the sweeter, softer, most sentimental chords. He is therefore the palest leaf, as well, of the independent Puritan tree which gave us Bryant, Emerson, Whittier, Lowell and Emily Dickinson.

Alfred Kreymborg
Our Singing Strength (New York:
Coward McCann, 1929), p. 140

With a personality such as Holmes had—sentimental, excessively sociable, incapable of vehemence except in matters strictly relating to his profession, so even-tempered that he missed both the great heights and the great depths—it is perhaps to be wondered at that he became an artist at all. But in finding the perfect medium for imparting his attitude toward life [the conversational essay], Holmes, without genius, or even an artistic temperament (if that is a help), succeeded in becoming a genuine artist. He established his own rules, evolved his own form. No one else can hope to do anything with the form he created, so peculiarly adapted is it to his own individuality. But he has form, and he has substance, and a perfect reconciliation of the one with the other. There are greater artists and greater men of whom this cannot be said.

Holmes's main shortcomings—the narrowness of his universe, his blindness . . . to the heterogeneous America that was growing up around him—make some of his views seem hopelessly limited and provincial. Few poets have lived who have had so much faith in the better things of the society they lived in. . . .

But his optimism is by no means a sad commentary on the quality of his mind, as our more disillusioned contemporaries have hastened to conclude. It is merely the expression of Holmes's temperament: the childlike simplicity of a candid heart, which believes eternally (if it can be said without superciliousness or disrespect) in Santa Claus. . . . Had he less charm, we might well be tempted to dismiss him (as most of us today dismiss the philosophical writings of John Fiske, whose optimism was not unsimilar to Holmes's) for what we cannot help regarding as his naivete. But we cannot, because he is one of the most winsome characters in literary history. It is impossible not to be impressed by the richness of his humane and scientific culture, and by the minuteness and sensitivity of his social perceptions. It is impossible, too, to resist the appeal of his central intellectual principle: "I don't want you to believe anything I say; I only want you to see what makes me believe it."

S. I. Hayakawa and Howard Mumford Jones
Oliver Wendell Holmes: Representative Selections
(New York: American Book, 1939), pp. cxi-cxiii

Both the *utile* and the *dulce* to Hawthorne were very much of his own time and place, the nineteenth century in New England. The timeless, universal quality which has enabled so much of Emerson to withstand the flooding changes of the past fifty years has not afforded anything like an equal protection to the writings of Holmes. . . .

. . . It is reserved for the very few to be the popular writers of more than one age. Yet there are many for whom [Holmes] still has, and through years to come must continue to have, much to say. Among these will be found the students, and the merely curious, who would inform themselves concerning American life and American letters in the nineteenth century, especially in New England. Lacking Holmes, they will lack the key to many doors of understanding. There are besides the lovers of writing illuminated by imagination, in familiar verse and serious poetry, and in wide-ranging prose. These will encounter many pages which, in manner and substance, will already appear outmoded. But the vein of true wit, true sympathy, true apprehension of many fundamental qualities in human nature, keeps cropping out in book after book, which refuses to take oblivion for its date or to write Finis on its title-page.

M. A. Dewolfe Howe
Holmes of the Breakfast Table (New York:
Oxford Univ. Pr., 1939), pp. 159-60

Holmes recalls England's neo-classical period in several ways. Like Addison and Steele, he based his admirable prose style upon the best of the talk—and that would be largely his own—that he could hear in his time. In verse his favorite form was the heroic couplet. Like Pope, although not to the same extent, he depended for his effects chiefly upon wit—a term within which he would have included both reason and good sense. His feeling for Boston, where a faint aroma of the eighteenth century still lingered when he was young, was like that of Dr. Johnson for London. Moderation, urbanity, and serene self-control meant as much to him as to Lord Chesterfield. He might have excelled in the writing of satire like that of Swift if his convictions had been more fervid and his heart less warm. Even his devotion to science makes one think of the eighteenth century Deists who saw in the laws of nature a second revelation of the Creator's mind and purpose. His prevailing optimism, based upon an assurance that the human mind can comprehend and in some degree control the physical world in which it finds itself, closely resembled that to be seen in the immediate followers of Sir Isaac Newton.

Odell Shepard
in *Literary History of the United States,* eds. Robert Spiller *et al,* Vol. I
(New York: Macmillan, 1948), pp. 598-99

Holmes is not the national, but the provincial poet. A descendant of Anne Bradstreet, a reader of Cotton Mather, he displays a New England homeliness, a Puritan familiarity with household detail. It is a pity that he could not have known the Colonial poet Edward Taylor (also a physician), with his spinning wheels, bowling alleys, coaches, and sugar cakes. Seldom achieving—or seeking—a grandiosity of conception, when Holmes looks for it he does not search among grandiose materials. Even his two best serious poems, *The Living Temple* and *The Chambered Nautilus,* are based upon materials becoming to a naturalist.

George Arms
The Fields Were Green (Stanford, Calif.:
Stanford Univ. Pr., 1953), p. 101

WILLIAM DEAN HOWELLS
1837-1920

Born March 1 in Martin's Ferry, Ohio. He did editorial work for the *Ohio State Journal* in 1856. In 1860, he took a trip to New England and met Emerson, Holmes, Hawthorne, and Lowell, and, in the same year, wrote a campaign biography for Abraham Lincoln. He was granted a consulate in Venice in 1861 and a year later married Elinor Mead. In 1866, he became a sub-editor, later editor, of the *Atlantic Monthly*. *Their Wedding Journey* was published in 1872 and *A Chance Acquaintance* in 1873. He gave up the editorship of the *Atlantic Monthly* in 1881 and wrote novels serially for *Century Magazine*: *A Modern Instance* (1882) and *The Rise of Silas Lapham* (1885). He became the editor of *Harper's Monthly* in 1886 and published *A Hazard of New Fortunes* (1890); *Criticism and Fiction* (1891); and *A Traveler from Altruria* (1891). He left *Harpers* in 1891, but wrote *"Easy Chair"* for the magazine from 1900-1920. *Literary Friends and Acquaintance* was published in 1900 and *Through The Eye of The Needle* in 1907. He died May 11.

No standard edition of collected works.

Van Wyck Brooks, *Howells, His Life and World* (1959)

PERSONAL

Modern novelists have discovered how highly organized is the nervous system of a duffer, how lacerating are his grief and joy; they have also discovered how many interesting things common men do in the course of a day's work. Mr. Howells does not get at all this, because he does not know people and their day's work; he has seen them from his front window and in parlours, offices and summer hotels. Or he is imaginatively unable to grasp those great moments in the soul (great to the experiencing if not to the observing, soul)—those moments which make the person whom the soul inhabits act in absorbingly interesting ways. Either Mr. Howells cannot or he dare not speak out about life. So that as the solitary, devoted protagonist of realism in these romantic United States he has been curiously ineffectual.

Is he not, after all, a feminine, delicate, slightly romantic genius, theoretically convinced that realism is "the thing," but not equipped with the skill and experience to practice it? Seeing that Tolstoy writes of social problems and the people, he would forthwith do likewise, but he does not understand social problems and the people. In short, he does not know life. He would not know how to sit down and eat his grub with a bunch of workmen and find out what they think of things. Yet, theoretically, avowedly, he is all on their side of the social battle.

John Macy
The Spirit of American Literature (Garden City, N. Y.:
Doubleday, 1913), pp. 287-88

[Howells] is almost the national ideal: an urbane and highly respectable old gentleman, a sitter on committees, an intimate of professors and the prophets of movements, a worthy vouched for by both the *Atlantic Monthly* and Alexander Harvey, a placid conformist. The result is his general acceptance as a member of the literary peerage, and of the rank of earl at least. For twenty years past his successive books have not been criticized, nor even adequately reviewed; they have been merely fawned over; the lady critics of the newspaprs would no more question them than they would question Lincoln's Gettysburg speech, or Paul Elmer More, or their own virginity. The dean of American letters in point of years, and in point of published quantity, and in point of public prominence and influence, he has been gradually enveloped in a web of superstitious reverence, and it grates harshly to hear his actual achievement discussed in cold blood.

Nevertheless, all this merited respect for an industrious and inoffensive man is bound, soon or late, to yield to a critical examination of the artist within, and that examination, I fear, will have its bitter moments for those who naïvely accept the Howells legend. It will show, without doubt, a first-rate journeyman, a contriver of pretty things, a clever stylist—but it will also show a long row of uninspired and hollow books, with no more ideas in them than so many volumes of the *Ladies' Home Journal,* and no more deep and contagious feeling than so many reports of autopsies, and no more glow and gusto than so many tables of bond prices. The profound dread and agony of life, the surge of passion and aspiration, the grand crash and glitter of things, the tragedy that runs eternally under the surface—all this the critic of the future will seek in vain in Dr. Howells' elegant and shallow volumes. And seeking it in vain, he will probably dismiss all of them together with fewer words than he gives to Huckleberry Finn. . . .

H. L. Mencken
Prejudices: First Series (New York:
A. A. Knopf, 1919), pp. 52-53

Mr. Howells was one of the gentlest, sweetest, and most honest of men, but he had the code of a pious old maid whose greatest delight was to have tea at the vicarage. He abhorred not only profanity and obscenity, but all of what H. G. Wells has called "the jolly coarseness of life." In his fantastic vision of life, which he innocently conceived to be realistic, farmers and seamen and factory-hands might exist, but the farmer must never be covered with muck, the seaman must never roll out bawdy chanteys, the factory-hand must be thankful to his good kind employer, and all of them must long for the opportunity to visit Florence and smile gently at the quaintness of the beggars.

Sinclair Lewis
Address . . . on the Occasion of the Award of the Nobel Prize
(New York: Harcourt, Brace, 1930), pp. 20-21

GENERAL

[Howells'] influence, by and large, was baleful. His greatest service was to taste; he turned American fiction toward realism. But this service was largely vitiated by his reservations both in precept and practice. . . . It is impossible to name a single figure upon whom he had any influence that was otherwise than unfortunate, or to name a single successor in fiction who, following his tradition, became one of the first-rate writers of the day. . . .

. . . He accepted the New England environment at Boston's evaluation and took Boston's judgments as his own. Consequently, he came to represent no more than a narrow class response to a disturbing society.

. . . He accepted the tolerance of a society he could not in his more thoughtful moments, respect, and won success by conformance to its attitudes and prejudices. He never cut through the surface and became a true portrayer of human life as it appeared in the United States. In the end he can only stand forth as the perfect exponent of the late Nineteenth Century bourgeois spirit in American literature.

C. Hartley Grattan
AM (May, 1930), p. 50

William Dean Howells was, I think, the most pathetic figure in [the] post-war gallery; he so narrowly missed out. If only he had not been so full of the bourgeois proprieties, if only he had not been so conscious of the smug audience he was writing for; if only he had not looked so conscientiously for the smiling side of life, which he thought of as particularly American. Could any one read Melville or Hawthorne and think that this was the characteristic touch of the American imagination? Impossible. The smile that Howells tried to preserve, undimmed by tears, undistorted by passionate emotion, was only the inane mask of the booster. One is all the more moved to pity for Howells because, believing in Tolstoi, he did not really love the America whose sensibilities he so carefully protected: he appreciated its snobbery, its pettiness, and its cruelty towards its financial inferiors. But social good will was in Howells' scheme the principal, the standard virtue: he could not see that outright animosity might be preferable, if it led to beauties and excellences that mere good will neglected to achieve.

Howells' characters were all life-sized, medium, unheroic; he painted no heroes, because he did not see them in life. Alas! that was the best reason in the world for painting them. Life exists in the possible as well as in the actual: the must and the maybe are equally valid. The conscientious littleness of Howells was painful: a man who saw as much as he did

should not lean on a gentlemanly walking stick. Mixing his love with prudence, Howells never went beyond the limits of conventional society: he
could admire Tolstoi but he was incapable of his splendid and terrible
folly. Howells had to a degree that should win for him forever the en-
comiums of our academic critics—the inner check. The inner elegance
and the inner check were complementary parts of his own personality;
and as a result, even the best of his novels, *The Rise of Silas Lapham*,
never quite reaches the marrow; for these checks and these elegances were
the marks of the spiritual castration which almost all his contemporaries
had undergone.

Lewis Mumford
The Golden Day (New York: Norton, 1926), pp. 167-69

Howells yielded without so much as an inner protest to Boston and this
pusillanimity of his is the worm that may hollow out the otherwise extraordinarily fine structure of his best work. There is in his treatment of
the major human emotions a shocking and contemptible moderation; there
is in his attitude to marriage, above all, an unbearable stuffiness and creeping prose which, being so obviously characteristic of his age, makes one
wonder that the Feminist revolt in America was not even more violent
and acute. The superstition prevails among the unthinking that Howells
and the genteel age took a high view of marriage. The contrary is true.
The view taken of marriage was revolting to every generous instinct; it
relegated married people, however young, to a situation that smelled of
ill-aired clothes-presses and kitchen soap; it assumed as impossible and
improper any poetry or passion in the relation of man and wife after the
honeymoon at Niagara Falls; it consented drily to the elimination between
people once safely married of gallantry, delight, even of courtesy and
delicacy; . . . But this was not all. Even of those superlatively innocent
relations which in his stories lead to marriage Howells' opinion was low.
"The whole business of love and love-making and marrying is painted by
the novelists in a monstrous disproportion to the other relations of life.
Love is very sweet, very pretty. . . ." Thus speaks the otherwise neither
foolish nor unmanly clergyman in *The Rise of Silas Lapham*. And this
view Howells shared or honestly thought he shared, declaring in *Criticism
and Fiction* that grief, avarice, pity, ambition, hate, envy, devotion, friendship have all greater part in life "than the passion of love." On his principle
that the sovereign virtue of art was truth to reality, he was forced of
course, in view of the inhibitions of his time and his personal practice, to
take precisely this attitude. It is needless to insist on the crushing handicap
imposed upon himself at the outset by a creative artist who regards as
trivial the instinct which, as psychology has demonstrated and the great

artists have always known, is implicated not only with our biological func-
tioning but in infinite ramifications with our higher nerve centers and is
thus a central element of every human activity from the humblest to the
most exalted. That Howells, with this handicap, comes off upon the whole
as respectably as he does, is a very high tribute to his native gifts.

Ludwig Lewisohn
Expression in America (New York: Harper, 1932), pp. 239-41

It does not matter that Howells was a visionary, that he was sentimental
and often confused, that his socialism had a little of Henry George, much
of William Morris, and more of Tolstoy in it. His intentions, his "instinct,"
were in the direction of the truest democracy. In the tradition of rebellion
and dissent that runs through American literature—from Sam Adams and
Tom Paine through Thoreau and Walt Whitman to Theodore Dreiser—
the name of Howells is not written small.

Bernard Smith
Sat (August 11, 1934), p. 42

. . . The society for which [Howells] wrote obviously expected the outward symbol of sexual possession to be treated with circumspection, and,
if portrayed at all, to be followed by marriage. But in Howells' novels the
ring did not always follow the kiss. . . .

Howells played somewhat daringly, then, with the outward symbol of
sexuality; and in many ways he seemed to have selected those incidents
of courtship which affected the subconscious sensitivities of his readers,
just as the convention of the kiss played upon their conscious; that he himself was probably but dimly aware of the full meanings of the actions he
chose to depict is not the point; what is important is that he sensed the
right thing to have his men and women do that might convey the undertones of the physical basis for their attraction.

. . . The foregoing is not meant to suggest that by the standards of our
own times or any other era, Howells was outspoken. Far from it. What
it does suggest is that within the farmework of the conventions and symbols of their times, Howells and the writers around him worked honestly
with the materials of the visible, conscious world of human relations with
which they were familiar. The life they wanted to portray was the expressed life, rather than the unexpressed, and their business was therefore
with outward social signs of sexual behavior which their admittedly restrained society produced.

Everett Carter
Howells and the Age of Realism
(Philadelphia: Lippincott, 1950), pp. 150-52

After the Haymarket riot in 1886 and the execution of five anarchists—
"the thing forever damnable before God and abominable to civilized men,"
he called it—he seldom again indulged in optimistic contentment. His
stories, for the next decade, have a somber note heretofore lacking; if the
vocabulary is less violent than that of Stephen Crane or Jack London, the
criticism is scarcely less fundamental. . . . [They] portray a society harassed by the irresponsibility of acquisitive capitalism, the evils of industrialism, and the disintegration of traditional standards of morality. For
all his timidity and quaint propriety, his almost feminine domesticity, no
one better understood or presented the transition from the old America
to the new than this dean of American letters who at the height of his
fame and influence cast his lot in with the protestants and rebels of his
generation.

Because Howells was content with familiar material and traditional
themes and with a style that was classical and chaste, the full force of his
originality and impact of his courage were not at once apparent. Though
his dissent from the accepted practices and standards of his day was
sharper than that of most of his contemporaries, he appeared less bold
than some of his own disciples. His break with the past was philosophical
rather than material, it was less an uprooting than a transformation. He
never permitted himself, except in some of his private letters, a violent
gesture or a raucous note, and he voiced regrets more often than hopes.
The gap that separated him from, let us say, F. Marion Crawford or
Thomas Bailey Aldrich was just as deep as that which separated the
spokesman of agrarian revolt or the recorders of urban growth or of political and social corruption from their predecessors, but it was less
ostentatious.

Henry Steele Commager
The American Mind (New Haven:
Yale Univ. Pr., 1950), pp. 59-60

Obviously there is room for difference of opinion about the way one reads
Howells' literature—or anyone else's literature. But there can be little
doubt that the use against Howells of his "smiling aspects" phrase—which
has been used to denigrate him ever since the early Van Wyck Brooks's
The Ordeal of Mark Twain—has been founded on a combination of misreading, ignorance, and an unknown variable. The misreading has been
of the essay in which Howells used the phrase. The ignorance has been
of Howells' temperament, the growth of his ethical sensibility and insight
into evil, and of the whole context of imaginative and critical writing in
which that essay appeared. The variable, requiring to be worked out for
each user of the phrase against Howells, has been the particular motivation of the critic. . . .

Howells took the risk of daring to commit himself to a new kind of tragedy. To pluralistic, relativistic, contingent tragedy—not politically, metaphysically, or hierarchically "of a certain magnitude," but only emotionally and morally, *psychologically* so as it operated by the realistic standard. The risk was that readers habituated to classical and romantic tragedy would refuse him the hospitality of learning to read him on these his terms.

Edwin H. Cady
The Realist at War (Syracuse, N. Y.:
Syracuse Univ. Pr., 1958), pp. 133, 137

. . . Howells was not a social or economic propagandist; he was an artist. Through the offices of literature he wanted to teach the value of a good life. The life that he admired, however, was to be achieved not through a wholesale condemnation of the civilization in which he found himself but through the preservation of those aspects of it already found to be good. He was thus in an admirable sense conservative. His moral appraisal of American life expressed itself most characteristically not in the socialistic outburst of *A Traveler from Altruria* but in a consistent awareness of values and responsibilities.

[A] remark from James's appraisal is apposite: "Other persons have considered and discoursed on American life, but no one, surely, has *felt* it so completely as he." Howells felt American life and characters deeply because he refused to accept the notion that the commonest occurrences of everyday life are any less subject to moral judgment than the most extraordinary. It is, as James noted, this steady hold on the significance of "the character and the comedy, the point, the pathos, the tragedy, the particular homegrown humanity under . . . [his] eyes" that characterizes Howells' moral sensibility. Howells would be content that we judge him by his own standards—"the simple, the natural, and the honest." He would insist, however, and properly, that this standard be understood as a statement of high artistic and moral purpose.

George N. Bennett
William Dean Howells: The Development of a Novelist
(Norman, Okla.: Univ. Oklahoma Pr., 1959), p. 214

. . . Each of Howells' domestic novels sets out to answer one unformulated question: how can sexual intercourse occur with pure women? How can even the sweetest of girls retain honor if she exudes even the faintest odor of what Melville called the savage musk? His solution . . . was to deny that sex had any role to speak of and to substitute for its shameful effects the corruption of a European education or a bad dream. His angel is of the "usual" American kind; that is to say, she turns out to be sick or vulgar, hysterically jealous or gratuitously cruel. She has "negro blood." She is loved by a fantastical husband, or, in still another version of this dilemma —*A Foregone Conclusion*—she innocently charms a decadent priest who offers to renounce his vocation and marry her.

The women who people Howells' imago, therefore, are not beautifully innocent ladies endowed with a special loveliness of the spirit. On the contrary, they are impelled by two opposing forces which are never reconciled and which, in the larger matters of American culture, Van Wyck Brooks has traced to an inexpungeable dualism in our life and letters. . . . [Women] are depraved innocents . . . betrayed as it were despite themselves by the very force of sex itself. Recalling Howells' opinion of Margaret Vance in *A Hazard of New Fortunes,* we recognize his abiding belief that only a virgin is really an angel. Other women, as he observed in *A Modern Instance,* are marked by an indelible stain.

William Wasserstrom
NEQ (December, 1959), p. 494

WASHINGTON IRVING
1783-1859

Born April 3 in New York City. In 1802, he became a clerk in the office of Josiah Hoffman. He visited Europe in 1804 and stayed two years. He passed his bar examination in 1806. *Salmagundi* papers were published in 1807 and *Knickerbocker's History* in 1809. In 1812, he became the editor of *Analectic Magazine.* He went to England in 1815 to aid his brother's business, but the firm was forced into bankruptcy in 1818, after which he remained abroad. *Sketch Book* was published in 1819-1820 and *Bracebridge Hall* in 1822. In 1826, he went to Madrid as a member of the American Legation and, in 1828, *Life and Voyages of Columbus* was published. He lived in the Alhambra during 1829, when *Conquest of Granada* was published. He returned to New York in 1832 and made a tour of the West. *The Alhambra* was published in 1832, *Astoria* in 1836, and *Adventures of Captain Bonneville* in 1837. He was appointed minister to Spain in 1841. The first volume of *Life of Washington* was published in 1855 and the final volume in 1859. He died Nov. 28.

The Works of Washington Irving (1860-1861), 21 vols.

Stanley T. Williams, *The Life of Washington Irving* (1935), 2 vols.

PERSONAL

. . . Irving's fame as a man of letters was inseparably joined with his roles of journalist, politician, diplomat. It may be said, I think, that no writer before 1850, with exceptions of Poe and Hawthorne, became eminent among Americans without their approval of his opinions on subjects far dearer to them than what Irving called "the gentleman-like exercise of the pen. . . ." When Irving was not orthodox, he was tactfully silent, and praise of him as an author was never drowned out, as in the case of Cooper, by abuse of him as a critic of his own people. His writings epitomized his compatriots' *bourgeois* culture and flattered their aspirations to be gentlemen, to write according to English models, to make money, to exploit the West, to found traditions, to be respected abroad. . . .

. . . In spite of his protests concerning his maladjustment to the world of men, Irving had his part in the events of his time. Few careers of American men of letters are more varied in background; few offer so many glimpses behind the scenes into the literary, social, and political worlds of five different nations. If Irving himself wearies us, mild-mannered, urbane, indecisive, discreetly ambitious, imitatively romantic, affectionate, and, at times, timid and dependent, the picturesque settings in which he moved, and which he repeatedly changed to satisfy his volatile temperament, do not.

Stanley T. Williams
The Life of Washington Irving, Vol. I
(New York: Oxford Univ. Pr., 1935), pp. xiv-xv

Rip Van Winkle

. . . The history of Rip Van Winkle shows that he has had a deep hold on the American mind: Irving's tale itself remains a popular legend, and the play that was written about him as early as the eighteen-thirties was remodeled by succeeding generations of American actors, until given its classic form by Joseph Jefferson. How did this happen? The reason, I think, was that Rip's adventures and disappointments stood for that of the typical American of the pioneer period. Inept at consecutive work, harried by his wife, and disgusted with human society, he retires to the hills with his dog and his gun. He drinks heavily, falls asleep, and becomes enchanted. At the end of twenty years he awakes to find himself in a different society. The old landmarks have gone; the old faces have disappeared; all the outward aspects of life have changed. At the bottom, however, Rip himself has not changed; for he has been drunk and lost in a dream, and for all that the calendar and the clock records, he remains, mentally, a boy.

There was the fate of a whole generation: indeed, is it not still the fate of perhaps the great majority of Americans, lost in their dreams of a great fortune in real-estate, rubber or oil? In our heroic moments, we may think of ourselves as Leatherstockings, or two-fisted fellows like Paul Bunyan; but in the bottom of our hearts, we are disconsolate Rips.

Lewis Mumford
The Golden Day (Oxford Univ. Pr, 1927), p. 68

Through the "sleeper" motif in ["Rip Van Winkle"] Irving attempts to cope with his castration and separation anxiety. Death is denied and changed into sleep, the loss of the person is denied and changed into disappearance. The disappeared person is able to return, the sleeping one to awake: Thus the finality of death is magically altered through resurrection. . . .

In the "sleeper" motif, the cave is a symbolic description of the geography of the female genital. The return to the cave, to mother, is important to Irving in several ways. His use of this motif is an expression of Irving's wish to be dead, of his wish to be united with mother oedipally and preoedipally thus coping with his castration anxiety and his separation anxiety, and it contains his wish for homosexual union with father via his identification with mother.

Through the story of Rip Van Winkle Irving deals variously with his wish for possession of his mother. His wish is achieved symbolically (by entering the earth), through regression (by identification with the baby Rip), by accepting castration (masochistic defence—being old and impotent), and identification with his father (upon his return Rip finds the father figure, Nicholas Vedder dead, and he himself becomes "reverenced as one of the patriarchs").

Marcel Heiman
American Imago (Spring, 1959), pp. 33-34

HISTORIES

. . . Because in order to speak for Federalist America he learned to write with a vanishing grace and a suavity not again to be attained on this side of the Atlantic, [Irving's] future is more secure than that of his successors in the historical vein, Motley and Prescott and Parkman, better historians than he, who transcended the "Washington" and the "Columbus," but could not write an "Alhambra." Cooper, crabbed republican aristocrat, came nearer the ruling passions of his country, but his loosely held romance of the frontier has already suffered from its slovenly diction and uneven texture. Hawthorne's didactic obsession stiffens the sombre beauty of his work, but Irving's lighter craft is well trimmed for the shifting gales of fame. He had a style, he had a temperament, he had an eye for the humors, he was born a New Yorker, he could say, as New Englanders would not say, as Philadelphians and Virginians and Carolinians could not say effectively: While we create a new society in a new republic, let us not forget the mellowness of the age we have left behind us overseas, let us not forget the graces of life, let us not forget to be gentlemen. And if this was all he said, it was put admirably, in a time of need, and with apposite and succinct example. He made Spain glamorous, England picturesque, and his own land conscious of values not to be found in industry, morals, or politics. A slight achievement beside Wordsworth's, a modest ambition by comparison with Byron's, but enough. Not a great man, not even a great author, though a good chronicler, an excellent story-teller, a skilful essayist, an adept in romantic coloring; not in accord with progress in America but the most winning spokesman for the Federalist hope; a musician with few themes, and the minor ones the best, and many played perfectly—that is Washington Irving.

Henry Seidel Canby
Classic Americans (New York: Harcourt, Brace,
1931), pp. 95-96

GENERAL

Irving inaugurated American literature not with the trumpets of rebellion, not with an epic elevation befitting a people who had conquered a wilderness, but with quiet, old-fashioned humour, a cultivated reserved accent, urbane manners, and a smiling indifference to certain local passions. Even at home he is a sympathetic and observant tourist, intimately acquainted with what he sees but not immersed in its currents of thought. He does not make us feel what most stirred the hearts and perplexed the minds of any considerable class of Americans in the year 1825. From the social contests, the clashing forces of mind and of economic necessities, the industrial and spiritual developments by reason of which we are now alive and what we are, Irving is almost as aloof as Poe.

John Macy
The Spirit of American Literature (Garden City, N. Y.:
Doubleday, 1913), pp. 21-22

The most distinguished of our early romantics, Irving in the end was immolated on the altar of romanticism. The pursuit of the picturesque lured him away into sterile wastes, and when the will-o'-the-wisp was gone he was left empty. A born humorist, the gayety of whose spirits overflowed the brim, he was lacking in a brooding intellectuality, and instead of coming upon irony at the bottom of the cup—as the greater humorists have come upon it after life has had its way with them—he found there only sentiment and the dreamy poetic. As the purple haze on the horizon of his mind was dissipated by a sobering experience, he tried to substitute an adventitious glamour; as romance faded, sentiment supplied its place. So long as youth and high spirits endured, his inkwell was a never-failing source of gayety, but as the sparkle subsided he over-sweetened his wine. This suffices to account for the fact that all his better work was done early; and this explains why the Knickerbocker *History* remains the most genial and vital of his volumes. The gayety of youth bubbles and effervesces in those magic pages, defying time to do its worst. The critic may charge the later Irving with many and heavy shortcomings, but the romantic smoke-clouds that ascend from Wouter Van Twiller's pipe cannot be dissipated by the winds of criticism.

Vernon Louis Parrington
Main Currents in American Thought, Vol. II
(New York: Harcourt, Brace, 1927), pp. 211-12

[T]he fact that Americans applauded because Englishmen did, while it may account for some of the early adulation, does not explain Irving's staying power; moreover, literary reputations, while they may be won, are not maintained, in that way. Equally inadequate is the reason advanced that he maintains his place simply because he was the *first*. Neither can his success be attributed to originality or profundity of thought, to insight into the great ideas that swept through the world, to superior ability in character portrayal or plot structure; for precisely in these provinces was he weakest. Reduced to essentials, his forte lay in (1) his temperament, and (2) his style:—a temperament that would vary from pure sentiment and romance to wit and urbanity, and a style that can best be described by the much-maligned word "elegant,"—in the sense that his manner was graciously suave and his expressions in gentlemanly good taste so that no one has yet fallen into the error of failing to recognize behind his words the soul of geniality.

Here, apparently, are qualities which do not loom very large but appear rather trivial by the side of the high seriousness of the Mathers, the intellect of Jonathan Edwards, the fecundity of Thomas Jefferson, or the ponderousness of Timothy Dwight. Nor is it patently clear, until the events and experiences and conditions of his life are scrutinized, how and by what means Irving came by the peculiar literary capabilities which have sustained him through the years while the writings of men built after a larger mould have been suffered to lie neglected for want of readers. For no other major American writer was so literally influenced and determined both by conformity with and by opposition to his "race plus place plus time" as was Irving.

Henry A. Pochman, ed.
Washington Irving: Representative Selections
(New York: American Book, 1934), p. xiii

. . . [Irving was] the first important American author to put to literary use the comic mythology and popular traditions of American character which, by the early nineteenth century, had proliferated widely in oral tradition.

The case for Irving's achievement in this direction rests primarily upon the personalities of Ichabod Crane and Brom Bones in "The Legend of Sleepy Hollow." There he gave our literature its first important statement of the clash of regional characters—the Yankee vs. the backwoodsman—who had already emerged as the dominant types in our regional folk traditions. The conflict between them was soon to become a major theme in our literature, as well as a continuing motif in a century and a half of folktales, and in our national history.

Daniel G. Hoffman
PMLA (June, 1953), pp. 425-26

Unable to achieve a satisfactory mode of imaginative expression from the stuff of the "commonplace realities of the present," Irving turned . . . to techniques which would give him the requisite imaginative latitude. He pretended both childishness and antiquity for America, then, in effect, stood back and saw these things fail before an always triumphant broad daylight which existed to celebrate the absence of childishness and antiquity. He handled his materials urbanely, with a diffused humor stemming largely from his use of the mock-heroic . . . ; this allowed him to maintain a stylistic, mannered, and gentlemanly distance from the resolution of his tales.

Terence Martin
AL (May, 1959), p. 147

HENRY JAMES
1843-1916

Born April 15 in New York City. His father moved to Europe in 1855, but moved again, to Newport, Rhode Island, in 1858. They spent the next few years moving between Europe and New England, finally settling in Cambridge in 1866. In 1862 he went briefly to Harvard Law School. He began writing criticism and stories for the *Nation* and *Atlantic* in 1865. In 1869, he traveled to Europe, dividing the next few years between Europe and the United States. He finally settled in Europe in 1875. A series of publications followed: *Roderick Hudson* (1876); *The American* (1877); *Daisy Miller* (1879); *The Portrait of a Lady* and *Washington Square* (1881); *The Bostonians* and *Princess Casamassima* (1886); and *The Tragic Muse* (1890). In 1891, *The American* was produced as a play, but failed. Other publications followed: *The Spoils of Poynton* and *What Maisie Knew* (1897); *The Awkward Age* (1899); *The Sacred Fount* (1901); *The Wings of the Dove* (1902); *The Ambassadors* (1903); and *The Golden Bowl* (1904). In 1904, he returned to the United States for a visit. The New York edition of his revised works was published with his prefaces in 1907-1909. In 1915, he became a British citizen. He died Feb. 28.

The Novels and Tales of Henry James (1907-1917), 26 vols.

Leon Edel, *Henry James* (1953-1962), 3 vols. (incomplete)

PERSONAL

It is, of course, in terms of his deracination that Henry James's unsatisfactory development is commonly explained. The theory is what we find, in its most respectable statement advanced by Mr. Van Wyck Brooks in *The Pilgrimage of Henry James.* The less delicate expositions more or less bluntly censure James for not having stayed in America and become a thoroughly American novelist. He should have devoted his genius to his own country and inaugurated modern American—the first truly American—literature. . . .

The obvious constatation to start from, when the diagnosis of his queer development is in question, is that he suffered from being too much a professional novelist: being a novelist came to be too large a part of his living; that is, he did not live enough. His failure in this respect suggests, no doubt, some initial deficiency in him. Nevertheless, the peculiarities in terms of which it demands to be discussed are far from appearing as simple weakness. It is no doubt at first appearances odd that his interest in manners should have gone with such moral-intellectual intensity. But the manners he was interested in were to be the outward notation of spiritual and intellectual fineness, or at least to lend themselves to treatment as such. Essentially he was in quest of an ideal society, an ideal civilization. And English society, he had to recognize as he lived into it, could not after all offer him any sustaining approximation to his ideal. Still less, he knew, could America. So we find him developing into something like a paradoxical kind of recluse, a recluse living socially in the midst of society. . . .

The same conditions . . . that drove him back on his art made him profoundly aware that his art wasn't likely to be appreciated by many besides himself. So he came to live in it—and not the less so for living strenuously—the life of a spiritual recluse; a recluse in a sense in which not only no novelist but no good artist of any kind can afford to become one. His technique came to exhibit an unhealthy vitality of undernourishment and etiolation. His technical preoccupation, to put it another way, lost its balance, and, instead of being the sharp register of his finest perceptions, as informed and related by his fullest sense of life, became something that took his intelligence out of its true focus and blunted his sensitiveness. . . .

But this is not the note to end on. It is a measure of our sense of the greatness of Henry James's genius that discussion should tend to stress mainly what he failed to do with it. But what achievement in the art of fiction—fiction as a completely serious art addressed to the adult mind— can we point to in English as surpassing his? Besides *The Europeans, The Portrait of a Lady, The Bostonians, Washington Square, The Awkward Age* and *What Maisie Knew*, there is an impressive array of things— novels, *nouvelles*, short stories—that will stand permanently as classics. [ca. 1948]

F. R. Leavis
The Great Tradition (Garden City, N. Y.:
Doubleday, 1954), pp. 197-98, 201, 210

As the years passed James's awareness of the American stake in the maintenance of civilization grew increasingly positive and imposing. In his later writings old Europe serves once more as the background for young America, and his restored interest in the nuclear fable of the passionate pilgrim is now worked out on a more ambitious scale and with more intricate artistic intentions. His last great novels are remarkable, too, for the resurgence in them of that native idealism—that "extraordinary good faith"— the effect of which in his early fiction was to link him with the classic masters of American literature. In *The Wings of the Dove, The Ambassadors*, and *The Golden Bowl* the motives and standards of this idealism are applied to the mixed disorder and splendor of the "great world," now no longer simply admired from afar but seen from within.

But the question whether the ultimate loyalty of James is claimed by Europe or America is hardly as meaningful as it has appeared to some of his interpreters. For actually his valuations of Europe and America are not the polar opposites but the two commanding centres of his work—the contending sides whose relation is adjusted so as to make mutual assimilation feasible. It is the only means by which the Jamesian idea of heritage can be brought to fruition. What his detractors can never forgive him, however, is his bursting the bounds of that autarchic Americanism of which Whitman is the chief exponent. Never having fallen into the habit of "glowing belligerently with one's country," he is able to invest his characters with an historic mission and propel them into spheres of experience as yet closed to them at home. They are the people named as the Ambassadors —and the nationalist critics who make so much of his expatriation should be reminded that there is a world of difference between the status of an ambassador and the status of a fugitive.

Philip Rahv
Image and Idea (Norfolk, Conn.: New Directions,
1949), pp. 46-47

"To be completely great," Henry James wrote in an early review, "a work of art must lift up the heart." His own novels do this in so eminent a degree as to leave him not indeed the greatest novelist who ever wrote the English language but certainly the greatest artist who ever became a novelist. "Here," cries Howells, "you have the work of a great psychologist, who has the imagination of a poet, the wit of a keen humorist, the conscience of an impeccable moralist, the temperament of a philosopher, and the wisdom of a rarely experienced witness of the world. . . ." It ought, one feels, to be enough. A generation after his death, the great expatriate who professed to have no opinions stands foursquare in the great Christian-democratic tradition. The men and women who, at the height of World War II, raided the second-hand shops for his out-of-print books knew what they were doing. For no writer ever raised a braver banner to which all who love freedom may adhere.

Edward Wagenknecht
Cavalcade of the American Novel (New York:
Holt, 1953), p. 105

For all his subtlety and tact, James is basically, hopelessly innocent, an innocent voyeur, which is to say, a child! And he is, indeed, the first novelist to do in full consciousness what Twain in *Huckleberry Finn* did just once unawares: present the complexities of adult experience as perceived by a pre-adolescent mind. In American literature and in English, writers have all along tended to make a virtue, even a fetish, out of what began as a necessity, treating the child's "pure" vision as the truest kind of vision, an ideal type of the artist's vision itself. The child character, made compulsory in our books by the restrictions of gentility and the fear of sex, is first used in *What Maisie Knew* to confront rather than evade experience. James's novel, like the later books which follow its pattern, is a kind of initiation story, though it deals not with a full-scale initiation from innocence to maturity but with a quasi-initiation that ends in a withdrawal from adult experience. The child in Anglo-Saxon literature learns the "mystery of iniquity" not as a participant but only as a witness of sin. In the Jamesian version of the Fall of Man, there are four actors, not three: the man, the woman, the serpent, and the child, presumably watching from behind the tree.

Leslie Fiedler
Love and Death in the American Novel
(New York: Criterion, 1960), p. 339

The Jamesian premises, like his "rules," "principles," and "laws" of art —or like the whole structure of the Jamesian "esthetics"—were almost always a rationalization of his own weaknesses and failures. His "triumph," in his own mind surely, and now, as it appears, in the mind of a whole bewitched generation of Jamesian explicators, analysts, and apologists, was simply that he converted every loss, every failure, every defeat, every debacle in his own career, into an imaginary victory. He is a supreme example of the Rationalizing Ego (in non- or pre-Freudian terminology) which must repress the least hint of danger, either in itself or in the world around it, by a series of ever ascending, ever more elaborate "explanations" which remove it farther and farther from any kind of troublesome reality. Henry James is indeed a whole course in the non-Freudian psychology of "survival," and of triumphant ascendancy, at the cost of all truth.

The great writers start first of all from self-knowledge, while James reveled in self-ignorance—which he then proclaimed and codified as "universal law." But how can a writer who is not "great," or "major," or even "important" in any important sense; or perhaps even *relevant* in the long workings of time for the majority of the human race—since James's vision of life was *so* singular, his experience so limited, his sensibilities so restrained: how can such a writer, finally, still remain so interesting? I have no intention here of destroying, or even debunking Henry James himself —that would be too easy, in a sense, and too cheap. When the present Jacobite cult has vanished from our literary scene (and no loss) James himself will remain as a remarkable phenomenon. Remarkable just because he is a phenomenon never before glimpsed on literary land or sea; and probably never to appear again. Henry James is indeed the most singular curiosity in the whole wide reach of literary history.

Maxwell Geismar
Henry James and the Jacobites (Boston:
Houghton Mifflin, 1963), pp. 12-13

GENERAL

The literature that he produced [in his early] period owes its superiority to his current product in general import and interest, I think, precisely to this factor of culture on which he now places so little reliance. It was inspired and penetrated with the spirit of cosmopolitanism, that is to say, culture in which the contemporary is substituted for the more universal element, and, if it does not quite make up in vividness for what it lacks in breadth, certainly performs the similar inestimable service of providing a standard that establishes the relative value and interest of the material directly dealt with. Out of his familiarity with contemporary society in America, England, France, and Italy, grew a series of novels and tales that were full of vigor, piquancy, truth, and significance. The play of the characters against contrasting backgrounds was most varied and interesting. The contrasts of points of view, of conventions and ideals, of customs and traditions, gave a richness of texture to the web of his fiction which, since it has lacked these, it has disadvantageously lost. His return to the cosmopolitan *motif* in *The Ambassadors* and (measurably) in *The Golden Bowl* is accordingly a welcome one, and would be still more welcome if the development of this *motif* were not now incrusted and obscured with mannerisms of presentation accreted in the pursuit of what no doubt seems to the author a "closer correspondence with life," but what certainly seems to the reader a more restricted order of art—an art, at any rate, so largely dependent on scrutiny as perforce to dispense with the significance to be expected only of the culture it suggests but does not illustrate. It is a part of Mr. James's distinction that he gives us so much as to make us wish for more, that he entertains us on so high a plane that we ask to be conducted still higher, and that his penetration reveals to us such wonders in the particular *local*, that we call upon him to show us "the kingdoms of the earth." [ca. 1909]

W. C. Brownell
American Prose Masters (New York:
Scribner's, 1929), pp. 392-93

Mr. James has two technical defects, one of style, the other of method. The defect of style is due to his habit of writing with his eye and his mind instead of with his ear. His great mind saves him perfectly when he is writing in his own person; but too often when he makes a character speak, he equips it with a peculiarly Henry-James sentence, a fault not un-like Browning's, but more pardonable in a poet than in a writer of realistic fiction. . . .

The James sentence, as a rule, will be found, upon scrutiny, to contain, admirably, each thing in its place, the entire idea; and whatever another writer, more naturally following the path of least resistance, which on the whole, is that path normally pursued by the human mind, would tag on, as who should say, as an afterthought, he cunningly, and true to an ideally more perfect intellectual arrangement, inserts, or more properly builds in, so that, in fine, to the English language is wonderfully restored, in him, some of the effect, so long lost, of the periodic sentence. But people don't talk that way, even the rather intellectual and delightfully clever human beings that he assembles.

The other defect, that of method, is the vice of his virtue. He is a critic of human life. He devises an interesting situation and then stands off and explains it. The good effect of this, which no other novelist quite so curi-ously affords, is a warrant of intellectual integrity, as if he wanted the reader to watch the story with him, discover things simultaneously with the author. The difficulty is that having assumed that he does not know all about it, but is a spectator too, he then, without any new action, gesture or speech to furnish new knowledge, plunges into the midmost mind of the character and tells things that are working there which only a god could know. . . .

John Macy
The Spirit of American Literature (Garden City, N. Y.:
Doubleday, 1913), pp. 332-33

Never was author more subjective and more enamoured of his own psychological processes than Henry James. Never does he lose sight of himself These characters of his are all of them Henry James. They slip out of their costumes at slightest provocation to talk with his tones, to voice his philosophy, to follow his mental processes. In externals they are true to model though not always deeply; the hands are the hands of Christopher Newman, but the voice is the voice of Henry James.

The tendency to self-consciousness has colored everything. Even his criticism has had its personal basis. It has consisted of studies in expatriation: the life of Story, that prototype of James; the life of Hawthorne, that exposition of the rawness of America and the unfitness of the new land for the residence of men of culture; *The American Scene*—that mental analysis tracing every shade of emotion as he revisits what has become to him a foreign land. His literary essays cover largely the experiences of his apprenticeship. They trace the path of his own growth in art. They are strings of brilliants, flashing, often incomparable, but they are not criticism in the highest sense of the word criticism. Few men have said such brilliant things about Balzac, Maupassant, Daudet, Stevenson as James, yet for all that a critic in the wider sense of the term really he is not. He lacks perspective, philosophy, system. He makes epigrams and pithy remarks. The ability to project himself into the standpoint of another, to view with sympathy of comprehension, he did not have. Within his limited range he could measure and the rules of art he could apply with brilliancy, but he could not feel.

Self-study, the pursuit of every fleeting impression, became in the author at last a veritable obsession. In his later books like *Notes of a Son and Brother*, for instance, and *The American Scene*, his finger is constantly upon his own pulse. He seeks the source of his every fleeting emotion. He does not tell us why he did not want to enter Harvard; he tries rather to trace the subtle thread of causation that could have led him not to *want* to want to go. When *A Small Boy and Others* appeared the world cried out, "Is it possible that at last Henry James has revealed himself?" whereas the truth was that few men ever have revealed themselves more. All this endless dissection and analysis and scrutiny of the inner workings is in reality an analysis of Henry James himself. Objective he could not be. He could only stand in his solitude and interpret his own introspections.

Fred L. Pattee
A History of American Literature Since 1870
(New York: Century, 1915), pp. 196-97

[James's] characters, besides being few in number, are constructed on very stingy lines.They are incapable of fun, of rapid motion, of carnality, and of nine-tenths of heroism. Their clothes will not take off, the diseases that ravage them are anonymous, like the sources of their income, their servants are noiseless or resemble themselves, no social explanation of the world we know is possible for them, for there are no stupid people in their world, no barriers of language, and no poor. Even their sensations are limited. They can land in Europe and look at works of art and at each other, but that is all. Maimed creatures can alone breathe in Henry James's pages—maimed yet specialized. They remind one of the exquisite deformities who haunted Egyptian art in the reign of Akhnaton—huge heads and tiny legs, but nevertheless charming. In the following reign they disappear.

Now this drastic curtailment, both of the numbers of human beings and of their attributes, is in the interests of the pattern. The longer James worked, the more convinced he grew that a novel should be a whole—not necessarily geometric like *The Ambassadors*, but it should accrete round a single topic, situation, gesture, which should occupy the characters and provide a plot, and should also fasten up the novel on the outside—catch its scattered statements in a net, make them cohere like a planet, and swing through the skies of memory. A pattern must emerge, and anything that emerged from the pattern must be pruned off as wanton distraction. Who so wanton as human beings? Put Tom Jones or Emma or even Mr. Casaubon into a Henry James book, and the book will burn to ashes, whereas we could put them into one another's books and only cause local inflammation. Only a Henry James character will suit, and though they are not dead—certain selected recesses of experience he explores very well—they are gutted of the common stuff that fills characters in other books, and ourselves. And this castrating is not in the interests of the Kingdom of Heaven, there is no philosophy in the novels, no religion (except an occasional touch of superstition), no prophecy, no benefit for the superhuman at all. It is for the sake of a particular aesthetic effect which is certainly gained, but at this heavy price. [ca.1927]

E. M. Forster
Aspects of the Novel (London: Arnold, 1944), pp. 205-7

In this outcome James transcended the nationalistic altogether—that obsession which had had so long a history. Yet in the aggregate of his novels he repeated a significant portion of the old fable. He showed that the American was in truth what the belligerent Yankee had always declared him to be, a wholly alien, disparate, even a new character. In the end the primary concern of James was with that character; and he kept a familiar touch of the fabulous in his narratives. "I had been plotting arch-romance without knowing it," he said of *The American*; and by romance he meant what Hawthorne had meant, life with a touch of the marvelous, an infusion which can be apprehended only imperfectly by the sense of fact. Romance appeared in the generality and scale which James gave to his characters and to his situations. Such titles as *The Wings of the Dove* and *The Golden Bowl* suggest a poetized conception completing the romantic character of the themes; and his handling is kept free from complicated circumstance. Poetry indeed overspread much of James's writing. Like that of the popular fabulists, it was packed with metaphor. "The morning was like a clap of hands." "She carried her three and thirty years as a light-wristed Hebe might have carried a brimming wine-cup." His figures could also be ironical; the romantic feeling is constantly enclosed by a close drawing. Recognition is fundamental in all of James's portraiture; yet a basic poetry of outline and expression remains clear, most of all in his later novels. Few writers have had so deep a sense of the poetry of character; and his poetical penetration was the rarer achievement because his approaches were not those of the primary emotions. [ca. 1931]

Constance Rourke
American Humor (New York: Doubleday, 1953), p. 203

There have been men who thought they understood James and tried to state the justification of his career. There has been a kind of James cult. But the majority of readers, however thoughtful and patient, have rejected him. Have they not been wise? No one can deny that considerable insight went into the writing of the earlier novels, and even in the later books there are moments when a subtle power of observation and understanding makes itself dazzlingly apparent; but for the most part James's novels and tales seem completely remote from the lives of the vast majority of men. And why should one read a novel if it does not give him a sense that he is moving, with enhanced powers of perception and a greater certainty as to direction, through the strange world of which he is part? It is all very well to praise James's technique, but could one not fairly characterize the literary processes we have been describing as a game? Is not James's world a world of almost complete abstractions, in which he invents the situations and the people, and only the technique is constant. Grant that he was a master of the game, and that the game, if one consents to abide by the rules, is fascinating to play; it is still a game.

Granville Hicks
The Great Tradition (New York:
Macmillan, 1935), pp. 121-22

James's great deficiency was his lack of sensuous awareness and participation. His viewpoint was always that of a passive and meditative spectator. He preferred to develop an emotional nuance into an elaborate metaphorical structure rather than to present a scene in its concrete immediacy; and he was incapable of dealing directly with physical passion. His habit of looking at his more positive characters from outside, as though he did not know what they were doing, has often exasperated his readers, and has sometimes been attributed to his expatriation; if he had remained in his own country, it has been suggested, he would have written as a participant and not as a puzzled spectator. It is more probable, however, that this deficiency was the result of certain peculiarities in James's own psychophysical constitution. He never married, and there are indications that he was physically incapable of a marital relationship.

Henry B. Parkes
The American Experience (New York:
A. A. Knopf, 1947), p. 262

. . . James's special moral quality, his power of love, is not wholly comprised by his impulse to make an equal distribution of dignity among his characters. It goes beyond this to create his unique moral realism, his particular gift of human understanding. If in his later novels James, as many say he did, carried awareness of human complication to the point of virtuosity, he surely does not do so here, and yet his knowledge of complication is here very considerable. But this knowledge is not an analytical one, or not in the usual sense in which that word is taken, which implies a cool dissection. If we imagine a father of many children who truly loves them all, we may suppose that he will see very vividly their differences from one another, for he has no wish to impose upon them a similarity which would be himself; and he will be quite willing to see their faults, for his affection leaves him free to love them, not because they are faultless but because they are they; yet while he sees their faults he will be able, from long connection and because there is no reason to avoid the truth, to perceive the many reasons for their actions. The discriminations and modifications of such a man would be enormous, yet the moral realism they would constitute would not arise from an analytical intelligence as we usually conceive it but from love. [ca. 1948]

Lionel Trilling
The Liberal Imagination (Garden City, N. Y.:
Doubleday, 1953), pp. 91-92

No one of [James's] books has the survival value, in and by itself, of the great masters of life in representative portraits—Dickens, Shakespeare, and in his limited field, Twain. But James did create a cult which gives his books a significance outweighing sometimes even their interest. It was not, as his enemies said, a cult of difficulty and obscurity. Difficulty was his personal choice. Obscurity is the fault of the reader who lacks, as James complained, the faculty of attention lost by the wayside in our modern flood of print. (Take ten per cent off this statement for Henry's vice— every writer has his vice—of verbosity.) The true cult that Henry founded was the cult of awareness. We have become sensitive, and largely through James and his followers, to depths and complications in quite usual courses of living where earlier novelists have been either unperceptive or blind. James has educated his readers and imitators in *seeing*, much as the psychologists and phychiatrists have educated us in *explaining*, new aspects of behavior. And it should be said that it was the literary man, and especially, in our times, Henry James who saw them first. In this his scope was broader than that of Proust. Awareness, intense, subtle, sympathetic, and unrelenting, has been Henry James's gift to the art of the novel.

Henry Seidel Canby
Turn West, Turn East (Boston:
Houghton Mifflin, 1951), p. 296

The dialectic of innocence and experience—usually, but not always, dramatized as the American and Europe—was so obsessive and constant a theme for Henry James that one is tempted to say it was not, finally, a theme at all: but rather the special and extraordinary sensitive instrument by which James gauged the moral weather of the life he was imitating. It was part of his technique as well as his content. An account of "innocence" in the fiction of Henry James, therefore, would be much the same as a book about James's fiction in general. . . .

But although James can be rewardingly examined in many different perspectives, one of the surest approaches to his work is that of the Adamic mythology I have been tracing. He saw himself in relation to French, Russian, and English novelists; but the form which life assumed in James's fiction reflected the peculiar American rhythm of the Adamic experience: the birth of the innocent, the foray into the unknown world, the collision with that world, "the fortunate fall," the wisdom and the maturity which suffering produced. The longer James lived abroad, the closer he moved toward a classic representation of the native anecdote. His initial treatment was realistic, in the Gallic manner; but his last novels shared the romantic, melodramatic, and mythic orientation of Cooper and Hawthorne and Melville. In *The Portrait of a Lady*, James took care to identify the social, domestic, and economic factors which led to Isabel Archer's entrance into the damaging world. In *The Wings of the Dove*, realities lie in the background; in the foreground, James enacts a singular combination of fairy tale and horror story. And the more James rehearsed the story, the more ambiguity he introduced into it. The later fiction reached sustained heights of narrative equivocation, and it is no longer possible to say that innocence is being either celebrated or exposed in its weakness; our allegiance is played with too cunningly, the wheel revolves too swiftly.

R. W. B. Lewis
The American Adam (Chicago: Univ. Chicago Pr., 1955), p. 153

The mind of Henry James was all-engrossing, imperial. He achieved a very nearly complete correspondence between the number and quality of things seen and the capacity to order them into an imaginative structure. His world is rendered wholly seamless and entire because it is quite literally the world which corresponds in every detail with the nature and the demands of the personality which apprehends it. The passages in *A Small Boy and Others* which emphasize James's concern with "others" as having a salience, an otherness that seemed much more satisfactory than simply being Henry James, suggest how fully the novelist entered into the world to grasp its every detail; but the consequence was that every alien detail underwent assimilation and transformation, so that James became the world, and the world became James. What his father predicted about the marriage of universality to particularity is an almost literal fact about the son's experience, and in the measure in which he succeeded as this sort of artist, it is a fact about his work as we experience it. One might make an anthology of observations about James which have this general purport. Many critics have said that James's characters approach the condition of impulses, natures, powers, symbolic constants, ideal limits of moral motion —to rehearse the terms used in the preceding chapters.

For James the whole middle ground of life which lies between the particulars observed and such universals as Maggie Verver's illimitable charity was swept bare for art. His father's taste for the unconditioned, which led to an explicit denial of the reality of sexuality and death, is present in the novelist, is, in fact, the very ground of his marvelous capacity for creating aesthetic order. As against the good European, delicately poised before the options of a complex culture, James is the good American, who succeeds in universalizing himself, finds the individual form which will contain totality. He became Constance Rourke's American Narcissus, intent on making a final image of the world as a reflection of consciousness, consciousness conceived as permeable throughout and rational through and through. In James the impulse of Emerson's generation to practice a Carthusian individualism came to artistic fulfillment.

Quentin Anderson
The American Henry James (New Brunswick, N. J.:
Rutgers Univ. Pr., 1957), pp. 352-53

In his essay "The Ambiguity of Henry James" Edmund Wilson outlines the meanings *The Turn of the Screw* would have if it *were* an allegory. The allegory would be Freudian, and we should read the story and understand the ghosts as the neurotic sex fantasy of the repressed governess. Wilson's account of the tale, which appeared in the 1930's, was a necessary correction to the older view that the ghosts were real diabolic agencies and that the governess, about whom there was nothing demented or sinister, was simply trying to protect the children from them.

Furthermore, it is astonishing how literally James uses the Freudian dream symbols. But a careful reading of the tale convinces us that the ghosts may really be there, marvelously adapted to but finally independent of the governess's fantasies. There are things about them, such as the physical appearance of Peter Quint, which the governess could not know and could not project out of her unconscious. The universe of meanings is bigger than the governess's own distraught mind, and the drama of the tale lies in her attempt to foresee and interpret with her frantic conscious-ness everything that can happen to her. Of course, she cannot do this, and if there is a moral in the book, it is that the attempt to live in a totally cognized world, in which all ambiguities are rationalized and symbolized according to the bias of one's own mind, is madness. However alert and imaginative it may be, the mind is narrow and obsessive compared with the infinite variety of experience. In the story James provides a tremendous dramatic irony by showing us reality in a guise that seems only slightly to vary from the governess's conception of it—but the variation is enough to suggest the abyss of difference.

Richard Chase
The American Novel and Its Tradition (Garden City, N. Y.:
Doubleday, 1957), pp. 239-40

SARAH ORNE JEWETT
1849-1909

Born September 3 in South Berwick, Maine. Her first story, "Mr. Bruce," was printed in the *Atlantic Monthly* in 1869. *Deephaven* was published in 1877. Following the death of her father in 1879, she spent most of the time in Boston and in travel abroad, always returning to Berwick. In 1896, *The Country of The Pointed Firs* was published. In 1901 she received the first LL.D. conferred on a woman by Bowdoin. She died June 24.

F. O. Matthiessen, *Sarah Orne Jewett* (1929)

[Sarah Orne Jewett's] power lies in her purity of style, her humorous little touches, and her power of characterization. Work like her "A White Heron," "Miss Tempy's Watchers," and "The Dulham Ladies," has a certain lightness of touch, a pathos and a humor, a skill in delineation which wastes not a word or an effect, that places it among the most delicate and finished of American short stories. Yet brilliant as they are in technique, in characterization and background and atmosphere, they lack nevertheless the final touch of art. They are *too* literary; they are too much works of art, too much from the intellect and not enough from the heart. They are Sir Roger de Coverley sketches, marvelously well done, but always from the Sir Roger standpoint. There is a certain "quality" in all that Miss Jewett wrote, a certain unconscious *noblesse oblige* that kept her ever in the realm of the gentle, the genteel, the Berwick old régime. One feels it in her avoidance of everything common and squalid, in her freedom from passion and dramatic climax, in her objective attitude toward her characters. She is always sympathetic, she is moved at times to real pathos, but she stands apart from her picture; she observes and describes; she never, like Rose Terry Cooke, mingles and shares. She cannot. Hers is the pride that the lady of the estate takes in her beloved peasantry; of the patrician who steps down of an afternoon into the cottage and comes back to tell with amusement and perhaps with tears of what she finds there.

Fred L. Pattee
A History of American Literature Since 1870
(New York: Century, 1915), pp. 234-35

That [a] "cheap streak" should have spread so far through American life, that the vulgar middle class should have taken over the rule of the country, gave [Miss Jewett] concern. To one brought up on Carlyle and Lowell and Arnold the ways of the plutocracy were abhorrent, and she clung the more tenaciously to the land of her memories, where the gentry ruled, where the plain people respected themselves and their betters, and where vulgar display was unknown. "I think as Mr. Arnold does," she wrote in 1884, "and as Mr. Lowell did, that the mistake of our time is in being governed by the ignorant mass of opinion, instead of by thinkers and men who know something." Though she disliked and distrusted the America that was submerging the old landmarks, she was as ignorant as her Maine fisherfolk of the social forces that were blotting out the world of her fathers, and she clung with pathetic futility to such fragments of the old order as remained. Like Lowell in his later years her heart was given to a Brahmin democracy where gentlemen ruled and where "the best traditions of culture and manners, from some divine inborn instinct toward what is simplest and purest," were held in universal respect.

> Vernon Louis Parrington
> *Main Currents in American Thought,* Vol. III
> (New York: Harcourt, Brace, 1930), pp. 65-66

[Sarah Orne Jewett's] delicate powers of perception . . . give to the best of her work a richness, an authenticity, and a dignity that are too rare to be scorned. It was precisely because she so placidly disregarded what lay outside her little world that she could concentrate so effectively upon it. It was because she instinctively rejected characters, situations, and emotions that were not congenial to her that she could let her imagination play so calmly and sympathetically over the lives she chose to record. We may grant that she is only a minor writer, that the kind of pleasure her work offers only remotely resembles the effect of great literature, that the insight she gives us into men and women is only fragmentary. We may grant her attitude is essentially elegiac, and that she writes of a dying world of old men and old women. We may even grant that her aims were virtually those of the other regionalists. But there is a difference. For a moment her people live and breathe. For a moment, as we yield to her art, we feel that here is a master, though a master of a tiny realm. Calmly, but with both instinctive determination and conscious artistry, she selected from the decaying New England about her the elements she admired, and out of them created a little world, not merely for the purposes of her stories but also for the needs of her personality. She found her refuge.

> Granville Hicks
> *The Great Tradition* (New York: Macmillan, 1935), pp. 104-5

The growth between *Deephaven* and *The Country of the Pointed Firs* can be measured by seeing how observation has matured to insight, and how her attitude toward both her people and her art has subtly deepened. In the early book the narrator seems (though she was not) a summer resident in search of the quaint and unique; without looking down on the people she is never quite at one with them, and her experiments with scenes are sometimes tentative and unsure. By the time of the *Pointed Firs* and its epilogue-story *The Dunnet Shepherdess*, she knows how to understand and therefore how to present her people; she has learned the great trick of true realism: to combine depth of sympathetic involvement with artistic detachment, reaching unity through the establishment of a point of view. Deeply responsive to a look or a word from people like Almira Todd the gatherer of pennyroyal, or William Blackett the taciturn islander, she can still see that look or word as only one thread in the fabric of her total impression. An emotional experience is thus never felt to be the end in view, but only an indispensable contribution to that end. One could cite among dozens of examples the farewell to Mrs. Todd, soon followed by the distant prospect of the same Antigone-like figure descending the profile of a hill as party to a walking funeral. One hears that Miss Jewett's was a limited and muted art. But the significant point—in an age of realism for social history's sake, or regionalism strongly dependent for its force on mere local color, where characters were sometimes embarrassed and stereotyped by being saddled with the responsibility of representing a particular region—is that her stories were works of art, and of a high order.

Carlos Baker

in *Literary History of the United States*, eds. Robert Spiller *et al*,
Vol. II (New York: Macmillan, 1948), pp. 846-47

Her own world may seem, at first blush, a small one, her people simple and often eccentric. Unsympathetically viewed, Miss Joanna, who believes herself to have committed the sin against the Holy Ghost, is as monstrous an egoist as Cowper was himself under the same delusion. Miss Jewett might well have denied this, for she was one of those rare writers who have achieved tenderness without sentimentality. Didacticism and a febrile aestheticism were equally impossible for her: she was a great lady, but she was not a prude. And that small world of hers was capable of producing a great lady because it had inherited a great tradition. Miss Jewett herself witnessed the decline of her country as a center of world trade; she saw the coming of the mills and of the Irish immigrants. "I remember so many of our pleasures of which I have hardly said a word," says the narrator of *Deephaven*, artfully. The material, one gathers, is inexhaustible; is it not human nature? Miss Jewett's own reading ranged from the classics to the modern French and Russian novelists. She relished every quaint provincialism of her people, but what she wanted most was for the world to know "their grand simple lives." And there is such simple dignity about them that the reader feels no straining for effect when William's anointing with penny-royal reminds the narrator of "A Dunnet Shepherdess" of "Medea's anointing Jason before the great episode of the iron bulls," or when Mrs. Hight's features are compared to those of "a warlike Roman emperor." Lowell compared Miss Jewett herself to Theocritus, and that was appropriate also. Kipling praised her for her grasp and vigor, and she was greatly admired by Henry James.

Edward Wagenknecht
Cavalcade of the American Novel (New York:
Holt, 1952), p. 173

. . . Ours is a literature that springs, when it springs at all, from violent contradictions of idealized feelings, that makes a specialty of sudden fruitions and melancholy aftermaths, that knows—with ambiguous exceptions like Henry James—no middle ground between extraordinary originality and equally extraordinary tastelessness, self-imitation, banality. A pragmatical literature, we might call it—one rarely able to live (and this is a source of strength as well as limitation) except in immediate contact with its undistilled and unprimed sources of feeling. . . .

Jewett's ultimate art in *Pointed Firs* is to sustain [a] creative balance of crossed feelings—to make for her materials a claim of value and permanence but to show it as hopeless. . . . Her judgments of present and past antedated her proving them in her art. But prove them she did—by making them as impersonal as the sympathy we are brought to feel for her characters; by suffusing them with the durable colors of legend, the solemnity of history. The *Country of the Pointed Firs* is a small work but an unimprovable one, with a secure and unrivaled place in the main line of American literary expression.

Warner Berthoff
NEQ (March, 1959), pp. 52-53

SIDNEY LANIER
1842-1881

Born February 3 in Macon, Georgia. He entered the sophomore class of Oglethorp University in 1857 and graduated at the head of his class in 1860. A year later he joined the Macon Volunteers of the Confederate Army and was captured in 1864 and imprisoned at Point Lookout, Maryland. He returned to Macon in 1865 and married Mary Day in 1867. *Tiger Lilies*, a novel based on his prison experiences, was published in 1867. In the years following 1874, he published various poems, treatises on music, and boys' books on legends of the Middle Ages. In 1879, he was made a lecturer in English literature at Johns Hopkins University, and, a year later, he published *The Science of English Verse*. He died Sept. 7 in Lyon, North Carolina.

Charles R. Anderson, ed., *The Centennial Edition of Sidney Lanier* (1945), 10 vols.

Aubrey H. Starke, *Sidney Lanier: A Biographical and Critical Study* (1933)

When [Lanier] died at thirty-nine he had made himself a technically excellent musician; within ten years (for his literary life had scarcely begun before he was thirty) he had fitted himself to give lectures on the English novel, Shakespeare and old English poets; he had written the most original treatise in existence on English verse, equalled, so far as I know that kind of literature, only by the studies of Poe and Coleridge; and he was the unapproachably best American poet of his generation. If ever there was a born genius since Keats, it was Lanier. Let there be no sentimentalizing over him, for he was a man of humour, he spoke always of his difficulties in a manly fashion, and when death strides into his pages it is an honest figure and not a personification of the tuberculosis against which the poet fought to victorious defeat. But if ever lamentation of a poet's death be justifiable, there may well be a cry of pain for the unfinished "Hymns of the Marshes." His voice was growing greater when he ceased to sing, and, like Keats,

> his angel's tongue
> Lost half the sweetest song was ever sung.   [ca. 1913]

> John Macy
> *The Spirit of American Literature* (New York:
> The Modern Library, n.d.), p. 312

Had Lanier lived long enough and freely enough, he would doubtless have perfected the instrument on which he played his original melodies: his poetry might now be recognized as pure poetry. For the most part, he achieved nothing more than a succession of beautiful tones and rhythms. What is wanting in Lanier, as in Poe and other artists in whom the critic surpassed the creator, is a little more of matter and less of manner, and a marriage so complete between subject and object as to make them indivisible. One has to make too many allowances for Lanier's intentions. They were superlative enough in themselves, but the performer falls too far behind his ideals. He is therefore too technical an artist ever to appeal to a large audience of divine average readers. He belongs to the studio, and to the musician's more than the poet's. The wide world can never take him completely to heart. He is not, except at persuasive moments, a companion, but a solitary. He speaks in a rather foreign tongue made up not so much of words as entrancing syllables. The soul of Lanier's musical scheme contained a didactic religionist. He was the most Christian and optimistic of poets, an optimism supremely brave in the worst of conditions. Like some of the Northern Puritans, he permitted a sustained flight of music aroused by Nature to be tainted with dogma. The preaching is forced, as with Longfellow, not implicit, as with Bryant. And so Lanier remains one of the tragic mysteries of American poetry, another victim of the general national inexperience with life and with letters.

Like other American originals, he needed a line of path-breakers to lay down the groundwork before him. His own failure as a pioneer is even more apparent in his thin school of followers. As compared with Poe, Emerson or Whitman, he had little influence on the future. His "Science Of English Verse" is a monument of stylistic criticism and as invaluable to poets as the documented system of Poe. But when one opens Lanier's poetry, one has to leave behind a great deal compact of theory alone, or of incommunicable music.

Alfred Kreymborg
Our Singing Strength (New York:
Coward-McCann, 1929), pp. 162-63

After a merely rudimentary education in what [Lanier] himself called "a farcical college" the war came, robbing him outright of four years of life, and fixing upon him a disease which made the few working days of his youth a piteous slow dying, reducing his artist life to the space of thirteen years. He was a beardless boy when he entered the Confederate Army, he was a broken and dispirited veteran when Lee surrendered to Grant— and yet, notwithstanding his pain and every other hindrance, the work which he did in the space of these few pain-filled years may be set against that of any Southern writer of his day or since. Certainly no artist ever followed an ideal more unswervingly in the midst of so many discouragements, and his story, to my mind, gives out a certain quiet sublimity. He had all that Poe lacked—patience, purity, constancy to a purpose, and perfect sanity.

Hamlin Garland
Roadside Meetings (London: John Lane, 1931), pp. 145-46

It is . . . the essentially American quality that makes Lanier's protest against capitalism so different from the protests of an English poet with whom, because of his love for the beautiful things of the past and his eagerness to give such things to the men of the present, he is sometimes compared—William Morris: an American quality in "The Symphony" may be difficult to define and impossible to illustrate by quotation, but it is there, as inescapably there as it is in "The Psalm of the West" where it is more apparent. It is this American quality that will perhaps prevent any very general appreciation of Lanier's poetry abroad, for his poetry is at once less descriptive of America—and therefore less easily appreciated— than that of Whitman, and more distinctly American than that of Poe. His appeal must ever be to those who love America, love the bright warmth of the sun on her broad fields, and understand the American spirit. One may well paraphrase the song of the good angel in his Centennial cantata and say that so long as we shall love true love, and truth, and justice, and freedom, and God, and our fellow men, admire bold criticisms and hold brave hope in good to come, no matter how dark the present may be, the name of Lanier—in whose poetry these virtues are manifest—shall shine, and his fame glow.

Aubrey H. Starke
Sidney Lanier (Chapel Hill, N.C.:
Univ. North Carolina Pr., 1933), p. 451

In his spontaneous lyrics and his sensuous descriptive verse Lanier achieves striking and original effects. I do not refer to his virtuosity in such a poem as "The Symphony," with its simulation of each instrument in an orchestra. That is only a clever experiment in technique by a dexterous artificer, which concentrates attention on the superficial form. In better and less obvious poems he skillfully used alliteration, tone color, vowel sounds and mixed rhythms to give musical effects and pictorial values: the ultimate effect is that of a richly embroidered sensuosity, which, unlike Swinburne's, never shades into sensuality. Only when he neglects his philosophy does he write authentic poetry. For that reason it is impossible to agree with John Macy that "only three volumes of unimpeachable poetry have been written in America, *Leaves of Grass,* the thin volume of Poe, and the poetry of Sidney Lanier. . . ." In Lanier's case the elimination of bad poems must be too drastic. Yet, in the six or eight which remain, there is the distinctive mark of a poet who wrote far better than he knew, who achieved a limited but fine body of work which in the main is unlike that which greater poets have done.

Edd W. Parks, ed.
Southern Poets: Representative Selections (New York:
American Book, 1936), pp. cxvii-cxviii

Fortunately, our two poets of sound, Poe and Lanier, were never able to fulfil their own elaborate aesthetic principles; in each, the inner poet was greater than the outward theorizer. Lanier, like Poe, to whom as an experimenter, he was closer than he realized, carries us along in the rush of an emotion which cannot be translated into exact meanings, fulfilling the dictum of Coleridge that poetry gives the greatest pleasure when only generally and not perfectly understood. Such power Lanier's poetry sometimes displays in spite of its opaqueness of thought or eccentricity of technique. All nature is tense at the moment of sunrise; or we are lost in the music of the soaring violins; the reality of our emotion mocks the inadequacy of intellectual meaning; momentarily at least we are rapt in his "strenuous sweet whirlwind." This was the musician Lanier's great, almost involuntary achievement in poetry; and parallels for this "indefinitiveness" of sensation, this communication of the excitement of music to verse, we shall find only in such poets as Poe and Swinburne.

Stanley T. Williams
in *Literary History of the United States*, eds. Robert Spiller *et al*,
Vol. II (New York: Macmillan, 1948), pp. 906-7

[Lanier] was dizzied by the high reaches into which the logic of his art threatened to take him—into a private, a "pure" art. He was at the end a latter-day Poe, though insufficiently free of his ties with a tradition of public poetry to move as far as Poe had in the direction of "pure" poetry. Moreover, he was insufficiently sure of himself as a person to move as far as Emerson, Whitman, and Emily Dickinson had in the direction of a poetry of the antinomian self. There was nothing in the Southern tradition which might have prepared him for such purity or such antinomianism. He came finally to distill the pseudo-Romantic lyric of the ante-bellum South into something genuinely his own. What made it his own was not theme or concept (of which he had little or nothing to add) but technique. He convinced himself that art's freedom was an essentially technical freedom, enabling the poet to push language into the condition of music. Music was process and movement, not statement, as it had to be with poetry. The inevitable subject for the poem was Nature, in whose mysterious processes even the poet was enmeshed.

The argument was circular. It armored Lanier against the threat of meaninglessness, as it trapped him, cutting him off from even the anti-poetic world of the ante-bellum South. History, tradition, ideas, human relations in the workaday world—for all these (which as a struggling literary man he had known well) he substituted Nature, wherein only might he comprehend the freedom of art sufficiently to bear its burden.

Roy Harvey Pearce
The Continuity of American Poetry (Princeton, N. J.:
Princeton Univ. Pr., 1961), p. 244

HENRY WADSWORTH LONGFELLOW

1807-1882

Born February 27 in Portland, Maine. He graduated from Bowdoin College in 1825 and traveled abroad in 1826 to study modern languages. In 1829, he was appointed professor of Modern Languages at Bowdoin. He married Mary Storer Potter in 1831. *Outre-Mer* was published in 1833, and, a year later, he was appointed professor of Modern Languages at Harvard. His wife died in 1835, while travelling in Europe. In 1839, *Hyperion* and *Voices of the Night* were published and, in 1842, *Ballads and Other Poems* and *Poems on Slavery*. He married Frances Appleton in 1843. The following works were published: *The Spanish Student* (1843); *Poems* (1845); *The Belfry of Bruges* (1846); *Evangeline* (1847); *Kavanagh* (1849); *The Seaside and the Fireside* (1850); and *The Golden Legend* (1851). In 1854, he resigned his professorship at Harvard and proceeded to publish *The Song of Hiawatha* (1855); *The Courtship of Miles Standish* (1858) and *The New England Tragedy* (1860). His second wife died in 1861. Other publications were: *Tales of a Wayside Inn* (1863); *Noel* (1864); *The Divine Comedy of Dante Alighieri* and *Household Poems* (1865-1867); *Flower de Luce* (1867); *The New England Tragedies* (1868); *The Alarm-Bell of Atri* and *The Divine Tragedy* (1871); *Three Books of Song* and *Christus* (1872); *Aftermath* (1873); *The Hanging of the Crane* (1874); *The Masque of Pandora and Other Poems* (1875); *Kéramos and Other Poems* (1877); *Bayard Taylor* (1878); *From My Arm-Chair* (1879); *Ultima Thule* (1880); and *In the Harbor; Ultima Thule, Part II;* and *Michael Angelo* (1882). He died March 24, 1882. *There Was a Little Girl* was published in 1888.

Samuel Longfellow, ed., *The Works of Henry Wadsworth Longfellow* (1886-1891), 14 vols.

Edward Wagenknecht, *Longfellow: a Full-Length Portrait* (1955)

PERSONAL

In the face of conventions which strutted as Fundamental Laws, and whose rigor we can hardly estimate nowadays, he was a bold innovator, who repeatedly showed the pioneer spirit in breaking with established traditions. "American" he assuredly was, and nothing could be more futile than the attempt to classify him among those who are passive reflections of European influence. He sought culture from European sources and defended this sort of cosmopolitanism in *Kavanagh,* where he praised the tenderness of the Germans, the passion of the Spaniards, the vivacity of the French, and the solid sense of the English—but this argues no tame subserviency. . . .

It requires a born aristocrat to rise above instinctive impulses: a "gentleman" Longfellow was. The older American type was pretty well submerged during the periods of immigration and frontier life, and has been well-nigh superseded, since the habit was formed of thinking of life in terms of business success, and of gentleness as emasculation. Mr. J. T. Adams holds that the pernicious type of unscrupulous business man began its detrimental development in New York. A highminded consideration for others, a generous wish to praise and recommend those who had not received recognition, a scrupulous reserve in regard to his own person and achievements—all these are eminently characteristic of this son of New England.

James T. Hatfield
New Light on Longfellow (Boston:
Houghton Mifflin, 1933), pp. 149, 155

Thinking of Longfellow in [a] comparative way, we see at once that he is by no means the Hamlet, but rather the Horatio, of his group—a "chorus character" voicing not so much his own idiosyncrasy as the normal, often the average, thoughts and feelings of his time. We find, also, that when standing in the company of his peers he looks somewhat pallid. In comparison with theirs, his thought lacks edge, his knowledge is lunar and literary, his moods are drowsy, and his opinions are vague. Unlike most of them, he does not seem to have earned but to have inherited his mental wealth. Seldom do we see him at work in the darkness of the mind, getting out his own ore. This man, we conclude, who never did a day's manual labor in his life, and who thought that he got enough physical exercise in putting on and off his overcoat, is somewhat deficient in mental muscle and in that spiritual strength which perhaps only the struggle with doubt can give.

Odell Shepard, ed.
Henry Wadsworth Longfellow: Representative Selections
(New York: American Book, 1934), p. xxxv

GENERAL

. . . Longfellow's reputation . . . was amply deserved in the poet's day, and rested in the main on his gifts as a story-teller in verse, on his power to transplant to American literature some of the colour and melody and romantic charm of the complex European literatures he had studied, and, more especially, on his skill in expressing in comparatively artless lyrics of sentiment and reflection homely and wholesome thoughts and feelings which he shared with his countrymen of all classes throughout a broad land the occupation of which proceeded apace during his own span of years. Whatever he accomplished beyond this as teacher and editor and writer of prose, and as self-conscious poet seeking success in the more elaborate traditional forms of his art, is worthy, to say the least, of as much praise as the similar work of his predecessors, contemporaries, and successors among American poets, and is not clearly doomed to a speedier death than the elaborate productions of his contemporaries and successors among the British world, or even of his century, as the admiration of the mass of his countrymen and the critical lucubrations of some of them might be held to imply; but it is, legitimately and permanently, in the forefront of the small band of important writers in verse and in prose who during the first century of the republic's existence laid firmly and upon more or less democratic lines the foundations of a native literature. (ca. 1917)

William Peterfield Trent
in *Cambridge History of American Literature*, Vol. II
(New York: Macmillan, 1946), p. 41

Whether or not [Longfellow's] influence upon the common people at the moment when they were at their most receptive stage was altogether good, is open to question. When America like a schoolgirl was hungry for culture and for poetry, Longfellow gave German romance and he gave little else. He came at the only moment in our history when he could have had a full hearing, or at least at the only moment when he could have been given the leading place to the exclusion of all others. His enormous popularity, his contagious sentimentalism, his breath of the Old World at this moment when America was peculiarly susceptible—all this, coming at the moment when a new group of poets was gathering, cast a shadow over a whole period of our poetic history. To Longfellow more than to any other cause may be traced the general lack of stamina in American poetry during two generations of poets.

Fred Lewis Pattee
Sidelights on American Literature (New York:
Century, 1922), pp. 247-48

Longfellow played an important part in the development of American letters in that he was one of the floodgates through which rushed a European culture that for a time swept before it any incipient autochthonous urges the effete East may have possessed. He undoubtedly believed in his heart that he was an American and so far as birth and tradition go he was one, but he had no conception of the duties—and they were duties—that devolved upon the American litterateur in those years of scanty culture when the basis of a national literature was being formed. Margaret Fuller knew. Poe suspected it. Walt Whitman gave dynamic evidence of it. But Longfellow without being quite conscious of it, was as much English as he was American. He was our great Victorian.

Indeed it is as a Victorian that I see him; not, perhaps, an American Tennyson, but, in some ways, an American Victoria. It would be decidedly frivolous to dub him "our late dear Queen" and yet his didactic obsessions, his insistence upon the purities of living, his careful abstention (congenitally necessary, of course) from passion of any sort, and the adulation bestowed upon him by vast masses of the American public and, in particular, by his ever-zealous personal friends, would seem to offer ample opportunity for so considering him. All this may be set down without losing sight of the facts that he was essentially lovable as a personality, valuable as an ornament to the American scene of his time, and, to some degree, distinguished as a scholar. It is unnecessary to insist too strongly on the many demerits and few virtues of his poetry, that unceasing output which percolated throughout the civilized world, for it is as a man that I choose to consider him, a representative figure of the dominant urge of his time.

Herbert S. Gorman
A Victorian American, Henry Wadsworth Longfellow
(London: Cassel, n.d.), pp. viii-ix

The present age, or any present age, has a tendency to look down from the fancied heights of sophistication upon the ages preceding it, and to judge them as stepping stones, or less than stepping stones. In our cocksure self-importance, we even assume we have sprung out of nowhere, and possess a divine right of intelligence straight from God, or whatever successor to God we believe in—if we believe in anything beyond our narcissism. To this ego, Longfellow seems absurd and laughable, and his former vogue incomprehensible. Nonetheless, the man was a pioneer, and the first American to bridge the sea between European culture and parochial barbarism. The latest Americans racing abroad after the latest continental culture are sailing liners not unrelated to the little ship the young Bowdoin student boarded nearly a century ago.

. . . The cultures he translated for America, mostly through his own poetry, were tastefully combed for their fairer aspects. He rarely yearned beyond the virtuous and the palatable. Inside these confines, he perfected his genius for a many-faceted facility. Evil books existed for him, but only once or twice did he permit their echoes to filter into his own work. . . . Naiveté was also the qualifying factor he addressed in his countrymen. He fed their ignorance on European books felt through his own, and the childlike public devoured him devotedly. The still youthful land was heaven-bent for education, and Longfellow, a teacher from his earliest conscious years, turned his didactic bent and training to the best account. His audience, like himself, believed in the goodness of life, a goodness the Quakers and Unitarians had introduced in driving out the evil-believing Calvinists. Opening with the "Psalm of Life," the poet of the people had arrived. In nine jingling verses, dripping with a larger number of clichés than any other poem in the language, Longfellow smote the heartstrings of the race.

Alfred Kreymborg
Our Singing Strength (New York:
Coward-McCann, 1929), pp. 98-99

Who, except wretched schoolchildren, now reads Longfellow? But people until but the other day read the verses of Henry Van Dyke and thousands are still reading those of Robert Service. The thing to establish in America is not that Longfellow was a very small poet, but that he did not partake of the poetic character at all. For minor poets have this in common with major poets—so far as such distinctions of magnitude are not in themselves absurd—that their business and function is the transmutation of impassioned experience into intelligible personal form. Such was evidently not the business and the function of Longfellow. Twice he came near poetic speech, once in the pathetic sonnet on his dead wife, once in "The Warning"—"There is a poor blind Samson in this land"—when the antislavery struggle roused even him. The ballads and the moralizing lyrics are all written from without, are all lacking the organic connection with one shaken soul and are therefore outside of the soul and of the world. . . . He never touches poetry. He borrows form and accepts content from without. The longer works are all strictly patterned upon the works of others. The plays are weary imitations of the Elizabethans. . . . He was really not unlike those minstrel artificers of the middle ages who borrowed freely from each other methods of dressing up a common substance and had not yet risen to the notion of expression as an individual act and therefore of literature as individual property. Doubtless this large body of narrative verse as well as certain lyrics of pleasant sentiment and easy rhythm still give pleasure to a sub-literary public. But men are not contemporaries though the same decades embrace their lives. To minds concerned with the imaginative interpretation of man, of nature and of human life, Longfellow has nothing left to say.

Ludwig Lewisohn
Expression in America (New York:
Harper, 1932), pp. 65-66

Just as Longfellow many times misses that perfection of mood which can have poetic pleasure for us, so his placid faith in mankind and his lack of profundity will leave us with a sense of inadequacy. In part our response is sound, but in part we seem to be making demands upon the poet that we have no right to urge. Though Longfellow does not go deeply into human experience, he sees with a good deal of clarity and poise that life which comes to his view. Without prophetic insight, he has perceptive everyday understanding, and he is willing to use diverse materials which show considerably larger spread than we might expect from our judgment of the genteel predilections of his background.

George Arms
The Fields Were Green (Stanford, Calif.:
Stanford Univ. Pr., 1953), p. 217

There was an element of pioneering in [Longfellow's] daring to devote himself when he did to the life of the creative writer. . . . He pioneered again when he rejected the law as an *ad interim* method of earning a living and turned instead to the teaching of modern languages. Even the uninitiated can still perceive the element of pioneering involved in his use of native American materials, as in *Hiawatha* and other poems, but it requires more knowledge of early American literature than most of us possess to be able to perceive as Van Wyck Brooks does, that even his first published book, his translation of the *Coplas* of Manrique, "an act of high talent, if there ever was one—sounded like full summer, in its music, beside the pallid poems of the thirties." Viewing the situation in comfortable retrospect, we find the *Poems on Slavery* tame, yet the book could not be reviewed in *Graham's Magazine* because the word "slavery" itself was taboo in its columns. In the 'forties, Longfellow's closest literary advisers felt that "The Skeleton in Armor" was too daring a departure from previous American didacticism; much later, a Boston paper lamented his use in *Hiawatha* of "the silly legends of the savage aborigines. His poem does not awaken one sympathetic throb; it does not teach a single truth. . . . In verse it contains nothing so precious as the golden time which would be lost in the reading of it." Even as late as 1882, the admiring F. H. Underwood was still confessing that he found *The New England Tragedies* "too depressing and painful."

Edward Wagenknecht
Longfellow: A Full-Length Portrait (New York:
Longmans, Green, 1955), p. 80

. . . There is everywhere in [Longfellow's] work that dimming over of detail; that subjugating of scene or incident to the similitude which it is to project; that forced melodiousness, wherein the rhyme word justifies its existence only as rhyme word. Such effects have their uses for the good, however. The poems mediate between the reader and the real world, helping him to accommodate that world to his dreams and fantasies. The new man in the new world, able to read before he could understand, was only too likely to be overwhelmed by such dreams and fantasies. In Longfellow's poems, nineteenth century *vox populi* spoke and thereupon heard its own echo, charged with all the rich resonances of places and tunes and rewards beyond its ken.

Roy Harvey Pearce
The Continuity of American Poetry (Princeton, N. J.:
Princeton Univ. Pr., 1961), p. 214

JAMES RUSSELL LOWELL
1819-1891

> Born February 22 in Cambridge, Massachusetts. He graduated from Harvard in 1838 and was admitted to the bar in 1840. In 1841, he published *A Year's Life* and established a literary journal, *The Pioneer*. He married Maria White in 1845. In 1848, he published *A Fable for Critics, The Vision of Sir Launfal,* and *The Biglow Papers.* He took his family to Europe in 1851, and, in 1853, his wife died. He was made Smith Professor of Modern Languages at Harvard upon the retirement of Henry Wadsworth Longfellow in 1855. He married Frances Dunlap in 1856. He was made editor of a new magazine, *The Atlantic Monthly* in 1857. *The Biglow Papers* (2nd Series) was published in 1866. In 1877, he was appointed Minister to the Court of Spain and, in 1880, United States Minister in London. He died August 12.

> Charles Eliot Norton, ed., *The Complete Writings of James Russell Lowell* (1904), 16 vols.
> Horace E. Scudder, *James Russell Lowell: A Biography* (1901)

PERSONAL

Psychologically, with his visions and his recurrent disturbing sense of secondary personality, [Lowell] was undoubtedly highly complex. So was he, also, temperamentally, with his conflicting inherited impulses toward idleness and action. He was complex and subtle in his intellect, with its vast variety of mental furniture, its odd irrelevancies, its unstable union of skepticism and faith. All these diverse qualities went to make up a "myriad-minded" humanist, who had in his own phrase something of the "multanimous nature of the poet" and longed for many lives and many careers. Yet, air-spun as the distinction may seem, the complexity in Lowell was only in his psychology, temperament, intellect; his character was all the while simple and sincere.

Ferris Greenslet
James Russell Lowell (London: Constable, 1905), pp. 239-40

The ultimate secret of Lowell's weakness did not lie, it is reasonable to maintain, in his own power to remedy. It belonged to his type of mind.

That precision in detail which a classical training might be supposed to foster and whose importance would be emphasized by the demands upon him as editor and professor, is for the most part wanting. That disregard of the unessential, that closeness of reasoning, that penetration to ultimate principles, all of which a course of legal training would inculcate in a mind receptive to such influence, left no perceptible traces on Lowell. His course in law seems to have fulfilled no purpose except that of equipping him with legal phrases for figurative use. *Porro unum est necessarium.* Lowell lacked philosophical depth of mind, the one thing so necessary that without it the total of his other endowments was inadequate.

Joseph J. Reilly
James Russell Lowell as a Critic (New York:
G. P. Putnam's Sons, 1915), pp. 209-10

POETRY

To be uncontemporaneous like Goethe, to rise to a region above the turmoil of the day, was the high ambition that impelled [Lowell] after his first residence in the scenes of European culture, and that lends to his writings on the great authors not merely a romantic enthusiasm but also an accent of genuine exaltation. His full realization of this ambition was thwarted, however, partly beause his native force was inadequate, and partly because he was sucked into the current of his times. At the most we may venture to say of him, as Dryden said of a poet that Lowell loved, that "he is a perpetual fountain of good sense," a fountain not unmixed with the waters of Helicon; or to declare that Dryden's praise was also Lowell's —that "amid the rickety sentiment looming big through misty phrase which marks so much of modern literature, to read him is as bracing as a northwest wind." At the least we may class him, as he classed Dryden, among those who impregnate rather than invent, among those "brokers of thought" who perform a great if secondary office in literature.

Norman Foerster
American Criticism (Boston: Houghton Mifflin, 1928), p. 156

Could [Lowell] have bent his restlessness to the art he loved best and given that art more of the critical power he bestowed elswhere, [he] would have left a richer collected song than the irregular, fitful flights so often destroyed by too many "isms tied together." One does not ask for fewer isms, but for more beauty.

Alfred Kreymborg
Our Singing Strength (New York:
Coward-McCann, 1929), pp. 128-29

Variable by temper and unstable in his intellectual backgrounds, Lowell faced the major disparities of his world like a weathercock, turning from one to another as the strength of each in turn pressed against his personal fortunes. Few poets have better exemplified the high-mindedness of the nineteenth century. All that poetry meant to Wordsworth, to Goethe, or to Carlyle he tried to make his own, naively confusing intention with accomplishment and piling ideal upon ideal in his effort to synthesize the old notion of the poet's contemplative life with the new fashion of activity. At intervals between his theorizing, he also attempted to make literature a profession to be followed through the doors opened to him by the new popular magazines which tried to make ladies pay the way for poets, and, although he would never have admitted the charge, much of the form and some of the substance of his verse were cut to the professional doors through which he hoped to pass. Lowell the ideal poet and Lowell the magazinist were both affected by the nineteenth-century desire to do good: he regularly pointed the direction from which the spirit of reform was blowing, and he was willing to sacrifice his high and his professional ambitions, and even, at times, his sincerity, to the major reform movement of his time and country. But in all his youthful works he was fighting wholeheartedly for a poet's place in a difficult world, straining at the restrictions of his environment and at the bonds of his own limitations, until he achieved for himself a place in American literature which somehow prevents his most hostile modern critics from speaking as disparagingly of his work as he himself often did when he looked back upon it.

Leon Howard
Victorian Knight-Errant (Berkeley, Calif.:
Univ. Californa Pr., 1952), p. 360

. . . In spite of an occasional achievement . . . which we neglect to our impoverishment, Lowell was a poor poet. To speculate upon the personal reasons behind this failure is for the psychologist rather than the literary critic. But neither Lowell nor the critics have abstained. . . .

Putting aside the personal reasons, we find public ones present throughout the whole body of verse. Most specifically we feel Lowell's habit of genteel romanticism (though this diminished with his growth . . .) and Lowell's inability to cultivate a particular kind of poetry with its obverse in a facile imitation of too many poets. . . . What emerges from this situation is a general weakness that one feels every time one comes to considering a literary characteristic. The language falls into prosiness or archaism, the morality into tidy didacticism, the ironies into pettiness. Lowell can seldom take an image from the concrete to the universal without diluting its earthi-

ness or muddying its ideal, and he regularly commits himself to form-
lessness.

George Arms
The Fields Were Green (Stanford, Calif.:
Stanford Univ. Pr., 1953), pp. 126-27

GENERAL

Whatever the critics may eventually come to say about Lowell, he was
certainly the ablest and most distinguished of the old Cambridge breed,
in the days when the Brahmin caste was disintegrating and Brahmin ideals
losing their hold on New England—a man of fine native abilities in whom
Harvard culture did its best to strike fire and light and understanding to
serve as a beacon to the rest of America. He was not of the Concord line
of transcendental individualists, nor of the militant strain of reforming en-
thusiasts; but of the true Brahmin line of Josiah Quincy and Edward
Everett and Oliver Wendell Holmes—men of sound culture who could
serve God valiantly in the social station in which He had placed them,
without wanting to pull down the old church to build a new. Like Charles
Eliot Norton—*clarum et venerabile nomen*—he had no plans of a new
building in his pocket, but was content to enlarge and embellish the old.
He would serve culture rather than causes. His gifts were Brahmin gifts,
his prejudices were Brahmin prejudices; and so in spite of a "certain
sprightliness of brain" that tempted him to rebel at the aridity of the scho-
lastic commons on which he fed, and in spite of certain youthful vagaries
and incursions into indiscreet places, he remained at bottom a Harvard
conservative, content with his birthright, hopeful that his ways were God's
ways. This suffices to explain the extraordinary reputation of Lowell in
Cambridge circles, and the difficulty with which it made headway elsewhere. Though he traveled much in his library—as Thoreau would say—
his prejudices remained narrowly local. To the last he remained extraordinarily parochial.

Yet the culture he served so faithfully never fruited in wisdom. He was
never quite certain of himself, of what he really believed. He was fond of
standing off and studying himself quizzically, to learn what sort of a person he was; yet he was swayed by so many impulses he was never quite
sure what sort of legs were under him. He was hopelessly bewildered by
his own vast disorder. His mind was as cluttered as a garret, filled with
an endless miscellany of odds and ends. Life puzzzled him, as it puzzles
every serious mind; but he allowed himself to be too easily discouraged by
his inveterate unwillingness to think. He never speculated widely or analyzed critically. Ideas, systems of thought, intellectual and social move-

ments, he had no interest in; he was content to remain a bookish amateur in letters, loitering over old volumes for the pleasure of finding apt phrases and verbal curiosities. With all his reading, history remained a blank to him; and science he would have none of.

Vernon Louis Parrington
Main Currents in American Thought, Vol. II
(New York: Harcourt, Brace, 1927), pp. 460-61

At the close of the war Lowell stood in the first rank of American poets, was highly esteemed as a critic, and was regarded as an authoritative student of political issues. His opportunity to guide the progress of American culture was threefold, and twenty-five years of life remained to him. Yet his failure was almost complete. As a poet he never conquered the diffuse romanticism that had marred his juvenilia; rather, he became increasingly derivative, and his major efforts, the various commemorative odes, are, despite the nobility of mood and the dignity of expression, palpably without either depth of thought or freshness of language. As a critic he was erudite, perhaps beyond all other American critics, and thoroughly familiar with the greatest writers of western culture. Nor was the range of his criticism narrow: he could speak as historian or philologist; he could write with the gusto of an epicure or assume the manner of a judge. But the incoherence of his critical studies, his preference for a casual attack in the manner of the informal essay, points straight to the deep-seated indolence of mind that prevented him from molding out of his insight and information a solid and consistent theory of literature. Principles he had in abundance, but, like all borrowed principles, they were a poor substitute for that organic body of fundamental ideas that the great critic cultivates, with the aid of his imagination, out of the soil of study and experience.

To the development of American literature he contributed almost nothing, except insofar as he may have furthered a thoughtful reading of the European masters.

Granville Hicks
The Great Tradition (New York:
Macmillan, 1935), pp. 16-17

The more one knows about [Lowell's] brilliant career, in so many ways so decidedly successful, the more one is inclined to call it a failure. What Lowell most deplorably lacks is coherence—and this not merely in the style of his prose and verse, but in his life, his thought, his beliefs, even his character. Lowell's mind was certainly one of the most brilliant that America has produced; but it was brilliant in the way of a shattered mirror, or, let us say, in that of the vividly colored bits of glass in a kaleidoscope that give the effect of a new geometrical pattern at every turn of the tube. . . . Continually while reading Lowell, and even when most delighted by the incessant glitter and glint of his style, one is perplexed and vexed that a man with such powers could not draw them together and so make more of them. . . .

Lowell's influence upon literary scholarship and criticism in America has been deep and pervasive, but it has not been the influence of a mind that reaches firm conclusions and renders consistent judgments in accord with them. It has been the influence of a sensitive and volatile temperament indulging itself in a lifelong intellectual vagabondage. In the sheer enjoyment of literature—hearty, robust, and, at any rate with regard to writers of the past, open-minded—Lowell has only such men as Lamb and Hazlitt for equals, and he has no superiors. His love of books was his nearest approach to a passion, and his devotion to them came nearer than any other of his enthusiasms to giving his life a shape and a focus. Moreover he did a great deal, by precept and example and by the contagion of his own delight, to spread the love of books in America. This was his main contribution to the task of "transplanting European culture." Thus, like Longfellow and Holmes, he did in his own way the indispensable work of all sound conservatism—conservation.

Odell Shepard
in *Literary History of the United States*, eds. Robert Spiller *et al*, Vol. I
(New York: Macmillan, 1948), pp. 603, 605-6

Instead of [transcendental] naturalism with its worship of newness, Lowell sought to substitute the solid wisdom of the human past. . . . From the confusion of modern thought, he turned to the "sane and balanced" writers before Rousseau. More liberal than his follower, Irving Babbitt, he agreed that Rousseau "is as consistent as a man who admits new ideas can ever be." But his conclusion is clear: what is new cannot be consistent, and what is traditional is good. "Democracy" is good, he said, because "properly understood, it is a conservative force." And America, the child of Great Britain, is "a democracy with conservative instincts." To strengthen this hereditary conservatism the genteel descendant of the Puritans preached a religion of humanistic culture: *Among My Books*.

Frederic I. Carpenter
American Literature and the Dream (New York:
Philosophical Library, 1955), p. 58

Lowell trimmed his sails before the winds of social change and came gradually to be the spokesman for a middle way of culture, in which the best of everything was to be cut down to the size of a people—an entirely new kind of popular audience—not yet up to the demands of the best.

. . . Lowell wanted to make poems which would help his great audience know [the] real world for what it was. He came to conceive of poetry as the product of neither the "natural" nor the "real" world, but of an "ideal" world. The ideal was there to give direction and coherence to men living in the real world and save them from their temptation to take seriously the natural world. The poet came to be not seer but schoolteacher; read not on railroad cars, but in schoolrooms; not by coarse men, but by well-scrubbed children and their anxious parents.

Roy Harvey Pearce
The Continuity of American Poetry (Princeton, N. J.:
Princeton Univ. Pr., 1961), pp. 193, 220

HERMAN MELVILLE
1819-1891

Born August 1 in New York City. He left Albany Academy to work as bank clerk on father's death in 1832. In 1837, he taught school near Pittsfield, Mass. In 1839, "Fragments from a Writing Desk" was published. In the same year, he shipped as a crew member to Liverpool, and, in 1841, he shipped aboard the Acushnet, a whaler bound for the South Seas, but he deserted ship in 1842 at Nuku Hiva. In 1843, he enlisted in the United States Navy at Honolulu. *Typee* was published in 1846 and *Omoo* in 1847. He married Elizabeth Shaw in 1847. A series of publications followed: *Mardi* and *Redburn* (1849); *White-Jacket* (1850); *Moby-Dick* (1851); *Pierre* (1852); *Israel Potter* (1855); *The Piazza Tales* (1856); *The Confidence Man* (1857) and *Battle-Pieces and Aspects of the War* (1866). In 1866 he was appointed inspector of Customs in New York. *Clarel* was published in 1876. In 1885 he resigned his position as inspector of Customs and subsequently published *John Marr and Other Sailors,* (1888) and *Timoleon* (1891). He died September 28. *Billy Budd* was published posthumously in 1924.

The Works of Herman Melville (1922-1924), 16 vols.

Leon Howard, *Herman Melville* (1951)

PERSONAL

[Herman Melville] would seem a prime example of the demonic writer, carrying all before him by what he *is* rather than by what he can *do.* He is often indifferent to the details of structure; his speculations are seldom profound and sometimes juvenile; he offers little variety of fictional character or situation. His greatest gift is a sense of tone and attitude, behind which we cannot help looking for an individual speaker; and this speaker, as it happens, can be taken as a very modern personality.

Yet Melville is no true case of the legendary writer whose life has enveloped his work. On the contrary, his work has been the most important source for his putative quality as a man. "Herman Melville (1819-91)" remains largely unknown, so that all attempts to identify the omnipresent voice of the novels with Melville as he lived and breathed have been self-defeating. What we have is a literary personality, a created figure who inhabits a created world. He is not a portrait of the man who lived in Pittsfield and New York, but a kind of presence—hardly a portrait—of the artist, the author; and his difficulties, whatever else they may include, are aesthetic quandaries. . . . From first to last, he presents himself as an artist, and a conscious artist. It is in this character that he seizes our attention.

The intimate connection between his "theme of the artist's problems" and the other themes of his work is in itself a modern quality. And the aesthetic issues that are raised within his books come very close to those that lie behind recent literature. Melville's appeal to the modern reader derives from a community of literary aim—a community of theory and of method and of the relationship between theory and method. At the same time his literary preoccupations help to explain the brevity of his professional career and the long silence that followed, which cannot be accounted for solely on personal grounds. He reached not only a personal, but also a technical, impasse. The logic of his career was the logic of his aesthetic premises; his concept of artistic truth was calculated to lead him into a skepticism of art.

Charles Feidelson, Jr.
Symbolism and American Literature (Chicago:
Univ. Chicago Pr., 1953), pp. 162-64

Moby Dick

[*Moby Dick*] is a book of esoteric symbolism of profound significance, and of considerable tiresomeness.

But it is a great book, a very great book, the greatest book of the sea ever written. It moves awe in the soul. . . .

What then is Moby Dick? He is the deepest blood-being of the white race; he is our deepest blood-nature.

And he is hunted, hunted, hunted by the maniacal fanaticism of our white mental consciousness. We want to hunt him down. To subject him to our will. And in this maniacal conscious hunt of ourselves we get dark races and pale to help us, red, yellow, and black, east and west, Quaker and fire-worshipper, we get them all to help us in this ghastly maniacal hunt which is our doom and our suicide.

The last phallic being of the white man. Hunted into the death of upper consciousness and the ideal will. Our blood-self subjected to our will. Our blood-consciousness sapped by a parasitic mental or ideal consciousness.

D. H. Lawrence
Studies in Classic American Literature (London:
Martin Secker, 1924), pp. 160-61

The absolute condition of present things was what Melville sought to track down in the fable and the myth of the White Whale. One may read Moby Dick as a story of the sea, and be irritated by the lengthy description of whales and whaling; one may read it as a treatise on the whaling industry, and be irritated by the irrelevant heroic figure of Ahab, or the innocent sinister beauty of Queequeg; and since it is also this, one may read it as an epic of the human spirit, and discover an equivalent of its symbolism in one's own consciousness. For me, the Whale is Nature, the Nature man warily hunts and subdues, the Nature he captures, tethers to his ship, cuts apart, scientifically analyzes, melts down, uses for light and nourishment, sells in the market, the Nature that serves man's purposes so long as he uses his wits and can ride on top. But with all this easy adventuring, there is another and deadlier Nature—the White Whale—a Nature that threatens man and calls forth all his heroic powers, and in the end defeats him with a final lash of the tail. That part of Nature cannot be harpooned, cannot be captured, still less drawn and quartered and sold. In sheer savagery —or was it perhaps in play?—the White Whale had once amputated Ahab's leg: with relentless vigilance Ahab follows the White Whale to its lair, impatient of baser catches on the way, as the great philosophers and poets have been impatient of the little harpoonings and dickerings of science and the practical life. The White Whale is not the kindly, milk-fed Absolute, in which all conflicts are reconciled and all contradictions united into a higher kind of knowledge; no, the White Whale is the sheer brute energy of the universe, which challenges and checks the spirit of man. It is only the lonely heroic spirit, who declares himself a sovereign nature, that dares follow the White Whale; and once he comes to close quarters with the creature, there is no issue but death. The White Whale is the external force of Nature and Destiny. In the end it conquers: it must conquer: until the spirit of man is itself Leviathan, and can meet its antagonist on even terms.

Lewis Mumford
The Golden Day (New York: Norton, 1926), pp. 149-50

Tragic though the theme was, comedy mapped the outlines of *Moby-Dick* and shaped its forms. Passages of comic fantasy are strewn through the narrative. The first encounter of Ishmael with Queequeg is pitched to the key of hilarious comedy, though penetrated by the gruesome and terrible. The comic touch is repeated again and again. . . .

Comedy remains in Moby-Dick like the strong trace of an irresistible mood. Even the movement of the narrative is that of comic travesty: it soars, circles, and rises to the persistent native form of rhapsody. But this primary resilience is stripped to its core. Humor becomes sardonic; that terror and sense of evil and impending death which had often been part of the comic legends of the country are relentlessly uncovered. Melville broke through the mask of comedy to find its ultimate secret, and gave Moby-Dick the final element which creates the epic: an encounter between gods and men. [ca. 1931]

Constance Rourke
American Humor (Garden City, N. Y.: Doubleday,
1953), pp. 155, 157

Melville was not a strong man defying the cruel order of the world; he was a weak man fleeing from his own soul and from life, a querulous man, a fretful man. It did not take reality—suffering, injustice, disease, poverty, public outrage or private wrong—to disillusion him. His life, as the lives of artists go, was not unfortunate. He was disillusioned from the beginning. He adopted all his life the regressive attitude of the neurotic—of the favorite child who wants the world to reconstitute for it the conditions of the nursery. Is that not evident even in *Moby Dick?* Much tried Prometheus does not defy the gods with that mad, sick violence, nor does he interrupt his defiance with babble about the brains of the sperm whale being accounted a fine dish. . . .

. . . It were generous to admit that the finest things in *Moby Dick* constitute one-fourth of that long book; it is certainly indisputable that of the rest what is not sound and fury merely is inchoate and dull. . . . No, Melville is not even a minor master. His works constitute rather one of the important curiosities of literature. He will be chiefly remembered as the inventor of a somber legend concerning the evil that is under the sun. But to embody this legend in a permanently valid form he had only half the creative power and none of the creative discipline or serenity.

Ludwig Lewisohn
Expression in America (New York:
Harper, 1932), pp. 189, 192-93

[Melville] could find no security in throwing over all the restraints of dogma, and exalting the god-like man. If the will was free, as the new faith insisted, Melville knew that it was free to do evil as well as to do good. He could not rest happy with Emerson's declaration that if he turned out to be the devil's child, why then he would live from the devil. For Melville had envisaged the fate of just such a man in Ahab. He had also seen in Ahab the destruction that must overtake the Man-God, the self-appointed Messiah. "Man's self-affirmation leads to his perdition; the free play of human forces unconnected with any higher aim brings about the exhaustion of man's creative powers." That sentence was to be written three-quarters of a century after *Moby-Dick*, by Berdyaev in *The Meaning of History*; but it bears unintentional relevance to what happened to Ahab. And the captain's career is prophetic of many others in the history of later nine-teenth-century America. Man's confidence in his own unaided resources has seldom been carried farther than during that era in this country. The strong-willed individuals who seized the land and gutted the forests and built the railroads were no longer troubled with Ahab's obsessive sense of evil, since theology had receded even farther into their backgrounds. But their drives were as relentless as his, and they were to prove like him in many other ways also, as they went on to become the empire builders of the post-Civil War world. They tended to be as dead to enjoyment as he, as blind to everything but their one pursuit, as unmoved by fear or sym-pathy, as confident in assuming an identification of their wills with im-mutable plan or manifest destiny, as liable to regard other men as merely arms and legs for the fulfilment of their purposes, and, finally, as arid and exhausted in their burnt-out souls. Without deliberately intending it, but by virtue of his intense concern with the precariously maintained values of democratic Christianity, which he saw everywhere being threatened or broken down, Melville created in Ahab's tragedy a fearful symbol of the self-enclosed individualism that, carried to its furthest extreme, brings disaster both upon itself and upon the group of which it is part. He pro-vided also an ominous glimpse of what was to result when the Emersonian will to virtue became in less innocent natures the will to power and conquest.

F. O. Matthiessen
American Renaissance (New York:
Oxford Univ. Pr., 1941), pp. 458-59

The voyage of the *Pequod* is . . . a voyage of discovery in the seas of experience for the writer as well as for the reader. Melville perhaps began with little more than the strong feeling that the whaling industry teemed with potential symbols, which if explored might lead to the leviathan it-self, that is, to the meaning of the leviathan—which "maketh a path to shine after him" like the monarch of all Drummond lights. With studied detail he presented the host of subordinate images—hooks, yards, trying vats, and stripping rigs—images of unfamiliar objects he had to make the reader visualize clearly if some of them were later to become small moons of light. These images, then, formed a frame in which he gradually made out his picture. As the picture grew, the images themselves began to re-veal their essential (symbolic) meanings, but so gradually that one cannot say whether these meanings make the growing picture or are drawn from it. In this world of dense reality, humanity, more abruptly symbolized, tries to assert itself. The trial and catastrophic failure comprise the tragedy; unlike most riddling tragedies, terror settles down as the meanings ray out toward the overwhelming ambiguity of the leviathan.

Melville's method, then, allows his symbols to accumulate meanings in the course of their use, as they knock about in his myth-world, and so a single meaning attached to them often has at least a partial validity. Allegorical interpretation of a medieval or puritanic sort, however, defeats the larger aspect of the work, for Melville's view of reality is a more oriental view, based upon a sense of the ultimate interdependence, rather than the isolation, of experiential units. By devices which serve his ends, even though they involve a considerable dehumanization of his characters, he makes his symbols blur through one another and take shape at that vanishing point where the one and the many become indivisible. His structure suggests a hierarchical arrangement of the interfused symbols, like Milton's arrangement of celestial beings in *Paradise Lost*, an arrangement difficult to justify in rationalistic (allegorical) language. Ahab contains all the qualities of his crew; but it cannot be said that the individuals of the crew contain all the qualities of Ahab, even as potentialities. And Ahab contains in tentative, frangible form all the qualities a mere "human" can contain of Moby Dick. [ca. 1948]

R. W. Short
in *Interpretations of American Literature*, eds. C. Feidelson, Jr., and
P. Brodtkorb, Jr. (New York: Oxford Univ. Pr., 1959), pp. 110-11

. . . The fate of the Pequod becomes a kind of prophecy of the fate of the democratic ship of state. Dedicated to a democratic God and manned by a democratic crew, sailing in search of profit, the Pequod is persuaded by an idealistic captain to give up its democratic rights in order to make total war against the forces of evil. To make the world safe for democracy, it abandons democracy, and to destroy evil, commits evil. Inevitably it sinks at last in "the final Pacific." And, as Ahab exclaims after seeing Moby Dick ram the Pequod: "The ship! . . . its wood could only be American!"

Thus the tragedy of Moby Dick prophesies (in the deepest sense of the word) the tragedy of the democratic dream. Its drama makes real the two great dangers inherent in all democracy: first, the actual danger that men may abandon their freedom of their own free wills; and second, the ideal danger that may confuse their democratic dream of freedom with the old romantic dream of absolute empire. For all historic democracies—the Roman, for instance—have perished thus: first by voluntarily accepting a Caesar, and second by seeking empire over all the evil of the earth. Thus —Melville had warned—"Romara's free eagles flew over all Mardi, and perched on the topmost diadems of the east."

In its own terms, therefore, the tragedy of *Moby Dick* is unanswerable: it is the tragedy of a weak and romantic democracy. The human weakness of its crew makes its tragedy probable, and the ideal falsity of its romantic purpose makes it inevitable. Unlike Hawthorne's *Scarlet Letter,* whose heroine was neither weak nor romantically deluded, Melville's *Moby Dick* suggests the tragedy of a weak and deluded democracy: if the American dream fails, it will fail either through the carelessness of the common people or through the confusion of its leaders. It will not fail because its freedom is inherently sinful (as Hawthorne often suggested), nor yet because its dream of goodness is wholly impossible (as Melville himself was to suggest, in *Billy Budd*).

Frederic I. Carpenter
American Literature and the Dream (New York:
Philosophical Library, 1955), pp. 78-79

In a democratic epic such as *Moby-Dick* avowedly is we would expect a celebration of the ideals of equality and brotherhood, on the one hand, and individualism, on the other. The ideal masculine attachment here is not the hierarchic relation of Achilles and Patroclus, tender as that is, but the perfect fraternal equality of persons of different race. Thus Ishmael and Queequeg join the much discussed company of Natty Bumppo and Chingachgook, Huck Finn and Jim. The different ideal of individualism is expressed in the really derring-do and self-respecting unconventionality of all the main figures. And Ahab becomes, as the "dark necessity" of the story sets in, a heightened example of independent man, as if Melville were out to test some of the extreme implications of the dominant Emersonian creed of self-reliance. . . .

For Melville there is little promise of renewal and reward after suffering. There is no transcendent ground where the painful contradictions of the human dilemma are reconciled. There is no life *through* death. There is only life *and* death, and for any individual a momentary choice between them. What moves Melville most powerfully is the horror that is the violent result of making the wrong choice. He is moved too by the comic aspect of the spectacle, the absurdity of such a creature as man, endowed with desires and an imagination so various, complex, and procreative yet so much the prisoner of the cruel contradictions with which, in his very being, he is inexorably involved. Finally, he is moved by the blissful, idyllic, erotic attachment to life and to one's ideal comrades, which is the only promise of happiness.

Richard Chase
The American Novel and Its Tradition (Garden City, N. Y.:
Doubleday. 1957), pp. 101-2, 107

Moby Dick is . . . Melville's great attempt to create order in a universe in which a break-down of the polarity between good and evil is threatened. This threat comes from Ahab, whose hatred of creation is the symptom, or perhaps the consequence, of that democratic disillusionment with the universe I have spoken of—that resentment of the spirit's betrayal of matter, and of God's betrayal of the world. In so far as Melville's own thought is to be equated with any particular person's, it is with Ishmael's. Ishmael represents Melville's resistance against the temptation to follow Ahab which was so powerful for him; he represents Melville's hold on the world of reality and of nature. But as Melville plunged almost immediately into the writing of *Pierre* when he had finished *Moby Dick*, the sanity and grace that had shaped the earlier of the two books was to vanish for good.

Marius Bewley
The Eccentric Design (London:
Chatto and Windus, 1959), pp. 210-11

[The essential themes of *Moby Dick*] are projected by two dark-skinned characters, supernumeraries in the action, who represent the polar aspects of the id, beneficent and destructive. The first is the Polynesian harpooner, Queequeg, whose relationship to Ishmael threatens to take over the entire book in its first portion; and the second is the Parsee, Fedallah, who is yoked to Ahab by a link as passionate, though quite different from that which joins the first two. . . . [These characters] are used to represent the basic conflict which lies at the heart of the book, the struggle between love and death. Queequeg stands for the redemptive baptism of water (or sperm), and around him the "Western" or sentimental story which is one half of Moby Dick develops; while Fedallah stands for the destructive baptism of fire (or blood), and around him the gothic or Faustian romance which is its other half unfolds. But it is Queequeg who wins, though the two never meet face to face, Eros which triumphs over Thanatos.

Moby Dick must be read not only as an account of a whale-hunt, but also as a love-story, perhaps the greatest love story in our fiction. In light of the development of the highbrow Western from Cooper to Hemingway, it is clear that the absence of women in *Moby Dick* indicates not the absence of love from the novel, but its presence in the peculiar American form of innocent homosexuality. . . .

In *Moby Dick*, the redemptive love of man and man is represented by the tie which binds Ishmael to Queequeg, while the commitment to death is portrayed in the link which joins Ahab to Fedallah; but the two relationships are disturbingly alike; both between males, one white and one colored. Indeed, the very darkness of Queequeg betrays a doubt about the angelic companion, oddly confuses him with the Satanic one! At some level, any sensitive reader is aware, even without the learned commentary of the analysts, that the dream of a dark-skinned beloved implies a sense of breaching a taboo, reaching out toward a banned erotic object. Melville is more conscious than he seems at first glance of the ambiguous nature of the love which he celebrates in *Moby Dick*, and which, beginning with the encounter of Ishmael and Queequeg, grows ever more general and inclusive, but never less suspect, as the story unfolds. . . .

It will not do to sentimentalize or Christianize Melville's pagan concept of love. It is not *caritas* which he celebrates; and his symbol for the redeeming passion is Priapus rather than the cross. Perhaps it is least misleading to think of the love which redeems Ishmael as Platonic, in the authentic historical sense of the word. Rising from the particular object to the universal, it remains suspect nonetheless; for like the ideal Eros of *The Symposium*, it is grounded in a relationship unequivocally rejected by the Judaeo-Christian tradition. Genteel or orthodox advocates of love should look hard at Melville's text before deciding to applaud the conquest of death he celebrates in *Moby Dick*. Yet it is love in the fullest sense which that book makes its center; not a brutal or casual relationship, but one which develops on the pattern of a marriage: achieving in the course of a single voyage the shape of a whole lifetime shared, and symbolizing a spiritual education.

Leslie Fiedler
Love and Death in the American Novel (New York:
Criterion, 1960), pp. 530-33

Although there are dim prefigurations in his earlier romances of what he was to do in *Moby Dick*, he found his mature purpose and the means of fulfilling it in the process of writing his greatest book. Consequently we cannot trace with exactness, as we could with Hawthorne, the gradual evolution of his mythical themes. They seem to leap fully formed from his mind. We may observe, however, that he draws together the mythical patterns of several cultures and of several levels within his own culture; the primitive ritual, the Greek myth, the Biblical legend, the folklore of supernatural dread and wonder (common to both the Old World and the New), and the specifically American folk traditions of comic glorification, of Yankee and frontier character. And in the "careful disorderliness" which is "the true method" of *Moby-Dick* these themes from myth, folklore, and ritual are ranged in a series of dialectical contrasts which dramatize and unify the several controlling tensions of the work. [ca. 1961]

Daniel Hoffman
Form and Fable in American Fiction (New York:
Oxford Univ. Pr., 1965), pp. 233-34

GENERAL

Broadly, the growth of Melville's comic artistry may be measured by its cumulative advance through four theoretical and somewhat arbitrary phases. The first, which we may label the *jocular-hedonic*, is instantly translatable into the simple idea of fun; more literally, joking in the most lighthearted vein merely for the shared pleasure involved. It is the most instinctive manifestation of humor. It has no axes to grind, no subtle overtones to convey. It is an unreflecting expression of the native play-spirit of the individual and his folk tradition. Next in the scale of artistic complexity is the *imaginative-critical* type of comedy, more literary in its origins, more sophisticated in its tone, more ulterior in its motives. This is the mode which enables the artist to increase the suggestive power of his comedy by enlarging the orbit of its implications. His object may be the favorable insights of humor or the unfavorable insights of satire. His interest in any case has passed beyond laughter—usually without sacrificing it—to the more serious business of casting balances and judging values. A third phase, the *philosophical-psychological*, is concerned neither with laughter nor with critical reflections on the passing scene, but with the ambiguous nature of values themselves, the interrelations of comedy and tragedy, and the bearing of both problems on the life of man. It is a stage which represents the artist's search for a balanced view of himself and his world. Finally, in the *dramatic-structural* phase, the artist who has mastered the other three deploys his comic forces to expose the vital interplay of character and situation and performs the successful act of creation that fuses the disparate elements of comedy and tragedy into a balanced work of art. As organic functions, these phases are not mutually exclusive, nor was Melville's exploration of the gamut always conscious and orderly. But his work, read in these terms, takes on an illuminating pattern of progress and retrogression, success and failure.

Edward H. Rosenberry
Melville and the Comic Spirit (Cambridge, Mass.:
Harvard Univ. Pr., 1955), p. 5

The consideration of Melville as a novelist should have shown . . . that it was precisely the practice of that craft that put his books, and himself, at a loss, and left him silent, stultified, and, before the great face of possibility, impotent for forty years of mature life. I trust that it will have been shown as at least plausible that Melville suffered the exorbitant penalty of his great failure, not as a result of the injuries inflicted upon him by his age, but because of his inability to master a technique—that of the novel—radically foreign to his sensibility. The accidents of his career, the worse accidents of his needs, brought him to a wrong choice. Yet had he made a right choice, the accident of his state of beliefs might well have silenced him altogether. Judging by the reception of his two serious books, he would have been anathema as a preacher and unpublishable as an essayist. We should be grateful for his ill luck in only a lesser sense than we are for

Dante's, or we should have lost the only great imagination in the middle
period of the American nineteenth century: a putative statement to which
all readers must assent.

Richard P. Blackmur
The Lion and the Honeycomb (London:
Methuen, 1956), pp. 143-44

We need not suppose that Melville "approved" of Ahab. He undoubtedly
"admired" this hero, this Titan of men (the creative artist is entitled to the
privilege of admiring his own creation), but he did not necessarily approve
of him, any more than Shakespeare necessarily approved of Macbeth, or
Milton of Satan. Ahab is diabolical, anti-Christian, and, like Macbeth and
Satan, he has a hellish fall.

From the moral standpoint, he is not an example, but a warning. He
illustrates both man's powers, and their misuse. He is romantic individualism carried to the last degree. He is the selfish monopolist, the dictator
with a genius for controlling people, an anti-social monster. . . . Ahab is
without laughter, and sick with the sickness of monomania. He is hopelessly, tragically self-involved. . . .

Some have regarded *Billy Budd* as Melville's own personal testament of
acceptance, and have reasoned that as *Moby Dick* reflects the rebellion of
Melville's youth, *Billy Budd* shows the reconcilement of his old age. This
view is open to the objection that it identifies rather too closely the author
of an imaginative work with his characters, thereby reducing the work to
mere autobiography. It is well not to confuse the critical question with the
biographical question. At the same time, both Ahab and Billy are portrayed with a good deal of sympathy, and it is reasonable to suppose that
each character, in his respective period, reflects something of the mood of
his creator. *Billy Budd* certainly is a brilliant and moving statement of the
ultimate Christian lesson of resignation to God's overruling Providence,
and it is pleasant, as well as reasonable, to think that Melville in his last
years felt the truth of this view. Perhaps he couldn't have written a book
like *Billy Budd* without feeling it.

Randall Stewart
American Literature and Christian Doctrine (Baton Rouge, La.:
Louisiana State Univ. Pr., 1958), pp. 96-7, 102

Melville's grand implication seems to be that all attempts to resist or deny
evil, no matter how they are rationalized, are maddeningly futile. Christianity may be gone, he says in effect, but evil is here to stay; no use trying to
idealize it out of existence, or conceal it with "costliest robes" or annihilate
it by main strength of will and resentment. It will abide and elude; and it

must be reckoned with. It is in us, even the deepest of us. Melville cites no text; he preaches no sermon on this head; he merely enunciates as best he can the critical moral predicament which his prophetic imagination apprehends.

Part of the extendibility of Melville's theme on this final level, of course, is due to the fact that he was truly prophetic, both in the sense of apprehending an incipient but suppressed conflict and dilemma of his own day (which only Hawthorne among his American contemporaries honestly confronted in his writings), and in the sense that historically the full reckoning with the problem was yet to come—*and just such an ill-starred solution was to be attempted* by modern man, who has tried philosophically and pragmatically to dismiss the notion of evil.

The problem has been with us now so long that there are many who have lost the capacity to be terrified by it; if an ever richer general response to this tragic novel can help us today or tomorrow to grasp and hold the reality of evil in our imagination, the book will have served as high a human purpose as any less "wicked" book in a time of more stable values. And if Ahab is to be the last of the race of great literary heroes (fittingly embodying the evil of evils and the highest spiritual splendor of man), why, even in the decline of our culture our pleasure in reading *Moby-Dick,* mixed with pain in a true purgation, will come in large part from our sense of participation in the magnificence and the richly deserved doom. [ca. 1955]

John Parke
in *Interpretations of American Literature,* eds. C. Feidelson, Jr. and
P. Brodtkorb, Jr. (New York: Oxford Univ. Pr., 1959), pp. 100-101

It may be said that the writing of fiction requires a certain discipline, and whether the writer is a "novelist" or a writer of "romances," to use Hawthorne's distinction, he "must rigidly subject himself to certain laws." Melville, however, consistently failed to do this, and yet, on the basis of technical deficiencies alone, it would be unjust to dismiss him as a bad writer. When he was bad, his defects certainly compounded the effect; but there is no denying that he produced at least one masterpiece—almost in spite of himself, it would seem. What is most regrettable is that inability to master a technique forced him into silence during those three decades when he was at his intellectual prime.

Herbert S. Donow
MLQ (June, 1964), p. 186

JOAQUIN MILLER
(CINCINNATUS HINER)
1839-1913

Born March 10 in Liberty, Indiana. He migrated with his family to Oregon in 1852. About 1856, he ran away from home and experienced many exciting (and perhaps apocryphal) adventures in pioneer Oregon and California. He married a Digger Indian girl in 1857 who bore him his daughter Cali-Shasta. In 1859, he attended school, taught and studied law. He was admitted to the bar in Portland, Oregon in 1861. He married Minnie Dyer about 1863, but she separated from him in 1866. In that year, he was elected judge of the Grant County court. *Specimens* was published in 1868. In 1870, he made a literary pilgrimage to London, where he was lionized as a pioneer poet. *Songs of The Sierras* was published in London in 1871. In 1871-1872, he traveled in South America and published *Life Amongst The Modocs,* in 1873. He married Abbie Leland in 1883 and settled permanently in Oakland, California in 1886. In 1897-1898, he went to the Klondike as a correspondent for the *N. Y. Journal.* He died February 17.

The Complete Poetical Works of Joaquin Miller (1897)

M. Marion Marberry, *Splendid Poseur; Joaquin Miller—American Poet* (1953)

Miller was by no means a satyr, as many have pictured him, delighting in wildness for the mere sake of wildness. He overflowed with humanity. No man was ever more sensitive or more genuinely sympathetic. In his later years he sat above the tumult a prophet and seer, and commented and advised and warned. Great areas of his poetry have nothing to do with the West, nothing at all with the manner and the material that are so naturally associated with his name. For decades his voice was heard wherever there was oppression or national wrong. He wrote sonorous lyrics for the Indians, the Boers, the Russian Jews; he wrote the ringing "Cuba Libre" which was read by the Baroness de Bazus in the leading cities before the Spanish war; he championed the cause of woman; and everywhere he took the side of the weaker against the strong. . . .

But almost all that he wrote in this pet field of his endeavor perished with its day. Of it all there is no single poem that may be called distinctive. He moralizes, he preaches, he champions the weak, but he says nothing new, nothing compelling. He is not a singer of the soul: he is the maker of resounding addresses to the peaks and the plains and the sea; the poet of the westward march of a people; the poet of elemental men in elemental surroundings—pioneers amid the vastness of the uttermost West.

Fred L. Pattee
A History of American Literature Since 1870
(New York: Century, 1915), pp. 111-12

After [Miller's] return to California in the middle 'eighties, there grew strong in him a sense that he was the leader of a native poetical movement, a spiritual seer with Messianic or at least prophetic mission, and in the flowing hair and beard of his last years, stalking majestically under the trees which he had planted by his monuments on The Hights, and gazing dreamily out over the Pacific, he looked the part.

Now, whatever one may think of Miller's actual contribution to poetry or to prose fiction, this evolution of an Indian fighter into the Moses of the Golden Gate is an extraordinary phenomenon. Considered merely as a detached individual, he is abundantly interesting to the biographer. But he repays sympathetic curiosity most generously perhaps when one regards and studies him as a register of the power exerted upon the individual by the American environment and the national culture, even at their thinnest and crudest. To study him in this fashion, the first requisite is a more coherent account of his career than has hitherto been available. Joaquin Miller was his own principal hero, but by a singular fatality his adventures have never been adequately written. Certain scenes and events he himself sketched repeatedly; but concerning many passages of his history he was extremely reticent. What is more serious, he had no steady narrative power. Lifelong an adventurous rover, in love with action, he finds it next to impossible to stick to the thread of his story. As soon as he grasps the pen, he overflows with sentiment and moralization, and he riots in description. Consequently his longer poems frequently produce the effect of panorama, and the feeling which they present remains obscure till the shifting pictures are connected and explained by the events of his own life.

Stuart P. Sherman
Americans (New York: Scribner's, 1924), pp. 188-89

Except for his influence, which was not lasting, and his reputation, always sightly tainted with ridicule, Miller seems of little account today. His long verse dramas, his panoramic and tempestuous narratives of the Indian country, Nicaragua, the mountains, and the deserts, are mainly sound and fury. The poet's own posturing, his bald self-aggrandizement, made him a character, though he was only in flashes a true poet. He wrote through a long life many books, but a very large proportion of what he wrote is chaff. Of the dramas, only *The Danites of the Sierras* offers much to a modern reader; and of his prose writings, cluttered with incredible lies, there is nothing likely to live except *Life Among the Modocs*, a fragment of what he called autobiography. Of his shorter poems, the anthologists neglect everything but "Columbus."

Wallace Stegner
in *Literary History of the United States*, eds. Robert Spiller *et al*, Vol. II
(New York: Macmillan, 1948), p. 868

The importance of Miller lies wholly in his contribution of new subjects from regions previously unexploited by the poets of the time. With Bret Harte he pulled the curtains and the Far West took its first bows upon the literary stage. Whitman, on his trip to Colorado in 1879, pondered the problem of giving expression to the grandeurs of deserts and mountains and wrote in *Specimen Days,* "I sometimes think that even the ambition of my friend Joaquin Miller to put them in, and illustrate them, places him ahead of the whole crowd." Like Whitman, he glimpsed the vastness of his country, and in a number of poems furnished picturesque fragments for the unwritten epic of the march of the white man to the Pacific. Despite his inferior verse on Europe and the Holy Land and the imitative accents of his measures, Miller was more of an *American* poet than most of his contemporaries.

Clarence Gohdes
The Literature of the American People (New York:
Appleton-Century-Crofts, 1951), p. 632

Joaquin was born neither in 1841 nor in 1842. For many years the 1841 date was accepted, but recently students of his career decided that the date was 1839. Actually, Joaquin was born on September 8, 1837. That he had managed to subtract not two but four or five years from his age came to light a few years ago with the publication of his secret *California Diary* which had been suppressed for a quarter of a century after his death. There is a sound explanation for Joaquin's insistence on the birth years of 1841 or 1842, one that will be accepted sympathetically (though why he preferred the month of November to September we shall never know). Joaquin was thirty-three when he became a Poet. Reasoning that he was far too elderly to be received by public and critics as a new lyrical genius, he chopped five years off his age and said he was twenty-eight, for while a budding Poet in his twenties is a symbol of hope and promise, a struggling beginner in his thirties is not. Even as an old man, Joaquin would casually subtract ten and even twenty years from his age.

Joaquin Miller may have fooled his biographers about his age (for after all there were no birth records kept in Indiana at the time, and when he explained that the family Bible containing the proper date had been lost, his word was taken), but it is doubtful if he fooled many of his friends. "That rascal is much older than I am," Ambrose Bierce, who was born in 1842, guessed correctly. But it is all the more puzzling that none of the chroniclers of Joaquin's life noticed the age of one of his brothers. If Joaquin actually had been born when he claimed, then his mother was a most unusual woman, capable of a prodigious feat, for she gave birth to another son five months before November 10, 1841, the date he gave most frequently for his own birth.

M. Marion Marberry
Splendid Poseur (New York: Crowell, 1953), pp. 2-3

FRANK NORRIS

1870-1902

> Born March 5 in Chicago. He moved with his family in 1884 to Oakland, California, and, in 1887, he traveled with them to Europe, where he enrolled in Atelier Julien for training in art. In 1890, he entered the University of California, where he wrote plays, stories, and poems. He went to Harvard as a special student in English in 1895 and, in the same year, was sent to South Africa as a war correspondent in the Boer War. After an illness, he returned to San Francisco in 1896. In 1898, he went to Cuba as a correspondent for *McClures Magazine* and published *Moran of the Lady Letty* the same year. In 1899 he became a reader for Doubleday Page and Co. *McTeague* was published in 1899 and *A Man's Woman* in 1900. He married Jeanette Black in 1900. *The Octopus* was published in 1901. He died October 5 in San Francisco of peritonitis.
>
> *The Complete Works of Frank Norris* (1928), 10 vols.
> Ernest Marchand, *Frank Norris: A Study* (1942)

[Norris] was one of the least sectional of American novelists, with a vision of his native land which attached him to the movement, then under discussion to "continentalize" American literature by breaking up the parochial habits of the local colour school. He had a certain epic disposition, tended to vast plans, and conceived trilogies. His "Epic of the Wheat"—*The Octopus* (1901), *The Pit* (1903), and *The Wolf* (never written)—he thought of as the history of the cosmic spirit of wheat moving from the place of its production in California to the place of its consumption in Europe. . . . Such conceptions explain his grandiose manner and the passion of his naturalism, which he was even willing to call romanticism provided he could mean by it the search for truths deeper than the surface truths of orthodox realism. He had a strong vein of mysticism; he habitually occupied himself with "elemental" emotions. His heroes are nearly all violent men, wilful, passionate, combative; his heroines—thick-haired, large-armed women—are endowed with a rich and deep, if slow, vitality. Love in Norris's world is the mating of vikings and valkyries. Love, however, is not his sole concern. The Pacific and California novels . . . are full of ardently detailed actualities; *The Pit* is a valuable representation of a "corner" on the Chicago Board of Trade. In all these his eagerness to be truthful gave Norris a large energy, particularly in scenes of action, but his speed and vividness are not matched by his body and meaning. [ca. 1917]

Carl Van Doren
in *Cambridge History of American Literature,* Vol. III
(New York: Macmillan, 1946), pp. 93-94

Norris at bottom was a fighter, and he fought his way clear of most of the vestiges of the romantic tradition which had survived. Like Garland, although he would never have used the term, he was a veritist at heart. He has been called by many a naturalist, but he was not. "I never truckled; I never took off the hat to Fashion, and held it out for pennies," he wrote in *The Responsibilities of the Novelists.* "By God, I told them the truth. They liked it or they didn't like it. What had that to do with me? I told them the truth." But the fact of he matter was he did not tell them the truth, or at least not all the truth. Like all the western writers, those native to the West as well as those influenced by the West—in fact, we might as well say like all the American writers of the nineteenth century—he never told the truth about sex. He told the truth about the sordidness of life, its brutality, its misery. He never hesitated to assail a social evil, never stopped short of trying to right a wrong. His novels were "naked truths," as one of his admirers described them, in every sense but the sexual. The sexual candor of Zola he never attempted. He was too clearly a product of the petty bourgeois environment in which he had lived to rise above the middle-class prejudice against sex in literature. His characters, unlike those of Howells, might not live moral lives, it is true, but the psychological consideration of the nature of their immorality, or even the nature of their morality, he never ventured to include within the province of his concern.

V. F. Calverton
The Liberation of American Literature (New York:
Scribner's, 1932), pp. 353-54

There was in Frank Norris a gusto for conflict that was typical of most Americans of the era of Theodore Roosevelt. The man loved a fair contest. "One good fight," he is quoted as saying, "will do more for a boy than a year of schooling." Yet it is Naturalistic dogma that the contestants are very badly matched; Nature can crack the bones of her victims without effort. In endowing his heroes with Homeric brawn Norris was unconsciously trying to equalize the contestants, to make a good fight of it. It is spectacle, however, rather than justice, which he has in mind. While Hardy was of a disposition to taunt the gods with cowardice and to enlarge the weaknesses of men to make the bitter inequality the more apparent, Norris could abandon without feeling this or that particular figure to seek out a new champion with better sinews and a tougher heart for another trial with the gods. . . . Yet because each merely provides spectacle, neither in victory nor in defeat do the supermen and superwomen of Norris move us. Like our pugilistic heroes, they are overtouted. We do not believe in their muscles, their jaws, their hearts. Never very real to us, they carry little conviction about life itself. Because we can attach no more feeling to them than we can to Odin or Frigga, they being quite outside the animal kingdom, we cannot generalize from their careers. Where Norris has employed supermen and superwomen, he has undeniably destroyed the illusion of life so essential to credence in determinism.

Oscar Cargill
Intellectual America (New York: Macmillan, 1941), p. 100

Norris's style is like the life he describes—vigorous, robust, often tumultuous. It is like a flood, sometimes a turbid flood, bearing the debris of its banks. But like a flood it moves, with a powerful impulse, sweeping along his mannerisms, his clichés, his rhetoric, which may encumber its surface but cannot seriously impede its movement or diminish its strength.

In him is neither any *fin de siècle* lassitude nor any wish to burn with a "hard gem-like flame"; when he burns it is with the red glare and the cracking roar of a forest fire.

His style is no unfit instrument for that symphony to whose profound harmonies his ear was ever attuned—"the symphony of energy, the vast orchestration of force, the paean of an indestructible life, coeval with the centuries, renascent, ordained, eternal."

Ernest Marchand
Frank Norris (Stanford, Calif.:
Stanford Univ. Pr., 1942), p. 192

. . . The key to Norris's mind is to be found in a naive, openhearted, and essentially unquenchable joy as radiant as the lyricism of Elizabethan poetry, a joy that is like the first discovery of the world, exhilarating in its directness, and eager to absorb every flicker of life. Norris wrote as if men had never seen California before him, or known the joy of growing wheat in those huge fields that could take half a day to cross, or of piling enough flour on trains to feed a European nation. It is out of the surge and greed of that joy that his huge, restless characters grow, men so abundantly alive that the narrow life of cities and the constraints of the factory system can barely touch them. He was the poet of the bonanza, teeming with confidence, reckless in the face of that almost cosmological security that was California to him. Every object in his books was huge, brought up to scale—the wheat fields in *The Octopus* that are like Napoleonic duchies, the eating and drinking in *McTeague*, the fantastic debaucheries in *Vandover and the Brute* (like a Boy Scout's dreams of ancient Egypt), the Renaissance prodigality in *The Pit*, and even the back-alley slugging and thievery in an adventure yarn like *Moran of the Lady Letty*, whose heroine, characteristically, is a Viking princess in blue jeans.

Alfred Kazin
On Native Grounds (New York:
Reynal and Hitchcock, 1942), pp. 99-100

. . . When all the legitimate criticisms of Norris have been made, they do not appear, when weighed against the solid worth of his writing, of major importance. The very need for pointing out that his imagination fell short of finality indicates that that imagination was a superior one indeed; and Norris's failures in philosophical consistency and in economy of style are failures in certain useful accessories of fiction, not in its absolute essentials. In those essentials, Norris is strong indeed. When all objections have been urged against him, certain conclusions about the solidity of his achievement remain unchanged. Those conclusions are (to speak summarily) as follows:—The aims Norris set up for himself are on the whole legitimate aims, to whose worth the history of fiction affords more than sufficient testimony. He had an uncanny knack of finding, recognizing, and telling good stories; and he equipped his stories with an abundance of characters, many of them curiously interesting, some of them racy and picturesque, most of them sharply individualized. Both his stories and his people he rendered through a medium of rich and vivid perception, the wide range of which includes the homeliest commonplace, the harshest ugliness, the most richly colored beauty, and an elusive mysticism. In fine, Norris succeeded abundantly in the proper work of the novelist—the creation of a large, credible, interesting, and significant imaginative world.

Walter F. Taylor
The Economic Novel in America (Chapel Hill, N. C.:
Univ. North Carolina Pr., 1942), p. 306

In addition to throwing into relief . . . certain significant aspects of Norris's last novel, *The Pit*, the idea that the romance between the hero and heroine of *A Man's Woman* was somehow a refraction of Norris's relationship with his mother furnishes the key to the mystery of why the heroines of his fiction are so tall and powerful: it is not so much that they are of abnormal size, but that the viewpoint from which they are described is that of a small boy looking at his mother. This idea is also helpful in understanding why Norris's women play the role of teacher and guide in the lives of the men they love and why physical contact between hero and heroine should be regarded as abhorrent, if not utterly unthinkable. And finally, it helps to relate Norris's fiction to one of the most widely and fiercely believed tenets of the success mythology, namely, "Everything I have I owe to my mother." However salient their jaws and broad their shoulders, Norris's fictional protagonists eventually find their effort to be a success in the world almost as harrowing as their creator had discovered it to be; in endeavoring to carve out a place in the sun for themselves, Norris's heroes thankfully draw aid and comfort and renewed strength from their surrogate mothers, their gigantic female pals.

> Kenneth Lynn
> *The Dream of Success* (Boston: Little, Brown,
> 1955), p. 184

Although a pioneer in forming a viable tradition of American naturalism, [Norris] displays at his best a precarious balance between the centrifugal pull of large abstractions and a centripetal interest in careful observation. It is the tension between these two approaches to reality—those of romance and realism—that contributes much to the vitality of his best work. When driven to ultimate formulations of that tension, he spins off into irrationality. When, as in *McTeague,* he finds a way to control its expression, he creates his monument. But the measure of his success is often the measure of his failure, the measure of his attempt to reconstitute romance in American letters.

> George W. Johnson
> *AL* (March, 1961), p. 63

THOMAS PAINE
1737-1809

Born January 29 in Thetford, England. After attending grammar school, he was apprenticed to a corset-maker in 1750. He shipped out as a privateer in 1756. He held various positions in the years following 1757 and had two brief marriages, the first ending within a year with the death of his wife and the second in a legal separation in 1774. In the same year, he left for Philadelphia with letters of introduction from Benjamin Franklin and wrote for the *Pennyslvania Magazine. Common Sense* was published in 1776 as well as the first of the *Crisis* papers. In 1787, he went to Europe to promote an iron bridge he had invented. In 1789, he went to Paris as a recognized revolutionist. *Rights of Man* was published in 1791, and, a year later, he was elected to the French Assembly. He was imprisoned in 1793 after the fall of Girondins but was released in 1794 at the request of James Monroe. Part I of *Age of Reason* was published in 1794 and Part II in 1796. *Agrarian Justice* followed in 1797. In 1802, he returned to

America, where he was vilified for *Age of Reason*. He died June 8 in New York.

Moncure D. Conway, ed., *The Writings of Thomas Paine* (1894-96), 4 vols.

Moncure D. Conway, *The Life of Thomas Paine* . . . (1892)

It would be idle to attempt to trace to their sources the major ideas of his philosophy. Probably Paine did not know where he got them. He was not a student like John Adams, familiar with all the political philosophers; rather he was an epitome of a world in revolution. He absorbed ideas like a sponge. He was so wholly a child of his age that the intellectual processes of the age were no other than his own. But he was very much more than an echo; he possessed that rarest of gifts, an original mind. He looked at the world through no eyes than his own. There is a curious remark in an early pamphlet which admirably expresses his method: "When precedents fail to assist us, we must return to the first principles of things for information, and *think*, as if we were the *first men* that thought." It was his remarkable ability to think from first principles that gave such freshness and vigor to his pen. He drew largely from French thought, but at bottom he remained English. If he was Gallic in his psychology of human nature and his passionate humanitarianism, he was English in his practical political sense and insistence on the economic sources of political action. In his political theory he was curiously like Roger Williams. A thoroughgoing idealist in aim, generous and unsparing in service to humanity, he was a confirmed realist in the handling of facts. He refused to be duped by imposing appearances or great reputations, but spoke out unpleasant truths which gentlemen wished to keep hidden. Clear and direct in expression, he seasoned his writings with homely figures and a frequent audacity of phrase that made wide appeal. He was probably the greatest pamphleteer that the English race has produced and one of its great idealists.

Vernon Louis Parrington
Main Currents in American Thought, Vol. II
(New York: Harcourt, Brace, 1927), pp. 340-41

Upon these four works, *Common Sense, The Crisis, The Rights of Man*, and *The Age of Reason*, Paine's literary fame must rest. Strictly speaking, he was not a literary man at all. He was a propagandist in wartime, a hurler of militant pamphlets before the opening of the newspaper age, a journalist who thought only in superlatives and who knew nothing of prudence. Always was he at the level of the common people, with a plan for Utopia founded always on the corner-stones of democracy, brotherhood, justice, equality—principles gathered principally from the New Testament which he knew by heart. He was a phrase-maker, a soap-boxer with a panacea, a man who knew the common people from whom he sprung and could speak with ease their language. He wrote as he thought, pell-mell, often in defiance of grammar, of logic, of elegance, but always so as to be instantly understood. He came at the one time in all history when he could have been a moving force, and the unprecedented success of the revolutions of which he was a part makes of him more of a prophet and philosopher than he really was. More and more his works must be relegated to the reference shelves rather than to the alcove for mere readers.

Fred L. Pattee
The First Century of American Literature
(New York: Appleton, 1935), p 24

Paine's literary method was that of the practical agitator and popular journalist. Not greatly concerned with aesthetic purposes, he sought first of all to persuade his audience. To achieve this end, he held that a writer should be candid, simple, clear, and bold; that he should arrange his work to obtain the maximum effect; and that he should not neglect appeals to feeling—"The mind of a living public feels first and reasons afterward." In realizing these principles in his own work, Paine avoided the use of cumbersome arguments from precedent, and eschewed any appearance of profound theorizing. With astonishing directness, with true "common sense," he cut to the center of every question. With an acute sense for practical effect, he spoke in an idiom absolutely plain and clear. He excelled in hitting off telling illustrations and climaxes, in fixing an idea forever in a single flash of eloquence: "O! Ye that love mankind! Ye that dare oppose not only the tyranny but the tyrant, stand forth!"

Walter F. Taylor
A History of American Letters (New York:
American Book, 1936), p. 52

His detractors succeeded in destroying [Paine's] reputation both before and after his death. For a hundred years, or thereabouts, his memory was held in contempt by most Americans. The young people were brought up either in ignorance of what Paine did to help in the War for Independence; or, on the other hand, they were taught all the slanders that have been tacked on to his memory. Public speakers and candidates for office made it a point never to quote from his writings in making their orations, even when such a quotation would be illuminating, for a mention of the disreputable Paine would have brought boos and sneers from their audiences. Histories of the American Revolution that did not contain even a mention of Thomas Paine were actually printed and circulated.

Paine should be in the Hall of Fame, of course, with Washington, Jefferson, John Adams and other founders of the republic, but his name was voted down. Theodore Roosevelt characterized him as a "filthy little atheist," a three-word phrase in which not one word is correct, for he was not filthy, not little, nor an atheist.

Will this patriot and fighter for human rights ever be restored to his proper place in the reverence and affection of the American people? No one can say for certain, for no one knows, but it is a fact that during the past decade much of the fog of slanders that dimmed his reputation has been dissipated by the sunlight of truth. Our grandfathers seldom mention him without some expression of contempt, but today men of understanding know better. Consider the words of Thomas A. Edison, who said, "I have always regarded Paine as one of the greatest of all Americans. Never have we had a sounder intelligence in this republic."

W. E. Woodward
Tom Paine: America's Godfather (New York:
Dutton, 1945), pp. 16-17

According to an old saying the secret of housewifery is to "simplify, classify, and glorify." This was Paine's literary formula. He reduces complex ideas to simple propositions, sometimes distorting them or omitting basic elements, but always producing a black-and-white lucidity. He then arranges his compact statements in neat categories and dins them into the reader's mind by repetition. The most important step, "glorification," he achieves by linking them with images which create an illusion of beauty and nobility. They are emotionally provocative, not because they "mean" much in any literal sense but because they are variations on clichés commonly associated with the good and the true.

"Government, like dress, is the badge of lost innocence," is a witty phrasing of a familiar notion; "the palaces of kings are built upon the ruins of the bowers of paradise" is effective because it is emotionally grateful. To revolt against George III seemed to many Americans a daring step; it was vaguely consoling, although not rationally reassuring, to be told that it would improve the landscape architecture of Heaven. Phrases like Paine's "summer soldier" and "sunshine patriot" live because they do the full work of metaphors and say more than literal statement could; usually, however, his images, for all their polish, reflect only a diffuse glow, attractive to hasty readers who wanted to believe that they basked in the light of truth rather than to absorb an intellectual demonstration of what truth was. Paine had the advertiser's talent, the knack of finding slogans which are easily remembered and quotable because they tickle the ear, and carried it to a pitch of expertness reached by only a handful of propagandists in all history.

Kenneth B. Murdock
The Literature of the American People (New York:
Appleton-Century-Crofts, 1951), p. 153

Most historians have assumed that Paine's great influence came as a result of his journalistic style—the compelling manner in which he wrote. It is worthy of considering whether his matter may not also have been universally appealing—that readers have been attracted by the sense of finality, of an approach to the absolute, in his works communicated by his notion of first principles.

Paine's concepts were revolutionary for his time, it is true, but they also rested on an appeal to a sense of permanence, of the absolute nature of things. In the political realm most of his principles are now considered axiomatic—and for that reason no longer associated with him. That is, of course, his democratic concepts, not his notion of politics as a precise science. The universal acceptance of his principles has paradoxically meant the decline of his popularity, for to the degree that they have been accepted and applied in society they have lost the aura of novelty and individuality. Paine made many mistakes in his career—and some of his applications of principles were grotesque—but his principles themselves have endured and triumphed and represent the most effective vindication of his life.

Alfred Owen Aldridge
Man of Reason (Philadelphia: Lippincott, 1959), p. 322

EDGAR   ALLAN   POE
1809-1849

Born January 19 in Boston. When his mother died in 1811 he was taken into the family of John Allan with whom he lived in England during 1815-1820. He attended the University of Virginia in 1826, but left in 1827 and enlisted in the U.S. Army. *Tamerlane and Other Poems* was published in 1827. He entered West Point in 1830, but was dismissed in 1831. *Poems* was published in 1831. In 1835, he became the editor of the *Southern Literary Messenger.* He married his cousin, Virginia Clemm, in 1836. *Narrative of Arthur Gordon Pym* was published in 1837. He edited and wrote for various magazines during 1838-1843. "The Raven" and *Tales* were published in 1845. His wife died in 1847. He died in Baltimore.

James A. Harrison, ed., *The Complete Works of Edgar Allan Poe* (1902), 17 vols.

Arthur H. Quinn, *Edgar Allan Poe: A Critical Biography* (1941)

PERSONAL

In instinctive recalcitrancy to the general constitution of things he passed his life in kicking against its pricks and produced his literature in the process. Inevitably the false, the ugly and the wrong attracted him, since the established standard is of the good, the beautiful and the true. But as the established is the only conceivable standard he was naturally forced to treat the former trinity in conjunction with, if not in terms of, the latter. The effect he aimed at being exclusively a sensational effect, he could best secure it by falsifying his material, and thus circumventing the reader's tranquility of expectation. The fact that such sensation is valueless was of no concern to a philosopher who attached value to sensation as such and to sensation only. Hence he devoted the powers of an extraordinary intellect to producing what is to the intellect of next to no interest. The abnormal, in its various manifestations, the sinister, the diseased, the deflected, even the disgusting were his natural theme. He could not conceive the normal save as the commonplace for which he had apparently the "horror" he could have liked to inspire in others by the presentation of the eccentric. Dread of the commonplace, as was pointed out centuries ago by a far otherwise penetrating critic than Poe, is fatal to the sublime. And there is assuredly no sublimity in Poe. [ca. 1909]

W. C. Brownell
American Prose Masters (New York: Scribner's, 1929), pp. 225-26

The testimony of unimpeachable quality has been given . . . to show that for long periods Poe was absolutely sober. His hard fight against a temptation, stronger to him than to normal people, and his remorse when he yielded, for the reasons he has given and for another which I have suggested [fear of insanity] leave much on the credit side to Poe.

Poe was not a drug addict. On this point we have direct testimony. Dr. English, who disliked him, gave his definite medical opinion to that effect. Thomas H. Lane, who knew him for several years, while acknowledging that "a drink or two" changed Poe from a mild man "in every way a gentleman" to a quarrelsome inebriate, insisted that Poe did not take drugs. . . . Those were days when opium was frequently given in small doses for pain, and Poe may well have taken it in that form. . . .

When his weaknesses have been catalogued, however, there rises above them the real Edgar Poe, the industrious, honorable gentleman whom Graham and Willis knew, the warm friend and courteous host whom Hirst, Mayne Reid and many others remembered. There was the brilliant thinker —whose charm came from that inner radiance that shone upon Helen Whitman and Susan Talley. Those who knew him best, loved him best. . . .

Of even more significance than Poe the man is Poe the artist. To bring to Virginia the few comforts she needed, he might harness his critical pen to drive a poetess, who could pay him. into temporary fame. But even the spectre of want could not force him into the prostitution of his genius as a poet and a writer of romance. Had he chosen to fill his pages with the sentimental twaddle then so popular, or to sully his creations of the beautiful with the suggestiveness that sells, he would have made a better living, and would now be forgotten. But he had his own lofty standards, and he lived up to them. For money he cared little, except as it provided for the wants of others. For fame he did care, but he was one of those souls who can see a prize, artistic, social, or financial, almost within their grasp, and, caring for something higher still, of which that prize is the price, can resolutely put it by. We can imagine him saying, with Browning's Duke,

> That would have taken some stooping—and I choose
> Never to stoop.

It is for this great refusal, for his willingness to lay all things upon the altar of his art, that Poe is most to be respected.

Arthur Hobson Quinn
Edgar Allan Poe (New York:
Appleton-Century, 1941), p. 695

[Poe] was the victim of neurotic compulsions in his writings as well as in his personal life. He is significant chiefly because his neuroticism assumed a characteristically American form. This becomes plain when he is contrasted with some European writer with comparable talents and similar emotional insecurity: for example, Coleridge. The European writer takes his bearings from the social order, and he may either rebel against it (like Coleridge in his youth) or idealize it and submit to it (like Coleridge in his old age). But Poe found himself in a void and could seek to make himself secure only by means of a fantastic exaggeration of the drive to power. He became pure will seeking omnipotence. In this respect he is comparable to Jonathan Edwards. In the poet, as in the theologian, the craving for omnipotence resulted both in a presumptuous attempt to explain the entire universe by logic (as in *Eureka*) and in fantasies of inhuman cruelty.

Henry B. Parkes
The American Experience (New York:
A. A. Knopf, 1947), pp. 196-97

. . . Mystery there will always be about [Poe], and perhaps it will always require a certain kind of temperament to feel on easy terms with him, but in this day and age anybody who considers him an atheist, a diabolist, an immoralist, or a Gothic monster is simply unwilling to consider the evidence at hand.

Few Americans have aspired more nobly than Poe, and, if he fell short of his ideal, this should bring him closer to us and help us to understand him better. His greatest fault was an instability which, despite all his capacity for work, made him unreliable in his personal relationships, and he could be very trying when he donned a mask of arrogance and bad manners to cover up this weakness. Whether his faults were born with him or developed through the evil conditioning of his life, it is not possible to say, for none of us has ever seen an unconditioned man or handled unparticled matter. With all his faults, however, and all the disadvantages he suffered, Poe did find those who loved him while he was alive, and legions of readers have remained loyal to him through the years, often in spite of the fact that they had no means of discovering how good a man he really was.

Edward Wagenknecht
Edgar Allan Poe (New York:
Oxford Univ. Pr., 1963), p. 221

POEMS

A taint of vulgarity spoils, for the English reader, all but two or three of [Poe's] poems—the marvelous "City in the Sea" and "To Helen," for example, whose beauty and crystal perfection make us realize, as we read them, what a very great artist perished on most of the occasions when Poe wrote verse. It is to this perished artist that the French poets pay their tribute. Not being English they are incapable of appreciating those finer shades of vulgarity that ruin Poe for us. . . .

The substance of Poe is refined; it is his form that is vulgar. He is, as it were, one of Nature's Gentlemen, unhappily cursed with incorrigible bad taste. To the most sensitive and high-souled man in the world we should find it hard to forgive, shall we say, the wearing of a diamond ring on every finger. Poe does the equivalent of this in his poetry; we notice the solecism and shudder. Foreign observers do not notice it; they detect only the native gentlemanliness in the poetical intention, not the vulgarity in the details of execution. To them, we seem perversely and quite incomprehensibly unjust.

It is when Poe tries to make it too poetical that his poetry takes on its peculiar tinge of badness. Protesting too much that he is a gentleman, and opulent into the bargain, he falls into vulgarity. Diamond rings on every finger proclaim the parvenu.

Aldous Huxley
Vulgarity in Literature (London:
Chatto and Windus, 1930), pp. 26-27

. . . Poe described the traditionally romantic dream of beautiful past times and far places, set in a world of fantasy. In the "misty mid-region of Weir," he imagined the beauty which he could not find in American actuality—in a "kingdom beside the sea," he and his ideal love would live a life of impossible perfection. His poetry described life as "A Dream within a Dream," for dreams were his only truth and his only beauty. Like all Americans he imagined and sought for "Eldorado". . . . He believed in the world of dream, and in its truth and beauty, more passionately than did either Emerson or Thoreau, but he wholly disbelieved in any possibility of its realization. In the intellect he conceived the absolute ideal, and even cried out a philosophical "Eureka." But his dream was unreal and his cry without conviction. Poe echoed the poetic despair of Byron, and prophesied the beautiful evil of Baudelaire, but his romantic nihilism found few counterparts in the American literature of his nineteenth century. Only later would the haunted heroes of O'Neill and Jeffers repeat his denial of hope and his celebration of violence.

Frederic I. Carpenter
American Literature and the Dream (New York:
Philosophical Library, 1955), p. 201

It is tragic that the value of Poe's poems lies primarily in their over-insistent exhibitions of an imagination trying in vain to demonstrate its power to reach beyond itself. But it is this fact, apparently, that helped French poets, not so sensitive to the vulgarities of that over-insistence as Americans can now be, to write poems of a seriousness which Poe could not attain. Moreover, it is the fact of Poe's poetic gift which set the pattern of his fiction— with its concern to explore the delicately harrowing relations between the world of common sense and that of the dream. Because his fiction has pattern, it is greater than his poetry, which has only force. Nonetheless, the life of the fiction seems to have been released by powers which could have been discovered only in the process of making poems. The poems take Poe's anti-poetic world as a given and strain to expose the mysterious poetic power which he feels informs it. That such a world exists is a prime assumption without which the poems would have little or no meaning. They depend for their force upon a dialectic of simple opposition to the world for which they are written. Yet they make little or no contact with that world. They exist, as it were, to remind their readers of a possibility, "Out of SPACE—out of TIME," which by definition is never actualizable in a "real," common-sense situation.

The authentic poet is Israfel, whose world is the simple negative of this one. Poe must strive to be Israfel, so to escape the very world in which even Israfel would "not sing so wildly well / A mortal melody. . . ." The poems project disembodied creativity, so to speak—the force of an imagination driven to be true to itself at all costs. (In his long prose treatise *Eureka*, Poe tried to construct a rationale for such disembodied creativity; the net effect of the work is at the least one of helpless megalomania, at the most one of wilful demonism.) The egocentrism of Poe's poems achieves its greatest value by being finally, in its very agonizing self-indulgent lyricism, an unsharable egocentrism. The poet is freed to be true to his sense of his self and his vocation, but at the cost of cutting himself off from his vulgarly substantial world. He shares the burden of the creative act with his readers and so would force them into releasing whatever potential for creativity is in them. In this he tends to be one with his major contemporaries. He is unlike his contemporaries, however, in that he wilfully pushes this conception of poetry to its extremest limits. For him the poetic act in the end signifies absolutely nothing but itself. Thus, from the perspective of those who can be only his readers, what that act means is considerably more than what it is. This perhaps is the inevitable fate of the work of a man who is more of a culture hero than an artist.

Roy Harvey Pearce
The Continuity of American Poetry (Princeton, N. J.:
Princeton Univ. Pr., 1961), pp. 152-53

STORIES

. . . It is plain that he was the most important figure in the history of the short story during his half-century. Hawthorne alone may be thought of as vying with him for this distinction; but although the New Englander is infinitely Poe's superior in some respects—as in the creation of character and in wholesomeness and sanity—he must yield place to him in the creation of incident, in the construction of plot, and in the depicting of an intensely vivid situation. Whether or not we allow Poe the distinction of having invented the short story will depend on our interpretation of terms; but at least he invented the detective story, and more than any other he gave the short story its vogue in America. . . .

His main limitations as a writer of the short story are to be found in the feebleness and flimsiness of his poorer work; in his all but complete lack of healthy humour; in his incapacity to create or to depict character; in his morbidness of mood and grotesqueness of situation. He suffers also in comparison with other leading short-story writers of America and England in consequence of his disdain of the ethical in art (though neither his tales nor his poems are entirely lacking in ethical value); he suffers, again, in comparison with certain present-day masters of the short story in consequence of his lack of variety in theme and form; and he was never expert in the management of dialogue. [ca. 1917]

Killis Campbell
in *Cambridge History of American Literature*, Vol. II
(New York: Macmillan, 1946), pp. 67-68

Poe turned to the writing of short stories because he needed to make money and because he discovered, perhaps all unaware even to himself, that poetry could not fulfill the high aims he had for it. Eventually the short story served Poe that office of necessary expression; it became a way for him of ordering an otherwise chaotic world; it also became a "poem" in its projection of some of those deepest impulses which had animated him as a poet but which, now that he had become more mature as a man and as an artist, Poe could delineate without the masquerade or the apparent embarrassment of his earlier years. . . .

A tale was like a poem in that it did not deal with ordinary life. Its range was the limitless reach of the imagination into the mysteries of existence. The one great mystery of life was the deep abyss of subconscious mental activity which lies beneath the otherwise placid surface of normal existence. Poe assumed in his tales one crucial condition: every mind is either half-mad or capable of slipping easily into madness. He was not so much concerned with precisely what madness was but with the conditions and stages whereby madness came to exist and evidenced itself in otherwise average, commonplace human beings. Therefore, he presented a number of protagonists who would not only go mad but who would, all the while, be aware that they were going mad; this introspective habit and self-knowledge would make all the more believable, and horrible, the stages in mental disintegration. . . .

In its way a short story is like a poem: it is not particularly *about* an action or a human situation, despite all the frenzy and sensationalism Poe wove into his action; it was the special, almost unique way whereby the action or situation is presented and understood. In its composition the writer engaged himself in a process moving toward an ordered comprehension of an idea; in its reading, the story is not something made by the artist: it is itself a separate entity, neither "didactic" nor the author's private biography, but capable of ordering and controlling the imaginative response of the reader. It contains, as Poe himself said, everything necessary to its explanation and understanding; it would be an exercise or journey of the responding imagination different every time it occurred; yet it should be, Poe maintained, reducible to certain known laws of art and the human mind. In such a way Poe became one of the first modern symbolists: symbolism was not merely one way but an infinitely variable means of presenting idea and meaning. Meaning and form were the elaborately complex ways the human mind made things known to itself.

Edward H. Davidson, ed.
Selected Writings of Edgar Allan Poe (Boston: Houghton Mifflin, 1956), pp. xiv-xv, xvii

"Everything in Poe is dead," Allen Tate has remarked. This does not controvert the tribute of Baudelaire, who ascribes Poe's special illumination to the phosphorescence of decay. The premise of knowledge is that all men are mortal, and the insights of tragedy culminate in the posture of dying. If Tolstoy's outlook could be summed up in his infantile effort to break through his swaddling bands, then it would be Poe's self-revealing gesture to assume the shroud. More than once he reminds us that Tertullian's credo, "I believe because it is absurd," was inspired by the doctrine of resurrection. And though Poe's resurrections prove ineffectual or woefully incomplete, we are reminded by the Existentialists that the basis of man's plight is absurdity. Poe's cult of blackness is not horripilation for horripilation's sake; it is a bold attempt to face the true darkness in its most tangible manifestations. If life is a dream, then death is an awakening. The dreamer coexists with another self, who may be his accuser or his victim, or his all too evanescent bride. His house may be a Gothic ruin or a home-like cottage; but any sojourn must be temporary; and the journey thence, though it ranges outward and upward, leads downward toward the very closest circumscription of space, the grave. Place and time, to sum them up in Poe's symbols, are his pit and his pendulum; the narrowing yet bottomless abyss that underlies the human condition, the ticking and tolling that measure and limit the heartbeat. Character, though it wears many masks, does not escape detection: it is the cowering spirit of underground man. Yet plot threads a lucid course through delirious labyrinths of grief and disaster, a mind encompassed by shadows, reason in madness.

Harry Levin
The Power of Blackness (New York: A. A. Knopf, 1958), pp. 163-64

The figures Poe created in his work were never as satisfactory, unfortunately, as the figure he composed with his life. Certainly Gordon Pym—though he moves into the first major scene "not a little intoxicated" and early confesses himself a member of the "numerous" race of the melancholy"—does not ever come alive as a significant character, much less assume the tragic dimensions attained by Poe himself. Poe lacks as a writer a *sense of sin,* and therefore cannot raise his characters to the Faustian level which alone dignifies gothic fiction. When he tries to treat in his tales (in the "Duc de l'Omelette," for instance) the Satanic pact, he is embarrassed and seeks refuge in the heavy-handed horseplay he took for humor. The relations of Pym with Peters suggest from to time the terrible bargain between Faust and Mephisto; but Poe will not permit Peters to become a real Devil, and Pym has obviously no soul to sell. Poe liked to boast that he had transformed the gothic from a "horror of Germany" to a "horror of the soul"; but by "soul" he seems to have meant only what we should call "sensibility." Certainly Pym, who in this respect resembles all of Poe's protagonists, responds even to torment aesthetically rather than morally; and for all his concern with evil, Poe provides only what Wallace Stevens would call an *Esthetique du mal*. If his own life seems to offer more genuinely metaphysical shudder, this is thanks not to him but to the Puritan conscience of Griswold, which made of him a kind of vulgar Faust for the American market, just as Baudelaire made of him a *poète maudit* for the French one. If there seem to be even now two Poes, it is because he left a half-finished self that has been completed in one way for the American middlebrow audience, and in quite another for the highbrow French public.

Leslie A. Fiedler
Love and Death in the American Novel (New York:
Criterion, 1960), pp. 413-14

CRITICISM

Poe's fame . . . can receive no aid from either his critical theories which are objectively considered absurd or from his technical inventiveness. It must continue to rest upon a handful of fantastic tales and poems and must, from the physical origin and character of these tales and poems, remain narrow. Having no commerce with either the human affections or the passions, sharing no fundamental instinct or concern or hope of the spirit of man, what is there left him but the faltering attention of some twilit hour? This hour and its mood are recurrent, especially in youth. In the reveries of late adolescence, which often have a touch of passing malady and perversity, the gloom and abstract cruelty of certain tales will probably always have their share. The maturer mind finds even these difficult to relish on account of their pretentious phrasing, their moments of tawdry melodrama, their constant use of the magniloquent *clichés* so familiar to all who know the older tradition of Southern eloquence. "Classical head," "snow-white and gauze-like drapery," "marble hand," "tumultuous vultures of stern passion," "fair England," "her lofty, her ethereal nature," "menials prepared her for the tomb," "yet I should fail in any attempt," "the fair page need not be sullied," "the wine flowed freely"—it is difficult to keep within the mood of stories broken by these phrases that smack of the provincial society column and of public celebrations of the fair Southland and its pure women. It has never been sufficiently observed how intimately

of his time and section—even to the declamatoriness of tone—was both
the critical and the imaginative prose of Poe.

Ludwig Lewisohn
Expression in America (New York:
Harper, 1932), pp. 166-67

[A]fter due allowance is made for [Poe's] pleasant deceptions and for his
deliberate cultivation of the "gothic" (the tale of horror in vogue when he
wrote), one must admit that there was something fundamentally wrong
about the man. His declaration, in "The Poetic Principle," that the tendency of passion is "to degrade, rather than to elevate the soul" and his
avowal that a dead woman is a more proper subject for a poem than a
live one should disturb the thoughtful critic. . . .

[H]is neurotic attitude toward love is a fact that cannot be denied. Out
of his renunciation of normal passion came his compensatory conception
of a supernal ideal beauty to be worshipped, which made him aver that
the death of a beautiful woman is the ideal subject for poetry. And from
this proceeds his theory that music best expresses this yearning for which
there can be no return. Bluntly, Poe's entire aesthetic can be traced to a
motivation not greatly different from that which inspires necrophilia—the
lust for the bodies of the dead. It is revelatory of the pretensions of
modern poetry and its supporting criticism that so much of both may be
traced directly to this one poor, warped mind. Yet such is the case.

Oscar Cargill
Intellectual America (New York: Macmillan, 1941), pp. 178-79

GENERAL

With no conscious connection with the life about him, Poe became nevertheless the literary equivalent of the industrialist and the pioneer. . . . Poe's
meticulous and rationalistic mind fitted his environment and mirrored its
inner characteristics far more readily than a superficial look at it would
lead one to believe. In him, the springs of human desire had not so much
frozen up as turned to metal: his world was, in one of his favorite words,
plutonian, like that of Watt and Fulton and Gradgrind: the tears that he
dropped were steel beads, and his mind worked like a mechanical hopper,
even when there were no appropriate materials to throw into it. It happened to be a very good mind; and when it had something valuable to
work upon, as in literary criticism, the results were often excellent. Left
to himself, however, he either spent his energies on small ingenuities like
ciphers and "scientific" puzzles, or he created a synthetic world, half-
pasteboard and half-perfume, whose thinness as an imaginative reality was
equaled only by its apparent dissociation from the actualities that sur-

rounded him. The criticism of Poe's fantasies is not that they were "unreal": Shakespeare's are equally so: the criticism is that they have their sources in a starved and limited humanity, the same starved and limited humanity in which Gradgrind devoted himself to "hard facts," and the frontier fighter to cold steel. Terror and cruelty dominated Poe's mind; and terror and cruelty leave a scar on almost every tale and anecdote about pioneer life. . . .

Poe, perhaps, had never heard one of these stories; but the dehumanized world he created gave a place for terrors, cruelties, and murders which expressed, in a sublimated and eminently readable form, the sadisms and masochisms of the pioneer's life. Man is, after all, a domestic animal; and though he may return to unbroken nature as a relief from all the sobrieties of existence, he can reside for long in the wilderness only by losing some of the essential qualities of the cultivated human species. Poe had lost these qualities, neurotically, without even seeing the wilderness. Cooper's generation had dreamed of Leatherstocking; in realization, the dream had become the nightmare world of Poe.

Lewis Mumford
The Golden Day (New York: Norton, 1926), pp. 76-78

. . . The problem of Poe, fascinating as it is, lies quite outside the main current of American thought, and it may be left with the psychologist and the belletrist with whom it belongs. It is for abnormal psychology to explain his "neural instability amounting almost to a dissociated or split personality," his irritable pride, his quarrelsomeness, his unhappy persecution complex, his absurd pretentions to a learning he did not possess, his deliberate fabrications about his life and methods of work, his oscillations between abstinence and dissipation, between the morbidly grotesque and the lucidly rational, his haunting fear of insanity that drove him to demonstrate his sanity by pursuing complex problems of ratiocination. Such problems are personal to Poe and do not concern us here. And it is for the belletrist to evaluate his theory and practice of art: his debt to Coleridge and Schlegel; the influence of the contemporary magazine on his conception of the length of a work of the imagination; the value of his theory of the tyrannizing unity of mood in the poem and short story; the provocation to the craftsman of the pretentiousness of contemporary American literature, joined to a flabby and crude technique; the grossness of the popular taste and the validity of his critical judgments. Whatever may be the final verdict it is clear that as an aesthete and a craftsman he made a stir in the world that has not lessened in the years since his death, but has steadily widened. Others of greater repute in his day have fared less prosperously in later reputation. He was the first of our artists and the first of our critics; and the surprising thing is that such a man should have made his appearance in an America given over to hostile ideals. He suffered much from his aloofness, but he gained much also. In the midst of gross and tawdry romanticisms he refused to be swallowed up, but went his own way, a rebel in the cause of beauty, discovering in consequence a finer romanticism than was before known in America.

Vernon Louis Parrington
Main Currents in American Thought, Vol. II
(New York: Harcourt, Brace, 1927), pp. 58-59

Perhaps there is no better instance in all literature of important achievement in despite of ethical weakness; which is but another way of saying that Poe just falls short of the heights because of ethical weakness. He was singularly wanting in interest in the actual life of experience which the great artists have represented and interpreted; he was as remote from the world of Shakespeare as any writer of his caliber could be. He was so indifferent to the phenomena and the problems of actual life that he barely managed to secure the materials for his own private house of art—his dream-world within the Shakesperian dream-world of actual life. While a writer like Shakespeare, as Coleridge rightly insisted, is in the march of the human affections, attuned to the law of human nature, a writer like Poe pursues his solitary way as if ignorant of the meaning of the human spectacle, and, although he orders his experience in shapes that are exquisite, leaves the major part of our human nature unresponsive. As a consequence of his lack of interest in humanity, his art is lyrical—limited to the re-creation of a mood, whether in his poems or in his tales. The subjective mood objectified and depersonalized is his almost unvarying substitute for the impersonal representation of life which is the aim of the realist and the impersonal imitation of the ideal which is the aim of the classicist. All high types of realism and classicism demand a grasp on man's "pathos" and "ethos," on the fluctuant life of emotion and the deeply established life of character, to both of which Poe was a stranger. His knowledge of character was obviously rudimentary (contrast Jane Austen, who was writing in his boyhood, or even Scott, another writer of his time, or the author of *The Scarlet Letter*), and his knowledge of the play of emotions in our reaction to the happenings of life was little more sophisticated—he knew only, or at least used only, a very few kinds of emotion, and used them broadly, elementarily, and not with subtlety, delicacy, or a sense of their multitudinous interrelations, as they are represented by Toystoy, or Meredith, or Henry James. It may be that he chose his materials deliberately; but this is not to say that he could have chosen otherwise had he so desired—the more one reads Poe, the more one feels that he used with supreme power the scant and inferior materials that he possessed. He was a master of creative imagination, but the chaos to which he gave form was but a small fragment of the whole.

Norman Foerster
American Criticism (Boston: Houghton Mifflin,
1928), pp. 14-15

Was this restless unbalanced person with his strange mentality wandering on the bounds of crime and genius a madman or a genius? "These distinctions in their absolute rigor," affirms Claude Bernard, "are only medical rubbish; genius and madness are only exaggerations of a healthy mediocrity." Nevertheless it is hardly to be doubted that towards the end of his career, beginning with his second stay in New York, and especially after the death of his dear Virginia, this poor superior degenerate was only a sort of partially reasoning madman, a half-insane person, whose circular, double-formed madness permitted the dipsomaniac impulses to graft themselves on the phases of melancholic depression and the flights of mystic erotomania on the crises of maniacal exaltation.

. . . The poetry made on this unstable basis, from the first lispings to the final divagations, sings its mournful melody, and, coming as it did from the depths of unconsciousness, survived the reason which it preceded. The criticism combines the sharp intolerance of an egotism as full of pride as of suspicions. The stories are prodigal in the most hallucinated visions of fear and the most obsessing impulse of crime, the most adventurous flights of intuition and the most inconceivable chimeras of imagination. His most grotesque humor only comes from behind the grin of a mask grimacing to hide its macabre ghosts and its depths of sadness, and the wildest of his dialectics only improvise boldly on a fragile basis of science and divination the most fantastic construction of an occult pantheism. The whole of this monstrous work quivers under the breath of madness, and sustains itself only through the invisible logic of happy proportion and the secret virtue of subtle artifices. But such is the prestige of so much art victorious over so great a frenzy that even the most recalcitrant judge must let slip the irresistible confession: "No, this extraordinary man who in several masterpieces has revealed in so masterly a way to humanity some of its most unusual aspects and some of the most supreme emotions was only a madman; or, if the word genius really means a superior originality, he had in his madness an inseparable as well as an undeniable share of genius."

Emile Lauvrière
The Strange Life and Strange Loves of Edgar Allan Poe
(Philadelphia: Lippincott, 1935), pp. 412-14

[I]n Poe, obscurantism has ceased to be merely an accident of inadequate understanding; it has become the explicit aim of writing and has begun the generation of a method. . . .

Poe . . . endeavors as far as may be to escape from a paraphrasable theme; he recognizes no obligation to understand the minimum of theme from which he cannot escape—in fact, he seems to recognize an obligation not to understand it; his historical training and understanding amounted nearly to nothing; so that there is nothing in his work either to justify his formulary expression and to give it content and precision of meaning, on the one hand, or, on the other, to give his work as a whole sufficient force and substance to make us forget the formulary expression—we merely have melodramatic stereotypes in a vacuum. The last instrument which, if well-employed, might to some extent have alleviated his phrasing, and which did, in fact, alleviate it in part in a few fragments . . . , the instrument of meter, he was unable to control except occasionally and accidentally. His theory of meter was false. Whether the theory arose from imperception or led to imperception is immaterial, but the fact remains that his meter is almost invariably clumsy and mechanical in a measure perhaps never equalled by another poet who has enjoyed a comparable reputation.

Yvor Winters
Maule's Curse (Norfolk, Conn.: New Directions,
1938), pp. 106, 118-19

. . . Poe had not made the major transition which the later nineteenth century would make, namely, that of lifting the burden of moral responsibility from the individual and imposing it on society. Poe's moral world was the "agony" of men who are morally responsible but who have somehow lost all awareness of and any reason for their responsibility. Guilt and evil are all the more appalling because they exist in the ever-worsening condition of the world, and yet no one is to blame. Men are forced to exist in this drama of terror and death as though there were some long-enduring and consistent regimen of action and judgment; all the while, however, they must improvise on the moment whatever is their action and moral justification. Roderick Usher, William Wilson, the man in the crowd, Montresor in "The Cask of Amontillado"—all these and others comport themselves and are necessarily judged as though there were a massive tradition or morality behind them, but they have themselves never known what it was. They are like Kafka's man in *The Trial* who never knows the charges contained in his indictment. . . .

. . . Poe . . . tried to swallow the new science whole and make it a substitute for the ritualized and dying faith in which he was reared. But what he thought was "science" was, after all, only his own private reconstruction of reality, not a system, not a logic, not even a moral scheme. It was a continued act of will which attempted to make reasonable a wholly irrational world. Thus "reality" and man's good and evil were not a science or an order at all but an imaginative construct; whatever moral or religious system there was must be contained only within a single knowing mind which faced a different situation every time it had a thought. . . . [ca. 1957]

Edward H. Davidson
in *Interpretations of American Literature*, eds. C. Feidelson, Jr., and P. Brodtkorb, Jr. (New York: Oxford Univ. Pr., 1959), pp. 81-82

HARRIET BEECHER STOWE
1811-1896

> Born June 14 in Litchfield, Connecticut. In 1832, her family moved to Cincinnati. She married Calvin E. Stowe in 1836. *The Mayflower* was published in 1843. In 1850 she moved with her family to Brunswick, Maine. She began *Uncle Tom's Cabin* in 1851 as a serial for *The National Era*, and it was published in two volumes in 1852. In 1853, *A Key to Uncle Tom's Cabin* was published. She visited Europe in the same year. *Dred: A Tale of the Dismal Swamp* was published in 1856 and *The Minister's Wooing* in 1859. She died July 1 in Hartford, Connecticut.
>
> *The Writings of Harriet Beecher Stowe* (1896), 16 vols.
>
> Forrest Wilson, *Crusader in Crinoline: The Life of Harriet Beecher Stowe* (1941)

Diminish it as one may by stressing its sentimentalities or juxtaposing against it gentler glimpses of slavery, there is no denying that *Uncle Tom's Cabin* presents an elementary human condition with all its stark humiliations and compulsions, the straits of mind and body and feeling to which man can reduce man. Viewed at a distance, apart from its inevitable association with a cause, its worth becomes that of the typical or prototypical; subtract it from literary history, and a certain evaluation of human experience would be gone. Slavery is, unhappily, a point of reference for many human judgments. . . .

[N]o doubt [Mrs. Stowe] was moved in the writing of her novel by an instinctive compassion; but she seems to have been pushed by another more personal motive, one which she touched upon again and again in her fumbling efforts at explanation. She had been caught in the toils of a [religious] formula as harsh and unyielding as any physical institution of bondage, in which torture was made the eternal destiny of a race whose earthly position at best was servile; the problem involved was one of first magnitude, one of the great type problems of human experience; she had confronted it without remission for more than thirty years; it had been personalized by the unflinching presence of Lyman Beecher; since her marriage she had found it forever at her side in the solid dogmatism of

Calvin Stowe; she had never truly resolved it. . . . In the midst of a bitter climax of revolt she had caught the dark image of the endless restraints imposed by the Fugitive Slave Law; that baffling snare was the final image of restriction. Ardent and tired and overwrought, in that sensitive state where the imagination grows fluid, where inner and outer motives coalesce, she had taken bondage as her theme, had become obsessed with its conditions, morbidly obsessed by the concomitant of punishment, the terrible infliction of pain; freedom at any cost, at the last cost, became her immense preoccupation. . . .

Then deep-laid patterns of escape, bondage, and rebellion were cloudy but familiar patterns for a public whose heritage in the main was identical with that of Mrs. Stowe, which had been bred largely in the same faith, and was breaking away from this with a prodigious sense of fortitude. The binding passionate, highly personalized emotion of the book seemed to envelop something elementary in the temper of the time. . . . At a swift turn Mrs. Stowe was hailed as the leader, even the creator of the contemporary movement against slavery. At a stroke she reaped the reward of the long and arduous labors accomplished through more than twenty years by that small group of iconoclasts whose leader was Garrison. Unwittingly she had written an abolition manifesto.

Constance Rourke
Trumpets of Jubilee (New York:
Harcourt, Brace, 1927), pp. 105, 107-9

Unquestionably Mrs. Stowe, a Northerner, did not know the Negro. The prototypes of George Harris and Eliza, mulattoes, she professed to have seen, and as a result they are more real than Uncle Tom, who is fairly canonized into sainthood, or the vaudeville Topsy, who never could have lived and yet who never will die. Her second phase of Uncle Tom, the Uncle Tom of the New Orleans aristocracy, is of *Godey's Lady's Book* texture. She knew no more of fashionable life in the creole city than the "females" of the thirties did of the Apennines where they found the villains for their romances. And the final Simon Legree climax is pure melodrama. Uncle Tom's religion now becomes fairly nauseating.

That Mrs. Stowe wrote the novel to placate the South, that she made of Simon Legree a Northern Yankee to forestall their anger, that she had no thought of any purpose save that of bringing North and South into harmony on the question that was bringing them to the brink of war, is disproved by the novel itself. To put forth such a claim is to confess to not having read the story straight through. The book was a stone from a sling; it was written with singleness of purpose; abolition is written on every page of it. And it accomplished its purpose. One need say no more. To analyze it for defects—and its defects are sophomoric—is totally useless. In the light of its amazing world-wide popularity, all criticism fades into nothingness. It came in the one moment of history when such success could have been possible. But come it did, and there is no escaping the fact that it will stand for long among the greatest masterpieces of fiction.

Fred L. Pattee
The First Century of American Literature (New York:
Appleton, 1935), p. 573

Cold figures tell that 300,000 copies [of *Uncle Tom's Cabin*] were sold the first year, but no figures can express the extent of its influence on the popular mind. Mrs. Stowe articulated what was already felt by millions, but she added new data so that vicariously her readers enormously extended the range of their experience. She could write with the authority and inspiration of a prophet, but she could also express herself on such a plane that her book could be "read equally in the parlour and the kitchen and the nursery of every house." Like Dickens she realized how slight a partition separates the fields of humor and pathos, and she moved freely in either area. If modern readers are inclined to feel that the deaths of Eva and Tom are touched with bathos, contemporary readers saw only tragedy in them. And even now, such was the flame of Mrs. Stowe's vehement ardor, the book is capable of enkindling the mind with strong feeling over issues that have long since become cold matter in most of the anti-slavery literature of the era, including much of Whittier's fierce invective. Imitations of Mrs. Stowe's work sprang up everywhere, but out of the immense body of "Uncle Tom literature" almost nothing has become permanent. Although structurally simple, Mrs. Stowe's book was essentially inimitable.

Alexander Cowie
Rise of the American Novel (New York:
American Book, 1948), pp. 449-50

With the exception of Hawthorne, she is the only very important New England novelist, and when we remember how little of New England actually found expression in Hawthorne's exquisite achievement, she is New England's most revealing native novelist. . . . Unlike Hawthorne, Harriet Beecher Stowe was precisely rather than loosely Puritan. Her whole life was a struggle with the premises Jonathan Edwards established with the authority of science and religion to return the spreading New England mind to those profound channels to salvation preached by Thomas Shepard and other seventeenth century divines. Original sin, predestination, freedom of the will, the burning necessity for a sincere conversion, grace, heaven, and hell: these were her primary points of reference as she carried out "symbolic action" in writing her novels.

She spoke, therefore, from far more deeply within the New England tradition than Hawthorne. . . . The essence of her achievement [is] her extraordinary talent for seeing Puritan New England steadily and for seeing it whole and for dramatizing it with vividly specific and often charmingly humorous detail. She can help us understand all varieties of New England character from the most granite-like stubbornness to the most mystical and loving submission; she can lead us credibly through the inner adventures of those blessed or cursed by Calvinism. Through her vigorously imagined world and through the inner history behind her fiction, we can experience afresh our New England past in its full human dimensions and its intellectual and emotional complexities.

Charles H. Foster
The Rungless Ladder (Durham, N. C.: Duke Univ..
Pr., 1954), pp. x-xi

Apart from a literary style that recalls (and probably influenced) the phthisic Sunday-school prizes which reconciled working class children to malnutrition and a premature transfiguration, *Uncle Tom's Cabin* has been chiefly neglected—in our own age—because it is hard to accept that an instrument of historical change should also be a work of art. The Victorian men of letters who were also liberals had to swallow *Uncle Tom's Cabin* whole without meanly regurgitating the style. But the book's popularity soon made it possible to discount the literary content altogether. It was eaten in fragments—tract-abridgements, school-selections, dramatic adaptations. As a barnstorming melodrama on tour (little Eva dragged heavenwards on a pulley) as a silent film (accompanied by the tunes of Stephen Foster), it held a large public till late in the nineteen-twenties. Even in Catholic Lancashire, where I was brought up, it was part of the pop-art of childhood, though the Church had placed it on the *Index* and enfranchisement had raised the price of cotton in our grandfathers' hard times. The vitality of the work is considerable. It survived its debasement as a bogus Siamese *wayang* in *The King and I,* recalling that Anna Leonowens had written to Mrs. Stowe about the Lady Sonn Klean's liberating all her slaves, saying: "I am wishful to be good like Harriet Beecher Stowe, and never again to buy human bodies, but only to let them go free once more." Now it seems, we have to take the whole book again, since there is little relevant to our age that can be taken out of it. Today's Negroes, who reject martyrdom and intend to overcome, are ashamed of bible-thumbing Uncle Tom; George Harris, prophet of a vital Africa, has become a demagogue with two gold Cadillacs. If the book is to mean anything now, a good deal of meaning must reside in the art.

Reading it, we find that all we have to forgive is the style. This is an un-American activity, a cluster of fashionable importations—chiefly from

Scott and Dickens, though in the Simon Legree episodes, Mrs. Stowe draws on the earlier Gothic which continues, in more sophisticated forms, to exert its appeal for Americans. Structurally, the book is very sound, and it even has a visual skeleton provided by the geography of slavery.

Anthony Burgess
Encounter (July, 1966), pp. 54-55

EDWARD TAYLOR

1645-1729

> Born in Leicestershire, England. He emigrated to Boston in 1668 and was admitted to Harvard as a sophomore, graduating in 1671. In 1679, he was ordained a minister in Westfield, Massachusetts. He wrote poetry throughout his ministry, but none was printed until 1939 (see below). He died June 24.
>
> Thomas H. Johnson, ed., *The Poetical Works of Edward Taylor* (1939) (contains biography)

Edward Taylor (1645-1729) broke through the restraints of strict Puritan literary doctrine in his best work, which is quite able to stand comparison with most of the major English religious poetry of the seventeenth century. He was born in England, came to Massachusetts in 1668, graduated from Harvard in 1671, and served as a physician and minister in Westfield until his death. He grew up when the poems of John Donne, George Herbert, and others of the English "metaphysicals," were still in vogue, and most of his own work is in their manner. It relies constantly on heavily charged metaphors and similes, prefers strength to smoothness in meter, plays with both the sound and sense of words, and deals constantly in hyperbole, sharp contrasts and even paradox. Taylor loved gems and perfumes as sources of imagery, his allusions to music suggest that he loved it, too, and his special affection for the *Song of Solomon* indicates his sensuous temperament. Throughout his work there is a feeling of conflict between that temperament and his Puritanical dread of encouraging the "Sensual Appetite" to carry off the "Reasonable Soule" on its back. Some of the strongest dramatic effects in his poems come from the conflict, and his request that his poems be not published may show that he realized that he had yielded sometimes to the affections' "hankering" after "Carnall things."

Some of his poetic virtues come, nonetheless, from his skilful and imaginative use of characteristically Puritan methods. By making the homeliest and most familiar images symbolize the loftiest spiritual realities; by constantly throwing his work into dramatic forms in which God, Christ, Satan, Mercy, Justice, and the soul are actors and speakers who often talk in the earthiest of dialects; by making bold and often startlingly effective juxtapositions of the most commonplace and the most exalted in language and matter; and by constantly lighting up doctrine by specific applications of it to human situations, just as the preachers were wont to do, he showed what admirable use a genuine artist could make of the Puritan literary code.

Kenneth B. Murdock
The Literature of the American People (New York:
Appleton-Century-Crofts, 1951), p. 57

Poetry with Taylor's peculiar quality could not, I think, have been written at all in England, even by Taylor himself. For the writer in England, wherever he may be living, works within a certain conditioning imposed by the context of that intimate island's culture; he knows the ways of other learned, literary men; he senses the current modes of writing; and even though he believes in freedom of language, as Baxter does, the writer is nevertheless tacitly and unconsciously influenced by the accepted conventions of public speech and writing in that culture. George Herbert lived in Bemerton, a country parson, and yet he could walk from there to the high and ancient culture of Salisbury. But in Taylor's frontier settlement these guide-lines fall away; cultivated conversation becomes rare; the minister's work is solely occupied with humble folk; his daily life is rude, simple, concerned with the bare stark facts of survival in a village that is at times little more than a stockade. Even the intellectual life must be limited to the essentials: Taylor's library at his death contained only one work of English poetry: the poems of Anne Bradstreet.

Thus the poet's conversations with God are spoken in a language that the meditative poet, living in England, would never use. For the soul, in meditation, is to speak as the man himself has come to speak; any other language would be dishonest and pretentious. So Taylor speaks in this peculiar mixture of the learned and the rude, the abstract and the earthy, the polite and the vulgar; for such distinctions do not exist in the wilderness.

The result is often lame and crude; in some respects the writer needs the support and guidance of an established culture; but since he in himself is almost the sole bearer and creator of whatever culture his village will possess, he must do what he can with whatever materials lie at hand. Out of his very deficiencies he creates a work of rugged and original integrity. The result helps to mark the beginning of an American language, an American literature.

Louis L. Martz
Foreword in *The Poems of Edward Taylor*, ed. Donald E. Stanford.
(New Haven: Yale Univ. Pr., 1960), pp. xxxvi-xxxvii

A number of Taylor's poems cannot be understood without an awareness of the typology behind them. Taylor's typology was the result of reading the entire Bible as a continuous history of God's chosen people; it had its origins in the Middle Ages, but it was emphasized and elaborated by the Puritans, who based their whole theology on the Bible and constantly sought in it answers to their spiritual and material problems; it was the result, in part, of constantly reading the Old Testament in terms of the New Testament, of looking for events in the Old Testament which foreshadowed events in the New Testament. Thus the ram which was sacrificed in place of Isaac foreshadowed Jesus who was sacrificed for man. The ram was the type; Jesus was the antitype. Similarly, Jonah's experience with the whale was a type of Jesus' burial and resurrection. Other types of Christ were Moses, Noah, and Joseph. The type of Christian baptism was Circumcision. The Jewish Passover was a type of the Lord's Supper.

Many of the Meditations were inspired by the Song of Solomon, always referred to by Taylor as Canticles and always understood according to the allegorical interpretation of the period. The two chief personages in Canticles are the bride and the bridegroom. Christ is the bridegroom and the Church (in Puritan terms, the Saints) is the bride.

Donald E. Stanford, ed.
The Poems of Edward Taylor (New Haven:
Yale Univ. Pr., 1960), p. liii

Taylor's relation to the mainstream of American literature raises an important issue. Some critics would have it that Taylor was merely a transplanted and "fossilized" Englishman or that his works might have been written anywhere in the world Taylor happened to be. But though in spirit and in form his work recalls writers of all times and many places, in motive and subject it belongs inescapably to seventeenth-century America. The Christ Taylor celebrated and imitated in his poems; the doctrines of his faith; the people and activities he valued; the terms he used and the concepts they held—all were defined and distinguished by the accumulated experience of colonial New England. Nowhere in the world did the Congregational system and Federal theology work out their implications and ideals so freely and fully as in Connecticut and Massachusetts. Admittedly, Taylor rarely treats his American situation directly; when he does, as in the elegies, the results are generally poor. The history of the New World was too recent and too little to provide the "stuff" of poetry. And his major poems almost never allude to his American locale. But these facts in no way minimize the influence of his American experience. Taylor transcended his frontier circumstances not by leaving them behind, but by transforming them into intellectual, aesthetic, and spiritual universals.

The curious thing about Taylor is that this transcendence resulted from no cosmopolitan ambition, but from his mystical introversion; his inward exploration of soul led him, deserving and fortunate, as Conrad would say, to speak like other artists "to our capacity for delight and wonder, to the sense of mystery surrounding our lives; to our sense of pity, and beauty, and pain; to the latent feeling of fellowship with all creation. . . ." Taylor's theology, his intense faith, and the American spiritual community in which he lived, combined to give a structure or form to his rapturous experience of reality; and they also provided a way of talking about it that is as valid now as it was for Taylor or for Plato. But the mystical experience, unfortunately, does not yield to the test of other experience at all. By tracing it, describing it, reacting to it, and praising it, Taylor limited his poetry; but he never relegated his verses to a minor activity. Unlike Milton, he could not have written poetry left-handed for fifteen years; for his poetry was to him a living act, his most prominent sign of the unitive life attained over a half century of painful endeavor and devotion. From time to time his writing moved him to think himself soaring above the stars to stand at heaven's door. But that mystical door always opened into the meeting-house at Westfield, admitting him to the society of Christ to whom he had a special calling in the suburbs of glory in America.

Norman S. Grabo
Edward Taylor (New York: Twayne, 1961), pp. 172-73

Taylor's work is the richest, freest, and most varied among Puritan poets. His imagination is funded with splendid exotic images as well as mundane, homely ones; and he can use them side by side. He shows evidence of having a larger sense of humanity than do his peers; he of all of them is the nearest to the English baroque poets. But he finally lacks the flexibility of a Herbert, not to say of a Donne or a Crashaw or a Vaughan. For all his luxuriating in "un-Puritan" images, he is nonetheless first and last a Puritan poet: concerned to show how his images speak for God, not for themselves; concerned not to image the situation of a man seeking, against all adverse forces, to know his God, but rather that of a man who has discovered that, in the sight of God to be a man—bound by human images —is to be at once everything and nothing."

Roy Harvey Pearce
The Continuity of Amercian Poetry (Princeton, N. J.:
Princeton Univ. Pr., 1961), p. 48

HENRY DAVID THOREAU

1817-1862

Born July 12 in Concord, Massachusetts. He entered Harvard in 1833 and graduated in 1837. In 1838, he opened a private school with his brother. In 1841, he took up residence at Emerson's home. He took over his family's business of pencil manufacturing in 1844. On July 4, 1845 he took up residence at Walden Pond and remained there until Sept. 6, 1847. In 1849, *A Week on The Concord and Merrimack Rivers* and "Civil Disobedience" were published. *Walden* was published in 1854 and "A Plea for John Brown" in 1859. In 1861, he went to Minnesota. He died May 6 at Concord.

The Writings of Henry David Thoreau . . . (1906), 20 vols. (Walden Edition)

Joseph Wood Krutch, *Henry David Thoreau* (1948)

PERSONAL

Those who really faced the wilderness, and sought to make something out of it, remained in the East; in their reflection, one sees the reality that might have been. Henry David Thoreau was perhaps the only man who paused to give a report of the full experience. In a period when men were on the move, he remained still; when men were on the make, he remained poor; when civil disobedience broke out in the lawlessness of the cattle thief and the mining town rowdy, by sheer neglect, Thoreau practiced civil disobedience as a principle, in protest against the Mexican War, the Fugitive Slave Law, and slavery itself. Thoreau in his life and letters shows what the pioneer movement might have come to if this great migration had sought culture rather than material conquest, and an intensity of life, rather than mere extension over the continent.

Lewis Mumford
The Golden Day (New York: Norton, 1926), pp. 107-8

Thoreau began, like most New England boys, with a gun and a fishing rod. He loved, as he says, the wild not less than the good, and his savage nature like his spiritual grew stronger in the woods. He had a taste for violence. But the wild thing captivated his imagination and stirred his mind. He sublimated his savagery into observation and comment. He sublimated his passions also into this single passion. As we find him in his Journal, he had apparently no amorous emotions which could not be satisfied by friendship, and indeed friendship with him seems to be synonymous with love, and is regarded as something to be won rather than enjoyed. He had dreamed of sexual intercourse as "incredibly beautiful, too fair to be remembered," * and had no patience with primness, though he was exasperated beyond measure by lewd talk. Yet love of woman for him was entirely sublimated into his passion for nature. I do not mean pantheism, or any ism, I mean a literal passion for wild experience. Hence the prime demand that society makes upon the individual meant nothing to him personally. He could love a sunset readily, but not a girl. His fright when one woman wanted to marry him is delicious.

*Letter to Harrison Blake, Sept. 1, p. 52.

The ferocity of sex pursuit bent away in him from sex to nature. He was clearly a lover in his walks, with a lover's jealousy for his solitude, and a lover's reticence as to his ends. I do not think this either morbid or pathological. The rather rarefied purity of his Concord circle made such a course easier than it would have been, say, in Italy, and it is more than probable that his rule of nonintercourse with mere society kept temptation away. But there is nothing surprising in his shift of love. It is a phase of the merging of the carnal into the divine familiar in other civilizations. There was nothing inhuman in Thoreau. With children he was delightful, and his fierce intolerance of polite conversation was unsocial perhaps, but certainly not true misanthropy.

He was, if you please, a "case" of the romantic movement, where nature becomes an obsession and loving observation a passion so satisfying as to engross the best energies. With Thoreau it was a permanent obsession. It is White of Selborne getting his love and his religion from the fruit of his sight. The "bliss of solitude" to such men is a passionate joy because the endless variety, movement, mystery, and beauty of nature satisfy every one of their emotions, absorbing their energies as fast as produced. Men in war and great adventure are so engrossed, and we take it with them as a matter of course. With Thoreau, it was doubly engrossing because his critical, philosophic mind hovered, like his favorite marsh hawk, above the sly coverts of his instincts, viewing each minute experience from on high as possible game for the soul—an ultimate secret slipping through the world's wild bush.

Henry Seidel Canby
Classic Americans (New York: Harcourt, Brace, 1931),
pp. 194-95

With all his aversion to distant movement [Thoreau] was not unrelated to the mythical figure of the Yankee peddler; he made the same calculations, many of them close and shrewd, often in the area of bargaining. He had that air of turning the tables on listeners or observers which had long since belonged to the Yankee of the comic mythologies; he used a wry humor in slow prose argument; he kept the habitual composure. Whoever might be his companion Thoreau seemed always alone, like the legendary Yankee. His tough and sinuous reveries were unbroken. "In any weather, at any hour of the day or night, I have been anxious to improve the nick of time, and notch it on my stick too; to stand on the meeting of two eternities, the past and the future, which is precisely the present moment; to toe that line." Here was the essence of self-consciousness, revealed in Yankee speech. Yet this always verged toward the abstract, slipping aside from personal revelation, and moving with increasing frequency toward another theme which had engrossed the Yankee, the land. That sense of wild land which had infused the Yankee monologues, creating a spare imagery and metaphor, was pressed by Thoreau back to its source until he obtained a whole subject. . . .

Whole passages of Thoreau's writing will have an unmistakable native authority, the true sound of native speech; others follow that are close and studied, narrow and purely literary. He produced no philosophy, though he obviously intended to construct a philosophy. His experience at Walden remains a singular experience; he is read for the aphorism or the brief description, for the Yankee character inadvertently revealed, for the shadowy impersonal soliloquy sounding even through the more prosaic talk like water underground. [c. 1931]

Constance Rourke
American Humor (New York: Doubleday, 1953), pp. 136-37

Walden

Very insignificant appeared Thoreau's little adventure in regional pioneering on the Walden frontier during the Golden Age of transcendentalism when his fellow transcendentalists were lending their praise to the American energy that swept the continent to open up a garden of plenty. Very foolish appeared Thoreau's adventure in spiritual pioneering, his experiment in a simple and satisfying life, to the ambitious scramblers for the spoils of the Gilded Age when Big Business was capitalizing the resources of a new west. It was not until the passing of the last American frontier, the disappearance of free land and easy fortune, that the American public, beginning to question the traditional concepts of "progress" and "success" read as a new discovery Thoreau's farsighted strictures against the passion for possession, that it read with new enthusiasm his invitation to build in the heart of the bustling trivialities a Walden of our own where we may pursue our private adventure in intensive pioneering.

And yet the modern reader, for all his admiration of Thoreau, doubts the complete adequacy of his solution. He cannot forget that Thoreau did his pioneering on the free land of Emerson's wood lot; that Thoreau's quarrel with the government was settled by Emerson's paying his poll tax; that the wages of the day labor by which Thoreau earned his living were fixed by men who worked not six weeks but twelve months a year. *Walden* is fascinating as the adventure of a solitary pioneer; it is fallacious as the guidebook for a general migration. An idyl of the golden age of transcendentalism, it is an ineffectual protest against the gilded age of industrialism. [ca. 1927]

Lucy Lockwood Hazard
The Frontier in American Literature (New York:
Barnes and Noble, 1941), p. 170

In his retreat in Walden, Thoreau came closer than any one in his age to putting into effect the doctrine of self-reliance which his friend Emerson preached and which most of his transcendentalist contemporaries advocated. There he achieved the comparatively untrammelled individual freedom which others talked about but never attained. Absurd as Thoreau's retreat may strike many to-day, it must be admitted that it was but a rational outcome of the individualistic philosophy which the frontier had inspired. If Emerson and others had literally believed in practising what they preached they would have followed Thoreau to the woods—and to jail. Emerson, however, preferred to remain the "seeing eye" but not "the working hand." Emerson loathed the crushing weight of institutions and the interfering power of the state; he maintained that "no law (could) be sacred to (him) but that of (his) nature"; but in the last analysis he preferred compromising with the state to fighting it. . . . If later events have tended to make Thoreau appear a little ludicrous, behaving and living as he did, we should remember that it is really not Thoreau but his doctrine that has come to look ludicrous. Emerson was saved from that ludicrousness because he never tried out what he advised, because he never tested what he taught. If there was a Quixotic element about Thoreau, it was the Quixoticism of the extremist—the man who, refusing to compromise, dauntlessly follows his logic where it leads.

V. F. Calverton
The Liberation of American Literature (New York: Scribner's, 1932), pp. 262-63

The meandering course of Thoreau's reflections . . . should not obscure his full discovery that the uneradicated wildness of man is the anarchical basis both of all that is most dangerous and most valuable in him. That he could dig down to the roots of primitive poetry without going a mile from Concord accounts for his ability to create "a true Homeric or Paphlagonian man" in the likeness of the French woodchopper. It also helps account for the fact that by following to its uncompromising conclusion his belief that great art can grow from the center of the simplest life, he was able to be universal. He had understood that in the act of expression a man's whole being, and his natural and social background as well, function organically together. He had mastered a definition of art akin to what Maritain has extracted from scholasticism: *Recta ratio factibilium*, the right ordering of the thing to be made, the right revelation of the material.

F. O. Matthiessen
American Renaissance (New York: Oxford Univ. Pr., 1941), p. 175

Walden is . . . a vast rebirth ritual, the purest and most complete in our literature. We know rebirth rituals to operate characteristically by means of fire, ice or decay, mountains and pits, but we are staggered by the amount and variety of these in the book. We see Thoreau build his shanty of boards he has first purified in the sun, record approvingly an Indian purification ritual of burning all the tribe's old belongings and provisions, and later go off into a description of the way he is cleansed and renewed by his own fireplace. We see him note the magic purity of the ice on Walden Pond, the fact that frozen water never turns stale, and the rebirth involved when the ice breaks up, all sins are forgiven, and "Walden was dead and is alive again." We see him exploring every phase and type of decay: rotting ice, decaying trees, moldy pitch pine and rotten wood, excrement, maggots, a vulture feeding on a dead horse, carrion, tainted meat, and putrid water.

The whole of *Walden* runs to symbols of graves and coffins, with consequent rising from them, to wombs and emergence from them, and ends on the fable of a live insect resurrected from an egg long buried in wood. Each day at Walden Thoreau was reborn by his bath in the pond, a religious exercise he says he took for purification and renewal, and the whole two years and two months he compresses into the cycle of a year, to frame the book on the basic rebirth pattern of the death and renewal of vegetation, ending it with the magical emergence of spring.

On the thread of decay and rebirth Thoreau strings all his preoccupations. Meat is a symbol of evil, sensuality; its tainting symbolizes goodness and affection corrupted; the shameful defilement of chastity smells like carrion (in which he agreed with Shakespeare); the eating of meat causes slavery and unjust war. (Thoreau, who was a vegetarian, sometimes felt so wild he was tempted to seize and devour a woodchuck raw, or yearned like a savage for the raw marrow of kudus—those were the periods when he wanted to seize the world by the neck and hold it under water like a dog until it drowned.)

But even slavery and injustice are a decaying and a death, and Thoreau concludes "Slavery in Massachusetts" with: "We do not complain that they *live*, but that they do not *get buried*. Let the living bury them; even they are good for manure." Always, in Thoreau's imagery, what this rotting meat will fertilize is fruit, ripe fruit. It is his chief good. He wanted "the flower and fruit of man," the "ripeness." The perfect and glorious state he foresees will bear men as fruit, suffering them to drop off as they ripen; John Brown's heroism is a good seed that will bear good fruit, a future crop of heroes. Just as Brown, in one of the most terrifying puns ever written, was "ripe" for the gallows, Thoreau reports after writing "Civil Disobedience," as he dwells on action and wildness, that he feels ripe, fertile: "It is seedtime with me. I have lain fallow long enough." On the metaphor of the organic process of birth, growth, decay, and rebirth out of decay, Thoreau organizes his whole life and experience.

Stanley Edgar Hyman
At (November, 1946), p. 140

GENERAL

Perhaps, in the end, what remains in the mind of the reader is the sense of constant expectancy that plays on almost every page of [Thoreau's] works. "Is not the attitude of expectation somewhat divine?" he asks in one of his letters, and always it is morning with him. The clearest expression of this buoyancy of the dawn may be found in the account of *A Walk to Wachusett*, but it is never long absent from the Journal and was a characteristic of his daily life. He walked the fields like one who was on the alert for some divine apparition, and Mr. M. D. Conway has observed that a strange light seemed to shine on his countenance when abroad. This, too, is a trait of the romantic spirit, no doubt; but its quality in Thoreau does not point to Germany. It came to him in part from his birth in a new land, and it was strengthened by his familiarity with English poets of the seventeenth century. In the works of Henry Vaughan more particularly you will find this note of expectation, rising at times to a cry of ecstasy for which there is no equivalent in the later American. I think of Vaughan as travelling his quiet rounds in his Silurian hills, with an eye open to every impression, and a heart like Thoreau's always filled with the waiting wonder of the dawn. If his mood strikes deeper than Thoreau's, it is because coming before the romantic worship of the individual, he never cut himself off from the Church and State, but moved in the greater currents of tradition. [ca. 1908]

Paul Elmer More
Shelburne Essays on American Literature (New York:
Harcourt, Brace, 1963), pp. 228-29

There is a hard pathos about Thoreau, the wanness of a stripped, unblossoming tree against a gray sky. He was intellectually one of the bravest men that ever lived, and also a clammy prig. He was a prose-stylist of singular and signal excellence and left no complete book behind him. The highest austerity assumes an inner fire; Thoreau did not even, like Emerson, recognize the necessary existence of warmth by regretting his want of it. He was wholly unaware of his human limitations, a bachelor and bachelor of nature from beginning to end. . . . Thoreau is a man and a writer, so to speak, in black and white. There is no color in him. A man like an etching. Nature had forgotten her drop of color in the jar. . . . Thoreau's style, for all its crystalline purity and lucidity, its happy balance, its exquisite moderation, does not continuously hold the reader. It is perhaps the best style yet written by an American. It slips from one's psychical grasp and is best tasted in single passages. It is the style of a great writer but of a defective man.

Ludwig Lewisohn
Expression in America (New York:
Harper, 1932), pp. 136, 140

Thoreau, like most other members of the hopeful party, understood dawn and birth better than he did night and death. He responded at once to the cockerel in the morning; the screech owls at night made him bookish and sentimental. And though their wailing spoke to him about "the low spirits and melancholy forebodings of fallen souls," the whole dark side of the world was no more than another guaranty of the inexhaustible variety of nature. Thoreau knew not evil; his American busk would have fallen short, like the bonfire in Hawthorne's fantasy, of the profounder need for the purification of the human heart. He would have burned away the past as the accumulation of artifice, in the name of the natural and the essential. But if the natural looked to him so much more wholesome and so much more dependable than others have since thought it, his account of the recovery of nature was never less than noble: the noblest expression, in fact and in language, of the first great aspiration of the age.

R. W. B. Lewis
The American Adam (Chicago:
Univ. Chicago Pr., 1955), p. 27

Thoreau, a Transcendentalist artist with unlimited faith in the symbolic resources and objective reach of his personal consciousness, conceived of his journal as a "song of myself" which theoretically, could have had as much objective artistic validity in its daily "nature notes" as other works that have come out of the romantic cult of the imagination. It is not absurd to say that Thoreau's Journals have the same broad intention—to show the meeting of the inner and external worlds—that Proust shows in erecting his great symphonic novel on the foundation of introspective analysis. Thoreau's favorite myth—the imagination (or "soul") in the material world is like Apollo condemned to work as a shepherd for King Admetus —was especially dear to Proust, who in the form of a quotation from Emerson used it as the epigraph to his first book, *Pleasures and Days*.

. . . Whether one thinks in terms of Proust or Joyce it is clear that like all the great twentieth-century writers whose concern with the stream-of-consciousness really starts from the romantic discovery of man's unconscious as a power of divination, Thoreau's whole literary faith is based on the mystic bonds between the private imagination and reality. Our generation is beginning to understand that Thoreau is not a "naturalist," and that the subject of his work is not the external scene, "nature," but the greater world of being with which the imagination claims affinities.

What makes Thoreau so different from the great modern Symbolist novelists is that he really had no subject but himself, and so had to strain for an "objectivity" that he could only simulate, not feel. Living in Concord with no real respect for anyone but himself, being a person with a shattering gift for holding his experience down to his image of what it should be, he let nothing grow wildly under his hand, allowed nothing to surprise him. He was always in control—in the Journals—and the life he held in such harsh control finally evaporated in his hands. He did not let the world flower under his benevolent gaze, as Whitman did—and Proust; he kept it as *his*, all the time, until there was nothing to possess but the Journals which the world rather tends to see as the dead records of his vanished love. [1958]

Alfred Kazin
Contemporaries (Boston: Little, Brown, 1962), pp. 49-50

MARK TWAIN (SAMUEL LANGHORNE CLEMENS)

1835-1910

> Born November 30 in Florida, Missouri. His father died in 1847, and he began to work as a typesetter in Hannibal, Missouri. In 1857, he became an apprentice pilot on the Mississippi River. He went to Nevada in 1861 as an assistant to his brother Orion, the Territorial Secretary. In 1862, he went to San Francisco, writing for newspapers there. *The Celebrated Jumping Frog of Calaveras County* was published in 1867. He sailed for the Holy Land 1867 and published *Innocents Abroad* in 1869. He married Olivia Langdon in 1870, and, in 1871, moved to Hartford, Connecticut. Many publications followed: *Roughing It* (1872); *The Gilded Age* (written with Charles Dudley Warner) (1874); *The Adventures of Tom Sawyer* (1875); *A Tramp Abroad* (1880); *The Prince and the Pauper* (1882); *Life on The Mississippi* (1883); *The Adventures of Huckleberry Finn* (1884); *A Connecticut Yankee at King Arthur's Court* (1889); *The Tragedy of Pudd'nhead Wilson* (1894); and *Personal Recollections of Joan of Arc* (1896). He received a Litt.D. from Oxford University in 1907. He died April 21 at Redding, Connecticut.

> Albert B. Paine, ed.,*The Writings of Mark Twain* (1922-25), 37 vols.
> J. De Lancey Ferguson, *Mark Twain: Man and Legend* (1943)

PERSONAL

[Mark Twain's personality] came into existence . . . through his mother's ruthless opposition to the poet in him, through the shock of his father's death; and every influence he had encountered in life had confirmed him in the pursuit of opulent respectability. . . . However, . . . this was not the real Mark Twain, this money-making, success-loving, wire-pulling Philistine; it was a sort of dissociated self, the race-character, which had risen in him with the stoppage of his true individuality. The real Mark Twain had been arrested in his development, the artist had remained rudimentary. . . .

. . . [H]is original submission to the taboos of his environment had prevented him from assimilating life: consequently, he was prevented as much by his own immaturity as by fear of public opinion from ever attempting seriously to recreate it in his imagination.

We can best describe Mark Twain therefore, as an improvisator, a spirit with none of the inner control, none of the self-determination of the artist, who composed extempore, as it were, and at the solicitation of influences external to himself.

Van Wyck Brooks
The Ordeal of Mark Twain (London:
Heinemann, 1922), p. 148, 164

At no time, except perhaps when he became so obsequious over the Oxford degree that was bestowed upon him, did Twain desert his forthright petty bourgeois point of view; at no time did he "sell out" his philosophy to the upper bourgeoisie of the East. In the twentieth century, if he had lived until our day, it is even likely that he might have joined in with Dreiser and taken a communistic stand. But living when he did, when all of America, even its labor movement, was dominated by a petty bourgeois instead of a proletarian psychology, the petty bourgeois position was the most advanced one of his type could take. To such as Twain it often seemed the stand of the revolutionary. In *Roughing It* he sarcastically condemned the American practice of not mining "the silver ourselves by the sweat of our brows and the labor of our hands, but to *sell* the ledges to the dull slaves of toil and let them do the mining." He was always enthusiastic about the French Revolution, and even defended the Terror without hesitation. . . .

Twain at least sought to make his philosophy inclusive. He tied up his art with his politics. . . . Even in *Huckleberry Finn*, the virtues extolled are those of the petty bourgeois frontiersman. Huck is a western lad, embodying the independent, dare-devil spirit of the region, a rapscallion type contemptuous of rules and regulations, scornful of Sunday-school and even of civilization—scornful of everything but himself and what he regards as right. Huck, an epic embodiment of the frontier in knee-pants, sticks by himself in defiance of what others think, in defiance even of institutions and all the moral paraphernalia of the conventional world.

V. F. Calverton
Liberation of American Literature (New York:
Scribner's, 1932), pp. 327-28

Mr. Brooks maintains that it was Mark Twain's pent-up genius, the un-expressed Shelley in him, that burst forth in the last two decades of his life in a terrible reaction against the materialism that had underlain his mature life. On the other hand, it is my belief that through a combination of circumstances, which have nothing to do with his hypothetical Shelley-ism, Mark Twain was totally unfitted to grow old; that the materialistic, "respectable" life he, a typical product of the unique atmosphere of the frontier, chose to lead among the "semi-rustic bourgeoisie" of New England denied him the philosophic background, the intellectual balance necessary to grow old gracefully. In a word, *Mark Twain's dilemma was the result of the failure of a dominant human trait he possessed to equip him for a normal human process.* Indeed, even at the risk of being unwarrantedly dramatic, it might be said that he was betrayed by his very humanity. It was a case chiefly of Tom Sawyer, of Hannibal, Missouri, growing old in Hartford, Connecticut.

What do Mark Twain's writings reveal of his intellectual processes—do they support my contention that his despair was only too natural to a Tom Sawyer who had attained his schoolboy's seventh heaven? They reveal, precisely what we should expect from the man whose "eternal youth" caused his books to sell into the millions of copies; the esthetic tastes of a fourteen-year-old; gravely delivered judgments on serious mat-ters which made up in naiveté what they lacked in profundity of thought; a delight in surreptitious obscenity, a yearning for revenge, a not infrequent conscious attempt to be funny which results only in flat artificiality—all very characteristic qualities of the average small boy! . . .

Thus Mark Twain remained throughout his life immature, socially, emotionally, intellectually; and thus when old age came he was totally unprepared for it.

Richard D. Altick
South Atlantic Quarterly (October, 1935),
pp. 361-62, 364-65

Huckleberry Finn

Mark Twain was a frontier humorist. His literary intelligence was shaped by the life of the frontier and found expression in the themes and forms developed by the humor of the frontier. Time's erosion simplifies much: it is now clear that Mark Twain, Henry James, and William Dean Howells wrote what is important of American literature in their period, and it is not Mark Twain's humor that gives him this permanence. For the future in America he is the author of *Roughing It, The Gilded Age, Life on the Mississippi, The Man Who Corrupted Hadleyburg, Pudd'nhead Wilson, The Adventures of Tom Sawyer,* and *The Adventures of Huckleberry Finn.*

But these books exist as satire and realism to which the frontier humorist attained. They are the humor of the frontier in its greatest incandescence, realizing its fullest scope and expressing its qualities on the level of genius. In them an American civilization sums up its experience; they are the climax of a literary tradition. But from the laughter of anonymous frontier story-tellers to the figure of Huckleberry Finn a clearly traced line exists, and Huckleberry Finn could have been arrived at along no other path.

Bernard De Voto
Mark Twain's America (Chautauqua, N. Y.:
Chautauqua Institution, 1932), pp. 240-41

Detailed study of the manuscript of his greatest book [*Adventures of Huckleberry Finn*] reveals no evidence of blighting censorship. The revisions show a skilled craftsman at work and show, too, that here as always he plunged at his writing with little preliminary planning, improvising as he went and frequently running into blind alleys. *Huck Finn* owes part of its superiority over *Tom Sawyer* to the fact that for its main outline it has only the familiar journey motif which always made Mark's thoughts flow most freely. As has been said, he simply took a clever and uninhibited boy, and let the whole world of the Mississippi happen to him. The great river itself bears Huck on from one experience to another, with none of the makeshift transitions that link Tom's adventures. After *Tom Sawyer* was finished Mark thought that he had perhaps made a mistake in not writing it in the first person; in Huck Finn he rectified that mistake, and gave the book the autobiographical form which is almost indispensable in successful picaresque romance.

J. De Lancey Ferguson
Mark Twain: Man and Legend (Indianapolis, Ind.:
Bobbs-Merrill, 1943), p. 227

In form and style *Huckleberry Finn* is an almost perfect work. Only one mistake has ever been charged against it, that it concludes with Tom Sawyer's elaborate, too elaborate, game of Jim's escape. Certainly this episode is too long—in the original draft it was much longer—and certainly it is a falling off, as almost anything would have to be, from the incidents of the river. Yet it has a certain formal aptness—like, say, that of the Turkish initiation which brings Molière's *Le Bourgeois Gentilhomme* to its close. It is a rather mechanical development of an idea, and yet some device is needed to permit Huck to return to his anonymity, to give up the role of hero, to fall into the background which he prefers, for he is modest in all things and could not well endure the attention and glamour which attend a hero at a book's end. For this purpose nothing could serve better than the mind of Tom Sawyer with its literary furnishings, its conscious romantic desire for experience and the hero's part, and its ingenious schematization of life to achieve that aim.

The form of the book is based on the simplest of all novel-forms, the so-called picaresque novel, or novel of the road, which strings its incidents on the line of the hero's travels. But, as Pascal says, "rivers are roads that move," and the movement of the road in its own mysterious life transmutes the primitive simplicity of the form: the road itself is the greatest character in this novel of the road, and the hero's departures from the river and his returns to it compose a subtle and significant pattern. The linear simplicity of the picaresque novel is further modified by the story's having a clear dramatic organization: it has a beginning, a middle, and an end, and a mounting suspense of interest.

As for the style of the book, it is not less than definitive in American literature. The prose of *Huckleberry Finn* established for written prose the virtues of American colloquial speech. This has nothing to do with pronunciation or grammar. It has something to do with ease and freedom in the use of language. Most of all it has to do with the structure of the sentence, which is simple, direct, and fluent, maintaining the rhythm of the word-groups of speech and the intonations of the speaking voice. [ca. 1948]

Lionel Trilling
The Liberal Imagination (Garden City, N. Y.:
Doubleday, 1953), pp. 116-17

Readers sometimes deplore the fact that the story [of *Huckleberry Finn*] descends to the level of *Tom Sawyer* from the moment that Tom himself re-appears. Such readers protest that the escapades invented by Tom, in the attempted "rescue" of Jim, are only a tedious development of themes with which we were already too familiar—even while admitting that the escapades themselves are very amusing, and some of the incidental observations memorable. But it is right that the mood of the end of the book should bring us back to that of the beginning. Or, if this was not the right ending for the book, what ending would have been right?

. . . For Huckleberry Finn, neither a tragic nor a happy ending would be suitable. No worldly success or social satisfaction, no domestic consummation would be worthy of him; a tragic end also would reduce him to the level of those whom we pity. Huck Finn must come from nowhere and be bound for nowhere. His is not the independence of the typical or symbolic American Pioneer, but the independence of the vagabond. His existence questions the values of America as much as the values of Europe; he is as much an affront to the "pioneer spirit" as he is to "business enterprise"; he is in a state of nature as detached as the state of the saint. In a busy world, he represents the loafer; in an acquisitive and competitive world, he insists on living from hand to mouth. He could not be exhibited in any amorous encounters or engagements, in any of the juvenile affections which are appropriate to Tom Sawyer. He belongs neither to the Sunday School nor to the Reformatory. He has no beginning and no end. Hence, he can only disappear; and his disappearance can only be accomplished by bringing forward another performer to obscure the disappearance in a cloud of whimsicalities.

T. S. Eliot
Introd. in *Adventures of Huckleberry Finn* (London:
Cresset Pr., 1950), pp xv-xvi

The conflict between what people think they stand for and what social pressure forces them to do is central to the novel [*Huckleberry Finn*]. It is present to the mind of Huck and, indeed, accounts for his most serious inner conflicts. He knows how he feels about Jim, but he also knows what he is expected to do about Jim. This division within his mind corresponds to the division of the novel's moral terrain into the areas represented by the raft on the one hand and society on the other. His victory over his "yaller dog" conscience therefore assumes heroic size: it is a victory over the prevailing morality. But the last fifth of the novel has the effect of diminishing the importance and uniqueness of Huck's victory. We are asked to assume that somehow freedom can be achieved in spite of the crippling power of . . . the social morality. Consequently the less importance we attach to that force as it operates in the novel, the more acceptable the ending becomes. . . .

Clemens did not acknowledge the truth his novel contained. He had taken hold of a situation in which a partial defeat was inevitable, but he was unable to—or unaware of the need to—give imaginative substance to that fact. If an illusion of success was indispensable, where was it to come from? Obviously Huck and Jim could not succeed by their own efforts. At this point Clemens, having only half escaped the genteel tradition, one of whose pre-eminent characteristics was an optimism undaunted by disheartening truth, returned to it. *Why* he did so is another story, having to do with his parents and his boyhood, with his own personality and his wife's, and especially with the character of his audience. But whatever the explanation, the faint-hearted ending of *The Adventures of Huckleberry Finn* remains an important datum in the record of American thought and imagination. It has been noted before, both by critics and non-professional readers. It should not be forgotten now.

Leo Marx
AmS (Autumn, 1953), pp. 435-36, 439-40

. . . Without advance planning, and spurred by momentary impulses, Mark Twain—in all probability unconsciously—constructed whole passages of *Huckleberry Finn* on an aesthetic principle of repetition and variation. Because the process was unconscious, it does not attain the regularity of Proust's employment of the Vinteuil theme [in *A la Recherche du Temps Perdu*] and we must also remember that Twain was working on a much smaller scale than the seemingly inexhaustible French analyst. . . .

. . . Just as such repetitions were conceived unconsciously or accidentally on the author's part, so their influence on the reader may be largely without his conscious attention to the means by which he is beguiled into finding the book somewhat ordered within his recollection, but by an order he cannot explain very clearly in terms of conventional plotting or symbols.

Frank Baldanza
AL (November, 1955), pp. 350, 354

In his relationship to his lot, his final resolve to accept what is called these days his "terrible freedom," Huck seems the first Existentialist hero, the improbable ancestor of Camus's "stranger," or the protagonists of Jean-Paul Sartre, or the negative characters of the early Hemingway. But how contrived, literary, and abstract the others seem beside Huck! He is the product of no metaphysics, but of a terrible break-through of the under-mind of America itself. In him, the obsessive American theme of loneliness reaches an ultimate level of expression, being accepted at last not as a blessing to be sought or a curse to be flaunted or fled, but quite simply as man's fate. There are mythic qualities in Ahab and even Dimmesdale; but Huck *is* a myth: not invented but discovered by one close enough to the popular mind to let it, this once at least, speak through him. Twain some-times merely pandered to that popular mind, played the buffoon for it, but he was unalienated from it; and when he let it possess him, instead of pretending to condescend to it, he and the American people dreamed Huck—dreamed, that is to say, the anti-American American dream.

Leslie Fiedler
Love and Death in the American Novel (New York:
Criterion, 1960), p. 589

Mr. Eliot and Mr. Trilling agree in their readings that the River is a god, presiding over the action, its divinity everywhere implied though nowhere stated outright. But there is a more explicit supernaturalism in this book. Or, more properly, there is an exemplification and a testing of three attitudes toward the imaginative fulfillment of life, and these are largely indicated in supernatural terms. Each typifies the moral nature of those who profess it. Two of these imaginary supernatural worlds prove morally inadequate;

the third—which pays homage to the river god—gives dignity to human life.

These attitudes, so compellingly dramatized by Mark Twain, are the conventional piety of the villagers; the irrelevant escape of the romantic imagination (as played by Tom Sawyer and an assorted adult cast of rapscallions and Southern gentlemen); and the world of supernatural omens which Jim, the runaway slave, best understands. Huck Finn is the sorcerer's apprentice. The superstitious imagination recognizes evil as a dynamic force; it acknowledges death. It is truer to the moral demands of life than is either the smug piety of Christian conformity or the avoidance of choice by escaping to fantasy and romance. [ca. 1961]

Daniel Hoffman
Form and Fable in American Fiction (New York:
Oxford Univ. Pr., 1965), p. 320

. . . There are a number of flaws in *Huckleberry Finn,* some of them attributable to Twain's refusal to respect the "work of art" and others attributable to his imperfect sense of tone. The downstream movement of the story (theme as well as action) runs counter to Jim's effort to escape. Life on the raft may indeed be read as implied criticism of civilization— but it doesn't get Jim any closer to freedom. . . .

For the downward movement of the novel, of course, the picaresque form serves the subject very well, allowing for innumerable and rapid adventures, afloat and ashore, and for the sort of ponderings that are peculiar to Huck. The picaresque form is also a clue to the kind of unity the book does have, a melodramatic mixture of reality and unreality and of comedy and horror. It is frequently theatrical in the good sense of the word. But the unity depends on Huck's mind, and too often there are bits of action, dialogue, and observation which are not appropriate to him. There are two sorts of theatricality in the novel, melodrama and claptrap.

. . . A more self-conscious artist would not have allowed such discrepancies to mar the tone of his novel. The truth is that Twain, however gifted a raconteur, however much genius he had as an improviser, was not, even in *Huckleberry Finn,* a great novelist.

William Van O'Connor
The Grotesque: An American Genre (Carbondale, Ill.:
So. Illinois Univ. Pr , 1962), pp. 110-11, 113

GENERAL

I have observed the literary career of "Mark Twain" unfolding itself with much interest. It has been a puzzle to me. It had always seemed to me impossible that a writer who violated all the canons of literary art, and whose themes were so thoroughly commonplace, should become so extensively known and so widely popular as Mr. Clemens has become. Of course, his fame is only of today, but it is wonderful that it is so widespread and hearty even if it is merely ephemeral. On what is it based?—that is the puzzle. He deals of the everyday and commonplace—he is often coarse (as in *The Adventures of Huckleberry Finn*), irreverent, if not blasphemous (as in the *The Innocents Abroad*), and unnatural and straining after effect (as in *The Adventures of Tom Sawyer*). He has not one tithe of the refinement of Lowell, the delicacy of Irving, or the spontaneous geniality of Holmes; and yet, in public estimation, he is greater, or at least, he is more popular, than all three combined!

. . . Mark Twain lacks the education absolutely necessary to be a great writer; he lacks the refinement which would render it impossible for him to create such coarse characters as Huckleberry Finn; furthermore, he is absolutely unconscious of all canons of literary art. "He amuses us—he makes us laugh. There is enough sorrow in the world," said a lady to me lately. Possibly, that is the secret of Mark Twain's immense popularity.

Alexander N. DeMenil
The Literature of the Louisiana Territory (St. Louis, Mo.:
St. Louis News Co., 1904), pp. 198, 199-200

In the presence of all beauty of man's creation—in brief, of what we roughly call art, whatever its form—the voice of Mark Twain was the voice of the Philistine. A literary artist of very high rank himself, with instinctive gifts that lifted him, in *Huckleberry Finn* to kinship with Cervantes and Aristophanes, he was yet so far the victim of his nationality that he seems to have had no capacity for distinguishing between the good and the bad in the work of other men of his own craft. The literary criticism that one occasionally finds in his writings is chiefly trivial and ignorant; his private inclination appears to have been toward such romantic sentimentality as entrances school-boys; the thing that interested him in Shakespeare was not the man's colossal genius, but the absurd theory that Bacon wrote his plays. Had he been born in France (the country of his chief abomination!) instead of in a Puritan village of the American hinterland, I venture that he would have conquered the world. But try as he would, being what he was, he could not get rid of the Puritan smugness and cocksureness, the Puritan distrust of new ideas, the Puritan incapacity for seeing beauty as a thing in itself, and the full peer of the true and the good.

H. L. Mencken
A Book of Prefaces (New York: A. A. Knopf, 1917), pp. 204-5

In the end Mark Twain's scope was nation-wide, because of the quality of his imagination, because of the regional elements which he freely mixed, the Yankee with the Californian, the backwoodsman with both of these. The wide reach may be unimportant for judgments of intrinsic quality, but its significance may be great among a people seeking the illusive goal of unity and the resting-place of a tradition. Through Mark Twain the American mind resumed many of its more careless and instinctive early patterns. The sense of legend was continued or restored, or at least the high comic legend again commanded the native fancy. The patterns might have been richer patterns: and Mark Twain's accent of a tense relationship with the older countries may seem deplorable; and much of his comic display has gone the transient way of comedy: he both gained and lost by a primitive vigor and by his adherence to the spoken and theatrical. But all these elements—the tense relationship with the rest—had long since joined in the making of the native character: to have abandoned or lost them would have meant an essential violence and disintegration. [ca. 1931]

Constance Rourke
American Humor (New York: Doubleday, 1953), pp. 174-75

[Twain] is our one folk-artist, both as a person and as a writer, comparable in office and function, in inspiration and accomplishment to the chroniclers and jesters and balladists of earlier ages. Regarding his voluminous works from this point of view one can with no great effort identify oneself with a type of mind and taste, no despicable one either, to which no sketch or jest or tale or essay has lost an element of freshness, wonder, liberation and delight. And one is happy that this is so and continues to be so. For Mark Twain is American in the older and permanently noble sense: no tyrant or moral meddler but sturdily and whole-heartedly for freedom and democracy, no cultivator of false and sinister reactionary subtleties but as in *A Yankee at King Arthur's Court* and *The Prince and the Pauper* and in an hundred other passages a strong defender of the better and freer life of the plain people, yet never flattering the people either, but valiantly and sharply castigating their hypocritic gestures, their moral delusions, their self-imposed limitations of heart and mind. Certain of their errors and follies he shares, for his spirit and theirs are essentially one. But this endears him to them and renders him accessible and makes him both guide and spokesman of their better possibilities.

Ludwig Lewisohn
Expression in America (New York: Harper, 1932), p. 230

. . . It is doubtful if [Twain] ever achieved all that he had given promise of doing or really deserved the high rank that was to so readily accorded him.

There is, it is at least clear, no one of his books that is wholly satisfactory, no one of his books that is quite so good as, while reading the opening chapters, one expects it to be. *Tom Sawyer*, at the outset, is not merely a glamorous evocation of the romance that boyish enthusiasm lends to life; it is a fine and subtle portrayal of the Missouri frontier. Yet it ends in the tawdry melodrama of conventional juvenile fiction. In the same way in *Huckleberry Finn*, after moving passages that celebrate the joys of loafing on a gently floating raft, after the swift narrative of the Sheperdson-Grangerford feud and the shooting of Boggs, after the robust humor of the episode of the Royal Nonesuch, comes the tedious and labored account of the rescue of Jim. We need not prolong the list, but who can forget the painfulness of the latter chapters of *Life on the Mississippi,* those commonplace notes on river towns, after the glorious record that, in the first part of the book, the author gives of his own river days? In book after book, after the most brilliant kind of beginning, Mark Twain crawls with undisguised weariness of soul to the closing page.

The imagination that can seize, as his so often and so effectively did, upon some trifling incident and catch its implications, is not necessarily an imagination equipped for the sustained development of a major theme. The literary attributes that lend brilliance to a descriptive paragraph or a brief narrative are not always able to maintain an entire novel upon a consistently high level. For what Mark Twain wanted to do, for the creation of a record of American life, for the expression of his own personality and experience, something was lacking. He had seen enough, and he could write, when he was at his best, much more eloquently than those contemporaries who rebuked him for his barbarism. But the imaginative power that sees hidden relations among the fragments observation reveals, that takes the fragments and shapes them into a whole, that builds towards some towering climax—that power was denied him.

Granville Hicks
The Great Tradition (New York:
Macmillan, 1935), pp. 43-44

. . . Two tendencies in Mark Twain, each of which impaired his work from the artistic point of view, can be followed through his writings to the point where they come into violent conflict with each other. De Voto . . . has suggested the need for an analysis of what he calls "the bases of Mark Twain's mind." This analysis . . . reveals a violent mental conflict, or logical dilemma, which forced much of his work into distorted patterns of both thought and structure, frequently making it impossible for him to achieve unity of any sort.

On the one hand, he was the rabid reformer, eager to uplift, instruct, and purify mankind. On the other, he was the dogmatic determinist, preaching as the text of his "Gospel" that the inborn disposition of mankind is "a thing which is as permanent as rock, and never undergoes any actual or genuine change between cradle and grave"—a doctrine which in effect renders useless all attempts to uplift, instruct, or purify mankind. The clash of ideas resulting from this logical dilemma was frequently great enough, the divergence in the two lines of thought was frequently wide enough, to furnish a plausible explanation for the structural defects, the lack of a norm, and the want of unity in tone which the critics have lamented as his chief failings as a literary artist.

Gladys C. Bellamy
Mark Twain as a Literary Artist (Norman, Oka.:
Univ. Oklahoma Pr., 1950), p. 56

. . . [There is] a tendency in America (and transatlantic fashions regarding American literature tend to be taken over uncritically in England) to suggest that the beginnings of the truly American in literary tradition come from the frontier and the West. According to this view Mark Twain is a more truly American writer than Hawthorne or Henry James. It is a view that, in offering to exalt him, actually denies his greatness, for it makes the attributed advantage in Americanness a matter of his being alienated from England and European tradition as Hawthorne and Henry James are not. Such an alienation could only be an impoverishment: no serious attempt has been made to show that any sequel to disinheritance could replace the heritage lost. Mark Twain is indeed "frontier" and Western, but in being greatly American he bears as close and essential a relation to England and Europe as that which we recognize in Hawthorne or in James (in some ways he strikes an English reader as being less foreign, less positively un-English, than either of them). The Americanness of alienation may be represented by Dreiser, Scott Fitzgerald, and Hemingway: The author of *Huckleberry Finn*, when we think of those writers, seems to belong to another world.

F. R. Leavis
Commentary (February, 1956), p. 130

. . . Writing about Bad Boys, virginal maidens, and precocious infants was not only an American tradition and the most fruitful expression of his imagination but Twain's means of adjusting to his immediate environment and a compromise with his far-flung electorate. To the degree that he felt both a part of and at odds with society—and I believe this was his normal frame of mind—writing about children permitted him both to escape and to confront some embarrassing problems. As a result, childhood became the characteristic mask, as humor was the typical mode, for communication with his world.

What happened, therefore, was that Twain largely resisted social and family pressures on his art that might have turned him into a second Charles Dudley Warner or Thomas Bailey Aldrich, and by playing both sides of the juvenile street, so to speak, made an opportunity of what might have proved a fatal danger. As a commercial writer, he made a fortune in this fashion. As a literary artist, he put children to his private purposes. These objectives were in essence threefold: to recreate in loving and honest detail the lost world of Hannibal before the War; to report and comment upon the money-crazed world of his own day; and finally, to reduce to simple terms the Darwinian intellectual revolutions which had made a shambles of his unsophisticated, post-Calvinist cosmology. These three concerns—all regarded by Twain as *moral* problems requiring *literary* formulation—achieved dramatic expression most typically and successfully through Mark Twain's childish figures.

Albert E. Stone, Jr.
The Innocent Eye (New Haven: Yale Univ. Pr., 1961), pp. 269-70

. . . Examples of Mark Twain's apprentice work illustrate Santayana's thesis that in the nineteenth century the United States was a country of two mentalities. Many of the comic devices presuppose a conflict between an established culture having for its focus the notion of ideality, and unrefined impulses originating in everyday experience, the vulgar world of the natural man. In the pastoral situation that Mark Twain took over from earlier humorists he found the means for dramatizing this conflict by bringing straight characters of conventional outlook face to face with vernacular characters who were indifferent or hostile to conventions and proprieties. The conflict could also be expressed through a contrast of styles: elevated rhetoric and diction versus colloquial speech and commonplace images. Although the vernacular impulse was potentially subversive of the traditional culture, Mark Twain did not perceive the issue abstractly. His mind was that of an artist; he thought in presentational rather than discursive terms. Nevertheless, his handling of comic situations and of contrasting styles shows an intuitive awareness of the cultural problem that Emerson and Santayana described. He was feeling his way toward the recognition that the traditional culture was decadent because it had lost the power to relate its values to actual experience.

Despite Santayana's charge that the humorists had no positive values to put in the place of the tradition they were attacking, Mark Twain's vernacular characters at least suggest the possibility of a view of life preferable to the attitudes implied by the notion of ideality—an integrated vision of the universe that could conceive ideal values within the realm of the commonplace. But it was no more than a hint.

Henry Nash Smith
Mark Twain, the Development of a Writer
(Cambridge, Mass.: Harvard Univ. Pr., 1962), p. 20

WALT WHITMAN
1819-1892

Born May 31 in Huntington, Long Island, N.Y. His family moved to Brooklyn, N.Y. in 1823. In 1842, he worked as a reporter, editor, and politician and published *Franklin Evans, or the Inebriate*. In 1846, he was editor of the *Brooklyn Eagle* but was discharged in 1848, after which he visited New Orleans. In 1850, he became a part-time carpenter with his father. The first edition of *Leaves of Grass* was published in 1855. In 1862, he went to Washington as a volunteer "visitor" in army hospitals and worked there in government offices. In 1865, *Drum Taps* was published and, in 1871, *Democratic Vistas*. He was paralyzed by a mild stroke in 1873 and moved to Camden, N. J. *Specimen Days and Collect* was published in 1882, and, in 1891-1892, the "Deathbed Edition" of *Leaves of Grass*. He died March 26 at Camden.

The Complete Writings of Walt Whitman (1902)

Gay Wilson Allen, *The Solitary Singer* (1955)

PERSONAL

. . . [Whitman] was neither sensual, nor rough and rugged, nor truly healthy, nor lusty, nor even very masculine. He was what is nowadays called a Narcissan, in love with himself, introverted, and so wrapped up in his own ego that he got no free delivery of energy except in his exhibitionism. . . .

Being himself far from normal, he gave voice to few of the normal emotions of America. "The home, the fireside, the domestic allurements are not in him," says John Burroughs. "Love, as we find it in other poets, is not in him." They are not in his poetry and they were not in him. He neither felt them, appreciated them, nor understood them. What he chiefly voiced was his own egotism—swollen to the dimensions of his country—his own morbidity, his own introversion. These are not typically American nor democratic, and the democracy has never accepted him.

Harvey O'Higgins
Harpers (May, 1929), pp. 704-707

They might have put on his tombstone: WALT WHITMAN: HE HAD HIS NERVE. He is the rashest, the most inexplicable and unlikely—the most impossible, one wants to say—of poets. He somehow *is* in a class by himself, so that one compares him with other poets about as readily as one compares *Alice* with other books. (Even his free verse has a completely different effect from anybody else's.) Who would think of comparing him with Tennyson or Browning or Arnold or Baudelaire?—it is Homer, or the sagas, or something far away and long ago, that comes to one's mind only to be dismissed; for sometimes Whitman *is* epic, just as *Moby Dick* is, and it surprises us to be able to use truthfully this word that we have misused so many times. Whitman *is* grand, and elevated, and comprehensive, and real with an astonishing reality, and many other things—the critic points at his qualities in despair and wonder, all method failing, and simply calls them by their names. And the range of these qualities is the most extraordinary thing of all. We can surely say about him, "He was a man, take him for all in all. I shall not look upon his like again"—and wish that people had seen this and not tried to be his like: one Whitman is miracle enough, and when he comes again it will be the end of the world. . . .

. . . Let me finish by mentioning another quality of Whitman's—a quality, delightful to me, that I have said nothing of. If some day a tourist notices, among the ruins of New York City, a copy of *Leaves of Grass*, and stops and picks it up and reads some lines in it, she will be able to say to herself: "How very American! If he and his country had not existed, it would have been impossible to imagine them."

Randall Jarrell
Poetry and the Age (New York: Vintage Books, 1953),
pp. 118-119, 120.

[Whitman's] most difficult battle . . . was not with illness, but with his wild homosexual desires, which never left him at peace and constantly menaced his balance. All who saw him admired his serenity and his perfect moral health; no one suspected the torments which lacerated him. It was probably his art which saved him by permitting him to express (in the etymological meaning of the word) the turbulent passions which obsessed him. Poetry was for him a means of purification which, if it did not make him normal, at least permitted him to retain his balance in spite of his anomaly. In this sense, . . . *Leaves of Grass* are "fleurs du mal," "flowers of evil." His poetry is not the song of a demigod or a superman, as some of his admirers would have it, but the sad chant of a sick soul seeking passionately to understand and to save itself. . . .

His anomaly, which in all likelihood was what drove him to write *Leaves of Grass*, also explains certain of his limitations, and notably his inability to renew himself as he grew older—unlike Goethe. He lived too much alone, too much wrapped up in himself. Nothing ever came to change the image of the world which he had made for himself between 1850 and 1855. He spent all his life in the solitude of his inner universe, "solitary, singing in the West." But his isolation weighed upon him (hence his compensatory dreams of democratic brotherhood), and it even drove him to despair sometimes. Hence the cries of suffering which escaped him and which often interrupt his hymn to life. As Frederico Garcia Lorca, who knew the same torments, so well understood, he is, despite appearances, the poet of anguish. . . .

Whitman had thus, at the very core of himself, a sense of defeat and frustration. He had had the ambition to create two masterpieces: a book of immortal poems and a life, the nobility and greatness of which would become legendary. He succeeded in one respect only, but his failure was, perhaps, the condition of that success. [ca. 1954]

Roger Asselineau
The Evolution of Walt Whitman (Cambridge, Mass.:
Harvard Univ. Pr., 1960), pp. 259-60

. . . The forty-two-year-old man who lies beneath [a gravestone in the Warwick, N.Y., cemetery] I have good reason to believe was one of the six illegitimate children whom the poet confessed to have fathered. What is incomplete in the inscription is the omission of any date of birth. This is all one reads there:

JOHN WHITMAN WILDER
Died Feb. 17, 1911. . . .

The preponderance of evidence—testimonial, documentary and circumstantial—points, I feel sure, to Whitman as the father of John Whitman Wilder. If such a conclusion seem damaging to a great poet's reputation, it is less so than his own confession to Symonds, which involved, not only an extramarital relationship and separation from the child that resulted, but five other such children. Charity will in its ignorance withhold judgment of whatever sudden impulse may have moved an impressionable nature to the first misstep, but persistent repetition in error is more difficult to believe or to extenuate. Whether or not there were other children now seems less a concern of ours.

Emory Holloway
Free and Lonesome Heart (New York:
Vantage Pr., 1960), pp. 144, 157-58

Leaves of Grass

. . . If we are uncomfortable these days with Walt Whitman, it is not because he pretended to be what he was not; our judgments are not so simple. "Above all to thine own self be true" was good enough advice in the mind of one surer than we are what *is* the self. It is because the motives of his masquerade were so literary and conventional, and the image of the poet he proposed himself such a ragbag of *Versunkenekulturgüte*, Rousseau, Goethe, George Sand, Carlyle, Emerson, and God knows what else, eked out with phrenology and Fourth of July rhetoric, that we hesitate to accept him. If Whitman were really the monster of health and sympathy he paints himself, really the solemn discoverer of a New Sex or even of a hypostasized America as his early followers came to believe, we should not abide him for a moment. It is the poet who feared literature, the sly old maid finally trapped by his own cunning who is *our* Whitman; and the point of *our Leaves of Grass* lies precisely in the distance between the poet and his eidilon. If that distance did not exist, Whitman would have been laughed out of existence by the first sophomore who snickered at "I dote on myself, there is that lot of me and all so luscious. . . ."

. . . Our Walt Whitman is the slyest of artificers, the artificer of "sincerity," and if this sounds like a joke, there is no reason why even the greatest poetry cannot be a joke on someone, not excluding its author. It does not seem enough to me to say, as G. W. Stonier has in one of the more perceptive comments on Whitman, "His duplicity staggers. He was a fine poet and a charlatan," because this implies that his fine poetry is based on something other than his charlatanism. Whitman's trickery is essential, not accidental, to his poems. Like the mannerists, like Shakespeare, who is the greatest among them, he is a player with illusion; his center is a pun on the self; his poetry is a continual shimmering on the surfaces of concealment and revelation that is at once pathetic and comical.

His duplicity is, I feel, a peculiarly American duplicity, that doubleness of our self-consciousness, which our enemies too easily call hypocrisy, but which arises from our belief that what we dream rather than what we are is our essential truth. The Booster and the Pharisee are the standard caricatures of the American double man, and Whitman was both Booster and Pharisee. Condemned to play the Lusty Innocent, the Noble Savage, by a literary tradition that had invented his country before he inhabited it, Whitman had no defenses. The whole Western world demanded of him the lie in which we have been catching him out, the image of America in which we no longer believe; the whole world cried to him, "Be the Bard we can only dream. Chant the freedom we have imagined as if it were real!"

But he was not "America"; he was only a man, ridden by impotence and anxiety, by desire and guilt, furtive and stubborn and half-educated. That he became the world's looked-for, ridiculous darling is astonishing enough; that he remained a poet through it all is scarcely credible. He has survived his images, and at last the outlived posturing, the absurd ideas, the rhetoric borrowed and misunderstood fall away, until only the poetry remains, and the poet, anonymous in the end as they were in the beginning.

I and this mystery here we stand.

Leslie Fiedler
In *Leaves of Grass One Hundred Years After,* ed. Milton Hindus
(Stanford, Calif.: Stanford Univ. Pr., 1955), pp. 58, 72-73

[Whitman] caught up and set to music the large contemporary conviction that man had been born anew in the new society, that the race was off to a fresh start in America. It was in *Leaves of Grass* that the optative mood, which had endured for over a quarter of a century and had expressed itself so variously and so frequently, seemed to have been transformed at last into the indicative. It was there that the hope that had enlivened spokesmen from Noah Webster in 1825 . . . to the well-named periodical, *Spirit of the Age* in 1849 . . . found its full poetic realization. *Leaves of Grass* was a climax as well as a beginning, or rather, it was the climax of a long effort to begin. . . .

. . . While European romanticism continued to resent the effect of time, Whitman was announcing that time had only just begun. He was able to think so because of the facts of immediate history in America during the years when he was maturing: when a world was, in some literal way, being created before his eyes. It was this that Whitman had the opportunity to dramatize; and it was this that gave *Leaves of Grass* its special quality of a Yankee Genesis: a new account of the creation of the world—the creation, that is, of a new world; an account this time with a happy ending for Adam its hero; or better yet, with no ending at all; and with this important emendation, that now the creature has taken on the role of creator.

R. W. B. Lewis
The American Adam (Chicago: Univ. Chicago Pr.,
1955), pp. 45-46

Leaves of Grass has just claim as America's epic. No attempt before it (and there were many) succeeded in becoming more than awkward imitations of the epics of the past. No book after it can ever again achieve its unique point of view. Coming shortly after the birth of the nation, embodying the country's first terrible trial by fire, prophesying the greatness to be thrust upon these states, *Leaves of Grass* possesses a position of intimate relationship with America that no other work can now ever assume. For better or worse, *Leaves of Grass* is America's, a reflection of her character and of her soul and of her achievements and her aspirations. If *Leaves of Grass* transfigures what it reflects, that is because its poet wanted to dwell not on the reality but on the ideal. If *Leaves of Grass* has its shortcomings and defects, so, surely, does the culture it attempted to embody. But after all the reservations are stated and the qualifications noted, we must confess that the book does measure up. If Whitman's vision exceeded his achievement, the scope of his achievement was still sufficient to win him just claim to the title of America's epic poet.

James E. Miller, Jr.
A Critical Guide to Leaves of Grass (Chicago:
Univ. Chicago Pr., 1957), p. 261

For me . . . the most important edition of *Leaves of Grass* is the 1860 edition; and its most important poem is "A Word Out of the Sea" (which, of course, became "Out of the Cradle Endlessly Rocking" in later editions). Here Whitman may be best justified: as a poet. . . . The structure and movement of this volume and of some of the principal poems in it (above all, "A Word Out of the Sea") are such as to furnish a valid and integral way for a poet dedicated to saving poetry for the modern world, thus—as poet, and only as poet—dedicated to saving the modern world for poetry. The Whitman of the 1860 *Leaves of Grass* would be a sage, a seer, a sayer. But he speaks of only what he knows directly and he asks of his speech only that it report fully and honestly and frankly, only that it evoke other speeches, other poems, of its kind. The poems in this volume do justify Whitman's claims for poetry in general—but in terms of what he may in fact give us, not of what he would like, or even need, to give us. The strength of the major poems in the volume is that they somewhat resist *our* need for more than they present, and make us rest satisfied —or as satisfied as we ever can be—with what they give. Above all, this is true of "A Word Out of the Sea"—as it is less true, and so less characteristic, of the later Whitman, the poet of "Out of the Cradle Endlessly Rocking." . . .

Meantime we must bring ourselves to say of the Whitman of 1892, the literatus, that he was driven to claim prophetic powers, not to put poetry to their service. Nothing could hold this Whitman back, not even the facts of a poet's life. Indeed, his life—his own and life in general—became less "factual," less "real" for him. And—since justification consists in deriving the necessary from the real, of tracing the necessary back to its roots in the real, of showing that the real is necessary—he no longer had a need to justify himself. . . . I daresay we need to recover the Whitman of 1860 —with his heroic sense of grounding the necessary in the real. He gave us permission to. I am suggesting that we *need* the poet of 1860, the poet of "A Word Out of the Sea." I mean to say thereby that our poets need him too. And justifying the need, we must justify him who contrived that his need be archetypal for ours.

Roy Harvey Pearce
The Presence of Walt Whitman (New York: Columbia Univ. Pr., 1962), pp 79, 108-109

GENERAL

. . . In an inextricably hodge-podge you find at once beautiful phrases and silly gabble, tender imagination and insolent commonplace,—pretty much everything, in short, but humour. In America this literary anarchy, this complete confusion of values, is especially eccentric; for America has generally displayed instinctive common-sense, and common-sense implies some notion of what things are worth. One begins to see why Whitman has been so much more eagerly welcomed abroad than at home. His conception of equality, utterly ignoring values, is not that of American democracy, but rather that of European. His democracy, in short, is the least native which has ever found voice in his country. The saving grace of American democracy has been a tacit recognition that excellence is admirable.

. . . In [the] decadent eccentricity of Whitman's style there is again something foreign to the spirit of this country. American men of letters have generally had deep artistic conscience. . . . The vagaries of Walt Whitman, on the other hand, are as far from literary conscience as the animals which he sometimes celebrates are from unhappiness or respectability. Whitman's style, then, is as little characteristic of America as his temper is of traditional American democracy. One can see why the decadent taste of modern Europe has welcomed him so much more ardently than he has ever been welcomed at home; in temper and in style he was an exotic member of that sterile brotherhood which eagerly greeted him abroad. In America his oddities were more eccentric than they would have been anywhere else.

. . . In one aspect he is thoroughly American. The spirit of his work is that of world-old anarchy; its form has all the perverse oddity of world-old abortive decadence; but the substance of which his poems are made—their imagery as distinguished from their form or their spirit—comes wholly from our native country. In this aspect, then, though probably in no other, he may, after all, throw light on the future of literature in America. As has been said before, "He is uncouth, inarticulate, whatever you please that is least orthodox; yet, after all, he can make you feel for the moment how even the ferry-boats plying from New York to Brooklyn are fragments of God's eternities. Those of us who love the past are far from sharing his confidence in the future. Surely, however, that is no reason for denying the miracle that he has wrought by idealizing the East River. The man who has done this is the only one who points out the stuff of which perhaps the new American literature of the future may in time be made." [ca. 1900]

Barrett Wendell
A Literary History of America (New York:
Scribner's, 1914), pp. 471, 477-79

From this side of the Atlantic I am for the first time able to read Whitman, and from the vantage of my education and—if it be permitted a man of my scant years—my world citizenship: I see him America's poet. The only Poet before the artists of the Carman-Hovey period, or better, the only one of the conventionally recognized "American Poets" who is worth reading.

He *is* America. His crudity is an exceeding great stench, but it *is* America. He is the hollow place in the rock that echoes with his time. He *does* "chant the crucial stage" and he is the "voice triumphant." He is disgusting. He is an exceedingly nauseating pill, but he accomplishes his mission.

Entirely free from the renaissance humanist ideal of the complete man or from the Greek idealism, he is content to be what he is, and he is his time and his people. He is a genius because he has vision of what he is and of his function. He knows that he is a beginning and not a classically finished work.

I honor him for he prophesied me while I can only recognize him as a forebear of whom I ought to be proud. [1909]

Ezra Pound
In *Whitman: A Collection of Critical Essays*,
ed. Roy Harvey Pearce (Englewood Cliffs, N. J.:
Prentice-Hall, 1962), p. 8

The indifference of democracy to its greatest poet seems a paradox, but the indifference does not exist. America is not a democracy; it is a vast bourgeoisie; the democracy which Whitman celebrates has not arrived on the earth. The men and women he saw and loved were the material of which he believed a democracy is some day to be born. So that when professors, deaf and blind to the life about them and especially to "democracy," which is as yet felt only by a minority, say that the ideals of the people are contrary to Whitman's ideals of the people, they are superficially right. The ideals of the people are bourgeois ideals inculcated by most of the "savants" in obedience to the economic powers that endow and dominate the universities. . . . Whitman's essential ideals must be ignored or comfortably misunderstood by the licensed thought-mongers, and the people must be taught that when any idea like Whitman's appeals to them as right and just and truly democratic, they are "being cheated by demagogues," as Professor Santayana puts it.

So much argument is necessary to account for the stupidity of learned doctors and acknowledged teachers of aesthetics in their treatment of Whitman. They are the voice of intrenched respectability against every voice of democracy. Whether Whitman becomes the poet of the people depends solely on whether the people rise from the economic and spiritual slavery and organize a true democracy. Then only will disappear the possibility that a professor of reputed authority in matters of art and philosophy can find an analogy "between a mass of images without structure and the notion of an absolute democracy."

Whitman's poetry is no more without structure than Shakespeare's; and "an absolute democracy" would be the most highly organized and well constructed government possible. The disorder which Whitman pictures is the world as it is; his democracy is an ideal, a society of the future which is to grow out of the visible disorder of the present.

John Macy
The Spirit of American Literature (Garden City, N. Y.:
Doubleday, 1913), pp 212-14

The one American writer who has left the genteel tradition entirely behind is perhaps Walt Whitman. For this reason educated Americans find him rather an unpalatable person, who they sincerely protest ought not to be taken for a representative of their culture; and he certainly should not, because their culture is so genteel and traditional. But the foreigner may sometimes think otherwise, since he is looking for what may have arisen in America to express, not the polite and conventional American mind, but the spirit and the inarticulate principles that animate the community, on which its own genteel mentality seems to sit rather lightly. When the foreigner opens the pages of Walt Whitman, he thinks that he has come at last upon something representative and original. In Walt Whitman democracy is carried into psychology and morals. The various sights, moods, and emotions are given each one vote; they are declared to be all free and equal, and the innumerable common-place moments of life are suffered to speak like the others. Those moments formerly reputed great are not excluded, but they are made to march in the ranks with their companions —plain foot-soldiers and servants of the hour. Nor does the refusal to discriminate stop there; we must carry our principle further down, to the animals, to inanimate nature, to the cosmos as a whole. Whitman became a pantheist; but his pantheism, unlike that of the Stoics and of Spinoza, was unintellectual, lazy, and self-indulgent; for he simply felt jovially that everything real was good enough, and that he was good enough himself.

In him Bohemia rebelled against the genteel tradition; but the reconstruction that alone can justify revolution did not ensue. His attitude, in principle, was utterly disintegrating; his poetic genius fell back to the lowest level, perhaps, to which it is possible for poetic genius to fall. He reduced his imagination to a passive sensorium for the registering of impressions. No element of construction remained in it, and therefore no element of penetration. But his scope was wide; and his lazy, desultory apprehension was poetical. His work, for the very reason that it is so rudimentary, contains a beginning, or rather many beginnings, that might possibly grow into a noble moral imagination, a worthy filling for the human mind. An American in the nineteenth century who completely disregarded the genteel tradition could hardly have done more.

George Santayana
Winds of Doctrine (London: Dent, 1913), pp. 202-3

[Whitman] cannot certainly be ranked among the greatest poets. There is a lack of co-ordination between his hopes and despairs that is quite different from the perplexity of an Æschylus before the spectacle of fate, and more resembles the shifting enthusiasms of the young. Philosophically he never grew up. "Do I contradict myself? Very well then I contradict myself (I am large, I contain multitudes)," has the bravado of a youth just past adolescence. Nor will his defects in form permit him the attribute of greatest. In poetic technique he remained, to the end, the gifted but dogmatic amateur, striking magnificent chords only when the fingers fell right. His perfect passages are not uncommon, but are always unsure. One holds one's breath lest he spoil them before they are said. Most dangerous of all to the supremacy of his art was his rôle of prophet self-imposed in which, with Carlyle and Emerson at his back, and an ever-present fondness for exhibitionism, he too often got out of hand.

Nor can he ever be ranked among the lesser men. He is a great poet, and a great man, when you have said your worst. Great because he shares the plenary inspiration that great poets must have. I do not refer to some reservoir of inner light to be tapped by the worthy, although Whitman would have liked that explanation. I mean rather a sense for the significance of the human in that blend of temporal and timeless which makes an age or an epoch. The great poets have this, and whether they are greatest depends upon the use they make of it. Such a sense is utterly denied to a Longfellow, for all his skill. He "ran errands" for the culture of his America (which is not to disparage him), but he could not feel the heartbeats of the society of which he was a part. Whitman had it. He had specifically the vision of ideal equalitarianism. Perhaps there never was and never will be even an approximate equalitarianism. What does it matter!

Such a term is only a name that never indicates a perfected state but only a tendency, a permanent possibility of the human race. The possibility of perfect comradeship, the possibility that faculties common to all men might be exalted, the possibility of democracy in a blend of the physical and the spiritual, the possibility that nothing human would be alien to the soul of emancipated man—that was Whitman's vision.

Henry Seidel Canby
Classic Americans (New York: Harcourt, Brace,
1931), pp. 348-49

To enter the world of Whitman is to touch the spirit of American popular comedy, with its local prejudices, its national prepossessions, its fantastic beliefs; many phases of comic reaction are unfolded there. Nothing is complete, nothing closely wrought; often Whitman's sequences are incoherent, like sudden movements of undirected thought or feeling. "No one will get at my verses who insists upon viewing them as literary performances," he said. The scale was large; Whitman possessed that sense of a whole civilization which must belong to the epic; his sweeping cadences could have held the heroic form; and though he lacked the great theme of gods and men his awareness of the country had a stirring animism, and his prototypical American was of far greater than human stature. Yet Whitman did not achieve the heroic, or only rarely, in broken or partial passages. Like those popular story-tellers who had often seemed on the verge of wider expression, he failed to draw his immeasurable gift into the realm of great and final poetry. For the most part he remained an improviser of immense genius, unearthing deep-lying materials in the native mind, in a sense "possessed" by the character of that mythical and many-sided American whom he often evoked. He was indeed the great improviser of modern literature. He had turned the native comic rhapsody, abundant in the backwoods, to broad poetic forms. [ca. 1931]

Constance Rourke
American Humor (Garden City, N. Y.:
Doubleday, 1953), p. 142

All Whitman's faults, though they may bar him from the first rank of poets, seem, when one considers his situation and his task, to have been virtues. A more disciplined mind would have been rendered impotent by the mere recognition of the impossibility of reducing to a system such conflicting elements. A less buoyantly optimistic mind would have sunk under the realization of the distance to be traveled before the great vision could be achieved. A less mystical mind, a mind more preoccupied with the steps by which the goal could be reached, would have narrowed itself down to concern with a small and malleable portion of American civilization. It was precisely the broad, unformed mind of a Whitman, undiscriminatingly affirmative, unhesitatingly hospitable, sharply perceptive of concrete detail, that could plunge into the wild jungle of a national life without political, economic, racial, religious, or social homogeneity.

Granville Hicks
The Great Tradition (New York: Macmillan, 1935), p. 28

No arrangement or rearrangement of Whitman's thoughts on . . . any . . . subject can resolve the paradoxes or discover in them a fully coherent pattern. He was incapable of sustained logic, but that should not blind the reader into impatient rejection of the ebb and flow of his antitheses. They possess a loose dialectic of their own, and a clue of how to find it is provided by Engels' discussion of Feuerbach: "One knows that these antitheses have only a relative validity; that that which is recognized now as true has also its latent false side which will later manifest itself, just as that which is now regarded as false has also its true." Whitman's ability to make a synthesis in his poems of the contrasting elements that he calls body and soul may serve as a measure of his stature as a poet. When his words adhere to concrete experience and yet are bathed in imagination, his statements become broadly representative of humanity. . . .

When he fails to make that synthesis, his language can break into the extremes noted by Emerson when he called it "a remarkable mixture of the *Bhagvat-Geeta* and the *New York Herald.*" The incongruous lengths to which Whitman was frequently carried in each direction shows how hard a task he undertook. On the one hand, his desire to grasp American facts could lead him beyond slang into the rawest jargon, the journalese of the day. On the other, his attempts to pass beyond the restrictions of language into the atmosphere it could suggest often produced only the barest formulas. His inordinate and grotesque failures in both directions throw into clearer light his rare successes, and the fusion upon which they depend.

F. O. Matthiessen
American Renaissance (New York:
Oxford Univ. Pr., 1941), p. 526

. . . Walt Whitman [is] a living force in the war against fascist barbarism as well as in the peace which America and the other United Nations seek to achieve through unconditional victory.

Our richest poetic interpreter of democracy, Whitman speaks directly to those who are battling today at the gates of a new era in which it will be possible, for the first time in history, to fulfill his vision of world liberty and fraternity. He inspires us to assert the imperishable dignity of man, to set our faces resolutely toward progress, to strengthen the concord of free peoples. Whitman teaches us that we shall surely prevail if only we have the will to unite and the courage to beat down the enemies of democracy wherever they may appear.

Samuel Sillen
Walt Whitman, Poet of American Democracy
(New York: International Publishers, 1944), p. 9

With his defective taste, his crudities of language, and his love for windy and pretentious rhetoric, Whitman was not a great poet, or even a poet at all, except in snatches. He was only a first rough sketch of an American writer—certainly not a finished portrait. Yet the critical opinion that places him at the center of American literary history is not unjustified. By attempting to make himself an embodiment, almost a mythical symbol, of the democratic way of life, he did succeed in uncovering some of the fundamental problems confronting American society. The fact that Whitman himself, as a private person, was not really so virile and carefree as his public role required him to be, does not invalidate his conclusions.

Henry B. Parkes
The American Experience (New York: A. A. Knopf,
1947), p. 194

Walt Whitman's "pose" and his literary deceptions may . . . be interpreted as a kind of "idealism"—as an attempt to realize his ideal in actuality. Progressively he struggled to reduce his stubborn, fractional flesh to spiritual unity. But if he had striven to do this only, it is doubtful whether he would have been misunderstood and attacked as he has been, for most of his attackers have themselves been moral idealists. The difficulty has been not so much the fact of his idealism as the character of the ideal which he sought to realize. Not only did the ideal "Walt" differ from, and come into conflict with, the actual Walter Whitman, but his ideal differed from and came into conflict with the genteel tradition which cultured Americans had been taught to revere.

For "Walt" Whitman personified, in poetry and in life, the American dream of popular democracy, in so far as that differed from, and came into conflict with, the genteel tradition of the American past, in which the young Walter had been reared. The conflict between Walter and "Walt" may therefore be interpreted as the conflict between two American ideals. The most bitter opponents of the poet have also been the most bitter opponents of that equalitarian dream which he sought to realize, both in life and in poetry.

Frederic I. Carpenter
American Literature and the Dream (New York:
Philosophical Library, 1955), p. 45

. . . Few nineteenth century poets had the epic touch, though many had epic ambitions. Whitman, however, had both the prophetic and the confessional strains in equal degree, and is unique among poets of the English language in his combination of them. He saw himself epically; his most trivial experience was thus potentially heroic, and his least observation could be presented as cosmic. He does not write epics, but he cultivates an epic pose in order to write lyrics. The result, in his more successful poems, is a remarkable counter-pointing of the individual and the social, the personal and the political, the confessional and the prophetic.

Whitman was a rhetorician and a poseur, and these are bad words in modern criticism. But there are good and bad ways of being rhetorical, and good and bad ways of posing. In his best poetry, Whitman's rhetoric was a device for expanding lyrical impressionism into epic design, and his posing was a means of giving moral scope to his observations. His own introductory statement of his theme—

> One's-self I sing, a simple separate person
> Yet utter the word Democratic, the word En-Masse—

does not represent his happiest form of expression, but it expresses an all-important point, the desire to speak for a civilization through self-expression. . . .

. . . This was Whitman's unique achievement: he created his own poetic conventions in response to his own poetic needs. In this sense he is the first truly original American poet. He wrote always as though he were the first poet, faced with the necessity of creating his own idiom and his own conception of poetry. This is perhaps a barbaric attitude—this view that solutions are to be found by examining the nature of the present case rather than by working through traditional forms. Whitman's "barbaric yawp" presented a challenge to the accepted view of the place of convention in art. But it was not uncontrolled, or merely exclamatory, or merely rhetorical. It was the idiom of a poet who had a complex vision which brought together himself, his country, and his world, thus uniting the egotist and the prophet, the patriot and the visionary, to end with a bodying forth of

> The melodious character of the earth,
> The finish beyond which philosophy cannot go
>   or does not wish to go
> The justified mother of men.

David Daiches
In *Leaves of Grass One Hundred Years After,* ed. Milton Hindus
(Stanford, Calif.: Stanford Univ. Pr., 1955), pp. 109-110, 122

His attempt to read into all men his own private eros was Whitman's pathetic fallacy—"pathetic" in more than one sense. If Whitman were naive, it was not because he failed to recognize his sexual inversion but because he was able to convince himself that it was normal among all healthy males. When he tried to elevate "adhesiveness" to a principle of national unity or of world brotherhood, his error was not only naive; it was grotesque. Yet his mistake, astounding as it seems, is of value to the student, for it marks the most sensitive spot in Whitman's self-image. It was his anomalous sexual yearnings which had, in the first place, imprisoned him within the walls of his own disapproval; if this part of himself could not be absorbed into the ego-image which was now to release him, all was lost. Whitman's attempt to universalize his inverted sexual desires was an error to which he was driven by the logic of his own self-redemption. . . .

It is a mistake to pretend that Whitman was a great mystic and religious prophet, to magnify his utterances concerning the soul and immortality and to minimize his celebration of nature in all its nakedness. He is obviously not a dependable moral or spiritual guide, for in the depths of his poetry he believed in no morals at all and the soul he really believed in was the uninhibited spirit of primeval energy. It was ironical that many of his fellow romantics should turn squeamishly away from his frank erotism. The history of primitive religions would seem to show that here Whitman was consistent as his critics were not; wherever and whenever nature has been worshipped, eros has always played a prominent part. Whitman's world was a pagan Eden, complete with the phallic serpent.

It was precisely Whitman's value that he is a great primitive poet; he gives us a rich poetic sense of primitive nature in all its luxuriance, prodigality, and power. His best poetry derives its unquestioned authority from his perception that this divinely created natural life is good, so good that it promises another life still better. His zestful songs in praise of nature's life and nature's death testify to a genuine poetic, if not a high religious, inspiration.

Ernest Sandeen
American Classics Reconsidered (New York:
Scribner's, 1958), pp. 243-44, 267

JOHN GREENLEAF WHITTIER

1807-1892

Born December 17 in Haverhill, Massachusetts. His first poem was published by William Lloyd Garrison's *Free Press* in 1826, the same year he attended Haverhill Academy. In 1828, he began to write for Boston newspapers. *Legends of New England* was published in 1831. In 1836, he settled on the family farm, "Amesbury." A series of publications followed: *Lays of My Home* (1843); *Voice of Freedom* (1846); *Leaves from Margaret Smith's Journal* (1849); and *Snowbound* (1866). He died September 7 in New Hampshire.

Horace E. Scudder, ed., *The Writings of John Greenleaf Whittier* (1888-1889), 7 vols.

John A. Pollard, *John Greenleaf Whittier, Friend of Man* (1949)

Whittier was not a great poet. He was not a poet of strong imagination or creative power. His view of life and his view of art were alike narrow. His thought never ran deep, and his sense of form and style was extremely defective. He produced nothing on a large scale which is in the least likely to survive, and even in the finest of his shorter poems he rarely rose to the supreme heights of lyric utterance. . . .

If Whittier was not a great poet, he was within his range a very true one. The beauty of a singularly pure and winsome personality irradiates his verse. His materials were homely, but his spirit was always noble. His touch upon the common chords of life was both tender and firm. Hatred of injustice and wrong, faith in God at once childlike and profound, these were his constant inspirations; and these he expressed with an exquisite sincerity, and at times with a simple felicity of phrase, which make us forget the limitations of his outlook, the triteness of his thought and imagery, and the frequent poverty of his technique.

William Henry Hudson
Whittier and His Poetry (London: Harrap, 1917), pp. 11, 13

In the history of English literature in the larger sense, Whittier is probably no more than a poet of the third rank. His native endowment was rich, but it was supplemented by neither the technical training nor the discipline required for the development of the artist. He was extremely careless about his rhymes—"good Yankee rhymes, but out of New England they would be cashiered," he once said of them. The construction of his stanzas was diffuse and often slovenly. The organ voice and the lyric cry were not, except at rare moments, his to command. But no American who lived in the shadow of slavery and internecine strife, none who grew to manhood in the generation succeeding those epic days, would dream of measuring his love and veneration for Whittier by the scale of absolute art. Whittier's verse is so inwrought with the nation's passion during that period of heightened consciousness that preserved the Union and redeemed it from the curse of slavery that it cannot be coldly and critically considered by any one who has had a vital sense of the agonies and exaltations of that critical time. . . . Fifty years ago, the verdict of thoughtful Americans acclaimed Whittier as the foremost American poet, with the possible exception of Longfellow, and while now there would be more dissentients from that judgment than there were then, his fame still rests upon a very solid basis of acceptance and esteem. And especially to those who have sprung from the soil of New England, he will always be the incomparable poet of their childhood home, of its landscape, its legendry, and the spiritual essence of its history. [1917]

William Morton Payne
in *Cambridge History of American Literature*, Vol. II
(New York: Macmillan, 1946), pp. 53-54

A great, even a noteworthy poet, Whittier certainly was not. Compared with Whitman he is only a minor figure. Among the better known American poets Bryant alone is so narrow in range and barren in suggestion. His austere and meager life bred too little sensuousness of nature and too few intellectual passions. An over-frugal watering of the wine of paganism had left the New England character thin. The sap of humor that ran so boisterously through the veins of the West, exuding a rough wit from Davy Crockett to Mark Twain, was quite gone out of the Yankee blood. His homely imagination was unquickened by a hearty village life as was the case with the English Bunyan and the Scotch Burns. He had become a bundle of Yankee nerves, responding only to moral stimuli. . . . Never a great artist, rarely a competent craftsman, he wrote for the most part impassioned commonplace, with occasional flashes that are not commonplace.

Vernon Louis Parrington
Main Currents in American Thought, Vol. II
(New York: Harcourt, Brace, 1927), pp. 366–67

Whittier's poetry is autobiographical. No man ever wrote more directly from his own experience. Though the bulk of his work begins to sound antiquated, the best of it is destined to survive, and to survive beyond the more popular works of his day or those more expert technically. His simplicity of character militated against any mastery of broader or subtler poetic media. He fell behind Poe and Longfellow in the manner of his writing. But in the matter, he outdistanced both, for he devoted himself to the things and themes of this life, and not to some nebulous lost love or sentimental transcriptions of foreign or domestic tales. Like Bryant, he was steeped in the native soil. Bryant's eye and ear were clearer and his hand more certain; but Whittier's instrument had more stops. He was not alone moved by Nature and immortality, but by the human race as well.

Despite the fate to which the bulk of his work has succumbed, enough
remains to give him a secure place in the American future.

Alfred Kreymborg
Our Singing Strength (New York: Coward McCann,
1929), p. 85

One should not censure Whittier, as critics often do, by over-emphasizing
his minor faults such as his misuse of rhymes, his limitations to few meters,
and his habit of introducing a moral; nor should one panegyrize him by
over-stressing such undoubted virtues as his adroitness in the portrayal
of rural life, his excellence as a balladist, and his merit as a composer of
consoling hymns. As a matter of fact he had more serious faults than using
bad rhymes, for he not only wrote poems untrue to life, but soulless effu-
sions in verse, some directed against scientific progress and some coun-
tenancing social abuses or suggesting feeble remedies for their cure; and
he had greater virtues than being merely a rural bard, since he was a prophet
whom the "strain" "of a higher mood" lifted into the position of a universal
poet of freedom. He was an accomplished lyricist who made his own noble
personality enhance the value of his poetry. He really deserves a place with
Walt Whitman among our great American poets.

Albert Mordell
Quaker Militant, John Greenleaf Whittier (Boston:
Houghton Mifflin, 1933), p. xvi

Whenever Whittier keeps in close touch with his Quaker piety and his
provincial folkways, he is a true poet; when he drifts on popular currents
of literary sentimentality, he writes badly. Precisely like Burns, he succeeds
as a spokesman of his provincial culture and fails as a conventional literary
poet. This accounts for the notable inequalities of his work. Of his five or
six hundred poems only a quarter have distinction, and of these but a score
hold memorable places in American literature. At first it is hard to see how
such an uncritical writer could produce that most modest of classics, *Snow-
bound*, or, producing that, could still write hundreds of mediocre verses.
The explanation lies simply in what he could and could not do. Whittier had
no ideas of his own. When he tried to think, he failed. Polite fashions in
literature sit ill upon his shoulders. Among the "Narrative and Legendary
Poems" are several in the fashionable exotic manner, with medieval settings, and almost all such are strikingly inferior. Similarly, his poems with
New England settings, which are in fact only thinly disguised romance in
Longfellow's vein, are much inferior to Longfellow's. Even in his best-

known poems the weak and strong features are divided between the romantic and the folk elements.

Henry W. Wells
The American Way of Poetry (New York:
Columbia Univ. Pr., 1943), p. 51

Significant also of a quality of mind that was rapidly becoming old-fashioned was the naïve directness of Whittier's poetic technique. With no obeisance to the method of suggestiveness illustrated by Whitman in "Out of the Cradle Endlessly Rocking," where a reminiscence of childhood is analyzed into its component sensuous images and then freely recomposed into a globed and harmonious work of art, Whittier developed *Snow-Bound* by a linear or melodic progression of one image after another. Very little is conveyed by hints or implications, but each mood and moment is defined with stark integrity. Behind this way of writing may be felt, not merely personal innocence, but a deep-seated racial conviction of the virtue of plain speaking, a conviction that for Whittier was reinforced by his Quaker breeding. As a man of undefeated spirit, he was not concerned to explore the devious hinterland of consciousness that could only be expressed by innuendo, suggestion, or symbol. What he felt he could say.

The virtue of Whittier's poetry at its best lies in its firm texture of sincerity. He wrote about things that he knew intimately. His feelings were based on sentiments tested by the strains of life and driven down until they rested on bedrock conviction. His religious perceptions especially rested on a very real sense of divine immanence.

George F. Whicher
in *Literary History of the United States*, eds. Robert Spiller *et al.*, Vol. I
(New York: Macmillan, 1948, rev. 1963), p. 580

In [*The Pennsylvania Pilgrim*] Whittier comes up to his best, liberating himself from merely topical interests and from a simplified code of good or bad. In attaining the first of these freedoms he has centered his focus upon the immediately personal, and in attaining the second he has given depth to his material. Of such paradoxes art is made, yet not without ultimate resolution; and in Whittier there emerges from the concentration and diffusion an essential poetry unaffected by formal loyalties.

In the relatively small groups of poems in which this happens, certain other qualities also emerge as distinctive values in his art. He successfully conveys a complex view of character, a control of narrative technique, and a just proportion of parts.

George Arms
The Fields Were Green (Stanford, Calif.:
Stanford Univ. Pr., 1953), p. 39

COPYRIGHT ACKNOWLEDGMENTS

467

Allan Poe by Arthur Hobson Quinn; from *Sermo Lupi Ab Anglos,* ed., D. Whitelock.

ARCHON BOOKS. THE SHOE STRING PRESS, INC. For excerpt from *The Victorian Sage* by John Holloway.

EDWARD ARNOLD (PUBLISHERS) LTD. For excerpts from *The Romantic Theory of Poetry* by Annie Edwards Doss; from *A Survey of English Literature 1780–1830* by Oliver Elton; from *Two Cheers for Democracy* and *Aspects of the Novel* by E. M. Forster; from *Piers Plowman: An Essay in Criticism* by John Lawler; from *On Writing and Writers and Wordsworth* by Walter Raleigh; from *The Cease of Majesty* by M. M. Reese; from *Edmund Spenser* by W. L. Renwick; from *Chaucer's: The Knight's Tale and the Clerk's Tale* by Elizabeth Salter; from *Early Shakespeare* by Norman Sanders; from *Criticism and Medieval Poetry* by A. C. Spearing.

ATHLONE PRESS OF THE UNIVERSITY OF LONDON. For excerpt from *Chaucer: The Franklin's Tale,* ed. Phyllis Hodgson.

THE ATLANTIC MONTHLY. For excerpts from "Emerson Re-Read" by James Trulow Adams; from "Young Boswell" by Chauncey Brewster Tinker, copyright © by The Atlantic Monthly Company, Boston, Mass., reprinted with permission.

ARTHUR BARKER LTD. For excerpts from *The Brontës* by Phyllis Bentley; from *Maria Edgeworth* by P. H. Newby; from *The Gothic Flame* by Devendra P. Varma.

A. S. BARNES & COMPANY, INC. For excerpts from *Shelley: The Man and the Poet* by Desmond King-Hele.

BARNES & NOBLE, INC. For excerpts from *The History of the English Novel* by E. A. Baker; from *The Enchanted Forest* by W. W. Beyer; from *Poets and Story-Tellers* by David Cecil; from *Chaucer and the Medieval Sciences,* 2nd ed., by Walter Clyde Curry; from *The Medieval Heritage of Elizabethan Tragedy* by Willard Farnham; from *The Background of English Literature* by H. J. C. Grierson; from *The Starlit Dome* by G. Wilson Knight; from *Humanism and Poetry in Early Tudor Period* by H. A. Mason; from *Paradise Lost and the 17th Century* by B. Rajan; from *Romantic Perspectives* by Theodore Redpath; from "Sir Thomas More" by A. W. Reed in *The Social and Political Ideas of Some Great Thinkers of the Renaissance and the Reformation;* from *Criticism and Medieval Poetry* by A. C. Spearing; from *Milton, Shakespeare's History Plays* and *The English Epic and Its Background* by E. M. W. Tillyard; from *A Dictionary of English Literature* by Homer A. Watt and William W. Watt.

B. T. BATSFORD LTD. For excerpt from *Preface to Shakespeare* (2nd series) by Harley Granville-Barker.

J. B. BEER. For excerpt from his *Coleridge the Visionary.*

G. BELL & SONS, LTD. For excerpts from *The American Novel and Its Tradition* by Richard Chase; from *The English Muse* by Oliver Elton; from *Swinburne* by Georges Lafourcade; from *Comedy of Manners* by John Palmer; from *The Age of Chaucer* (1346–1400) by F. J. Snell; from *The Age of Tennyson* by Hugh Walker.

ERNEST BENN LIMITED. For excerpts from *Chapman* by Havelock Ellis; from *Chaucer and His Times* by Grace Hadow; from *English Literature: Medieval* by W. P. Ker; from *A Literary History of Scotland* by J. H. Millar; from *Shakespeare's Workmanship* by Arthur Quiller-Couch.

RONALD BOTTRALL. For the excerpt from his "Byron and the Colloquial Tradition in English Poetry", which appeared in *Criterion*.

BOWES AND BOWES LTD. For the excerpt from *Amphibian* by H. C. Dufferin.

BRANDT & BRANDT. For excerpts from *Hawthorne: A Study in Solitude* by Herbert Gorman; from "Henry Thoreau in our Time" by Stanley Edgar Hyman, first published in *Atlantic Monthly,* copyright, 1946, by the Atlantic Monthly Co.; from *Samuel Butler* by Clara G. Stillman.

CURTIS BROWN LTD. For excerpts from *Elizabethan Lyrics* by Catherine Ing; from *The Life of John Stuart Mill* by Michael St. John Packer.

BROWN UNIVERSITY PRESS. For the excerpt from *Samuel Johnson* in Grub Street by Edward A. Bloom.

THE BRUCE PUBLISHING CO. For excerpts from *Francis Thompson: In His Paths* by Terence Connolly; from *A Cheerful Ascetic and Other Essays* by James J. Daly.

BUCKNELL REVIEW. For the excerpt from "Andrew Marvell and the Winged Chariot" by John Wheatcroft.

BURNS AND OATES LTD. For the excepts from *Newman as a Man of Letters* by Joseph J. Reilly; from *Shelley* by Francis Thompson.

DOUGLAS BUSH. For the excerpt from his article on Andrew Marvell in *The Sewanee Review*.

M. C. BRADBROOK. For excerpt from his *The Growth and Structure of Elizabethan Comedy* and *Shakespeare and Elizabethan Poetry*.

THE BRITISH COUNCIL. For excerpts from the following titles in the series *Writers and Their Work: Charles Lamb* by Edmund Blunden; from *Sir Thomas Malory* by M. C. Bradbrook; from *George Crabbe* by R. Brett; from *Geoffrey Chaucer* by N. Coghill; from *Andrew Marvell* by C. Devlin; from *John Skelton* by Peter Green; from *Sir Walter Scott* by Ian Jack; from *Robert Herrick* by John Press.

J. B. BROADBENT. For excerpt from his *Some Graver Subject*.

UNIVERSITY OF CALIFORNIA PRESS. For excerpts from *The Art of Beowulf* by A. G. Brodeur; from *Studies in the Comic* by Bertrand H. Bronson; from *Essays Critical and Historical Dedicated to Lily Campbell* by Alexander H. Chorney; from *Shakespeare's Tragic Frontier* by Willard Farnham; from *The Idea of Coleridge's Criticism* by R. H. Fogle; from *Kipling the Story Writer* by Walter Morris Hart; from *Victorian Knight Errant* by Leon Howard; from *De Quincey to Wordsworth* by John E. Jordan; from *Studies in the Comic* by B. H. Lehman; from *Steele at Drury Lane* by John Loftis; from *The Anatomy of Robert Burton's England* by William R. Mueller; from *Christina Rossetti* by Lona Mosk Packer; from *Tennyson's Maud: The Biographical Genesis* by Ralph W. Rader; from *John Lydgate* by Walter F. Schirmer; from *The Varied God* by Patricia M. Spacks; from *Tristram Shandy's World* by John Traugott; from *The Poacher from Stratford* by Frank W. Wadsworth; from *The Rise of the Novel* by Ian Watt; from *17th Century Prose* by F. P. Wilson; from *Jane Austen's Novels* by Andrew H. Wright; also from the articles on Chaucer and the excerpt from Jonson and Boswell by Bertrand Bronson which appeared in *Publications in English;* from *"Wuthering Heights and the Critics"* by Melvin R. Watson, © 1949 by the Regents of the University of

California, reprinted from *The Trollopian* (now called *Nineteenth-Century Fiction*) III, pp. 243–63, by permission of The Regents.

CAMBRIDGE UNIVERSITY PRESS. For excerpts from *English Literary Criticism: The Medieval Phase* by J. W. Atkins; from *Women Writers of the Nineteenth Century* by Marjorie Bald; from *Four Metaphysical Poets* by Joan Bennett; from *George Eliot* by Joan Bennett; from *Sir Thomas Browne* by Joan Bennett; from *Shakespeare Survey* by S. L. Bethell; from *Of Paradise and Light* by Muriel C. Bradbrook; from *Themes and Conventions of Elizabethan Tragedy* by Muriel C. Bradbrook; from *Andrew Marvell* by M. C. Bradbrook and M. G. Lloyd Thomas; from *Beowulf* by R. W. Chambers; from *Shakespearean Tragedy* by H. B. Charlton; from *Light and Entertainment* by Rosalie L. Colie; from *Shelley and Other Essays* by George Cowling; from *Medieval Panorama* by G. G. Coulton; from *The Lollard Bible* by Margaret Deanesly; from "The Introduction of Printing into England and the Early Works of the Press" by E. Gordon Duff, in *Cambridge History of English Literature,* Vol. II, eds. G. W. Ward and A. R. Waller; from "The Earliest Scottish Literature" by Peter Giles, in *Cambridge History of English Literature,* Vol. II; from "Pearl, Cleanness, Patience and Sir Gawayne" by Sir Israel Gollancz, in *Cambridge History of English Literature,* Vol. I; from *John Skelton* by Ian A. Gordon; from an article on Sir Thomas Malory by Alice D. Greenwood, in *Cambridge History of English Literature,* Vol. II; from "English Prose in the 15th Century" by Alice D. Greenwood, in *Cambridge History of English Literature,* Vol. II; from *The Canon's Yeoman's Prologue and Tale,* ed. Maurice Hassey; from an article on Keats by C. H. Herford, in *Cambridge History of English Literature,* Vol. XII; from an article on William Shakespeare by Harold Jenkins, in *Shakespeare Survey;* from *Tennyson* by William Paton Ker; from *Thomas Gray* by R. W. Ketton-Cremer; from "The End of the Middle Ages" in *The Religious Orders in England,* Vol. II, by David Knowles; from "Barclay and Skelton: Early German Influence on English Literature" by A. Koelbing, in *Cambridge History of English Literature,* Vol. III; from the Introduction by F. L. Lucas to *George Crabbe: An Anthology;* from *Dante Gabriel Rossetti* by F. L. Lucas; from *Eight Victorian Poets* by F. L. Lucas; from *Ten Victorian Poets* by F. L. Lucas; from an article on John Wyclif by Bernard L. Manning, in *Cambridge Medieval History,* Vol. VII; from *The Problem of John Ford* by H. J. Oliver; from *Preaching in Medieval England* by J. R. Owst; from *Of Paradise and Light* by E. C. Pettet; from *Studies in Literature* by Arthur Quiller-Couch; from *The Sense of Glory* by Herbert Read; from *Towards the Twentieth Century* by H. V. Routh; from *William Cowper of the Inner Temple* by Charles Ryskamp; from an article on Radcliffe by George Saintsbury, in *Cambridge History of English Literature,* Vol. XI; from an article on Hunt by George Saintsbury, in *Cambridge History of English Literature,* Vol XII; from "Chaucer" and "The English Chaucerians" by George Saintsbury, in *Cambridge History of English Literature,* Vol. II; from articles on Charlotte Brontë, Collins, and Thomas Hoccleve by George Sampson, in *The Concise Cambridge History of English Literature;* from "The Scottish Chaucerians" by G. Gregory Smith, in *Cambridge History of English Literature,* Vol. II; from *Marlowe, A Critical Study* by J. B. Steane; from *English Satire* by James Sutherland; from *Essays in Criticism and Research* by Geoffrey Tillotson; from *The Miltonic Setting* by E. M. W. Tillyard; from *A Study of Elizabethan and Jacobean Tragedy* by T. B. Tomlinson; from *Paradise Lost and Its Critics* by A. J. A. Waldock; from *The Third Part of King Henry VI* (new Cambridge ed.) by John Dover Wilson.

MRS. HENRY S. CANBY. For excerpts from *Classic Americans* by Henry Seidel Canby.

JONATHAN CAPE LTD. For excerpts from *Man's Unconquerable Mind* by R. W. Chambers; from *Skelton* by H. L. R. Edwards; from *John Ruskin* by Joan Evans; from *The Elect Nation* by William Haller; from *Poetry and Humanism* by M. M.

Mahood and Kennikat Press, Inc.; from *Jonathan Swift* by John Middleton Murry, with the permission of the Executors of The John Middleton Murry Estate; from *The Last Attachment* by Iris Origo, with the permission of John Murray; from *The Pre-Eminent Victorian* by Joanna Richardson; from *Rejoice in the Lamb* by William Force Stead; from *Blue Ghost* by Jean Temple.

THE CARNEGIE INSTITUTE OF WASHINGTON. For the excerpt from *Lydgate's Fall of Princes,* Henry Bergen, ed.

ARTHUR J. CARR. For the excerpt from his article on Alfred Lord Tennyson in the *University of Toronto Quarterly.*

CASSELL AND COMPANY LTD. For excerpts from *Young George Farquhar* by Willard Connely; from *A Victorian American, Henry Wadsworth Longfellow* by Herbert S. Gorman; from *Elizabeth Barrett Browning* by Dorothy Hewlett; from *Scottish Poetry: A Critical Survey* by James Kinsley, ed.; from *Studies French and English* by F. L. Lucas; from *George Eliot* by Charles S. Olcott; from *Charles Dickens and His Friends* by W. Teignmouth Shore.

CHATTO AND WINDUS LTD. For excerpts from *Coleridge the Visionary* by J. B. Beer; from *The Complex Fate* by Marius Bewley; from *The Eccentric Design* by Marius Bewley; from *The Growth and Structure of Elizabethan Comedy* by M. C. Bradbrook; from *Shakespeare and Elizabethan Poetry* by M. C. Bradbrook; from *Some Graver Subject* by J. B. Broadbent; from *The Spare Chancellor* by A. Buchan; from *Seven Types of Ambiguity* by William Empson; from *Some Versions of Pastoral* by William Empson; from *English Emblem Books* by Rosemary Freeman; from *The Background of English Literature* by H. J. C. Grierson; from *Cross-Currents in 17th Century English Literature* by H. J. C. Grierson; from *Essays and Addresses* by H. J. C. Grierson; from *Poems of Lord Byron,* edited by H. J. C. Grierson; from *A Critical History of English Poetry* by H. J. C. Grierson and J. C. Smith; from *The Poetry of Crabbe* by L. Haddakin; from *Charles Dickens* by Una Pope-Hennessy; from *On the Margin* by Aldous Huxley; from *Vulgarity in Literature* by Aldous Huxley; from *Drama and Society in the Age of Jonson* by L. C. Knights; from *Explorations* by L. C. Knights; from *The Common Pursuit* by F. R. Leavis; from *The Great Tradition, New Bearings in English Poetry,* and *Revaluation* by F. R. Leavis; from *The John Fletcher Plays* by Clifford Leech; from *John Ford and the Drama of His Time* by Clifford Leech; from *The Life of Bret Harte* by Henry C. Merwin; from *The Broken Compass* by Edward Partridge; from *Paradise Lost and the 17th Century* by B. Rajan; from *The Field of Nonsense* by Elizabeth Sewall; from *Books and Characters* by Lytton Strachey; from *The English Epic and Its Background* by E. M. W. Tillyard; from *Five Poems* by E. M. W. Tillyard; from *Poetry Direct-Oblique* by E. M. W. Tillyard; from *Poetry and Its Background* by E. M. W. Tillyard; from *Shakespeare's History Plays* by E. M. W. Tillyard; from *Shakespeare's Last Plays* by E. M. W. Tillyard; from *The Herculean Hero* by Eugene M. Waith; from *Byron and the Spoiler's Art* by Paul West; from *The 17th Century Background* by Basil Willey; from *Jane Austen's Novels* by Andrew H. Wright.

THE UNIVERSITY OF CHICAGO PRESS. For excerpts from *More Contemporary Americans* by Percy Boynton; from *Matthew Arnold: A Study in Conflict* by E. K. Brown; from *Symbolism and American Literature* by Charles Feidelson, Jr.; from *Henry Vaughan: The Experience and the Tradition* by Ross Garner; from *The Structure of Literature* by Paul Goodman; from "An Interpretation of Chaucer's Legend of Good Women" by D. D. Griffith, in *Manly Anniversary Studies;* from *The Sister Arts* by Jean H. Hagstrum; from *William Blake, Poet and Painter* by Jean H. Hagstrum; from *Tobias Smollett, Traveler-Novelist,* from *The*

Modernity of Milton by Martin A. Larson; from *The American Adam* by R. W. B. Lewis; from *Heralds of American Literature* by Annie R. Marble; from *A Critical Guide to Leaves of Grass* by James E. Miller; from *Daniel Defoe* by John Robert Moore; from *The Road to Tryermaine* by A. H. Nethercot; from *Speculative Instruments* by I. A. Richards; from *Coleridge, Opium, and Kubla Khan* by Elisabeth Schneider; from *Dr. Johnson's Dictionary* by James J. Sledd and Gwin J. Kolb; from *The Political Philosophy of Hobbes* by Leo Strauss; from *Elizabethan and Metaphysical Imagery* by Rosamund Tuve; from *A Reading of George Herbert* by Rosamund Tuve; from *Rage for Order* by Austin Warren; from *The Seneca Amble* by George Williamson; from *17th Century Contexts* by George Williamson.

Also for the following articles in *Modern Philology:* on Geoffrey Chaucer by J. V. Cunningham (Feb. 1952); on John Milton by Northrop Frye (LIII); on Alexander Pope by Elder Olson (XXXVII); on Jonathan Swift by George Sherburn (LVI); on Geoffrey Chaucer by James Sledd (Nov. 1953); on Thomas Shadwell by John Harrington Smith (XLVI); on William Shakespeare by Theodore Spencer (XXXVI); on Thomas Gray by John H. Sutherland (LV); and on Geoffrey Chaucer by J. S. P. Tatlock.

THE CLARENDON PRESS. For excerpts from *Poets and Poetry* by John Bailey; from *English Classic Drama 1700–1750* by F. W. Bateson; from *Chaucer and the 15th Century* by H. S. Bennett; from *The Parliment of Foules* by J. A. W. Bennett; from *An Introduction to the 18th Century Drama* by Frederick S. Boas; from "The Hoole Book" by D. S. Brewer, in *Essays on Malory,* ed. J. A. W. Bennett; from *Political Ideas of the English Romanticist* by Crane Brinton; from *Alexander Pope* by Reuben A. Brower; from *English Literature in the Early 17th Century* by Douglas Bush; from *Essays on the 18th Century* by John Butt; from *English Literature at the Close of the Middle Ages,* 2nd ed., by E. K. Chambers; from *Samuel Taylor Coleridge* by E. K. Chambers; from *Arthur Hugh Clough* by Catherine Churley; from *Selections from Gavin Douglas* by David F. C. Coldwell; from *Essays in the 18th Century* by Herbert Davis; from *English Literature in the Early 18th Century* by Bonamy Dobrée; from *The Lamp and the Lute* by Bonamy Dobrée; from *Henry Fielding: His Life, Works, and Times,* 2nd ed., by F. Homer Dudden; from *Essays and Studies,* Vol. XXI, by T. S. Eliot; from *Robert Henryson, Poems,* ed. Charles Elliott; from an article on W. S. Landor by Oliver Elton, in *Walter Savage Landor,* ed. E. K. Chambers; from *Shakespeare's Comedies* by Bertrand Evans; from *Essays on Middle English Literature* by Dorothy Everett; from *The Study of Poetry* by H. W. Garrod; from *Wordsworth: Lectures and Essays* by H. W. Garrod; from *The Pearl,* ed. E. V. Gordon; from *Shakespearean Comedy* by George Gordon; from *The Poetry of Donne,* Vol. II, by H. J. C. Grierson; from *Introduction to Browning's Men and Women* by G. E. Hadow; from *The Structure of Allegory in "The Fairie Queene"* by A. C. Hamilton; from *Henry Vaughan* by F. E. Hutchinson; from *Augustan Satire* by Ian Jack; from *The Dream of Learning* by D. G. James; from *William Dunbar, Poems,* ed. J. Kingsley; from *Jane Austen and Her Art* by Mary Lascelles; from *Anglo-Norman Literature and Its Background* by M. Dominica Legge; from *The Metaphysical Poets* by J. B. Leischman; from *The Allegory of Love* by C. S. Lewis; from *English Literature in the 16th Century* by C. S. Lewis; from "The English Prose Morte" by C. S. Lewis in *Essays on Malory,* ed. J. A. W. Bennett; from *Geoffrey Chaucer* by John Livingston Lowes; from *"Gewain and the Green Knight"* by Laura Hibbard Loomis, in *Arthurian Literature in the Middle Ages,* ed. R. S. Loomis; from *Tennyson: Poetry and Prose* by F. L. Lucas; from *The Complete Works of John Gower,* Vol. II, by G. C. Macaulay; from *The Earlier Tudors 1485–1558* by J. D. Mackie; from *The 14th Century 1307–1399* by May McKisack; from *Wordsworth* by Mary Moorman; from *Complaint and Satire in Early English Literature* by John Peter; from *Six Essays on Johnson* by Walter Raleigh; from *Shelley at Work* by Nevill Rogers; from *Oxford Lectures on Poetry* by E. de Selincourt; from the Introduction by E. de Selincourt to *The Prelude* by William Wordsworth; from an article on Hazlitt by E. de Selincourt in *Walter Savage Landor,* ed. E. K. Chambers; from "Caxton and Malory" in *Essays on Malory* by Sally Shaw; from the Introduction by John Shawcross to *Biographia Literaria* by S. T. Coleridge; from *The Letters of Jonathan Swift to Charles Ford* by David Nichol Smith; from *On the Poetry of Pope* by Geoffrey Tillotson; from *Pope and Human Nature* by Geoffrey Tillotson; from *Novels of the 1840's* by Kathleen Tillotson; from *Sir Gawain and the Green Knight,* eds. J. R. R. Tolkien and E. V. Gordon; from *Malory* by Eugene Vinaver; from *Audience of Beowulf* by Dorothy Whitlock; from *The English Poetic Mind* by Charles W. S. Williams; from *Elizabethan and Jacobean* by F. P. Wilson.

CLARKE, IRWIN & CO. LIMITED. For excerpts from *Shakespeare and Elizabethan Poetry* by M. C. Bradbrook; from *The Herculean Hero* by Eugene M. Waith.

COLLEGE ENGLISH. For excerpts from articles on The Gawain-Poet by William Goldhurst and on Geoffrey Chaucer by Charles A. Owen, Jr.

D. E. COLLINS. For excerpts from "A Turnpoint in History" by G. K. Chesterton in *The Fame of Blessed Thomas More.*

WILLIAM COLLINS SONS & CO. LTD. For excerpts from *The Imagination of Charles Dickens* by A. O. J. Cockshutt; from *Alfred The Great* by E. Duckett; from *Born under Saturn* by Catherine M. MacLean; from *Southey* by Jack Simmons.

UNIVERSITY OF COLORADO PRESS. For the excerpt from the University of Colorado Studies: *Elizabethan Studies and Other Essays in Honor of George F. Reynolds* by George R. Kernodle.

COLUMBIA UNIVERSITY PRESS. For excerpts from *Mr. Cibber of Drury Lane* by Richard H. Barker; from *English Institute Essays 1946* by Cleanth Brooks; from *Milton's Blindness* by Eleanor Brown; from *Studies in the History of Ideas* by John Dewey; from *Matthew Prior* by Charles K. Eves; from *Religious Trends in English Poetry,* Vol. I and II, by Hoxie Neale Fairchild; from *The Romantic Quest* by Hoxie N. Fairchild; from *Diderot and Sterne* by Alice G. Fredman; from *English Institute Essays 1948* by Northrop Frye; from *Sir Walter Scott, Bart.* by H. J. C. Grierson; from an article on Ben Jonson by Ray L. Heffner in *English Stage Comedy,* ed. W. K. Wimsatt Jr.; from the Introduction by L. H. and C. W. Houtchens to *Leigh Hunt's Dramatic Criticism 1808–1834;* from *Ben Jonson: Poet* by George Johnstone; from *Richard Brome, Caroline Playwright* by R. J. Kaufman; from *Medieval Story,* 2nd ed., by William Witherle Lawrence; from *John Skelton Laureate* by William Nelson; from *The Poetry of Edmund Spenser* by William Nelson; from *The Breaking of the Circle* by Marjorie H. Nicolson; from *Vergil and the English Poets* by Elizabeth Nitchie; from *The Psychiatric Novels of Oliver Wendell Holmes* by Clarence P. Obendorf; from *The Broken Compass* by Edward Partridge; from *The Presence of Walt Whitman* by Roy Harvey Pearce; from *A Critique of Paradise Lost* by John Peter; from *The Language of Tragedy* by Moody E. Prior; from *George Gascoigne* by C. T. Prouty; from *The Background of Gray's Elegy* by Amy L. Reed; from *Hudibras in the Burlesque Tradition* by Edward A. Richards; from *The Darkening Glass* by John D. Rosenberg; from *Human Dignity and the Great Victorian* by B. N. Schilling; from *Middleton's Tragedies* by Samuel Schoenbaum; from *A History of American Philosophy* by Herbert W. Schneider; from *The English Ode from Milton to Keats* by George N. Shuster; from *The Poetry of Thomas Hardy* by James G. Southworth; from *Shakespeare and the Allegory of Evil* by Bernard Spivak; from *Reason and the Imagination* by Miriam K. Starkman; from *Robert Henryson* by Marshall W. Stearns; from *Sir Walter Raleigh: A Study in Eliza-*

bethan Skepticism by Ernest A. Strathmann; from *The Novels of George Eliot* by Jerome Thale; from "Leigh Hunt as Man of Letters . . ." by C. D. Thorpe, in *Leigh Hunt's Literary Criticism,* eds. C. W. and L. H. Houtchens; from *John Bunyan, Mechanick Preacher* by William York Tindall; from *The Herculean Hero* by E. M. Waith; from *Hardy of Wessex* by Carl J. Weber; from *The American Way of Poetry* by Henry W. Wells; from *The 17th Century Background* by Basil Willey; from "Leigh Hunt as Political Essayist" by Carl R. Woodring, in *Leigh Hunt: Political and Occasional Essays,* eds. C. W. and L. H. Houtchens and Lawrence Huston.

THE COMMONWEAL. For the excerpt from "On Reading Thomas More" by Padraic Colum.

COMPARATIVE LITERATURE. For the excerpts on Geoffrey Chaucer by Stephen Manning and on Sir Thomas Wyatt by D. G. Rees.

TRUSTEES OF THE JOSEPH CONRAD ESTATE. For the excerpt from his *Notes on Life and Letters.*

CONSTABLE AND CO. LTD. For excerpts from *The Characters of Love* by John Bayley; from *William Blake, His Philosophy and Symbols* by S. Foster Damon; from *Sir Walter Scott, Baronet* by H. J. C. Grierson; from *Lewis Carroll* by Derek Hudson.

THE CONTEMPORARY REVIEW. For the excerpt from the article on Thomas Dekker by Constance Spender.

CORNELL UNIVERSITY PRESS. For excerpts from *Poor Collins* by Edward G. Ainsworth, Jr.; from *Charles Kingsley* by Stanley E. Baldwin; from *Fielding's Theory of the Novel* by Frederick O. Bissell, Jr.; from *Paradise Lost in Our Time* by Douglas Bush; from *John Marston: Satirist* by Anthony Caputi; from *The Dickens Critics* by Lauriat Lane; from *Mountain Gloom and Mountain Glory* by Majorie Hope Nicolson; from *The Making of Walton's Lives* by David Novarr; from *Thomas Lodge by Edward A. Tenney.* Copyright, Cornell University used by permission of Cornell University Press.

COWARD-MCCANN, INC. For excerpts from *Sir Walter Scott* by John Buchan; from *Our Singing Strength by Alfred Kreymborg,* copyright 1929 by Coward-McCann, Inc.

THE CRESSET PRESS, LTD. For excerpts from *Louisa May Alcott* by Katherine Anthony; from *Introduction in the Life of George Crabbe by His Son* by Edmund Blunden; from *Francis Bacon, First Statesman of Science* by J. G. Crowther; from *Adventures of Huckleberry Finn* by T. S. Eliot; from *James Thomson* by Douglas Grant; from *Introduction in the Autobiography of Leigh Hunt* by J. E. Morpurgo; from *The Beginnings of English Literature to Skelton 1509,* 2nd ed., by W. L. Renwick and Harold Orton.

THE CRITICAL QUARTERLY SOCIETY. For the excerpts on Thomas Traherne by Margaret Bottrall and on Geoffrey Chaucer by Rosemary Woolf.

THOMAS Y. CROWELL CO. For the excerpts from *The Poetry of Robert Browning* by Stopford Brooke; from *Splendid Poseur* by M. M. Marberry.

CROWN PUBLISHERS, INC. For the excerpt from *John Milton, Englishman* by James Holly Hanford, © 1949 by James Holly Hanford.

PETER DAVIES LTD. For the excerpt from *The Life* by Mona Wilson.

DELAWARE NOTES. For the excerpt from Marion N. Green "Christian Implications of Knighthood and Courtly Love in Chaucer's *Troilus*", *Delaware Notes*, 30th Series, 1957.

DELL PUBLISHING CO., INC. For the excerpt on Shakespeare reprinted from *The Laurel Shakespeare: Much Ado About Nothing*, ed. Francis Fergusson. Copyright © 1960 by Western Printing and Lithographing Company and reprinted by permission of the publishers, Dell Publishing Co., Inc.

J. M. DENT & SONS LTD. For excerpts from *Notes on Life and Letters* by Joseph Conrad; from *Thomas H. Huxley* by J. R. Ainsworth; from *Robert Browning* by Edward Dowden; from *Scottish Poetry from Barbour to James VI*, ed. N. M. Gray; from *Winds of Doctrine* by George Santayana; from *Le Morte D'Arthur of Sir Thomas Malory* by Vida D. Scudder; from *An Introduction to the Study of Browning* by Arthur Symons; from the introduction in *The Life of Percy Bysshe Shelley* by Humbert Wolfe.

THE DIAL PRESS. For the excerpts from *Literary Criticism in America* by George E. De Mille; from *Milton: Man and Thinker* by Denis Saurat.

DISCOURSE. For the excerpt on Thomas Carew by Francis G. Schoff.

DODD, MEAD & CO. For excerpts from *Thomas Henry Huxley* by Edward Clodd; from *Robert Browning* by C. H. Herford; from *William Makepeace Thackeray* by Charles Whibley.

HENRY W. DORMER. For the excerpt from his introduction to *Utopia*.

DOUBLEDAY & COMPANY, INC. For excerpts from *Blake's Apocalypse* by Harold Bloom, copyright © 1963 by Harold Bloom, reprinted by permission of Doubleday & Company, Inc.; from *The American Novel and Its Tradition* by Richard Chase, copyright © 1957 by Richard Chase, reprinted by permission of Doubleday & Company, Inc.; from *Emerson* by Robert M. Gay, copyright 1928 by Doubleday & Company, Inc., reprinted by permission of the publisher; from *Hawthorne: A Study in Solitude* by Herbert Gorman, copyright 1927 by George H. Doran Company, reprinted by permission of Doubleday & Company, Inc.; from *A Victorian American: Henry Wadsworth Longfellow* by Herbert S. Gorman, copyright 1926 by George H. Doran Company, reprinted by permission of Doubleday & Company, Inc.; from *Bitter Bierce* by C. Hartley Grattan, copyright 1929 by Doubleday & Company, Inc., reprinted by permission of the publisher.

THE DUBLIN REVIEW. For excerpts from articles on Alexander Pope by J. M. Cameron; on Sir Thomas More by P. E. Hallett; on Thomas More by J. S. Phillimore.

GERALD DUCKWORTH & CO. LTD. For excerpts from *George Eliot* by Anne Fremantle; from *The Last Romantics* and *A Preface to the Faerie Queene* by Graham Hough; from *Thomas Moore* by Seamus MacCall; from *Samuel Butler* by R. F. Rattray; from *The English Utilitarians* by Leslie Stephen.

DUKE UNIVERSITY PRESS. For excerpts from *Chaucer: A Critical Appreciation* by Paull F. Baum; *Ten Studies in the Poetry of Matthew Arnold* by Paull F. Baum; from "Coleridge on the Seventeenth Century" by Louis I. Bredvold; from *Coleridge on the Seventeenth Century* by R. F. Brinkley; from *The Development of English Humor* by Louis Cazamian; from *Charles Brockden Brown* by David Lee

Clark; from The *Indian Summer of English Chivalry* by Arthur B. Ferguson; from *The Rungless Ladder* by Charles H. Foster; from *John Gay* by William Henry Irving; from *English Verse Between Chaucer and Surrey* by E. P. Hammond; from *Inward Sky* by Hubert H. Hoeltje; from *Swinburne's Literary Career and Fame* by Clyde Kenneth Hyder; from *Desire and Restraint in Shelley* by Floyd Stovall; from *George W. Cable* by Arlin Turner.

For excerpts from articles in *American Literature:* "The Structure of Huckleberry Finn" by Frank Baldanza; from "Lafcadio Hearn's Twice-Told Legends Reconsidered" by Beong-Cheou-Yu; from "Rip, Ichabod, and the American Imagination" by Terence Martin; from "Frank Morris and Romance" by George W. Johnson; from "Cable and the Creoles" by Edward L. Tinker. From *South Atlantic Quarterly,* from "Mark Twain's Despair: An Explanation in Terms of His Humanity" by Richard D. Altick.

T. A. DUNN. For the excerpt from his *Philip Massinger.*

E. P. DUTTON & CO. INC. For excerpts from *The English Novel* by Walter Allen; from *Arthur Tennyson* by A. C. Benson; from *Ephemera Critica* by John Churton Collins; from *Edward Lear* by Angus Davidson; from *Browning* by F. R. G. Duckworth; from *Here Lies Richard Brinsley Sheridan* by Kenelm Foss; from *Vision and Gesture* by Charles Gardner; from the Introduction in *Letters of Lord Byron* by André Maurois; from *An Introduction to the Study of Blake* by Max Plowman; from *Le Morte D'Arthur of Sir Thomas Malory* by Vida D. Scudder; from *Blake's Innocence and Experience* by Joseph Wickstee; from *Tom Paine: America's Godfather* by W. E. Woodward.

WILLIAM EMPSON. For excerpt from his *Some Versions of Pastoral.*

ENGLISH STUDIES. For excerpts from articles on George Peele by M. C. Bradbrook; on William Wycherley by T. W. Craik; on Sir Thomas More by W. A. G. Doyle-Davidson; on George Peele by Inga-Stina Ekeblad; on Jeremy Taylor by J. R. King; on Andrew Marvell by Maren-Sofie Rostvige.

THE ENGLISH UNIVERSITIES PRESS LTD. For the excerpt from *John Wycliffe and the Beginnings of English Nonconformity* by K. P. McFarlane.

ESSAYS IN CRITICISM. For excerpts from articles on Geoffrey Chaucer by John F. Adams; on Thomas Gray by A. E. Dyson; on Sir Thomas Wyatt by J. D. Hainsworth; on Sir Walter Scott by Joyce Horner; on Andrew Marvell by Frank Kermode; on William Dunbar by Edwin Morgan; on John Gower by Peter Rison; on Geoffrey Chaucer by Roger Sharrock; on Daniel Defoe by Ian Watt.

ENGLISH ASSOCIATION. For excerpts from articles in *Essays and Studies* on John Lydgate by H. S. Bennett; on Samuel Richardson by F. S. Boas, published by the Clarendon Press.

EYRE & SPOTTISWOODE LTD. For excerpts from *Erasmus, Tyndale and More* by W. E. Campbell; from *A Portrait of Thomas More* by Algernon Cecil; from "Sir Thomas More" by R. W. Chambers in *The Great Tudors;* from *The American People* by Henry B. Parkes.

FABER AND FABER LTD. For excerpts from *Poetic Diction* by Owen Barfield; from *Chaucer* by G. K. Chesterton; from *Medieval Lyrics,* ed. R. T. Davies; from *The Use of Poetry and the Use of Criticism* by T. S. Eliot; from *Selected Essays* by T. S. Eliot; from *Elizabethan Essays* by T. S. Eliot; from *Mrs. Browning* by Althea Hayter; from *Dante Gabriel Rossetti* by R. L. Mégroz; from *Francis Thompson* by R. L. Mégroz; from *The Life and Letter of Tobias Smollett* by

Lewis Melville; from *Reason and Romantics* by Herbert Read; from *Wordsworth* by Herbert Read; from *The Scots Literary Tradition* by John Speirs; from *Chaucer The Maker* by John Speirs; from *Medieval English Poetry the Non-Chaucerian Tradition* by John Speirs; from *A Reading of George Herbert* by Rosamund Tuve; from *Dunbar the Poet and His Period* by Rachel Annand Taylor; from *Seventeenth Century Contexts* by George Williamson.

FARRAR, STRAUS & GIROUX, INC. For excerpts from *Jane Austen* by Elizabeth Jenkins; from *Keats* by J. M. Murry; from *The Pleasures of Peacock* by B. R. Redman; from *The Donne Tradition* by George Williamson.

LITERARY EXECUTOR OF MR. REGINALD FARRER. For excerpt from article on Jane Austen by Reginald Farrer in *Quarterly Review*.

DE LANCEY FERGUSON. For excerpt from his *Pride and Passion: Robert Burns*.

LESLIE FIEDLER. For excerpts from his *Love and Death in the American Novel*.

UNIVERSITY OF FLORIDA PRESS. For excerpt from *SAMLA Studies in Milton* by Ants Oras.

THE FOLGER MEMORIAL LIBRARY. For excerpt from article on Sir Thomas More by Giles E. Dawson and Edwin E. Willoughby.

THE FOLGER SHAKESPEARE LIBRARY. For excerpt from *Joseph Quincy Adams Memorial Studies* by George Winchester Stone, Jr.

ROSEMARY FREEMAN. For excerpt from her *English Emblem Books*.

GLASGOW UNIVERSITY PUBLICATIONS. For excerpts from an article on William Shakespeare by R. W. Chambers; from "Thomas Campbell: An Oration" by W. Macneile Dixon.

HERBERT GOLDSTONE. For excerpt on George Peele from *Boston University Studies in English*.

VICTOR GOLLANCZ, LTD. For excerpts from *Blake's Apocalypse* by Harold Bloom; from *Literature and Society* by David Daiches; from "Note on Milton" in *The Divine Vision* by Northrop Frye; from "The Theme and Structure of William Blake's Jerusalem" in *The Divine Vision*.

JOHN E. GRANT. For excerpt from his "On Blake's Tyger" in *Discussions of William Blake*.

LITERARY ESTATE OF H. J. C. GRIERSON. For excerpt from *Poems of Lord Byron*, ed. H. J. C. Grierson.

FLORA GRIERSON. For excerpt from *Essays and Addresses, Cross-Currents in 17th Century English Literature, A Critical History of English Poetry,* and *Lyrical Poetry from Blake to Hardy* by H. J. C. Grierson.

GROVE PRESS. For excerpt from the Introduction by John Berryman to *The Monk* by M. Lewis.

L. HADDAKIN. For excerpt from her *The Poetry of Crabbe*.

permission of the publishers from Sir Maurice Bowra *The Romantic Imagination*
Cambridge, Mass.: Harvard University Press, Copyright 1949, by the President
and Fellows of Harvard College); from *Matthew Arnold, Poetry and Prose* by
John Bryson; from *Tennyson* by Jerome Buckley; from *Jonathan Swift and the
Anatomy of Satire* by John W. Bullitt; from *Mythology and the Romantic Tradi-
tion in Poetry* by Douglas Bush; from *The First Part of King Henry IV* (Arden
Edition) by Andrew S. Cairncross; from *Shelley and His Circle,* Vols. I and II by
K. N. Cameron and Eleanor L. Nicholes; from *Shakespeare's Roman Days* by
Maurice Charney; from *Chaucer's Early Poetry* by Wolfgang Clemen; from *Poe:
A Critical Study* by Edward Davidson; from the Introduction by H. W. Donner to
Plays and Poems of Thomas Lovell Beddoes; from *The Use of Poetry and the
Use of Criticism* by T. S. Eliot; from *The Evolution of Keats Poetry,* Vol. II, by
C. L. Finney (reprinted by permission of the publishers from Claude L. Finney
The Evolution of Keats' Poetry, Cambridge, Mass.: Harvard University Press,
Copyright, 1936, by the President and Fellows of Harvard College, Copyright,
1964, by Claude Lee Finney); from *Poetry and the Criticism of Life* by H. W.
Garrod; from *Emily Dickinson, the Mind of the Poet* by Albert J. Gelpi; from
The Writings and Life of George Meredith by Mary Sturge Gretton; from *Thomas
Nashe: A Critical Introduction* by G. R. Hibbard; from *Abraham Cowley's World
of Order* by Robert B. Hinnan; from *The First Modern Comedies* by Norman N.
Holland; from *John Lyly. The Humanist as a Courtier* by G. K. Hunter (reprinted
by permission of the publishers from G. K. Hunter *John Lyly: The Humanist as
Courtier,* Cambridge, Mass.: Harvard University Press, Copyright, 1962, by G. K.
Hunter); from *Thomas Gray, Scholar* by William Powell Jones; from *Chaucer
and His Poetry* by George Lyman Kittredge; from *A Study of Gawain and the
Green Knight* by George Lyman Kittredge; from *The John Fletcher Plays* by
Clifford Leech; from *The Overreacher* by Harry Levin; from *Paradise Lost as
"Myth"* by Isabel Gamble MacCaffrey; from *De Quincey: A Portrait* by J. C.
Metcalf (reprinted by permission of the publishers from J. C. Metcalf *De Quincey:
A Portrait,* Cambridge, Mass.: Harvard University Press, Copyright, 1940, by the
President and the Fellows of Harvard College); from *The Disappearance of God*
by J. Hillis Miller; from *The Estate of Poetry* by Edwin Muir; from *Collected
Poems of Sir Thomas Wyatt,* ed. Kenneth Muir; from *Sir Philip Sidney as a
Literary Craftsman* by Kenneth O. Meyrick; from *On Rereading Chaucer* by
Howard Rollin Patch; from *Emerson's Angle of Vision* by Sherman Paul; from
A Life of Matthew Gregory Lewis by L. F. Peck; from *The Quest for Permanence*
by David Perkins; from *Wordsworth and the Poetry of Sincerity* by David Perkins;
from *Melville and the Comic Spirit* by Edward H. Rosenberry; from *Piers Plow-
man: An Introduction* by Elizabeth Salter; from *Elizabethan Poetry* by Hallett
Smith; from *Mark Twain, the Development of a Writer* by Henry Nash Smith;
from *Virgin Land* by Henry Nash Smith; from *The Gay Couple in Restoration
Comedy* by John H. Smith; from *English Biography before 1700* by Donald A.
Stauffer; from *Milton and Science* by Kester Svendsen; from *Carlyle: Selected
Works* . . . by Julian Symons; from *John Bunyan* by Henri Talon; from *Images
and Themes in Five Poems by Milton* by Rosamund Tuve; from *The Subtle Knot*
by Margaret L. Wiley; from *Macaulay Prose and Poetry* by G. M. Young.

D. C. HEATH AND COMPANY. For excerpt from *Beowulf* by Fr. Klaeber.

WILLIAM HEINEMANN LTD. For excerpts from *Emily Dickinson's Poetry* by Charles
R. Anderson; from *Bret Harte* by Henry W. Boynton; from *The Ordeal of Mark
Twain* by Van Wyck Brooks; from *Poems by John Skelton* ed. Richard Hughes;
from *In Defence of Shelley* by Herbert Read.

GEORGE C. HESELTINE. For excerpt from "John Wyclif" in *Great Yorkshiremen.*

DOROTHY HEWLETT. For excerpt from *Elizabeth Barrett Browning.*

send. Also for excerpts from articles in *Journal of English and Germanic Philology:* on Geoffrey Chaucer by Robert J. Allen; on The Gawain-Poet by John Conley; on Nathaniel Lee by A. L. Cooke and Thomas B. Stroup; on Geoffrey Chaucer by Robert Estrich; from "Blake and the Druids" by Peter F. Fisher; on William Shakespeare by Allan H. Gilbert; on John Skelton by Judith Seitzer Larson; on Thomas Otway by William H. McBurney; on Geoffrey Chaucer by Arthur K. Moore; on Tobias Smollett by Ronald Paulson; on William Shakespeare by Irving Ribner; on Geoffrey Chaucer by J. Burke Severs; on Geoffrey Chaucer by Gardiner Stillwell.

INDIANA UNIVERSITY PRESS. For excerpt from *Charles Lamb. The Evolution of Elia* by George L. Barnett; from *The Novels of Thomas Deloney* by Merritt E. Lawlis; from *Apology for the Middle Class: The Dramatic Novels of Thomas Deloney* by Merritt E. Lawlis; from *Strange Seas of Thought* by N. P. Stallknecht; from *Walter Bagehot* by Norman St. John Stevas.

INTERNATIONAL PUBLISHERS. For excerpts from *Thomas More and His Utopia* by Karl Kautsky; from *Walt Whitman, Poet of American Democracy* by Samuel Sillen.

THE JOHNS HOPKINS PRESS. For excerpts from articles in *Journal of English Literary History:* on John Lyly by Jonas Barish; on Geoffrey Chaucer by Paull F. Baum; on George Eliot by George T. Bissell; on Thomas Hobbes by Donald F. Bond; on William Shakespeare by Adrien Bonjour; on John Dryden by Reuben A. Bower; on Sir Walter Raleigh by C. F. Tucker Brooke; on Oliver Goldsmith by Curtis Dahl; on Geoffrey Chaucer by Bernard I. Duffy; on Sir Thomas More by Robert C. Elliot; on Sir John Suckling by O. H. Fletcher; on William Dunbar by Denton Fox; on Geoffrey Chaucer by Denton Fox; on Oliver Goldsmith by Morris Golden; on Charles Lamb by Richard Haven; on Geoffrey Chaucer by Arthur W. Hoffman; on Geoffrey Chaucer by C. Hugh Holman; on John Dryden by Edward N. Hooker; on Andrew Marvell by Lawrence Hynan; on Henry Fielding by W. R. Irwin; on Thomas Hobbes by Martin Kallich; on Thomas Shadwell by William M. Milton; on Samuel Butler by Ricardo Quintana; on Matthew Prior by Monroe K. Spears; on Samuel Pepys by Hazelton Spencer; on Sir Philip Sidney by Theodore Spencer; on Andrew Marvell by Joseph H. Summers; on John Lyly by Robert Y. Turner; on Geoffrey Chaucer by Dale Underwood; on Andrew Marvell and Thomas Traherne by John Malcolm Wallace; on Thomas Shadwell by Charles S. Ward; on Robert Herrick by Thomas R. Whitaker. For excerpts from *The Harmonious Vision* by Don C. Allen; from *Malory's Originality "The Tale of the Death of Arthur": Catastrophe and Resolution* by Wilfrid L. Guerin; from *The Mind of a Poet* by R. D. Havens; from *Essays in the History of Ideas* by Arthur O. Lovejoy; from *Chapters on Chaucer* by Kemp Malone; from *Milton's Debt to Greek Tragedy in Samson Agonistes* by William Riley Parker; from *Paradise Regained and the Tradiiton of Poetry* by Elizabeth Marie Pope; from *The Subtler Language* by E. R. Wasserman; from *The Finer Tone* by E. R. Wasserman; from *Pope's Epistle to Bathurst* by E. R. Wasserman. For articles from *Modern Language Notes* on Gavin Douglas by J. A. W. Bennett; on Alexander Pope by R. E. Hughes; on The Gawain-Poet by D. W. Robertson; on John Milton by John T. Shawcross; on Robert Herrick by Leo Spitzer.

JOURNAL OF AESTHETICS AND ART CRITICISM. For excerpts from articles on John Milton by Robert Durr; from "Poetry and Design in William Blake" by Northrop Frye.

L. C. KNIGHTS. For excerpt from *Explorations* and *Drama and Society in the Age of Jonson.*

DAVID MCKAY COMPANY, INC. For excerpts from *Charles Dickens, a Critical Introduction*, by K. J. Fielding; from *The Tudor Age* by James A. Williamson.

MACDONALD & CO. LTD. For excerpts from *The First Romantics* by Malcolm Elwin; from *Lord Byron's Wife* by Malcolm Elwin.

MCGRAW-HILL BOOK CO. For excerpts from *Young Sam Johnson* by James L. Clifford; from *Apes, Angels and Victorians* by William Irvine; from *Thackeray: The Age of Wisdom* . . . by Gordon N. Ray.

ALEXANDER MACLEHOSE & CO. For excerpt from *A Historical Survey of Scottish Literature to 1714* by Agnes Mure Mackenzie.

MACMILLAN & CO. LTD., London. For excerpts from *Walter Pater* by A. C. Benson; from *Shakespearean Tragedy* by A. C. Bradley; from *Oxford Lectures* by A. C. Bradley; from *Heroic Poetry* by C. M. Bowra; from the Introduction in *A Treasury of Irish Poetry in the English Tongue* by Stopford Brook and T. W. H. Rolleston; from *Sir Philip Sidney and the English Renaissance* by John Buxton; from *Robert Browning* by G. K. Chesterton; from *John Keats* by Sidney Colvin; from *A History of English Poetry* by W. J. Courthope; from *George Eliot* by Anne Fremantle; from *Form and Style in Poetry* by W. P. Ker; from *Essays on Medieval Literature* by W. P. Ker; from *Swinburne* by Harold Nicolson; from *George Meredith* by J. B. Priestley; from *A History of English Prosody* by George Saintsbury; from *A History of English Prose Rhythm* by George Saintsbury; from *Christina Rossetti* by Dorothy Margaret Stuart; from *Anthony Trollope* by Hugh Walpole.

THE MACMILLAN COMPANY, NEW YORK. For excerpts from *English Literary Criticism* by J. W. H. Atkins; from *The Mount of Vision* by William Muir Auld; from *Literary History of the United States* by Carlos Baker; from *Garrick* by Margaret Barton; from *Early Tudor Poetry* by John M. Berdan; from *Edward Fitzgerald* by A. C. Benson; from the Introduction in *A Treasury of Irish Poetry in the English Tongue* by Stopford Brook and T. W. H. Rolleston; from *The Young Shelley, Genesis of a Radical* by K. N. Cameron; from *Intellectual America* by Oscar Cargill; from *A History of English Literature* by Louis Cazamian; from *Carlyle* by Louis Cazamian; from *Robert Browning* by G. K. Chesterton; from *The Aesthetics of Walter Pater* by Ruth C. Child; from *Medieval Panorama* by G. G. Coulton; from *A History of English Poetry* by W. J. Courthope; from *The Development of the English Novel* by Wilbur T. Cross; from *The Satire of Jonathan Swift* by Herbert Davis; from *Lectures on the Relation between Law and Public Opinion* by A. V. Dicey; from *The American Novel* by Carl Van Doren; from *Cambridge History of American Literature* by Carl Van Doren; from *Cambridge History of American Literature* by Norman Foerster; from *Roadside Meeting* by Hamlin Garland; from *Studies in Shakespeare, Milton and Donne* by James Holly Hanford; from *The Great Tradition* by Granville Hicks; from *The Romantic Image* by Frank Kermode; from *Memoirs of a Southern Woman of Letters* by Grace King; from *Shakespeare's Problem Comedies* by William Witherle Lawrence; from *Cambridge History of American Literature* by William E. Leonard; from *Literary History of the United States* by Harry T. Levin; from *The Social Mode of Restoration Comedy* by Kathleen M. Lynch; from *Literary History of the United States* by Kenneth B. Murdock; from *The Sun at Noon* by Kenneth B. Murdock; from *Cambridge Literature of American History* by Fred L. Pattee; from *Cambridge History of American Literature* by William Morton Payne; from *Howells, James, Bryant and Other Essays* by William Lyon Phelps; from *In Selected Poems of* . . . *Hardy*, ed. John Crowe Ransom; from *Newman as a Man of Letters* by Joseph J. Reilly; from *A Companion to Shakespeare Studies* by George Rylands; from *Literary History of the United States* by Odell Shepard; from *Cambridge History of American Literature* by Stuart P. Sherman; from *The*

Life of Robert Burns by Franklyn B. Snyder; from *Shakespeare and the Nature of Man* by Theodore Spencer; from *Literary History of the United States* by Wallace Stegner; from *Shakespeare Studies* by E. E. Stoll; from *Horace Walpole* by Dorothy M. Stuart; from *Cambridge History of American Literature* by Algernon Tassin; from *Alfred Tennyson* by Charles Tennyson; from *Shakespeare's Last Plays* by E. M. W. Tillyard; from *Studies in Milton* by E. M. W. Tillyard; from *Cambridge History of American Literature* by William Peterfield Trent; from *Cambridge History of American Literature* by Samuel M. Tucker; from *Literary History of the United States* by George F. Whicher; from *Sir John Vanbrugh* by Laurence Whistler; from *George Eliot* by Blanche Colton Williams; from *Literary History of the United States* by Stanley T. Williams; from *John Bunyan* by Ola Elizabeth Winslow; from *Ralph Waldo Emerson* by George E. Woodberry; from *The Paradise of Oscar Wilde* by George Woodcock; from *The Paradox of Oscar Wilde* by George Woodcock.

M. M. MAHOOD. For excerpt from his *Poetry and Humanism*.

KEMP MALONE. For excerpt from his *Widsith*.

MANCHESTER UNIVERSITY PRESS. For excerpts from *Patience*, ed. Hartley Bateson; from *The Phoenix,* ed. N. F. Blake; from *Three Old English Elegies,* ed. R. F. Leslie; from *Alliterative Poetry in Middle English* by J. P. Oakden.

JOSEPH ANTHONY MAZZEO. For excerpt on Andrew Marvell from *Journal of the History of Ideas.*

METHUEN & CO. LTD. For excerpt from *English Literary Criticism: The Medieval Phase* by J. W. H. Atkins; from *English Literary Criticism: The Renaissance* by J. W. H. Atkins; from *New Light on Pope* by Norman Ault; from *The Lion and the Honeycomb* by Richard P. Blackmur; from *Chaucer's Pilgrims* by Harold F. Brooks; from *The First Part of King Henry the Sixth* by Andrew S. Cairncross; from *Shakespearean Comedy* by H. B. Charlton; from *The Development of Shakespeare's Imagery* by W. H. Clemen; from *Chaucer's Early Poetry* by W. H. Clemen; from *Essay on Books* by A. Clutton-Brock; from *Chaucer and His England* by G. G. Coulton; from *The Comic Tales of Chaucer* by T. W. Craik; from *The Personality of Jonathan Swift* by Irvin Ehrenpreis; from *Christopher Marlowe* by Una M. Ellis-Fermor; from *The Jacobean Dream* by Una M. Ellis-Fermor; from *Tradition and Romanticism* by B. Ifor Evans; from *Beowulf and the Seventh Century* by R. Girvan; from *The Blazon of Honor* by Margaret Greaves; from *George Meredith* by Sturge Henderson; from *Middle English Literature* by George Kane; from *The Crown of Life* by G. Wilson Knight; from *The Wheel of Fire* by G. Wilson Knight; from *The Burning Oracle* on John Milton (Poets in Action) by G. Wilson Knight; from *Elizabethan Love Sonnet* by J. W. Lever; from *Shakespeare's Wordplay* by M. M. Mahood; from *Widsith* by Kemp Malone; from *Macbeth* (Arden ed.) by Kenneth Muir; from *Shakespeare* by Allardyce Nicoll; from *Music and Poetry in the English Renaissance* by Bruce Pattison; from *Jacobean Tragedy* by Irving Ribner; from the Introduction in *The Poems of John Keats* by E. de Selincourt; from *Three Northumbrian Poems,* ed. A. H. Smith; from *Sermo Lupi Ad Anglos,* ed. D. Whitelock; from *Pope's Dunciad* by Aubrey L. Williams.

UNIVERSITY OF MICHIGAN PRESS. For excerpts from the Papers of the Michigan Academy of Science, Arts and Letters on Sir Francis Bacon by Edmund Greeth and on Joseph Addison by Clarence D. Thorpe; from *The Intellectual Millieu of John Dryden* by Louis I. Bredvold; from *Sir Thomas Browne* by Frank R. Huntley; from *The Bow and the Lyre* by Roma A. King; from *New Bearings in English*

Poetry by F. R. Leavis; from *The New View of Congreve's Way of the World* by Paul and Miriam Mueschke.

THE MICHIGAN STATE UNIVERSITY PRESS. For excerpts from *The Spare Chancellor* by Alistair Buchan; from *Sanity in Bedlam* by Laurence Rabb.

UNIVERSITY OF MINNESOTA PRESS. For excerpts from *Mythology and the Renaissance Tradition* by Douglas Bush; from *Sir Thomas Browne: A Study in Religious Philosophy* by William P. Dunn; from *The Background of Thomson's Seasons* by Alan D. McKillop; from *Heroic Knowledge* by Arnold Stein; from *The Byronic Hero* by Peter L. Thorslev, Jr.; from *American Literary Naturalism* by Charles C. Walcutt.

UNIVERSITY OF MISSOURI PRESS. For excerpts from *Essays on Shakespeare and Elizabethan Drama in Honor of Hardin Craig* by Arthur Brown, Philip Edwards, Paul H. Kocher, and Irving Ribner; from *Christopher Smart* by Edward Answorth and Charles E. Noyes, © Board of Curators of the University of Missouri.

MODERN LANGUAGE QUARTERLY. For excerpts from articles on Robert Burton by Robert M. Browne; on Nicholas Rowe by Donald B. Clark; from "The Paradox of Francis Jeffrey" by J. R. Derby; from "Hermann Melville and the Craft of Fiction"; on The Gawain-Poet by George J. Engelhardt; on Thomas Heywood by P. M. Spacks; on Andrew Marvell by Leo Spitzer.

THE MODERN LANGUAGE REVIEW. For excerpts first published in the *Modern Language Review* from articles on George Peele by Harold Jenkins, XXXIV(1939); on Samuel Pepys by W. Matthew, XXIX(1934); on John Donne by B. F. Nellist, LIV(1964); on Samuel Daniel by Cecil C. Seronsy, LII(1957) and here reprinted by permission of the Modern Humanities Research Association and of the editors.

THE MONTH. For excerpts from articles on Sir Thomas More by Alban Goodier; on William Langland by Stanley B. James; on John Barbour by T. H. Kean.

MOREHOUSE-BARLOW CO. INC. For the excerpt from *A History of the Church of England* by J. R. H. Moorman.

WILLIAM MORROW AND CO. INC. For excerpts from *Emily Dickinson* by Richard Chase; from *Voyage to Windward* by J. C. Furnas; from *Sheridan: His Life and His Theatre* by Lewis Gibbs; from *James Fenimore Cooper* by James Grossman; from *In Defense of Reason* by Yvor Winters.

HARRY MORRIS. For excerpt from article on Robert Southwell.

MRS. WILLA MUIR. For excerpts from *The Politics of King Lear*, from *The Structure of the Novel*, and from *Essays on Literature*, all by Edwin Muir.

LEWIS MUMFORD. For excerpts from his *The Golden Day*.

JOHN MURRAY. For excerpts from *Every Man a Phoenix* by Margaret Bottrall; from *Byron in England* by Samuel Chew; from *Robert Browning* by Betty Miller; from *The Last Attachment* by Iris Origo.

EXECUTORS OF JOHN MIDDLETON MURRAY'S ESTATE. For excerpt from *Jonathan Swift* by John Middleton Murry.

UNIVERSITY OF NEBRASKA PRESS. For excerpts from *Pamela-Shamela* by Bernard Kreissman; from *Introduction in the Life of Dryden* by Bernard Kreissman; from

JOHN PETER. For excerpt from his article on Richard Crashaw in *Scrutiny*.

A.D. PETERS & CO. For excerpts from *Leigh Hunt and His Cricle* by Edmund Blunden; from *Shelley: A Life Story* by Edmund Blunden; from *Rossetti* by Evelyn Waugh.

PHILOSOPHICAL QUARTERLY. For excerpts from articles on John Milton by Arthur E. Barker; on Daniel Defoe by Edwin B. Benjamin; on Alexander Pope by Thomas R. Edwards, Jr.; on John Milton by Allan H. Gilbert; on Henry Vaughan by Merritt Y. Hughes; on John Cleveland by John L. Kimmey; on John Milton by H. V. S. Ogden; on John Skelton by Alan Swallow.

PHILOSOPHICAL LIBRARY INC. For excerpts from *American Literature and the Dream* by Frederic I. Carpenter.

POETRY. For excerpts from article on William Cullen Bryant by Harriet Monroe.

LAURENCE POLLINGER LTD. For excerpts from *The Lambs* by Katharine Anthony; from *Studies in Classic American Literature* by D. H. Lawrence.

PONTIFICAL INSTITUTE OF MEDIAEVAL STUDIES. For excerpt from an article on The Gawain-Poet by Charles Moorman.

JOHN POPE-HENNESSEY. For excerpt from Una Pope-Hennessey's *Charles Dickens*.

PRINCETON UNIVERSITY PRESS. For excerpts from *Citizen Thomas More and His Utopia* by Russell Ames; from *Literature of Anglo-Saxons* by G. Anderson; from *Smollett's Reputation as a Novelist* by Fred W. Borge; from *Elizabethan Revenge Tradedy* by Fredson T. Bowers; from an article on Wordsworth by Douglas Bush in *Wordsworth Centenary Study*, ed. G. J. Dunklin; from an article on Wordsworth by O. J. Campbell in *Wordsworth and Coleridge*, ed. E. L. Griggs; from *Four Essays on Gulliver's Travels* by Arthur E. Case; from *Suffering and Evil in the Plays of Christopher Marlowe* by Douglas Cole; from *Gulliver's Travels: A Critical Study* by William A. Eddy; from *The Cycle of Modern Poetry* by G. R. Elliott; from *Prophet against Empire* by David V. Erdman; from *Fearful Symmetry* by Northrop Frye; from *The Restoration Comedy of Wit* by Thomas H. Fujimura; from *Chaucerian Essays* by Gordon Hall Gerould; from an article on Samuel Butler by Dan Gibson, Jr., in *17th Century Studies*, ed. Robert Shafer; from *More's Utopia: The Biography of an Idea* by J. H. Heter; from *The Alien Vision of Victorian Poetry* by E. D. H. Johnson; from *The Great Argument* by Maurice Kelley; from *Old English Elegies* by C. Kennedy; from *Tobias Smollett* by Lewis M. Knapp; from *Religious Humanism and the Victorian Novel* by J. C. Knoepflmacher; from *Milton's Samson and the Christian Tradition* by F. Michael Krouse; from an article on Wordsworth by Emile Legouis in *Wordsworth and Coleridge*, ed. E. L. Griggs; from *On Being Human* by Paul Elmer More; from *Jane Austen as Defense and Discovery* by Marvin Mudrick; from an article on Wordsworth by F. A. Pottle in *Wordsworth Centenary Study*, ed. G. J. Dunklin; from *The Continuity of American Poetry* by Roy Harvey Pearce; from *The English History Play in the Age of Shakespeare* by Irving Ribner; from *A Preface to Chaucer* by D. W. Robertson, Jr.; from *Piers Plowman and Scriptural Tradition* by D. W. Robertson, Jr., and Bernard F. Huppé; from *The Poetical Career of Alexander Pope* by Robert K. Root; from *Swift's Satire on Learning in a Tale of a Tub* by Miriam Kosh Starkman; from *Charles Kingsley* by Margaret Farraud Thorp; from *Thomas Traherne* by Gladys I. Wade; from *Perilous Balance* by W. B. C. Watkins; from *Shakespeare and Spencer* by W. B. C. Watkins; from *The Court Wits of the Restoration* by J. Harold Wilson.

PROCEEDINGS OF THE BRITISH ACADEMY. For excerpts from articles on William Langland by Nevill Coghill; on John Milton by T. S. Eliot; on Beowulf by R. Girvan; on Thomas Carlyle by H. J. C. Grierson; on John Skelton by John Holloway; on Andrew Marvell by J. B. Leishman; on William Shakespeare by C. S. Lewis; on Beowulf by J. R. Tolkien.

PUBLICATIONS OF MODERN LANGUAGE ASSOCIATION. For excerpts from articles on George Gascoigne by R. P. Adams; from "Emerson and the Organic Metaphor" by Richard P. Adams; on Robert Greene by Don Cameron Allen; from *Topographical Poetry in 18th Century England* by Robert A. Aubin; on Sir Thomas More by Nellie Slayton Aurner; from "Congreve's Plays on the 18th Century Stage" by Ammett L. Avery; on Laurence Sterne by Theodore Baird; on John Milton by Millicent Bell; on Geoffrey Chaucer by Dorothy Bethurum; on Geoffrey Chaucer by Earle Birney; on Edward Young by Isabel St. John Bliss; from "Dialectic in *The Marriage of Heaven and Hell*" by Harold Bloom; on The Gawain-Poet by Marie Padgett Hamilton; from *Musae Anglicanae* by Leicester Bradner; on George Gascoigne by Leicester Bradner; on John Gay by Wallace Cable Brown; from "The Stage History of Shelley's *The Cenci*" by K. N. Cameron and Horst Frenz; from *Henry Howard, Earl of Surrey* by Edwin Casady; from "Hazlitt as a Critic of Art" by S. P. Chase; on Henry Vaughan by Wilson O. Clough; on John Gower by George R. Coffman; on Andrew Marvell by John S. Coolidge; on Alfred Lord Tennyson by Allan Danzig; on Gavin Douglas by Bruce Dearing; on Geoffrey Chaucer by E. Talbot Donaldson; on Jonathan Swift by Irwin Ehrenpreis; from "The Meaning of 'Fellowship with Essence' " by N. F. Ford; from *History of the Pre-Romantic Novel in England* by James R. Foster; on Geoffrey Chaucer by Robert Worth Frank; on Oliver Goldsmith by W. F. Gallaway, Jr.; from "Coleridge and the Luminous Gloom" by E. B. Ghose, Jr.; on The Gawain-Poet by Marie Padgett Hamilton; on John Milton by James H. Hanford; on Geoffrey Chaucer by Walter Morris Hart; on Shelley by R. D. Havens; from "Southey's *Specimens of the Later English Poets*" by R. D. Havens; on Sir Thomas More by A. R. Heiserman; from *William Congreve, the Man* by John C. Hodges; from "Irving's Use of American Folklore: 'The Legend of Sleepy Hollow' " by Daniel G. Hoffman; on Collins by Clyde K. Hyder; on Andrew Marvell by Lawrence W. Hynan; on John Milton by Sears Jayne; on Henry Vaughan by Alexander C. Judson; on Geoffrey Chaucer by Helge Kökeritz; on Thomas Nashe by D. J. McGinn; on Alexander Pope by Elias F. Mengel, Jr.; on Geoffrey Chaucer by Arthur Mizener; on Thomas Otway by John R. Moore; on John Vanbrugh by Paul Mueschke and Jeanette Fleischer; on Geoffrey Chaucer by Charles Muscatine; on Sir Thomas More by William Nelson; on John Lydgate by Pierrepon Herrick Nichols; from "The Case of Shelley" by F. A. Pottle; on Tobias Smollett by Rufus Putney; on George Peele by A. M. Sampley; on John Marston by Samuel Schoenbaum; from "Milton and Forbidden Knowledge" by Howard Schultz; from "Keats, Milton and the Fall of Hyperion" by S. M. Sperry; on Richard Hooker by Sister M. Stephanie Stueber; on Newman by Martin Svaglic; on David Garrick by Elizabeth P. Stein; on Coleridge by E. E. Stoll; on Keats by C. de W. Thorpe; on Andrew Marvell by John M. Wallace; from *The English Romantic Poets* by Bennett Weaver; from "Samuel Rogers: Man of Taste" by Donald Weeks; on William Langland by Henry W. Wells; on Henry Fielding by John Edwin Wells.

G. P. PUTNAM'S SONS. For excerpts from *John Ruskin* by A. C. Benson; from *William Morris* by Elizabeth Luther Cary; from *Studies in Literature* by Sir Arthur Quiller-Couch; from *The Earnest Atheist* by Malcolm Muggeridge.

THE QUARTERLY REVIEW. On William Caxton by K. N. Colville; from "Coleridge's Conversation Poems by George McLean Harper.

from *The Charted Mirror* by John Holloway; from *Story of the Night* by John Holloway; from *John Lyly: The Humanist as Courtier* by G. K. Hunter; from *The Romantic Image* by Frank Kermode; from *The Burning Oracle* by G. Wilson Knight; from *Humanism and Poetry in the Early Tudor Period* by H. A. Mason; from *Collected Poems of Sir Thomas Wyatt,* ed. Kenneth Muir; from *The Place of Hooker in the History of Thought* by Peter Munz; from *ABC of Reading* by Ezra Pound; from *The Mind and Art of Coventry Patmore* by John Cowie Reid; from *Coleridge of Imagination* by I. A. Richards; from *The Darkening Glass* by John Rosenberg; from *Divided Image* by Margaret Rudd; from *Reason and the Imagination* by M. K. Starkman; from *Hardy of Wessex* by Carl Weber; from *Mrs. Gaskell* by A. Stanton Whitfield; from *Carlyle Till Marriage* by David Alex Wilson.

RUSSELL & RUSSELL, INC. For excerpts from *Carlyle* by Emery Neff [1932], New York, Russell & Russell, 1968; from *Wordsworth* by George McLean Harper [1916], 1960; and for their cooperation in matters pertaining to several other excerpts.

RUTGERS UNIVERSITY PRESS. For excerpts from *Franklin's Wit and Folly* by Richard E. Amacher; from *The American Henry James* by Quentin Anderson; from *Piers Plowman as a Fourteenth-Century Apocalypse* by Morton W. Bloomfield; from *That Rascal Freneau* by Lewis Leary; from *Mary Shelley* by Elizabeth Nitchie.

THE JOHN RYLANDS LIBRARY. For the excerpt from an article on William Caxton by W. Wright Roberts.

ST. MARTIN'S PRESS, INC. For excerpts from *Oxford Lectures on Poetry* by A. C. Bradley; from *Early Shakespeare* by Norman Sanders.

JOHN SALY. For excerpts from his "Keats' Answer to Dante."

MRS. VERONICA SANAKARIAN. For excerpts from *Poetry and Its Background* and *Milton* by E. M. W. Tillyard.

THE SATURDAY REVIEW. For excerpt from an article on William Dean Howells by Bernard Smith.

CHARLES SCRIBNER'S SONS. For excerpts from *American Prose Masters* by W. C. Brownell; from *The Liberation of American Literature* by V. F. Calverton; from *Sir Richard Steele* by Willard Connely; from *Brawny Wycherley* by Willard Connely; from *A Companion to Victorian Literature* by Thomas Parrot and Robert B. Martin; from *American Classics Reconsidered* by Ernest Sandeen; from *Americans* by Stuart P. Sherman; from *The Showman of Vanity Fair* by Lionel Stevenson; from *This Was a Poet* by George F. Whicher; from *Axel's Castle* by Edmund Wilson.

MARTIN SECKER & WARBURG LIMITED. For excerpts from *Thomas Hardy* by Lascelles Abercombie; from *The Life of William Hazlitt* by P. P. Howe; from *The Life of John Stuart Mill* by Michael St. John Packer; from *Critical Essays* by George Orwell; from *Algernon Charles Swinburne* by Edward Thomas; from *The Opposing Sex* by Lionel Trilling.

THE SEWANEE REVIEW. For excerpts from articles on Charles Brockden Brown by Warren B. Blake; on Andrew Marvell by Douglas Bush; on William Shakespeare by Francis Fergusson. All copyrighted by The University of the South.

ELIZABETH SEWELL. For excerpt from her *The Field of Nonsense.*

by Aline Grant; from *Jane Austen* by Margaret Kennedy; from *Sir Walter Scott* by Una Pope-Hennessy; from *On the Limits of Poetry* by Allan Tate; from *Maule's Curse* by Yvor Winters.

FRANK SWINNERTON. For excerpt from his *R. L. Stevenson.*

SYRACUSE UNIVERSITY PRESS. For excerpts from *William Caxton and His Critics* by Curt F. Bühler; from *The Realist at War* by Edwin H. Cady; from *The Sin of Wit* by Maurice Johnson; from *Design in Chaucer's Troilus* by Sanford B. Meech.

UNIVERSITY OF TEXAS PRESS. For excerpts from *Studies in English* by Frances Barbour; from *Sir Thomas Elyot, Tudor Humanist* by Stanford E. Lehmberg; from *Of Sondry Folk* by R. M. Lumiansky; from *Hawthorne's Tragic Vision* by Roy R. Male; from *Symmetry and Sense: The Poetry of Sir Philip Sidney* by Robert P. Montgomery, Jr.; from Byron's Don Juan by Truman G. Steffan; from articles in *Texas Studies in Literature and Language* on Sir John Suckling by L. A. Beaurline; on William Dunabr by A. M. Kinghorn; on Robert Henryson by A. M. Kinghorn.

ANGELA TILLYARD. For excerpts from *The English Renaissance: Fact or Fiction* and *Shakespeare's Last Plays* by E. M. W. Tillyard.

STEPHEN TILLYARD. For excerpts from *The English Epic and Its Background, Poetry Direct and Oblique, Five Poems 1470–1870,* and *Shakespeare's History Plays* by E. M. W. Tillyard.

THE TIMES LITERARY SUPPLEMENT. For its generous permission to quote from several studies and reviews.

HAROLD E. TOLIVER. For excerpt on Thomas Dekker in *Boston University Studies in English.*

UNIVERSITY OF TORONTO PRESS. For excerpts from *Milton and the Puritan Dilemma* by Arthur Barker; from *The Renaissance and English Humanism* by Douglas Bush; from *The Infinite Moment* by William O. Raymond; from *Matthew Arnold* by Carleton Stanley; from *On English Prose* by James R. Sutherland; from *The Apocalyptic Vision in the Poetry of Shelley* by R. G. Woodman; from articles in *University of Toronto Quarterly* on John Wilmot, Lord Rochester by Fredelle Bruser; on Alfred, Lord Tennyson by Arthur J. Carr; on Samuel Richardson by A. E. Carter; on William Shakespeare by F. David Hoeniger; on William Dunbar by John Leyerle; on Geoffrey Chaucer by G. G. Sedgewick; from "The Mariner and the Albatross" by George Whalley; on John Milton by A. S. P. Woodhouse.

LIONEL TRILLING. For excerpts from his *Matthew Arnold.*

TULANE DRAMA REVIEW. For excerpts from four articles on Christopher Marlowe by C. L. Barber, Alfred Harbage, Harry Morris, E. M. Waith, copyright Tulane Drama Review; first printed in *Tulane Drama Review's* special Marlowe issue, Vol. 8, No. 4 (Summer 1964, T24).

TULANE UNIVERSITY. For excerpts from articles in *Tulane Studies in English* on Thomas Otway by Aline Mackenzie; on Robert Southwell by Harry Morris.

TWAYNE PUBLISHERS, INC. For excerpts from *In Search of Stability* by Morris Golden; from *Edward Taylor* by Norman S. Grabo; from *A Tennyson Handbook* by George O. Marshall.

C. V. WEDGWOOD. For excerpts from an article in *The Listener* on John Cleveland. Wellesley College. For excerpt from *The Art of Newman's Apologia* by Walter Houghton.

WESLEYAN UNIVERSITY PRESS. For excerpts from *The Moral Basis of Fielding's Art* by Martin C. Battestin, copyright © 1959 by Wesleyan University, reprinted by permission of Wesleyan University Press; from *The Limits of Mortality* by David Ferry, copyright © 1959 by Wesleyan University, reprinted by permission of Wesleyan University Press.

WEST VIRGINIA UNIVERSITY PHILOLOGICAL PAPERS. For excerpt from an article in *W. V. U. Studies* on John Wilmot; on Lord Rochester by S. F. Crocker.

BASIL WILLEY. From excerpt from his *The 17th Century Background*.

UNIVERSITY OF WISCONSIN PRESS. For excerpts reprinted by permission of the copyright owners, The Regents of the University of Wisconsin, from *Jonson and the Comic Truth* by John J. Enck; from *Romantic Narrative Art* by Karl Kroeber; from *The Moral Vision of Jacobean Tragedy* by Robert Ornstein; from *Richard Crashaw* by Ruth C. Wallerstein; from *Tudor Book of Saints and Martyrs* by Helen C. White; from *Politics in the Poetry of Coleridge* by C. R. Woodring.

H. F. & G. WITHERBY. For excerpts from *The History of the English Novel* by E. A. Baker.

YALE UNIVERSITY PRESS. For excerpts from *Shakespeare: A Biological Handbook* by Gerald Eades Bentley; from *The Allegorical Temper* by Harry Berger, Jr.; from *Sir Gawain and the Green Knight* by Marie Boroff; from *Coleridge as a Religious Thinker* by J. D. Boulger; from *The American Mind* by Henry Steele Commager; from *Piers Plowman and the Scheme of Salvation* by Robert Worth Frank, Jr.: from *The Politics of Samuel Johnson* by Donald J. Greene; from *The George Eliot Letters* by Gordon Haight; from *Hawthorne: Critic of Society* by Lawrence S. Hall; from *Otway and Lee* by Roswell G. Ham; from *Browning's Character* by Park Honan; from *The Life and Minor Works of George Peale* by David H. Horne; from *The Poetry of Clough* by Walter Houghton; from *The Voices of Matthew Arnold* by Wendell Stacy Johnson; from *Thomas Carlyle . . .* by William Savage Johnson; from *The Swinburne Letters* by Cecil Lang; from *The Excursion: A Study* by J. S. Lyon; from *Pepys on the Restoration Stage* by Helen McAfee; from *Pope and His Contemporaries* by Mayard Mack; from *Three Studies in the Renaissance* by William G. Madsen; from *The Later Career of Tobias Smollett* by Louis L. Martz; from *The Poems of Edward Taylor* by Louis L. Martz; from *The Poetry of Meditation* by Louis L. Martz; from *Purity* by Robert J. Menner; from *Thomas Lodge: The History of an Elizabethan* by N. Burton Paradise; from *Theme and Structure in Swift's Tale of a Tub* by Ronald Paulson; from *The Key of Remembrance* (New Haven and London) by Robert O. Payne; from the article on James Boswell by Frederick A. Pottle in the *Yale Review*, XXXV (1945–46); from *Swift's Rhetorical Art: A Study in Structure and Meaning* by Martin Price; from *The Flourishing Wreath* by Edward I. Selig; from the article on Edward Taylor by Donald E. Stanford in *The Poems of Edward Taylor;* from *The Innocent Eye* by Albert E. Stone, Jr.; from *The Complete Works of Thomas More*, Vol. II, ed. Richard S. Sylvester; from *Etherege and the 17th Century Comedy of Manners* by Dale Underwood; from *The Pattern of Tragicomedy in Beaumont and Fletcher* by Eugene M. Waith; from *The Hero of the Waverly Novels* by Alexander Welsh; from *New Light on Dr. Johnson* by W. K. Wimsatt, Jr.; from *Complete Prose Works of John Milton* by Don M. Wolfe.

CROSS-REFERENCE INDEX TO AUTHORS

Only significant references are included.

499

INDEX TO CRITICS

*Selections from the Times Literary Supplement, always unsigned,
are indexed under the publication title.*

LEECH, Clifford
Beaumont, I, 267–268; Fletcher, I, 267–268; Ford, I, 329–330
LEGALLIENE, Richard L.
Kipling, III, 125–126
LEGGE, M. D.
Gower, I, 166–167
LEGOUIS, Emile
Chaucer, I, 71; Wordsworth, II, 523–524
LEHMAN, B. H.
Sterne, II, 206–207
LEHMBERG, Stanford E.
Elyot, I, 326
LEISHMAN, J. B.
Donne, I, 319; Traherne, I, 489–490; Vaughan, I, 496–497
LEONARD, William E.
Bryant, III, 244–245
LESLIE, R. F.
Elegaic Poetry, I, 38–39
LEVER, J. W.
Sidney, I, 451 453; Surrey, I, 476; Wyatt, I, 512–513
LEVI, Joseph
Hawthorne, III, 316
LEVIN, HARRY
Bierce, III, 238; Hearn, III, 329–330; Marlowe, I, 390–391; Poe, III, 412
LEVIN, Michael H.
Kyd, I, 380–381
LEVISON, Wilhelm
Bede, I, 9–10
LEWALSKI, Barbara K.
Milton, II, 127–128; Shakespeare, I, 540
LEWIS, C. S.
Campion, I, 284–285; Chaucer, I, 82; Daniel, I, 302–303; Douglas, I, 124–125; Drayton, I, 325; Dunbar, I, 139; Gawain Poet, I, 150; Gower, I, 159–160; Greene, I, 346; Langland, I, 184–185; Lodge, I, 384; Lydgate, I, 200–201; Malory, I, 213; Milton, II, 115–116; More, I, 233; Morris, III, 152; Shakespeare, I, 553–554; Shelley, II, 474, 492; Sidney, I, 448–449; Skelton, I, 235–236; Southwell, I, 455–456; Surrey, I, 476
LEWIS, R. W. B.
Cooper, III, 259–260; Holmes, III, 332; James, III, 359–360; Thoreau, III, 433; Whitman, III, 451
LEWIS, Sinclair
Howells, III, 338
LEWISOHN, Ludwig
Bierce, III, 237; Crane, III, 263; Emerson, III, 286; Freneau, III, 304–305;

Hearn, III, 328–329; Holmes, III, 331–332; Howells, III, 340–341; Longfellow, III, 374; Melville, III, 385; Poe, III, 413–414; Thoreau, III, 432–433; Twain, III, 443
LEYBURN, Ellen D.
Butler, II, 20–21
LEYERLE, John
Dunbar, I, 142–143
LINDBERG, John
Carlyle, III, 55
LINDSAY, Maurice
Burns, II, 18
LLOYD, L. J.
Skelton, I, 239
LOFTIS, John
Fielding, II, 80; Steele, II, 200, 201, 201–202
LOOMIS, Laura H.
Gawain Poet, I, 148
LOOMIS, Roger S.
Chaucer, I, 93–94; Gawain Poet, I, 151; Malory, I, 213
LOVEJOY, Arthur
Milton, II, 118
LOVELL, Ernest J., Jr.
Byron, II, 307–308, 313, 319
LOWELL, Amy
Hunt, II, 377–378; Keats, II, 386, 389, 393
LOWES, John L.
Chaucer, I, 92–93; Coleridge, II, 330–331, 336
LUCAS, F. L.
Arnold, III, 8–9; Browning, R., III, 39; Clough, III, 61; Crabbe, II, 352; Langland, I, 192; Rossetti, D. G., III, 171–172; Tennyson, III, 199–200, 200–201
LUMIANSKY, R. M.
Chaucer, I, 91–92
LUND, Mary G.
Chatterton, II, 23
LYNCH, Charles A.
More, I, 227
LYNCH, Kathleen M.
Dryden, II, 60; Etherege, II, 63; Shadwell, II, 184; Suckling, I, 473–474
LYNN, Kenneth
Norris, III, 400–401
LYON, J. S.
Wordsworth, II, 518–519

MacCAFFREY, Isabel
Milton, II, 122–123
MacCALL, Seamus
Moore, II, 430–431

229; Wycherley, II, 242–243

PARADISE, N. B.
Lodge, I, 382–383

PARKE, John
Melville, III, 392–393

PARKER, George
Defoe, II, 48

PARKER, William R.
Milton, II, 128–129, 130, 139–140

PARKES, Henry B.
Edwards, III, 279–280; Emerson, III, 287–288; Franklin, III, 298–299; James, III, 358; Poe, III, 407; Whitman, III, 459

PARKS, Edd W.
Lanier, III, 368; Shirley, I, 445

PARNELL, Paul E.
Cibber, II, 28–29

PARRINGTON, Vernon L.
Bryant, III, 247; Cooper, III, 253; Edwards, III, 278–279; Franklin, III, 296; Freneau, III, 302; Hawthorne, III, 322; Irving, III, 347–348; Jewett, III, 362–363; Lowell, III, 379–380; Paine, III, 402; Poe, III, 415–416; Whittier, III, 463

PARROT, Thomas M.
Brontë, E., III, 25; Chapman, I, 294; Hardy, III, 102; Shakespeare, I, 550

PATCH, Howard R.
Chaucer, I, 70

PARTRIDGE, Edward
Jonson, I, 376

PATTEE, Fred L.
Bierce, III, 235; Brown, III, 240–241; Cable, III, 249–250; Crane, III, 262; Dickinson, III, 271; Franklin, III, 297; Hawthorne, III, 315; Hearn, III, 327–328; James, III, 355–356; Jewett, III, 362; Longfellow, III, 372; Miller, III, 394; Paine, III, 402–403; Stowe, III, 420–421

PATTISON, Bruce
Campion, I, 282–283

PAUL, Sherman
Emerson, III, 288–289

PAULSON, Ronald
Smollett, II, 196–197; Swift, II, 221

PAYNE, Robert O.
Chaucer, I, 86

PAYNE, William M.
Whittier, III, 462–463

PEARCE, Roy H.
Bryant, III, 246–247; Dickinson, III, 273–274; Holmes, III, 333–334; Lanier, III, 369; Longfellow, III, 375–376; Lowell, III, 381–382; Poe, III,

409–410; Taylor, E., III, 426; Whitman, III, 452–453

PEARSON, Hesketh
Scott, II, 455

PECK, Louis F.
Lewis, II, 427

PERKINS, David
Shelley, II, 470; Wordsworth, II, 526

PERRY, Bliss
Carlyle, III, 57

PERRY, Henry T. E.
Congreve, II, 32; Etherege, II, 66; Farquhar, II, 69; Vanbrugh, II, 230; Wycherley, II, 238–239

PETER, John
Crashaw, I, 299–300; Gower, I, 160–161; Marston, I, 404–405; Milton, II, 124

PETERS, Robert L.
Swinburne, III, 191–192

PETERSON, Houston
Huxley, III, 120–121

PETTET, E. C.
Greene, I, 341–343; Shakespeare, I, 533, 572–573; Vaughan, I, 493, 499–500

PHELPS, William Lyon
Browning, R., III, 38–39; Bryant, III, 245

PHILLIMORE, J. S.
More, I, 229

PICK, John
Hopkins, III, 112, 114

PINTO, Vivian de Sola
Rochester, II, 178

PITT, Valerie
Tennyson, III, 202, 209–210

PLOMER, Henry R.
Caxton, I, 59–60

PLOWMAN, Max
Blake, II, 274, 277, 290

PLUMMER, Charles
Alfred The Great, I, 3–4

POCHMAN, Henry A.
Irving, III, 348

POLLARD, Arthur
Crabbe, II, 355–356

POPE, Elizabeth M.
Milton, II, 125

POPE-HENNESSY, Una
Dickens, III, 75; Scott, II, 454

POTTER, George R.
Thomson, II, 225

POTTLE, Frederick A.
Boswell, II, 8; Shelley, II, 493; Wordsworth, II, 504